Psychology
in the Work Context

Psychology
in the Work Conte

Ziel C Bergh • Antoinette L Theron (Ed

OXFORD
UNIVERSITY PRESS

OXFORD
UNIVERSITY PRESS

Great Clarendon Street, Oxford ox2 6DP

Oxford University Press is a department of the University of Oxford.
It furthers the University's objective of excellence in research, scholarship,
and education by publishing worldwide in

Oxford   New York

Athens Auckland Bangkok Bogotá Buenos Aires Calcutta
Cape Town Chennai Dar es Salaam Delhi Florence Hong Kong Istanbul
Karachi Kuala Lumpur Madrid Melbourne Mexico City Mumbai
Nairobi Paris São Paulo Shanghai Singapore Taipei Tokyo Toronto Warsaw

with associated companies in Berlin Ibadan

Oxford is a registered trademark of Oxford University Press
in the UK and certain other countries

Published in South Africa
by Oxford University Press Southern Africa, Cape Town

Psychology in the Work Context
ISBN 0 19 571845 3

© Oxford University Press Southern Africa 1999

Previously published by International Thomson Publishing
Southern Africa (Pty) Ltd (1 86864 068 X)

First published 1999
Reprinted 1999, 2000, 2001

Cover design by Collage Graphics
Illustrations by Dr Jack

Published by Oxford University Press Southern Africa
PO Box 12119, N1 City, 7463, Cape Town, South Africa

Set in 10 pt on 12 pt Souvenir
Typesetting and reproduction by PG&A, Western Cape
Printed and bound by NBD, Drukkery Street, Goodwood, Western Cape

Authors: Ziel Bergh

Antoinette Theron

Linda Albertyn

François Badenhorst

Dirk Geldenhuys

Leona Ungerer

Frans Cilliers

Theo de Koker

Abridged Table of Contents

Contents

Preface

In the context of the work situation, psychology involves various processes that together constitute an open system. The essence of an open system is that it is dynamic and characterised by change: the processes function as inputs to the system. Their interrelated functioning generates outputs by both the individual and the work situation, for example, productivity, job satisfaction and organisational effectiveness. The outputs can provide feedback to the system, thereby eliciting renewed or maintained inputs.

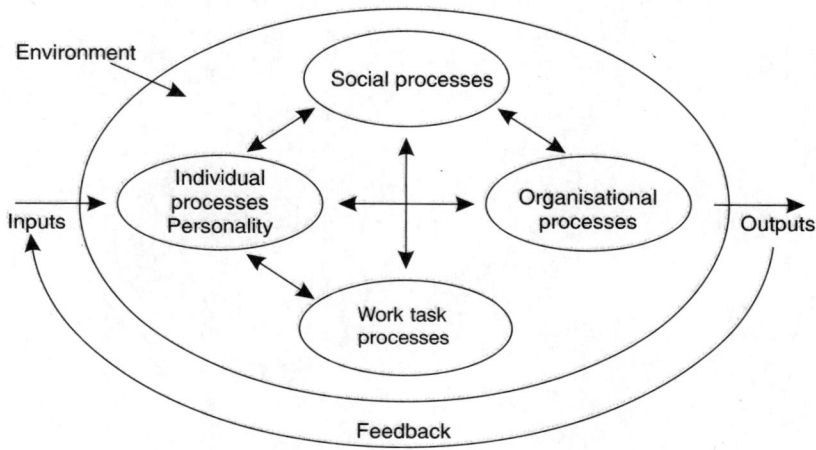

Inputs to the system include:
- individual processes within the individual
- the personality of the individual, which is the unique organisation of processes within the individual
- social processes that involve the interaction between individuals
- organisational processes that affect individual as well as social processes
- processes that have to do with the execution of work tasks

All these processes are influenced by environmental factors that affect the system, for example technological, economic, socio-cultural and political factors.

A systems model for studying psychology in the work context is akin to information technology, in which the computer is the processor of information. Studying individuals and groups and their work in terms of a systems model (that is, an information processing model) is aimed at holistic thinking, which implies recognising and understanding the interrelatedness of psychological and work processes, rather than their separate functioning.

The systems model presented here can be used as a guide for studying the text. The text is not, however, written in close adherence to the model. The main emphasis in this book is on individual processes, social processes and personality. A chapter introducing the student to organisational processes is included and the significance of work task processes is dealt with in a chapter on the biological basis of behaviour. Examples throughout the book allude to organisational and task processes, but these extensive fields of psychological study are fully covered only in specialised texts.

Part I
Introduction

Introduction

As a science and academic discipline, psychology has evolved from general philosophical enquiry to different theoretical approaches, each incorporating premises on the content of psychological enquiry. These approaches constitute the historical foundations of the subject, but are significant beyond their historical influence, in that they give direction to the generation of psychology as a dynamic, evolving science per se, as well as an applied science incorporating the work context.

The object of a science is establishing methods for explaining and predicting phenomena. This is accomplished by the methodology in which theoretical knowledge is systematised scientifically by means of description, analysis, comparison and classification.

Perspectives on general and work behaviour

1

Antoinette Theron

CONTENTS

Learning outcomes

After studying this chapter you should be able to:

- describe the subject matter and methods in structuralism, functionalism, behaviourism, Gestalt psychology, psychoanalysis and humanistic or phenomenological psychology
- explain the concerns of cognitive psychology
- explain what metapsychology involves
- give a synopsis of the history of industrial psychology
- describe applied fields of industrial psychology
- relate schools of thought to fields of study in industrial psychology

Key concepts

mechanism, natural science, consciousness, introspection, adaptation to the environment, individual differences, control, prediction, conditioning, organisation of meaningful wholes, unconscious, free association, eidetic reduction, "knowing", systems, holistic

1.1 INTRODUCTION

Psychology in the work context is the field of study of *industrial psychology*. Different terms are used in different countries for this field of study. In South Africa it is called industrial psychology, in Britain occupational psychology, in the United States industrial and organisational psychology and in European countries it is work and organisational psychology.

Industrial psychology is an applied field of psychology and therefore shares a common history with the developmental history of psychology.

Psychology originated from philosophical theorising in the 5th century BC in ancient Greece. Greek philosophers concerned themselves with understanding the structure and functioning of the psyche, which in Greek refers to the mind or soul (Meyer et al. 1989). Pythagoras and Plato maintained that the soul is structurally and functionally different from the body. Plato distinguished three parts of the soul, namely the rational soul, which involves knowledge, the spirited soul, which involves courage and pursuing honour, and the passionate soul, which involves bodily pleasure. Aristotle maintained that the soul is part of the body and is the essence or self of the individual which determines the purpose of the body (Leahy 1992).

The relation between body and mind, and the extent to which they influence each other, was debated for centuries when studying and attaining knowledge of humans.

In the 17th century, knowledge provided by the growth of natural science, in particular physics, paved the way for psychology as an experimental science. Scientific knowledge brought about a spirit of mechanism, in which it was believed the universe had been perfectly designed and that natural processes are mechanically determined and can be explained as well as predicted by the laws of physics. An example of mechanistic functioning is the clock, which in the 17th century was akin to the importance of the computer in the 20th century. Clocks are characterised by precision, regularity, and predictability. These mechanisms became likened to the functioning of the human, whose mind and body was seen as functioning inherently lawfully, and is therefore understandable in terms of knowledge gained by observation and experimentation, rather than mere philosophical inquiry (Schultz & Schultz 1996).

In the second half of the 19th century psychology became an experimental science in its own right. It was seen as a *natural science*, relying on the knowledge and methods of physics, chemistry and physiology. It was studied in laboratories and became a formal academic discipline, taught at universities.

Wilhelm Wundt

The first psychology laboratory was founded in Leipzig, Germany, in 1879 by Wilhelm Wundt, a German physiologist. Wundt is regarded as the founder of experimental psychology. His book, published in two parts in 1873 and 1874, *Grundzüge der physiologischen psychologie (Foundations of physiological psychology)* became an influential text. Wundt's laboratory served as a model for psychology and drew students from all over the world.

1.2 SCHOOLS OF THOUGHT

As new currents in science and culture emerged, psychology, influenced by the spirit of the times, also changed, incorporating new currents of thought. Theoretical propositions on what the subject matter of psychology should comprise, and what methods should be used, became incorporated in schools of thought. A school of thought was an intellectual movement whose adherents shared more or less the same ideology. Towards the end of the 19th century and over the course of the 20th century different schools of thought were established, contributing different theoretical and methodological propositions for studying humans. Contemporary psychology is built on the frameworks provided by the schools (Schultz & Schultz 1996).

1.2.1 Structuralism

The first school of thought, structuralism, was influenced by the establishment of Wundt's laboratory, the publication in 1860 of a book on psychophysics by Gustav Fechner, *Elemente der Psychophysik (Elements of Psychophysics)*, and the work of Edward Bradford Titchener, who came from Oxford University in England to work in Wundt's laboratory. Between 1893 and 1900 he developed a laboratory at Cornell University in America, establishing experimental psychology, with structuralism as its focus, in America.

The subject matter of structuralism was *consciousness*. By studying the structural elements of conscious experience, the structuralists attempted to understand psychological processes such as sensation, attention, perception, reaction, feeling and emotion. Titchener, for example, found that the elements consistently experienced in emotions such as love, hate and sadness comprise feelings of pleasure or displeasure. Wundt maintained that besides pleasure and displeasure, emotions also involve feelings varying from relaxation to tension and from excitement to depression (Schultz & Schultz 1996).

The method used in structuralism was called *introspection,* which refers to self-observation of one's immediate experience of a stimulus, to ascertain the feelings or thoughts that the stimulus evokes. It was assumed that conscious experience could best be described by the person having the conscious experience. Introspection was seen as a method which would reveal the elements of the mind – in Titchener's words, the atoms of the mind – analogous to methods in natural science in which the structural components of, for example, light and sound could be revealed. Whereas in physics the interest was in studying the physical processes involved in light and sound, in psychology the interest was in studying the experience of the individual when exposed to such factors. Under the guidance of a person trained to apply introspection, subjects had to give detailed reports of the immediate sensations aroused by a stimulus such as a sound or a light or a colour, a taste or smell, or stimuli such as pressure, pain, heat or cold applied to the skin by laboratory apparatus. The reports had to be impartial, free of any interpretation or meaning that the subject associated with the stimulus on the strength of past experience. If the subject was shown a red flower, the researcher would be interested in sensations elicited by the colour red, and not the subject's existing knowledge of the flower. In his experiments using introspection, Titchener discovered more than 44 000 sensations, of which 21 820 were identified as of a visual nature and 1 600 as auditory, that is, involving hearing (Schultz & Schultz 1996).

As a method, introspection reflected the spirit of mechanism, which influenced the view of humans functioning as machines. Although introspection could yield detailed information, it could not provide comprehensive understanding of the content of the mind. Not all behaviour, for example, habits or even performance at work, occurs with the individual being conscious of it. Furthermore, the process of introspection can change the content of consciousness, in that the subject becomes an observer and when he or she experiences the same stimuli again, the experience is different. Thus introspection can be too subjective to be entirely reliable and has limited value for providing generally accepted scientific knowledge. It cannot be

applied to the study of children, and individuals trained to apply introspection must be mature and sophisticated enough to eliminate the possibility of personal bias.

Despite criticisms of the methodology, structuralism was and is significant in the study of psychology by virtue of its focus on conscious experience. Subject matter such as sensation, feeling and attention, as well as introspection, found in verbal reports based on subjective experience, is still prevalent in psychology.

In industrial psychology, for example, the notion, although not the original method, of introspection is implied in employees' reports on their personal experience of the work situation, such as the use of computers as it concerns the development and refinement of computer equipment. Introspection is also implied in self-reports assessing personality or determining attitudes (Schultz & Schultz 1996).

1.2.2 Functionalism

Functionalism developed in America as a reaction against structuralism. Psychology was seen as a practical science with its subject matter the *functions* of the mind rather than the structure or content of the mind. The focus was on the mind, as it is functional to the individual's adaptation to the environment. Of significance was not, for example, the structure of emotions, but the role that emotions play in social adaptation. William James, an American physician, philosopher and psychologist, discussed this topic in his book, *Principles of psychology,* published in 1890. James also wrote about the functions of religion in *Varieties of religious experience,* published in 1902. A well-known statement of James, which indicates that consciousness should not be understood in terms of elements, was his description of time perception as "a stream of consciousness" (Gorman & Wessman 1977:40). James maintained that the individual's adaptation to the environment is influenced by his or her conscious awareness of the continuity and meaning of the merging of past, present and future, which is the basis of experiencing time.

The major influence on functionalism was Charles Darwin's book on evolution, *The origin of species*, published in 1859. This work influenced the spirit of the time in general, and psychology in particular, toward interest in the adaptation of organisms to the environment.

Implicit in evolution theory is that living organisms change through progressive advance, which enables species and new forms of species that emerge, to survive. According to Darwin's theory, natural selection, adaptation to the environment and variability contribute to survival. The process of natural selection favours living organisms that have certain attributes which enable them to survive in a given environment. Thus those which are best equipped biologically have the best chance of adapting. Those best adapted to the environment survive and reproduce. Over many generations genetic transformations occur through adaptation to the environment. Because of the law of variability in heredity, offspring differ from their preceding generations. New attributes evolve through genetic change that provide individual differences, i.e. variations between members of a species or between different species.

Attributes that influence adaptation and have been shown to be common to both man and certain animals, particularly the primates, are will, reason, instincts, sensations, emotions, imagination, curiosity and the ability to imitate. The difference between man and animal is merely that human behaviour is governed more by will and reason, while that of animals is ruled more by instinct (Darwin 1970).

Because of similarities between humans and animals, the functionalists' methods included experiments with animals, by which they attempted to explain human behaviour.

Darwin's work also turned the focus of psychology to *individual differences*. This became a fundamental concept in psychology through the work of Sir Francis Galton, an English scientist, who worked on heredity and mental abilities. Galton contributed particularly to the methodology of psychology, by compiling and applying ability tests, questionnaires and statistical techniques. He also fostered interest in genetic twin studies, child development, mental deviation and the relation between heredity and the environment.

Although functionalism no longer exists as a school, it has a lasting legacy in the spirit of pragmatism in industrial psychology. The application of tests, questionnaires and statistics is of major importance in industrial psychology. In personnel selection, one of the specialist fields in industrial psychology, the basic premise is that individuals differ with regard to intelligence, aptitude, skill, interests and other characteristics. Selection aims at identifying personal characteristics in an applicant, and to predict whether he or she will become a competent and satisfied worker in an occupation that requires that individual's characteristics.

1.2.3 Behaviourism

In 1913 John B. Watson, an American psychologist, launched behaviourism, which became known as the First Force in psychology. Watson advocated an entirely objective psychology, which aimed at developing general principles of behaviour based on *control* and *prediction* of overt behaviour. For Watson the subject matter of psychology was *observable behaviour*, since only what is observable, according to him, could be studied objectively. Watson was totally opposed to the structuralist focus on consciousness and the functionalist focus on heredity. He maintained that the environment determines behaviour. Humans are merely reactive beings and what they are and become is determined by causes outside themselves. Thus behaviour can be predetermined by the control of environmental factors.

Watson made no distinction between humans and animals and his methods were based on animal psychology. Studying an animal's or a human's behaviour objectively meant that it could be described in terms of stimuli and responses. This became known as the *stimulus-response (S-R) approach* in psychology.

John B. Watson

A precursory influence on the behaviourist method was the work of Ivan Pavlov in Russia. Pavlov was a physiologist who specialised in animal psychology and won the Nobel prize in 1904. Through experiments with dogs Pavlov showed that behaviour can be *conditioned*, that is, learned by mental associations that occur mechanically by stimulus-response relations. Pavlov found, for example, that dogs learned to associate food with other stimuli that were present at the same time, such as a light or sound, or even the footsteps of the person who fed them (Schultz & Schultz 1996). They eventually reacted in the same way to these stimuli, even in the absence of food. Thus the same response was elicited by stimuli that a dog had learned to associate with food.

Watson's methods were also influenced by the work of Vladimir M. Bekhterev, a Russian psychiatrist who specialised in animal psychology and focused on the role of reflexology in mental functioning.

The notion that the association of stimuli or events is the basis of mental processes stems from earlier philosophical thinking. In the 17th century, John Locke, a British philosopher, described the human psyche as a *tabula rasa* (a blank tablet) on which associations are imprinted through sensory experience. These associations combine to form larger units which comprise the contents of the mind.

This view is echoed in Watson's celebrated statement that, through conditioning, he could train any given infant, regardless of his or her talents or abilities, to be a doctor, lawyer, architect, beggar or thief.

Watson also applied his belief that behaviour can be controlled and predicted to consumer behaviour. He devised techniques in advertising aimed at manipulating people's needs, motives and emotions to create incentives to buy products (Schultz & Schultz 1996).

Watson's theory of behaviourism was influential in America until approximately 1930. After this, up to about 1960, a new kind of behaviourism, called neo-behaviourism, became influential through the work of Edward C. Tolman, Edwin Guthrie, Clark Hull and B.F. Skinner. They adhered to conditioning being the learning process in psychology but extended the subject matter from observable behaviour to include *unobservable behaviour* as well.

This is called the *stimulus-organism-response (S-O-R) approach*. Tolman inferred that factors within the organism such as memory, thinking, emotions and needs are intervening variables, i.e. factors that come between the direct relationship between the stimulus and response and therefore influence the response. Applied to a training programme (the stimulus) in the work situation, the influence of individual factors such as previous knowledge, existing skills and motivation (organismic factors) could result in various degrees of competency (the response).

After 1960 the notion of consciousness was introduced into behaviourism theories. Social learning theories were developed which focused on learning in social situations. Social learning occurs by implementing cognitive processes, i.e. processes by which the individual becomes conscious of the environment, such as recognition and perception of other people's behaviour.

Behaviourism in all its forms is highly influential in industrial psychology. The emphasis on learning, for example, has become the basis of personnel and management training.

1.2.4 Gestalt psychology

"Gestalt" is a German word which means "form" or "configuration".

Gestalt psychology developed in Europe as a reaction against the elementist approach of structuralism. Gestalt psychology thinking did not accept that the mind could be studied by breaking it up into elements, because it functions as an interconnected whole. It could also not be studied in terms of cause and effect, as was done in behaviourism. It could only be studied in terms of how experience is perceived meaningfully. The subject matter of psychology was thus the *wholeness of experience*, since the mind combines elements into patterns or configurations that have a meaning which is not present in the elements themselves. When we hear music we do not "hear" the structural elements of the composition, but the rhythm or melody that the organisation of the elements provide. When three matches are arranged in the shape of a triangle, we do not perceive the configuration as three matches, but as a triangular form.

The Gestalt school evolved from the research of German psychologists Max Wertheimer, Kurt Koffka and Wolfgang Köhler.

Max Wertheimer

Wertheimer got the idea of investigating the phenomenon of apparent motion when travelling on a train taking him on holiday. The apparent movement of nature as seen from the moving train made him realise that the mind perceives stimuli differently to what they actually are. He interrupted his holiday and conducted an experiment which brought to light what is called the *phi-phenomenon* (Schultz & Schultz 1996).

The experiment involved sitting in a darkened room watching two bars of lights flashed on and off alternately. If the time interval between the flashes was more than 0,2 seconds the lights were seen alternately, but if the time interval between flashes was less than 0,2 seconds, what was perceived was one moving light. This apparent motion is the phenomenon experienced in motion pictures, which are based on a quick succession of still pictures (Leahy, 1994).

The phi-phenomenon showed that perception is not the sum total of sensory elements, but more than the sum of the parts. The organisation or combination of the sensory elements comprising a structure gives rise to a new perception which is perceived in such a way as to be meaningful.

The Gestalt psychologists believed that all aspects of a human's experiential field are interrelated and that it is an inherent and universal quality of humans to perceive any stimulus field as a balanced, simplified and organised whole (Arnheim 1947).

As the school gained momentum, the Gestalt concept was also incorporated in the study of learning, memory, motivation and thinking. A well-known experiment of Köhler on thinking illustrates problem-solving in chimpanzees. A chimpanzee was placed in a room with a banana hanging out of reach from the ceiling and boxes scattered randomly over the floor. After several trials the chimpanzee stacked the boxes to create a "ladder" to reach the banana. The chimpanzee thus reorganised the stimulus field (the boxes) into a meaningful useful whole (a "ladder").

In the work situation, the Gestalt concept can be applied to organisational culture. Organisational culture is a shared perception that the members of an organisation have of its meaning. Aspects that constitute its meaning include allowance for motivation and risk-taking, attention to detail and precision, competitiveness, people orientation and team orientation (Robbins 1998). The way in which such aspects are organised can constitute different meanings of organisational culture, for example a culture of rules and regulations in a work group, or a culture of innovative teamwork.

Wertheimer saw the Gestalt movement as more than mere psychological explanation – he saw it as a world-view encompassing the idea that the world can be a coherent whole and that the realities of life can be organised into meaningful parts (Leahy 1994).

The Gestalt movement was the antecedent of psychology as a human science rather than as a natural science (Meyer et al. 1989).

1.2.5 The psychoanalytic school

The psychoanalytic school had its foundation in the publication in 1895 of a book *Studies on hysteria*, written by Sigmund Freud, a medical doctor who specialised in clinical neurology, and Joseph Breuer, a physician. Both lived and worked in Vienna, Austria.

Although psychoanalysis overlapped in time with other schools of thought, its concerns were totally different. Its subject matter was the role of the *unconscious* in mental disorders, and the methodology used was clinical observation, not laboratory experimentation.

Freud is regarded as the mastermind of the psychoanalytic school, which became known as the Second Force in psychology.

According to Freud (in Russell 1970) the mind consists of not only conscious mental contents, but *unconscious* mental contents as well. Unconscious contents include the same type of mental activities that are consciously experienced, such as ideas, memories, feelings and emotions, except that the individual is not aware of the unconscious activities. The nature of the unconscious cannot be explained in terms of physiological or chemical processes or a locality in the brain, but there is enough "proof" that the unconscious exists: for example the altered states of consciousness in hypnosis, ideas that suddenly occur in the mind without one knowing where they came from, the psychic contents of the minds of mentally ill individuals, and the dreams of normal people.

Unconscious processes are accessible, i.e. they can become conscious through the psychoanalytic method of *free association*. Some processes come to consciousness more readily than others, depending on how "deep" they are in the unconscious. They are inferred through free association, in which the individual says anything that comes to mind, and the unconscious activities come to mind by "entering" the conscious. Initially these activities may seem strange and incomprehensible, even alien to the person undergoing analysis, but eventually they can become understandable and contribute to an understanding of the behaviour (Freud in Russell 1970).

Freud found that in the process of psychoanalysis, most patients reported unconscious activities concerning childhood experiences and that the experiences had sexual overtones.

This can be explained in terms of the spirit of the time. In 19th century Victorian society "proper" behaviour was valued and sexuality posed a problem. The lower classes were sexually free, producing many offspring to look after them in their old age. In a society becoming more industrialised, the middle and upper classes regarded children as economic liabilities who drained income, in that they had to be looked after until they could enter the workforce. In their concern to avoid reproduction, men became impotent or consorted with prostitutes, leaving their wives frustrated by the disappointments of matrimony and often neurotic. Most of Freud's patients were middle-class women, whom he identified as suffering from hysteria caused by sexual problems. He also found that some patients had suffered sexual abuse as children, while others fantasised about sexual experiences. This Freud interpreted as referring to a childhood sexuality, which he saw as universal, applicable to all human beings. This childhood sexuality involved the child's fantasy of falling in love with the parent of the opposite sex and being jealous of the partner who possessed this parent. This experience was hidden in the unconscious and gave rise to neurotic behaviour. The implication is that childhood experiences, whether real or mere fantasy, operate actively in the unconscious, influencing overt behaviour, because the mind is dynamic, not static, and by discovering these unconscious experiences, the individual's behaviour can be understood.

In industrial psychology Freud's theory is relevant to the psychodynamics of organisations. The study of behavioural dynamics and unconscious processes leads to a deeper understanding of organisational issues. A worker may approach the work situation with unfulfilled family needs which he or she wants to fulfil there, for example, the need for a father figure to provide recognition and affection. If these needs do not fit the reality of the work situation, the individual experiences anxiety. To cope with anxiety, which involves feelings of loneliness and alienation, the individual bonds with groups or powerful individuals to establish some meaningful relationship, and satisfy the fantasy that relationships involve pairs.

In consultancy and training, the psychoanalytic approach involves making sense out of non-sense and the view that there are no coincidences in life (Cilliers & Koortzen 1996). The implication is that unconscious mental contents continually affect consciousness.

Approximately 20 years after Freud proclaimed his beliefs, different views of the psychoanalytical approach emerged. Splinter groups accepted Freud's views of the unconscious, but placed less emphasis on sexuality, focused on the future as well as childhood experience, and accentuated the role of social relations and social institutions.

1.2.6 Humanism or phenomenology

A school of thought which became known as the Third Force in psychology was called humanism in America and phenomenology in Europe. The movement developed early in 1960 as a reaction against behaviourism and psychoanalysis. Adherents maintained that people cannot be seen as machines that simply react to external stimuli, as behaviourism claimed, and they saw Freudian psychology as too negative, with its focus mainly on maladjustment. The subject matter of psychology was seen as focusing on the positive aspects of conscious mental activity, incorporating humans' striving for psychological growth, self-actualisation and autonomy. It thus embraced psychology as a human science.

Phenomenological views originated in the thinking of existentialist philosophers in Europe, including Franz Brentano, Søren Kierkegaard, Martin Heidegger, Karl Jaspers, Edmund Husserl and Jean-Paul Sartre. The basic tenet of existentialism is *free will*, that is, humans are free to set their own goals in life and are responsible for their own choices. Free will cannot be measured in quantitative terms in laboratories by natural science methods. Rather than seeking for causal factors to explain human behaviour, behaviour and experience should be understood in qualitative terms within the framework of humans' own way of experiencing.

The school of thought developed against the background of mass societies and bureaucratic structures that undermine human individuality and freedom, as well as the effects of technological development, which can involve an impersonal, mechanised way of living, with individuals becoming alienated from themselves.

The thinking was that psychology should be concerned with assisting individuals in becoming their authentic selves, to have a positive view of themselves and find meaning in being. The assumption is that humans have an innate inclination towards psychological growth and self-fulfilment, and with their will can overcome environmental limitations. Victor E. Frankl, an Austrian psychiatrist, while interned in a war-time concentration camp, noted that in the direst of physical conditions humans still strive for dignity and ways of finding *meaning* in life. He survived spiritually by developing a theory of self-actualisation and therapy to reorient individuals toward finding meaning in their existence.

While Gestalt psychology focused on the meaning of the whole of perception, humanists (phenomenologists) focused on the whole of the person. Thus to understand what has meaning for individuals at a given time, not only behavioural acts, but also thinking, feelings and perceptions, i.e. personal experience, should be understood, and the individuals themselves should understand these aspects, because humans understand themselves through personal experience.

The original phenomenological method, which was also applied in humanism and in therapy in Gestalt psychology, was that of Husserl. It amounts to looking "into" oneself by means of systematically directed thought. This is established by *eidetic reduction* (eidetic means images of anything seen or experienced). By systematically reducing the images in a person's mind, i.e. images pertaining to thoughts, feelings or perceptions, the individual can be helped to "see" the real issue at stake for what it really is. The past is not regarded as significant. The difference between the phenomenological method and introspection is that, while the latter attempted to unveil the elements of the mind, phenomenology attempted to eliminate conscious content that is irrelevant at a given time or in a given situation.

This approach has also become applicable in the work situation. Industrial psychology, with its emphasis on human resource development, traditionally operates mainly from a humanistic framework in that it incorporates consciousness as an explanatory concept (Cilliers & Koortzen 1996), reflects the optimistic view of human striving in humanism, and in the study of motivation, takes into consideration the role of the will (Cilliers 1991).

An assumption in human resource development is that it is as natural for humans to work as it is to rest and to play. They have the ability to take responsibility and if provided with the right opportunities, such as challenging work and participation in decision-making, through, for example, power-sharing, they will be effective and satisfied workers. This can apply to all workers, irrespective of background, education and occupational status (Furnham 1997).

1.2.7 Cognitive psychology

Gestalt and humanistic (phenomenological) psychology culminated in the cognitive movement. This movement gained impetus in approximately 1960 and is still a major force in psychology.

It is assumed that humans are basically problem-solvers and that they can be understood by taking cognisance of the way in which they evaluate and process stimuli, make plans and react. The term "cognitive" stems from the Latin word *cogitare*, which means "to know". Thus in cognitive psychology the emphasis is on factors by which one "knows", such as thinking, intelligence, memory, learning, expectancy and perception. Perception, for example, is not seen as the mere passive registering of information, but as the processing of information through the active participation of the person (Leahy 1994). This implies that perception is a process of knowing rather than seeing.

As in Gestalt psychology, cognitive psychology emphasises the organisation of stimuli, but the subject of this psychology is seen more as understanding how information is organised in the mind.

The development of computer science has influenced this approach. The mind is seen as similar to a computer, as an information processor that can *actively process* and *integrate inputs*. The individual's sense of time, for example, is explained in terms of the integrated functioning of cognitive processes that together function as an internal clock, characterised by coherence and continuity. In a psychological sense this may be due to an innate need of humans to regulate,

plan and integrate their behaviour (Toda 1975).

In an analogy to a computer, cognitive psychology can be seen as incorporating the view of man as a machine. The simplistic mechanistic view of man as a machine in behaviourism, however, gives way to the view of man as a *complex machine* in cognitive psychology. It presents a new model of man as a machine by replacing the concepts of "stimulus" and "response" with the concepts "inputs" and "outputs" and the association between stimuli and responses is replaced with the terms "computational states" and "internal computations" (Leahy 1994). Schultz and Schultz (1996:19) indicate that whereas in behaviourism psychology had "lost its mind", it regained it through the study of consciousness in cognitive psychology. Consciousness is not, however, studied in terms of the structural elements of the mind, as it was studied in structuralism, but as a function of the mind as a coherent structure.

The view of humans as complex involves the variability and changeability of individuals. Their motivation, for example, is influenced by various interchangeable factors, and at different times. Individuals may enter the workplace with particular needs, but as they and the organisation interact, the needs are modified (Furnham 1997). This results in changes in the individuals' subsequent inputs and outputs.

Organisations are also seen as complex in that they are systems consisting of interrelated parts. They function in terms of various inputs, involving the individual, work groups, the work itself and economic and technological factors, which are transformed to outputs reflecting the organisation's effectiveness as shown in figure 1.1. The outputs also represent the outputs of individuals and groups. All the outputs can again and again be transformed to new inputs, as the organisation functions as a dynamic system.

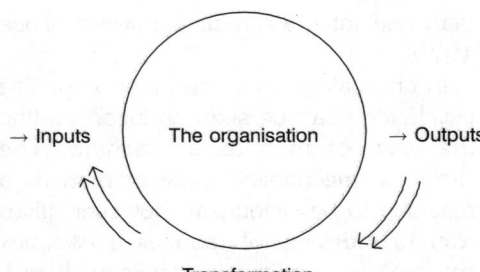

Figure 1.1   A basic system model of an organisation

1.2.8 Metapsychology

The contemporary approach in psychology is not to adhere rigidly to one or other school of thought, but to combine concepts and methods from different schools.

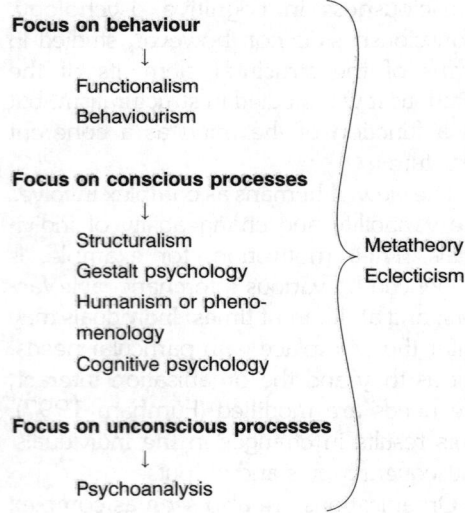

Figure 1.2   Schools of thought

This is an eclectic approach involving metatheories. Metatheories are integrative approaches that overcome the limitations of adhering to one particular theoretical point of view (Jordaan & Jordaan 1989). An example of a metatheory is a theory of motivation that incorporates a behaviourist term, "reward", as well as a cognitive term, "expectancy".

The aim of metapsychology is to place the human behaviour and experience in a holistic perspective. In a *holistic perspective* the assumption is that a human is an organised whole, functioning in totality through the interaction of structures and processes. Studying these interactions has more informational value than studying the structures and processes in themselves (Magnussen 1990). Together they can be complimentary in contributing to new theories.

Metapsychology is also characterised by dialectics and contextualism in that it engages in dialogue on different concepts and methods in different contexts of human life and experience. Psychological factors are, for example, placed in their physical, social and cultural context (Altman 1990). As these contexts are characterised by diversity, metapsychology incorporates concepts from psychology, sociology, and economics. Metapsychology not only studies humans in relation to their physical environment, but also in relation to their transcendental environment, which includes theology and philosophy (Meyer et al. 1989).

The boundaries of psychology are constantly being expanded by absorbing new types of content, recognising the complexity of the phenomena in studies, and using more varied research strategies (Pervin 1990).

1.3 INDUSTRIAL PSYCHOLOGY

1.3.1 History of industrial psychology

Industrial psychology became a legitimate, specialist field of psychology in 1910 (Muchinsky et al. 1998). Major contributions to its development reflected the pragmatism of functionalism with the focus on individual differences and measurement.

The first application of psychological principles in advertising was presented by

Walter Dill Scott, a student of Wundt's, in a series of lectures on advertising at an American university. Scott published two books on the subject in 1903 and 1908. He also became interested in personnel psychology and made contributions to the selection of salespeople, executives and military personnel.

A scientific approach to management was heralded by Frederick W. Taylor, a mechanical engineer, in the publication of his book *The principles of scientific management* in 1911.

Frederick W. Taylor

Taylor's premise was that the organisational goal of high production at low cost, and workers' expectations of high wages, could be reconciled by analysing every component of a job to determine the most efficient method, by selecting the best worker for a job, training him or her in the correct methods of executing the job and paying incentives for greater efficiency (Vlok 1967). Taylor's principles were first applied by the Bethlehem Steel Company in America. His work gained wide acceptance in industry and became known as Taylorism.

Taylorism was based on the view that man is a rational-economic being. It held the view that humans are inherently lazy, inefficient and undependable, that only

financial incentives will induce them to work and their fallibility can be counteracted by training them according to clearly set standards.

Criticism of Taylorism included seeing it as exploitation of the worker, without consideration of individual psychological needs. It was also seen as fostering unemployment, because individuals became specialists in a particular job, which made them stay in their jobs, not making room for others. This also negated their personal growth and innovation.

In 1913 the publication of a book by Hugo Münsterberg, a German psychologist who also studied under Wundt and later went to America, illustrated the differences between natural science and applied science as it applies to selection of workers, designing work situations and sales jobs. A well-known laboratory experiment that Münsterberg conducted was to simulate the operation of a trolley car to ascertain what contributed to the operator's conducting the job safely. The conclusion was that it required the ability to simultaneously comprehend all the operations of the trolley car (Muchinsky et al. 1998).

During the First World War (1914-1918) industrial psychology gained more recognition when psychologists were employed in screening recruits and selecting them to the best advantage for jobs in the army. Army psychologists devised a test, the Army Alpha Test, for measuring intelligence. After discovering that 30% of recruits were illiterate, the Army Beta Test, for people who could not read, was developed (Muchinsky et al. 1998). During the war psychologists gained knowledge of collapse under stress and after the war, of readjustment to civilian life.

In 1924 a series of experiments, which took several years, were launched at the Hawthorne Works of the Western Electric Company in America. Psychologists from Harvard University, under the direction of

Elton Mayo, conducted the experiments. The objective was to determine the influence of environmental working conditions, such as different levels of illumination and different lengths of rest periods, on productivity. The research revealed that factors other than environmental factors influenced productivity. Production did not decrease and even improved as conditions became unpleasant. The results were interpreted as suggesting that the workers worked harder because of the interest taken in them. This was seen as satisfying their needs for recognition, for feeling important and useful. During the experiments the workers also formed informal friendship groups, which gave rise to higher group morale, and was interpreted as satisfying their needs for affiliation.

Criticism of the Hawthorne experiments came after findings that the positive effects suggested by the experiments were not necessarily lasting – they could last for a few days or two years, depending on the type of work situation (Muchinsky et al. 1998).

Nevertheless, the experiments had an impact on the development of industrial psychology and influenced the rise of the human relations approach. This approach emphasised the importance of social needs, which were seen as more motivating than financial incentives.

When the Second World War (1939-1945) broke out, psychologists had more refined selection and placement techniques and these were used for officer training as well as for employee selection in civilian life.

In South Africa, industrial psychology had its origin as an experimental science in 1946, with the establishment in Johannesburg of the National Institute for Personnel Research. South African contributors to the development of industrial psychology include R.W. Wilcocks, who developed intelligence and aptitude tests in the 1970s and P.R. Skawran, who worked on the selection of pilots for the armed forces (Raubenheimer 1987). Major contributions to the field are made by the Human Sciences Research Council in Pretoria, where the focus is primarily on the development of psychometric instruments.

The interests of psychologists in South Africa are coordinated by a professional association, the Psychological Society of South Africa (PsySSA). It has institutes for the various fields of psychology, including the Institute for Industrial Psychology. PsySSA publishes a journal, the *South African Journal of Psychology,* which publishes research findings in psychology. Another journal, the *Journal of Industrial Psychology,* focuses mainly on publishing research in the context of the work situation.

To qualify as a professional industrial psychologist a master's degree and registration with the South African Professional Board of Psychology is required, in terms of the Medical, Dental and Supplementary Health Service Professions Act. The function of the board is to set requirements for professional training and conduct.

1.3.2 Applied fields of industrial psychology

The fields that must be studied before registration as a professional psychologist are the following:

1.3.2.1 Research methodology

In this field the student becomes skilled in applying scientific methods, including testing and statistical evaluation of data.

1.3.2.2 Personnel psychology

This field is concerned with recruitment, selection, placement and training of employees, as well as the study of factors that affect the utilisation of personnel (also known as human resources). It focuses on individual differences and predicting a fit between the employee and the organisation. Personnel psychology is also called human resources management.

1.3.2.3 Organisational psychology

This field is concerned with the organisation as a system involving individuals and groups, and the structure and dynamics of the organisation. The basic aims are fostering worker adjustment, satisfaction and productivity, as well as organisational efficiency. Organisational psychology also includes management psychology.

1.3.2.4 Career psychology

This field is concerned with career and organisational choice, career issues that affect individuals in the course of their careers and changes in organisations that affect careers. The focus includes career counselling and career planning and development.

Other fields that must be studied in order to practise as an industrial psychologist are the following:

1.3.2.5 Ergonomics

This field is concerned with understanding human performance in man-machine systems. The focus is on the design of the structure of equipment and of work itself, including the interaction of physical and human factors. It is also referred to as human factors psychology and engineering psychology.

1.3.2.6 Consumer psychology

This field is concerned with decision-making and motivation in searching for, purchasing, using and evaluating products and services. It aims at facilitating communication between producers and consumers.

1.3.2.7 Labour relations

This field is concerned with problems between employers and employees and issues presented and handled by labour unions. The focus is on conflict, restructure of conflict and negotiation with regard to employee rights according to legislation.

1.3.2.8 Occupational mental health

This field is concerned with the psychological wellbeing of the worker, involving adjustment and maladjustment in the work context. The focus is on psychological conditions and behaviour that thwart optimal functioning in work roles and methods of evaluating and managing psychological health.

1.4 CONCLUSION

Psychology has a history of divergent theoretical approaches. Some approaches have similar orientations, such as the orientation in functionalism and behaviourism to explain behaviour in practical natural science terms, and the orientation in Gestalt and humanistic (phenomenological) psychology to understand experience in psychological, human terms.

Some approaches also have directly opposing orientations. For example, the focus on behaviour in functionalism and behaviourism is in opposition to the focus on consciousness in structuralism, Gestalt psychology, humanism (phenomenology) and cognitive psychology. Cognitive psychology is also in opposition to the focus on the unconscious in psychoanalysis.

Some approaches emphasise past experience, while others consider only present experience as significant. Structuralism, Gestalt psychology and humanism (phenomenology) focus on the present, while behaviourism and psychoanalysis focus on the past.

This diversity provides various orientations for studying humans in the work context. The basic aim of industrial psychology is understanding and explaining, as well as predicting and influencing, human behaviour and experience in the work context, while psychology in general is concerned with all the various contexts in which humans function. Although industrial psychology has developed its own theories and methods, it remains an applied field of psychology, incorporating the theories and methodology of psychology. In every profession knowledge and insight of the basic discipline from which it evolved serve as underpinning for the fields of professional practice. Therefore, the professional study of psychology in the workplace requires insight in the theory, subject matter and methodology of general psychology.

Self-evaluating questions

1. Describe the subject matter and methods in approaches that view psychology as a natural science.

2. Describe the subject matter and methods in approaches that view psychology as a human science.

3. Apply the variables in the S-R and S-O-R approaches to the work situation.

4. Explain the origins and aims of psychoanalysis.

5. Describe the assumptions in cognitive psychology and indicate their relevance to the work context.

6. Briefly explain the differences between the schools of thought.

7. Discuss the statement "industrial psychology is an applied field of psychology" with reference to schools of thought in psychology.

Methodology 2

Ziel Bergh _____

CONTENTS

Learning outcomes

After studying this chapter you should be able to:

- describe the goals and principles of scientific thinking
- illustrate the difference between inductive and deductive modes of thinking
- describe the steps in scientific research
- differentiate between different types of variables
- explain different types of research strategies
- describe different types of research methods or techniques
- differentiate between descriptive and inferential (non-descriptive) statistics
- illustrate four levels of measurement with examples
- illustrate and describe a normal distribution
- differentiate between the mean, median and mode
- give the meaning and value of correlation and regression in words
- describe the terms validity and reliability
- identify possible errors in research and assessment
- understand ethical codes for psychological research and assessment
- describe the issues of test bias and fairness in test use

Key concepts

research, scientific thinking, verification, empirical, logical thinking, hypothesis, variables, measurement scales, descriptive, inferential, distribution, central values, variance, correlation, regression, ethical codes, bias

2.1 INTRODUCTION

Research implies the systematisation of knowledge, in which philosophy, common sense, speculation and hypotheses are tested in objective ways and the logical coherence of phenomena becomes accepted as scientific truth.

The goals of research in psychology are the systematic inquiry of human behaviour to describe, explain and predict behaviour and solve problems of a human nature. These scientific goals endeavour to make the fit between individuals and groups and the various contexts in which they function (environments), such as the workplace, as optimal as possible. In the work context this is found in applications such as job design and job description, personnel selection and placement, assessment of potential

and work performance, improvement of productivity, managerial assessment, training and development, career counselling, physical, occupational and mental health and organisational development.

2.2 SCIENTIFIC THINKING

The primary objective of a science such as psychology is to establish rules to describe, explain and predict phenomena using analysis, comparison, classification and description (Mouton & Marais 1990; Kerlinger 1973; Mark 1996). In this regard a science can be defined as a system of concepts (constructs or statements), theories, findings and methods that is generally accepted by other scientists or supported by other scientific findings. Because of its verified theory and methods, industrial psychology is a science in many respects, compared to pseudo and unscientific psychological knowledge like our own subjective ideas and theories, folklore, prejudices and superstition.

A science is not about the topics or contents being studied, but rather the underlying thinking processes and approaches utilised in studying and solving problems. In this regard, although much controversy and untested speculation still exist, many concepts and methods from the various psychological approaches can be regarded as scientific truths, because they have stood the test of unbiased and objective research. At the same time we must heed the warnings that much research in psychology is plagued by poor research processes. Sources of non-scientific knowledge often used to make decisions in organisations, are personal experience, so-called reliable sources and authorities, intuition, untested logical reasoning, analogies and cultural norms and values (Dipboye et al. 1994). Other sources are the many subjective measurement errors which people make in their judgements, because they are human and are influenced by their own values and prejudices. The following attributes characterise a scientific approach (Mouton & Marais 1990; Rosenberg & Daly 1993; Dipboye et al. 1994).

2.2.1 Empirical thinking

"Empirical" generally refers to "tested" knowledge and conclusions based on direct, sometimes indirect, but systematic, repeated and incontrovertible observation. Empirical scientific thinking differs from pure speculation or guessing, in which conclusions are based on own ideas, intuition, casual observations and even our own subjective preferences and prejudices.

2.2.2 Verification and objectivity

Verification means that research and its reported findings must be of such a nature that other researchers are able to repeat the research under more or less the same circumstances using similar methods. Verification ensures certainty about, and extension of knowledge, and even allows for previous findings and mistakes to be rectified.

2.2.3 Testability

Testability means that research questions must be realistic and possible to assess. The concepts or variables being researched must be precisely defined and measured against our current knowledge and available assessment methods. Some concepts in psychology are difficult or even impossible to measure, such as metaphysical aspects, dreams and unconscious states. In science, and in psychology, pseudo-science sometimes results because of poor application of assessment and research knowledge and practices.

Kerlinger (1973) supports these principles when he asserts that scientific methods differ from common sense in that they force scientists to be systematic, exert control, look for relationships between things and avoid speculative or metaphysical explanations.

2.2.4 Logical thinking and reasoning

Different types of problems demand different problem-solving and decision-making skills.

Logical thought is not a scientific method in itself, but logic must be the basis of all scientific thinking. It allows for hypotheses to be logically derived and for the systematic and realistic interpretation of data and results. By dint of logical principles, facts or truths, singly or jointly, may yield new truths, which implies that any recognised truth is and must be based on unimputable grounds.

Induction and deduction are modes of logical thinking.

Deduction is arriving at a specific conclusion from general principles. For instance, fair remuneration promotes work satisfaction, therefore the organisation pays fair wages, therefore workers in the organisation are satisfied.

Most definitions and hypotheses are derived through the process of deduction. Definitions are statements of "what things are" based on what is already known about things. If, for instance, we deduce that "personality is the result of the interaction between hereditary or biological factors and environmental influences after birth", we have arrived at a truth that is widely accepted.

Induction is deducing general rules from specific principles, the latter being accepted as existing truths. For instance, workers in the organisation are satisfied, the organisation pays fair wages, therefore remuneration affects work satisfaction.

Induction is applied when hypotheses are tested, because we generalise from specific research findings.

Both deductive and inductive reasoning, though quite logical, can produce unrealistic or unreasonable conclusions, especially if biased by hidden agendas, prejudices, opinions and emotions.

Other forms of thinking and reasoning are represented by the processes of imagery, conceptualisation (the forming and classification of concepts), judgement, problem-solving, decision-making and creativity.

In most scientific journals, for instance the *South African Journal of Psychology* and the *South African Journal of Industrial Psychology*, the criteria for publication are in accordance with these standards for scientific research, ensuring scientific control and a scientific way of reporting on and communicating about research processes and results.

2.3 STEPS IN THE RESEARCH PROCESSES: RESEARCH DESIGN

Research in the social or behavioural sciences includes many disciplines, such as psychology, sociology, education, ethnology, criminology, social work, management and economic behaviour, communication, nursing, psychiatry, geria-

trics and health sciences such as sport and recreation.

Researchers from different disciplines or schools of thought have their own preferences for the methods used, for instance for more qualitative or quantitative methods or different research models. In general, however, researchers follow a systematic method comprising certain steps. Research design is really a decision-making process in which the investigator must take decisions to solve the what, how and why of the specific research problem, all aimed at making the process of research and the findings as unbiased and objective as possible (Kerlinger 1973; Leedy 1989).

When studying the following sections, apply the concepts, principles and methods to the following work-related problem.

> You are a training consultant and want to market the best method for training managers on all levels to use PCs effectively.

In the following sections answers are provided to some of the questions you might have while doing your research, for instance which process and steps must be followed, which research strategy is best, which variables must be identified and controlled, how the necessary information will be obtained, what research hypotheses will be arrived at, how the data will be organised and analysed, which research errors are to be avoided and which ethical aspects must be considered.

The process and steps in research, which are really interdependent, are reflected in figure 2.1.

This process indicates that research design is a cyclical or systemic process in which all aspects interact to determine effective research and valid findings.

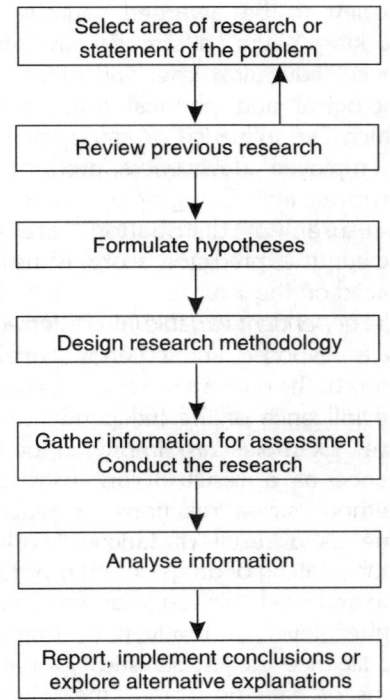

Figure 2.1 Steps in the research process

2.3.1 Defining or stating the problem

In broad terms this means establishing the macro field and goals of research, for instance organisational or personnel psychology, but more specifically defining the precise research problem or research question in terms of a soluble problem such as "what is the relationship between the method of training and training success or learning" or "how will employees react when losing their jobs or when working on a computer". An early decision must be taken as to whether basic or applied research will be undertaken.

Basic research is directed at obtaining knowledge about a subject, studying topics and verifying and building theory. In clinical psychology, theories are constructed by using, among other things, case studies, as in the case of Freud's psychoanalytical theory, which was based on observations of client behaviours. In the psychometric method the trait or factor models on aspects of personality, for instance Cattell's trait theory and various factor models on abilities, are the result of correlational research or the relationship between variables.

Applied research is directed at establishing whether concepts and methods are valid and applicable in practice, such as when managerial training courses are offered according to, for instance, situational leadership theory, decision-making theory or contingency theory; or when management tries to improve work performance by attempting to motivate employees according to equity theory or needs theory; or when we try to assess persons or treat maladjustment according to the assumptions and practices of psychoanalysis, behaviouristic theory or by following a more humanistic approach. Boehm (1980) describes the differences between academic research and practical research in organisations. In the latter, research is often directed at work problems and where it is difficult to have efficient controls.

2.3.2 Identification of variables

In a research project it is crucially important to isolate and define the relevant variables, since they will influence the research design (for instance working with one or two groups; which variables should be controlled, and how; and the selection of assessment and statistical procedures).

Variables in research refer to those characteristics of humans which vary and can be allocated numerical values in some way. Behaviour and processes are derived from the various theories and concepts of human behaviour and are used in the various application areas. The researcher must conceptualise or describe variables precisely in order to be able to measure them. Variables are controlled and manipulated by the investigator in order to assess possible relationships. Examples of variables are personality traits such as intelligence, motivation, anxiety, self-efficacy, self-concept and independence; socioeconomic factors such as education, income, job levels, employment status (e.g. unemployment); biographical factors such as gender, age, matrimonial status; environmental variables such as pollution, noise, working hours, supervision and factors such as attitudes, values and political and religious affiliations. These variables are either in the person (intrapersonal), between people (interpersonal), about the person (personal information such as age) or in or from the environment (interactional).

Research is used to establish whether phenomena exist, are related, stay consistent or change (variability), and enables people to explain, describe and predict behaviour in many areas of human conduct. Statisticians refer to this variability as variance, meaning the amount of observed change (or consistency) in behaviour within a person over time or in various situations (intrapersonal), between persons (interpersonal), or as a result of environmental influences (interactional).

An important classification of variables in research, especially in experimental research, divides variables into dependent and independent variables. This relates to the relationship of cause and effect between variables.

- *An independent variable* (also referred to as a stimulus or predictor variable) refers to an antecedent state, event or phenomenon, or what may cause changes in other phenomena. In this sense the independent variable in work settings is mostly applied as a predictor variable, inasmuch as its relationship with occupational performance is established. The independent variable is measured and controlled by the researcher, for instance the type of training to be given, the amount of

money to be awarded, number of working hours, differences in intelligence, education level and other psychological and physical traits, all of which can influence or cause variance in employee effectiveness, productivity, turnover etc. On graphs where the measurement distributions are depicted, the predictor score is usually placed on the x-axis.

- *The dependent variable* (also referred to as a response and criterion variable) refers to the outcome or consequence of the influence of the independent variable. Examples are improved performance as a result of an instruction method, stress reactions or reaction time as a result of fatigue (working hours), taking of drugs or better production and academic results as a result of a higher level of motivation, training, intelligence etc. In statistical presentations of data on graphs the criterion variable is usually shown on the y-axis. In statistics the relationship between predictors and criterion scores are measured according to inferential statistical methods such as correlation, regression and variance analysis. Criteria or standards for decision-making is an important issue in the work context, for instance to find personality-related criteria or work behaviours which can be predicted by various types of personality measurements.

If you want to determine whether "a relationship exists between training success and the type of training programme on PCs for managers" you will work with the following variables: the job level of the subjects – they must all be managers – is a constant which you must control, as is the type of computer and the scoring system, which must be the same for everyone, and possible variables such as age and education. The type of training programme is the independent variable, which will be manipulated by you by using different types of instruction. The type of training programme is supposed to influence training success, which is the dependent variable. If differences in management level, age and education exist or if different types of computers are used, these uncontrolled factors are intervening or moderator variables which can influence the relationship between the independent and dependent variables.

An *intervening variable,* or moderator or confounding variable, is any extraneous variable, usually uncontrolled or unexpected, that intervenes in or moderates the relationship between the stimulus and response variables. It is, for example, possible that work motivation is not only an effect of financial reward but can be moderated by factors such as gender, culture, interest, work attitudes, health, management policies and the type of work.

Another classification of variables is based on the nature of the numerical values that variables assume. Broadly speaking we can assume that some psychological and related variables take on definite values in whole (round) numbers, while others can assume any value, including fractions and decimals.

- A *discrete variable* is, for example, the number of books, people, cases, number of men or women, age groups or occupational groups. Discrete variables can only be expressed in whole numbers. It is meaningless to speak of 1,05 people, although this is sometimes done to indicate average numbers of people in census surveys.
- A *continuous variable* can assume any value between certain points. A person can be 17, 23 or 55 years of age; 1,23 m tall; attain an IQ score of 110,50 or have an average score on a work performance task of 3,5 on a seven-point scale.

2.3.3 Reviewing the literature

A study of relevant literature (theory and research) will inform the researcher of existing knowledge and research needs, applicable concepts and theory, as well as research findings on the chosen topic, besides revealing methodologies utilised in previous research and possible weaknesses and problems experienced.

In this regard the importance of theory in a science must be realised. A theory is a set of assumptions or propositions, together with relevant concepts, used to explain and predict psychic and behavioural phenomena and processes and possible relationships between such variables in a systematic way (Kerlinger 1973). Theories provide concepts, generate research questions and hypotheses, support research findings and explain and even predict behaviour. Research topics and methods are embedded in a comprehensive theoretical frame of reference. If, for example, you are researching the effects of conditioning on employees' job performance, you are working within the behaviouristic frame of reference, and may possibly use direct observation as an assessment method.

2.3.4 Formulating hypotheses

Is it possible for you to state research hypotheses in your task of training managers to use PCs?

It is necessary to state research hypotheses, which are developed from the research objectives and the research problem or question. Hypotheses are the application of deductive and inductive reasoning in order to formulate specific research questions, either from general or very specific information about the variables in question. Hypotheses also serve to subdivide the problem into various related questions.

A hypothesis is a provisional, assumed or tentative statement or guess about the relationship between independent and dependent variables, for instance "training methods will not affect training success in managers". Hypotheses may be formulated from existing theory or from previous research.

Hypotheses are general statements only, and must still be verified by the findings of a research project. In this respect hypotheses are stated as a statistical hypothesis in which a relationship is assumed or a null or alternate hypothesis in which a "non-relationship" is postulated, which is done to have a standard to test the initial hypothesis. The purpose of research essentially is to prove whether stated hypotheses are correct or not.

2.3.5 Research strategies

The research strategy is the overall or broad approach, incorporating the type and location of research being utilised. It is important to consider whether the research will be executed in natural or experimental settings, and the amount of control researchers want to exert over variables, conditions and research participants. In general experimental research findings are more valid. However, due to the small numbers of research participants and the unnaturalness of the research location, it is more difficult to apply the findings to other situations. Research in the field or in natural settings may have more numbers and is more generally applicable, but, because of less control, the findings are often less valid.

Experimental research, such as laboratory research, is done in contrived or "unnatural" settings in which there can be very strict controls. The investigator is able to control and manipulate the measurements to be certain about the cause and effect relationship between the dependent and independent variables. A research design decision has to be taken whether to use only the experimental group or more groups, for instance a control group for comparison purposes.

Field research, however, is preferred in the work context, because it is undertaken in natural situations such as a factory, home or school.

Action research designs are related to field research and involve researchers and participants in obtaining information in the workplace. In the process of the research and from the feedback of results, problems are solved as they unfold. In South Africa, as in many developing and changing countries, many transformation problems are solved in the process of working.

In *survey designs* people are asked on questionnaires and in interviews how they feel about or perceive things, their attitudes on issues, what complaints they have, what they are satisfied with, etc. The aim of survey research is to gather quantitative information about human behaviour at a specific time and place (cross-sectional surveys) or over longer periods (longitudinal surveys). In organisational diagnostic surveys employees' attitudes to various organisational issues are investigated by asking questions about work satisfaction, feelings about remuneration and fringe benefits, supervision, physical working conditions, organisational communication, opportunities for promotion, and prejudices in the workplace. Survey researchers try to use as many measurements (samples) as possible from the available employees (population). A problem in survey research is the intentions or response styles of respondents when answering questionnaires, for instance agreeing on all items, providing incomplete answers, etc.

The researcher must also decide if the information required must be qualitative or quantitative in nature. This will determine whether more subjective methods, such as observations or interviews, are used, with the interpretation consisting of subjective opinions and descriptions; or whether "hard", objective measurements such as standardised tests and ratings are used to gather data, with statistical procedures and norms to interpret findings. For research findings to be accepted as valid for people in all situations (generalisability), the researcher must do sampling to obtain a representative sample of cases or measurements from what is available (population). In research on personality and psychopathology, it is possible to use case study designs involving only one participant, or a few.

2.3.6 Specific methods to gather data

Except in strict experimental procedures where causes of behaviour are researched, techniques are directed at finding relationships or links between variables by using correlational types of research.

There are many methods to assess human behaviours and related information.

2.3.6.1 Natural observation

The observation of behaviour can be in experimental or natural situations. The researcher could be an active participant, as in an experiment, while other observation can be unobtrusive, such as watching the driving habits of motorists. The research subjects can be aware or unaware of being assessed or observed. Observations can be made using various methods, such as rating scales, questionnaires, physiological measurements and technologies such as video recordings and computerised assessments.

2.3.6.2 Interviews

An interview is essentially a technique for discourse or interaction between two or more people, in which verbal, but also non-verbal, communication is usually used to achieve a certain purpose, such as gathering or giving information or influencing behaviour. To assess and observe the variables in the research design or assessment plan, a suitable

atmosphere must be created in which the right questions can be asked and appropriate responses given.

In *unstructured interviews* the researcher usually only facilitates communication, observing behaviour and not asking too many direct questions.

Assessing employee attributes

Structured interviews are planned in detail beforehand. The topics to be discussed and even specific questions to be asked are prepared in advance, and situations in the interview to which the subject must react are catered for. Structured interviews are often conducted according to an interview schedule in which the interviewer asks the questions and records the answers. During interviews the researcher plays a very active role and has a strong presence, and must not allow his or her own values and attitudes to influence answers or actions.

2.3.6.3 Archival sources

Researchers can utilise existing information and prior or historical knowledge to apply to a research design. Personnel and organisational records on productivity, absences, promotions and accidents is one source. For more general research, for example on aspects of a country or prominent persons, information can be obtained from articles in newspapers and books, reports from parliament, government documents, letters, speeches and financial analyses. Simonton (1986) analysed personal, biographical and performance information from archival sources to assess and compare the management styles of American presidents. The Truth and Reconciliation Commission in South Africa is using historical data and experiences in the quest to resolve people's conflicts.

2.3.6.4 Physiological measurement

A definite relationship exists between bodily processes and psychological behaviours and vice versa. Personality and other psychological disorders are related to many physical and psychological diseases. In work psychology this knowledge is important when assessing the causes and consequences of fatigue and work stress and in designing an optimal fit between the physical workplace and the employee in terms of physical and psychological needs. Measurements of bodily reactions and reflexes, muscular tension, perspiration, brain activities, blood pressure, heart rates, skin temperatures and nervous system functions are taken to determine work adjustment. The lie detector apparatus used in criminal and insurance cases tests biological reactions to assess the honesty of people.

2.3.6.5 Psychological tests

Psychological tests are standardised methods to assess broad or specific aspects of behaviour. Standardisation means that instruments are constructed for a specific purpose and people use standard procedures in administration and for scoring and interpretation (Owen & Taljaard 1989; Gregory 1996). Questionnaires, projective techniques and behavioural or observation techniques are mostly used in psychological testing.

Psychological questionnaires or self-report inventories consist of sets of prior constructed questions, usually in multi-choice format, directed at obtaining specific information to assess a certain domain of personality or other specified behaviour as reported by the person. The use of psychological questionnaires is restricted to qualified psychologists and to those specified in law and by governing bodies.

Many non-psychological questionnaires are used freely, especially in survey research on human behaviour and organisational processes for organisational diagnosis.

Psychological tests can assess the following:

- *Personality* (non-cognitive tests), which consists of behaviours, emotions, characteristic traits, motivation, how the person acts and copes in various situations, as well as factors that influence how behaviour is shaped and develops. Personality testing is subdivided into assessment through standardised psychological questionnaires, projective techniques, behavioural methods such as observations, interviews, rating scales and check lists and physiological measurements.
- *Cognitive or mental abilities,* which refer to the thinking, reasoning and problem-solving capabilities of personality. Such tests usually include testing of intelligence, aptitudes and achievement as well as creativity and cognitive development, and are done using various types of verbal and non-verbal tests as well as practical performance tests.

- *Values, interests and attitudes* are tested to assess various aspect of career choice and development. Questionnaires are mostly used.
- *Environments and the fit between people and their environments.* This is based on the assumptions that human behaviour is a function of interactions of personal and environmental characteristics. For this reason, career choice for instance, has been coupled to the congruence between personality type and a certain occupational or environmental type. In the workplace, it is now general practice to design the physical and social aspects of work to suit the total profile of employees as far as possible. Practitioners continually monitor the psychological culture and climate of institutions and organisations by keeping track of employees' and even customers' feelings and attitudes towards management and the organisation.

2.3.7 Levels of measurement scales

It is important to know what type of information the measurement of certain variables by certain instruments will provide, and what types of mathematical and statistical manipulations can be executed when using a certain type of measurement scale. One of the tasks of researchers is to assign numerical values to the responses from subjects. Some information may have "real" value, such as answers on an IQ or achievement test. Such answers can be mathematically or statistically manipulated by addition, multiplication or more involved calculations. Other numbers assigned to information from subjects don't have "real" value except to classify or order data, and they must be calculated and interpreted as such.

Four levels of measurement scales, each with unique characteristics, can be distinguished:

- *Nominal measurement,* the simplest type of scale, refers to the classification of people or things without there being an order and quantitative value, so that similarities or differences with respect to variables can be indicated only by categorising. This is the case when numbering the players in a rugby team, classifying employees as either male or female, classifying persons into certain types of jobs and recording incidences of diseases. If numerical values are allocated, say one for male, two for female or one to 15 for the various rugby team positions, the numbers merely have a labelling or naming value. Such figures are purely qualitative data with no numerical value and are unsuitable for mathematical calculations, except for counting.
- *Ordinal measurement* scales contain all the characteristics of the nominal scale, but indicate rank and order, such as highest to lowest. Employees may be ranked on job performance from highest to lowest or job preferences ranked from most to least preferred. Note, however, that although increasing precedence is indicated, such as more or greater than, the ranking is relative and the real quantitative differences or intervals are not known, for example between the first-placed and last-placed employee on their performance rankings. Mathematical manipulations do not make much sense in ordinal scales, except if special statistical tools are utilised.
- *Interval measurement comprises* all the characteristics of nominal and ordinal scales, and includes *numerical values of definite intervals.* Zero (0) values, however, cannot be indicated. Because the exact zero point is not known, the exact distance of any score from the zero point can also not be determined, and for this reason one interval score cannot be divided into another. Most measurements of psychological variables in tests

and questionnaires of IQ, personality traits, attitudes, aptitudes and values are done according to the interval scale method. On a few IQ scores, e.g. 70, 80, 90, 100, 110 and 120, it is known that the higher scores indicate more of the trait, and the intervals or differences between 70 to 80 and between 110 to 120 are the same; the same holds for temperature as measured on Fahrenheit and Celsius scales. It is meaningful to say that an increase of 10° (20 to 30) is equal to a decrease of 10 (40 to 30) and that this increase is the same as an increase of 50 to 60. Since absolute zero points do not apply to interval scales, it cannot be said that an IQ of 120 is twice as much as an IQ of 60 or that a temperature of 60° is twice as warm as 30° or that 0° C or 32° F indicate an absence of temperature. It is impossible in the assessment of human behaviour to say that a person has zero of a trait, even if a scale might indicate it as such. Interval scales are suited to certain statistical calculations like adding and subtracting, which enables us to determine averages (mean scores), standard deviations and correlations and to transform raw scores into various types of other derived scores which can be interpreted more meaningfully.

- *Ratio scales* represent the highest level of measurement and integrate all the characteristics of the previous three levels of measurement, but can indicate absolute values and definite zero points and permit the application of all mathematical functions and more advanced statistical techniques. Few, if any, psychological variables are suited to be measured by ratio scaling techniques. Physical measurements like time, distance and weight are suited to these scales. In ergonomics as well as in health psychology, physical and physiological measurements are sometimes used to assess the relationship between physical aspects and psychological behaviours in the workplace.

2.3.8 Analysing data: basic statistics

Statistical techniques are used to systematise information quantitatively in order to summarise, interpret and draw meaningful conclusions from vast amounts of data on human behaviour. Generally speaking data can be depicted and interpreted by either descriptive statistics and non-descriptive or inferential statistics.

Descriptive statistics are used to organise and summarise data. It comprises frequency distributions of scores, the normal distribution curve, measures of central tendency (mean, median and modus), measures of variability or dispersion and even correlation in some instances.

Inferential statistics or non-descriptive statistics like correlation, regression and factor analysis enable the researcher to make certain inferences, conclusions or predictions with reference to probability laws or degrees of significance.

2.3.8.1 Descriptive statistics

When measurements of individuals or groups are conducted on a certain measuring scale the data should be arranged and processed so that the numerical values can eventually be interpreted meaningfully. In most cases a summary of data will start with a *raw data matrix* (data as gathered) which is really only a presentation of each subject's scores in rows and columns. Raw data, however, cannot be interpreted meaningfully and must be accurately summarised.

Tables, graphs and figures are popular ways to present numerical summarised data.

Frequency distributions

Frequencies (*f*) refer to the number of times (incidence) that a measurement occurs in a group or with an individual. When a number of frequencies are depicted or arranged, the presentation is known as a frequency distribution. Note the following percentages obtained in a test after an on the job training course:

66, 69, 68, 66, 68, 74, 69, 69, 67, 69, 72, 70, 70, 68, 67, 73, 72, 68, 70, 69, 71, 70, 69, 72, 71, 68, 67, 69, 72, 71.

These scores can firstly be presented from lowest to highest in the form of a table, to indicate how the marks obtained in the training test are distributed.

Marks (%)	Cases	f (frequency)
66	11	2
67	111	3
68	~~1111~~	5
69	~~1111~~-11	7
70	~~111~~	4
71	111	3
72	~~111~~	4
73	1	1
74	1	1
		N = 30

Table 2.1 Frequency table of marks obtained in training test

You can see at a glance how scores are distributed. Another important advantage of a frequency table is that large numbers of measurements can be divided into class intervals or a grouped frequency distribution for a more orderly presentation. In the case of 100 students (N = 100) we can classify their marks as shown in table 2.2 where the class interval size of 10 is used.

From table 2.2 it is immediately clear that half of the students obtained marks between 50 and 59 and that the marks of most students were between 50 and 69. Such information is important to, say, a training officer or a lecturer, because it can be seen that the test was rather easy. From table 2.2 it is also clear that the marks increase or decrease more or less equally or symmetrically to either side of the frequency of 50.

Marks (%)	Frequency (f)
90 – 99	1
80 – 89	3
70 – 79	5
60 – 69	13
50 – 59	50
40 – 49	8
30 – 39	8
20 – 29	6
10 – 19	5
0 – 9	1
	N = 100

Table 2.2 Grouped frequency table: class intervals

Statistically no further meaningful deductions can be made from such a table.

Such distributions can, however, be presented more clearly visually through graphs. In graphs the frequencies are represented by means of areas rather than entries. The following are merely simple presentations of two kinds of graphs, namely the histogram or bar graph (fig. 2.2) and the frequency polygon (fig. 2.3). These graphs (and the bar diagram) all have a vertical left-hand line (y-axis) or ordinate and a horizontal base line (x-axis) or abscissa axis that meet each other at a 90-degree angle. The variables or class intervals are entered on the x-axis and the frequencies on the y-axis. In the following two graphs the data from table 2.2 are used.

In figure 2.2 each block or area represents the number of people (f) who obtained a certain mark; six people fall into the measurement class of 20-29, 50 into the measurement class of 50-59, etc.

In addition, it is clear that the graph declines approximately symmetrically to the left and right from the middle. On closer examination it is clear that the distribution inclines slightly to the right because most cases, namely 72, occur in the interval 50-99 and only 28 in the

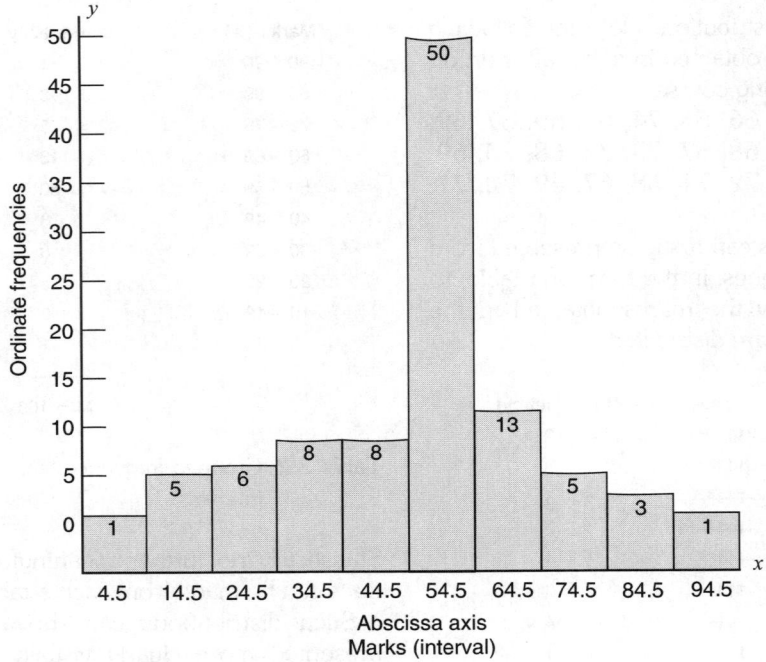

Figure 2.2 Histogram

interval 0-49. If exactly the same number of cases occurred in all the intervals on both sides of the centre, it would then have formed an absolutely normal, symmetrical or bell-shaped distribution (this is discussed later).

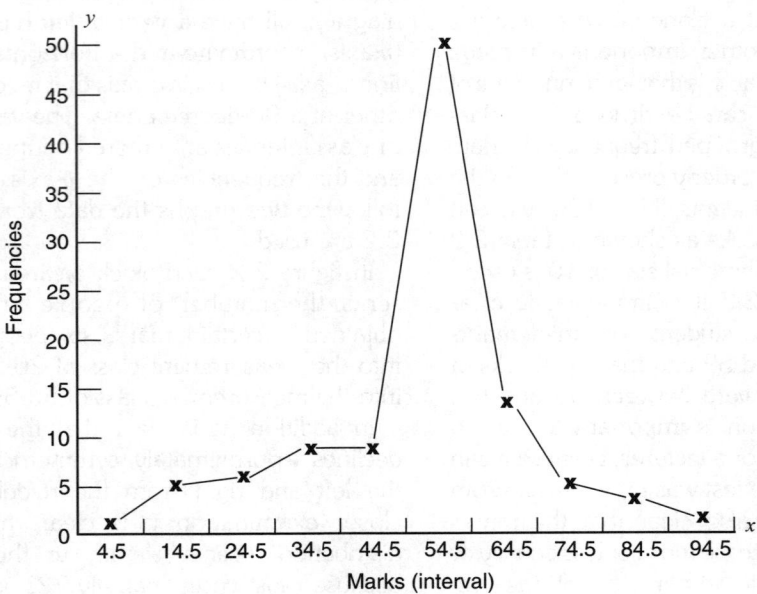

Figure 2.3 Frequency polygon

In figure 2.3 dots are connected to give a graphic line, instead of columns, to indicate the frequencies of intervals and the distribution. The data on the frequency polygon in figure 2.3 resemble those in figure 2.2.

All deductions from the histogram can be done in the same way from the frequency polygon.

The normal distribution curve

It has been pointed out that a distribution can be absolutely symmetrical or bell-shaped, in other words it can be a *normal distribution* if an equal number of cases occur to the left and the right of the centre. A normal distribution has the following unique characteristics:

- It is symmetrical, bell-shaped, with a single peak in the middle and an even decline to each side.
- The distributions of the areas in the curve are of constant proportion, that is, the distributions are within certain distances from the mean $(\overline{X})$. In the normal distribution formula, mean and standard deviations are used to describe the nature of score or case distributions.

With most human characteristics, particularly when a great number of measurements are taken, we can expect to find a normal distribution.

The ratios of the normal distribution curve (as in fig 2.4) apply to any normal distribution. The normal distribution and its special characteristics (constant proportions or ratios) are very important to psychological measurement (e.g. for the calculation of norms). Note that not all distributions are normal. In research, sets of data are often smoothed to adapt irregular distributions to a normal distribution curve.

Two types of deviations from normal distributions often occur, namely a skew distribution and kurtosis.

Skewness refers to the degree of symmetry or asymmetry of the distributions. Two forms of skewness exist:

- *Skewness to the left* (negatively skew) occurs, for instance, when a test was too easy and most of the marks are above the average as in figure 2.5.
- *Skewness to the right* (positively skew) occurs when the test was too difficult and the marks are therefore predominantly below the average as in figure 2.6.

Such skewness in distributions in test marks can be rectified by revising the questions and setting them so as to suit the subjects' capacities.

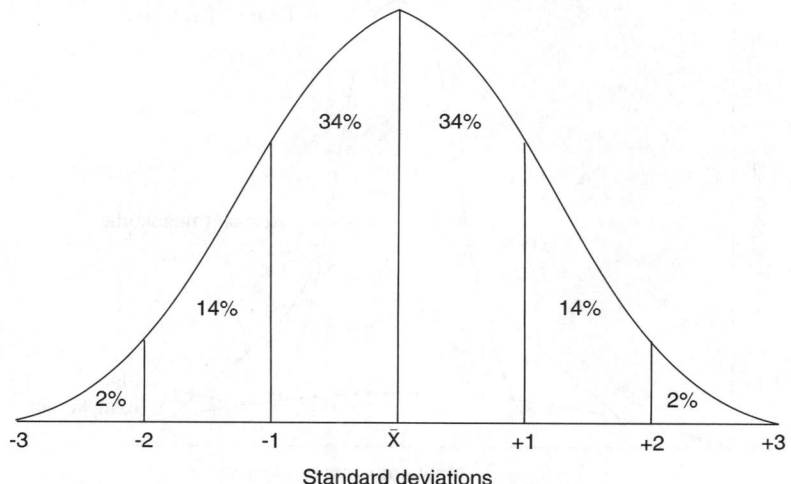

Figure 2.4 The normal curve: area ratios, mean and standard deviations

Kurtosis refers to the flatness or pointedness of a distribution curve, even if it is symmetrical. *Pointedness* is found where almost all the scores are found in the middle. *Flatness*, on the other hand, is the result of scores distributed over the whole spectrum (see figure 2.7).

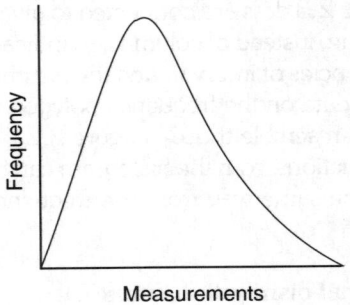

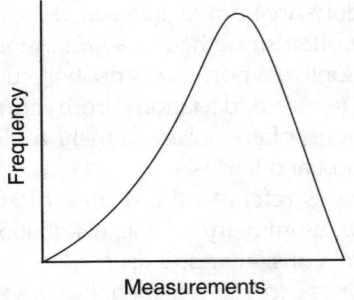

Figure 2.5 Skewness to the left (negatively skew)

In addition, there are other kinds of distributions, such as bimodal distributions.

Measurements of central tendency
When we seek to briefly describe a certain distribution or its main characteristics without giving the whole distribution,

Figure 2.6 Skewness to the right (positively skew)

we can use quantitative statistics such as central values. A central value is a single value which best represents or summarises the total distribution. Such values or numbers enable us to compare various distributions of data.

The *mean* $(\overline{X})$ is the arithmetic mean or average of a group of scores or measurements. In our example in table 2.1 the mean of the 30 marks is 69,466 (approximately 69,47). We write it as $\overline{X} = 69,47$. The calculation is done by using the following formula in which we add (Σ) the individual scores (X) and divide it by the number of cases (N).

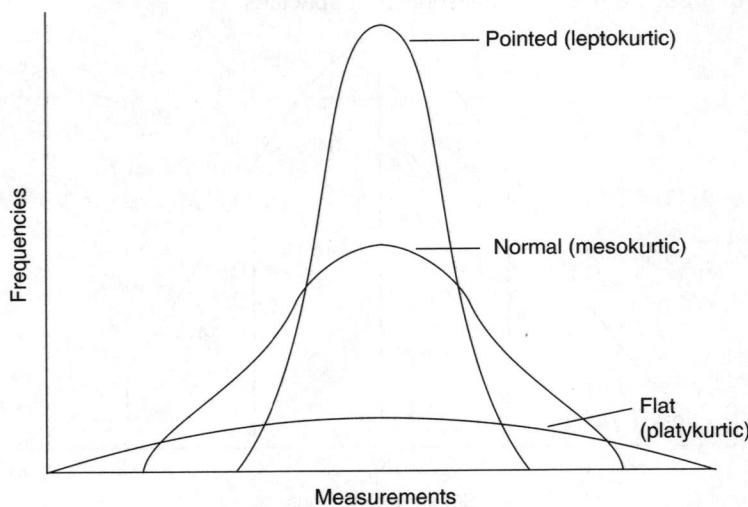

Figure 2.7 Kurtosis

$\overline{X} = \Sigma \frac{X}{N}$ where

$\overline{X}$ = symbol for arithmetic mean

Σ = symbol for sum of

X = scores

ΣX is therefore the sum of the scores and

N = number of measurements or persons.

The equation in table 2.1 is therefore as follows:

$$\overline{X} = \frac{2\,084}{30}$$

$$= 69,47$$

Each of the scores or measurements contributes to the mean. This means that extreme scores, either very high or very low, can greatly influence the mean and actually give a somewhat inaccurate picture of all the other scores.

Note that the sign X is used to indicate scores (such as marks), and x is the symbol for deviations from the mean.

The *median (mdn)* is a midpoint on a collection of scores above or below which half of the measurements are located, that is, the middle score of a distribution. Another definition for the median is the 50th percentile. In smaller groups of measurements, in which clashes between scores do not occur, the median calculations are simple. For instance, in the series 2, 3, 4, 6, 7, 9, 10, 11, 14 (N = 9), the median is merely the score which is in the middle position when the scores are classified from low to high. In this case the median is the *fifth* score because:

$$\frac{N+1}{2}$$

$$9 + 1 = \frac{10}{2} = 5$$

Therefore 7 is the median for the above series because 7 falls exactly in the middle (5th score) of the series (4 figures are below and 4 above 7).

For grouped data as in table 2.2, the calculations are somewhat more complex.

In most cases where the distribution is reasonably normal, $\overline{X}$ and the median are approximately equal, for instance, in our example above, $\overline{X} = 7,33$.

The *mode* is the point or value in a distribution which occurs most often. In table 2.1, 69 occurs most often, thus the most frequent score mode is 69.

In general, the $\overline{X}$ is the most reliable central value for comparison because calculations of it in random samples will vary less than those of the median and the mode. The arithmetic mean also lends itself to more advanced arithmetical and algebraic processing and is often an important factor in psychological statistics, particularly because of the fixed relations in the normal distribution. The median is, however, preferable in skew distributions and when there are greatly deviant values in a distribution, while the mode has limited value, except in cases of nominal data such as the size of families. In other types of measuring scales (ordinal, interval and ratio) the median and $\overline{X}$ are the appropriate central values.

Measures of dispersion (variability) or spread

Measures for *variability* indicate the degree to which scores vary or are spread around the central tendency or to what extent scores in a distribution differ from one another. If all scores are the same, there is no variability or spread.

Central values indicate the most representative value or point in a distribution, yet they do not describe a distribution adequately. Thus two sets of scores could, for instance, have the same means and both be symmetrical, yet in a histogram or polygon, they would look totally different. This could be the case in pointed and flat distributions (kurtosis). Such distributions differ in the *distribution range or variability* of scores. Compare the following two series of scores:

(a) 40, 41, 38, 39, 38, 42, 41, 39, 40, 42
(b) 5, 40, 30, 50, 15, 10, 25, 15, 25, 35

Although there are various indexes for variability or range of distribution, range, variance (S^2) and standard deviations (S) are discussed only briefly.

Range is estimated by simply calculating the difference between the highest and lowest values in a distribution. In (a) above, the range is therefore $42 - 38 = 4$ and in (b) the range is $50 - 5 = 45$. Range is a reasonably unreliable indication of distribution dispersion since extreme scores can sometimes be located far from the other scores in a distribution. Suppose that in (a) above an extreme score of 8 occurred. The range would then changed to 34 ($42 - 8$).

A better indication of dispersion is the *variance (S^2)* of a distribution where all the scores are included in the calculation. Variance is calculated by obtaining all the squared deviations from the arithmetic mean. Remember that $\overline{X}$ stands for arithmetic mean, X = scores, x = deviations and x^2 stands for squared deviations. In (a) and (b) above, variance is calculated as shown in table 2.3:

	(a)			(b)	
X	$x =(X-\overline{X})$	x^2	X	$x =(X-\overline{X})$	x^2
40	0	0	5	−20	400
41	1	1	40	15	225
38	−2	4	30	5	25
39	−1	1	50	25	625
38	−2	4	15	−10	100
42	2	4	10	−15	225
41	1	1	25	0	0
39	−1	1	15	−10	100
40	0	0	25	0	0
42	2	4	35	10	100

Table 2.3 Calculation of variance

(a)	(b)
$\overline{X} = 40$	$\overline{X} = 25$
$\Sigma\, x^2 = 20$	$\Sigma x^2 = 1\,800$
$N = 10$	$N = 10$
$S^2 = \dfrac{\Sigma x^2}{N-1}$	$S^2 = \dfrac{\Sigma x^2}{N-1}$
$= \dfrac{20}{10-1}$	$= \dfrac{1\,800}{10-1}$
$= \dfrac{20}{9}$	$= \dfrac{1\,800}{9}$
$= 2,22 \rightarrow$	$= 200 \rightarrow$

From the above variances (2,22 and 200) it is clear that the distribution range of (a) is far smaller than that of (b), something that was not clear when range was calculated.

Standard deviation (S or SD) is a calculation that logically follows the calculation of variance. Standard deviation is defined as the positive square root of the variance of a distribution or collection of scores. S is preferred to S^2 because the standard deviation is expressed in the same unit of measurement as the original score in a distribution, unlike variance, which is expressed in squared values. In examples (a) and (b) above S is calculated as follows:

(1) $S = \sqrt{\dfrac{\Sigma(\overline{X}-X)^2}{N-1}}$ or $S = \sqrt{\dfrac{\Sigma x^2}{N-1}}$

$= \sqrt{\dfrac{20}{10-1}}$

$= \sqrt{\dfrac{20}{9}}$

$= \sqrt{2.2}$

$= 1,48$

(2) $\sqrt{\dfrac{1\,800}{10-1}}$

$= \sqrt{\dfrac{1\,800}{9}}$

$= \sqrt{200}$

$= 14,14 \rightarrow$

Here, too, the larger distribution range of (b) is indicated by its larger S value (14,14). Standard deviation (S) is useful because it attributes more significance to scores in a distribution. We know that the arithmetic means in examples (a) and (b) are 40 and 25 respectively. We also know how many standard deviations make each individual score fall above or below the mean. Hence a score of 41 in example (a) lies one S above the mean and a score of 39 one S below the mean, and so forth.

Both variance (S^2) and standard deviation (S), like the arithmetic mean, are fundamental concepts for calculations in virtually all statistical processing.

Measurement of relationship (correlation)

Correlation indicates the numerical degree of relationship, association or predictability between two or more variables. Thus one speaks of the *relation* between IQ and school performance or the *prediction* of school performance on the basis of scores in an IQ test. These aspects are important in work, especially in selection decisions on future job behaviour on the basis of different variables such as aptitude tests and criteria for job effectiveness.

In statistical terminology correlation between two variables is referred to as the extent to which two variables co-vary linearly; in other words how variance or change in one variable correlates with variance in another. As a rule, there is a direct correlation between age and height, which means that as a person grows older we can expect him or her to grow taller. Hence by knowing age we can predict the specific heights that should be attained.

The inference or deductions made by using relationships is based on the laws of probability or significance, which is another example of logic in scientific research. We cannot generalise findings if they are not significant. The higher the statistical significance the more confident we can be that our research hypothesis will be correct, for instance, that a significant relationship does

exist between two variables and is not a chance event.

The magnitude of a relationship is expressed as a *correlation coefficient (r)*, a numerical value from $-1,00$ to $+1,00$, to indicate to what extent two variables correlate either negatively or positively, and gives the *direction* of a relationship.

A positive or direct correlation means that the scores or measurements on two variables are either both high or both low.

Figures 2.8 and 2.9 illustrate visually a perfect positive ($+1,00$) and a perfect negative correlation ($-1,00$).

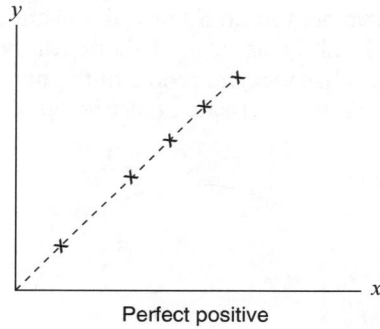

Figure 2.8 Perfect positive correlation

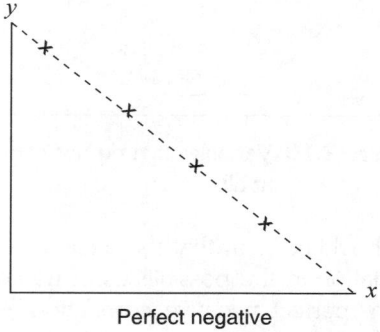

Figure 2.9 Perfect negative correlation

In figure 2.8 all the scores correlate exactly – the larger the score on the x-axis, the larger will be the score on the y-axis. In figure 2.9 the perfect negative correlation means that the larger the x score, the smaller the y score. In both cases, therefore, the relationships will be perfect and fall precisely on a straight line. Perfect scores of this kind are seldom encountered in practice. However, in the field of statistics certain requirements are laid down for a relationship or correlation to be significant. Validity correlations higher than 0,35, and reliability higher than 0,70 are usually accepted as significant. This is particularly important when one wishes to determine whether or not differences between, for example, groups, are significant.

When two variables do not manifest any relation (vary) at all, for example height and achievement in an IQ test, the distribution range will be large and there will be no pattern because the scores of the two variables do not correlate at all (see fig. 2.10).

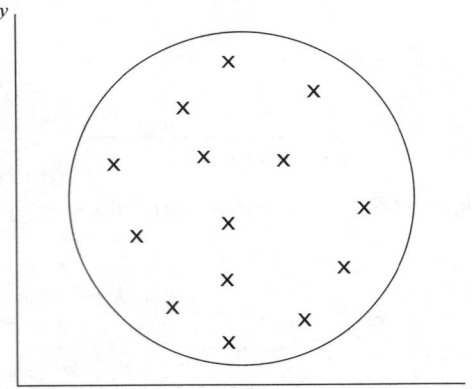

Figure 2.10 Variables that do not correlate at all

It should be clear that there can be infinite variation in the possibilities of no correlation, perfect negative correlation (−1,00) and perfect positive correlation (+1,00), depending on the relation between the variables. The type of correlation can always be expressed visually in the line of best fit. As indicated earlier, it is always a straight line in the case of +1,00 and −1,00. The further the correlation deviates from these perfect relations, the further the distribution will lie from the straight line.

Remember that although a correlation coefficient indicates the relation between variables, it does not provide an explanation for definite cause and effect. Hence correlation coefficients on their own cannot be used to predict behaviour, only to indicate a relationship.

2.3.8.2 Inferential statistics

If we use correlations to indicate a relationship between variables in a group, we use them as descriptive statistics. When we generalise a correlation between specific variables and apply that to other variables, groups or situations, or when we predict the scores on one test or task as the basis of our knowledge of the scores of another test, we use relationship or correlation, and specifically regression analysis, as inferential statistical methods to draw conclusions.

Regression analysis involves statistical methods in which correlation coefficients are used to predict behaviour. Regression analysis involves determining the *line of best fit* (prediction or regression line) based on the type of correlation between the two variables. On the basis of regression lines one can calculate regression equations and make predictions about variables within certain margins of certainty or uncertainty.

In figure 2.11 the line of best fit is represented by a correlation 0,70, which means that the correlation is positive but not perfect – hence errors of measurement may occur. A person with a test score of 60, for example, will obtain a job performance score of about 50, yet persons with test scores of 40 or 50 may obtain job performance scores of 45 or 55. For this reason one or other measurement error index is calculated in most psychological tests, which can be taken into consideration in the test scores obtained.

Decision-making theories in industrial psychology (on selection, for example) are based primarily on regression equations. Following regression analysis, expectancy tables are often compiled, from which

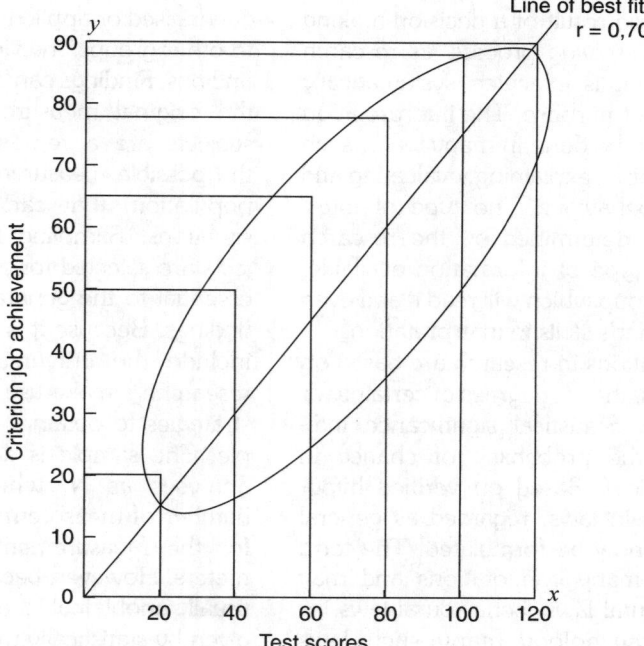

Figure 2.11 Regression analysis

scores on one variable can be used to predict expected scores on another.

In more advanced research calculations methods such as multivariate statistics, for example, factor analysis may be used. The latter is a statistical technique whereby, on the basis of correlations between variables, one can determine what variables have common properties, or the underlying structure or basic factors of a set of variables. The primary function of factor analysis is to reduce the number of variables in a vast number of measurements by identifying the overlap between the various measures. Thus Cattell (researching personality) and Thurstone (researching intelligence) used factor analysis of various test scores and other data to determine that personality basically comprises 16 primary factors, and intelligence is composed of seven group factors. Factor analysis is usually depicted in a factor matrix, showing the clusters of factors which belong together. Another technique, meta-analysis, is used to analyse the data and

results of many research projects, allowing researchers to do deeper analysis and make finer inferences because they consider more measurements. Using this method, researchers recently established that personality is a better predictor of occupational behaviours than was indicated in earlier studies (Barrick & Mount 1991; Tett et al. 1991).

2.3.9 Conclusions and generalisation in research

Making correct interpretations and drawing accurate conclusions from research data and assessment results really depends on the rule of "garbage in – garbage out", as nothing can make up for poor research design, errors in assessments or incompetencies of researchers! Interpretation is based on logical thinking, probabilities and the integration of findings, as determined by the stated research or assessment questions, the meaning of the research variables and the statistical or other methods of processing data. Interpretation is also the end result of a decision-making and problem-solving process, as research or assessment is executed systematically and with a set purpose. The interpretation of results can be done in many ways, such as by describing, explaining, evaluating and predicting behaviour. The type of interpretation is determined by the research design, the type of information available, the target group which will read it and even the researcher's skills in interpretation.

Interpretations in research are based on probabilities, that is, degrees of certainty or significance. Statistical significance indicates that the probability of chance in findings is low. Based on verified hypotheses, certain laws, regarded as general truths, can now be formulated. The term "law" has many connotations and may refer to natural laws, behavioural laws, or rules. In psychology many such laws evolved from research, such as the Law of Effect and the Gestalt laws, which were formulated on the basis of experimental research. A set of laws becomes a theory once it is integrated into a system incorporating a specific topic which describes the relationships between different aspects of such a topic. In this way many theories evolved, for instance, on personality, motivation, perception, intelligence, leadership and learning. In most cases accepted theories and concepts evolved progressively through logical reasoning, hypothesising, verification, data collection and processing, interpretation and the formulation of laws, which give such knowledge considerable predictive value. In this respect, although many so-called theories and concepts or aspects of them may provide handy tools to understand human behaviour, they remain unverified hypotheses or speculation until verified by scientific research.

Conclusions in research really involve generalisation of findings. Generalisation, also referred to as external validity, means that statistically significant findings may be generalised or applied in a broader context to other groups, individuals, situations and findings. Findings can only be generalised if the original measurements or research subjects are a representative sample of the possible measurements (universum or population) that can be made in such situations. Sampling (how research subjects are selected for a research project) is essential to the generalisation of research findings. Because it is often impractical to include the universum or population, researchers make use of various sampling strategies to obtain a representative sample. The sample is depicted in statistical analyses as N, which represents the number of measurements. Possible values for the measurements are called parameters. However, because parameters are usually unobtainable, an estimate has to be given by statistically manipulating the data from samples for significance. If, for instance, 300 South African businesses need to be selected in order to do a survey on affirmative action practices, random sampling may be utilised to give every business an equal chance to be included in the sample. Many of the same psychological tests are used on adults, although the tests were constructed and standardised on only a sample of adults. Validity generalisation is also applied in a variety of cognitive tests used as valid predictors of job and training performance criteria over a broad spectrum of jobs, groups and individuals (Walsh & Betz 1995).

Generalisation is necessary to achieve the scientific requirements of empiricism, verification and testability, in order to build a science of psychology on sound theories and practices. Valid conclusions and representative findings are essential. Too many instances exist where group averages, for example, do not make provision for individuals, or where certain groups are discriminated against when a theory, concept or test is applied to them because they were excluded from the original research. Such unscientific thinking often forms the basis of prejudices, bias and unfair practices which cause suffering for those involved and lead to bitter disputes to rectify injustices.

Analysis of applied research often leads to the results being rejected, in which case new hypotheses must be researched, data must be analysed again or findings must be applied in other ways.

The results of research and assessment may be divulged or reported on through verbal communication, papers read at conferences, advising a client in a counselling session, etc. Findings can be summarised and described in various types of reports, in articles or in books. The various forms of reporting or communicating research and assessment results and processes are specialised topics and demand adherence to principles of scientific writing (Tallent 1989; Sternberg 1994).

2.4 RESEARCH AND ASSESS-MENT EFFICIENCY: SOURCES OF ERROR

When evaluating research and assessment, the most important criterion is that phenomena are true or real, or that the relationship between variables, and therefore between people, is real. Errors in measurement cause findings to be random in nature. The more errors there are, the more unlikely it becomes to say that findings are really accurate or that the relationship between variables is really what we expect it to be. Errors also make it difficult to determine statistical significance. Measurement errors may create the false belief that research findings are the truth, when in fact such results may merely give a false impression of the truth.

Measurement errors are the difference between obtained results and real results.

Errors in measurement do occur as a result of the research process, the nature of psychological concepts, weaknesses in the psychological measurement techniques,

rating or observation errors during the research and subjective errors by researchers. Measurement errors can be *constant errors* if they always influence measurements; for example, some scales for measuring a trait may always measure somewhat higher or lower than other methods. Some errors, however, may be *random,* in that they only occur occasionally due to circumstances or human errors. Some errors can be reduced and even in some way corrected when statistics are compiled. However, many errors, especially those caused by subjective influences such as prejudice and bias, cannot be corrected by statistical manipulation.

2.4.1 Reliability and validity

Reliability and validity are expressed as correlation coefficients (r), to express the effectiveness of measurements and the magnitude of constant or random errors in measurement (Kerlinger 1973).

Reliability concerns the consistency of measurements, i.e. a process or measurement repeated in various situations or by different persons will provide more or less the same measurement results. The higher the reliability coefficient (preferably higher than 0,70) the less chance there is of inconsistent measurement. Reliability coefficients can be expressed in measurements of stability, equivalence and internal consistency. Rater reliability refers to the degree of agreement between researchers and assessors, for example similar observations by participants of similar techniques on the same behavioural dimensions.

Validity is the psychometric requirement for a measurement technique to measure what it is designed to measure. If we use an IQ test, we must be sure that the questions represent aspects of intelligence and not another construct. A measurement may have high reliability, but low validity.

Validity, like reliability, is expressed by means of a correlation coefficient (preferably higher than 0,35). Various types of validation indexes can be calculated, depending on the type of research, for instance for content, construct and criterion validities. The latter involves determining whether or not a particular predictor variable, for example self-esteem, relates to an external criterion such as job achievement. Another form of validity is face validity. However, it is not a technical or scientific form as are those mentioned earlier. It refers to the extent to which a certain instrument appears relevant for the user. If employees believe or perceive a measure such as performance appraisal or a personality test to be job-related, they may be more honest in their responses.

Reliability and validity are the most important criteria for research and assessment effectiveness and may be part of and reflect all or most sources of measurement error.

2.4.2 Specific measurement errors

Errors in obtaining data derive from many sources, such as inadequate research design, poor administration, mistakes by the assessor or researcher, errors by the research subjects or persons being assessed as well as weaknesses in measuring instruments.

2.4.2.1 Errors in research design

If a research project is not planned and executed according to a systematic and logical process and in terms of the objectives of the project, the scientific and research objectives cannot be achieved, and results may be unreliable and invalid. Researchers may lose control if existing data is used and rewritten or reinterpreted. If a research sample is biased, unrepresentative or too small, with too few measurements, or drafted incorrectly, generalisations made from the findings could be invalid. Experimental research findings, for instance, are not necessarily transfer-able or generalisable to predict human behaviour in occupational settings. By the same token correlational research cannot be used to explain causes of behaviour.

2.4.2.2 Administration and scoring errors

Examples of the poor administration of measuring devices are:
- using nonstandardised procedures and techniques, i.e. different procedures in different situations and with different research participants
- vague or incorrect instructions
- poor research conditions (noise, poor lighting, incorrect or incomplete measuring material and interruptions)
- errors in time limits or other controls

Examples of scoring errors are:
- errors in observation and scoring, for instance clerical or calculation errors
- errors in interpretation of values such as norms
- distortions of data by research subjects and researchers

2.4.2.3 Errors by researchers and assessors

Errors made by researchers could be due to insufficient skills and competencies and subjectiveness in attitudes, values and behaviours. Researchers must realise their power to influence research, assessments and findings. Being human, it is very difficult not to reflect some aspects of their own preferences, expectancies, values and attitudes in research. This is borne out by the fact that many, if not all, theories in psychology also reflect something of the relevant theorists personal views and experiences. Researchers must as far as possible be objective in research and assessment practices. Behaviour patterns of researchers that might cause uncontrolled error variance could be low integrity; being untruthful; wishing to establish something or to prove a certain point by distorting data and findings; or reporting on nonexistent data.

Subjective influences which can cause invalid findings include the following rating effects:

- *Halo effect.* This occurs when the assessor gives the same level of score or rating over all dimensions. This usually happens when the rater forms an impression on one outstanding aspect only and this influences all subsequent scoring. For example, an employee who is very friendly during an interview or test may be rated high or positively in all dimensions.
- *Context effects.* This refers to situations where employees, for example, are rated similarly to the rest of their work group (assimilation effect) or when employees are either rated much higher or lower than their work group (contrast effect).
- *Central tendency, severity or leniency effect.* This occurs when a rater tends to allocate only average scores, say three on a five-point scale, or tends to only give very low (negative) or very high (positive) marks.
- *Order effect.* This occurs when the order of available information influences ratings. For instance, raters may score what they have seen, heard or experienced last (recency error) more positively, negatively or accurately. In the same way first impressions, for instance an applicant arriving late, or physical attractiveness, may influence ratings even more than recent information.
- *Negative information.* This tends to influence raters more than positive aspects, for instance when assessors look for mistakes, rather than assess strong points, in performance appraisals.
- *Rating errors.* These may occur because of personal preferences. We often like a person who resembles us in some respects. Physically attractive assessees can influence raters to assess more

positively, and ratings may also be biased for reasons such as age, race, gender and other demographic variables.

All of the above can cause rating errors and prevent research from differentiating between attributes. These rating effects may also influence the interpretation of assessment results.

Other aspects of research efficiency are related to how economical research is in terms of time; finances and the use of human resources; participants' awareness of their role; changes and even mortality in research participants; whether the research achieves its predetermined goals; and how research relates to ethical principles and sensitive social issues.

2.5 ETHICAL AND SOCIAL ISSUES IN RESEARCH AND ASSESSMENT

Although psychological research and assessment and the decisions and actions resulting from them are used to benefit people, these processes also have pitfalls and can be misused.

2.5.1 Professional and ethical standards

In South Africa, as in many other countries, the training and practices of psychologists are controlled by law and various controlling bodies. All professional and practising psychologists must be registered with the South African Dental and Medical Council which, through the Professional Board for Psychology, controls and applies the laws regarding psychological training and professional actions. The Psychological Association of South Africa (PsySSA) and its various institutions, such as Industrial Psychology, Counselling Psychology, Clinical Psychology and Educational Psychology, and other interest groups to which psychologists can voluntarily subscribe, are bodies which through conferences, training, publications, newsletters, marketing actions and other efforts try to facilitate the interests of psychologists. PsySSA manages the code published as *Ethical codes for psychologists* which stipulates values and norms for psychologists with respect to both professional actions, such as testing, therapy and research, and their own actions, as well as behaviour towards colleagues and especially clients.

2.5.2 Basic assumptions and ethical principles

The *basic ideals* and *assumptions* underlying psychological practices are based on the recognition of the worth and dignity of the individual irrespective of race, creed, sex, status and language. This includes the understanding that people are all alike in some respects; that some people are alike in some respects and that every individual is also unique in some respects. In summary these assumptions entail the responsibility of psychologists to objectively and in an unbiased way utilise research knowledge, methods and skills to understand human behaviour better and to facilitate the welfare of people.

The *ethical principles* to which all psychologists and human resources practitioners (assessors, researchers, therapists, counsellors and other human resource workers) should adhere can be summarised as follows (PsySSA 1992; APA 1992):

- *Professional and scientific responsibility* entails psychologists, in their different roles and through their knowledge, skills and activities, serving the best interests of the profession and their clients and taking responsibility for actions.
- *Competency* refers to psychologists maintaining high standards by reflecting qualifications and experience accurately; where necessary staying up to date in their sphere of practice; and executing tasks professionally and in a planned and responsible way.

- *Moral and legal standards* compel psychologists to be aware of and sensitive to prevailing standards and issues and not to act, or use methods, in a way that will offend or not be in the best interest of clients. Psychological tests, and other processes and decisions involving people, must be fair and undiscriminating.
- *Confidentiality* implies that any information about any client will be respected as private; such privileged information will not be divulged, except with the client's consent, in any way or to any person, or used for any reason other than the original objective of the action. The psychologist must, however, be alert to possible dangers for the client if information is withheld.
- *Informed consent* refers to the client's autonomy and freedom of choice in what actions will take place and the client's right to be informed about any overt or covert procedures. The client's privacy must not be invaded, except if the client is aware of it, as when observing a client's behaviour. If covert observations are necessary, participants must be debriefed. Clients must not be coerced or forced to take part in any action.
- The *welfare* of individuals and groups is always paramount. Clients must be subjected to no physical or mental discomfort, or the minimum which is realistic in the situation; no action, procedure or type of relationship must harm the integrity of the professional contract between psychologist or researcher and client; psychologists must steer clear of consulting with family and close friends; not be romantically involved with clients; and be open to clients about fees and termination of services if no progress is being made.
- *Benefits of research* refer to the careful consideration and planning for research to determine the benefits for the research participants; financial implica-

tions; possible psychological consequences or health risks for participants;
benefits for the researcher and the
objectives of the research, i.e. what
type of knowledge or outcome is to be
achieved.

- The making of *public statements* and the
marketing of services by psychologists
must only be done according to policy
and in such an unbiased and noncom-
mercialised way as to not degrade other
professional people and to give the
client the freedom to choose. Psychologists may not use or receive favours in
any way to enhance their services and
may not advertise directly or receive
commercial gain in advertisements.
- *Professional relationships* must be upheld at all times. The status of colleagues
and other professions must be respected; relationships with clients, students or research participants must
never be on a personal, romantic level
and sexual harassment of any nature is
inexcusable; psychologists must only
take credit for contributions they have
really made and must not intervene,
without agreement, in the practices of
other psychologists; psychologists must
have the moral duty to report any
misconduct which will harm the interests of the profession.
- In *animal research*, if necessary, psychologists will apply all scientific and
legal demands and be sensitive to any
societal or ecological norms; research
with and on animals will be carried out
according to scientific and planned
research procedures; minimal or no
harm or degradation will be done to
animals.
- *Conflicts* over ethical principles or
dilemmas may arise when psychologists
have to make decisions that might seem
contradictory. Divulging confidential
information, for instance, about a client's dishonesty, may represent an
invasion of privacy. However, it may

be in the client's best interest to do so,
provided such a decision is not taken to
cause harm.

2.5.3 Social issues in assess-
ment and research

Part of the psychologist's professional
and scientific responsibility is to serve the
best interests of the client and the
community. This is done best if the
psychologist has an objective and unbiased attitude, and knows the relevance,
strengths and limitations of psychological
knowledge, practices and methodologies
to use these responsibly. Psychologists
and their practices do influence, and can
change, people's lives and they must
accept accountability for this.

One of the critical issues in psychological
research and assessment is using psychological data scientifically and in an unbiased
and fair manner. Duckitt (1992) discussed
in some detail prejudice in psychology
across time in various practices. Two of
the sensitive areas in which the use of
psychological research findings and assessment data has spurred controversy and
even legal action are personality attributes
related to gender and race, selection and
promotion decisions and legal cases in
which psychologists appear as expert
witnesses.

The controversy of test bias originated in
the fact that individuals and groups from
different cultural and ethnic backgrounds,
as well as males and females, obtained
different scores on ability tests, like IQ tests.

The issue of bias in testing practices can
be divided into two interdependent but
separate controversies, test *bias* and test
fairness (Gregory 1996). For many reasons, especially ideological-political and
emotional reasoning, confusing and often
incorrect interpretations surround these
issues.

Test bias exists when statistical indices
indicate that a test is differentially (not the
same for all) valid for different groups of a

population. Usually this happens when people, because of differences such as culture, education, age and gender, understand test items differently, or find the test items not equally difficult. If a numerical reasoning test is set in English for comparable males, but a number of them cannot understand English well, and the test scores predict success differently for the two groups, test bias exists. In this case the score differences can be attributed to the differences in language, or cultural differences, rather than differences in numerical ability. Test bias may also exist if test items are about a subject of which a specific person or a subgroup has no knowledge, and is scored without taking this into account. Some persons will find such items difficult to answer, though they may be very intelligent. If computer-related questions are used to test IQ in 12-year olds in South Africa, they will for many reasons be biased in favour of city children as opposed to rural children, and probably between white and black children. In the same manner test bias can exist if the underlying construct (e.g. numerical reasoning) which the test is supposed to measure is measured differently for different subgroups or by two different tests.

In general, however, research on test bias, using statistical indices such as factor analysis, regression analysis and intergroup comparisons, indicates that in the domain of ability tests, little test bias exists between different cultural groups and between the sexes (Gregory 1996). In South Africa the same might be true, but much more research is necessary to verify this assumption and to discard the cognitive and emotional misconceptions on ability and other forms of testing in and between groups (PsySSA 1992).

Test unfairness, mentioned earlier, is a socially defined concept (Walsh & Betz 1995; Dipboye et al. 1994). Test unfairness occurs in unfair personnel policies and strategies, incorrect test administration and prejudiced decisions based on test scores, whether the test is statistically biased or not. Many such unfair policies and uses of test procedures and test scores are vested in ideological, political and emotional attitudes and prejudices directed at consciously favouring certain persons or groups. If an individual or group, for instance in job selection, is excluded from selection and is not given the same chance as other comparable persons because of unfair personnel policies and testing procedures, or the fact that a test is culturally or sexually biased, then such procedures amount to discrimination and unfair testing.

Such actions have led to the introduction of affirmative action and personnel policies to correct the injustices of the past. Emotional pleas for the banning of all employment testing have been made. Such pleas imply that the introduction of other techniques, which ought to be fair and scientific, also harbour the seeds of prejudice. It will always be better to use testing; however, it is undesirable to use or not use it for the wrong reasons. Psychological research and testing based on sound scientific, theoretical and practical principles require vigilance in order to be used fairly and correctly. Materials must be updated to remain relevant.

Practical applications of courtroom testimony by psychologists include crime cases in which the psychologist must not only determine character profiles, but also testify in pleas of insanity at the time of the crime, the determination of competency to stand trial and the prediction of possible violent or other dangerous behaviour. Other examples are testimony in divorce and child custody cases and the determination of trauma due to injuries in accidents or other mishaps, and even the determination of career development implications and loss of income potential in cases of unfair job dismissals. In legal actions assertions are made that psychological diagnoses and predictions of human behaviour often lack reliability and validity, and that expert psychological testimonies do not really assist in legal decisions (Faust & Ziskin 1988). Contrary arguments are offered by, for one, Matarazzo (1990), who asserts that psychological practices have sufficient credentials in these matters.

2.6 CONCLUSION

Methodology in psychology is essential to assess, verify, integrate and even expand the assumptions and concepts of theories on human behaviour. In work organisations, ongoing research on occupational behaviours is a necessary outcome, but also a stimulus to improve existing thinking and practices and to accommodate changes in the work environment. In many instances theory, assessment and research in psychology are now integrated into supportive tools to explain, describe and predict, and to systematise knowledge of human behaviour in various contexts and in all its complexities (Pervin & John 1997). However, the variation in concepts and methodologies allows researchers and practitioners to use the most applicable variables and methods in specific situations. Potentially influential in human behaviour, research and assessment methodologies in psychology will have to strive for unbiased and objective research processes, results and conclusions.

Self-evaluating questions

Take a research problem in your work or community and do the following:

1. Describe the possible steps which you will follow to conduct this project.
2. Give a hypothesis or a research question for your research.
3. Explain your thinking in deriving a hypothesis.
4. Identify the type of variables and show how you are going to measure and control variables.
5. Describe the type of research and the research methods you are going to use.
6. Consider what possible errors you must control and the possible ethical and social issues which you will have to check.
7. Show how your research adheres to the principles of scientific thinking.

Part II

Individual Processes

Individual processes

Individual processes include inherited and acquired factors that affect the individual in the work situation. Knowledge of these processes contributes to understanding individuals as human beings and as contributors to economic life. Biological factors provide the quantitative and qualitative perimeters within which individuals develop. Development is the ultimate, continual process in which the individual's biological and psychological functioning is expressed, influencing his/her personal growth and goals and his/her cognisance of information in the environment.

Biological basis of behaviour

3

Antoinette Theron & Theo de Koker

CONTENTS

Learning outcomes

After studying this chapter you should be able to:

- distinguish between mitosis and meioses
- describe the functioning of DNA
- explain how meioses occurs
- indicate differences between identical and nonidentical twins
- explain how sex is determined
- distinguish between dominant and recessive traits
- explain the meaning of genotype and phenotype
- explain the heredity of intelligence, personality traits and behavioural deviations
- describe the nervous system as an integrated functional entity, taking into account all component parts
- describe the structure and functioning of the muscle system and explain muscle fatigue
- discuss job design, taking into account body posture, body size, and repetitive strain injuries
- provide ergonomics recommendations for work station design

Key concepts

genetics, cells, mitosis, meiosis, human behaviour, heredity, nervous system, brain, spinal cord, muscles, fatigue, ergonomics, job design, work station design

3.1 INTRODUCTION

Humans are extremely complex biological entities. Careful study of the complex interactions characterising the human organism is essential in understanding normal human behaviour, functioning and performance.

3.2 GENETICS
3.2.1 Foundations of development (cells)

Fundamentally all living organisms are composed of functional units, or *cells*, which reproduce themselves through a unique process of division in order to maintain the organism from conception until death. The human body is made up of trillions of cells. Each cell is a living unit in itself, capable of existing, performing chemical reactions and contributing to the overall functioning of the human body. The cells in the human body, while they vary in form and function, all have certain structural features in common, as well as functional properties such as metabolism, respiration, growth, receptiveness to stimuli, movement and reproduction (Guyton 1996).

Cells are the building blocks of the body organs, and each of the organs performs its own specialised function. Before one can understand how any of the organs function or how the organs function together to maintain life, a prerequisite is to understand the inner workings of the cell itself.

3.2.1.1 Mitosis

A human originates with the fertilisation of the female egg (ovum) by the male sperm to form a single cell known as a *zygote*. By means of sequential cell division the zygote develops into the various types of cells of which bodily organs are composed, such as muscle, glandular, bone, blood and nerve cells. The actual process by which the cell splits into two new cells is called mitosis. Mitosis is a process that sustains growth and maintains the organism throughout its lifetime. In the event of tissue injury, such as a scratch or cut, the organ regenerates by means of mitotic cell division, whereby identical new cells are formed from damaged ones (Guyton 1996).

Mitosis is a continuous process which typically takes two hours from start to finish.

3.2.1.2 DNA (genes)

The genetic origin of all organic life is contained in the *deoxyribonucleic acid* (DNA) molecule. DNA is the functional unit known as a *gene*, derived from the Greek word meaning "to give birth". Thousands of DNA molecules combine to form a *chromosome*. Each human cell contains 46 chromosomes, arranged in 23 pairs, which together constitute anything from 50 000 to one million DNA molecules, i.e. genes. The DNA molecules replicate and divide to maintain the genetic material. They are reproduced identically in new cells formed by mitosis (Davis et al. 1985; Guyton 1996).

Genes control heredity from parents and the same genes also control day-by-day functions of all the cells. The genes control cell function by determining what substances will be synthesised within the cell – what structures, enzymes and chemicals.

3.2.1.3 Meiosis

On reaching puberty humans are capable of reproducing, due to a type of cellular division known as meiosis, which occurs in the germ cells to produce ova and spermatozoa. Germ cells are also propagated by mitosis. By means of mitosis new daughter cells contain the same quantity of DNA and chromosomes as the parent cell. By means of meiosis, however, each daughter cell has only half (23) the number of chromosomes of the parent cell (Davis *et al.* 1985; Guyton 1996).

In much simplified terms, meiosis involves the following (see figure 3.1):

- The chromosomes arrange themselves in homologous pairs, thus termed because each chromosome in the pair carries genes producing similar bodily attributes.
- It may happen that a part of a single chromosome breaks off and exchanges places with a corresponding part of a homologous chromosome, thereby altering the DNA composition of a single chromosome. This exchange of DNA is a factor that contributes to differences between parents and their offspring.
- The two members of the chromosome pair move to opposite poles on either side of the equator of the cell, the choice of the pole being random.
- A cleavage furrow forms around the centre of the cell and each cell divides into two daughter cells, each containing 23 single chromosomes.

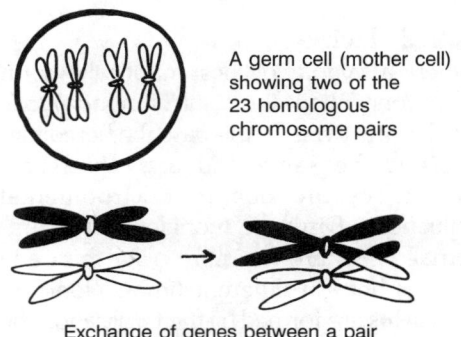

A germ cell (mother cell) showing two of the 23 homologous chromosome pairs

Exchange of genes between a pair of homologous chromosomes

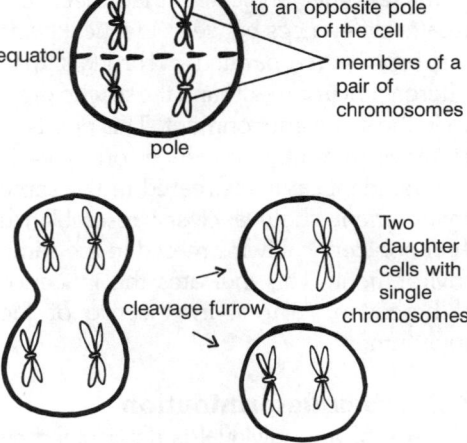

pole

Each member of the chromosome pair moves to an opposite pole of the cell

equator

members of a pair of chromosomes

pole

cleavage furrow

Two daughter cells with single chromosomes

Figure 3.1 Meiosis (simplified)

The daughter cells divide through mitosis into two new daughter cells apiece, keeping the chromosome and DNA quantities constant. A total of four cells is therefore produced by the original germ cell.

In females three of these cells usually disintegrate, and the fourth cell develops into an ovum. The two female ovaries normally produce an ovum each every alternate month. In males these cells develop into sperm cells. One ejaculation may release up to 200 million sperm cells. The number of sperm cells varies according to age and the physical and psychological state of the individual. Only one of the sperm cells fertilises the ovum. If not fertilised, the ovum is discharged in the menstrual cycle.

3.2.2 Twins
When a zygote divides mitotically soon after conception, the result is *monozygotic* or identical twins. In this case the hereditary basis is the same and any observable differences are due to environmental influences. *Dizygotic* (nonidentical or fraternal) twins are no more alike than any siblings born at different times. Nonidentical twins are formed by the fertilisation, by different sperm cells, of two ova produced at more or less the same time (Guyton 1996).

Studies have indicated that there are greater differences between identical twins who have been separated and brought up in different environments and those who grew up in the same environment. This points to an environmental influence on genetic factors. Identical twins reared in the same environment show a closer resemblance than nonidentical twins reared in the same environment. This indicates the influence of hereditary factors, irrespective of the environment.

3.2.3 Sex determination
The sex of an individual is determined by only one pair of the 23 pairs of chromo-

somes in the germ cell. Sex chromosomes may be either X chromosomes or Y chromosomes. Two X chromosomes produce a female, while the XY combination produces a male. On the segregation of chromosomes during meiosis the daughter cells of the male cell may contain either a X or a Y chromosome, while the female daughter cells will each contain a X chromosome. Should the ovum be fertilised by a sperm with a Y chromosome, the new organism will be a male, whereas a combination of two X chromosomes from both parents produces a female. Sex is therefore determined by the male cells (Davis et al. 1985).

3.2.4 Dominance and recessiveness
Genes control specific characteristics, either separately or in conjunction with other genes. Each member of a pair of homologous chromosomes contains a gene, in the same place or locus, which controls a particular characteristic. These paired genes are called *alleles*. Segregation of the chromosomes during meiosis thus means separation of the alleles also. The zygote which is formed receives single genes from each parent which together form new alleles (Marieb 1989).

The combination of similar, but not identical, genes does not have an intermediary effect on the offspring. However, some genes have a dominant effect which manifests itself, while others are only manifested in observable characteristics if two identical genes derive from both parents respectively. These latter are known as *recessive* genes. Examples of recessive characteristics are blue eyes, blonde, red or straight hair, baldness, night blindness, congenital deafness and albinism.

If a zygote receives a gene for straight hair from one parent and a gene for curly hair from the other, the child will have curly hair, as the latter gene has the dominant character. However, the recessive gene for straight hair is retained in the genetic constitution and transmitted to its descendants. If the zygote receives a gene for straight hair from both parents, the child will have straight hair, since there is no dominant gene to counteract the effects.

3.2.5 Genotype and phenotype

The actual genetic constitution of an individual is his or her genotype and his or her manifest characteristics are his or her phenotype. As a result of dominance and recessiveness of the genes, genotypes and phenotypes are not identical in every aspect. Phenotype refers not only to observable physical attributes, but also to psychological traits which manifest themselves because of environmental experience. The genotype comprises the genetic content which is passed on to an individual's descendants, whereas the phenotype refers to the observable effects of dominant genes and paired recessive genes, as well as the manifestation of genotypical characteristics due to environmental stimulation.

An individual may be genotypically endowed with an aptitude for original combinations of given ideas, but if his or her environment offers no scope for developing this ability, it may remain latent and be lost in terms of productivity. Theoretically all phenotypical characteristics will develop, given an optimal environment, but in practice individual development remains an unknown quantity to some extent, because a person with his or her experience amounts to more than the sum of the component parts.

3.2.6 Multiple determination (polygenic heredity)

In most cases characteristics are determined not by the dominance or recessiveness of pairs of genes but by the combined influence of various genes and different loci in the chromosomes. This applies to a number of personality traits as well as to

temperament and intelligence. *Temperament* refers to the prevalence of certain moods typical of the individual, such as whether his or her reactions are slow or quick, or whether he or she is predominantly active or passive. *Intelligence* comprises various factors including verbal fluency, verbal comprehension, reasoning ability, abstract thinking, ability to see spacial relations and number facility.

As a rule these characteristics are not definable in simple terms, because of both the complexity of genetic influence and the complex interaction between heredity and environment, which determines the functional value of characteristics. A single gene may influence the development of more than one attribute. For instance, a gene may have a primary effect on one characteristic, at the same time exercising a secondary influence on others that are largely determined by other genes. Genes also differ in the degree to which they influence the phenotype, that is, their penetration and time of expressivity. For example, cataracts on the eyes are attributed to genetic causes but they are manifested at different ages and in differing degrees of severity.

3.2.7 Sex-linked genes

The same chromosomes that determine sex also carry genes which control other physical characteristics. These genes are almost invariably carried by the X chromosome and only rarely by the Y chromosome. The inheritance patterns controlled by such genes deviate from the dominance-recessiveness rule and are *different for the phenotypes of the two sexes.* Among males such a gene on a X chromosome manifests dominantly, whereas females require the presence of two identical sex-linked genes for the quality to be manifest.

Examples of such characteristics are haemophilia and colour blindness. Haemophilia is a blood disorder that prevents the plasma from coagulating, so that the slightest scratch may cause excessive bleeding. Colour blindness is a defect of the retina, restricting the ability to distinguish between certain colours, notably red and green. Haemophiliacs are constrained to work and live in situations where risks of injury are marginal, while colour-blind individuals cannot perform work where colour discrimination is vital, as it is in advertising or the fashion world.

3.3 THE NERVOUS SYSTEM
3.3.1 Structure of the nervous system

The human nervous system consists of different parts operating on various levels. These parts should, however, all be seen as one integrated whole, hierarchically interacting by means of neuron association, so that higher levels are affected by lower levels and vice versa.

The human nervous system relies upon specialised cells to carry out its function. The nervous system is comprised of two major cell types, *neuroglial* cells and *neurons*. The neuroglial cells comprise the interstitial tissue of the nervous system, which gives organs of the nervous system their characteristic shapes. The neurons are dispersed among the neuroglial cells, and they are specialised to conduct electrochemical impulses. It is this conduction of impulses by the neurons that allows the nervous system to transmit information to and from various parts of the human body (Guyton 1996; Marieb 1989).

3.3.2 The neuron

The neuron or nerve cell is the basic unit that integrates internal processes by means of its unique function of conducting electrochemical impulses. Neurons transmit stimuli originating either in the environment or within the individual to the brain and other parts of the body, where these stimuli acquire functional significance. Even without the presence of external stimuli, the nervous system is a hive of constant

spontaneous electrochemical activity. Some neurons, for example, are more active while the individual is asleep, becoming less so during waking hours.

A neuron consists of a cell body extending into nerve fibres called dendrites, which receive impulses, while the fibre which conducts impulses from the cell body to adjacent neurons and organs is called the axon (see figure 3.2). Most neurons have only one axon, although some are ramified.

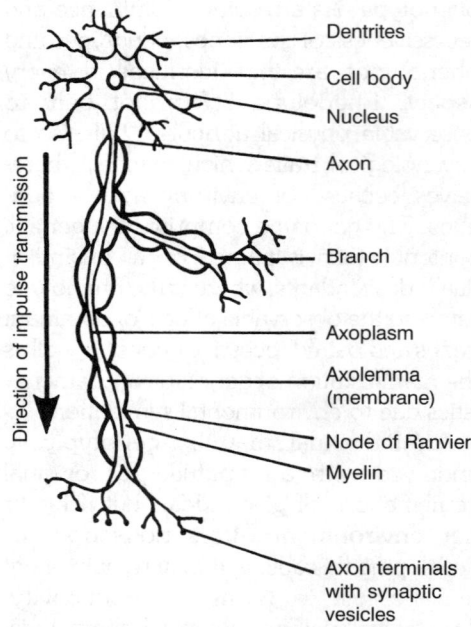

Figure 3.2 A neuron

The axon consists of a central core, the *axoplasm*, which is semi-fluid and surrounded by a thin membrane, and the *axolemma*, which is polarised, that is, it carries a negative electrical charge on the inside and a positive charge on the outside. The electrical charges on both sides of the membrane are carried by chemical solutions containing molecules called *ions* (Davis et al. 1985; Guyton 1996).

Some axons are enveloped in a fatty substance called *myelin*. The myelin sheath which acts as an insulation to prevent the loss of electric messages is interrupted at intervals by constrictions called the *nodes of Ranvier* (see figure 3.2). Impulses are conducted more rapidly along myelinated axons than others, since they leap from one node to the next. Stimuli are conducted in one direction only, from the dendrites to the axon via the cell body. This ensures the orderly organisation of nerve activity (Davis et al. 1985; Guyton 1996).

When the neuron is stimulated by some form of energy, for example thermal, kinetic or chemical energy, there is a change in the electrochemical potential of the neuron, resulting in a selective influx of positively charged ions through the membrane. This potential is known as the spike or action potential – alternative terms for a nerve impulse.

To trigger a nervous impulse a stimulus must be of a minimum intensity. It must reach an arousal threshold which depends on the threshold of the neuron. Any stimulus with an intensity too low to trigger an impulse is below the threshold of that neuron. The thresholds of different neurons vary, while that of a specific neuron usually remains fairly constant. However, the threshold can be artificially changed, by drugs for instance. The action of pain-

killing drugs raises the thresholds of neurons in a particular part of the body, making it less sensitive to pain stimuli. Stimulants have the reverse effect.

The transmission of impulses from one neuron to another occurs at a synapse, a space of about 0,00002 cm between the axon of one neuron and the dendrites of the next. The axon terminates in tiny branches on which appear small vesicles. When an impulse is transmitted to the next neuron these vesicles release the chemical substances they contain (e.g. acetylcholine) into the synaptic gap (see figure 3.3).

Some of these chemicals may have an excitatory effect on the post-synaptic neuron while others have an inhibitory effect which arrests the impulse at that point.

The inhibition of impulses helps to control the functioning of the nervous system and hence the functioning of behaviour. Insufficient inhibition may cause abnormal physiological behaviour. Alcohol, for example, affects the higher brain centres responsible for normal inhibiting behaviour. When the percentage of alcohol in the blood rises from 0,10 % to 0,65 %, the blood supply to the neurological centres causes confusion, loss of coordination and stupor due to lack of inhibition.

Epilepsy is caused by excessive discharges of stimuli by neurons which, depending on the type of epilepsy, may be accompanied by abnormal muscular spasms due to excessive muscular stimulation. Although epileptic attacks can be chemically controlled, some epileptics are limited in their choice of vocation; for instance, they cannot operate machinery or drive vehicles which will endanger life when their nervous activity disturbs their control over bodily functions.

A single axon and its branches can transmit impulses to a number of neurons and several neurons can convey stimuli to one neuron, thus involving a great many neurons in nerve activity. Should the

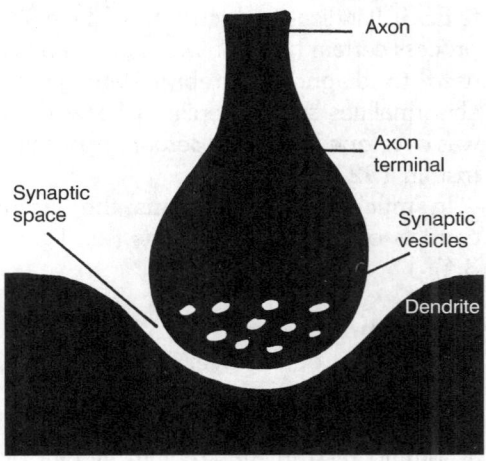

Axon

Axon terminal

Synaptic space

Synaptic vesicles

Dendrite

Figure 3.3 A synapse

chemicals released by one neuron be inadequate to activate the next neuron, impulses from other neurons combine to provide a stimulus strong enough to exceed the threshold of the post-synaptic neuron. This is known as *spatial summation*. Successive impulses from one axon may, however, collectively activate the post-synaptic neuron, in which case we speak of *temporal summation*.

The axon of a single neuron may be in contact with as many as 100 post-synaptic neurons while the dendrites of a neuron may link with up to 1 000 pre-synaptic neurons.

3.3.2.1 Classification of neurons

Neurons differ in shape, size and function and are assembled in various structured groups. The following types of neurons are distinguished:

- *Receptor neurons* form receptors of vision, sound, smell, taste, cold, heat, pressure and touch on the basis of their sensitivity to different forms of stimuli or energy from either the external or the internal environment within the body.
- *Sensory neurons* (afferent) conduct information from the receptors to the central nervous system. The nerve fibres of a number of sensory neurons combine to form a sensory nerve, for example the optic nerve or the auditory nerve.
- *Motor neurons* (efferent) conduct information from the central nervous system to the effectors – muscles and glands. The fibres of a group of motor neurons together constitute a motor nerve.
- *Association neurons* serve to connect sensory and motor neurons, thus effecting numerous nerve connections by which information is integrated.

3.3.3 The central nervous system

The central nervous system consists of the brain and the spinal cord.

3.3.3.1 The brain

The adult human brain has a mass of approximately 1,5 kg, which represents less than 3% of total body mass. Despite its small mass, the human brain makes humans unique amongst all other living animals. It is the brain that allows us to think, to feel emotions, to remember and to process all the sensory information gained from the environment. The brain enables humans to monitor changes in both their internal and external environment and to produce the appropriate responses to these changes (Davis et al. 1985).

The brain is composed of some 10 billion nerve cells grouped in different structures, for instance concentrations of the bodies of clusters of neurons called *nuclei*, and groups of axons constituting the nerves which link the various parts of the nervous system. Cerebral activity is sustained by oxygen and nutrients which are conveyed to the brain by the blood, in the same way that the blood conveys these substances to the rest of the body. Fainting is caused by a deficient supply of oxygen to the brain.

The electrical activity of the brain can be measured by an electroencephalograph (EEG). This device registers brain waves graphically by means of electrodes linked to the scalp. The graphic report is known as an electroencephalogram (also abbreviated to EEG). It indicates which parts of the brain process certain types of information and is used to diagnose cerebral damage or abnormalities such as epilepsy. The EEG was developed by Hans Berger, a psychiatrist, in 1921.

In much simplified terms the brain consists of the following parts (see figure 3.4):

The cerebral cortex

This is the outer layer of the brain, comprising approximately 80% of the total brain capacity of humans. It is accommodated in the cranium by dint of convoluting and folding. It is the seat of

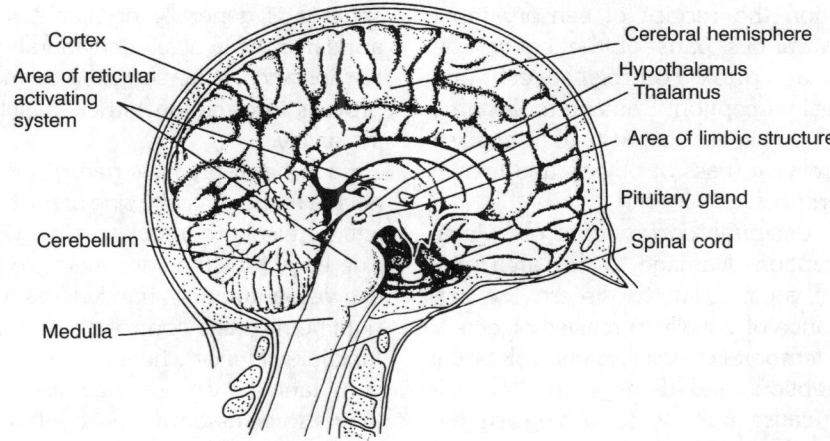

Figure 3.4 Vertical brain section

sensory, motor and association centres which integrate and interpret information, thus constituting the highest level of nerve activity.

The cerebral cortex gives meaning to behaviour through cognition, the higher mental processes that process data, which permit more subtle responses than the merely reflex.

In humans the association centres occupy approximately three-quarters of the cortex – which explains the complexity of human behaviour as opposed to that of animals. They serve to integrate certain activities, for example reading and hearing (sensory functions), writing and speaking (motor functions), language and functions of intelligence, emotional control, memory and perceptual organisation.

Four association areas can be distinguished: the frontal, parietal, occipital and temporal cortical areas (see figure 3.5). Each of these areas is responsible for certain specialised functions. These areas constitute the outer part of the *cerebrum*, which makes up the bulk of the brain and is surrounded by the cortex. The cerebrum consists of two symmetrical halves or *hemispheres*, the left and right hemispheres. Each hemisphere is divided into

a frontal, parietal, occipital and temporal lobe (see figure 3.5).

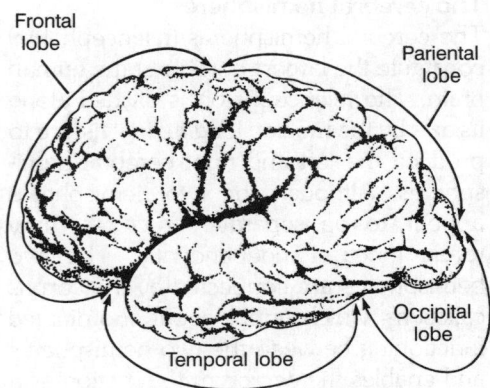

Figure 3.5 Cerebral hemispheres

- The *frontal cortex* has diverse functions, including the control of relative functions like planning, perseveration and motor behaviour, or movements of parts of the body. Injury to this area may cause reduced initiative and reduced purposive behaviour, diminished intellectual functioning, and the tendency to perseveration, which means offer-ing the same response repeatedly, regardless of consequences.

- The *parietal cortex* has as its primay function the receipt of sensory input from various parts of the body. The parietal cortex controls speech and tactual perception. Damage to this area may result in an incapacity to distinguish the relative mass of objects and textual differences.
- The *occipital cortex* controls visual perception. Damage to this area may cause an inability to discern the significance of visually perceived objects.
- The *temporal cortex* also controls visual perception, and damage to this area may cause inability to distinguish between shades. The temporal area would appear to have a memory function as well, as stimulation of it causes the individual to recall experiences from the past.

The cerebral hemispheres

The cerebral hemispheres (telencephalon) constitute the largest portion of the human brain. The telencephalon is divided along its axis by the median longitudinal fissure to produce the left and right cerebral hemispheres. Although the two hemispheres appear to be separate structures, they rarely function independently. The two hemispheres are connected by the corpus callosum, which brings about coordinated functioning between the two hemispheres and enables the cerebrum to function as a unit (Davis et al. 1985).

Besides coordinated functioning, the two hemispheres also control independent specialised functions. The left hemisphere is specialised for language functions, logical thinking and analytical and mathematical tasks. The right hemisphere is responsible for spatial visualisation, imagination, intuition and musical and artistic activities.

Some researchers believe that not only is a particular hemisphere more dominant than the other when the activities which it controls are being carried out, but also that in certain individuals one of the hemispheres is generally dominant, as would appear from typical behavioural activities. For instance, a person may be inclined to process information either analytically or intuitively.

Each hemisphere is neurologically connected to the opposite side of the body. The left hemisphere regulates the right-hand side body functions, for example the right eye vision and right-handedness, while the right hemisphere controls the left-hand side functions. Hence where one hemisphere is dominant, the various specialised functions may also be associated with left- and right-handedness, depending on the degree of domination.

Notwithstanding the different functions which the hemispheres control, most human behavioural functions cannot be reduced to a single structure of the nervous system, since its functions are complex and integrated.

The thalamus

The basic function of the thalamus is as a relay station from which impulses are routed to and from the cerebral cortex. Except for the sense of smell, all sensory impulses arriving at the brain must pass through the thalamus before being projected upward to specific areas of the cortex. The thalamus also helps to interpret simple sensations, such as pain, temperature and crude touch and pressure sensations.

The hypothalamus

The hypothalamus is one of the primary brain regions that control the unconscious activities of various organs of the body, such as the heart, lungs, digestive tract and excretory system. The hypothalamus controls body temperature, appetite and feeding behaviour, thirst, sleep and wakefulness, psychosomatic events and activities of the endocrine system. The hypothalamus also controls the pituitary gland, which in turn controls other glands affecting emotional and motivational aspects of behaviour.

The limbic system
The limbic system consists of a number of structures linked to the thalamus and hypothalamus. Electric stimulation of different parts of the limbic system evokes emotional responses such as excitement, despondency, mobility, passivity and anger. The cerebral cortex also contains a limbic area which would appear to store past emotional experiences, for example experience related to pain, smell or sexuality.

The hypothalamus, a major integration area for involuntary, visceral activity, is a central part of the limbic system. Thus, involuntary physiological activities of various organ systems are often associated with emotional states. For example, feelings of guilt or anxiety often cause elevations in blood pressure and heart rate, as well as changes in respiratory rhythm and the electrical conduction of the skin.

The reticular activation system (RAS)
The RAS consists of a variety of neural pathways and brain stem nuclei, as well as the thalamus, which communicates with all areas of the central nervous system. The RAS serves as a coordinating centre consisting of diffused cells with inhibitory or facilitating (excitatory) functions involving activation, sleep and wakefulness. This mechanism brings the whole body to a state of alertness and readiness.

Sensory stimuli from the receptors activate the RAS, which transmits impulses to the cerebral cortex, thereby enhancing its receptivity to sensory messages. The RAS sifts the impulses so that not every stimulus from the immediate environment is registered.

The cortex in turn transmits impulses to the RAS, inhibiting or facilitating its functioning. For example, an employee's attitude to a superior (information stored in the cortex) determines whether he or she will act on the instructions of the superior (activation of the RAS by the motor areas of the cortex) or conveniently fail to notice them (inhibition of the RAS by the sensory cortex). This may also explain why the recollection of stressful situations can cause increased anxiety levels.

The RAS consists of two parts. Electrical stimulation of the lower part appears to be inhibitory, inducing somnolence and fatigue. The degree of weariness depends on a balance between inhibitory and excitatory effects. When the inhibitory action predominates, motor readiness is reduced. Monotony, which plays a part in fatigue, is caused by insufficient or inadequate stimulation from the environment. This means that there is little stimulation of the excitatory part of the RAS. Increasing activity of the inhibitory RAS results in somnolence, fatigue and reduced alertness.

The medulla oblongata
The *medulla oblongata*, or myelencephalon, is the lowest portion of the brain stem. The medulla contains nerve cells controlling vital functions such as respiration and blood pressure. It also acts as a relay station for the transmission of actual information such as a skin sensation caused by contact with a person or object (Davis et al. 1985).

The cerebellum
The cerebellum receives sensory information from receptors in the skin, muscles, joints, balance mechanism and visual and auditory organs. The primary function of the cerebellum is the coordination of muscle activity, muscle tone and balance. The cerebellum receives information on the state of muscles as well as on planned muscle action. Damage to the cerebellum results in uncoordinated movement, affecting actions like walking, writing and balance.

3.3.3.2 The spinal cord

The spinal cord is situated in the spinal column and enclosed by 31 vertebrae. In an adult, the spinal cord is approximately 45 cm long and weighs about 30 g. The spinal cord connects many of the nerves that make up the peripheral nervous system to the brain. Although the spinal cord constitutes only about 2% of the central nervous system, its importance far outweighs its size. Through this connecting structure, sensory impulses from the body reach the brain and motor impulses from the brain descend to control motor activities of the body. Thus the brain provides a link between reflex behaviour and the higher mental processes it controls.

The spinal cord is the site of the lowest level of nerve activity, as it is concerned with reflex behaviour that is not under the control of higher mental processes like volition or reason. A reflex is a stereotyped reaction following almost instantly on a specific stimulus. It constitutes the basis of simple stimulus-response relations in the learning process. In a simple reflex a nerve impulse is transmitted from a receptor along a sensory neuron to the effector, which responds to the message, for example through muscle activity. The axon branches of sensory neurons can also be connected with various motor neurons as well as association neurons and this gives rise to more complex reflexes. Pavlov's research on the learning process was based on the interconnection of various reflexes.

Motivation, which is based on higher cerebral processes like insight, problem-solving and planning, can affect the acquisition of reflex behaviour.

3.3.4 The peripheral nervous system

Although the brain and spinal cord make up the central nervous system, information is fed into and out of the central nervous system by means of peripheral nerves. These peripheral nerves connect the sensory receptors and motor effectors of the body with the central nervous system. This peripheral network of nerves makes up the peripheral nervous system, which is subdivided into the autonomic and somatic nervous systems.

3.3.4.1 The autonomic nervous system

The autonomic nervous system is responsible for the regulation of visceral organ activities, among which are heart rate, smooth muscle contraction, glandular secretion, gastrointestinal motility and secretion and urinary bladder emptying.

This system is controlled by the hypothalamus, which is, in turn, subject to the limbic system. The autonomic system functions chiefly by reflex, triggering processes of which we need not be aware. Under normal circumstances, the autonomic nervous system operates outside the realm of consciousness. For this reason, one does not have to think in order to control visceral functions as they are under "automatic" control by the autonomic nervous system.

The autonomic nervous system is subdivided into the sympathetic and the parasympathetic systems. Most organs are connected to the autonomic system through both these systems. The two systems affect such organs in opposite ways, the sympathetic system activating them and the parasympathetic system inhibiting them. This counteractive effect of the two systems serves to maintain a physiological balance. In emotional crises, such as fear, the sympathetic system triggers activity, for example accelerated heartbeat, which causes a physiological imbalance. The parasympathetic system then restores the balance by reducing cardiac activity.

Balance or equilibrium in bodily organs is maintained by fluctuations in the two subsystems of the autonomic system. This state of equilibrium is called homeostasis.

Because homeostasis is arrived at reflexively without conscious cerebral intervention, the body automatically adjusts to emotional states. This homeostatic control enables humans to do other things, for example think, work and play, without constantly having to be on guard to control their bodily processes.

In some people one of the two autonomic systems is more active than the other. When the sympathetic system predominates, the individual is usually physically tense, and consequently he or she is prone to be easily excitable and emotional, and can have difficulty in concentrating on one subject. When the parasympathetic system dominates, the individual suffers from lassitude, lack of drive and motivation, and poor powers of concentration. However, most people have an autonomic balance with only sporadic bursts of dominance by one system or another. When balanced, such people have a moderate level of tension and therefore are tranquil, calm and able to concentrate.

3.3.4.2 The somatic nervous system

The somatic nervous system is connected with receptors in the skin, inner tissue, joints and skeletal muscles. The latter are termed voluntary muscles, as they are controlled by volition through contact with the central nervous system, which thus controls the operation of the somatic nervous system, for example to produce changes in posture.

Somatic reflexes do not involve the autonomic nervous system. However, even those reflexes that are primarily somatic have an autonomic component. For example, if the skin of an extremity is painfully stimulated, there is a somatic reflex withdrawal of the limb. This withdrawal reflex is accompanied by a rise in blood pressure and heart rate. These events result from autonomic reflexes activated along with somatic reflexes.

3.4 THE MUSCLE SYSTEM
3.4.1 The structure and functioning of muscles

Human movement is made possible by a muscle system which extends over the whole body and makes up about 45% of the total body mass. Each separate muscle consists of a large number of muscle fibres which vary between 0,5 cm and 14 cm in length, while the average diameter of muscle fibre is 0,1 mm. A single muscle may contain between 100 000 and 1 million fibres attached to bones by means of sinews. These consist of groups of specialised fibres known as collagen fibres (Grandjean 1988).

Muscles are connected to both motor and sensory nerves. Each muscle fibre is synaptically connected with a branch of a motor nerve axon by means of specialised terminal structures called motor end plates (see figure 3.6). These plates release a chemical transmitter substance which causes the muscle fibres to contract. The number of muscle fibres stimulated (and hence the force and speed of movement) is related to the frequency of motor impulses, but the nature of the contraction is also determined by the type of muscle tissue, its location and its arrangement. For example, some muscles can contract to half their length, so that the length of a muscle also determines its work potential.

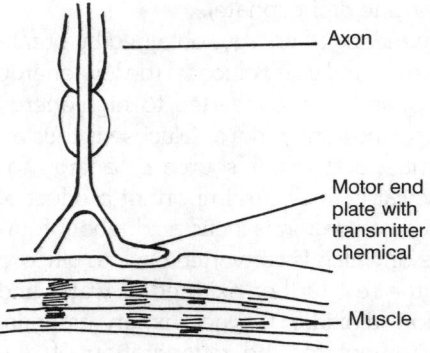

Figure 3.6 Nerve-muscle synapse

The frequency of motor impulses to a muscle depends on reflexes from the spinal cord on the one hand, and nerve activity generated in the brain on the other. Spinal cord reflexes are also controlled by the RAS, in that some of its neurons have long axons extending down the spinal cord, among other things to activate muscles for the physical posture which initiates movement. The brain can grade the frequency of stimuli to muscles so that muscle strength is more or less proportionate to the action to be executed.

Brain centres like the cerebellum and cortex are informed of the state of the muscle system by sensory nerves connected to the muscle. These convey sensations of the position, force and tension of the muscles which are interpreted by the brain, which then transmits motor impulses for the appropriate action to the muscles.

The energy necessary for muscle contraction comes from the chemical energy reserves stored in the muscle. Muscular work therefore depends on the conversion of chemical energy into mechanical energy. Chemical reactions release energy which changes the structure of the protein molecules in the muscle fibres, thereby shortening them. The immediate source of energy is phosphate compounds which, in the course of chemical action, are changed from a high-energy state to a low-energy state (e.g. adenosine triphosphate to adenosine diphosphate).

By means of energy, obtained by breaking down and using glucose, the low-energy compounds are converted to high-energy compounds once more. Glucose is thus an essential and major source of energy for muscular activity. An important product of glucose oxidation is lactic acid, about four-fifths of which is converted back to glucose and the rest further oxidised to water and carbon dioxide. Oxygen is an essential requirement for the regeneration of glucose and high-energy phosphate compounds. It constitutes a second vital prerequisite for muscular activity.

Glucose and oxygen are stored in muscles in limited quantities only, necessitating constant supplies from the blood. Because of this, blood supply can place restrictions on muscular activity. During strenuous exertion the demand for blood increases 10 to 20 times. The mechanisms by which this increased supply is secured are an accelerated heart rate, heightened blood pressure and dilation of blood vessels.

3.4.2 Dynamic and static muscular activity

We distinguish between dynamic (rhythmic activity) and static (fixed position) muscular activity. The former comprises a rhythmic succession of muscular contractions followed by relaxation, whereas static activity requires prolonged spells of contraction.

In everyday life various parts of the body perform diverse static muscular activities. For instance, standing requires continuous contraction of whole groups of muscles in the legs, hips, back and neck to maintain different parts of the body in the desired position. Sitting requires no static activities from the legs and as a result imposes less overall muscular strain. A reclining position demands hardly any muscular contraction, which makes it most suitable for resting.

There are certain basic differences between static and dynamic muscular activity. Static exertion causes compression of blood vessels owing to increased muscular pressure and consequent decreased blood supply. Dynamic muscular activity, on the other hand, means an increased blood supply, the muscle receiving ten to twenty times more blood than during static muscle activity. Successive contraction and relaxation during dynamic activity ensures regular blood supply during this phase. In this way the muscle is adequately furnished with glucose and oxygen during dynamic activity while waste is effectively removed. Intense static contraction cuts off the supply of oxygen and sugar from the blood, with the result that waste products accumulate.

During static muscular activity the blood supply is reduced proportionately to the strength of the contraction. When the contraction reaches 60% of its maximum strength, the blood supply is cut off entirely. At lower intensities some measure of blood is supplied and during static exertion of between 15% and 20% of maximum strength, the blood supply is said to be normal. Static effort exerting 50% or more of maximum strength can be maintained for one minute at the utmost, implying that, in job design, exacting static activity should be confined to a minimum or eliminated altogether.

3.5 JOB DESIGN

Jobs and work environments are designed in the light of muscle functioning and the part this plays in the integrated functioning of the various systems of the human body. In view of the physiological infrastructure of muscular activity, industrial psychologists have established principles of job design to ensure optimal utilisation of human ability while allowing for limitations and weakness. Ergonomics principles are applied in the design of jobs and work environments. Some of the concerns in job design are body posture, body size, and repetitive strain.

3.5.1 Working body posture

Standing and sitting are the most frequently adopted working postures, but other postures, such as lying down, are also used, for instance in repair work. There are many tasks which oblige people to remain sitting or standing in a fixed position for long periods. Activities such as machining, industrial inspection, dentistry, driving or just sitting at a desk or computer workstation are typical.

The posture adopted by a person is determined by the need to reach controls, to keep the feet on pedals, or to keep the eyes in positions from which the task can be seen. When the task is very dangerous or demanding, as it might be for a pilot or an astronaut, the consequences of making things too difficult for the operator are serious and may be life threatening for a large number of people. In such cases, great efforts are made to minimise the discomfort and difficulty of reaching for controls and reading displays. In many tasks, however, when the consequences of error are neither as serious nor so obvious, people are often expected to adapt to a working posture, even though this may cause discomfort and difficulty.

The ability of people to adapt themselves to difficult situations, and their willingness to accept the challenge of tasks that are more difficult than they need be, should not blind us to the costs of adaptation. Among these costs are injuries and strains from bad working postures, less spare capacity to deal with emergencies, and a greater probability of accidents and errors.

The work space of the hands depends on body posture and task requirements, hence various suitable work space envelopes can be described. However, vision requirements at work also determine the working volume. Operation of controls is usually done either with the hands or the feet. Foot operations are stronger but slower, and should be required from seated operators only. Hand operation of controls is faster and weaker but more versatile. Tools and equipment should be designed to properly fit the hand. This requires not only proper sizing of a handle, but also its arrangement, so that the wrist or arm is not brought into straining positions.

Improper posture and repeated and forceful operations may lead to "overuse" disorders, often associated with the repetitive use of hand tools, particularly if they vibrate. Another common source of overuse disorders is the frequent use of keyboards.

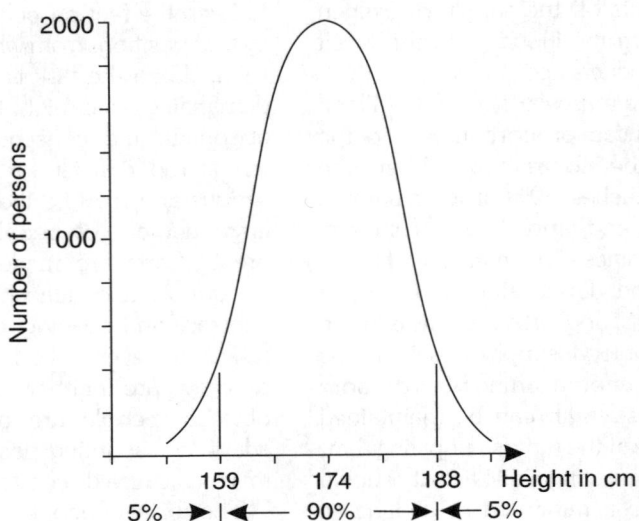

Figure 3.7 Normal distribution curve (frequency distribution of body height)

3.5.2 Body size

There is an enormous variation in body size between individuals, the sexes and different races. Two people of the same height and sex are almost certain to differ in arm or leg length, sitting height, hand size or any body dimension. Body size means not just height but any body measurement which is important for the equipment or work space being designed.

To design a work space properly, the range of body sizes of the anticipated user population must be known. The users of a piece of equipment may form a large group, such as all men, for example miners, or all men, women and older teenagers who are motorcar drivers, or may be a more restricted group, such as children under the age of 12 who are users of primary school furniture. Knowledge of the average body dimensions of the group of users is not sufficient; the distribution and range of sizes within the group must be known or estimated. Fortunately, it has been shown that in the case of most body dimensions, this distribution is known and can be closely approximated by a known

mathematical formula, called the *normal distribution*. In figure 3.7 the normal distribution curve for body height is shown. Most people in a group are near the average for the group, but a sizeable proportion are appreciatively above or below the average, and a few people will be far from the average. It is common in ergonomics solutions to cater for 90% of the user population, and to exclude the 5% furthest above and the 5% furthest below the average, as shown in figure 3.7 (Galer 1987). The figure depicts the frequency distribution of body height among South African males.

3.5.3 Repetitive strain

Repetitive strain refers to overuse of certain body elements.

In the early 1980s, an epidemic of so-called *repetitive strain injuries* (RSI) occurred in offices where keyboards were used. An understanding of the injury mechanisms is necessary, so that they may be prevented by ergonomic measures at work.

An overuse disorder is the result of

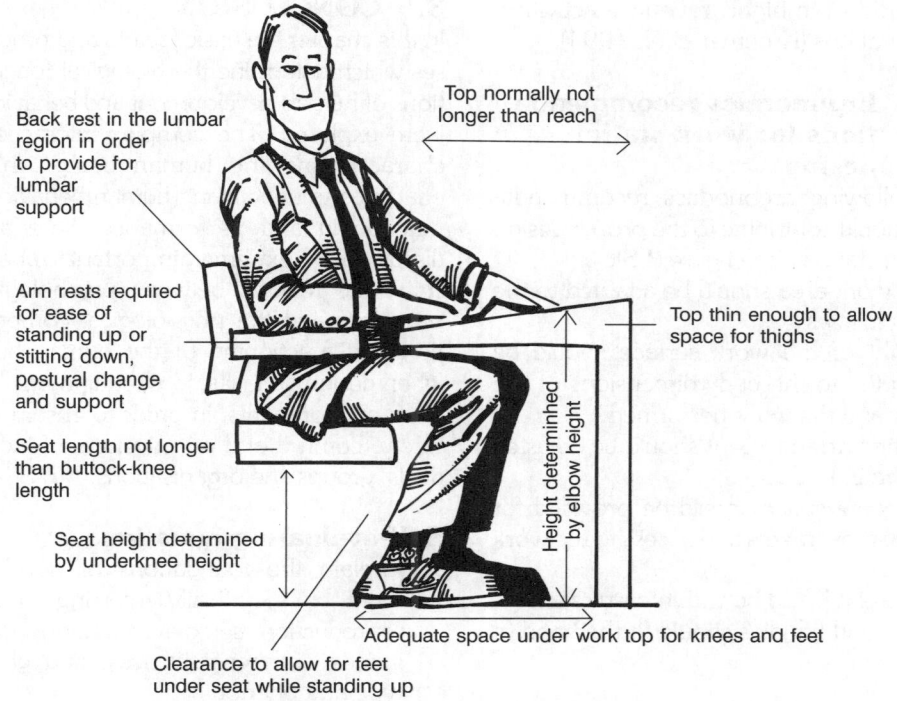

Back rest in the lumbar region in order to provide for lumbar support

Top normally not longer than reach

Arm rests required for ease of standing up or stitting down, postural change and support

Top thin enough to allow space for thighs

Seat length not longer than buttock-knee length

Height determinhed by elbow height

Seat height determined by underknee height

Adequate space under work top for knees and feet

Clearance to allow for feet under seat while standing up

Figure 3.8 The work station

excessive use of a body element, often a joint, muscle or tendon. In contrast to a single-event injury, called acute or traumatic, the overuse disorder stems from sustained efforts or from often repeated actions which are not harmful when they occur once or infrequently, but whose time-related cumulative effects finally result in an injury. These effects are usually related to body posture or motion, energy or force exerted and duration or repetitiveness. Different terms have been used to describe these phenomena, such as occupational overuse disorder (or injury, or syndrome); regional musculo-skeletal disorder; work-related disorder; repetitive stress or strain or motion injury; cumulative trauma disorder; rheumatic disease and osteoarthrosis (Kroemer et al. 1994).

Overuse disorders or repetitive strain injuries often occur in connective soft tissues, particularly to tendons and their sheaths. They may irritate or damage nerves and impede the blood flow through arteries and veins. They are frequent in the hand-wrist-forearm area (for example, in the carpal tunnel) and in the shoulder and neck. Repetitive loadings may even damage bone, such as the vertebrae of the spinal column.

Among the best-known repetitive strain injuries is the *carpal tunnel syndrome* (CTS). People who suffer from CTS are normally employed in work requiring light, highly repetitive movements of the wrists and fingers, for example typists. In the early 1980s, CTS was well recognised as a frequently occurring, disabling condition of the hand that can be caused, precipitated or aggravated by certain work activities in the office and on the shop floor. Critical activities include a flexed or hyperextended wrist, especially in combination with forceful exertions, in highly repetitive activities, and vibrations (Kroemer et al. 1994).

3.5.4 Ergonomics recommendations for work station design

The following ergonomics recommendations should contribute to the proper design of work stations (see figure 3.8).

The work area should be adapted to the user as follows:
- height of the work surface should be adapted to the body dimensions of the user and the work performed
- seating arrangement should be adjusted to the individual
- adequate space should be provided for body movements and access to the work station
- controls should be within easy reach
- grips and handles should fit the hand of the user

The work should be adapted to the user as follows:
- unnecessary strain should be avoided
- strength requirements should be within desirable limits
- body movements should follow natural rhythms
- posture, strength and movement should be harmonised
  Particular attention should be paid to:
- alternating in, and between, sitting and standing postures
- sitting is preferable to standing (if one must be chosen)
- keeping chain of force vectors through body short and simple
- allowing suitable body posture and providing appropriate support
- providing auxiliary energy if strength demands are excessive
- avoiding immobility, preferring motions

3.6 CONCLUSION

In this chapter the basic factors and processes which determine the biological foundations of human development and behaviour were explored. The complex interactions characterising the human being which enable us to understand human behaviour, functioning and performance were also discussed. It is extremely important to understand the relation between psychological processes and the physiological composition and functioning of the human body when designing tasks, jobs, equipment and work environments, in order to ensure the safety, comfort and effectiveness of individuals, groups and organisations.

Self-evaluating questions

1. Explain the foundations of development by specifically referring to cell reproduction, sex determination, dominance and recessiveness, and genotype and phenotype.
2. Make a list of factors that would explain why blood relatives can be genetically different.
3. Explain the structure and functioning of the central and peripheral nervous systems.
4. Explain the structure and functioning of the muscle system.
5. Explain how static and dynamic muscular activity involves fatigue, with reference to particular types of work.
6. Discuss the causes of repetitive strain injury.
7. Evaluate your work area, furniture and activities at work according to the ergonomics recommendations for work station design provided in this chapter. Indicate how certain aspects can be improved.

Human development

4

Ziel Bergh

CONTENTS

Learning outcomes

After studying this chapter you should be able to:

- describe the field of study in human development
- give examples to illustrate the characteristics of human development
- discuss the domains of human development in various stages
- explain how genetic and learning factors determine human development
- observe how critical periods influence human development
- discuss people's development over the life span
- analyse adult career development as part of human development

---

Key concepts

development, maturation, growth, ageing, maturity, evolution, differentiation, complexity, predictability, cognitive, physical, psychosocial, moral, genetic, learning, environment, critical periods, attachment, ego-identity, career transitions, tasks, occupational identity, early life, adulthood, old age

4.1 INTRODUCTION

The study of human development, in personality and career psychology, incorporates age-related or sequential changes from a person's conception to death, due to genetic and learning influences. Human development is about maturation, growth and ageing in a person's physical characteristics, thinking processes and social and emotional behaviours. Human development also involves transitions during the life span in which the individual, at every stage, must reach a certain level of maturity in order to socialise in and fulfil various life roles, such as in education, love and marriage, friendships, work, parenting, religion, recreation and society.

Changes resulting from genetic attributes are termed *maturation*. They are inborn and "pre-planned", will occur at certain stages and ages, but can be hindered by influences such as faulty nutrition and illness. *Ageing* refers to chronological increase in years and biological and physical changes. Ageing may result in a decline of functions, but may also relate to improvement in some functions. *Growth* may refer to increases in the physical size of biological structures, but also to improvement in mental and psychosocial competencies. *Maturity* refers to the integration of physical, cognitive, social and psychological (emotional) tasks at a level where a person can function or live as a fully functioning person at every stage. People can be defined as mature if they show "physical and social independence and autonomy, independent decision-making and some degree of stability, wisdom, reliability, integrity and compassion" (Craig 1996:474). Maturity may apply to various stages of life or to specific aspects of human functioning; for instance, it is said that sexual maturity occurs during puberty or early adolescence; "school readiness" (about 7 years) at a stage when children are sufficiently developed to attend school; and career maturity when a person is ready to make responsible occupational choices from time to time. Maturity may be defined in many ways and has many cultural nuances. A clear demarcation in time is not a simple matter, but maturity is often coupled to being an adult (about 21 years and older). *Readiness* may refer to a point in development where the individual has matured sufficiently to benefit from learning or experiences.

The study of human development is necessary for the following reasons:

- Development results in a repertoire of competencies (knowledge, abilities, skills, behaviours, attitudes and values) needed for life roles.
- Development enables people to determine timelines or schedules and norms on what to expect of people, when and how certain types of physical, cognitive and psychological behaviours are supposed to occur and how to act accordingly.
- Development provides continuity and identity in people's ways of living and behaviour, for instance with respect to family ties, cultural habits and values, interpersonal styles and attachment behaviours, types of jobs and socio-economic standards.

4.2 CHARACTERISTICS OF HUMAN DEVELOPMENT

The processes of development can be explained by identifying some of their characteristics, which incorporate elements of both maturation (genetics) and learning (environment).

4.2.1 Hierarchical evolution of phases

All theories generally agree on the various life and career stages, each marked by qualitative differences in behaviour. Although more specific and overlapping phases are distinguished, they can usually be grouped into four overlapping main stages: *early life stage*, from infancy through childhood to adolescence, and involving occupational choice and preparation (birth to about 22); *young adult stage*, involving entry and establishment in a career (about 22 to 45); *middle adulthood stage*, involving career consolidation, maintenance and change (about 45 to 60); and *late adulthood life stage* (60 and older), involving career decline and retirement. Adult occupational life concerns the adult stages, but the importance of the formative earlier stages especially,

and even late adulthood stage, cannot be ignored.

The progression or evolution of phases is predetermined by the *maturation of biological systems*, such as the central nervous system. Gesell (in Craig 1996) asserts that under normal conditions behaviours evolve in orderly and predictable sequences; i.e. certain physical, cognitive and psychological behaviours emerge at certain ages and stages. In contrast to the newborn baby, whose behaviour is largely reflexive, the developing child acquires greater control over its behaviour and becomes increasingly susceptible to the host of environmental influences as the higher cortical brain centres develop.

Skeletal growth also produces changes in shape, size and weight. An imbalance between physical and *emotional maturation* causes problems of adjustment. Thus adolescents may suffer mental stress because they are sexually mature, yet emotionally still children, unable to handle the dimensions of socio-sexual adaptation. Among many teenagers, and women, physical appearance or body image constitutes a major norm for acceptance by the group. Youngsters and women who are retarded in their physical development and differ conspicuously from their peers may give vent to antisocial behaviour, avoid group activities (appearance anxiety) as a defence against possible rejection, or behave aggressively to compensate for feelings of inferiority. A child whose relatively early physical maturity is accompanied by healthy emotional maturation may develop qualities of self-control and responsibility which could culminate in leadership attributes during adult life.

Phases of development are, however, not discrete, separable entities. Each phase emanates from preceding ones and is inextricably linked with the next. In later phases certain elements of early behaviour are either eliminated as ineffectual or transformed into higher patterns of

The cycles of life

adaptation. Hence we speak of evolution from elementary to higher behaviour, which is accompanied by an involution of various behavioural elements.

There are different orders or rates of development for different types of behaviours. Structure primarily precipitates function. An infant is unable to talk until the relevant neurological speech centres have matured, yet is able to understand language before it has mastered it as a means of communication. Speech development progresses relatively slowly compared to control over body movements like walking. Once the infant has learned to speak, its orientation is more cognitive, and motor development slows down.

The same may hold for evolution of career decision tasks; people may experience career indecision because certain tasks have not developed in earlier phases. In recent times, due to changes in labour markets and work ethics, strict adherence to the stage idea is questioned. For instance, people now have to create their own vocations, more so than in the past, or youths are forced to study longer and be dependent on parents for longer periods.

The years up to puberty constitute a relatively long period of parental dependence, which continues to influence the individual's adjustment after reaching adulthood. Thus some adults fail to develop healthy, self-managing independence, remaining relatively dependent on symbolic parent or authority figures to control their actions. The impact of youthful experience is evident from research on many personality disorders, like sociopaths (people whose behaviour deviates from social and moral norms), which shows that, despite attempts to eradicate antisocial behaviour through psychotherapy, these trends still surface under stress, because the roots of such behaviour in early childhood cannot be entirely removed.

4.2.2 Differentiation from the general to the particular

At birth the cortex is still poorly developed and behaviour follows mainly reflexive, motor-sensory patterns. Babies react to diverse physical and emotional stimuli in rather general ways, such as undirected and diffuse physical movement with the whole body, and general excitement. Gradually the baby's responses become recognisable as particular gestures or emotions. By three or four months any human action will occasion a smile, but by six months the baby is able to discriminate and its smiles are reserved mainly for its mother or caretaker. Initially any unfamiliar stimulus or stranger provokes fear, but eventually, with increased powers of discrimination, fear is prompted only by particular people, objects or situations.

Cortical maturation gives rise to greater selectivity with regard to effective behaviour in situations demanding choice. As indicated in the next section, the developing person's problem-solving skills develop from very concrete to more abstract, becoming evaluative, allowing diverse thinking and recognising relationships between things.

4.2.3 Increased complexity

At birth motor neurons are mainly small, with long axons transmitting impulses at low speed, evoking only diffuse general responses. With age the development of an insulating myelin layer around the axons of some neurons causes speedier and more continuous transmission of impulses and hence more complex behaviour.

The complexity and quality of motor development is also reflected in more intelligent behaviour. The progressive development of abilities for association, complex thought, reasoning and language enables people to learn and internalise knowledge from their culture. Through learning and maturation the baby's "cooing" communication with its mother becomes language communication with the world, just as its primitive biting and sucking reflexes change to the traditional eating habits of its culture.

Infants' first emotional bonds with their mothers form the basis of their subsequent emotional ties (attachment behaviours) with other children and other adults, as in friendship and love, relationships with co-workers, superiors and with groups in the work or social, cultural and political associations. The variety of behaviour codes with regard to marriage alone indicates the complexity of motivations in modern man. More and more, babies' largely physiological needs are supplemented and changed by social needs of ego and self-actualisation until, by the time they are adults, all these needs are integrated and expressed in balanced ways.

Increased complexity and sophistication is also evident in other physical and psychosocial functions as a result of maturation and learning. In this respect babies' sleep patterns change into more time spent in exploring the "world", while the secretion of certain hormones in males and females, and social norms, allows for sexual interest, stimulation and ways to express these urges. Deficiencies in certain hormones, for instance thyroxin (secreted by the thyroid gland), result in hypothyroidism, a condition of general underdevelopment in physical, cognitive and emotional attributes

4.2.4 Predictability

As a rule most individuals follow a recognisable, similar pattern of development. This is one of the advantages of the stage theories, which allow us to more or less determine norms or time schedules and what to expect from people at different ages and transitions. Such predictability applies not merely to simple responses to a single stimulus, but also to successive patterns of diverse behaviours. Behaviour is to some extent predictable, because its development is partly automatic, irrespective of the limitations of learning. Physiological functions are important for the survival of the individual and for the species. As far as the individual is concerned, it is necessary to know when the person is ready for both formal and informal learning and for emotional experience.

General forms of behaviour provide criteria for normality whereby individuals can be assessed. The average infant starts walking at 14 months, retarded ones at between 30 and 80 months. Bright infants start talking at 11 months, average ones at 16 months and retarded children at between 30 and 80 months. Here development is seen mainly as a function of maturation, but environment must always be a consideration.

Motor development can be retarded by both physical and emotional factors; examples of the latter are emotional overprotection and deprivation. In a study of children in institutions and in dysfunctional families, it was found that although their motor development at two months was normal, by the end of the first year they became progressively retarded. However, between the ages of four and six their motor behaviour once more corresponded to the norm. Early motor retardation was attributable to restricted stimulation and experience, but with maturation they eventually improved. In another study it was found that twin girls, who at the age of two months were placed in a restricted environment without social interaction or maternal nurture but with good physical care, at 13 months differed in no way, either emotionally or cognitively, from children who had received all the necessary positive stimulation. Maturation had been automatic (Craig 1996; Kennedy 1971).

Research suggests that the correlation of physical with mental traits is also predictable. Outstanding qualities tend to be combined in one individual. Mental development occurs mostly between the ages of one and 18 while the body is growing.

Development can be predicted in the light of biological and environmental factors like parent-child relationships and culture. This is easier to determine during childhood if one allows for factors like nutrition, emotional stimulation or deprivation, and learning opportunities, but further research is needed. Environments constantly change, introducing new experiences and attitudes as well as unpredictable chance incidents.

4.3 DOMAINS OF HUMAN DEVELOPMENT

Human development involves changes in three broad interdependent areas of human functioning: physical, cognitive and psycho-social. Development, changes and integration in all domains are important for the progressive development of the individual over his or her life span, but also for effective functioning in each stage and with respect to specific areas, e.g. as scholar, worker, parent and member of society. A child in grade A will only be ready for school and cope with the school situation if the necessary mental, physical and emotional developments are in place and complement one another. The child must not only think, understand and remember, but also speak and perform practical tasks, as well as adjust to pressures and responsibilities of a new situation and the emotional demands of peers and groups. This applies to the university student, the human resources manager or the technician. Effective occupational fit is not only about intellect, but also about competencies of problem-solving, logical reasoning, judgement, emotional control, social skills and adapting to the physical demands of the job. A fourth domain, *career development*, could be added, which is part of life span development, possibly integrating all previous development and which also results from progressive changes and growth in the physical, cognitive and psychosocial domains.

4.3.1 Physical or biological domain

The physical or biological entails *maturation, growth and ageing* and primarily refers to changes in the person's body as a result of innate biological processes. Maturation processes are quite similar for most people, but exceptions and differences are evident. Motor and physical attributes like walking, talking, reproductive capacities, ageing, contracting certain diseases, aspects of perception, even certain intellectual and psychological processes, like learning, and personality traits, may develop quite similarly or universally in all people and not altogether influenced by social learning. It seems as if intelligence, as measured by intelligence tests, reaches its peak somewhere between the 20s and 30s, and declines after the age of 45.

Bio-psychological approaches to personality, which emphasise the role of genetics in human development and in psychosocial behaviours, are related to ethnology, the study of animal behaviour, and often finds commonalities with humans. Researchers such as Lorenz and Harlow (cited in Craig 1996) found similar types of attachment behaviours in humans and monkeys. An indication of biological determination is that even retarded and isolated individuals still demonstrate certain sequential development in physical, cognitive and psychological behaviours. Behaviour patterns in humans, such as affiliation and nurturing, mating, dominance, aggression and territoriality, may have biological elements, in addition to learning or cultural influences.

4.3.2 Cognitive development

This refers to the progressive development of .*thought processes*, mental abilities and the capacities to obtain, process, interpret, retrieve and use information. These attributes change over time, from being simplistic, concrete and self-centred to more complex, organised, integrated and holistic.

Recognised theories on cognitive development are Piaget's theory on cognitive development, Schaie's theory on adult thinking, information-processing theories such as Sternberg's, and Kohlberg's notions on moral development (Craig 1996; Cloninger 1996). Cognitive development is based on growth and maturation of genetically determined processes (such as brain and other neurological structures) and the development of cognitive competencies at certain age-related transitions. As the person grows and matures, it is expected that certain intellectual and other cognitive abilities will develop and become available to the individual, and the person is thus expected to perform certain tasks. Progression in a specific job or in a career also depends on development of cognitive skills, which become more advanced with higher job levels. In this respect, it is assumed that a manager must be able to show more initiative and think more creatively and integratively than subordinates.

The characteristics of development discussed up to now are reflected in many ways in Piaget's much recognised and researched theory on the development of cognition.

Piaget indicated how cognition in all children develops in predictable hierarchic phases through interaction between maturation and learning experiences. During these phases the cognitive processes together with the emotional experiences form categories of information (cognitive structures) or "schemata", which can change in quantity and quality. As thinking processes become more complex, individuals' ability to adapt to the environment and to organise information also progresses through the mechanisms of assimilation and accommodation.

Through *assimilation* quantitative development takes place, new information and experiences are interpreted and integrated with the existing mental processes, without the mental structures changing. *Accommodation* promotes qualitative development, in that cognitive processes are changed to handle new experiences. In the work situation accommodation contributes to adaptation through the learning of new concepts, or being able to solve more complex problems from all the separate sources of information.

Cognitive adaptation is effected through integration of various schemata and balance between assimilation and accommodation. An important contribution of Piaget's theory is the implications for adult thinking, specifically the finding that thinking patterns progressively develop from very concrete to complex and abstract.

The phases through which cognitive development progresses are given in table 4.1.

Stages and ages	Characteristics
Sensory (Birth – 2 years)	• knowledge through looking at and touching, holding and manipulating objects • coordination, sensory-motor perception becomes more complex, e.g. perception of feeling, weight, texture, taste and sound • distinguish self and environment • the concept of "object permanence", that is, objects exist even though not directly visible • little ability to understand symbols
Pre-operational (2 – 7 years)	• learn through own actions • increasingly able to remember and anticipate • internalise the concrete world through language and visual images • concepts of mass and constancy of objects • still many problems with relationships, things still seem irreversible; not all elements are considered • still egocentric in thinking
Concrete operational (7 – 11 years)	• more progress in concrete thinking • handle problems more logically and in various ways, consider more aspects • insight into the views of others • development of the concepts of number, relationships and reversibility • steady progress towards adult ways of thinking
Formal operational (11 – through adulthood)	• make use of abstract thought in addition to concrete, imagine things, metaphors, formulate and test hypotheses • logical thinking (inductive and deductive), systematic and diverse in problem-solving

Table 4.1 Piaget's stages of cognitive development

Schaie (1986) asserts that *adult thinking* develops in different progressive stages.

- In the acquisition stage, during childhood and adolescence, the individual acquires progressively more complex ways of thinking, of which the formal operations stage represents the highest level.
- The achieving period during young adulthood involves problem-solving and decision-making, through which, for example, the individual uses intellectual competencies to prepare for a career (studying and choosing a career).
- Growing from the achieving stage, the individual moves into a stage of responsibility, which means that such an individual must be an independent thinker, able to use his or her own solutions not only for personal and career problems, but also towards family, employer and the wider community.
- The executive stage, during middle adulthood, also involves responsibility, and enables people, through an increase of knowledge, such as how organisations function, to serve in responsible positions.
- In the final stage of reintegration, the individual at an old age must use his or her accumulated repertoire of intellectual skills to assess life and to give meaning to what has passed.

In terms of integration of cognitive competencies, Kegan (1982) asserts that cognitive development in every stage and throughout the life span has to do with ways of giving meaning to things and experiences. These *meaning systems* determine how people think and feel about things and how they behave. Every individual has a unique way of solving problems, though some aspects will be similar for some people at certain stages. As the adult matures, these meaning systems become progressively more complex and sophisticated, and unique to each individual, although similarities with other people also occur.

An important aspect of cognitive development is *moral development* or reasoning, indicating a person's progressive acquisition of a perception of right and wrong (a conscience). This usually develops in stages: the young child who thinks about right and wrong in terms of rewards and punishment from external sources such as parents; the older child who uses rules to create an own perception of morality; the adult who has an internalised or personal set of rules and ethics which are used to judge own and other behaviours and events (Kohlberg, in Craig 1996).

4.3.3 Psychosocial development

This involves the self-concept and self-identity of who and what the person is. All aspects of personality development are concerned: the self in various roles, such as a private person, a worker, a family person and as a member of society. It also involves personality characteristics, social skills and emotional reactions. Many approaches, especially the psycho-dynamic (psychoanalytic), humanistic theories (e.g. self theories) and learning (behaviouristic) approaches, explain much of how psychological characteristics, adjustment and maladjustment develop as a result of internal and external influences from the environment, such as important other people and groups.

4.3.4 Career-related tasks development

The development of these competencies as part of a person's life span development are as important as any of the other developmental domains; all domains, physical, cognitive and psychosocial, contribute to career choice to enable the individual to make appropriate career-related decisions at certain stages, whether it be choice of school subjects, a study direction, a first job, maintaining relationships at work, decisions to stay in or change a job or to retire. Developing a work ethic, attitudes about productivity and performance, and values as to what issues in work life to emphasise, should also be facilitated in human development. This is especially important if we consider that work, together with family life and religion, is one of our most important central life interests. Work gives meaning to life in many respects. It is most important that people find meaning in work and provide for themselves economically.

Development and changes in these four domains seldom occur separately, but rather interdependently and holistically and causes human growth and behaviour changes in people. Development in one area will influence change or adjustment in another. Development in one area or during one phase is often critical or a prerequisite for development or change in another area.

4.4 DETERMINANTS OF HUMAN DEVELOPMENT

Developmental influences are classified as inherited, and learning or experience as a result of various environmental influences. It is widely accepted that human development is the product of the interaction between genetic potential and social learning, and the latter often determines how the genetic characteristics manifest themselves.

4.4.1 Hereditary determination

Many human similarities and unique behaviours are influenced by our inborn or genetic inheritance. Maturation due to genetic potential is a predetermined series of biological and related processes that occur as the individual grows physically and increases in age, without environmental and even illness and nutrition factors having a marked influence on the natural course of events. Absolute favourable environmental factors, such as physical health, nutrition and psychosocial conditions, do not necessarily increase the tempo of maturation.

Genetic determination has a more dominant influence on the physical domains of behaviour, such as the rate of physical growth, muscles, glands, the brain and sense organs, the development of motor skills and even the manifestation or potential manifestation of physical diseases and psychological disorders. Although some put the extent of genetic dominance in intelligence higher or lower, a consensus estimate of authorities in this field is about 60% (Snyderman & Rothman 1987). Some also believe that the level of intelligence and specific talents, such as music, are the result of genetics. Genetic influence on psychological and social behaviour is connected to attachment behaviours and aspects of perception, while personality factors and psychological and physical disease patterns are increasingly connected (Eysenck 1991; Friedman & Booth-Kewley 1987).

4.4.2 Environment and learning

Environmental influences involve all non-genetic factors that may come into play before birth, such as nutrition, substance uses, happiness and stress, and which influence the pregnant mother and unborn child, and those experienced after birth, when the new-born is subjected to an array of planned and unexpected environmental influences and learning experiences. Environmental factors are related to psychosocial and emotional development and also to cognitive and physical development. The impact of influences is determined by many factors, such as the intensity and frequency of the influence, how a person perceives events and the person's ability to cope with possible influences.

Physical factors include nutrition, toxic chemical substances in the air and medicine, radiation, sound and pollution which, as well as directly influencing an individual's health and growth processes, may even influence body cells and, in serious cases, the genetic make-up of a person, causing mutations and severe immune deficiencies similar to those found in sufferers from AIDS.

Psychosocial determinants include all social and psychological influences on learning throughout life, which become part of the individual's socialisation and self-concept as a person and as a member of social groupings such as children, parents, marital partners and workers. These influences may come from experiences in the family context, as between parent and child; other children and extended family members; experiences about parenting and being married; experiences in school and with peer groups; occupational experiences; and the quality of the broader social environment, for instance general socioeconomic and political stability. All these determinants are the building blocks for an individual's behaviours, feelings, attitudes, values, thoughts and actions in different life roles. In this way individuals develop concepts and values about work and career maturity and acquire a productive or unproductive work orientation. Faulty learning of the productive role results in types and degrees of work dysfunction.

Environmentally acquired behaviours are "learned or socio-cultural genetics", the latter term depicting behaviours being "grained in" and carried over as a result of social learning. We develop and acquire certain behaviours, because we have practised or experienced such behaviours repeatedly. Such behaviours are moulded into lasting behaviour patterns by various methods of learning, such as conditioning, association, imitation and modelling.

4.4.3 Interaction between person and environment

The interaction between maturation and learning is accepted and illustrated by many theoretical approaches and extensive research. The interaction between person and environment is perhaps best explained by Bronfenbrenner's ecological-systems model of human development (Craig 1996:12). This model views development as a dynamic process in which the individual and the environment mutually and reciprocally influence development. Figure 4.1 shows an adapted presentation of Bronfenbrenner's model indicating the multiple environmental and external influences as well as the circular influence between person and environment.

According to this model the *microsystem* is the person in his or her living environment, consisting of those persons and organisations with whom the most intimate and frequent contact occurs. The individual, in terms of personality and frame of reference, influences and restructures this immediate environment to an important degree and creates new sources of influence for himself or herself and others. The second level of influence or *mesosystem* is created by the interactions between elements of the microsystem; for example, if the schools, churches, employers and neighbours exclude certain people because of language or ethnic group, such interactions will have serious consequences in more than one domain of development. The *exosystem* may involve aspects outside the individual's immediate contacts that may still influence him or her. These may be the family members' workplace, institutions in the community such as health facilities, extended family members, friends, social clubs and professional organisations. You may, for example, work from home for a company, which could influence not only your career development, but also the organisation's way of personnel management, while your presence at home may influence your children's development as well as the way your wife goes about her career and parenting role. The fourth system, the *macrosystem*, represents a fluid type of influence in that it focuses on specific cultural and societal

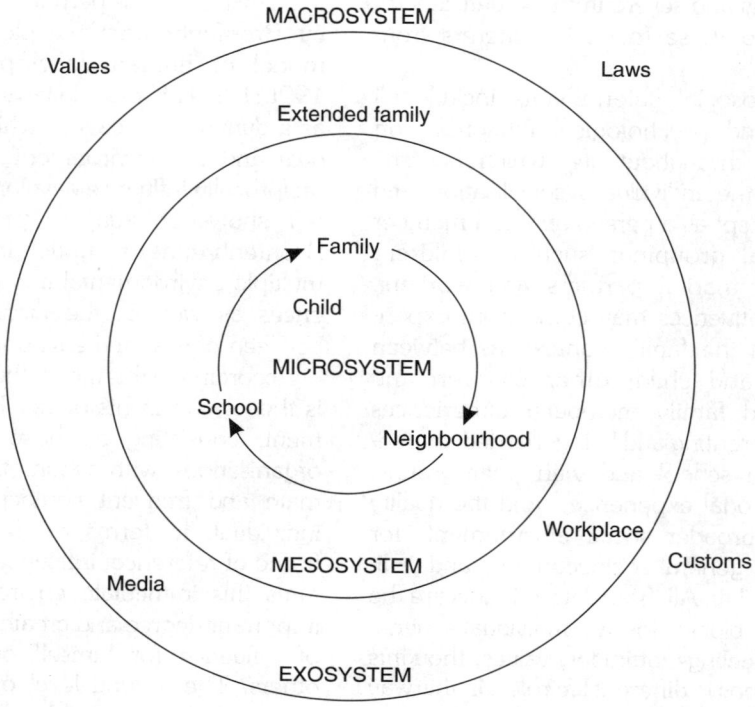

Figure 4.1 Systemic environmental influences in human development
Source: Craig, 1996

values, habits, laws and socioeconomic and political systems. These influences may be the most powerful in human development, as they often regulate exactly how the individual or groups can, must or may live. In our world there are many examples of the dire consequences for individuals and groups, for instance in education, finances, housing and career life, when actions exclude certain people from participating and sharing.

A further indication of how life span development is influenced by multiple determinants is given in the work of Hernandez, Stoller and Gibson, as well as Baltes (in Craig 1996). These authors emphasise the extreme influence of historical and life events, cultural aspects and opportunities on personality, ageing, development and ways of coping with life's problems. In this respect the time in history

and the type of opportunities people of different groups have will be influenced in different ways, as will their life and coping skills. Watkins and Mauer (1995), in a study in South Africa on the meaning of work, found that black managers experience a stronger sense of entitlement than white managers, which is ascribed to previous inequalities and prejudiced management systems. Baltes (1987) believes that life span development is influenced by more factors than just the interaction between development and history. He identified three broad factors which interactionally influenced development. During the *normative age-graded influences*, the usual biological and social changes take place at certain ages. These include aspects such as going to school, puberty, menopause, marrying and certain physical changes due to ageing. *Normative history-graded influences* concern historical events and traumas like war, natural disasters and other events which influence all or many people at the same time, to more or less the same degree. *Non-normative influences* refer to events that happen to certain people only, or to people in different ways, such as first loves, first employment, job loss, divorce, illnesses, promotions, moving house and death in the family. Personal circumstances and demographic variables, such as age, gender, race and social class determine how these factors influence each individual.

4.5 CRITICAL PERIODS IN DEVELOPMENT: VARIOUS VIEWS

A critical period refers to a certain *point in time* when particular factors, especially environmental factors, will or can have positive or negative effects, for instance factors such as lack of food, pollution or deprivation of parental love in the first year of life. If an individual fails to encounter the critical experiences that are part of normal development for his or her group, or undergoes an unusual experience, this may give rise to problems at a later stage. By implication this means that the more a child's environment deviates from the norm for his or her group, in respect of parents, other adults, siblings and friends, the greater the chances of maladjustment. Critical periods in childhood do not mean that early experience is irrevocably embedded in the personality. Later experiences may be equally influential, or even more so. Harmful early experience may be neutralised by subsequent positive experience. In contrast to critical events, *optimal periods* refer to experiences when maturation and learning are responsible for successful development, or the points at which people will be sufficiently ready or mature to benefit from certain experiences.

Some aspects of psychological and biological growth are fairly stable as regards environmental influence, being little affected by external variation, while others may be more sensitive to environmental factors. Biological factors cause a predisposition which makes the organism receptive to particular types of stimulation at a specific age. Given this stimulation new forms of behaviour arise, but without it the organism will only acquire such behaviour with great difficulty, if at all. Usually periods of sensitivity to environmental change occur early in life and are of limited duration; they are therefore critical. One period is relatively insensitive to the specific influences of another critical period. The functional significance of an early period may not affect the individual till much later; for instance the mother-infant relationship may only manifest in emotional relations at a subsequent stage.

Research findings indicate that patterns of behaviour may be transferred across families and from childhood to adulthood (Derlega et al. 1991).

4.5.1 The first five or six years

Several writers, such as Bowlby, Ainsworth and Freud, consider the first five or six years to be the most critical for development, on the grounds that at this stage the relatively immature neurological or physiological systems are not yet able to respond effectively to the complexities of the environment. Mental development occurs predominantly while the individual is still immature and is thus more vulnerable to harmful environmental factors, which may impair healthy development.

For the child between one and six the critical identity development areas and changes are in the development of: small and gross physical skills; thinking patterns from concreteness only to understanding time, order and symbols; learning and remembering; language formation; and the identification and modelling of parents, family and media influences, to express feelings and act in a disciplined and socially appropriate way. Children's natural curiosity, fantasy, games and parental identification are ways in which information, attitudes and interest in occupations are established.

Important close relationships

A critical development task of infants during the first and second years of dependence on parents, especially the mother, is to form healthy *attachment behaviours*, i.e. feelings of interdependence, mutual feelings of devotion and emotional ties. Bowlby and Ainsworth (quoted in Craig 1996) believe that it is critical for babies to form emotional ties with a single mother figure. Initially babies only become involved with one person at a time. By the time they learn to discriminate more, usually after the first year, they form attachments to others as well.

The role of a working mother often necessitates a number of substitute mothers, such as nursemaids and crèche staff, and this may mean the lack of a continuous, consistent, qualitative relationship; in other words, a breach of the one-to-one relationship with an adult. Other investigators attach less importance to a relationship with a single mother figure, maintaining that it is feasible to have a number of qualitative relationships.

The quality of early attachment behaviours may be transferred to adult attachment behaviours, types of interpersonal communication, falling in love and marriage, attachments to own children, friendships and relationships at work.

Research with infants (Bowlby 1988; Ainsworth et al. 1979) and adults (Hazan & Shaver 1994; Sperling & Berman 1994) found various types of intimate behavioural styles. These types are referred to as secure and insecure patterns of attachment behaviour.

Insecure attachment is presented as three types. The ambivalent attachment type shows mixed feelings of acceptance and rejection and in relationships may demand extra attention; the avoidant attachment type is characterised by fear and rejection of close relationships and may avoid commitment in relationships; in the disorganised or disoriented type of attachment the person is confused and contradictory and may feel secure with one person, but show insecurity with another.

Insecure attachment experiences in infancy are also related by research to over-dependence and emotional sensitivity, fewer social skills and less competence in older children (in Cloninger 1996). Higher levels of empathy were found in adults who reported higher involvement with parents at a very young age (Koestner, Franz & Weinberger 1990). Psychological maladjustment, depression and various other factors in adulthood were associated with insecure attachment behaviours in early childhood (Acklin et al. 1989; Acklin et al. 1991).

Secure attachment type people have positive, unthreatened relationships with others. Secure relationships are important in all stages of life, therefore consistency of such experiences in a family's life time may be as important, or even more so, than secure attachment experiences at a certain stage only. Secure attachment experiences during childhood will most probably lead to well-adjusted adults, for instance with regard to mental health and intimate adult relationships. Ainsworth et al. (1979), for instance believes that secure infant bonding behaviour will characterise affectionate adult bonds. This means that the adult will be able to be loyal to a chosen person, but also feel safe to share such relationships. This would be the case when the young adult enters a career and also marries. Both parties in such a marriage have to feel and know that they are in a loving, respected and enduring relationship, but they must also trust each other in working away from each other and relate to other people of the same and opposite sexes in the workplace.

With reference to performance behaviour and career efficacy, secure attachment in childhood will probably produce higher intellectual achievements in older children and adults (Jacobsen, Edelstein & Hofmann 1994). Better achievements are also related to first-borns, because parents often spend more time with their first-born or only child. The development of self-esteem in all people, especially the young, must be severely hampered in South Africa, a country plagued by high unemployment, labour unrest and ethnic and racial disputes, and with some of the highest crime, divorce, rape and child abuse rates in the world. Many young people will go through life without exemplary role models in family and work life.

Freud (Carver & Scheier 1996) differentiates between five so-called *psychosexual stages* of personality development: oral (first year), anal (age two to three), phallic (three to seven), latent (five to twelve) and genital (from puberty onwards). Each stage, especially the first three, is related to a specific area of the body (mouth, anus, genitals) through which sexual energy is set free.

The manner in which needs are gratified in each stage by parents and others, i.e. whether behaviours are realistically allowed or frustrated, may cause fixations which will be manifested in later personality traits and behaviours. *Fixations* occur when experiences at a certain stage get stuck and do not develop beyond that stage, are threatening, provoke anxiety and stay unresolved. This causes the child or adult to keep on seeking satisfaction for unresolved conflicts by using inappropriate, immature behaviours from previous stages. This is referred to as regression.

Freud believes that anxiety-based disorders (neuroses) originate in early childhood when the ego is not mature enough to resist stress. Adult behaviours, including work behaviours, are also related to the type of development during the early psychosexual development phases, although little research exists. The development of independence, self-control, a healthy sexual identification and a moral conscience, healthy heterosexual relationships, as well as the ability to love unselfishly, are some of the important consequences of the first six years for adult occupational behaviour. Some of the problematic behaviours of employees could possibly be explained by Freudian theory, for instance passiveness, verbal aggressiveness and manipulative behaviours may convert from the oral stage's early behaviours of sucking and biting; rebelliousness and untidiness from the anal stage's expulsion of faeces, while men who will do anything to achieve in their careers might be thought of as having phallic fixations, trying to prove their masculinity by being very ambitious and superior in work performance.

4.5.2 Life span development

In contrast to Bowlby and Freud who emphasised the first five years, Erikson (1963) regards human development as a process of psychosocial development in eight stages, but over a life span towards the acquisition of *ego-identity*. Ego-identity is obtained by resolving conflicts in eight consecutive phases, from birth to maturity. Each phase constitutes a critical period, during which certain ego attributes are developed which determine the individual's self-concept and may influence behaviour for the rest of the person's life. Although early phases do influence later phases, possible wrong developments can be rectified if an individual in a later stage receives what he or she was deprived of in an earlier stage. Parental, social and cultural factors are important influences. Many of the critical aspects and characteristics of human development are incorporated in Erikson's theory. This theory may be the most influential theory in human development literature, and also contributes greatly to career development concepts, though many criticisms are also levelled at its inability to explain the many differences between people's development.

4.5.2.1 Trust versus mistrust (first year of life)

During infancy trust and an inner security develop as a result of satisfactory maternal care. Trust is the infant's first social achievement, in that the mother is trusted, even if she is occasionally absent.

Mistrust is manifested in a sense of rejection, with concomitant scepticism towards life and people. These attitudes, either mistrust or trust and optimism, remain with the individual throughout life. This stage is similar to attachment as described by Bowlby, Ainsworth and Freud.

4.5.2.2 Autonomy versus shame and doubt (2-3 years)

Maturation of physical functions, for instance control over excretory functions, teaches the child self-control and adequacy, which fosters a sense of self-esteem, pride and autonomy.

Frustrations in these areas may, in the adult, foster feelings of inadequacy, inability to control, self-doubt and unassertiveness.

4.5.2.3 Initiative versus guilt (4-5 years)

The toddler learns initiative by sharing responsibilities, such as the care of younger children, and by manipulating toys and exploring the environment. He or she internalises the qualities of the provider he or she will in due course become.

If he or she fails to develop initiative and is criticised too much, he or she grows into an adult who inhibits potential or develops psychosomatic ailments to evade responsibility, or else overcompensates for lack of initiative, for instance by boasting.

The following stages are especially relevant for adult occupational behaviours.

4.5.2.4 Industry versus inferiority (6-11, through puberty)

At school-going age the child is ready to acquire qualities of productivity such as perseverance and task completion, and developing a sense of learning, accomplishment and competency. He or she is introduced to the concepts of division of labour and specialisation and learns the significance of status and roles through the opinions of peers. In preliterate societies children learned industry through getting to know the basics of their technology and economy, for example how to use tools for hunting and fishing.

Lack of opportunity for industry, inability to do what is expected or negative assessment by others gives rise to feelings of inferiority, as in the case of people who are not even willing to try because they think they are not worthy. This may be the breeding ground for what is known as the "fear of success" and "learned helplessness", found in people who out of fear can't be self-sufficient.

4.5.2.5 Identity versus ego confusion (12-18 years, adolescence)

During adolescence all the qualities and roles developed during the previous phases find expression in a broader social context. Teenagers test their identity by belonging to groups and gangs and by falling in love with heroes and members of the opposite sex. Here others provide a criterion for the development and recognition of one's own identity.

If individuals feel that they do not have the same identity in other's eyes as they have in their own, they become confused as to their roles in life and who and what they really are.

4.5.2.6 Intimacy versus isolation (early adulthood)

Young adults share their identity with others through affiliation and friendship. This is accompanied by a strong ethical awareness and the ability to commit themselves in intimate relationships. The ideal form of intimacy is a relationship based on mutual trust, sharing spheres of work and recreation, and mutual, simultaneous sexual satisfaction.

Lack of intimacy creates a sense of isolation and consequent self-absorption and produces people wrapped up in themselves. Successful resolution of intimacy conflicts is based on the development tasks during the previous phases.

4.5.2.7 Generativity versus stagnation (adulthood)

As individuals proceed into adult life, they need to feel needed, especially in relationships with others and family. They may satisfy this need by, for example, caring for children or by societal involvement. This desire to give is not the same as the mere desire to have children. Generativity may also find expression in spiritual work, in the sense of caring for God's creatures, chari-table work and even in career efforts, but in Erikson's view this can never compensate for genuine involvement with offspring.

Lack of such self-fulfilment leads to preoccupation with self, as, for example, in someone who sees himself or herself as only a child, like a helpless invalid, or who becomes so wrapped up in a marriage partner that he or she regards the other person as his or her only child.

4.5.2.8 Ego-integrity versus despair (ageing/maturity)

If all the conflicts of the previous phases have been resolved and healthy ego-characteristics have developed, the aged individual accepts his or her life cycle with a spiritual sense of order and meaning, which provides emotional integration and softens the fear of death.

Despair in people is manifested by a feeling that life is too short. Such people are inclined to regard others with disapproval, which is merely a form of self-reproach. This may be the case in many older people or even in younger ones, when people experience their life, relationships and activities as meaningless.

4.6 CAREER TRANSITIONS AND TASKS

Career maturity is the progressive maturation and growth in physical, cognitive, and psychosocial domains which enables people to cope with development tasks at each life stage, for instance career choices and societal roles. Career maturity is influenced by every life stage and differences are related to people's different attributes and circumstances. A related concept is career self-efficacy (Lent & Hackett 1987), which refers to people's belief in their abilities and expectations of being successful in jobs and to do specific career-related tasks.

Much of what transpires positively or negatively in adult personal and vocational behaviours may be related to the formative early years and physical, cognitive, social and emotional behaviours. Attachment behaviours during the critical periods in infancy and the establishment of career concepts in childhood are important for adult career transitions.

During life span development and integration in the domains of physical, cognitive, moral and psychosocial development, people must acquire certain development tasks or competencies related to learning, work and career choice. Havighurst (in Herr & Cramer 1972:103) defines a *development task* as a task which arises at or about a certain period in the life of the individual, successful achievement of which leads to happiness and success with later tasks, while failure leads to unhappiness in the individual, disapproval by society, and difficulty with later tasks.

Such competencies could be to make choices between tasks that they like and dislike, accept responsibility to do tasks and to complete tasks within certain time limits, make initial career choices in selecting certain subjects or study directions and be able to enter a first job.

There are many theories which explain career development, for example those of Ginsberg et al., Super, Levinson, Roe, Holland and Havighurst (Craig 1996; Sharf 1997; Schreuder & Theron 1997; Möller 1996). Most of these theorists are in agreement with regard to the different career stages and the relevant development tasks.

For Super, career development, career adjustment and career maturity are related to expressions of self-concept, while Havighurst emphasises the development of skills and attitudes. Table 4.2 integrates the views of Super and Havighurst on stages and necessary development tasks.

Ages and phases	Tasks and transitions
0 – 14 Growth phase	**General physical and mental growth**
0 – 3 Pre-vocational	• no or little career interest
4 – 10 Fantasy	• fantasy or games about work, based on identification with parents
11 – 12 Interest	• likes and dislikes basis for job and career interest
13 – 14 Capacity	• abilities as basis for thinking about jobs and careers
	• through schoolwork learns priorities, organising time and completing tasks
15 – 24 Exploration phase	**Broad exploration of work**
15 – 17 Tentative	• various attributes (ability, values etc.) become basis for occupational choices
18 – 21 Transition	• more specific and realistic about career choices, study and job entry
22 – 24 Trial	• study and first job entry, identity as a worker

Ages and phases	Tasks and transitions
25 – 44 Establishment phase	**More permanent job or career, creative years**
25 – 30 Trial	• possible changes of jobs and career
31 – 44 Stabilisation	• productive, stable work in a given job and career
	• moving ahead, maintain income and life style and societal roles
45 – 65 Maintenance phase	**Progress and continuation in a given career line**
	• holding job, updating and innovating
	• maintaining societal roles and possibly planning for retirement
65+ Decline phase	**Preparation to retire**
65 – 70 Deceleration	• if work, deceleration and decline in capabilities, plan to retire
71+ Retirement	• cease work, contemplates life

Table 4.2 *(continued)* Career stages and tasks: the views of Super and Havighurst
Sources: Super and Havighurst in Craig 1996; Weiten 1995 and Sharf 1997.

The following is a discussion of development tasks in adult career transitions, as reflected in table 4.2.

4.6.1 Early life – occupational choice and preparation (birth to 22)

The critical issue of early life development towards adult career adjustment is whether the adolescent or young adult has achieved integration of self-identity, and is prepared to fulfil various roles. Career maturity, the responsibility to choose a career identity and career entry, might be most important. This involves growing independent and autonomous from parents, but keeping supportive relationships. Identity formation at adolescent level may also be different for men and women. While young men are busy with career issues, many young women at this stage are more involved in relationship issues, because they believe that marriage is more important to their identity than occupational choices.

Important career development tasks for career maturity at this stage, just before career entry or tertiary studies, are given by Super and Crites, as summarised by Sharf (1992) and Craig (1996). These tasks include the competencies to make choices and decisions, and the development of certain attitudes:

• *Career orientation* is the person's active involvement and commitment in the process of career choice, i.e. knowing what is expected and using information and abilities to solve career choice problems.

- *Career information and planning* require the ability to explore and gather the necessary information to plan for and decide on a certain career.
- *Consistency of career preferences* relates to constancy of choice over time, but also to choices within career directions.
- *Certainty or crystallisation* of concepts and attitudes about work and careers.
- *Wisdom of vocational choices* relates to a realistic choice, based on an assessment of abilities and interests compared to the demands of possible jobs or careers. This is especially important during the transition stage (18-21) when the young adult must decide on a study and career direction and even start in a job.

According to Marcia (in Craig 1996) and Erikson's identity versus identity confusion stage, adolescents may experience four types of ego identity states in career choice issues.

If adolescents are able to explore many possibilities and seek information about themselves before making choices on study and career issues, they may be said to have achieved occupational *identity* with no identity diffusion. In the case of the adolescent who cannot make a choice as yet, he or she may be said to be in a *moratorium*, an ongoing state of uncertainty. An adolescent who cannot make or avoids making any career decision, such as what subject to major in or what type of job to enter, may experience vocational *identity diffusion*, which in turn may lead to trying a number of jobs without success. Such individuals may become failures in society, with all the accompanying problems. Identity diffusion may even exist in the adolescent who thinks he or she has made the right career choice, say to be a pilot, just because he or she always wanted to be a pilot or because others wanted that occupation chosen. Such an individual's

vocational identity is *foreclosed* or rigid, because he or she cannot consider other options and may make an incorrect choice, although such decisions may not cause a crisis or anxiety.

The development of these career-related tasks must be considered in terms of the physical, cognitive and emotional changes during this youthful stage.

Adolescents' primary characteristics are physical and body image awareness, sexual maturity and experimentation, a search for self-identity and adult levels of thinking. However, due to long periods of study, financial and emotional dependence on parents, as well as the pressures to make the first "real" career choices, adolescents often experience emotional turmoil and identity confusion. Unresolved conflicts from previous stages and events like intimate relationships, unwanted pregnancies, substance use and law enforcement problems may intensify the difficulties in personal and career adjustment.

Adolescents' rebellious behaviour, self-criticism and criticism of parents' and other norms, can also be interpreted as quests to behave, feel and think more independently. However, emotional insecurity may result in overreaction, impulsiveness or poor choices. Greater analytical powers would enable the adolescent to make early career decisions and to assess the overload of information on careers which they encounter at this stage. By career entry, youths must have learned to accept authority, working in groups and the value of synergy or cooperation.

Adolescents' sense of self-identity is not only increased by experimenting sexually and emotionally in new attachments and critically using adult cognitive powers, but also in the process of separating from their families. Hoffman (1984) described the process of separation from families in adolescents and young adults according to four types of independence which the person must acquire: emotional (less dependent for acceptance and affect); attitudinal (develop own attitudes and values); functional (solve own problems and be financially more independent); and conflictual (separating without guilt feelings and remorse). Craig (1996) asserts that part of the adolescents' adjustment lies in the type of agreement and mutual support which exist between them and their parents as they search for an own identity and greater freedom.

Mentor, executive and novice

4.6.2 Young adulthood – entry and establishment in the workplace (22-45)

Adulthood is often regarded as the period beyond 20 years of age. Avery and Baker (1990) classify adulthood in five stages: building a workable life (22-28); crisis of questions (29-34); crisis of urgency (35-43); attaining stability (44-50); and mellowing (50 years and older).

Levinson's theory on career development emphasises four development tasks for the young adult or "novice" (17-33) to grow into adulthood (40-60). They are: define a dream (set life goals); find a mentor (an adult of stature to facilitate growth towards independence away from parents and family); develop a career (all activities to find a stable career pattern); and establish intimacy (find a supportive intimate relationship, such as a spouse

in marriage). Craig (1996) refers to research indicating that women experience more difficulty than men in realising their dreams, the biggest being to adjust to their husband's aspirations, and to split themselves and their dreams between marriage, having children and a career.

Much of early adulthood's development tasks are about adjustment to the realities of adult roles. Consolidation or stability implies ongoing identity formation as a person, and involves tasks such as getting married, finding a stable occupation, establishing family and home, friendships, relationships, participating in recreation activities and assuming societal roles. A partner for marriage or intimacy, and the responsibilities of parenthood, seem to be crucial parts of adulthood in all stages and in many roles. These demands require many changes and adjustments. In this respect Freud saw success as an adult as being successful in love and work, while Erikson and others proposed ideas such as intimacy and generativity, which means that the adult found self-identity in personal goals such as marriage, children, family, work and community. The adult's quality of relationships is important in many spheres, such as nurturing one's own children, managing one's romantic affiliations and influencing other persons in the work context, either as a manager or mentor or working in a team with colleagues. The focus of this involvement differs for every individual. Unresolved attachment crises from childhood may be powerful determinants of unsuccessful relationships in adulthood.

Many unusual changes and influences may mark this stage, such as starting late or very early with a career, family, the addition and loss of family members, divorce and the problems of being a single parent, children separating from home, possible unemployment and the family having to move for work purposes, which in itself can influence family stability in many respects. A redefinition of many issues will often be necessary, as in marriage, arrival of children, divorce and career changes.

Cognitively the adult's study, work and general life experience results in a more mature, committed, responsible and integrated approach to problem-solving. In the assessment of managerial cognitive skills, the aspect of strategic thinking, i.e. to be able to do forward planning, while considering many factors and having a total view of things, is considered to be of crucial importance. Riegel (in Craig 1996), for one, asserts that, in addition to the formal operations quoted by Piaget, the adult also develops a mode of dialectical thinking: the ability to consider and integrate opposing ideas and to be more realistic about issues than the adolescent or very young adults. According to Schaie adult intelligence develops in a few stages, which evolves into the adult being able to use all acquired skills in a flexible and responsible manner, in order to solve problems over the life span. Work roles in early adulthood may be recognised by growth in loyalty and commitment, but may require a mentor to give direction.

The nature of work in families also demands career adjustment. This is needed, for instance, in the case of many dual-career couples, and often demands a redefinition of family roles. However, the possibility of role conflicts in families, and between work roles and family roles, exists (Greenhaus & Parasurman 1989). The mere fact that children of all ages are left at home while parents work has implications for family wellbeing and the development of children. The changing nature of work and the labour market also influence interactional patterns at home and in the family. For instance, many individuals and families use their homes as a workplace.

4.6.3 Middle adulthood and old age – consolidation, maintenance and change (45-60)

Middle adulthood might be the years from 45 to about 60. These are the stages of stability (45-50) and mellowing (50 and older).

The main development tasks of middle age are to maintain career standards, a standard of living, marriage and family relationships, to assist children into adulthood, uphold societal roles and develop leisure activities. In occupational activities specifically, the employee is busy with holding a job or position, updating knowledge and skills and innovating work methods to be more efficient. Having consolidated and being still creative, people can now direct their energies to the service of others, such as family, and as mentor to junior employees. The person still wants to be generative and make contributions, but starts to look for other forms of recognition. The emphasis shifts from physical powers to mental powers or wisdom; from sexuality in human relationships to socialising, which is an important aspect in marriages but could be a source of conflict, especially for unevenly aged married couples; a shift from a very strong emphasis on work to themselves and their involvement in family life (Craig 1996).

During middle adulthood physical changes and problems of age become more evident. Decreases in visual acuity, hearing, motor skills, reaction time, as well as internal physiological and hormonal changes, start to show in the mid-40s and early 50s, though these changes should not influence work performance in a critical sense. Both men and women at age 45-50 may experience so-called midlife crises, including menopause in women, with its related hormonal and health changes, and being sexually less active.

In general cognitive abilities show a steady decline with an increase in age (especially after 50), notably in the more basic (inherited) aspects of intelligence, such as memory, inductive reasoning, speed of learning, doing tasks quickly and accurately and the ability to learn new contents and new relationships. However, decline in old age, for instance of memory, is often not as extreme as many people would have us believe.

Older people's cognitive styles are often associated with "wisdom" or being experts, based on much work and life experience, a bigger variety of, and more integrated, knowledge of things, judgement, reasoning and practical problem-solving skills. In this respect older persons may often be more suited to adjusting to quick changes in the work environment, because of their integrated ways of thinking, varied knowledge, and flexibility in problem-solving and reasoning. Schaie (in Craig 1996), for instance, indicates that persons who in general have a lot of opportunities, ongoing environmental and cultural stimulation, and a satisfying social and emotional life, may well experience a high level of maintenance and growth in cognitive skills. It is not surprising that most management and executive jobs are filled by persons in the middle adulthood group, and also that in many fields such as writing and research such persons have their most productive years after 40 or 50 and even as late as the 70s.

Psychosocial development in middle adulthood (45-60) will, in many respects, overlap with developmental tasks of early adulthood (20-45) and with old age (over 60), for instance in the level of financial independence, amount of social support from friends, family, work colleagues and health. For many reasons, adults in their 40s and even 50s may start or restart marriage, have young children and start, or change to, a new career. This means that some middle-aged are still busy with establishing a career in order to have a good standard of living, to facilitate marriage and spouse relationships, help older and younger children grow, contribute in societal life, develop a pattern of recreation, adjust to growing physical and health concerns and get more involved with ageing parental systems as well as making provision for their own old age needs.

An important aspect of the greater involvement in family and other social relationships is helping their adolescent children and family to find a place in the adult world. Some adults find this separation process and living with their children as equals easy, others experience some conflicts, often resulting in family stress. When all the children have left the home to make their own way, some parents may have the so-called "empty nest" experience. This is a time when man and wife must find new ways to relate to each other, and other interests to give meaning to their lives and to fill their time. Reassessment of careers is an important aspect of the midlife development stage, especially if there are unresolved conflicts or changed values and circumstances. In South Africa, where major sociopolitical transformation is taking place, many people, especially whites, elect or are forced to reassess their careers. Others, due to job loss, have to set out on a new career direction, such as starting their own business. Black South Africans have to start totally new careers, also in managerial positions which were unavailable in earlier times.

Many authors suggest the so-called *midlife crisis* is an age-related or normative development which occurs at about age 40. Other researchers assert that this stage is no more critical than other life transitions.

Barnett and Pleack (1992) proposed that the mid-career stage manifests differently in four types of man:

- The transcendent-generative man experiences no midlife crisis. Such individuals find accomplishment and happiness in life.

- The pseudo-developed man is not really in control, has a lot of unsolved problems, is confused, but will often role play as if everything is in order.
- The typical midlife crisis man is really confused and cannot cope with life's problems. This could be a temporary or a permanent way of life.
- The punitive disenchanted man is totally unhappy for the most part of his life, feels alienated and can seldom cope with life's demands.

In women these conflicts differ for reasons such as childbirth, late or later career entry and role conflicts in the family, due to assuming multiple roles as employee, spouse and mother, as well as factors such as being widowed or divorced and the socioeconomic pressures due to these events.

4.6.4 Old age and disengagement

For the aged the main development tasks are to uphold or defend some form of personal identity, dignity and integrity rather than despair, find new meaning in life and evaluate their spent lives, amid many changes and forced adjustments. Old peoples' main concerns are about health care, being financially independent, having social support and not being lonely. Maintaining a sense of identity must coexist with changing attitudes, yielding control to others and being more dependent on family and other persons. The negative scenario for the older adult could be stagnation and despair if they are unable to develop and be content with an identity that helps them cope with crises.

Old age is often misunderstood. For many reasons it is generally characterised by a steady decline in all domains; physically, cognitively, socially and emotionally, especially in the late 60s and 70s. Many of the aged do not experience physical and cognitive losses as being serious, because they adjust to changes by "working clever", doing less better in more time, or applying "selective optimisation with compensation" (Baltes 1993).

For many older people retirement from work presents big adjustment problems, especially if retirement is not planned and prepared for; for instance in terms of income, social relationships and leisure activities. For others their assessment of a

Social support in old age

life well spent may provide feelings of satisfaction and completeness. When persons have stability, they may apply their wisdom as mentors of others and spend more quality time with their own, extended families and friends, a state which Erikson refers to as ego-integrity. Many "young" elderly (60-69) and "middle-aged" elderly (70-79) stay active in some way, still practising their physical, cognitive and social abilities. A serious problem for old people is being too focused on themselves, too busy complaining about the ills of old age and having a preoccupation with retirement and death, which could render them unable to still enjoy life and to adapt to younger generations.

4.7 CONCLUSION

The diversity of human behaviours, which finds expression in human development, include the integration and interdependence of heredity and environment, of physical, cognitive, moral and psychosocial domains, of structure and function, of self and the outside world, and of the individual, work and society. Development in one area only, or inadequate integration of the different areas, could lead to dysfunctionality or meaninglessness.

The biggest challenge for future generations is not only to understand and recognise natural differences and similarities between people and groups, but also to create the social conditions in which all individuals have a fair chance to realise their potential. Much research is necessary to further understand the interactions between maturation and social learning processes. In the midst of changing work opportunities and attitudes about work, the changing nature of the working environment and jobs, we have a huge task to redefine career concepts and career development. Do the assumptions of progressive life and career stages or transitions still apply, if for many meaningful life and a secure job may always only be a dream? Reassessing development concepts is also necessary in the light of the increasingly prominent role in working life of women and disadvantaged groups, for whom existing career development concepts may not adequately provide. Moreover, many people will retire earlier, others will be forced to work into old age, and millions of people will earn a living in "informal labour markets", outside the formal structures of established positions and organisations. It seems as if career psychologists and other "educators" have a role to play in establishing new "mind sets" in people, to enable them to be creatively and "entrepreneurially" oriented, and more responsible for their own career training and development.

Self-evaluating questions

1. If you compare yourself to an infant or child, do you think the characteristics of development are true?
2. Describe developmental domains and refer to critical development influences.
3. In assessing your own way of thinking, do you think that some of the principles on cognitive development apply?
4. If you assess the behaviour of a child or adult whom you know well, do you find the assumptions or principles proposed in Erikson's theory valuable?
5. Explain critical periods in human development and also refer to attachment behaviours.
6. Make a list of those things in work and a career which you think are important or unimportant and indicate where or how you think you acquired these tasks and attitudes?
7. Analyse your own career development transitions and describe the critical constraints and facilitating factors.

Learning

5

Dirk Geldenhuys

CONTENTS

Learning outcomes

After studying this chapter you should be able to:

- give a clear definition of the learning concept
- explain, compare and apply the principles of classical and instrumental conditioning to practical examples
- describe the social learning theory as a combination of the behaviouristic approach and the cognitive approach
- describe the nature and effectiveness of different reinforcement schedules
- describe the effectiveness of punishment
- explain the concept "adult learner"
- describe the different learning principles, and provide practical examples
- distinguish between the different training techniques
- explain what is meant by transfer of learning
- describe the evaluation of training as the last phase of the training process

Key concepts

performance, behaviourism, conditioning, reinforcement, punishment, cognitive learning, cognitive map, social learning, adult learner, training, need analysis, instructional objectives, learning principles, transfer, learning techniques, experiential cycle, experiential techniques, nonexperiential techniques, evaluation

5.1 INTRODUCTION

Unemployment is one of the major problems in South Africa, but despite the vast supply of labour, significant shortages in certain professional and skilled worker categories are experienced. The obvious solution to the problem is the enhancement of education and training levels of all the citizens of the country. It is therefore not surprising that the government is placing so much emphasis on the training and development of employees by their employers. To make a meaningful contribution to industry, it is of the utmost importance that people providing training are well equipped for the task. This chapter provides you with a basic knowledge of

learning concepts on which training theories and models are built.

5.2 WHAT IS LEARNING?

We often hear people say "I saw them learning". Can we really see somebody busy learning? What if the person is tested afterwards and it turns out that no learning seems to have taken place, for instance when the person fails the test so badly that he or she would probably have attained the same results in a test before the "learning"? It is clear that the learning process cannot be observed or studied. All that can be measured is performance in the execution of some task, the solving of a problem or some other activity where the individual draws on what has been learned. Hence the activities derived from learning, rather than the learning process itself, are visible.

From a psychological perspective, we study behaviour, so that we can make inferences concerning the process (learning) believed to be the cause of the behaviour. If we want to know if learning has taken place, we determine if behaviour has *changed* as a result of an experience. It is, however, important that the behavioural changes observed not be attributed to temporary body states caused by illness, fatigue, etc. Although such factors may modify behaviour, their effects don't last long, whereas what is learned is only forgotten over time, or until new learning displaces old learning (Hergenhahn & Olson 1993). Thus with learning the change is relatively permanent. Another question that needs to be answered is whether what is learned results in changed behaviour immediately. To answer this question we can use the example of paramedics, who learn how to save lives at the scene of a collision by watching videos and listening to lectures, but do not translate that learning into behaviour until they are involved in a real emergency. We can say that the potential to save lives resulted from learning, although behaviour was not immediately affected. This form of learning is called *latent learning*.

It is important to distinguish between learning and performance. Learning refers to the potential change in behaviour, whereas *performance* refers to the translation of this potential into behaviour (Hergenhahn & Olson 1993). Thus, while behaviour is necessary to determine whether learning has occurred, its absence does not imply that learning has not occurred. Even when trainees have demonstrated learning by means of performance in the training environment, the learning will not necessarily transfer to the work situation.

The concept of learning is therefore defined as a relatively permanent change in behaviour (or behaviour potentiality) that results from experience (Hergenhahn & Olson 1993; Robbins 1998).

5.3 THE LEARNING PROCESS

The learning process is described from different viewpoints, based on the different schools of thought in psychology.

From a *behaviouristic* point of view the learning process is described in terms of classical conditioning or operant conditioning. Other approaches to the learning process are the cognitive approach and a social learning approach or observational learning.

5.3.1 Classical conditioning

The term classical conditioning is commonly associated with I.P. Pavlov, whose experiments with dogs illustrated the importance in learning of the association of stimuli and resulting responses.

Classical conditioning

A hungry dog was shown food which was termed the *unconditioned stimulus*. The dog's saliva began to flow. This was called the *unconditioned reflex*, as it happened automatically, independent of prior learning processes. A bell was then rung just before or while the food was shown to the dog. The dog's saliva flowed again. The process was repeated several times. In the third stage the bell was rung without any food being given. Salivation still occurred. The bell was called the *conditioned stimulus* and the flow of saliva a conditioned reflex.

An association had been established between stimuli in which the conditioned stimulus, initially unrelated to salivation, triggered the same response as the un-conditioned reflex. The bell evoked an anticipation of food. Thus the conditioned stimulus served to reinforce the conditioned reflex. However, when the food was repeatedly withheld, the ringing of the bell in the absence of food ceased to cause salivation. Extinction of the association between the two stimuli, as well as the conditioned reflex, had occurred either because of insufficient repetition or exces-sively long intervals in the process of conditioning.

During a storm some of Pavlov's dogs ended up in floodwater and this traumatic experience caused the *extinction* of condi-tioned reflexes. In humans trauma or shock can also cause extinction of learned behaviour. A temporary loss of condi-tioned responses may result in inhibition of behaviour, for instance in cases of extreme stress and temporary amnesia. After a while (e.g. a period of rest) there may be spontaneous recovery; in other words, the conditioned response may recur after having been extinguished. This shows that the extinction of conditioned reflexes is not necessarily permanent. The condi-tioned response can be facilitated by a fresh stimulus similar to the unconditioned stimulus. Various stimuli and types of situations can evoke the same response through stimulus generalisation. The closer the resemblance between stimuli, the greater the generalisation, e.g. an emo-tional response learned through contact with one person is generalised to include all members of the nation or race to which the person belongs.

Discrimination between stimuli is learned through *differential reinforcement* of the response. This is achieved through alter-nating stages where, *first*, the uncondi-tioned stimulus (e.g. food) follows the conditioned stimulus (e.g. a bell with a certain pitch), and secondly, where the unconditioned stimulus (e.g. food) does not follow another, though similar, stimulus

(e.g. a bell with a different pitch). After the repetition of this procedure, the response follows only the stimulus that was rein-forced.

A form of classical conditioning in which a third stimulus produces the same re-sponse as the conditioned response is known as *higher-order conditioning*. The conditioned stimulus (e.g. a bell) serves as the conditioned stimulus for a new stimulus, (e.g. a light). By pairing the two stimuli, the light also becomes a conditioned stimulus producing the response. Classical condi-tioning can be used to explain emotional behaviour. In humans, however, the ex-planation of behaviour in terms of this learning process is speculative, as there are factors involved which are not always easy to identify. Human behaviour is not purely reflexive; one type of emotional response can have different manifestations, and stimulus generalisation is not always ob-vious.

5.3.2 Operant or instrumental conditioning

Classical conditioning paved the way for the operant approach to learning. The term is chiefly associated with B.F. Skinner, whose experiments with rats and pigeons demon-strated how behaviour can be changed by controlling the learning process. *Operant conditioning* (instrumental conditioning) differs from classical conditioning in that the latter merely consists of an association of stimuli that elicits a particular response without necessarily achieving anything, whereas instrumental learning implies the acquisition of a reaction to obtain mean-ingful results. For instance, a young child may express frustration by throwing a tantrum, but through parental rebukes learns that this behaviour is not profitable and solves no problems. Through the reward of "correct" behaviour the child acquires acceptable modes of social conduct and learns how to utilise its environment effectively. In essence instrumental learning means that individuals gain control over their environment.

Reinforcement in the form of reward or punishment is of cardinal importance in this method of learning. The initial stimulus triggers a particular response, because this response is consistently reinforced by reward during the conditioning process. Reward is a second stimulus which is pleasurable or positive. Conversely, a first stimulus may result in inhibition or avoidance of a specific response, because the response was repeatedly negatively reinforced by a second stimulus which was unpleasant.

In addition to the positive or negative reinforcement of the response through a second stimulus (primary reinforcement), a third stimulus, associated with the reinforcing stimulus, can strengthen the response further. This is known as *secondary reinforcement*. For instance, a person learns to fulfil a work role (first stimulus) effectively (response), as it is primarily reinforced by constructive guidance and praise from the supervisor.

The latter's attitude towards the person and his or her performance has a secondary effect, namely the respect of colleagues, which gives him or her more status in the work group. On the one hand secondary reinforcement results from the response, which may cause the response to recur, and on the other hand it enhances the value of primary reinforcement. Higher status in the work group gives even more weight to the praise of the supervisor.

5.3.2.1 Reinforcement schedules

The role of reinforcement in learning was formulated primarily by E.L. Thorndike in his *Law of effect*, which posits that behavioural reactions are acquired when the consequences are agreeable, but are not learned when the consequences are disagreeable.

The acquisition of various responses can be effected by scheduling reinforcement in accordance with a *fixed ratio* schedule, where reward is offered only after a certain number of responses, for example payment of a bonus on completion of a task, and a *fixed interval schedule*, where reward comes after a specific time has elapsed, irrespective of the number of responses, for example annual salary increases, whether merited or not.

The two schedules may be combined or varied through *variable ratio* and *interval* schedules, in which case the number of responses rewarded or the periods of reinforcement fluctuate.

The four different schedules are presented in table 5.1.

Schedule		Description
F I X E D	ratio	rewards after constant number of actions
	interval	rewards after constant amount of times
V A R I A B L E	ratio	rewards after a variable number of actions
	interval	rewards after a variable amount of time

Table 5.1 Reinforcement schedules

The schedules have different effects on the learning process or work situation to which they are applied. A fixed ratio schedule generally gives rise to relatively high performance – the sooner a task is completed, the sooner the reward is received, and the more tasks are done, the more rewards there are. Consider, for example, the work of a farm labourer paid for piecework.

A fixed interval schedule tends to result in behaviour which offers a measure of resistance to extinction and shows fluctuations during the interval.

Performance tapers off directly after reinforcement, while it peaks just before reinforcement is offered again. Consider the office worker who has the habit of allowing files to pile up until just before a report on them has to be compiled at the end of the week or month.

A variable ratio schedule usually gives rise to high, consistent performance over long periods, as the worker is uncertain when reward will be given and therefore perseveres with the task. A salesperson will persevere with efforts at door-to-door selling in spite of the fact that he or she is not successful with every client. As a rule a variable interval schedule results in relatively high uniform performance with high resistance to extinction, for example in the case of a person who does not know when merit assessments are going to be conducted and therefore continues to produce work of a high quality.

In the application of all four schedules a tapering off of performance may occur, as they encourage evasion or withdrawal from the situation. It occurs in the case of both fixed and variable ratio schedules if tasks are overloaded, i.e. too many responses are expected too quickly with too few breaks in between, as for example in the case of a secretary who is overloaded with work. Fixed and variable interval schedules reveal this tapering off when overlong periods pass between reinforcements, such as the number of years between promotions.

Behaviour learned through scheduled reinforcement is usually more resistant to extinction than behaviour which is continuously reinforced by means of reward after every correct response. Behaviour learned in childhood through various reinforcement schedules will continue to occur in adulthood although it is no longer rewarded.

Skinner also believes that the causes of behaviour are to be found in the environment and not in the individual. He rejects concepts like self and autonomy as behavioural determinants. He describes an imaginary utopian society where human behaviour is regulated in accordance with the principles of instrumental learning (Hergenhahn & Olson 1993). The implication is that people can be wholly manipulated by those who have the power to do so. Instrumental learning has been criticised on the grounds that it generalises a method of learning which is not necessarily applicable to all individuals and underestimates the role of cognitive factors in the learning process.

5.3.2.2 The effectiveness of punishment

In instrumental learning punishment refers to a stimulus which diminishes the probability or strength of a response preceding it. Not only does it comprise the administering of unpleasant stimuli, but the withholding of stimuli may also be experienced as punishment, for example the retraction of fringe benefits or emotional support, and the disapproval of people whose approval is desired.

The *effectiveness of punishment* is often questioned because it may cause emotional reactions which harm the learning process. Intense punishment stimuli that are painful or terrifying may also be queried from a moral point of view because they conflict with humanistic principles. Individuals also differ in their reactions to and interpretation of punishment. The following findings with regard to punishment are generally valid:

- The more intense the punishment, the more effective it is. This may sometimes be true to the extent that the effect is irreversible. The danger of intense punishment is that it could cause associated conditioned emotional reactions, which in the long term may have more far-reaching implications than the behaviour which was originally punished, for example a child's negative feelings towards the parent meting out the punishment.
- Light punishment may suppress undesirable behaviour temporarily, but it will occur again later.
- The more consistent the punishment, even though it may be light, the more effective it appears to be.
- The closer the punishment is in time and place to the undesirable behaviour, the more effective it is.
- The deeper a pattern of behaviour is entrenched as a habit, the less effective will punishment be.
- People can adapt to punishment and this lessens its impact.
- Punishment for an undesired response may be effective if it is followed by positive reinforcement (reward) for an alternative response. In this way behaviour is shaped so that not only does one learn what not to do but also what should be done in a given situation.

5.3.3 Cognitive learning

The cognitive approach to learning is primarily based on the learning model of E.C. Tolman. According to his model, objects in the environment are perceived as means toward desired goals. Between the perception of a stimulus and the acting out of a response, a series of cognitive activities take place. The response to the stimuli depends on the *perception* whether such a response will lead to the achievement of the desired goal or not. People learn what is in their environment and gradually develop a picture of it. This picture is called a cognitive map. The *cognitive* map thus represents past relationships between stimuli, behaviour and goal accomplishment (Hergenhahn & Olson 1993).

The cognitive approach relates closely to contemporary theories of motivation, such as the expectancy theory of V.H. Vroom (Camp et al. 1986). Vroom's theory implies that we are able to store the relationships between past behaviour and its consequences in combination with current information to make inferences about the consequences of future behaviour. Cognitive theories are thus concerned with how and why people decide to do things, and psychologists attempt to determine this by studying the way people view various activities as perceived opportunities to pursue desired goals.

To differentiate between the operant approach and the cognitive approach, it can be said that the operant approach describes the physical events surrounding behaviour and its modification, while the cognitive approach attempts to describe the mental processes through which learning and behaviour are connected (Camp et al. 1986). The difference can be illustrated by the following example: a bus driver helps an elderly person to get on the bus and is complimented by the passengers on the bus. Thereafter he makes an effort to help all elderly persons. From a behaviouristic approach the helping of the elderly person was positively reinforced by the compliments of the passengers. Having been positively reinforced, the behaviour is repeated whenever the bus driver sees an elderly person getting on the bus. From a cognitive perspective, however, we would conclude that the bus driver helps elderly persons in order to be complimented by the passengers, because being complimented is highly valued.

5.3.4 Social learning

Social learning is primarily based on the work of A. Bandura and his associates. Their perspective incorporates both behaviourist and cognitive ideas in the description of the learning process. It shares with operant conditioning the notion that behaviour is affected by its external antecedents and consequences. On the other hand, these antecedents and consequences must be processed cognitively before they can have an impact on the individual's behaviour.

According to the social learning theory, also known as observational learning, vicarious learning or modelling, behaviour is learned simply through *observation* of other people's behaviour, without necessarily performing the behaviour. It is remembered as visual images and later appears in applicable situations. Parents, older siblings, teachers, popular friends, group leaders and television and film stars may all be "models" for this type of learning, which occurs particularly in the acquisition of social behaviour, in other words, behaviour which is influenced by the "presence" of others. Affection or aggression evident when parents communicate with each other serves as a model for a teenager's communication with the opposite sex. In the work situation, the model might be a manager or colleague who demonstrates desired behaviour. Mentors or senior workers may also act as important models, especially for new employees. In the South African situation, it can be asked if the shortage of experienced black managers to act as models is not a constraint to the progression of black managers in the hierarchy.

For someone to learn by observing a model, four types of processes must take place (Camp *et al.* 1986; Greenberg & Baron 1993; Robbins 1998).

5.3.4.1 *Attentional processes*
The learner must pay attention to the model. Models who are more likely to get the learner's attention will be imitated more frequently and more precisely than other models. Models can also purposefully call attention to themselves or to key learning points to facilitate learning.

5.3.4.2 *Retentional processes*
The information being observed is then processed for retention. The initial phase of retention is the coding of information into cognitive symbols that can be stored, retained and retrieved. It can then be manifested behaviourally in a language. This provides us with a model that specifies how relationships between behaviour and its consequences can be retained and recalled to influence future behaviour, even if the behaviour was not reinforced, or performed by the learner (Camp *et al.* 1986). After the learner has symbolically coded the observed behaviour, he or she can visualise or imagine himself or herself actually engaging in the behaviour. The learner thus develops a verbal description or *mental image* of the model's actions in order to remember them. This process is called symbolic rehearsal. It is akin to practising in the mind. Although symbolic rehearsal may not always occur, the transfer of learning will be improved if it is practised by learners and if they are assisted to develop their own symbolic codes.

5.3.4.3 *Behavioural reproduction processes*
After the learner has observed the behaviour of the model and imagined himself or herself doing the same, the behaviour must then actually be practised. This practise proves that the learner can perform the modelled behaviour. While the final manifestation is affected by the environment in which it occurs, part of the behavioural reproduction is also internal to the learner, because the reproduction of the learned behaviour sequence improves its retention (Camp et al. 1986).

5.3.4.4 *Motivational processes*
Learners must have some motivation to learn from the model. Learning thus finally depends on the feedback from the environment in response to the

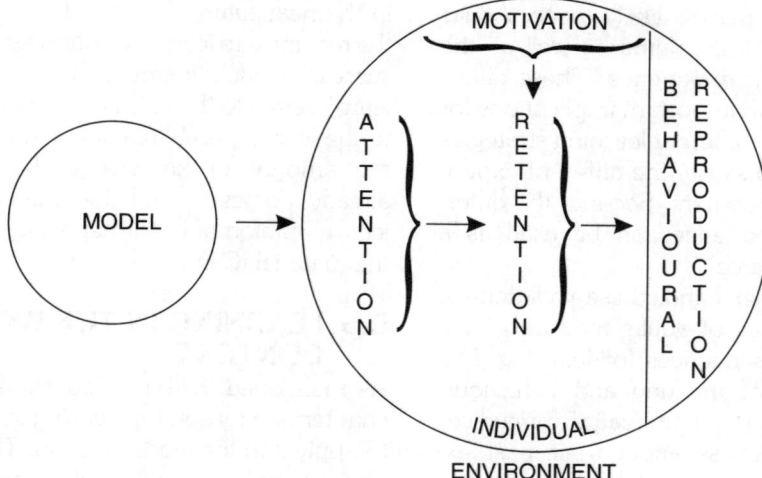

Figure 5.1 Social or observational learning
Source: Adapted from Camp et al. (1986)

behaviour. Whether the environment produces positive, negative or no consequences in response to the behaviour, that feedback will influence that behaviour in the future.

The processes of social learning are illustrated in figure 5.1.

Social learning plays an important part in many formal training programmes of organisations. It also occurs in an informal manner, for example when the traditions, culture and norms of organisations are learned and integrated in the behaviour of employees, especially during the socialising process of new employees (Greenberg & Baron 1993).

5.4 THE ADULT LEARNER

In organisations, we mostly have to do with a specific type of learner, the adult learner. This has led to the development of a learning model that differs from the well-known pedagogical model and is based on adult learning principles, also called *andragogy*. The assumptions

inherent in the andragogical model (Camp et al. 1986; Knowles 1984) are the following:

5.4.1 The self-concept of the learner

Adult learners are self-directing. Once adults have developed a self-concept of being responsible for their own lives, they develop a psychological need to be perceived and treated by others as capable of carrying out this responsibility. If adults then experience an "education" or "teaching" situation, they hark back to their conditioning from school days, assume a dependent role and demand to be taught. If they are then really treated as children, this conditioned expectation conflicts with their need to be self-directing, and instead of learning, they use their energy to deal with this conflict.

5.4.2 The experience of the learner

Adults come into a learning situation with a fairly well-defined cognitive map. This map is based on their experience of the world, and the older they are, the more detailed their map is likely to be. Adults thus differ in the volume as well as the quality of their experience. These differences have two important implications for training. First, different learning strategies are needed to satisfy the different experiences of the learners. Second, the differences in experience can be used as a learning resource.

On the other hand, these well-defined cognitive maps of adults may also have negative consequences for learning. Habitual ways of thinking and behaviour, preconceptions about reality, prejudices and defensiveness about their past experiences have developed that have served them for a long time. They are therefore reluctant to interpret new information as signalling a need for cognitive change. If a new concept or principle has to be learned, all of those parts of the cognitive map that relate to the new concept must be unlearned or reintegrated. It is this unlearning that is difficult for an adult learner. The learning process takes longer with adults for this reason and not necessarily because of a decline of intellectual capabilities (Camp et al. 1986).

Another consequence of an adult's greater experience is that it increasingly becomes the source of the adult's self-identity. If it is ignored, it is not the experience that is rejected, but the person. This is especially important to remember when working with undereducated adults, because they have little to sustain their dignity other than their experience.

5.4.3 Motivation to learn

Adults are motivated to learn when they experience a need to know or do something in order to perform more effectively in some aspects of their lives. For the most part, adults do not learn for the sake of learning or curiosity. Learning must be useful to enable them to perform a task or

to solve a problem, or to be applied at least in the near future. The need to learn and the readiness to learn are critical aspects for successful adult learning. The "need to learn" refers to the value of the knowledge to the learner, and "readiness to learn" to the amount of knowledge the trainee already possesses and the trainee's subjective opinion of his or her ability to learn the material (Camp et al. 1986).

5.5 LEARNING IN THE WORK CONTEXT

As mentioned in the introduction of this chapter, the reason for studying learning is to apply it in the work situation. The most obvious application of learning concepts in the work situation relates to the training and development function of organisations.

5.5.1 The training process

Although vast amounts of money are spent annually on training, the impact of the training efforts on the performance of organisations is poor. This is mainly a result of the haphazard manner in which training and development efforts are often undertaken. In order to achieve better results with training and development efforts, training models have recently been developed that are based on a so-called *systems approach* (Dipboye et al. 1994; Camp et al. 1986; Goldstein 1993). A basic assumption of most of the models is that training must consist of an orderly, planned sequence of events in order to be effective. According to Goldstein (1993) the first phase of the training process is an assessment of training needs and the development of training objectives. The second phase consists of the training-development phase and the third phase is called the evaluation phase. The different phases are now discussed in more detail in order to elaborate on the different learning principles in the process. The training process is illustrated in figure 5.2.

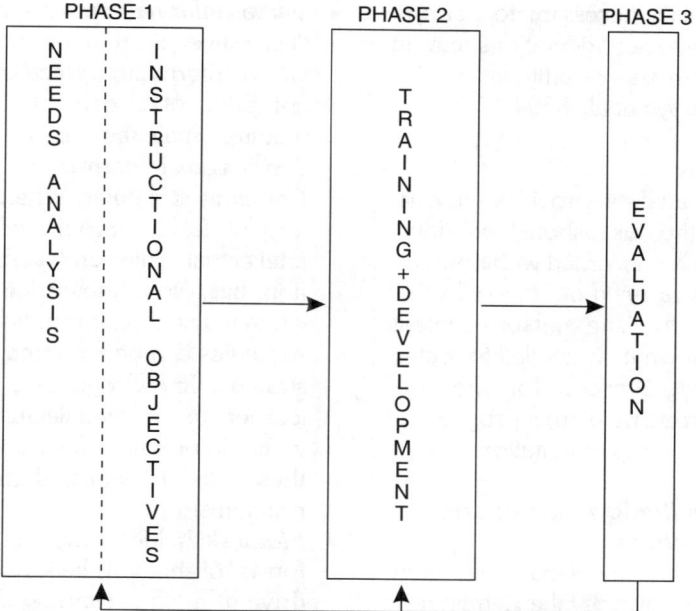

Figure 5.2 The training process

5.5.1.1 Need analysis

This phase of the training programme provides the information that is necessary for the design of the entire programme. It consists of the analysis of the organisation; the analysis of the task, including knowledge, skills and abilities; and person analysis (Goldstein 1993).

Organisational analysis

Training in organisations is regarded as a subsystem of the organisation. No training can be done in isolation. It is therefore first of all necessary to analyse the organisation.

The first step is to examine the short- and long-term goals of the organisation. This will ensure that training programmes are developed that will not become obsolete because of changes in the organisation, for instance the use of new technology in the near future. Organisations must also ensure that there is a positive climate to enable transfer of learning from the programme to the job. An aspect to consider is whether training is the best solution to fulfil a specific need. An alternative to training can be provided by selection and employment of persons who already possess the skills required for jobs.

Task analysis

The second stage of assessing training needs involves task analysis. The first step in conducting a task analysis is to compile a *job description* in behavioural terms. The job description specifies the duties as well as the conditions under which the job is performed. The second step is called task specification. This consists of a list of tasks providing information about what the worker does and how he or she does it, to whom or why (Goldstein 1993). The task specification enables the determination of what knowledge, skills, abilities and orientations (KSAO) are necessary to perform the job effectively. Knowledge can be defined as an organised body of factual or procedural information that is applied in performing a job; skill is the psychomotor capability to perform job operations; ability is the cognitive capability necessary to perform the job; and employee orientations refer to specific temperaments or attitudes needed for the job (Dipboye et al. 1994).

Person analysis

While the task analysis provides information on how the task should be done, person analysis is concerned with how well an employee is carrying out the tasks that comprise the job. The person analysis provides the information needed for determining the target group for the programme, the content of the programme and its design and implementation.

5.5.1.2 Specifying instructional objectives

After a needs assessment has been completed, a decision must be taken if training is needed. Training is not always the best option. Costs can be saved through work design, for example redesigning a particular task in such a way that it can be broken down into a number of smaller units requiring fewer skills. If a decision is finally taken in favour of training, the training needs must be described in terms of objectives. These objectives not only provide the input for the design of the programme, but also serve as measures of success that will be used in the evaluation of the programme.

When setting learning objectives, the learning outcomes that are the target of the training must be defined. Gagné, quoted by Goldstein (1993), has identified the following five major categories of learning outcomes or capabilities:

- *Intellectual skill.* This is also called procedural knowledge and includes concepts, rules and procedures. It presumes that one already knows the concepts that constitute the procedures. The learning of a principle is demonstrated when it can be applied in different situations, for example when using a rule to determine instalments on a loan at a specific interest rate.

- *Verbal information.* This is also called declarative information and refers to factual information. Recalling the different parts of a computer (disk drive, monitor, main board) is a demonstration of verbal information.

- *Cognitive strategies.* When performing a new task, learners not only use intellectual skills and verbal information, but also a knowledge of how and when to use the information. Cognitive strategies can be regarded as a type of strategic knowledge that enables the learner to use intellectual skills and verbal information (Goldstein 1993). It thus helps to learn, think and solve problems.

- *Motor skills.* Motor skills refer to obvious forms of human behaviour, such as driving a car, running a computer program and mowing a lawn.

- *Attitudes.* The different preferences of learners for particular activities reflect the differences in attitudes. These attitudes are learned, for example from the different commercial messages we get from the mass media. Organisations often try to influence the attitudes of their employees. One method is by creating a specific culture.

Objectives can generally be specified in two different forms, namely learning objectives and performance objectives. Learning objectives state what the trainee will know, while performance objectives state what a trainee will be able to do (Dipboye et al. 1994).

5.5.2 Training and development phase

Only after the training needs have been identified and the objectives specified can a training programme be developed or purchased and conducted. During the development phase, an environment must be designed that is conducive to achieving the objectives. This entails selecting a blend of learning principles and techniques that are based on the tasks the trainees have to perform (Dipboye et al. 1994; Goldstein 1993). Although it is not always feasible to apply all the learning theories to all training situations, certain valuable learning principles have been identified that can be used to improve the effectiveness of training programmes. Different theories on the way people learn were discussed earlier. Concepts such as the role of models and the value of positive reinforcement are important learning principles that should be incorporated in the training process.

5.5.2.1 Learning principles

Some of the important learning principles to facilitate the acquisition of knowledge, skills, abilities and orientations during training are as follows:

Trainee readiness

The extent to which learning will take place depends first on the basic potential or intellectual ability of the trainee, and second on the strength of his or her motivation to pursue the goal of learning. Generally speaking, the stronger the motivation the more effective the learning will be. Although a great deal of research has been done on different kinds of motivation in groups, such as reward and punishment, praise and rebuke, social recognition and competition, it is difficult to determine which form of motivation is best for any particular situation or individual. Reward seems to be more effective than punishment, yet a combination of the two produces better results than either on its own; praise is on the whole more efficacious than rebuke and some competition in learning is better than none. A crucial aspect of motivation in learning is a purposeful orientation towards learning a particular action, memorising something or solving a problem.

Practice and recitation

On the strength of his experiments with animals Thorndike formulated a *Law of Exercise* which posits that learning and retention (memory) of a response depend on how regularly and how recently the response has been paired with the stimulus situation. The more frequently it is practised, the better the chances that the correct response will be learned.

According to Dipboye et al. (1994), research indicates that if information has to be learned (memorised), the learners must recite the material, and if the training is focused on the acquisition of a skill, the learners must also demonstrate the skill. Findings further indicate that overlearning can be highly effective and efficient in the learning of complex skills. Overlearning means that practice should continue past the point where additional gains are made. Overlearning can, however, be problematic. The repetition of simple tasks may lead to boredom and a decline in motivation.

Distribution of practice

Although massing practice often leads to better short-term performance than the distribution of practice, it leads to poorer long-term performance of the task. As a rule it is more effective to distribute learning activity over a period of time than to learn a mass of material at once. The most effective distribution of periods for learning and relaxation must be established for each learning situation, as ultimately the optimal duration will depend on the individual learner and his or her powers of concentration. The effective distribution of learning may lead to reduced fatigue because of adequate rest periods, as well as improved motivation, opportunity for the activity of the nervous system to persevere with learning, and occasions for the learner to eliminate defective approaches to learning.

Knowledge of results

Knowledge of results (feedback) of learning is important, especially in learning motor skills. Individuals ought to know not only what is ultimately expected of them, but also how well they have done in each attempt. Knowledge of results stimulates a desire to repeat successful actions as well as to correct unsuccessful ones, and fosters a conscious attitude which encourages accuracy in learning. On the other hand, too much feedback may cause anxiety and embarrassment. Feedback on successes tends to be more effective than feedback on failures. The feedback must be specific and should be provided immediately after the response.

Whole versus part learning

The relative effectiveness of whole versus part learning is of special significance. When a substantial amount of material has to be learned, such as a part in a play, it is important to know whether it will be easier to memorise the material as a whole, or to subdivide it into separate components and combine it afterwards. Blum and Naylor, quoted by Dipboye et al. (1994), proposed that whole-task learning is more efficient when the task is both highly organised (components of the task are highly interrelated) and *complex* (difficulty of each task component). On the other hand, part learning becomes increasingly more efficient with tasks that are low in organisation and high in complexity.

Working on a computer is an example of a task that is highly organised and relatively complex. The task involves an interrelated sequence of actions: switching on the computer, entering the password, entering the program, etc. It would be more efficient to learn these actions in a sequence rather than learn them as individual tasks. Learning to play cricket is an example of a task that is low in organisation. The learner can learn the various tasks – batting, bowling, etc. – independently.

5.5.2.2 Transfer of learning

When designing a training programme, the generalising of training from the training situation to the work environment is of the utmost importance. In the discussion of conditioning we referred to the generalisation of stimuli in Pavlov's experiments: the phenomenon whereby association triggered by a conditioned stimulus in a particular conditioning situation can be transferred to other, similar stimuli which then elicit the same response. In an analogous way learning can be transferred from one situation to another. Transfer is regarded as positive when what is learned in training improves learning or performance in the workplace. On the other hand it may be that training does not affect performance in the work setting. The worst scenario is negative transfer, in which training impedes or hinders performance.

A typical experiment to study transfer of learning requires the subject to trace a pencilled outline of a star shape while only watching the movements of his or her hand in a mirror. Using an experimental group and a control group, it was established that acquiring dexterity with the right hand benefits the performance of the left hand as well. Such transfer of skill from one part of the body to another is called bilateral transfer.

Similarity of stimuli and responses is a basic principle in transfer. The greater the similarity between stimuli in the learning situation and stimuli in the work situation, the stronger the transfer from the learning to the work situation will be. Equally, the greater the similarity between the responses required in two different activities, the more readily transfer will occur. For instance, if a person is able to drive one make of car, he or she will not have much difficulty in driving another make, as the main controls (stimuli) in both vehicles are much the same, while the type of responses required also correspond to a great extent. For similar reasons a proficient pianist will learn typing more easily than someone without such finger dexterity.

Transfer of learning from one situation to another, similar situation can be illustrated in the learning of a verbal skill. Memorising a list of meaningless syllables usually facilitates the learning of a second list, as if the subject has learned how to master this kind of material. On the other hand, the ability to memorise meaningless syllables seems to have an adverse effect on learning, for example, a piece of prose, in which case negative transfer occurs.

5.5.2.3 Training techniques
In the training of employees specific techniques must be used. The different training techniques are categorised as nonexperiential and experiential (Camp et al. 1986). *Nonexperiential techniques* are more cognitively oriented and therefore try to stimulate learning through their impact on thought processes. *Experiential techniques* are more behaviourally oriented and focus on learning by means of concrete experiences.

Nonexperiential techniques include the following:

The lecture
There are different formats for lectures, depending on the role of the trainee in the process. Unlike the traditional straight lecture, the ideal lecture should be a two-way flow of information by which knowledge is transmitted from trainer to trainees. Trainees can actively learn from lectures by listening, observing, summarising, questioning and taking notes. The format may vary, based on the feedback of trainee understanding. A lecture makes economical use of time, as it can cater for large groups, but its scope is limited in terms of active participation, feedback and determining the learning tempo of each individual. Furthermore, it does not guarantee insight. Unfortunately, there is no agreement among researchers regarding the relative value of the lecture.

Effective learning, or not?

Audiovisual aids
Tape recordings, overhead projectors and closed-circuit television are invaluable and may be used in a lecture room or independently by students. In the industrial setting audiovisual aids are normally used in combination with other techniques. This promotes learning, as attention is heightened by the change of pace from the other technique. Audiovisual aids are also effective in cueing or focusing trainees' attention on a specific issue (Camp et al. 1986). Multisensory approaches are also encouraged by researchers.

Programmed instruction (PI) and computer-assisted instruction (CAI)
PI is a form of self-instruction that uses the principles of reinforcement, while CAI can be defined as the application of PI in a computerised format (Camp et al. 1986). It is claimed by advocates of PI that the technique complies with the following principles (Dipboye et al. 1994):
- Learners must be actively involved in the process.
- Learners must be able to progress at their own pace.
- Learners must be given immediate feedback on their responses.
- Learners must be rewarded frequently with experiences of success.

Programmed instruction is regarded as effective for the learning and retention of factual knowledge, but relatively less effective in terms of developing problem-solving skills. It is, however, time-consuming and expensive to develop a good program, and in the case of computer-assisted instruction, some learners still have a resistance to using computers. Some individuals also need personal contact and therefore it is recommended that PI be combined with other techniques such as lectures or discussions.

Experiential learning techniques are primarily based on the experiential learning theory of Kolb (Camp et al. 1986). According to this theory, learning is a cyclical process consisting of four steps. It starts with a *concrete experience*. The experience must be observed and reflected on to identify its elements. A concept is formulated to express the experience in relation to previous experiences and we then generalise by predicting if similar consequences are likely to recur if we repeat certain behaviours in other situations. These predictions are then tested, a new experience is constituted, and the process starts all over again. The learning cycle is illustrated in figure 5.3.

The following experiential techniques are often used in organisations:

Simulators

Simulations involve the use of equipment that requires trainees to use the same procedures and actions that are necessary when operating the actual equipment in the workplace. Simulators are often used to save costs, or when human lives would be at stake, for instance when training pilots. It is recommended that the equipment and the psychological conditions resemble as closely as possible the actual equipment and environment in which the tasks will be done (Camp et al. 1986).

Case studies

Case studies are often used in a small group situation. The group is provided with a written description of the background to, and problems of, a real or realistic situation. The group is expected to organise the information, identify the decision issue, determine a diagnosis, find a rational solution and develop a plan of action (Camp et al. 1986).

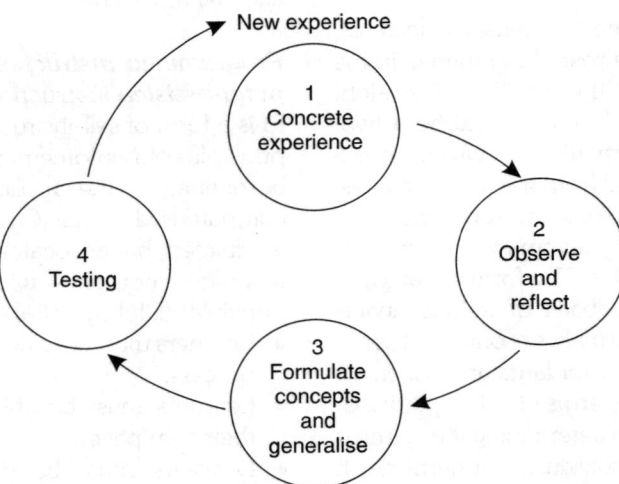

Figure 5.3 The experiential learning cycle
Source: Adapted from Camp et al. (1986)

Role-playing

Emotional involvement, attitude change, and possibly also empathy, can be fostered by assuming the role of a person in a hypothetical problem situation, or in a simulated interview situation. The student is required to handle a situation he or she has not hitherto experienced, and may be compelled to formulate and adopt arguments which entirely contradict the view normally held. It is suggested that role-playing accomplishes learning by doing, through imitation, through observation and by feedback as well as through analysis and conceptualisation. Role-playing also provides the opportunity to practise skills that are transferable to the work situation (Camp et al. 1986).

Business games

Games are developed to represent the functioning of an organisation. After being given information on aspects such as organisational problems, managerial functions and policy decisions, trainees are asked to make input decisions and are then provided feedback on the consequences of their decisions. Business games are very popular and are especially used in management training. The more realistic the game is, the more effective it will be, especially in the transfer of learning.

In-basket technique

With this technique the in-basket of a manager is simulated. The trainee is provided with memos, phone messages, letters and requests that a manager will typically have to address in a short amount of time. Although the primary purpose of the technique is to develop decision-making skills, it is also used to increase other skills, such as time management, as well as for assessment purposes.

Sensitivity training

Sensitivity training, also called T-groups (training-groups), is primarily used for training in human relations. Unstructured real-life opportunities are provided to study behaviour as it occurs during training. Although trainees develop insights into their interpersonal relationship styles, a disadvantage is that there is not often the opportunity to apply the training in the work situation. A similar technique is used to study group processes and dynamics. Because of the misuse of sensitivity training in the past, it has fallen into disfavour. It is, however, again gaining popularity with psychologists for use as an intervention in organisational development.

In conclusion, nonexperiential techniques should be used when needs assessment indicates a *knowledge deficiency*, while experiential techniques should be considered in the case of a *skill deficiency*. It is evident that the role of the trainer will differ, depending on the technique that is used. Using a nonexperiential technique, the trainer's role is basically to provide learning. The trainer therefore manages the learning process by controlling the flow of information. Using experiential techniques, the trainer is more a facilitator. The trainer provides opportunities for trainees to learn and guides the process in a collaborative effort.

5.5.3 Evaluation phase

Organisations are not really interested in the learning process or the training as such. They want to know what the return on their investment in training is. This can only be determined by evaluating the outcomes of the training. Although the importance of this last phase is never denied, it is the most neglected phase of the training process.

5.5.3.1 Criteria for evaluation

For a systematic approach to training, the criteria to be used for evaluation purposes must be based on the needs assessment. The choice of criteria should thus be guided by the analysis of the needs of the organisation, the task requirements and the current deficiency of the trainee regarding knowledge, skills and orientations.

Kirkpatrick (1977) developed the following criteria for the evaluation of training:

- *Reactions of participants.* This is obtained by asking the trainees for their opinion of the programme. A questionnaire about the skills of the trainer, the use of audiovisual aids, etc. is a typical example of how to obtain this information.
- *Learning.* Learning is normally evaluated by means of paper-and-pencil tests to determine if principles, facts and techniques that were taught are understood.
- *Behaviour changes.* An assessment is made to determine if the training has led to changes in behaviour on the job.
- *Results.* The measurement of results includes aspects such as increases in work performance, labour turnover, absenteeism and a reduction in costs.

Although this approach is valuable in determining the criteria for evaluation, it also has some shortcomings. One of them is that it is not always necessary that a programme be enjoyed (reaction of trainees) for learning to take place. The unlearning of certain behaviours may for instance be very painful.

5.5.3.2 Summative versus formative evaluations

Trainers are not only interested in the outcomes of training programmes; they also want to know what process factors influence the success of the training. This information can be obtained by observing the trainees and trainer or by monitoring the process at certain intervals. An evaluation that incorporates the mediating factors is called *formative evaluation*, while evaluation that only measures the outcome of a programme is called *summative evaluation* (Dipboye et al. 1994).

5.5.3.3 Evaluation design

The evaluation phase must also focus on the design to assess the training programme. Approaches in conducting research also apply to the evaluation of training programmes (Camp et al. 1986). The evaluation must determine *internal validity*, i.e. whether the results obtained from the training programme can be ascribed to the programme as such, and not to factors such as history, maturation and mortality. The evaluation should be designed to achieve this.

It is also important to determine the *external validity* of the programme. Can the findings be generalised to performance in other situations, for instance the work situation, other groups, and to other organisations (Goldstein 1993)?

5.6 CONCLUSION

The perception was created in the past that employees who did not perform in their jobs were transferred to training positions. Fortunately, things have changed to a great extent in many organisations in South Africa today. It is now apparent that no efficient and effective training can be done if trainers are not well equipped and qualified for their task. A thorough knowledge of learning theories and principles is necessary, as well as the skills to apply it in the development, conducting and evaluation of training programmes. For certain techniques, such as sensitivity training, advanced training in psychology is necessary.

Self-evaluating questions

1. Identify the aspects that should be taken into account when defining the learning concept.
2. Explain how knowledge of the different learning theories can help to improve training in the work context.
3. Determine the similarities between behaviouristic theories of learning and the experiential learning theory of Kolb.

4. Define the concept of "adult learning" and explain how a trainer can incorporate its principles in training programmes.

5. Discuss the different learning principles and describe, with examples, how these principles can be applied in the development of a training programme.

6. Distinguish between the different training techniques.

7. Explain how the proper evaluation of training can help to ensure that money spent on training is well spent.

Perception

6

Leona Ungerer

CONTENTS

Learning outcomes

After studying this chapter you should be able to:

- describe concepts in psychophysics and indicate how these influence everyday life
- find examples of advertisements in which stimulus attributes are used to get the reader's attention
- provide examples explaining four laws of grouping
- distinguish between monocular and binocular cues in depth and distance perception
- explain the various types of illusions
- point out the role of perceptual constancies in your life
- explain extrasensory perception
- distinguish between impression formation and attribution
- discuss the role of impression formation in our lives, with special reference to short cuts people use
- describe the ways in which other people's behaviour is explained by attribution theory
- distinguish between prejudice and discrimination
- provide some explanations of how prejudice and discrimination develop
- indicate how prejudice and discrimination can be reduced

Key concepts

psychophysics, threshold, signal detection, subliminal perception, sensory adaptation, selective attention, shape perception, Gestalt laws, pattern recognition, depth perception, movement, perceptual constancy, extrasensory perception, illusions, person perception, impression-formation, attribution, perceptual short cuts, self-fulfilling prophecy, stereotypes, halo effect, contrast effects, projection, group dynamic effects, prejudice, discrimination

6.1 INTRODUCTION

Perception is a process by which we understand reality. Perception helps us to recognise objects and scenes in our environment, to interpret this information and to extract meaningful and useful representations of our world from it. Perception is not possible without sensation, which entails the registration and coding of light, sound and other energies that impinge on the sense organs (Gray 1994). *Sensation* can be said to be the stimulation of sense organs and perception the selection, organisation and interpretation of sensory input (Weiten 1995). In essence, perception is the ultimate purpose of sensation.

The senses are separately and mutually involved in perception. For example, one can smell food, and see and smell food. Without hearing, we would not be able to hear somebody call out a warning or participate in a conversation. Without touch and the other skin senses, we would expose ourselves to objects that are too hot and heavy. Without a sense of smell, we would enter rooms filled with smoke or poisonous gases and without taste, we might not be motivated to eat.

Because vision can be regarded as the most prominent sense, this chapter focuses more on visual perception, but includes references to the other senses.

6.2 PSYCHOPHYSICS: BASIC CONCEPTS AND ISSUES

The early experimental psychologists were interested mainly in sensation and perception. They were interested in *psychophysics* – the study of how physical stimuli are translated into psychological experience. Gustav Fechner, a German scientist, was an important contributor to psychophysics. Some of the issues and concepts which have been studied in psychophysics over the years are thresholds, the just-noticeable difference, signal-detection theory, subliminal perception and sensory adaption.

6.2.1 Thresholds

Sensation begins with a stimulus, or any detectable input from the environment. The weakest detectable stimulus for any given sense (for example the minimum amount of light needed to see) is a threshold, also referred to as limen. A threshold is a dividing point between energy levels that do and do not have a detectable effect (Weiten 1995).

An absolute threshold for a specific type of sensory input is the minimum amount of stimulation that an organism can detect. Absolute thresholds, however, differ from person to person, among senses, and even for the same person under different situations. Therefore researchers, such as Fechner, arbitrarily define the absolute threshold as the stimulus intensity which is detected 50% of the time. Using this definition, researchers found that under ideal conditions, human abilities to detect weak stimuli are better than expected. Disturbances from the environment will influence people's perceptual thresholds.

6.2.2 The just-noticeable difference

A just-noticeable difference (JND) is the smallest difference in the amount of stimulation between stimuli which senses can detect (Weiten 1995). The JND has different values for different objects and senses, as Weber detected. For instance, the JND is higher for heavy objects than for light ones. The smallest detectable difference, however, is a fairly stable proportion of the mass of the original object. This principle came to be known as *Weber's law*. Weber's law states that the size of a just-noticeable difference is a constant proportion of the size of the initial stimulus. In general, as stimuli increase in magnitude, the JND becomes larger.

6.2.3 Signal-detection theory

Signal-detection theory proposes that detection of stimuli involves not only raw sensory processes, but also higher mental processes and decision-making processes (Egan, in Weiten 1995). An air space controller monitoring a radar screen for enemy aircraft must not only detect visual signals, but also realise how accurate or certain he or she has to be, and consider the consequences of incorrectly reacting and giving a false alarm.

6.2.4 Subliminal perception

The concepts of thresholds and detectability also serve to explain sensory stimuli that fall beneath the threshold of awareness. This is known as subliminal perception, which is the registration of sensory input without conscious awareness (Weiten 1995).

Researchers studying a variety of phenomena, such as implicit memory, unconscious learning (for example, self-help tapes which supposedly contain subliminal messages to help the person concentrate) and memory illusions, have found evidence that perception can take place without awareness (Greenwald, in Weiten 1995).

It is believed that subliminal perception or persuasion can be especially useful in advertising. In a survey of American consumers it was found that almost two-thirds believe in the existence of subliminal advertising and over half are convinced that this technique can get them to buy things they do not really want (Lev, in Solomon 1996).

The American public's fear of unconscious manipulation probably began with a widely popularised experiment performed in a drive-in movie theatre in September 1957. During a showing of the movie Picnic, a firm called the Subliminal Projection Company inserted messages that said "Drink Coca-Cola" and "Eat popcorn" for 1/3 000 second every five seconds. This rate was too fast for viewers to be aware that they had seen the images. Supposedly, sales of popcorn increased by almost 20% and consumption of Coke grew by almost 60%. This experiment was never replicated and has repeatedly been criticised. The design of the study was flawed because other possible effects on consumption, such as the movie itself and the weather during the showing, could not be ruled out (Solomon 1996).

Although research by clinical psychologists suggests that people can be influenced by subliminal messages under very specific conditions, it is doubtful that these techniques are of much use in most marketing contexts. Some of the factors discouraging the use of subliminal messages are the following:

- There are strong individual differences in threshold levels.
- Advertisers lack control over consumers' distance and position from a screen.
- The consumer must be paying absolute attention to the stimulus.
- Even if the desired effect is induced, it operates only at a very general level. A message might, for example, increase a person's thirst, but not necessarily for a specific drink.

In summary, there is no evidence that subliminal stimuli are especially powerful, and can lead people to buy specific products or improve themselves by using tapes with subliminal messages.

6.2.5 Sensory adaptation

Sensory adaptation is an automatic process that keeps us aware of the changes, rather than the constants, in our sensory input. This is because, like most organisms, humans are interested in changes in their environment that may signal threats or unpleasantness.

Sensory adaptation is a gradual decline in sensitivity to prolonged stimulation (Weiten 1995). When one takes a cold shower, the water temperature feels warmer after a few moments. Our sense of smell will adapt to the perfume or aftershave we use in the morning, after which others may smell it, but we do not.

The rest of this chapter deals with basic principles that influence perception.

6.3 PERCEPTION: THE FOCUS OF ATTENTION

Due to various limitations, our attention, or mental focus, captures only a small portion of the visual and auditory stimuli available at a given moment, while ignoring other aspects (Baron 1996). Thus, we selectively attend to certain aspects of our environment while keeping others in the background (Johnston & Dark, in Baron 1996).

Selective attention has obvious advantages, because it allows us to maximise information gained from the object of our focus, while reducing sensory interference from other, irrelevant or threatening sources. As perceivers we are subject to attention fluctuations, for example being busy with one task when our name is mentioned. Shifts in attention are often referred to as the "cocktail party phenomenon": listening and talking to one person or group, but also becoming aware of some of the other conversations taking place around one.

MARTELL **5** STAR BRANDY

IT'S A QUESTION OF STYLE

Size and stimulus attribute
© *Hunt-Lascaris*

Movement as stimulus attribute
© *Nestlé, SA*

ABSOLUTELY CLASSIC WIGS

m'lady
EXCLUSIVELY DESIGNED WIGS
1st FLOOR MEDICAL CENTRE
HEERENGRACHT CAPE TOWN
TEL: (021)253986/7

Contrast (unusual association) as stimulus attribute
© M'lady

Attention fluctuation illustrates one way in which we deal with the demands of divided attention. Although we control the focus of our attention, at least to some extent, certain characteristics of stimuli can cause our attention to shift suddenly. Advertisers have capitalised on attention-getting strategies. Some stimulus attributes that are particularly relevant to the design of advertisements and packaging, because of their impact on attention and perception, are features such as contrast, novelty, stimulus intensity, colour and sudden change.

The advertisement on p. 119 shows a bottle which is small compared to the roulette wheel. In terms of the "square root law" (a special version of Weber's law) the size of an object must increase or decrease fourfold to double its attention value. Increases in intensity (for example of sound and colour) are subject to the same exponential ratio. It has also been found that colour advertisements attract more attention than monochrome advertisements. Other factors may, however, also play a role here, such as the type of publication and the proportion of colour advertisements it contains. The position of the stimulus is another factor. The upper half of a printed page attracts more attention than the lower half, and the left more than the right, in conformity with normal reading patterns.

Movement makes objects conspicuous in the perceptual field and this is often used or suggested in advertisements (see p. 120). In this advertisement implied movement is used – it seems as if the water is moving from glass to glass. Contrast is introduced by the variation of stimuli, for example large or small, or unusual associations (see p. 121). In this advertisement an unusual image, that of a bald-headed woman, is used to get the reader's attention. The same effect can be obtained by isolating a stimulus, for example a small object in an empty space.

Additionally, the attention focus is dramatically effected by higher-level cognitive processes, such as motivation, expectancy and interest.

6.4 SHAPE PERCEPTION

If we lacked shape perception, our visual world would consist of random patches of light and dark and a disorderly mass of coloured and colourless fragments. If you look up from this book, however, you will notice that your visual world contains objects that have distinct borders and clear-cut shapes. Two important aspects of shape perception are organisation and pattern recognition.

6.4.1 Organisation

According to the Gestalt approach we perceive objects as well-organised, whole structures, instead of separate, isolated parts. The Gestalt psychologists stressed that our ability to see shape and pattern is determined by interrelationships among the parts.

Looking from a window, you will realise that the visual world is organised; for instance, you can distinguish a car from its surroundings. This component in our perceptual world is called the *figure-ground relationship*. When two objects or areas share a common boundary, the figure is the distinct shape with clearly defined edges, while the ground is simply the part that is left over, forming the background in the scene. The car that you see through the window is the figure, while everything that surrounds it is the ground or background.

In addition to ground, we also organise visual stimuli into patterns and groups. The Gestalt psychologists discovered that the following laws of grouping influence perception (see figure 6.1), known as the laws of perceptual organisation.

- The *law of proximity* indicates that objects near each other tend to be perceived as a unit or pattern.
- The *law of similarity* indicates that objects similar to each other tend to be seen as a unit.

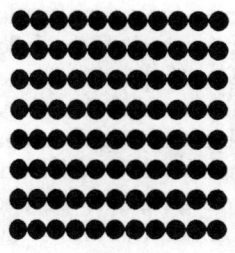

Proximity
Elements that are close to one
another tend to be grouped together.

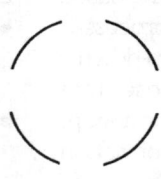

Closure
Viewers tend to supply missing elements to close or
complete a familiar figure.

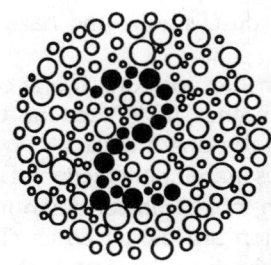

Similarity
Elements that are similar tend to be
grouped together.

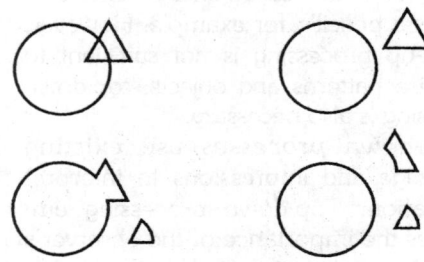

Simplicity
Viewers tend to organise elements in the simplest way
possible.

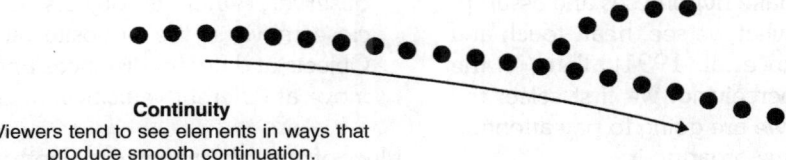

Continuity
Viewers tend to see elements in ways that
produce smooth continuation.

Figure 6.1   Laws of perceptual organisation
Source: Weiten 1995:141

- The *law of continuity* indicates that we tend to perceive smooth, continuous lines, rather than discontinued fragments. Elements that follow the same general direction are perceived as forming a unity.
- The *law of closure* indicates that a figure with a gap will be perceived as a closed, intact figure. We tend to fill and connect the disconnected elements in visual information that are full of gaps.

- The *law of simplicity* indicates that we tend to organise elements in the simplest way possible.

Each of these laws is illustrated in figure 6.1.

6.4.2 Pattern recognition
Psychologists acknowledge that it is a major challenge to explain how we manage to recognise patterns and forms in objects so readily. Some perceptual psychologists

believe that the ability to perceive objects represents a form of problem-solving based on two categories of mental processes simultaneously: bottom-up and top-down.

Bottom-up processes are those that register and integrate sensory information. These processes depend on the information from the senses at the bottom (lowest or most basic) level of perception. The lowest level of the information-processing conti-nuum, the sensory system, takes in pat-terned stimuli and passes them along through successively higher stages of pro-cessing until the brain finally concludes, "This is a pencil", for example. However, bottom-up processing is not sufficient to recognise patterns and objects; top-down processing is also necessary.

Top-down processes use existing knowledge and impressions to interpret information. Top-down processing em-phasises the importance of the observer's concepts, expectations and prior knowl-edge – the kind of information stored at the top (or highest level) of perception. When we look at an object, information flows downward too, in that our experience leads us to make hypotheses and assump-tions about what we see, hear, touch and taste (Bootzin et al. 1991). Thus, in the process of perceiving, we first select the information we are going to pay attention to and then we organise it.

6.5 DEPTH AND DISTANCE PERCEPTION: HOW FAR AWAY IS IT?

Except when reading, most of our visual activity requires looking at objects that are solid and have depth and distance dimen-sions, such as viewing television.

There is no single explanation for depth, distance, height and width perception (Matlin 1992), as we use many cues (Baron 1996). These cues are divided into two categories, *monocular* and *binocular*, depending on whether stimuli are seen with one eye or both eyes.

Monocular cues (one eye) for depth or distance perception include the following:

- *Size cues.* The larger the image of an object on the retina, the larger and closer the object is judged to be.
- *Linear perspective.* Parallel lines ap-pear to converge in the distance; the greater this effect, the farther away an object appears to be.
- *Texture gradient.* The texture of a surface appears to become smoother as distance increases.
- *Atmospheric perspective.* The farther away objects are, the less distinctly they are seen – dust, smoke and haze may interfere.
- *Overlap* (or interposition). If one object overlaps another, it is seen as being closer than the one it covers.
- *Height cues* (aerial perspective). Below the horizon, objects lower down in our field of vision are perceived as closer; above the horizon, objects higher up are seen as closer.
- *Motion parallax.* When we travel in a vehicle, objects far away appear to move in the same direction as the observer, whereas objects that are close move in the opposite direction. Objects at different distances appear to move at different velocities.

Much of our ability to perceive depth is based on the use of monocular cues. However, we also rely heavily on binocular cues – depth perception based on both eyes.

Binocular cues for depth perception stem from two primary sources:

- *Convergence.* In order to see close objects, our eyes turn inward, toward one another; the greater this movement, the closer such objects appear to be.
- *Retinal disparity* (binocular parallax). Both eyes observe objects from slightly different positions in space; the differ-ence between the two images is inter-preted by our brain to provide another cue to depth.

Binocular information is clearly useful in depth perception, and is more accurate than monocular information only (Foley, in Matlin 1992).

6.6 PERCEPTION OF MOVEMENT

So far we have considered perceived movement as caused by the motion of objects in the environment. We now discuss perceived movement when the object perceived to be moving is actually stationary.

The phenomenon by which the illusion of motion is created when non-moving stimuli are presented in rapid succession in such a way as to imitate real movement, is called *apparent movement*, stroboscopic movement or the phi-phenomenon. Apparent movement can be perceived in some neon signs when adjacent bulbs are turned on and off in sequence to create the impression of movement.

Earlier we have described the perception of movement in terms of a change in the position of an object relative to the observer. An observer, however, also has another frame of reference against which to judge movement, namely the normally stationary scene surrounding the object. If an object is seen moving against a stationary background, its motion will generally be perceived correctly. But if a stationary object is seen against a moving background, movement of the surrounding scene may be perceived as movement of the object. This is known as induced movement.

Induced movement may have caused your fright when you were seated in your car at a traffic light next to a large truck, and thought your car was rolling backwards. After braking quite hard, you may have discovered that you were not moving backwards at all. The truck, instead, was moving forwards. In this situation, the truck filled your field of view and your perceptual system interpreted its movement to be the result of your movement.

6.7 PERCEPTUAL CONSTANCY

When we move around, we perceive a stable world in which objects do not change haphazardly, but retain their characteristics under many different viewing conditions, which makes our world simple and more predictable. This happens because of the phenomenon called *constancy*, which is the tendency for qualities of objects (such as size and shape) to seem to stay the same, despite changes in the way we view the objects (Matlin 1992).

A number of different constancies have been identified.

Size constancy means that an object seems to stay the same size despite changes in the distance between the viewer and the object. The reason for this is that we are familiar with the usual sizes of objects and take distance into account. For instance, whether a bus is close, two blocks or two kilometres away, we "perceive" it as large.

Shape constancy means that an object seems to stay the same shape, despite changes in its orientation toward the viewer. A compact disc, for instance, is not distorted into an oval when we view it from an angle; it remains round.

Lightness and colour constancy is demonstrated in our visual system. An object seems to stay the same lightness and colour despite changes in the amount and colour of light falling on it. A pair of black shoes, for instance, continue to look black in bright daylight or artificial light.

6.8 ILLUSIONS

Perceptual constancies, depth cues and principles of visual organisation (e.g. the Gestalt laws) help people perceive the world accurately. Sometimes, however, perceptions are based on inappropriate assumptions, caused by optical illusions. An optical illusion involves an apparently inexplicable discrepancy between the appearance of a visual stimulus and its physical reality (Baron 1996). In short, it can be said that illusions are incorrect perceptions, or false interpretations of sensory information.

According to Baron (1996) there are two types of illusions: those due to physical processes and those due to cognitive processes.

Illusions due to distortion of *physical processes* include mirages, in which one perceives images that are not really there – such as the "water" one often seems to see on the dry road ahead.

Illusions related to cognitive processes fall into two categories: illusions of *size* and illusions of *shape* or *area*. Figure 6.2 shows the most famous visual illusion – the Müller-Lyer illusion, which is an example of an illusion of *size*. The two vertical lines in this illusion are really the same length. However, the "wings outward" version looks about 25% longer than the "wings inward" version.

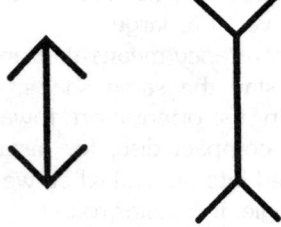

Figure 6.2   The Müller-Lyer illusion
Source: Weiten 1995:147

According to Corin (in Matlin 1992) several factors may explain why the "wings outward" version looks longer. One of the most likely explanations is that people judge it to be longer because the eyes move a longer distance to perceive the whole figure.

According to Schiffman (in Baron 1996) evidence suggests that illusions generally have multiple causes. One explanation is provided by the theory of misapplied constancy, suggesting that some parts are farther away than others. Our powerful tendency toward size constancy then comes into play, with the result that we perceptually distort the length of various lines.

According to Greist-Bousquet, Watson and Schiffman (in Matlin 1992), learning seems to affect the extent to which our perception is influenced by illusions, since many visual illusions decline in magnitude following extended exposure – although they do not decline altogether.

Another type of illusion is that of area, illustrated vividly by the well-known moon illusion, or the phenomenon that the moon looks bigger at the horizon (about 30% bigger) than at its highest point in the sky (Baron 1996). A possible explanation for the moon illusion is that when the moon is near the horizon, we can see that it is farther away than trees, houses and other objects. When it is overhead at its zenith, such cues are lacking. Thus the moon appears larger near the horizon because there are cues available that cause us to perceive that it is very far away. In this case, our tendency towards size constancy again leads us astray.

Shape illusions (see figure 6.3) can also influence perception. In this illusion, the Poggendorf illusion, a line disappears at an angle behind a solid figure, reappearing at the other side at what seems to be the incorrect position. Use a ruler to assess for yourself which of the three lines on the right continues the line on the left in the figure.

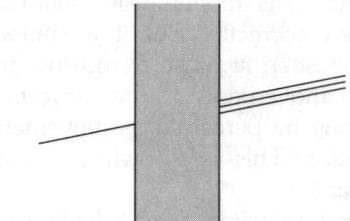

Figure 6.3   The Poggendorf illusion
Source: Weiten 1995:147

Cross-cultural studies have uncovered differences among cultural groups in their propensity to see certain illusions. Segall, Campbell and Herskovits (in Weiten 1995) found that people from a number of non-Western cultures are less susceptible to the Müller-Lyer illusion than Western samples.

The most plausible explanation for this phenomenon is that in the West, we live in a "carpented world" which is dominated by straight lines, right angles and rectangular rooms, buildings and furniture.

Illusions explain real and induced inconsistencies in perception and may have practical consequences. According to Matlin (1992) the Poggendorf illusion (see figure 6.3) was responsible for a plane crash near New York in 1965, resulting in four deaths and forty-nine injured. Two planes were about to land in the area, but a cloud formation was between them, and because of the Poggendorf illusion they perceived that they were heading directly towards each other. Both pilots changed direction to correct what they perceived as an error and collided.

According to Weiten (1995) optical illusions illustrate that perceptions of objective reality may be largely wrong and subjective, resulting from misperceptions and even illusions due to the influence of many personal and contextual factors.

6.9 THE INFLUENCE OF LEARNING AND HEREDITY ON PERCEPTION

Evidence suggests that perception is influenced by learning (nurture) as well as heredity (nature). Evidence that perception is innate has been obtained from research on blindness. People born blind (or blinded soon after birth), whose sight was later restored through medical procedures, could make at least partial sense of the visual world, such as following moving objects (Von Senden, in Baron 1996). Furthermore, research on very young babies by Adam and Doty, cited in Baron (1996) and Schiffman (1990), suggests their ability to perceive and distinguish colour, sounds and smells at birth or soon after.

Considerable evidence substantiates the view that key aspects of perception are learned. Experiments were carried out in which human volunteers wore special goggles that inverted their view of the world and reversed right and left. The volunteers initially experienced difficulty in carrying out normal activities with their goggles on, but soon adapted and did everything from reading a book to flying a plane (Kohler, in Baron 1996).

Heredity and learning in combination also influence perception (Wiesel, in Baron 1996). Sacks (in Baron 1996) mentions the case of Virgil, a 50-year-old-man who regained his sight after 45 years of blindness. The fact that Virgil could immediately detect visual features, such as letters, objects and colours, suggested the influence of nature. However, Virgil could not "see" in the true sense. Learning even simple visual relationships required great effort, since most of his knowledge of the world had come to him though the sense of touch. It is therefore clear that both biology and learning play critical roles in perception.

6.10 FACTORS INFLUENCING PERCEPTION

A number of factors in the perceiver, perceived objects and the situation (context) may shape and sometimes distort perception.

6.10.1 The perceiver

The cliché "beauty is in the eye of the beholder" suggests that perception is subjective. Subjective factors include attitudes, motives, interests, prejudices, preferences, past experiences and expectations. A surgeon will more readily notice an "imperfect" nose than an engineer, who again will more easily notice errors in the construction of a building.

Subjective perception can, however, change as social or cultural factors change. In South Africa people are becoming more used to women from all ethnic groups being in managerial positions as it becomes more and more common.

Our expectations can distort our perceptions, because we are inclined to see what we expect to see. If we expect policemen to be rude and young people to be rebellious, we may perceive them this way regardless of their actual traits or how they behave.

6.10.2 The perceived object or target

Characteristics in the object being observed can affect what is perceived. Loud people are more likely to be noticed in a group than quiet ones. Motion, sounds, size and other attributes of objects influence the way we see them. People's attributes, however, are also coloured by the perceiver's subjectivity. Judgement errors in decisions to select one applicant and not another may result from such subjective attributions of the perceiver to the perceived.

6.10.3 The situation

Human behaviour, like perceptions, can seldom be interpreted without considering the context in which it occurs. Persons who have just terminated a relationship are more likely than others to notice the happy couples around them, until they adjust to their loss or are in a new relationship. The time at which an object or event is seen can influence attention and therefore perception, as can situational factors in the work situation.

The factors influencing perception are shown in figure 6.4.

6.11 EXTRASENSORY PERCEPTION

We sometimes refer to a person's "sixth sense", that is, knowing something without the use of our five basic senses. In more scientific terms this refers to extrasensory perception (ESP) – literally, perception without a basis in sensation.

According to Baron (1996) a more recent concept, psi, is currently used instead of the older term, ESP. Bem and Honorton (in Baron 1996) define psi as unusual processes of information or energy transfer that are currently unexplained in terms of known physical or biological mechanisms.

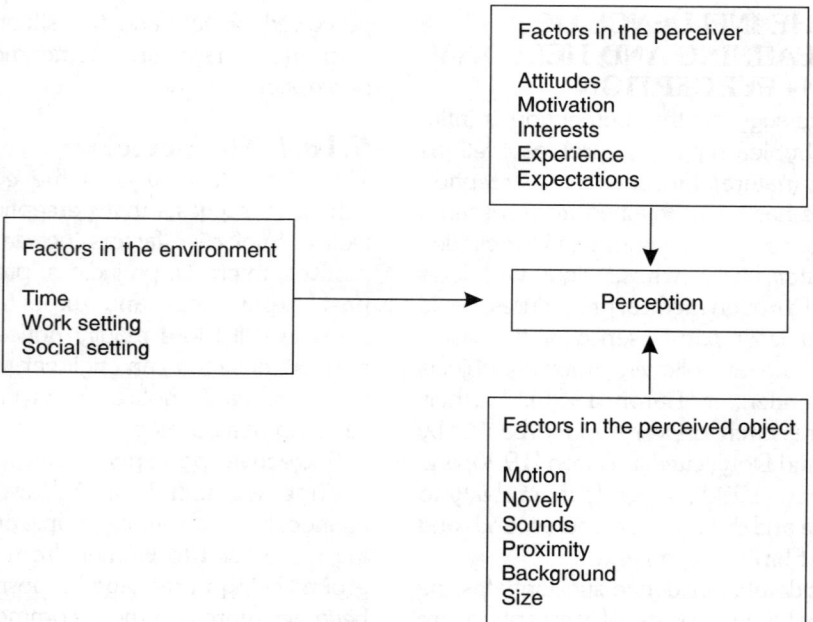

Figure 6.4   Factors that influence perception
Source: Adapted from Robbins (1993)

Parapsychologists, who study psi and other paranormal events, suggest there are actually several distinct forms of psi (or ESP). One form of psi is pre-recognition, the ability to foretell future events. Fortune-tellers earn their living from the supposed ability to make such predictions. Clairvoyance, the ability to perceive objects or events that do not directly stimulate sensory organs, is another form. Telepathy, a skill used by mind-readers, involves the direct transmission of thought from one person to the next. Another phenomenon that is often associated with psi is psychokinesis, or the ability to affect the physical world purely through thought. Bending spoons or moving objects with the "mind" or performing feats of levitation (making objects rise into the air) are examples of psychokinesis.

Most psychologists are sceptical of the existence of psi, for several reasons. The first, and probably most important reason for doubting its existence, is the repeated failure to replicate instances of psi and thus adhere to the principles of scientific thinking. According to Blackmore (in Baron 1996), it even appears that the more studies of psi are controlled, the less evidence they provide. Second, scientific understanding states that all aspects of our behaviour must ultimately stem from biochemical events, yet it is not clear what physical mechanism could account for psi. Third, much of the support for psi has been obtained by persons already convinced of its existence. Until satisfactory evidence emerges, critics will remain sceptical.

6.12 INTERPERSONAL PERCEPTION

When we interact with people, we are constantly engaged in person perception, the process of forming impressions of others. This process of forming impressions of others is universal and is very important, as it is the basis for further social interaction. Our initial impression forms the basis for organising further information, and while we may find that our initial impression is incorrect, it is much more likely that it will serve as the foundation on which our lasting impression is built (Tyson 1987).

Although our perception of people and of physical objects involves some of the same general perceptual processes, person perception is more complex, for at least three reasons. First, in forming impressions of others we try to "perceive" qualities that we cannot observe directly but must infer from their appearance and behaviour. Second, we see people as being causal agents, that is, as having motives and intentions that underlie their observed behaviour. Consequently, in person perception we assess what the person's motives and intentions might be. Finally, we know that individuals can try to manipulate our impressions of them and even deceive us. For these reasons, the "figuring out process" involved in person perception is especially subtle and challenging (Goldstein 1994).

However, our impressions are often inaccurate because of the many biases and fallacies that occur in person perception. Both impression formation and attribution form part of person perception. Impression formation involves integrating various pieces of information about a person. Attribution involves the explanations we create about the reasons for our own behaviour and the behaviour of other people (Matlin 1992).

Prejudice and discrimination are also powerful factors that shape our perceptions.

6.12.1 Impression formation

Impression formation is critical in our relationships with others. We constantly form opinions of other people and act on these opinions.

We tend to use a number of shortcuts when judging others. These shortcuts may be useful for quickly forming accurate perceptions and for making predictions. However, they can involve distortion. The following are forms of shortcuts.

6.12.1.1 Schema

Individuals tend to categorise one another in terms of schema. A schema is a generalised idea about a frequently encountered object, event or person. According to Weiten (1995) there are a number of different types of social schema in interpersonal perception, which correspond with the various aspects of the social world. A person schema consists of selected bits of information about a person, organised into a coherent picture (Matlin 1992). In this way people are labelled and put in categories such as social climbers, materialists, individualists, collectivists. A second type of schema is our self-schema, a cognitive framework of the way we think about ourselves, such as being ambitious or motivated.

We also have role schema about how people in particular positions, jobs or roles should behave, for example be conformist or innovative. Finally, there is the type of schema which is concerned with events and their usual sequence over a period of time, which are called event schema or scripts. These schema are generalised expectations about how we or other people should behave in particular situations and the sequence in which the behaviour should occur (Tyson 1987), for example protocol at formal official meetings.

Once a schema has been formed or activated, it influences both what people perceive and remember. Thus, simply identifying a new neighbour as a politician can lead to assigning characteristics such as "outgoing" and "power-loving" to the person, without necessarily being correct. You may tend to observe and remember the person's behaviours that are consistent with your schema, while filtering out or forgetting information that doesn't fit your schema.

6.12.1.2 The primacy effect

The primacy effect is the tendency for early information to be considered more important than later information (Matlin 1992). We use cues based on attributes that are immediately apparent, such as talkativeness, grooming, smiling, gender and general appearance. This prevents us from paying close attention to later information.

An important by-product of the primacy effect is the self-fulfilling prophecy. A self-fulfilling prophecy operates in situations where our expectations about someone lead him or her to act in ways that confirm our original expectation (Jussim, in Matlin 1992). A supervisor's initial treatment of employees, based on high expectations, may influence the employees to live up to these expectations.

6.12.1.3 The negativity bias

An effect called the negativity bias predicts that impression formation is more strongly influenced by a person's negative traits than his or her positive traits. According to a current explanation (Skowronski & Carlston, in Matlin 1992) we tend to judge or expect good people to be consistently good and we expect bad people to be sometimes bad and sometimes good.

6.12.1.4 Effects of physical appearance

Studies have shown that people's judgements of other people's personalities are often influenced by their appearance, especially their physical attractiveness. People tend to ascribe desirable personality characteristics to those who are good-looking, seeing them as more sociable, friendly, poised, warm and well-adjusted than those who are less attractive (Eagly, Ashmore, Makhijani & Longo, in Weiten 1995). Some research findings, however, suggest that there is little correlation between attractiveness and personality traits (Feingold 1988).

6.12.1.5 Stereotypes

Stereotypes are widely held beliefs that people have certain characteristics because of their membership in a particular group.

The most common stereotypes are those based on sex and on membership in ethnic or occupational groups. Preconceived notions that Jews are mercenary, that blacks have rhythm and that Italians are passionate, are examples of common ethnic stereotypes (Weiten 1995). People who hold traditional gender stereotypes may assume that women are emotional, submissive, illogical and passive, while men are unemotional, dominant, logical and aggressive. Occupational stereotypes include perceiving lawyers as manipulative, accountants as conforming, artists as moody, unionists as aggressive and defiant.

Stereotyping is a normal cognitive process that saves the time and effort required to understand people individually (Macrae, Milne & Bodenhausen, in Weiten 1995). Stereotyping, because it generalises and integrates a lot of information, therefore saves energy by simplifying our social world and makes it easier to understand people and events. Stereotypes, however, are often broad overgeneralisations that ignore the diversity within social groups and lead to inaccurate perceptions of people.

6.12.1.6 Halo effect

When we draw a general impression about a person based on a single characteristic, such as intelligence or appearance, a halo effect is operating (Robbins 1998). Thus someone may be considered intelligent simply because he or she speaks well while his or her social or arithmetic inadequacies are not taken into consideration. If impressions are based on a positive trait, the person will most likely be overestimated, whereas a negative trait may result in a general underestimation of the individual.

6.12.1.7 Contrast effects

Contrast effects can also distort perceptions. This is because we don't evaluate a person in isolation; our reaction to one person is often influenced by other persons we recently encountered. This is especially true in an interview situation, where a candidate may receive a more favourable evaluation if he or she is preceded by mediocre applicants, rather than by strong applicants (Robbins 1998).

6.12.1.8 Projection

The tendency to attribute own characteristics to other people, called projection, can distort perceptions about others, because people are not perceived as they are (Robbins 1998). In some personality tests projection is used to assess how people assess themselves while projecting about situations and other people.

6.12.1.9 The in-group and out-group dynamic

As the process of stereotyping illustrates, schema are activated when we identify a person as belonging to a specific group. Another related phenomenon, called the in-group and out-group dynamic, refers to the tendency to see people differently, depending on whether they are members of our in-group (that is, any group we belong to) or not. Not only do we tend to favour members of the in-group, but we tend to see members of the out-group (any group we don't belong to) differently in other ways. Whereas we may see in-group members as unique individuals with diverse qualities, we may see out-group members as being similar to one another. This dynamic may even create greater perceptual distortions or differences when factors such as gender (male or female), ethnicity (races) and nationality (countries) are part of group comparisons, as such groups may have less contact and therefore share less information about each other (Goldstein 1994).

6.12.1.10 Selectivity in person perception

When judging other people, we tend to do so selectively, according to our own schema, interests, background, experience, attitudes and even bias. Selective perception allows us to "speed-read" others, but we run the risk of forming inaccurate impressions and confirming our negative expectations of others. Because we see what we want to see, we can draw unwarranted conclusions from an ambiguous situation. If, for instance, a rumour circulates in one's organisation that lay-offs are going to take place, and a senior executive visits the organisation, it can be interpreted as a step in this direction, while the executive may be just on a routine visit to the organisation.

The discussion so far indicates that our judgements about others are seldom accurate, even though we would like to believe that we are good judges of people. Not only do various attributional biases distort our judgements, there are also a number of judgemental errors which result from the way in which we organise and store information.

The process of "figuring out" people involves not only creating an impression of their characteristics, but also making judgements about why they behave as they do. In the next section cognitive processes that affect the way we interpret the causes of people's actions are considered.

6.12.2 Attribution theory

When judging other people we all have our own personal or hidden theories about them. These are formed and influenced by our personal experiences and attributes, which in turn influence the behaviours we attribute to others.

Our perceptions of people differ from perceptions of inanimate (lifeless) objects, because we make inferences about the actions of people (Robbins 1998). The result is that when we observe people, we attempt to develop explanations, we want to give an "attribute" of why people behave in certain ways. Making attributions in our social life serves important functions. According to Fiske and Taylor (in Goldstein 1994), we make attributions because of a need to predict the future and exert some control over events. Understanding why things happen places us in a better position to achieve our goals.

People don't attempt to explain everything that happens around them. Generally people are more likely to make attributions when unusual events catch their attention; when events have personal consequences for them; others behave in unexpected ways and if they are suspicious about the motives underlying people's behaviour (Weiten 1995).

Attribution theorists specify the kinds of attributions people make, the information they use to do this, and the errors and biases that tend to influence these processes.

6.12.2.1 Types of attributions

According to Heider (in Goldstein 1994) we assign two general kinds of causes to people's behaviour. *Internal attributions* are based on causes of behaviour within the person. *External attributions* are based on causes of behaviour outside the person, in the environment.

We also apply these two types of attributions to ourselves. If you explain the fact that you failed a training test by telling yourself that you're not very good when it comes to using training technology, you are making an internal attribution. If, on the other hand, you explain your performance in terms of the difficulty of the apparatus or an instructor's incompetence, you are making an external attribution.

Determining whether the cause of a behaviour is external or internal depends largely on three factors: consensus, distinctiveness and consistency (Kelley, in Goldstein 1994). According to Kelley, people arrive at causal attributions by asking three types of questions about a specific behaviour:

- *The consensus question.* How does the person's behaviour compare with that of other people in the same situation?
- *The distinctiveness question.* How does the person's behaviour vary across situations or with other people?
- *The consistency question.* How does the person behave at different times and in different situations?

People arrive at either internal or external attributions weighing all three of these factors. Research evidence indicates that people often think in this way when making attributions (Zuckerman, in Goldstein 1994). However, the task of weighing consensus, distinctiveness and consistency is complex and time-consuming. Given the number of attributions we make daily, it seems unlikely that we go through such an elaborate process every time. We tend to reserve this deliberate attribution process for situations in which events are unexpected or have an unpleasant outcome (Weiner, in Goldstein 1994). Various errors or biases may distort attributions.

6.12.2.2 Attributional errors and biases

Social psychologists found that attributional errors and biases sometimes lead to inaccurate judgements of whether the cause of a behaviour is internal or external. In some situations these biases cause us to make erroneous internal or external attributions. Attributional errors and biases are the following:

The fundamental attribution error

The fundamental attribution error is the tendency in people to overestimate internal factors, such as a person's traits or attitudes, and to underestimate situational factors in explaining behaviour (Ross, in Goldstein 1994). Thus, we may assume that a trainee who performs poorly is unintelligent or lazy, while overlooking possible environmental explanations such as inhibiting family problems.

The actor-observer effect

Research has shown that our bias shifts, depending on whether we are observing other's behaviour or explaining our own – a phenomenon called the actor-observer effect.

The actor-observer effect is the tendency for the actor (the person performing a behaviour) to attribute the behaviour to the situation and the observer (the person watching the actor behave) to attribute the same behaviour to the actor's disposition. (Nisbett, in Goldstein 1994). This means that bias in favour of internal causes – the fundamental attribution error – is stronger when people explain another's behaviour rather than their own. If you trip while walking down an office corridor, colleagues are more likely than you are to conclude that you're clumsy or uncoordinated (an internal cause). You are, however, more likely to look for some external cause, such as the polish on the floor.

Blaming the victim

A third type of attributional bias occurs when we try to explain unfortunate events that occur to others, such as being sexually harassed or fired from a job. Circumstances such as these intensify the tendency to look for internal causes, an effect called blaming the victim. An example of a blaming-the-victim reaction to a report of sexual harassment is that "it was the secretary's fault because she dressed provocatively". If a person is dismissed, the reaction might be "he had it coming".

One possible explanation for blaming the victim is that it protects us from the notion that bad things could just as easily happen to us (Thornton, in Goldstein 1994). Blaming the victim also allows people to maintain their belief in the just-world hypothesis – the idea that life is basically fair, so that good things happen to good people and bad things happen to bad people. By blaming victims, we allow ourselves to think that because we do not share their attributes, we will escape similar misfortunes (Lerner & Miller, in Goldstein 1994).

The self-serving bias

A fourth cognitive tendency applies to attributions we make about ourselves: the self-serving bias. This is the tendency to distort attributions about our own behaviour to make ourselves look good. We accomplish this by giving ourselves credit for good outcomes ("I did well in the test because I am clever") and by blaming the situation for poor outcomes ("I did poorly because the test was unfair").

One possible reason why we slant our attributions to favour ourselves is to protect our self-esteem by seeing ourselves in a positive light. Another reason is that self-serving biases allow us to present ourselves favourably to others.

6.12.3 Prejudice and discrimination

Prejudice and discrimination are two closely related concepts and have become nearly interchangeable in popular use. Social scientists, however, prefer to define their terms precisely. Prejudice is negative attitudes held toward members of a group (Weiten 1995). Like other attitudes, prejudice includes three components: beliefs ("Afrikaners are conservative"), emotions ("I despise men") and behavioural dispositions ("I wouldn't appoint a woman"). Racial prejudice receives most publicity, but prejudice is not limited to ethnic groups. Women, homosexuals, the aged, the handicapped and the mentally ill are also targets of widespread prejudice. With changing situations new prejudiced groups may be created: in South Africa "rumours" circulate about "white males" being in-creasingly uncertain about obtaining jobs in certain sectors. Thus, many people hold prejudicial attitudes toward one group or another, and many have been victims of prejudice.

Prejudice may lead to *discrimination*, which involves behaving differently, usually unfairly, toward the members of a group. Prejudice and discrimination tend to go hand in hand, but attitudes and behaviour do not necessarily correspond (Weiten 1995).

The behavioural component of prejudice consists of tendencies to act in negative ways towards members of another group. Often these behavioural tendencies cannot be acted on directly because of social pressure, fear of retaliation or even legal constraints. When such constraints are absent, prejudice may be directly ex-pressed and this behaviour is termed discrimination.

Discrimination comes in various forms. Sometimes it is obvious, for example giving jobs to certain groups. In other instances it can be much more subtle and disguised, especially when social norms and law prohibit prejudice and discrimi-nation. Examples of more subtle discrimi-nation are a reluctance to assist members of other groups, avoidance of contact with members of other groups and tokenism, meaning taking some trivial positive action and using this as sufficient justification for not engaging in more meaningful behaviour.

6.12.3.1 The development of prejudice

The psychological explanations of preju-dice fall into the following broad cate-gories: those that focus on direct intergroup conflict, the authoritarian per-sonality, the sociocultural learning ap-proach and cognitive processes. These approaches, on their own or in combina-tion, have value in explaining prejudice in certain instances.

Direct intergroup conflict

According to this theory, hostility develops between the members of two groups if they compete for something. Tyson (1987) for example believes that the prejudice between Jews and Palestinians results from the fact that they feel entitled to the same land.

The authoritarian personality

The authoritarian personality refers to people who accept authority figures unquestioningly, if these figures are from their own group. They believe strongly in obedience and respect for authority, and also in traditional values – those who disobey them should be punished severely. Futhermore, these people are obsessed with power and toughness. The authoritarian type of personality is inclined to believe there is only one right or wrong, and no in-between. This is because they think rigidly and in absolute terms. Experts believe authoritarian personalities show these traits because they are normally exposed to very harsh child-rearing practices, which result in aggression towards their parents, that cannot be expressed. When they reach adulthood, this aggression is displaced by exerting authority over members of out-groups and their subordinates.

Sociocultural learning approach

According to this approach, prejudice is learned through socialisation. Children can therefore learn prejudice from their parents, friends, the mass media and in school.

Parents, through education and punishment and rewards, play an important role in children's acquisition of prejudice. It can grow from being punished or prohibited from playing with children from other groups. More subtle ways of children acquiring prejudice are through observing and imitating the behaviour of parents. In this way children may also make deroga-tory remarks about another group, without really understanding their meaning. These early attitudes are often later reinforced by friends of a similar background with similar attitudes.

Cognitive processes

According to Tajfel (in Tyson, 1987) when people are introduced, they immediately label others as belonging to their own group or to another recognisable group. Two further processes, namely *assimilation* and *contrast* are associated with this *social categorisation*. Assimilation results in our seeing people in our own groups as being more similar than they really are. We also tend to see people in other groups as being more different than they really are (contrast). When we process information about other groups, these processes distort our perceptions and we do not get the opportunity to reconsider any existing stereotypes and feelings. According to Tajfel (in Tyson, 1987) this explains why simply dividing people into groups can lead to biased evaluations and discrimination.

6.12.3.2 Reducing prejudice and discrimination

Three ways of reducing prejudice and discrimination which are frequently suggested are education, intergroup contact and legislation (Tyson 1987).

Education

The main source of prejudice is parental education, which outside influence can't change much. Prejudices learned at home, however, are further reinforced by the mass media and society in general. According to Tyson (1987) attempts can be made to reduce the degree of stereotyping which occurs in books, television programmes and films.

Approaches which have attempted to teach people about other groups, in the hope that more information will lead to greater understanding and acceptance, have been notably unsuccessful. This is probably because such campaigns are directed at the cognitive component of prejudice. They largely ignore the affective (emotional) component, which is probably more important to change.

Intergroup contact

Originally it was thought that contact between members of different groups would decrease prejudice. This was one of the main reasons for the abolishment of segregation in America during the 1950s. This is also the motive in South Africa for enforcing equality and having different groups share the same amenities. However, it is apparent that mere contact does not necessarily reduce prejudice.

According to Amir (in Tyson, 1987) a number of conditions have to be met for intergroup contact to be successful in reducing prejudice. Firstly, the people involved should be of equal status. Secondly, the contact should not be formal or superficial in nature, but rather close and intimate. Thirdly, the situation must be conducive to mutual cooperation and interdependence and this cooperation should preferably have a positive outcome.

It is not always possible to fulfil all the above conditions, especially in a country such as South Africa. Tyson (1987) believes that if only some of these conditions are met, it may result in some changes, which in turn will make it easier to fulfil more of the conditions. This may then lead to further change.

Legislation

According to Tyson (1987) it is generally accepted that legislation cannot change attitudes and that laws should not be passed before the majority of people support them. Tyson (1987) points out that a dramatic change in racial attitudes, however, took place in America when legislation regarding segregation and dis-crimination was changed. A possible explanation for this is the fact that people usually do not like to behave contrary to what is expected of them or what they themselves expect. If a law is changed and people are expected to behave in a way that does not match their current attitudes, it may motivate them to change their attitudes. An approach like this will possibly be most successful with the authoritarian personality type person, because they tend to regard the law highly and are thus likely to obey it.

6.13 CONCLUSION

Sensation and perception through all the senses allows people to perceive reality in a unified manner and in a unique way. Perceptual phenomena explain possible variations in people's everyday experiences, as well as the many possibilities for inaccurate perceptions in all areas of life. Although experience of the physical realities might be more or less accurate, illusions, for one, clearly illustrate that in some instances no one-on-one correspondence between sensory input and perceived experience of the world exists. This is even more true for social and person perception, where many personal attributes and external factors sometimes subjectively influence judgements of other people to create inaccurate perceptions, biased attitudes, insensitive and even discriminating behaviours.

The principles involved in perception are powerful in *every* aspect of people's lives. In business they can be valuable in influencing employees' self-perceptions, their perceptions of social work rules and their positive attitudes towards customers. Customers' behaviours and attitudes can be assessed by using their perceptions of products, services and organisations. Most important, however, is the social scientists' and human resources practitioners' use of perceptual psychology and practices, to not only facilitate positive social behaviours, but also to influence attitudes and prejudices among individuals, societies and work groups in a diverse country like South Africa. This includes not only testing and verifying existing assumptions, but also creating a theory and practice unique to a specific society.

Self-evaluating questions

1. Describe ways in which you can benefit in general or in your work from knowing ways in which people receive and process sensory information.
2. Apply practical examples to indicate why selective attention is important.
3. Explain how Gestalt principles influence perceptual processes and give practical examples.
4. Describe perceptual constancies.
5. Using examples in your own world, illustrate how to judge depth and distance.
6. Explain what attribution is and how it can be used to understand human behaviour.
7. Explain how you can apply the information on person perception, stereotypes, prejudice and discrimination to improve relations at work or in any group to which you belong.

Cognition

7

Leona Ungerer _____

CONTENTS

Learning outcomes

After studying this chapter you should be able to:

- distinguish between the different components of thinking
- discuss the role of heuristics in decision-making
- explain the relationship between language and thought
- explain what a syllogism is
- indicate the connection between creativity and intelligence
- describe the nature of sensory, short-term and long-term memory
- give explanations for forgetting
- outline ways of promoting memory
- differentiate between the functional, structural, process and pragmatic approaches to intelligence
- indicate factors which affect intellectual abilities
- describe extreme levels of intellectual behaviour

Key concepts

cognition, mental imagery, concepts, prototypes, schemas, algorithm, problem-solving, trial and error, means-end analysis, mental set, confirmation bias, oversight bias, hindsight effect, creativity, divergent thinking, heuristics, decision frames, escalation of commitment, sensory memory, short-term memory, long-term memory, rehearsal, mnemonics, mental age, mental retardation, genius

7.1 INTRODUCTION

The ability to think and to reason are distinguising characteristics of humans. Thinking is the basis for our knowledge of the world and for our actions based on that knowledge. Furthermore, we have a language in which we can communicate the contents of our consciousness.

We acquire knowledge by means of our perceptual systems. This chapter emphasises the use of knowledge and explains how humans combine, manipulate, store and transform that stored knowledge during thinking. Underlying the study of thinking is the view that the brain is a complex information processing mechanism which, among other things, mediates our grasp of phenomena in our field of experience. Thinking is a component of intelligence and by studying facets of both we can understand and predict behaviour.

Cognition is a more formal term for thinking. It refers to the way in which we internally process and use information about the world around us. Cognitive activity takes many different forms, e.g. reasoning, planning, deciding, problem-solving, remembering, imagining and speaking.

The biggest difficulty psychologists face when studying cognition, is that it consists mainly of private, internal experiences, which are very subjective. They therefore have to, for example, observe people's behaviour and make use of reaction time measurement and recordings of the brain's neutral activity to make inferences about cognition. As a result, thinking is studied in an abstract way.

When looking at the mental structures used for thinking, one realises just how abstract cognitive analysis is. We tend to talk about thoughts, ideas and memories as if they really exist, but in reality this is not true. Cognitive psychologists also use quite abstract terms, like *schemas*, *concepts*, *mental maps* and *mental images*, to help them refer to the different aspects of cognition, which are representations of reality (Simons, Irwin and Drinnin, 1987).

7.2 COMPONENTS OF THINKING

Thinking is a complex but cardinal field in the study of human behaviour. In any industrial situation people have to think: a manager must think before coming to a decision; a manufacturer must think about how to manufacture and market a product; a secretary must think how to organise tasks. The important components of thinking are mental imagery, concepts and problem-solving.

7.2.1 Mental imagery

Mental imagery refers to mental representations of things that are not physically present. Unlike a perceptual image, a mental image is not produced by stimulating the sensory receptors. Mental images rather represent events and objects that we merely imagine, as well as those we have actually experienced.

Mental imagery is also used to create cognitive maps. A cognitive map is a mental representation of the world as we believe it to be, or mental representations of physical space (Garling, in Matlin 1992). Like other forms of imagery, cognitive maps have practical significance. We use our internal maps to find the department in the building we work in and to give directions to people.

7.2.2 Concepts

Mental imagery focuses on the mental manipulation of spatial arrangements, while concepts focus on the mental manipulation of the properties of items in order to appreciate their similarities. A concept is a mental category of objects, ideas and events that share the same properties. We use concepts whenever we group similar items together: for example: typists, secretaries, co-workers are all employees or a team.

Such concepts are not formed from a set of common features but are built around a representative sample, or prototype. A *prototype* exhibits the typical features of a particular category: for example, a suit and tie typifies many people's concept of a boss. Bosses are more easily recognised as superiors than are others as subordinates. The prototype is usually the concept member that has the most features in common with other concept members and shares the fewest features with other concepts. It is the most representative example of the particular concept.

The *prototype* indicates what is typical about a specific category, while the *schema*, another mental structure, indicates what is essential about a specific category. A schema is a more general term than a prototype. It is a mental structure that can be used to organise information. Schemas are plans or procedures for classifying people, events or objects. You may, for example, have a schema for deciding which colleagues would enjoy working on a project. When the plans deal with expected sequences of events and actions, the term *script* is used (Abelson, in Simons et al., 1987). Schemas and scripts are the most important systems of plans for cognitive processing.

We use *conceptual grouping* to organise our lives. If, for instance, you work with files, think how you group other files. Any collection, whether it is files or books in an office, or consumer items in a grocery shop, quickly become overwhelming unless organised according to concepts.

The fact that we tend to group together similar items simplifies our lives in many ways. It makes it easier to find things, and helps us to remember more facts than if we did not have this tendency. When one groups together the items that one has to remember in a concept, it is easier to remember the attributes of the concept than having to remember each separate object or event. If we were not able to conceptualise, we would not be able to generalise or even think. This is because concepts help us to categorise different objects and events according to their similarities.

7.2.3 Problem-solving

We use problem-solving to reach a goal that is not readily achievable. In our interpersonal relationships as well as our occupations, problem-solving is a major human activity.

7.2.3.1 The problem-solving process

The typical problem-solving sequence is familiar to most people. Generally, after you recognise that you have a problem, you define it, plan a strategy for solving it, carry out the strategy and evaluate the effectiveness of your solution. The solution can be found by chance, by trial and error, or mechanically.

Problem-solving can also involve creative thinking. In this case the stages in creative problem-solving are:

- *Preparation*. During this stage you become aware that you have a problem and start collecting information to solve the problem. You try to make sense of the problem and try to solve it a few times.
- *Incubation*. Incubation takes place when you set the problem aside because at first you did not succeed in solving it. You no longer concentrate on the problem, but unconsciously your mind may still be occupied with it.
- *Illumination*. It sometimes happens that you get the solution to the problem with a sudden burst of insight called the "Aha-experience".
- *Verification*. Sometimes these "Aha-

experiences" turn out not to be the correct solution. You therefore have to verify the information to determine whether it is an appropriate solution.

7.2.3.2 Problem-solving strategies

Once you have presented the problem, you can pursue a variety of strategies to solve it. Some methods are very time-consuming, but they always produce an answer – perhaps immediately or perhaps several years later. Other methods require less time, but they may not produce a solution. Some methods to solve problems are trial and error, algorithms, means-end-analysis and analogies.

Trial and error strategies are relatively inefficient random searches for solutions. Problem-solvers make use of trial-and-error methods when the solutions are not readily apparent. However, according to Simons et al. (1987), people still rely on trial and error, even when more efficient methods are apparent.

When trial-and-error searches become systematic rather than random, the strategy is called an *algorithm*. An algorithm is a method that always produces a solution to a problem sooner or later. Following a fixed agenda at a meeting is one example of an algorithm – following the steps precisely produces a solution.

Algorithms are useful, but we are more likely to use *heuristics* when trying to solve problems. In problem-solving, heuristics are selective searches that examine only the options most likely to produce a solution. They are based on knowledge and past experience with problem-solving. Heuristics, unlike algorithms, do not guarantee a solution, but they do make a solution very likely. For instance, an open agenda at a meeting may lead to a solution of a problem, but cannot guarantee it. If you search for your pen, you may adopt a two-step heuristic. First you look where you usually put it and then search all the flat surfaces. Two problem-solving strategies that use heuristics are means-end-analysis and analogies.

In *means-end-analysis* the problem-solver divides the problem into a number of smaller problems (or tasks). Each of these is solved by assessing the difference between the original solution and the goal and then reducing that difference. In other words, you first determine what "ends" you want and then what "means" you will use to reach the ends. If your manual for a training course is stolen, you may decide to borrow a manual from a colleague who took the course last year. In this case the problem can be divided into several subtasks:

- make a list of colleagues and acquaintances of colleagues
- contact these people
- fetch the manual

In an *analogy* we use a solution to an earlier problem to help solve a new one. As with the means-end approach, the analogy usually, but not always, produces a correct solution. Analogies are useful in mathematics. Unfortunately, people are often reluctant to transfer what they learned previously to the solving of new kinds of problems (Mayer, in Matlin 1992).

7.2.3.3 Barriers to problem-solving

Solving problems would be easier if we just had to choose the best strategy. Unfortunately, we also have to overcome barriers to effective problem-solving. Two important barriers to problem-solving are functional fixedness and mental set. In both cases, old ideas persist and inhibit the development of new ideas.

Functional fixedness means that the function for which we use an object remains fixed or stable. Successful problem-solving often requires overcoming functional fixedness, for example using a grocery trolley to convey books, or even children.

Functional fixedness focuses on a characteristic of an object in problem-solving. A related concept, *mental set*, describes a characteristic of people when they solve problems. With a mental set problem-solvers keep using the same solution they have used with previous problems, even though there may be easier ways of approaching the problem.

Functional fixedness and mental sets both demonstrate that mistakes in cognitive processing are usually rational. Functional fixedness occurs because we apply our mental sets too rigidly and fail to realise that objects in our world can have other functions. It may be a wise strategy to apply the knowledge that we learned in earlier problems when solving future problems. However, in the case of mental sets, we apply the past experience too rigidly and fail to notice more effective solutions.

7.3 REASONING

Reasoning and thinking are interchangeable terms in everyday usage. However, in the study of thinking, reasoning refers to thinking for the purpose of making decisions, forming judgements, solving problems and drawing conclusions from available information.

7.3.1 Formal versus everyday reasoning

First, it is important to draw a distinction between formal reasoning and everyday reasoning. In formal reasoning, all the required information is supplied, the problem to be solved is straightforward, there is typically only one correct answer and the reasoning we apply follows a specific method. One important type of formal reasoning is *syllogistic reasoning* – reasoning in which conclusions are based on two propositions called premises. For example, consider the following syllogisms:

(1) All businessmen are men.
(2) All men are moral.
(3) Hence all businessmen are moral.

(1) Increased production means more pay.
(2) More pay means more inflation.
(3) Hence increased production must be combatted.

The second example indicates that reasoning, while it may proceed logically, can produce unreasonable or unrealistic results. The third statement is a deduction based on the conclusion that greater production promotes inflation – a conclusion following logically on the first two statements. Although the deduction that production has to be restricted is based on logical reasoning, it is nevertheless an unrealistic conclusion.

This simple example illustrates an important point: formal reasoning can be a powerful tool for processing complex information, but only when its initial premises are correct.

In contrast to formal reasoning, *everyday reasoning* involves the kind of thinking we do in our daily lives: planning, making commitments and evaluating arguments. In such reasoning, some of the premises are implicit and others may not be supplied at all; the problems involved often have several possible answers, which may vary in quality or effectiveness and the problems themselves are not self-contained – they relate to other issues and questions of daily life. Everyday reasoning, then, is far more complex and far less definite than formal syllogistic reasoning.

7.3.2 Sources of error in reasoning

Unfortunately, we are not as good at reasoning as we like to believe we are. Several factors, working together, seem to reduce our ability to reason effectively.

Confirmation bias, our tendency to test conclusions or hypotheses by examining only, or primarily, evidence that confirms our initial views, can cloud our reasoning. Because of confirmation bias, people often become locked into flawed conclusions. It prevents people from even considering information that might call their premises, and thus their conclusions, into question.

Oversight bias causes us to be selective in overlooking flaws, depending on the perceived importance of the issue at hand.

After specific events have occurred, we often feel as though we could have prevented them. This is known as the *hind sight effect*.

7.4 CREATIVITY

According to Matlin (1992), creativity is the ability to perceive original, new and significant relationships in existing ideas and phenomena, and to transform them into useful and functional methods and techniques for problem-solving. It involves finding a solution to an open-ended task in a way that is both unusual and useful. Creative thinking leads not only to new ideas, knowledge, products, etc., but also to new problems. Darwin's theory of evolution, Freud's psychological theories and Pavlov's experiments on conditioning are examples of creative intellectual pursuits.

Although creativity is frequently (even stereotypically) associated with physical science and art, it can be found in any field and in all walks of life. Most people, experts included, associate creativity with creative solutions to problems, responses on creativity tests, scientific explanations and music or the visual arts. However, people can also be creative in applying an idea or designing a new building or work project.

Creativity means innovative thinking which will produce better, more ingenious or more aesthetic results. It differs from originality in that original thinking implies simply innovation without any considerations of value or utility (Baron 1996).

Although creativity is usually associated with a specific (high) level of intelligence (even with brilliance), high intelligence or a high IQ score is not necessarily a predictor of creative behaviour. It is better to describe creativity as the total cognitive style of a person, a combination of how he or she has learned to be intellectually effective in his or her environment and use of special intellectual abilities. Creativity therefore can occur over a broad range of intellectual functioning.

People who score high on creativity tests also tend to score high on intelligence tests (Sternberg & Davidson, in Matlin 1992). Still, some people are highly intelligent but not very creative. All in all it can be said that creativity overlaps with intelligence, but the two are certainly not identical. An individual may, but will not necessarily, possess both qualities.

Research findings on the connection between creativity and intelligence include the following:

- Creativity coincides with high intelligence more often than with low intelligence.

- Creative people are unconventional in their occupational aspirations, for example choice of career, whereas highly intelligent people without creativity evince a need for conventional occupations and avoid insecurity and risk.
- Creative people rate a sense of humour high among desirable attributes they would like to possess, whereas highly intelligent people regard it as of minor importance.
- Teachers prefer intelligent pupils to creative pupils.
- High creativity does not correlate highly with job performance.
- Creative people tend to be impulsive, but are able to control and manipulate their behaviour realistically.
- Creative people have rich fantasy thinking and tend to use their own judgement despite social pressure.

Attempts are often made to assess creativity in everything from designs for buildings to poetry, fashion and even doctoral dissertations, yet there is no single agreed on psychological test for measuring creativity.

Who thinks convergently and who thinks divergently?

One measure of creativity developed by Guilford (in Baron 1996) is based on the distinction between convergent and divergent thinking. *Convergent thinking* applies existing knowledge and rules of logic to narrowing the range of potential solutions and focusing on a single correct answer. Although such thinking is productive in many situations, it does not appear to foster true creativity. In contrast, *divergent thinking* moves outward from conventional knowledge into unexplored paths and unconventional solutions. A creative person using divergent thinking processess information in diverse ways, finding a new solution or a variety of solutions. It is from such thinking that creative breakthroughs seem to derive. In Guilford's *divergence production test*, persons are asked to list the number of uses they can generate for common objects – for example bricks. The more uses a person can list and the more unusual they are, the higher the score. Thus, responses like "build a wall" or "make a chimney" are scored as being lower in creativity than ones like "grind them up to make emergency face powder". The unusual answers often reflect thinking that breaks out of the ordinary cognitive channels most people follow most of the time.

7.5 DECISION-MAKING

We make lots of decisions, for example which route to take to work, what to eat, what job to accept and where and how to spend our money. If you were a perfectly rational decision-maker, you would make each of these choices in a cool, almost mathematical way, taking into consideration the utility or value to you of the outcomes each alternative might yield and the probability that such results would actually occur. However, people do not usually reason in such a systematic way.

Decision-making requires us to make a choice about the likelihood of uncertain events. Like other cognitive tasks, it requires us to combine, manipulate and transform our stored knowledge. However, we often lack clear-cut guidelines on how to make the best decision.

When we have no rules or step-by-step procedures to use in decision-making, we tend to rely on heuristics. Heuristics are rules of thumb or strategies that are likely to produce a correct solution. Heuristics are typically very useful, especially because they help us to simplify the overwhelming amount of information we could potentially consider when we need to make a decision. A problem arises, however, because we fail to appreciate that heuristics have their limitations. Even good rules-of-thumb should be applied with caution. We tend to make errors in decision-making when we take these normally useful heuristics and apply them inappropriately (Simons et al. 1987).

7.5.1 The role of heuristics in decision-making

Three important heuristics, namely availability, representativeness and anchoring and adjustment, can influence our decision-making. Decision-making can also be influenced by the way a question is asked or framed and by escalation of commitment.

7.5.1.1 *Availability*

We use the availability heuristic whenever we estimate frequency or probability in terms of how easy it is to think of something. If you have to say which individuals are the most popular members of your work group, you would most probably be influenced by your own views and those of colleagues you are friends with. The availability heuristic is useful, in so far as the availability (or ease with which examples are remembered) is correlated with true, objective frequency. However, there are other factors that influence memory retrieval but are not correlated with objective frequency.

One factor that influences memory retrieval is recency. In general we can recall an event better if it happened yesterday, rather than a year ago. Familiarity is another factor that influences memory retrieval. It distorts frequency judgements in the same way that recency distorts these judgements. Specifically, we are likely to recall items better if they are familiar rather than unfamiliar to us. If you have to learn a new list of names, and there are a number of familiar names on the list (names of people that you know), you will most probably remember them more easily.

7.5.1.2 Representativeness

Representativeness is probably the most important of the decision-making heuristics. When we use the representativeness heuristic, we decide whether the sample we are judging matches the appropriate prototype. For instance, a sample of coin tosses should have 50% heads and no systematic order in the pattern of heads or tails.

According to Matlin (1992), representativeness usually leads to the correct choice in everyday decisions. It is generally a useful heuristic that produces wise decision-making. However, when we overuse it, we can make incorrect decisions.

The tendency to misuse the representativeness heuristic suggests that we should pause whenever we have to decide which of two options is best. One option may sound much more attractive because the description is so very representative, or typical. However, before selecting this option, one must be sure one has paid sufficient attention to other important information.

7.5.1.3 Anchoring and adjustment

When we make an estimate, we often start off by guessing a first approximation – an anchor – and then make adjustments to that number on the basis of additional information. This strategy is called the anchoring and adjustment heuristic. Like the two other heuristics we have examined, this heuristic often leads to a reasonable answer. However, people typically rely too heavily on the anchor, and their adjustments are usually too small (Toersky & Kahneman, in Matlin 1992).

Keep the anchoring and adjustment heuristic in mind when next you need to estimate a quantity. Provide an educated guess as a first anchor. Then make adjustments to that anchor, based on other information. However, urge yourself to make appropriately larger adjustments. Suppose that you are trying to decide how many bottles of beverage to order for an office party to which about 12 people will come. You bought 12 bottles for six people last June, so twice that, or 24, would be a first approximation, or anchor. But now it is December and people are likely to be thirstier. You are serving spicy food and the party is likely to last longer. If you rely too strongly on the anchor, you are likely to run short. Therefore keep in mind that each of the new pieces of information requires a substantial adjustment.

7.5.2 Decision frames

In the case of decision frames people are influenced by the wording of a question and they may underestimate the importance of other relevant information.

Researchers have discovered many applications of decision frames in various professions. Credit card companies found that customers preferred the phrase cash discount rather than credit card surcharge even though the amount was the same (Thaler, in Matlin 1992). When people were asked to narrow the pool of applicants for a job, they eliminated more applicants when they were told to accept the most suitable applicant than when they were told to reject the least suitable applicants

(Hunter, in Matlin 1992). This information on framing should encourage you to analyse whether a decision you are making is inappropriately influenced by the question's wording.

7.5.3 Escalation of commitment

It sometimes happens that people who have made a bad decision stick to it even as the evidence of failure mounts. They may even commit additional time, effort and resources to a failing course of action in order to try and turn the situation around. This tendency to become trapped in bad decisions, known as escalation of commitment, helps to explain why some people remain in unsatisfactory work situations or relationships (Brockner & Rubin, in Baron 1996).

Staw and Ross (in Baron 1996) suggest that escalation of commitment stems from several different factors. Early in the escalation process, initial decisions are based primarily on rational factors. When things go wrong and negative results occur, it is at first quite reasonable to continue, because temporary setbacks are common and there may be a lot of costs involved in changing a decision too soon.

As negative outcomes continue to mount, however, psychological factors come into play. Persons responsible for the initial decision may realise that if they back away from it, they will be admitting that they made a mistake. These people may indeed experience a growing need for self-justification as negative results increase.

In later phases of the process, external pressures from other persons or groups affected by the bad decision may come into play. For example, people who did not originally make the decision but have gone along with it may now block efforts to reverse it because they too have become committed to the actions it requires.

Fortunately, researchers have found that under certain conditions people are less likely to escalate their commitment to a failed course of action, for instance when available resources to commit to further action are limited and the evidence of failure is very obvious.

7.6 LANGUAGE AND THOUGHT

Most scientists agree that what truly sets us apart from other species of animals is language – our ability to use an extremely rich set of symbols, plus rules for combining them, to communicate information.

According to Sharrat (1987), language and thinking are intrinsically related and interdependent. Because of this interdependence, some theorists started to believe that language is necessary for thinking to take place. This belief became known as the *linguistic relativity hypothesis*, or the *Whorfian hypothesis*. According to this hypothesis, language structures, thought and the structure of your language cause you to think of the world in certain ways. As a result the thought patterns of people from different cultures (who speak different languages) differ.

According to Sharrat (1987) this hypothesis cannot be entirely true, if one thinks about it realistically. If it were true, young people and the higher apes would not be able to think, because no thinking would have been possible without the medium of language.

7.6.1 Theories of the relation between language and thought

According to Sharrat (1987) there are four possible ways in which thoughts and language are related:

- Language is necessary for, and determines, thoughts (the Whorfian hypothesis).
- Thought precedes language and is necessary for its development.

- Language and thought have separate origins.
- Language and thought have a common cognitive basis.

All these ideas have been incorporated into a number of theoretical views.

7.6.1.1 The behavioural view

The behaviourists believed that language and thought are actually the same phenomenon. According to them, thought is internalised speech. Watson (in Sharrat, 1987) postulates that people are just talking to themselves when they are busy with mental activities. Smith, Brown, Toman and Goodman (in Sharrat, 1987), however, found by means of an experiment that thought must be an internal non-motor activity.

7.6.1.2 The linguistic relativity view

According to Sharrat (1987) Whorf's hypothesis is probably one of the best known hypotheses on language and thought. It underscores the idea that language dominates thought.

A lot of research has been done on Whorf's hypothesis, or the linguistic relativity theory, and experts in general seem to accept that there are no empirical grounds for this hypothesis. Researchers acknowledge the fact that people can see the world in the same way, irrespective of their language.

7.6.1.3 The Piagetian view

In Piaget's view of the conceptual development of children's language, language is regarded as secondary and playing a supportive role in the development of thinking. According to this theory language is one of the symbols through which thought works, but it is not the only one. Piaget's view of the role of language in thought is therefore almost the opposite of Whorf's.

7.6.1.4 Chomsky's view

Chomsky (in Sharrat, 1987) believed that language and thinking are independent of one another. He was especially intrigued by the fact that children manage to acquire language so rapidly and efficiently at a stage when their cognitive functioning still seems to be relatively undeveloped.

Chomsky explained this by pointing out that children have a capacity to extract and identify grammatical rules. This has to be an innate capacity because simple learning cannot account for it. Chomsky called this hypothetical genetically determined capacity for recognising and producing grammatically structured speech, a *language acquisition device* (LAD). He proposed that this capacity is uniquely human; no other animals can use language the way humans do, and no other species has a LAD. Only humans, therefore, have linguistic ability and they acquired it through evolution.

Chomsky's view was quite popular in the 1960s and early 70s, but according to Sharrat (1987), this strongly nativist view of human language acquisition has more recently been reassessed and evidence is being found to question his theory.

7.6.1.5 The cognitive view

Cognitive psychologists believe that humans have cognitive mechanisms for recognising internal consistency and structure in all the stimuli to which they are exposed and that these mechanisms are genetically determined. They also maintain that is not necessary to propose a separate language structuring mechanism.

According to Sharrat (1987) the cognitive view on the common origins of linguistic and cognitive behaviour cannot be substantiated by direct empirical evidence. At the moment, however, there is no evidence against it. Furthermore, it intuitively makes sense, as well as being consistent with general evolutionary beliefs about the continuity of function from animals to humans.

7.6.2 Language, thought and metacognition

According to Simons et al. (1987), it would seem as if psychologists are faced with an unanswerable question about the relationship between language and thought. Although findings in cross-cultural research suggest that thought controls language, everyday instances of language influencing thought are numerous. Descriptions and job titles are often changed so that people can think differently about the job (we now refer to an air hostess as a flight attendant and do not refer to someone as a chairman any longer, but as a chairperson).

Some of the similarities between thinking and language are that both thinking and language production involve the integration of many separate processes; neither activity occurs without the accompanying processes of attending, perceiving, learning and remembering; both thinking and language production involve conscious and unconscious processes and both are monitored by a higher-order process called *metacognition*.

Metacognition is our capacity to monitor our own thoughts. In metacognition, we analyse what we know and how well we know it. When you read an examination question, you are probably metacognitively aware if you know the answer. When you make a speech, you are probably simultaneously monitoring what you say and how well you say it. According to this approach, language and thought emerge as integrated processes monitored by metacognition (Simons et al. 1987).

7.7 MEMORY

Memory, according to *Hutchinson's Encyclopedia* (in Higginson 1993), is the ability to store and recall observations and sensations. Memory therefore concerns the retention and recall of information.

The exact nature of memory is still the subject of a great degree of research and debate, but it is generally agreed that different parts of the brain deal with and store different sorts of memory.

Research into memory processes has identified many different types of memory. Semantic memory deals with how the world in general works, and involves such aspects as language or social rules and customs. There is episodic memory of particular moments in which we were personally involved, declarative memory which can give a name to a car, and our kinaesthetic or muscle memory which enables us to know how to drive it. We may lose our memory for words through illness, but usually remember how to drive a car, ride a bicycle or play the piano if earlier we had learned the skill.

A human's memory is not fixed like the memory in a computer, waiting to be used. Rather it is in a constant state of flux as new connections are made and pathways opened or closed. At this stage of scientific discovery the duration of information storage and the modes of processing data seem to indicate three stages of memory: sensory memory, short-term memory and long-term memory.

7.7.1 Stages of memory

The stages of memory are the following:

7.7.1.1 Sensory memory

Sensory memory provides temporary storage of information supplied by our senses. It holds representations of information from our senses very briefly – just long enough, it appears, for us to determine that some aspect of this input is worthy of further attention.

Data processing is quick, automatic and we are not consciously aware of it. Researchers differ on the duration of sensory storage. It is estimated at a fraction of a second or a few seconds. If you have ever watched someone wave a flashlight in a dark room and perceived what seemed to be trails of light behind it, you will have an idea of the operation of sensory memory.

7.7.1.2 Short-term memory

From the receptors, information proceeds to short-term memory where it is decoded. This is accompanied by selective attention, which is the registering of some stimuli while ignoring others. Much information is lost during short-term storage, but it appears to be an adjustment process to prevent overloading the long-term memory with unnecessary information.

Because short-term storage lasts no longer than 20 or 30 seconds, only a limited amount of information can be stored. This brief span is necessary to simultaneously permit fresh information being registered and newly received information being stored. A practical illustration is that of an interpreter at a conference, speaking and listening simultaneously, translating (speaking) one sentence while listening to the next. When pronouncing the first sentence he or she verbally repeats the information. This probably allows some of the information to be stored long enough to reach the long-term memory.

Short-term memory lasts just long enough for most people to be able to repeat a seven-digit number immediately after they have heard it. If this information is not transferred in some way to long-term memory, it will be forgotten unless it is actively rehearsed (constantly repeated).

According to Baron (1996), it seems as if short-term memory can hold seven to nine separate pieces of information. However, each of these "pieces" can contain several separate bits of information – bits that are somehow related and can be grouped together in meaningful units. Each piece of information is described as a chunk, and the amount of information held in chunks can be quite large.

Because of the process of *chunking*, short-term memory can hold a large amount of information, even though it retains only seven to nine separate items at a time.

7.7.1.3 Long-term memory

Long-term memory allows us to retain vast amounts of information for a long time. From the point of view of duration and capacity, our long-term memory is impressive.

For information to enter long-term memory, elaborative rehearsal seems to be required (Baron 1996). This is rehearsal requiring significant cognitive effort, including thinking about the meaning of new information and attempting to relate it to information already in memory. For instance, if you wish to enter the facts and findings presented in a section of this chapter into long-term memory, it is not sufficient to just state them over and over again. Instead, you should think about what they mean and how they relate to things you already know.

According to Baron (1996), long-term memory has a seemingly limitless capacity, and it can retain information for very long periods, perhaps indefinitely. In spite of this, quite often we are unable to remember something when we need to. The cause of such difficulties lies in the process of *retrieval* – our ability to locate information that has been stored in memory.

It is difficult to separate retrieval from the issue of storage – the way information is initially placed in long-term memory. Storage plays an important role in determining how easily information can later be retrieved. In general, the better organised materials are, the easier they are to retrieve. One key to the effective retrieval of information from long-term memory, then, is *organisation*. Organising information requires extra effort, but it appears that the benefits in terms of later ease of retrieval make this effort well worthwhile.

When information is stored in long-term memory, actual physical changes occur in the brain, whereas short-term memory, which only lasts for seconds, depends on a temporary biochemical change.

In long-term memory information is recoded. Hebb (in Hockenbury & Hockenbury 1997) believes that long-term storage is based on combinations of various groupings of neurons functioning on a reverberating basis. Adjacent neurons grow closer together to form a group, whereupon groups draw together, effecting structural changes in complex groupings of neurons to form permanent memory units.

Other researchers believe that memory is attributable to chemical changes within neurons rather than interaction between them. In their opinion the existence of innumerable synaptic connections alone cannot account for the vast amount of knowledge retained to a greater or lesser extent throughout a lifetime. They regard long-term memory as the recoding of information which is chemically stored in the cells of the cortex (Higbee 1988).

7.8 FORGETTING

If we have all these memory stages and processes, why do we still forget? Several theoretical explanations attempt to explain the phenomenon.

- *Decay of memory* traces. Perhaps the simplest explanation of forgetting is that information entered into long-term memory fades or decays with the passage of time (Baron 1996). The nerve groupings caused by synaptic connections in the brain during learning are also called memory traces, or engrams. If the information contained in these traces remains unused, the traces decay and the information is lost. According to Kalat (1990) this concept of quantitative decay does not hold water, for then all unused information would be forgotten, yet we know that something to which one has not given a thought for many years is recalled. According to Baron (1996) considerable research evidence suggests that decay is probably not the key mechanism in forgetting.

- *Inability to retrieve stored information.* According to Baron (1996) the key problem in long-term memory is retrieval of information, or finding a specific piece of information in such a huge storage system. Too much information is stored to be readily retrieved and recalled, implying that *storage and retrieval are separate processes.* Retrieval is limited by insufficient cues (activating stimuli) from the environment or the individual. Such a dearth of cues could be attributable to the limited attention span of the human mind, which is unable to register an indefinite number of stimuli at a given moment.

Retrieval is further influenced by the organisation of information in the long-term memory. Information is stored in categories, such as a number of words with the same meaning, or a number of words with different meanings but a similar sound.

Sometimes one sees a familiar object or one remembers something without being able to "retrieve" the correct word for it at once. In the process of retrieval one recalls a number of words organised in this category, all providing cues to the right word. Brown and McNeill (in Kalat 1990) call this the tip-of-the-tongue phenomenon.

- *Repression.* Freud used the word repression to describe the suppression of ideas and feelings, recollection of which would be disagreeable to the individual. For this reason they remain in the unconscious mind. Hence the inability to retrieve such stored information is due to motivated forgetting.

- *Distortion of memory traces.* This implies that both the structure of memory traces and the quality of the original information change in the course of time. It may relate to subjectivity of perception, meaning that every individual perceives things in a unique way, and that one person will perceive the same object differently on various occasions. At *every* recall these differences in perception add to the distortion, as when some elements of knowledge are overemphasised and others are overlooked.

- *Interference.* Forgetting is also ascribed to the interference of other subject matter in the period between a learning attempt and the recall of specific information.

When newly learned information impairs the recall of previously learned matter we speak of *retroactive inhibition*. Imagine a student who has to write an examination in industrial psychology on Thursday and another in business management on Friday. Before the examination both subjects are studied. Industrial psychology is studied first, then business management. If the learning of business management interferes with the recall of industrial psychology while writing the latter, this would be due to retroactive inhibition.

It seems, however, that information learned first is more likely to impair recall of subsequently learned information than interpolated activity. This phenomenon is known as *proactive inhibition*, which means that the study of industrial psychology prior to the learning of business management would interfere with recall of the latter. (The example is purely hypothetical. Quite apart from memory, positive transfer may play a part in related fields of study.) Generally speaking, proactive inhibition means that existing knowledge, attitudes, habits, etc. affect those learned subsequently. Over a 10-year period we acquire more knowledge which may interfere with fresh knowledge, than the knowledge we are able to acquire within a single month between learning and recalling fresh knowledge.

7.9 PROMOTING MEMORY

Some of the ways in which memory can be promoted are the following:

- *Insight.* Memory is facilitated if subject matter is properly understood when it is studied the first time, that is, when it is learned with insight.
- *Rehearsal* lengthens the span of short-term memory and facilitates recoding in long-term memory, promoting subsequent recall. Research has shown that rehearsal is mostly verbal, that is, using words, but it may also be done by means of visual or auditory (sound) images.

Repetition applies not only to things we want to imprint in our long-term memory but also to quickly recalling such vital facts as where we parked our car. Repetition should be combined with visualisation in situations similar to this. You should see your car parked in bay E and see the third-floor sign as you leave the car park, then think of it all again when you are a short distance away.

- *Mnemonics.* These techniques, once used by Greek and Roman orators to improve their memories, are being researched in laboratories today and involve association of facts with visual images.

Facts are arranged in sequence, each being associated with some aspect of a familiar visual field such as a room or a street. Each fact is allocated a "place" in the street, and on recall one merely "walks" down the imaginary street where every window, door, wall and tree provides a cue to a specific fact.

Mnemonics are particularly useful in learning unrelated facts such as numbers, but Kendler (in Kalat 1990) points out that it may simply facilitate concrete, associative learning without fostering abstract insight. Abstract reasoning is a hallmark of cognitive development and formal training is also directed at developing powers of abstraction.

- *Organising information.* Defective organisation of initial learning impedes retrieval. Organisation reveals relations between facts. For instance, a lecture on deviant behaviour organised according to a scheme of causes, symptoms and treatment will be easier to remember because the facts are not learned as isolated units. It could also promote transfer in the study of other forms of deviant behaviour through association of categories within the scheme.

- *Making meaningful associations.* According to Higbee (1988) most things we want to remember have meaning to us in some way, otherwise we would not try to remember them. If, for instance, we look hard for the interest and meaning in every task our work involves, we are likely to remember all our duties as they are related to the whole.

Linking something you want to remember with something you already remember well is an excellent way to assist memory. If, for instance, you meet someone with an unfamiliar name, the name may remind you of a familiar object, or the person may even remind you of a certain animal, for example a cat. You can then visualise the person holding the object or moving like a cat to remember the name.

- *Remember in pictures (visualisation).* When we hear something we want to remember, we should take time to picture it in our imagination. We can also work at making the pictures as clear as possible.

Many people think visualisation is difficult, but we all visualise all the time, sometimes quite unthinkingly. When we recall an occasion, the main sense used is that of sight. For example, we see with our inner eye the moment we were told we were being promoted.

- *Use exaggeration and humour.* Exaggeration can be combined with visualisation to form a very powerful aid to memorising. We remember best things

that stand out from the ordinary for any reason and exaggeration is a good way to make something ordinary seem extraordinary. It would therefore help if we make the important parts of our visualisation large and out of all proportion to the rest of the scene, and make it look funny.

Exaggeration

- *Use as many senses as possible.* Seeing things in our mind's eye is only the start. We have five senses and the more of them we use, the more places in our brain the memory is stored right from the start, which facilitates retrieval.
- *Take time to store the information.* Unless circumstances make it absolutely impossible, we must always allow ourselves as much time as we need to make the necessary associations and visualisations to store the memory efficiently. Sometimes this is easy, but in some situations, for example at a conference, when one is introduced to lots of people in quick succession, it is difficult.
- *Break material to be remembered into small sections.* If you need to remember a long number, break it into groups of two or three. When learning a speech or procedure, learn a small section at a time, having first read the whole several times to familiarise yourself with the content, then keep adding small sections to the whole one at a time.

- *Do not try to memorise too much at once.* There is evidence that it is much more valuable to spend several short sessions on memory work than one long one. Such an approach gives the brain time to assimilate the material and the person doing the memorising the opportunity to realise which parts are proving most difficult. Taking breaks in between memorising sessions also keeps different parts of the material from being muddled up with each other.

Some people remember better what they see and others remember better what they hear. Although most people may not consciously think about it, they probably know whether they take in things better if they see them rather than hear them or vice versa. It is unusual for someone not to be biased in favour of one method or the other, so when you realise your type, you can make sure you present yourself with material to remember in the mode which suits you best.

According to Higbee (1988), remembering is a learned skill. For this reason, improving memory is like developing any other skill. One must work at it by learning the appropriate techniques and practising them, just like learning to be good at golf.

Some people believe that an intelligent person (one with a high intelligence quotient, i.e. IQ) will naturally remember more easily than a person with a lower IQ. According to Higbee (1988) some relationship does exist between intelligence and memory ability. One reason for this may be that intelligent people are more likely to learn and use effective memory techniques on their own.

7.10 INTELLIGENCE

Intelligence is one of the concepts used to describe the cognitive functions of human personality and to indicate individual differences. Intelligence broadly refers to humans' global ability to conduct themselves competently in different situations by means of understanding, the acquisition of knowledge, reasoning, judgement, memory and practical skills. In practice, human behaviour – especially work and other achievement behaviour – is frequently judged in terms of ability requirements.

7.10.1 Definition of intelligence

Although there are many definitions of intelligence there is no generally accepted one. Authors agree, however, that intelligence refers to general ability and to specific abilities which enable humans to adapt to their environment.

It is very important to realise that intelligence is not a concrete entity which a person possesses in absolute quantities. The concept of intelligence is merely an abstraction to describe intellectual and performance behaviour. Furthermore, the term IQ and other quantitative indexes are simply numerical values for all the abilities, skills and knowledge which a person has learned or possesses at a given point in development.

Researchers now agree that heredity (or inborn potential) and environmental influences (learning behaviour) contribute to the quality and level of intellectual behaviour at any given time. In practice direct measurement of intelligence, aptitude or potential is impossible; we can only infer from observing or assessing behaviour, by means of ability tests, whether or not a person behaves intelligently.

Another point of consensus among authors is that intelligence is not merely the sum total of a number of abilities. Intellectual behaviour is influenced by many other factors, such as the way abilities are combined for a specific task, as well as nonintellectual aspects such as motivation, interest, personality factors and emotional condition.

Intelligence is usually explained from a functional, structural or pragmatic point of view. These approaches are not necessarily mutually exclusive. In the actual measurement of abilities all three are often integrated, as shown in the following discussion.

7.10.1.1 Functional definitions

These definitions approach intelligence from the angle of observably intelligent and effective behaviour, rather than regarding it as an inherent quality. Hence the emphasis in many definitions is on intelligence as the ability to *adapt effectively to the environment*. According to this approach, humans can solve problems and adapt to new situations through conscious processes of thought. Their intelligent behaviour is organised and controlled by a variety of cognitive processes through which they are able to solve problems and control, change, and adapt to the environment. Criticism of these definitions is based on the fact that emotional factors also determine adaptive behaviour.

Differences between people with regard to their ability and rate of learning and their ability to *learn from experience* seems an acceptable explanation for intelligence. In fact people learn differently, perform tasks differently, their achievements are different and they occupy different jobs. Correlations between intelligence and learning behaviour are frequently reported. Industrial psychology also tends to link success at work to functional work behaviour.

Definitions which regard intelligence as the *capacity for abstract thinking* – in other words, the ability to cope efficiently with symbols in the consciousness – see this ability as functional intelligence. Intelligence is therefore linked to creativity, judgement, imagination and insight, among others. However, the essence of things such as abstract thinking, creativity and judgement, and how to judge or measure them, remain problematic to psychologists.

Intelligence is frequently associated with *practical behaviour*. Several researchers, including Thorndike and Guilford, refer to practical or nonverbal behaviour as an important aspect of intelligence. In intelligence tests such as the Wechsler scale for adults, a total intelligence score is calculated by combining practical (nonverbal) and verbal (theoretical) subtests.

There is also a connection between social or interpersonal behaviour and functional or intellectual behaviour. Thorndike speaks of "social intelligence", and Guilford refers to social situations as an area where intelligence can be determined.

Functional views on intelligence are well represented in more comprehensive definitions such as the one formulated by Wechsler (in Simons et al. 1987). He regards intelligence as the *aggregate or global ability of the individual to act purposively, to think rationally, and to act effectively in and towards his environment.* In other words, Wechsler asserts that intelligence involves the individual's behaviour as a whole, that cognitive and behavioural factors determine intelligence and that intelligence is a general ability but that it may also be manifested in more specific, relatively independent and distinguishable abilities. His view is reflected in the rationale, composition, application and interpretation of the famous Wechsler intelligence scale for adults.

Associated with this view, that intelligence is more than just a number of abilities, is the emphasis often placed on what are known as *noncognitive factors* of intelligence. Research shows that intellectual achievement should be considered within the context of a definite phase of development. Authors who stress environmental influences and learning behaviour underline factors such as cultural, social and educational background, position among siblings, possible physical deprivation and diseases, and domestic circumstances such as parents' educational practices and attitudes and emotional deprivation. Many of these factors may contribute to the individual's personality, values, attitudes, interests and motivation, which may in turn influence intellectual performance in a particular field.

7.10.1.2 The structural approach

This approach to intelligence is aimed at determining and analysing the elements of intelligence. It has been established by means of factor analysis (a statistical method using large quantities of data or measurements of human behaviour to establish whether there are specific correlations to indicate a common or underlying factor or factors) that intelligence comprises various elements. On the whole structural views on intelligence tend towards two extremes, seeing intelligence either as a *general factor* or as a *specific factor*. Supporters of a middle course propose proving, by means of factor and multiple factor analysis, that intelligence actually consists of general plus specific plus group factors.

The notion that intelligence depends on one general factor was first stressed by Simon and Binet in their pioneer individual intelligence test. Both this test and later versions, such as the Stanford-Binet, which are still being used (as well as the Wechsler scales) for measuring adult intelligence, contain sets of heterogeneous items covering various intellectual factors (mainly verbal and numeric) and express IQ in a single overall score for various age groups. Although Binet acknowledged that intelligence comprises various facets, for example imagination, memory, attention and understanding, he insisted that intelligence was the sum total of these elements.

Spearman also developed his two-factor theory by means of factor analysis. In this theory all achievement behaviour is explained by two main factors, *a general or G factor and specific or S factors.*

Spearman regards the G factor or general ability as a function of the whole cortex, which can cause the individual to maintain the same level of achievement in several fields. The rationale of the G factor argument is that all intellectual processes are interrelated; there is a common element or G factor which characterises all intellectual achievement.

Spearman explains that the achievements of people with different intellectual abilities will not be the same in terms of specific (S) factors which are functions of specific cortical areas. Spearman therefore explains intelligence as a function of the G and S factors, of which the ratios may be different in every activity. For instance, in arithmetic the ratio between G and S can be 80:20, in Latin 50:50.

Most of the tests concerned with general intelligence, for instance the Wechsler test are based on Spearman's rationale. They offer one total score for intelligence, but also contain separate subtests which can attain specific or multiple meaning through interpretation and processing.

Thurstone explains intelligence in terms of a multifactor or *group factor theory.* He identifies seven primary or group factors which he regards as distinct and special abilities, but which also imply the existence of a general factor because of the interrelationship among them. However, Thurstone does not explicitly acknowledge the existence of a G factor. He identifies the following seven *primary factors* (Simons et al. 1987):

- Spatial visualisation (S) means the ability to identify proportions in shapes, and to form and handle visual-spatial images.
- Numerical ability (N) refers to the operation of numerical functions.
- Perceptual speed (P) refers to the ability to identify and perceive visual detail rapidly and accurately.
- Verbal comprehension (V) involves the ability to understand spoken and written language (words and sentences) in context.

- Word fluency (W) is the ability to use language and words rapidly and flexibly (in speech and writing).
- Memory (M) is the ability to store and productively retrieve information, for instance words, figures and symbols.
- Reasoning (R) refers to the ability to think logically, to enable problems to be solved through planning and the use of principles.

In job analysis, intellectual job or task requirements are predominantly linked to constructs which correspond to Thurstone's primary intelligence factors.

Thurstone established by means of factor analysis that certain test items correlate, that is, measure the same or approximately the same quality. Thus vocabulary, word fluency, spelling, reading comprehension, etc. may be interrelated to form the factor verbal ability (aptitude), which Thurstone recognises as a group factor, and which agrees with Spearman's idea of the G factor.

Guilford (in Simons et al. 1987) developed his famous theory on the structure of intellect (SI), the so-called three-dimensional model, which tries to furnish a systematic integration of all intellectual factors (figure 7.1). He accounts for intellectual functioning by means of the interrelation of three dimensions: *operations* (what one can do or the process by which the intellect functions), *contents* (type of material, for example items in a test which prompt certain operations) and *products* (the outcome of actions prompted by one or more contents). A

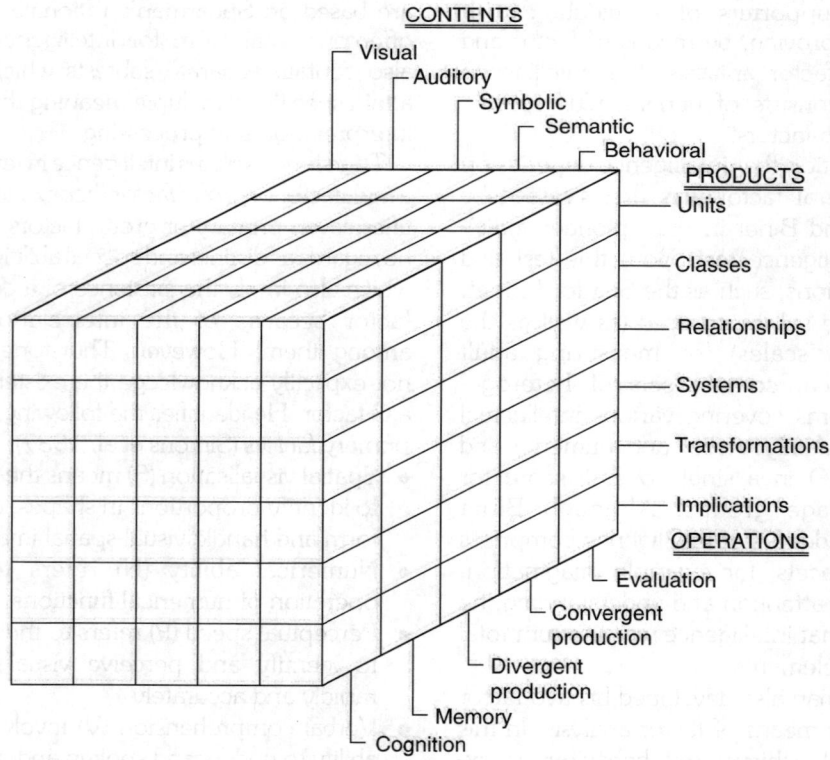

Figure 7.1   Guilford's structure of intellect model

combination of an operation and content results in a product which can be regarded as an ability, for example the individual answers (operation) items in various verbal tests accurately (good verbal ability), or items in mechanical aptitude tests well (good mechanical-spatial aptitude). Guilford represented his three dimensions on a $5 \times 5 \times 6$ cube.

The five intellectual processes or operations are the following: cognition, memory, divergent production, convergent production and evaluation.

The five stimulus or content processes refer to what the act is based on, for instance the tasks involved in a job or the items in a test. They are the following: visual, auditory, symbolic, semantic and behavioural content.

Abstract intelligence

Verbal intelligence

Concrete intelligence

Social intelligence

Intelligence is complex

Spatial intelligence

The six products refer to what a person has to produce, for instance his or her response to a test. They are: units, classes, relationships, systems, transformations and implications.

Guilford therefore sees intelligence as comprising at least 150 abilities ($5 \times 5 \times 6 = 150$), most of which have been measured and used in numerous ability tests, though not necessarily under the same names. According to Lindzey (in Weiten 1995) more than 100 of Guilford's assumed factors have been determined empirically.

Guilford's theory has far-reaching implications for psychological theory, and for research on learning, memory, problem-solving and decision-making. His model also has great potential for the construction of vocational tests, especially with regard to four types of intellectual behaviour: the *concrete intelligence* (figural content) needed by technicians, operators, engineers, artists, etc.; two types of *abstract intelligence* (symbolic and semantic content) needed by linguists, mathematicians, geometricians, etc.; *social intelligence* (behavioural content) needed by teachers, social workers, therapists, leaders, politicians, etc.

According to Weiten (1995) Guilford's theory illustrates the complexity of intelligence, the interdependence of abilities, and the fact that overall personality forms the basis of intellectual behaviour.

Vernon's hierarchical model (in Weiten 1995) combines the concepts of *general intelligence, specific factors* and *group factors*, while showing the interrelation between them. He attaches primary significance to the general factor (G), from which proceed two major group factors, verbal-numerical-educational (V:Ed), and practical-mechanical-spatial (K:M), less important group factors, for example word fluency and numerical ability, and a number of specific abilities.

Generally it can be said that the most important difference between the functional and structural approaches to intelligence is

that the former regards intelligence and thus intellectual behaviour or performance not merely as the sum of a number of abilities. It involves the total person, including his or her adaptive reactions and factors such as motivation, interest and personality.

7.10.1.3 The pragmatic or operational view

This view, which grew out of the structural approach to intelligence, is concerned with the design and use of various ability tests. Intelligence is regarded as a *measurement concept* and is reflected by performance in a specific test. This view finds application in the existence and use of various types of intelligence and ability tests, and in the phenomenon that one person obtains different scores when repeating the same test and that one person or group obtains different scores in different tests.

The pragmatic approach to intelligence constitutes the basis of *psychometrics*, a branch of psychology which studies the principles and practice of psychological measurement. Psychometricians endeavour to refine measurement techniques technically and statistically in order to provide useful psychological descriptions, diagnoses and predictions based on test scores. The usefulness of test scores is determined by factors such as psychometric requirements for standardisation, namely objectivity, validity and reliability.

7.10.1.4 Other views

In the *process theories* of intelligence the emphasis is on cognitive processes, and the quality of intellectual achievements is regarded as merely the structure or quantity of intelligence. These approaches are the result of strong resistance to the structural models, where the emphasis is mainly on various abilities and their psychometric measurement.

All *developmental theories* on intelligence date back to Binet's concept of intelligence as something which increases with age. Piaget discovered through research in Binet's laboratory that at different ages children often make the same mistakes in tests and assignments. On the basis of this Piaget postulated his theory of intellectual development, which stresses three primary stages of development.

The developmental approach also links with a view of intelligence as a lifelong process of development and change (Weiten 1995).

The *cognitive theories* of researchers such as Sternberg (1996) stress the processing of information to explain intellectual behaviour. According to this theory intelligence must be measured and explained in terms of cognitive processes: sensorial functions, grouping ability, memory processes, classification ability, encoding methods, methods of learning, and reasoning, which the individual employs in the performance of intellectual tasks, such as in a job or performance in an intelligence test.

Sternberg identifies six types of information processing: encoding, deduction, mapping, application, verification and response. He regards the ability to reason analogously as a good indication of the level of general ability (IQ).

According to the *process* theories, intelligence need not only be measured by tests. It is preferable to note how the individual uses his or her cognitive style to perform tasks and how he or she functions in and adapts to the environment. Scales have been designed for this purpose which, in terms of Piaget's theory, evaluate sensory-motor skills. Scales based on the principle of "learning from experience" are used for mentally retarded children (Weiten 1995).

There are also authors who emphasise *biological* and *neurological processes* in the explanation for intelligence. This view covers a broad spectrum, from those who regard intelligence as a hereditary factor and abilities as absolute, unchangeable and immeasurable, to those who believe that hereditary qualities determine one's potential for development because of environmental influences. Cattell (in Weiten 1995) speaks of "fluid" and "crystallised" intelligence; the former refers to innate potential ability and the latter to intellectual ability as affected by environmental, educational and cultural factors. Hebb's A and B types of intelligence and Vernon's (in Weiten 1995) concepts of "constitutional" intelligence and "intelligence C" also refer to the respective roles of heredity and environment.

7.10.2 Growth and stability of intelligence

It is commonly accepted that intelligence develops steadily up to about the age of 16 from inherent potential and the influence of learning and environmental factors. This relatively predictable development varies greatly between individuals and groups.

Although time and development may make a difference to IQ test ratings, research has shown that there will be drastic differences only if the individual or his or her environment undergoes drastic changes. In practice testing constancy of IQ is determined by comparing the increase in mental age with the increase in chronological age.

Mental age can be defined as the level of intellectual development achieved by a person in terms of chronological or real age. If a person's mental age is significantly higher than his or her chronological age, it can be assumed that his or her intelligence is above average. On the other hand, the mental age of a person with below average intelligence is lower than the chronological age. A person is intellectually normal or average if his or her performance equals that of the average person in his or her age group, for instance a mental age of 16 means that the person succeeds in all the test items passed by other 16-year-olds.

It has been found that the ratio between mental age (MA) and chronological age

(CA) develops fairly consistently; a three-year-old child with a MA of two will have a MA of four by the time it is six years old and a MA of six by the time it is nine years old. Comparison between children of different age groups is difficult, as one cannot state unequivocally that the degree of development between two and three years of age is the same as that between the ages of, say, 16 and 17. It has also been discovered that young children between two and three develop at a faster rate than those between 12 and 13. For this reason, intelligence measurement of children under the age of eight may fluctuate, and IQs taken at the age of five may bear little resemblance to those taken at the age of 18.

Stern (in Weiten 1995) evolved the concept of "intelligence quotient" (IQ), which expresses intelligence as the ratio between MA and CA in the formula:

$$\frac{MA}{CA} \times \frac{100}{1}$$

A mental age equal to chronological age means an average IQ

(e.g. $\frac{10}{10} \times \frac{100}{1} = 100$)

while a MA higher than CA results in an above average IQ

(e.g. $\frac{13}{10} \times \frac{100}{1} = 130$)

and a lesser MA in a below average IQ

(e.g. $\frac{8}{10} \times \frac{100}{1} = 80$)

A mental age far below chronological age means an IQ far below average, for example:

$\frac{16}{50} \times \frac{100}{1} = 32$

This use of mental age to determine intelligence does not provide for the measurement of adult IQ, as it would wrongly imply that the growth of intelligence diminishes at the age of approximately 16. This would mean that the older the individual, the "duller" he or she becomes.

Most current tests use deviation IQ, a concept created by Wechsler and imple-

IQ score	Descriptive category	% of population	
140 +	extremely gifted	0,38	2,28
130 – 139	highly gifted	1,90	
120 – 129	gifted (superior)	7,40	
110 – 119	high average	15,46	
90 – 109	average	49,72	
80 – 89	low average	15,46	
70 – 79	borderline mental retardation	7,40	
55 – 69	slight mental retardation	2,03	
40 – 54	moderate mental retardation	0,14	2,28
25 – 39	serious mental retardation	0,08	
0 – 24	extreme mental retardation	0,03	

Table 7.1 The classification of IQ scores   *Source: Adapted from Louw (1982:148)*

mented in the well-known Wechsler intelligence scales. Deviation IQ is a type of test score (a normalised standard score) with a mean value and a standard deviation applying to all age groups. In this way an individual's test score can be compared with a specific group in so far as it deviates from the mean.

Because of the volume of research done on intelligence, it becomes possible to speak in terms of a normal distribution (see table 7.1). Scores can be classified in categories such as highly gifted, gifted, high average, average, low average, borderline cases, mentally deficient, etc., which allows for individual treatment. We know approximately what to expect from a person with a given IQ, and can therefore place him or her correctly as regards treatment, training, a job, etc.

7.10.3 Extreme levels of intelligence

Extreme levels of intelligence refer to extreme or extraordinary manifestations of intelligence, for instance in mental retardation and genius.

7.10.3.1 Mental retardation

The cut-off point used as a criterion to classify intellectual behaviour as mentally retarded is an IQ of 70 or lower. It is estimated that approximately 3% of the population can be regarded as mentally retarded. A person should not, however, be classified solely on the basis of one IQ score in one specific test. There are many errors of measurement in psychometric tests and numerous other factors must also be considered, for instance the person's development, social adaptability, emotional state and family influences.

The categories of mental retardation are more or less as follows:

- extreme mental retardation: less than 25
- serious mental retardation: 25-39
- moderate mental retardation: 40-54
- slight mental retardation: 55-69

Various people may use different classifications, the differences, however, are not drastic.

The emphasis today is on educating the mentally retarded and not just categorising them. It has been found that a person who is slightly mentally retarded (an IQ of 55-69) is able to perform simple reading and writing tasks and do practical work. In sheltered employment such adults can play an economically productive and worthwhile role, but they must be assessed in their own right, because they function at a level of approximately eight- to 12-year-olds.

Individuals in the 40-54 IQ group can be taught to perform simple tasks and to take care of their personal hygiene. Because of their handicaps, for instance unintelligible speech and physical clumsiness, they should perform sheltered labour and receive considerable support for their own safety. They function, as adults, at the level of four- to seven-year-olds.

It is commonly accepted that persons with an IQ of lower than ±25 are ineducable. They are completely dependent on others and are sometimes referred to as "dependent retarded".

The inability of the mentally retarded to benefit from training, education, and experience can be attributed to the problems they experience in focusing their attention productively, their inability to learn, understand and remember concepts – factors which complicate progressive learning – and the attitude some acquire of "I can't". This attitude can sometimes also be blamed on other people who do too much for them.

7.10.3.2 Genius

Approximately 2% of the population are regarded as exceptionally gifted, and authors are inclined to set their own criteria for the classification of these people. Genius seems to be individuals with a measured IQ of 130-140 and higher. Possibly the best source on genius is the long-term study (from 1930 to 1977) by Burks (in Weiten 1995) involving 1 500 high and primary school pupils with measured IQs of 140 and higher.

These and other studies have produced the following findings:

- Genius is characterised by very high intelligence and creativity.
- Child geniuses do better in their academic studies than their peers, and they read a lot. Of the experimental group, 90% received university training and two-thirds of them graduated. A professional career was followed by 70% and they all occupied management jobs.
- Child geniuses are usually better developed physically than their peers. They have a higher mass at birth, above-average height at primary school, are able to speak and walk sooner as infants and are in better physical shape.
- Child geniuses do well in positions of leadership, are socially adaptable and accepted, although it is regarded as "normal" for geniuses to be "eccentric".
- In evaluating aspects of personality, teachers rate these children higher than a comparative peer group. These aspects include sound judgement, diligence, achievement motivation, eagerness to learn, group integration, modesty, leadership, originality, perseverance, and popularity.
- The parents of geniuses also do better in IQ tests than the population mean, and are better qualified than parents in comparative groups. Most of the fathers of these geniuses occupy professional or semiprofessional jobs or are businessmen, while a smaller number are skilled workers, and only a few are semiskilled or unskilled workers.

In later comments on these findings it was pointed out that genius was not a prerequisite for academic or job success and that a successful child genius had not necessarily inherited the ability to succeed. In fact, some geniuses fail to make a success of their school or professional careers. In most of these cases their failure or poor adaptation can be attributed to poor social environments where positive social, emotional and intellectual stimulation is absent or inadequate.

7.11 CONCLUSION

Cognition concerns processes by which the individual "knows", that is, processes information. This involves different processes which interactively determine individual differences with regard to acquiring, understanding and utilising knowledge. Cognition thus influences differential performance of different individuals in the work situation.

Cognitive competencies are the result of the interaction of inherited factors with learning, training and experience. Human resources professionals have to be skilled in identifying, developing and utilising cognitive competencies to facilitate and predict the best fit between the worker and the work.

Self-evaluating questions

1. Describe the basic components of thinking and explain the functioning of problem-solving and reasoning with reference to the work situation.
2. Describe the role of heuristics in decision-making with reference to making choices in the work situation.
3. Explain the statement: creative thinking can be distinguished from intelligence.
4. Explain how and why forgetting occurs.
5. Explain how memory can be facilitated.
6. Distinguish between the structural, functional and pragmatic approaches to explain intelligence and evaluate their application.
7. Describe extreme levels of intelligence, indicating how they apply to work.

Motivation 8

Antoinette Theron

CONTENTS

Learning outcomes

After studying this chapter you should be able to:

- describe the characteristics and aims of purposive behaviour
- explain how motivation can be facilitated by reinforcement, job content and job design
- list characteristics of self-actualisation with reference to different authors
- explain Allport's view of adult motivation
- discuss expectancy and related concepts in the motivation process
- describe how perception of self-efficacy influences behaviour
- identify dimensions of attribution
- describe equity as a process of comparison
- describe how emotions have functional value in personal and interpersonal contexts
- describe Frijda's model of emotional intensity
- explain how emotion influences work performance
- describe the concept emotional intelligence
- explain Freud's view of unconscious motivation, and describe its application to humour and in career choice

Key concepts

purposiveness, reinforcement, positive motivation, negative motivation, job satisfaction, job dissatisfaction, rotation, enlargement, enrichment, self-actualisation needs, propriate autonomy, perseverative autonomy, expectancy, valence, instrumentality, self-efficacy, locus of causality, fairness, emotion process, unconscious contents

8.1 INTRODUCTION

Motivation is a process that involves the *purposiveness* of behaviour. The process is brought about by factors that activate behaviour and influence the direction, and perseveration, that is, the sustained effort, of behaviour.

The aims of purposive behaviour are varied. It may be aimed at psychological balance or at psychological renewal. Psychological balance can be understood in terms of the Law of Effect and homeostasis, while psychological renewal can be understood in terms of heterostasis.

The *Law of Effect*, originally formulated by E.L. Thorndike, refers to acquiring behaviour because it has agreeable consequences. An individual may, for example, acquire competence in his or her job because it has the agreeable consequences of recognition by the boss and the approval of colleagues.

Homeostasis is a concept originally formulated by W.B. Cannon to explain the bodily tendencies to maintain physiological equilibrium, that is, balance. Physiological imbalance, caused by emotions such as fear or anger, automatically triggers the autonomic nervous system to restore physiological balance, thereby facilitating stable or optimal bodily functioning. In a psychological sense, homeostasis means that the aim of purposive behaviour is to maintain optimal psychological balance. The individual who has acquired competence motivation, for example, will persevere in being competent because it provides a balance between his or her purposive behaviour and its consequences.

In a broader motivational context this can be interpreted as indicating that once the individual has accomplished certain goals, the behaviour that facilitated it will remain the same. Since individuals are capable of psychological growth and change, obtaining psychological equilibrium should not be seen as a final motivational state, but as conducive to exploring new and different directions that facilitate optimal psychological functioning. This incorporates the term heterostasis.

Heterostasis motivates different states of equilibrium that provide psychological renewal. Competency motivation, for example, may lead to the individual seeking new means of competency by exploring different skills involving different aims. The aims of purposive behaviour may go beyond merely seeking agreeable consequences towards seeking novelty, stimulation and complexity in one's work.

As the aims of purposive behaviour vary, the factors that activate it also vary. Factors that have been shown by research to play a part in the direction and perseveration of motivated behaviour include various external and internal activators.

8.2 EXTERNAL ACTIVATORS

External activators refer to factors in the environment, rather than factors within the individual, that play a part in motivated behaviour. Recognition of such factors is based on the assumption that the individual is not necessarily always self-motivated and that motivation can be induced by external factors.

8.2.1 Reinforcement

The factor generally seen as the most significant external activator is reinforcement.

Reinforcement is the cardinal factor in instrumental conditioning, through which behaviour is acquired because it is reinforced by *reward,* a consequence which is pleasurable and serves as a stimulus for repeating the behaviour. Behaviour can also be inhibited because it is reinforced by *punishment,* a consequence which is unpleasant and serves as a stimulus to inhibit the behaviour.

In the context of motivation, reinforcement involves the learning process in acquiring purposive behaviour. In the work situation, consequences perceived by the individual as rewarding and constructive denote positive motivation, while consequences that the individual does not perceive as having constructive value denote negative motivation.

In *positive motivation* the emphasis is on rewarding correct behaviour and not on punishing incorrect behaviour. The assumption is that the worker should or does know what is expected of him or her and how to accomplish it. A supervisor can implement positive motivation by allowing a worker to engage in more challenging tasks and offering constructive guidance on how to handle challenges when required. A prerequisite in this situation is that the supervisor has enough knowledge to offer constructive advice.

In *negative motivation* the emphasis is on punishing incorrect behaviour which is not conducive to effective performance. Although negative motivation can be effective in learning avoidance behaviour, it has limitations, because the motivational objective of activating purposive behaviour is not considered. A supervisor may find fault with, for example, a worker's unprofessional conduct in a professional situation, without pointing out what professional conduct entails.

Besides not being constructive, negative motivation can have the following undesirable effects (Maier & Verser 1982):

- Hostile and childish behaviour resulting from rebuke for poor quality work can be generalised to other work-related factors, resulting in a negative attitude toward the entire work situation.
- Punishment can lead to avoiding the person who implements punishment, rather than avoidance of the behaviour that caused it. This can amount to continuing the undesirable behaviour and merely avoiding being caught.

- Focusing only on the negative aspects of a worker's behaviour can provide stimulation for continuing with the unacceptable, in that hearing only what not to do suggests alternative ways of causing trouble.
- Negative motivation can instigate fear, which in turn reduces the willingness to accept new ideas.

In general reinforcement has value for predicting the perseverance of effort, as well as the quality and quantity of work, but it does not contribute adequately to explaining why a worker leaves the job or how job satisfaction is involved in work motivation (Robbins 1998).

8.2.2 Job content

Job content has been found to be related to motivation and job satisfaction (Herzberg et al. 1959).

In the literature job content is generally associated with internal motivation, stemming from needs intrinsic to the individual. It can, however, be seen as an external motivator, in that it involves the structure or design of the work, that is, the components and requirements of the job itself which can be described in objective terms, but have an effect on the intrinsic motivation of the individual doing the job.

The significance of job content in motivation is illustrated in Herzberg's motivation/hygiene theory (Herzberg et al. 1959). Herzberg and his colleagues found that two different sets of variables were related to job satisfaction and job dissatisfaction.

Job satisfaction was deduced from factors in the research subjects' work about which they felt positive. These factors were all related to job content, and included responsibility, achievement, recognition and growth. Herzberg called them *motivators,* and motivators were seen as intrinsic factors, in that subjects saw them as characteristics of themselves in doing their work.

Job dissatisfaction was deduced from factors about which subjects felt negative. These were not factors intrinsic to the individual, but external factors such as physical working conditions, company policy, salary, supervision and relationships with co-workers. Herzberg called them *hygiene factors,* because if they were not adequate, subjects would be dissatisfied with their work. Their being adequate, however, did not make subjects satisfied with their work, because satisfaction was derived from motivators. If motivators were inadequate, subjects did not feel job dissatisfaction, and neither were they motivated.

Herzberg's theory has stimulated extensive research, some of which confirms it and some of which refutes it. The theory nevertheless has had wide popular appeal and may be seen as providing an impetus for designing jobs vertically, that is, expanding jobs to provide workers with more individual responsibility in planning and controlling their work (Robbins 1998).

8.2.3 Job design

Job design includes job rotation, job enlargement and job enrichment, which are procedures in organisations aimed at facilitating employee motivation.

In *job rotation* it is assumed that employees need change to broaden their interests and capabilities. By shifting them periodically from one job to another which is on the same level, their work activities become diversified. Rotation can have a training effect in that employees acquire a larger range of skills. Nurses, for example, acquire more skills by being rotated between different wards in a hospital. Rotation can benefit the organisation as well as the employee. A section or department becomes self-sufficient, because more employees can do more jobs and can provide more varied inputs when the need arises, such as when absenteeism affects the productivity of the whole section. Rotation can, however, be demotivating for employees who seek to acquire specific responsibilities in their chosen fields of specialisation (Robbins 1998).

In *job enlargement* it is assumed employees need change from routine to reduce repetition and monotony. A job is enlarged by providing a variety of tasks within the job, thereby expanding the job on a horizontal level. For example, a typist's work may be enlarged by alternating typing with administrative tasks. Some workers experience enlargement as satisfying, but others see it as merely an increase from one job to additional jobs, which do not add interest or challenge. To have motivating effects, enlargement procedures should be revised constantly.

In *job enrichment* it is assumed employees need responsibility, independence, autonomy and complexity. A job is enriched by the addition of more complex tasks, thereby expanding the job content vertically. An administrative officer's job can be enriched by giving him or her more authority over his or her work procedures, including planning, executing and evaluating his or her own work. Of vital importance is accountability, in which employees have self-responsibility, which makes them feel they are achieving something worthwhile (Moorhead & Griffin 1989). Although enrichment reduces absenteeism and turnover, and increases job satisfaction, it does not inevitably increase productivity (Robbins 1998).

Some individuals eventually feel that more responsibility should be rewarded by increased benefits, including financial benefits.

Individual differences with regard to the motivational effects of job design are taken into consideration by the *job characteristics model* propounded by Hackman and Oldham, cited in McKenna (1994). The authors present the following five basic characteristics of a job that are likely to improve its motivating effects:

- *skill variety,* which focuses on the number of skills and talents a job requires
- *task identity,* which focuses on the extent to which a job is identifiable with an obvious outcome, or whether the worker is responsible for the whole
- *task significance,* which focuses on the impact the job has on other people
- *autonomy,* which includes freedom, discretion and independence
- *feedback,* which involves information on one's work performance

The extent to which these characteristics are significant to employees depends on whether they are motivated toward psychological growth or not.

Generally job design can be motivating if the worker sees his or her performance as fulfilling intrinsic needs.

8.3 INTERNAL ACTIVATORS

Internal activators are psychological processes within the individual that determine, or influence, his or her motivation. Focusing on these processes is based on the assumption that the individual can be self-motivated, in that he or she is a cognitive being who is rational, has a will, who understands his or her needs and goals and personally contributes to the outcomes of his or her behaviour.

8.3.1 Self-actualisation

Self-actualisation is an inner-directed process, by means of which individuals express and fulfil their inner self (Maslow 1970; Rogers 1978; Shostrom 1976).

Shostrom (1976) describes it as a process which is never completed, for it is not an end that individuals achieve, but a process of becoming, through which they find inner balance. Inner balance is achieved when individuals integrate opposing polarities such as strength/weakness and love/fury into complementary wholes. Such polarities are akin to the two powers in Eastern philosophy, Yin and Yang, which respectively symbolise darkness and light as complementary forms in the universe. By achieving inner balance, individuals actualise themselves according to their inner orientation, through which they express what they really feel, want and prefer, that is, achieve a state of being what they really are.

Carl Rogers distinguishes between self-actualisation and a tendency toward actualisation.

Actualisation indicates optimal functioning, a rewarding state that the individual achieves through optimal adjustment and growth. The tendency to self-actualisation, however, refers to a dynamic process in which the individual strives for autonomy by actualising a part of the self (Guthrie Ford 1991). It is the tendency the individual has to maintain and enrich himself or herself by an active growth process, akin to plant life that is self-generating, despite favourable or unfavourable conditions. Actualisation is not aimed at fulfilling all the individual's potential, but forms the substratum of all human motivation, which can selectively and constructively provide self-enrichment in diverse forms of life. The need for food, sex, play, and exploration of the self and the environment can be behavioural activities in which self-actualisation manifests.

Frankl (1969) sees humans' primary striving as the will-to-meaning. Fulfilling the will-to-meaning leads to self-actualisation. The *will-to-meaning* is personal and unique to every individual. Finding meaning can be facilitated by actualising three types of values: *creative values* are realised when an individual creates something; *experiential values* are realised by experiencing the good, the real and the beautiful; *attitudinal values* are realised, for instance, when an individual sees meaning in something which seems to have no meaning, such as unavoidable suffering (Frankl 1957).

Finding meaning involves decision-making. The individual has inner freedom to choose what to actualise, that is, deciding in

which life sphere or work sphere to find meaning, and whether what is chosen will provide self-actualisation. One individual may find personal meaning in teaching others, while another may find meaning in developing a business enterprise.

Maslow (1970) sees self-actualisation as a motivational level at which individuals develop their individuality in a unique way, according to their own individual style. It is a growth process in which individuals become what they really are and express the self. Maslow maintains self-actualisation acquires motivational force only when individuals have relative satisfaction of lower level needs, which have to be satisfied in a specific hierarchical order.

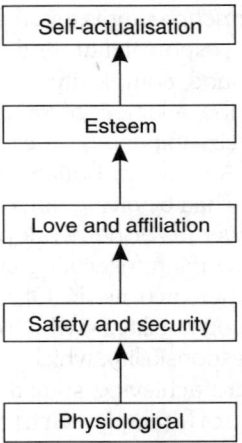

Figure 8.1 Maslow's hierarchy of needs

The hierarchy starts with *physiological needs,* for example the need for enough food to eat and the need to survive on one's income. When these needs are relatively satisfied, *safety and security needs* emerge, for example the need to feel that there are adequate safety measures in the physical work environment and that one has job tenure or job prospects and a pension fund. After relative satisfaction of these needs, the next level that emerges is *love and affiliation needs,* such as for close relationships and affiliation to work groups. Relative satisfaction of this level is followed by *esteem needs,* such as needing to feel that one has prestige, and respect from other people.

The individual is relatively dependent on external factors in the physical, socio-economic and socio-cultural environment for satisfaction of these four need levels, to the extent that he or she needs other people and societal or work structures to help satisfy them. Deprivation at any of these four levels can lead to emotional disturbances, which are, however, not necessarily consequences of lack of self-actualisation.

Self-actualisation involves what Maslow called *being needs.* Being needs include needing as well as valuing the following: goodness, truth, unity, beauty, elegance, playfulness, awareness of life and meaningfulness.

Maslow (1970) found that a selected group of eminent public and historical figures he regarded as self-actualising individuals shared the following important characteristics, among others:

- autonomy, in the sense of being relatively independent of the physical and social environment
- a democratic orientation
- a feeling of connectedness with people
- human "weaknesses" such as pride, selfishness and conflict
- resistance to acculturation and high conventionality
- feeling peak experiences, that is, high levels of consciousness in certain situations
- the ability for fresh appreciation and wonderment
- a naive, childlike type of creativity
- an eye for the unobvious and the ostensibly confusing
- feeling at ease with the ambiguous, the inexact and the disorderly
- an orientation that does not evaluate truth in terms of order and certainty

Mittleman (1991) maintains that the characteristics of self-actualising individuals can be reduced to a single characteristic, namely *openness to experience.* This does not primarily refer to fulfilling one's potential, but to an existential openness that is "good" for the individual in that it involves the *authenticity* of the individual.

8.3.2 Functional autonomy

Gordon W. Allport's view of motivation focuses on the *transformation of motives* (Allport 1970).

As the individual matures the instincts and drives of childhood become transformed into more distinctive contemporaneous motivational systems. These systems are functionally autonomous, in that they emerge as motives with their own driving power and are different from childhood motivation in character and aim.

Although adult motivation can be traced to an origin in childhood, the relation is not relevant to understanding adult motivation, because adult motivation is always contemporary, that is, significant to the present.

Adult motives also become self-sustaining, in that activities that were previously means to ends become ends in themselves. For example, a student may initially study a subject only as a means to improve his or her qualifications. In the course of the study the student becomes absorbed in the subject to the extent of wanting to build a career on it. Knowledge initially acquired for instrumental purposes then becomes a self-propelling interest.

Motives form plural systems, in that they can be expressed in various ways despite originating from a particular cause. A business person, for example, who has successfully reached his or her initial aim of economic security, may develop a strong propensity to taking risks and facing new challenges, which he or she channels into various entrepreneurial pursuits that may even involve lack of economic security.

The above examples illustrate what Allport referred to as *propriate functional autonomy,* which evolves from the individual's values and interests. The word "propriate" is derived from the Latin word "proprium", which means "characteristic" or "own" (Meyer et al. 1989).

An example of perseverative functional autonomy

Allport also distinguished *perseverative functional autonomy,* which indicates behaviour that is circular and repetitive, continuing automatically without remaining dependent on the antecedents from which it developed. Hunger, fatigue, lust, and the need for exercise, which have their origins in physiological causes, may become mental habits that recur in behaviour patterns and rituals. Perseverative functional autonomy is illustrated in the case of a person for whom jogging has become a ritual, something that *must* be done (see above).

Perseverative autonomy can also apply to good workmanship. Motivated perhaps by a need for recognition, good workmanship can become an end in itself that persists even if recognition is not forthcoming. Likewise, task completion may become a need with a force of its own that sustains the individual's work tempo irrespective of the urgency or triviality of the task.

Of vital significance in functional autonomy is that motivated behaviour does not require reinforcement, as it stems from within the individual and is self-sustaining.

8.3.3 Expectancy

In Victor H. Vroom's theory expectancy refers to the individual's subjective beliefs about the outcomes of his or her behaviour. Motivated behaviour is not only influenced by the outcomes of the behaviour, but also by the extent to which the individual believes that the behaviour will have particular outcomes. Expectancy applies to behavioural choices that have uncertain outcomes and can vary greatly in strength between the belief that particular behaviour is certain to have a particular outcome, and the belief that the behaviour will not have a particular outcome (Vroom 1964).

An individual may, for example, believe that effective performance will certainly or probably result in promotion, or can subjectively believe that promotion is unlikely, despite effective performance, because of factors beyond his or her control, such as having to compete with colleagues, changing company policy, or lack of availability of higher-level jobs in the future.

Expectancy is a useful concept for explaining why workers are not motivated to do more than the minimum (Robbins 1998).

Vroom maintained that expectancy in conjunction with valence activates and sustains behaviour.

Valence refers to the relative attractiveness that outcomes have for the individual. Just as expectancy can vary in strength, so valence can have a wide range of subjective significance for the individual. An outcome has positive valence if the individual prefers to attain the outcome rather than not attain it, which means he or she has a positive attitude concerning the outcome. An outcome has negative valence if the individual prefers not to attain it, which means he or she has a negative attitude, and it has zero valence if the individual is indifferent to the outcome. One individual may attach positive valence to being promoted to a general managerial level in the organisation, while for another it will have negative or zero valence because he or she prefers to be proficient at technical skills in his or her specialist field.

An implication of valence is that it concerns the individual's expectation of whether the outcomes of his or her work activities will provide satisfaction or dissatisfaction.

Valences and experiences together provide the motivational force that determines the individual's choice (Vroom 1964). Force may be seen as the intention to perform in a certain way (Steers & Porter 1987).

Vroom further incorporated the concept of *instrumentality* in motivated behaviour. Instrumentality means the valence of a performance outcome is also determined by its instrumental relation to other outcomes. Effective performance can, besides leading to promotion, facilitate networking with other groups, and provide fringe benefits that improve the quality of work and family life.

Besides seeing performance as instrumental in attaining outcomes, an individual may also see it as instrumental in avoiding certain outcomes. He or she may work hard at certain job activities mainly to avoid demotion or dismissal or being transferred. Valences can also change. Activities that an individual would have preferred to avoid can eventually become satisfying (Vroom 1964).

Vroom's views gave rise to a number of theoretical formulations classified as VIE, for valence-instrumentality expectancy theories.

Lawler and Porter's model is based on Vroom's terminology, but also incorporates the terms efforts, abilities and role perception (Steers & Porter 1987).

The effort that the individual puts into performance is determined by the value (valences) of rewards expected, and the probability that rewards are dependent on effort (perceived instrumentality). The actual performance is, however, also influenced by the individual's ability to do the job and the perception of the role he or she has in executing the job. Ability includes skills and personality traits required to do the job, and role perception refers to the individual's understanding of what the job entails.

Besides being a motivational factor in performance, expectancy is also a motivational factor in occupational choice and organisational choice. An individual may choose a type of occupation in terms of his

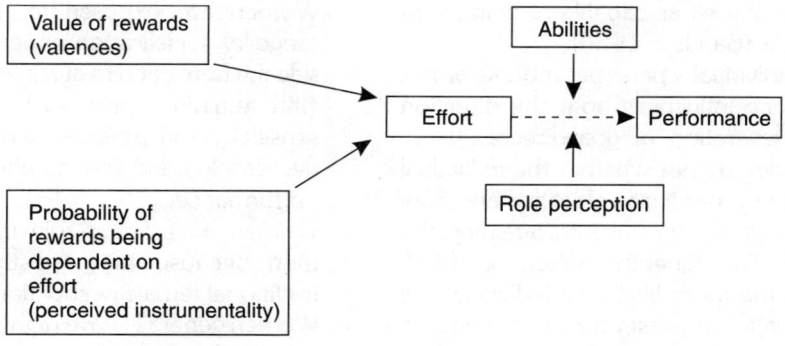

Figure 8.2 Lawler and Porter's model of expectancy theory
Source: Adapted from Steers & Porter (1987)

or her expectancies of accomplishing desired success, and choose an organisation in terms of the outcomes that the individual believes will be forthcoming. Research has shown that in general most individuals expect an organisation to provide minimally acceptable economic gains, as well as challenging, novel activities (Moorhead & Griffin 1989).

Expectancy is also known to be related to acquiring an *achievement motive*. David C. McClelland maintains that the motive to achieve derives from growing expectations in childhood. Children develop achievement motivation if they are challenged with toys and tasks that require mastery beyond their present knowledge and existing expectations. They should be given toys and tasks that become progressively more novel and complex, to the extent that the child is not certain of mastering the task. If mastery is a certainty, the child becomes bored and loses interest. An implication is that the child might become an adult who is not interested in achievement (McClelland et al. 1970).

8.3.4 Self-efficacy

Self-efficacy refers to the sense of having more or less control over events that affect one's life. It involves the perception of one's personal capacity to use one's skills effectively. It does not involve judging one's skills as such, but judgement of what one sees oneself as capable of doing with one's skills (Bandura 1986).

The individual's perception of his or her self-efficacy influences both the direction and perseveration of goal-directed behaviour. It determines whether the individual will pursue a particular objective and how much effort will be put into attaining the objective. The higher the perception of self-efficacy, the more likely the individual will be motivated to persevere in attaining an objective, even if the pursuit involves overcoming obstacles. If the pursuit has negative consequences, the individual will

not necessarily have a negative view of his or her skills if he or she has high perceived self-efficacy.

Perception of one's self-efficacy influences behaviour in conjunction with personal dispositions such as values, preferences, goals and social prototypes, which are perceptions of other people and events. These dispositions form self-regulating mechanisms according to which the individual determines his or her own behaviour and sets his or her own standards of self-efficacy (Mischel 1970).

Hackett and Betz (1981) postulate that men and women differ with regard to their self-efficacy perceptions. Women, in contrast to men, have low self-efficacy expectations because their socialisation experiences result in low expectations of success. This gives rise to internal barriers that prevent them from fully realising their capabilities and talents. Consequently they limit their career choices to a narrow range of options.

Differences between men and women are ascribed to factors including the following:

• Men are exposed to successful performance associated with masculine roles – which are seen as instrumental to effective performance – such as assertiveness, activity, competition and dominance, as well as a variety of socialisation experiences outside the home. Women are exposed to a narrower range of socialisation experiences outside the home and to qualities associated with feminine roles, such as nurture, sensitivity and passivity, which are not necessarily conducive to effective work performance.

• Women have fewer role models than men because they mostly work in traditional female occupations.

• Women generally have higher stress and anxiety levels than men, which can influence their self-efficacy expectations.

- Women generally receive less encouragement from parents, teachers and friends toward career achievement in work that is not traditionally associated with women.

A South African study (Millar 1995) showed that men have significantly higher self-efficacy expectations with regard to traditional male occupations, while women have significantly higher self-efficacy expectations for traditional female occupations. No differences were shown between men and women for neutral occupations. In the study traditional male occupations included chartered accountant, physician, architect, lawyer, engineer, chemist, pastor, draughtsman. Traditional female occupations included nurse, social worker, primary school teacher, occupational therapist, dietician, beauty and health therapist, fashion designer. Neutral occupations included psychologist, journalist, secondary school teacher, copy writer, musicologist, tourist guide, managerial consultant, interior designer.

8.3.5 Attribution

Attribution involves trying to understand, by localising the causes, why events and one's behaviour have certain outcomes. Causes are attributed to either internal factors within the individual or external factors in the situation. Rotter (1966) calls this dimension in attribution the *locus of causality*. An internal or an external locus of causality can be a characteristic of individuals.

In applying attribution to achievement motivation Weiner (1972, 1980, 1986) found that individuals localise their successes and failures according to a locus of causality, as well as a stability dimension. Stability refers to the consistency of causes over time. Individuals who attribute the outcomes of their achievements to internal factors, seek further attributions in either their ability, a stable factor which does not show much variation, or in their effort, an unstable factor subject to variation. Individuals with high achievement motivation use these two stability dimensions to explain the outcomes of their behaviour.

Contemporary and traditional female role models

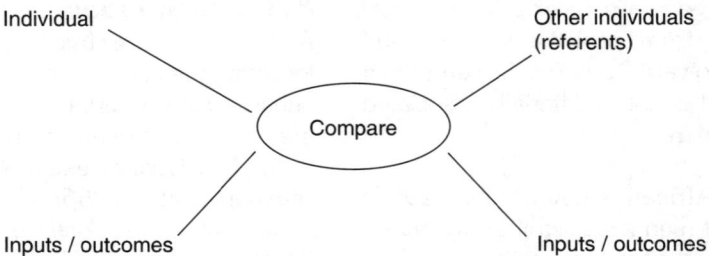

Figure 8.3 Perceiving equity

Individuals with low achievement motivation use ability and effort as well as two stability factors associated with an external locus of causality, task difficulty and luck. Task difficulty is seen as a stable factor, while luck is seen as an unstable factor.

The implication of attribution theory is that individuals may have a motivational orientation by which they see themselves as responsible for decisions that can affect the outcomes of behaviour, or an orientation by which outcomes are attributed to factors beyond the self, including the possibility of fate.

8.3.6 Equity

Equity concerns the perception of *fairness* in the work situation. Individuals compare the relation between their job inputs and job outcomes to the relation between job inputs and job outcomes of other individuals (see figure 8.3). An individual may compare what he or she puts into the job, for example skills, qualifications, experience and effort, in relation to what he or she gets out of the job, for example remuneration, to similar factors pertaining to other employees.

Equity is perceived if the ratio of his or her inputs to outcomes corresponds to that of other individuals, such as co-workers working on the same job, that he or she uses as referents for comparison. Inequity is perceived if the outcomes in relation to inputs are either too low or too high in comparison to referents.

Adams (1965) proposed that inequity results in tension which motivates individuals to correct it and establish equity. If employees perceive their remuneration as too low in relation to their inputs when compared to co-workers, they may lower their inputs by putting less effort into the work. They may also attempt to change the outcomes by lowering the quality of their work but increasing the quantity. If they are working on a piece-rate basis, this will result in more payment. If they perceive their remuneration as too high for their input in comparison to co-workers, they may increase input by working harder or acquiring new skills.

To establish equity, individuals may also change their perception of a referent, such as reasoning that the referent's job situation excludes benefits that are favourable, or they may choose other referents, for example individuals doing similar work in other organisations.

Research on equity has mostly focused on pay but other aspects of the work situation can also involve equity. Outcomes can include various rewards that result from inputs, such as the freedom to act, interesting and challenging work, and status symbols (Muchinsky et al. 1998). Status symbols are outcomes of the individual's status and may vary in different occupational groups. Business executives, for example, may perceive personal income and growth of the company as status symbols, while blue-

Emotion	Elicitor	Function in self context	Function in interpersonal context
Sadness	Loss of valued object by self or by others	Serves to immobilise the individual by withdrawal and decreased effort (possibly to forestall further trauma); promotes empathy and concern for losses of others	Elicits empathy, nurturing and support from others
Fear	Perception of anger	Serves to identify threat, instigate flight or attack	Signals submission, wards off attack
Anger	Frustration of goals, pain	Effects removing barriers or sources of frustration	Signals warding off possible attack by avoidance, compliance, submission or aggression
Joy	Familiarity, pleasurable stimulation	Signals to continue with present activities	Promotes social bonding through contagiousness of good feeling
Interest	Novelty, expectancy, discrepancy	Opens the sensory system to absorb information	Signals receptivity, promotes interaction

Table 8.1 Functions of emotions as indicators of motivated behaviour
Source: Adapted from Magai (1996)

collar workers may see their seniority, and professional people their autonomy, as outcomes of their status (Robbins 1998).

In essence, equity does not concern equality, in that everyone should be treated the same, but involves perceptions and feelings in relation to particular referents (Muchinsky et al. 1998).

8.3.7 Emotion

Emotions have motivational value in that they are activators of behaviour towards functional ends. They are psychological constructs that are inferred from behaviour, such as physiological reactions and expressive behaviour, including facial and verbal expressions, tone of voice, gesticulations and gesture. They have functional, that is, adaptive, value for the individual in a personal and an interpersonal sense, that is, in relation to others, as they influence the reactions of others to the individual (Frijda 1996; Magai 1996; Oatley & Jenkins 1996).

8.3.7.1 Functions of emotions

Table 8.1 illustrates the functions of five emotions: sadness, fear, anger, joy and interest, as indicators of motivated behaviour. The table shows factors that elicit a particular emotion, the adaptive function that the emotion has for the individual personally and the function of the emotion in the interpersonal context.

Because emotions are functional in the individual's personal and interpersonal adaptation, the recurrence of certain emotions may lead to emotions becoming embedded in the individual's personality as traits. Traits are personality characteristics that are relatively stable over time and become typical of the individual's behaviour. Magai (1996) indicates that the repeated activation of anger, for example, may result in a hostile personality type, while repeated activation of interest may result in a personality type motivated by striving for functionally autonomous goals as Allport conceptualised in functional autonomy.

8.3.7.2 Intensity of emotions

Intensity of emotions involves the strength with which emotions feature as activators in motivation. Individuals differ with regard to particular emotions that they experience, as well as the intensity with which they experience particular emotions.

The occurrence and intensity of an emotion may best be understood by viewing emotion as a process involving parti-cular steps that influence behaviour. Frijda (1996) conceptualises the steps of the emotion process as encompassing events, appraisal, action readiness, mood and regulation processes (see figure 8.4).

An *event* involves anything that personally concerns the individual, such as his or her values, goals and sense of identity. An event may affect personal concerns such as self-esteem, social prestige, sense of competence, self-determination, fairness or acceptance by a group.

Appraisal concerns the meaning that the event has for the individual. It involves cognitive processes by which the individual perceives or evaluates the extent to which the event is significant. Appraisal determines whether an event will activate an emotion or not. It can involve clear perception of an event as a reality, or it may merely involve a feeling of heightened sensitivity that one's concerns are touched, or the individual may be unaware of the real significance of the event. For example, an individual may not realise that a colleague's behaviour towards him or her concerns his or her deep sense of self-esteem and only experience a sense of being hurt.

Action readiness is part of the individual's action repertoire which indicates the capacity for certain emotions. An individual may, for example, have a stronger capacity for anger in comparison to other individuals, and be more likely to become violent when anger is felt intensely. Action readiness does not only refer to readiness to

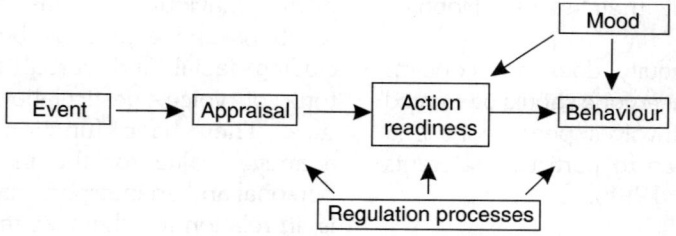

Figure 8.4 The emotion process
Source: Adapted from Frijda (1996)

act, but also to a lack of readiness to act. Anxiety may have the emotionally paralytic effect of apathy, and grief may lead to despair and breakdown of action (Frijda 1996).

The next step that influences emotional intensity is the individual's *mood state*, which refers to the prevailing state of excitation at the time of the event. It can be based on a previous event that the individual associates with the present event, making him or her more sensitive to the present event. Mood state can also be influenced by excitement, exhaustion, irritation and the individual's state of health, which makes him or her more or less disposed to respond emotionally in a particular way. It may last for hours, days or weeks, without the individual necessarily realising it, but in essence maintaining the readiness for action or resisting change. Research findings cited by Oatley and Jenkins (1996) suggest that mood dimensions include positive moods such as feeling contented, cheerful, happy, pleased, satisfied, warmhearted, and negative moods such as feeling blue, depressed, downhearted, gloomy, sad and unhappy.

The last step that Frijda (1996) distinguishes in the emotion process is regulation. *Regulation* concerns the control that the individual has over the emotion being experienced, that is, whether it is inhibited or subject to lack of inhibition. Lack of inhibition intensifies emotional behaviour, such as anger escalating to violence in quarrels, and anxiety leading to panic.

Frijda maintains that the social environment in particular influences regulation, in that social norms shape, condone and reinforce certain expressions of emotion. In some societies it is common to express love, jealousy and hatred by overt display, while in other societies it is more inhibited. In some groups in society, aggression is condoned to the point of endorsing violence. Group norms may also induce emotions that the individual does not really feel, such as aggression induced by a group. In riots and disturbances, for example, a mass emotion spreads over the group which goes beyond the individual's real motives. The emotion manifests in collective behaviour that provides a sense of psychological unity, despite the reasons for the behaviour (Kolasa 1969). Such mass displays of emotion supersede the individual's normal adaptive behaviour and he or she loses control over his or her individual responsibility and awareness of the consequences of the actions.

8.3.7.3 Emotion and performance

Emotional intensity influences work performance, as it involves different levels of activation. The effects of different levels of activation on performance efficiency are illustrated by the inverted U-curve (figure 8.5).

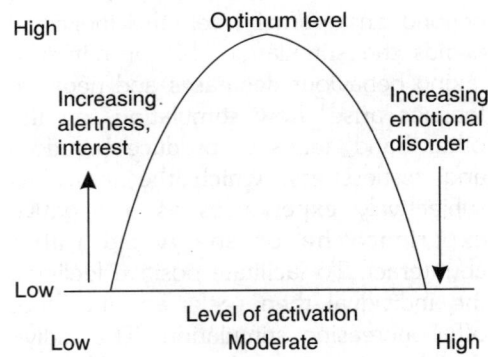

Figure 8.5 The relation between performance and level of activation

At a low level of activation performance efficiency is low, while at a moderate level of activation performance is at its optimal level, that is, the individual is most efficient, but as activation increases, performance decreases. These effects can be due to emotion experienced in challenging situations, competitive situations, pressing time schedules and in executing complex tasks that require stimulus discrimination and differential responses for effective performance.

Activation involves psychophysiological tension, which can be low, moderate or high, depending on the extent to which the individual perceives a situation or task as stressful. Low tension facilitates low performance, moderate tension facilitates optimal performance and high tension results in lower performance. In emotional stress situations the individual feels confused, attention fluctuates and anxiety, panic, anger or euphoria arise, which have the effects of lowered efficiency and the disintegration of the balance between emotional, intellectual and decision-making functions (Jordaan & Jordaan 1989).

Psychophysiological tension is also influenced by the stimulation a situation or task involves, which is not necessarily perceived as stressful, but affects performance. When a situation is stimulating beyond an optimal level, the individual avoids the stimulation, his or her risk-taking behaviour decreases and negative feelings arise. Low stimulation, on the other hand, tends to produce boredom and restlessness, which the individual subjectively experiences as a negative experience he or she would rather counteract. To facilitate positive feelings, the individual then seeks activities that offer increasing stimulation. The individual may work toward an optimal level of stimulation by taking risks, or become attracted to challenging situations that stimulate his or her curiosity (Reeve 1992).

8.3.7.4 *Emotional intelligence*

Emotions may be seen as skills in themselves that play a part in motivation. Emotional skills are seen as involving emotional intelligence, which Salovey (quoted by Goleman 1995) sees as including the following:

- knowing one's own emotions, that is, being certain of what one's real feelings are when making decisions
- managing one's own emotions, that is, being able to handle feelings of distress, anxiety and gloom, and soothe oneself
- motivating oneself towards mastery and creativity by setting goals to accomplish
- recognising emotions in others by being empathic (having the ability to feel what they are feeling and what their needs are) and being able to handle relationships with social competence.

8.3.8 Unconscious factors

Some activators of motivation can be unconscious, such as appraisal in the emotion process, which can occur without the individual being consciously aware of the real significance of the event he or she is appraising.

Freud emphasised the role of the unconscious in motivation. According to Freud (1970) the content of the unconscious includes instincts, ideas, memories and emotions of which the individual is not aware, because they are inhibited in the unconscious by the mechanism of repression. They can, however, become conscious in substitute forms of behaviour, which disguise them to the extent that the individual does not know what the real reasons for his or her behaviour are.

Repression occurs because some of the contents of the unconscious are not socially acceptable. This unconsciously causes conflict in the individual, because the contents of the unconscious are embedded in an energy which functions according to a pleasure principle seeking direct satisfaction. Conflict between satisfying unconscious contents and adhering to societal norms causes anxiety and consequently the unconscious contents manifest in masked forms such as defence mechanisms, dreams and humour.

Freud sees *humour* as a liberation from anxiety in which the pleasure principle manifests in forms that mask unpleasant emotions. Humour can, for example, mask the emotional pain of tragedy.

Grotjahn (1957) maintains that a sense of humour evolves gradually over the life span as the individual learns to master anxiety caused by conflict. Grotjahn considers humour as a characteristic by which a personality type can be identified, such as the practical joker, the tease, the clown, the mocker, the cynic, the optimist and his or her opposite, the pessimist, who are all members of a "family" struggling to find an acceptable outlet for aggression.

Unconscious motivation involving the pleasure principle is implied in Bordin's theory of career choice (Bordin 1990). Bordin sees the urge to play as inherent in career choice. The urge to play may be unconscious and unarticulated, but it motivates the individual to seek a self-satisfying occupation. This stems from childhood experience. In childhood play is spontaneous, but as the individual develops, play becomes linked to effort and becomes more directed. Due to parental or societal pressure effort may become a compulsion. If a compulsion is extreme, work may become a self-alienating experience in which the fusion between work and play is severed. Compulsion can, however, be a part of normal work life if it has intrinsic meaning for the individual and provides intrinsic satisfaction.

8.4 CONCLUSION

Motivation has been defined as purposive behaviour instigated by activators that determine the direction and purposiveness of behaviour. As a dynamic process motivation is subject to change in that activators, direction and purposiveness can change. At different times and in different situations in his or her career different factors have significance for the individual and the factors also vary in the degree of significance they have. Purposeful behaviour is not necessarily aimed at achieving a particular recognisable goal, but can involve a self-sustaining process that is a goal in itself and is a means of expressing the inner self. As such, goal-directed behaviour refers to behaviour that is meaningful for the individual.

Self-evaluating questions

1. Explain how external activators can facilitate motivation.
2. Motivation is a self-sustaining process through which the individual expresses his or her inner self. Explain this statement in terms of self-actualisation and functional autonomy.
3. Explain how expectancy, self-efficacy and attribution are involved in the individual's perception of the outcomes of his or her behaviour.
4. Discuss the statement, Equity involves fairness.
5. Discuss emotion as an activator in motivation.
6. Explain the relation between emotion and performance.
7. Explain how the pleasure principle operates in motivation in general and career choice in particular.

Part III
Social Processes

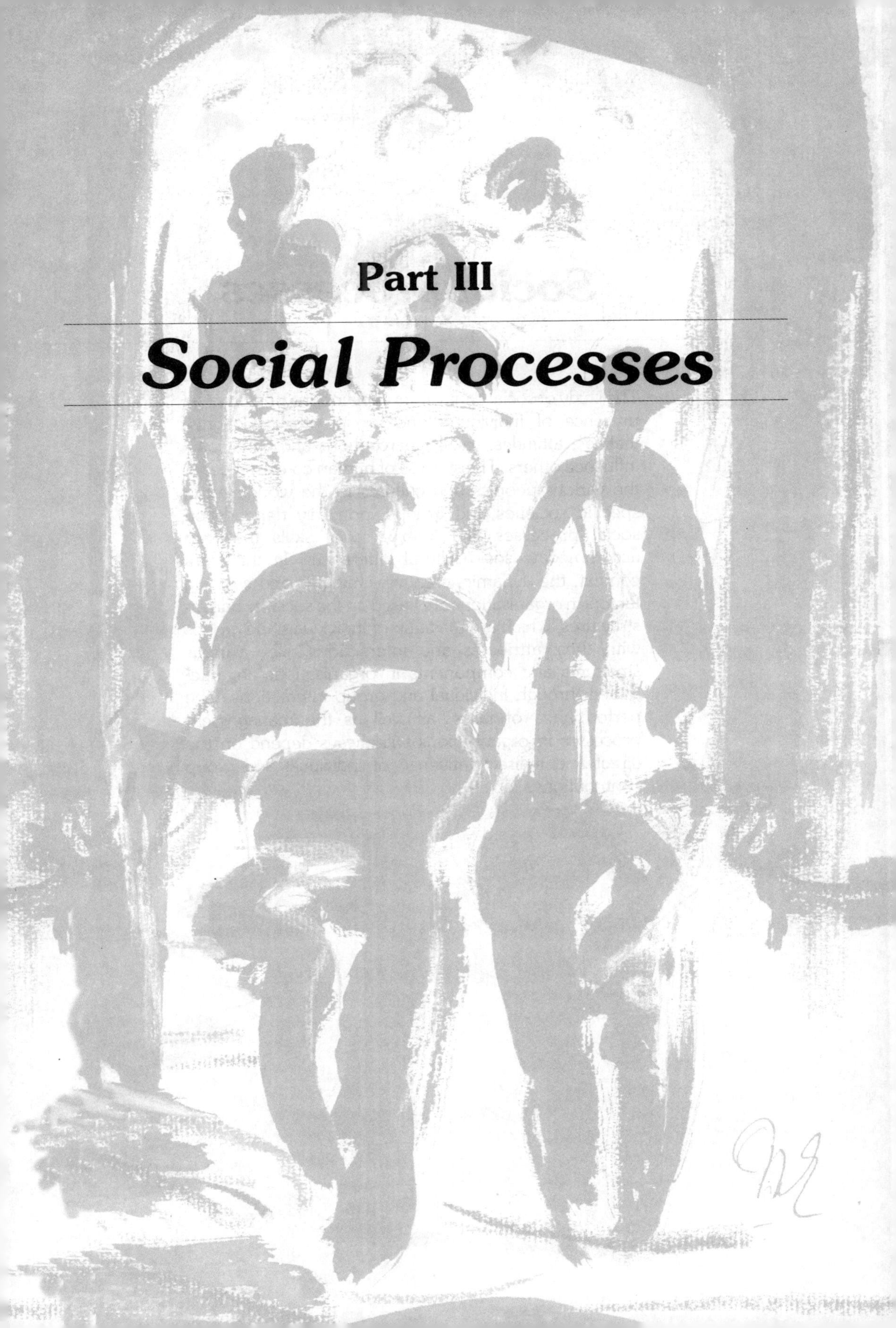

Social processes

The study of social behaviours explains how the physical presence of individuals and groups, their thoughts, feelings, attitudes, values, perceptions and behaviours influence others. The success of human co-existence, of the various peoples and cultures in the world and in specific societies and groups, primarily depends on social processes and interpersonal skills that can accommodate socio-cultural differences. In the work context, the dynamic, creative, changing and evolving factors in organisations are based on the social or human structures, which are made up of individuals and groups with their attributes and interactions. The various structures and components in organisations are integrated through individual and group interactions. The performance of tasks, as well as the management processes in organisations will always depend on the direct and indirect influence of individual and group contributions.

Attitudes and values

9

Antoinette Theron

CONTENTS

Learning outcomes

After studying this chapter you should be able to:

- explain the nature of attitudes
- describe the functions of attitudes
- differentiate between individual and external factors as agents of attitude change
- explain how cognitive dissonance is handled in attitude change
- explain how self-perception contributes to attitude change
- explain how the credibility of the communicator, the organisation of communications and the situation influence attitude change
- discuss work-related attitudes
- explain the nature of values
- explain how socio-cultural factors influence the development of values
- discuss Spranger's six value-orientations as part of personality
- discuss the organisational value systems related to culture as presented by Hofstede
- discuss the role of values in the meaning of work with reference to work centrality and international and national research findings

Key concepts

selective orientation, beliefs, opinions, cognitive dissonance, self-perception, credibility, messages, job satisfaction, intrinsic values, personal value-orientation, cultural values, organisational values, work versus working, work centrality, self-fulfilment, difference

9.1 INTRODUCTION

Attitudes and values are orientations that are distinguished by definition, but are also used interchangeably as related concepts. Attitudes can be based on the individual's value system. Values are denoted as referring to attitudes, interests, norms, principles, beliefs, needs and aims (Hattingh 1991; Williams 1979). These terms, as well as other terms associated with values such as ideology, code, standard, cultural orientation, life philosophy and reality conception can all be accommodated by the term orientation (Joubert 1986). Such terms indicate *selective orientations* (Williams 1979). Attitudes and values, as well as other related concepts

of significance in work context, such as interests, can thus be seen as selective orientations that direct the individual's preferences and modes of behaviour.

9.2 THE NATURE OF ATTITUDES

Generally an attitude is defined in terms of three components distinguished by Secord and Backman (1964): cognitive, emotional and behavioural. The nature of the attitude may vary according to the extent to which it is more cognitive or more emotional, which is reflected in the behavioural component, through which the attitude becomes perceptible. An employee may have a negative attitude to the boss, incorporating a strong emotional component; yet as the employee gains better understanding of the boss, the attitude can become more cognitive and manifest in evaluative rather than emotional behaviour.

Some attitudes are relatively stable and difficult to change. These attitudes can be regarded as *central attitudes,* as they form part of the individual's personality structure and can be related to the individual's self-concept. Other attitudes are regarded as *peripheral attitudes,* as they are temporary and subject to change. Central attitudes incorporate, for example, placing high value on justice and fairness. Peripheral attitudes can incorporate placing high value at particular times on certain consumer goods, physical work conditions and the climate in the work group.

The relative permanence or changeability of attitudes depends on their origin and on the intensity and duration of the factors that gave rise to them. Attitudes develop through interaction between parent and child; critical periods of development; ways of learning; social, cultural and educational influences; information transferred through mass media; personal experiences which may have a profound influence on an individual's attitudes and socialisation in the work situation.

From a learning perspective, attitudes can be acquired by classical and instrumental conditioning, and social-cognitive learning.

Attitudes may be based on *beliefs,* or a belief may be the cognitive component of an attitude. The cognitive aspects of an attitude are related to the individual's value system, that is, the internal frame of reference which directs his or her behaviour. An individual with a humanistic value system, for example, will have a favourable attitude towards democracy and related beliefs on social and political issues. In the work situation this value system may affect his or her attitudes to co-workers and subordinates in that these attitudes will be based on beliefs upholding human dignity, liberty, equality and solidarity.

Beliefs can be realistic, true or false in terms of external realities and changing situations. For a given individual, his or her beliefs are subjectively true at a given point in time, irrespective of whether they are realistic or rational or not.

Although an individual's beliefs are truths in which he or she firmly believes, another individual with different beliefs may regard them as mere opinions. An *opinion* is specific in the sense that it is the interpretation of given facts, for example the opinion that the wages in a firm are unfair. An opinion, like a belief, can be either true or false, and has emotional content. The more emotional it is, the smaller its relation to a belief. In this context it may form the emotional component of an attitude. A person's attitude towards democratic supervision may be based on strong feelings and opinions. However, opinions may be based on facts and therefore have little connection with attitudes.

The more strongly an opinion is based on facts, the easier it will change if the facts are changed. If an opinion is based on an attitude, it offers more resistance to change. The emotional nature of a negative attitude may persist even though the negative facts become positive. For example, if a supervisor is suspicious of workers generally, his or her attitude toward an unproductive worker in his or her group will not necessarily change if the worker becomes more productive; the supervisor will be more inclined to look for faults, to confirm the negative attitude taken.

9.3 FUNCTIONS OF ATTITUDES

The functions of attitudes are seen as determining the meaning of facts and situations, organising facts and selecting them (Maier & Verser 1982) as well as defending and expressing the self (Katz 1960; McKenna 1994). These functions can be understood as follows:

- Attitudes determine the *meaning of facts and situations.* For example, an individual may protect his or her attitude by rationalising about facts that conflict with the attitude. This function is illustrated by research that shows that male employees ascribe the success of male managers to intelligence and competence, while they ascribe the success of female managers to luck and favourable circumstances.

- Attitudes become substantiated *by the organisation of facts*. For example, a supervisor with a negative attitude towards older workers will maintain this attitude by regarding a group of older workers, who are just as productive as younger workers, but less sociable, as unsatisfactory in that they do not foster communication in the work department. A supervisor who is unbiased, on the other hand, may regard the older group as satisfactory because they are more task-oriented than socially oriented.
- Attitudes *select facts*. An individual perceives and communicates facts which confirm his or her attitude and ignores facts that do not. In an attempt to strengthen the attitude, the individual may see the facts relevant to his or her attitude as causal to the attitude. A political attitude, for example, is confirmed by facts which the individual perceives as proving it to be correct, and in a meeting the individual will mention only the facts which communicate his or her attitude and remain silent about other facts.
- Attitudes *defend the self*. They affirm and protect self-esteem, as well as protect individuals from acknowledging undesirable realities in themselves. Individuals may affirm their self-esteem by, for example, valuing and accumulating luxury consumer goods beyond their practical use because it enhances their self-image. Individuals may protect their self-esteem by persistently holding to political attitudes that were majority attitudes, but have become minority attitudes due to transitional structures. Individuals may deny an undesirable aspect of themselves, such as lack of commitment to work demands that require independent effort to update knowledge, by holding the attitude that the major function of the boss is to provide knowledge and support.
- Attitudes *express the self* in that they can express the individual's central values and incorporate self-concepts. An individual who inherently values justice may express this aspect of his or her self by supporting causes or mechanisms in organisational decision-making that incorporate democratic principles. An individual who values having power over others may seek occupational positions in which he or she is concerned with political issues affecting the organisation.

9.4 ATTITUDE CHANGE

Attitude change can be the result of changes in individuals' cognitions or behaviour, which means individuals themselves are the *active agents* in attitude change. Change can also be induced by external factors, which means individuals are the *recipients* of communications that influence their attitudes (Hogg & Vaughan 1995; Stephan & Stephan 1990).

9.4.1 The individual as active agent

Factors involved in the individual changing his or her attitudes include cognitive dissonance and self-perception.

9.4.1.1 Cognitive dissonance

Cognitive dissonance refers to an imbalance in two or more of the individual's cognitions, that is, thoughts or beliefs, or cognitions and actions, which should logically be consistent with each other. Cognitive dissonance can occur when an individual who values pacifism is involved in military strategy in his or her work situation, and when an individual who acknowledges that smoking is detrimental to health works for a tobacco company. This imbalance causes tension which the individual tries to reduce by employing mechanisms that can provide consonance.

The theory of cognitive dissonance was originally developed by Leon Festinger in

1957 and has generated much research. It brought attention to the significance of beliefs as components of attitudes (Hogg & Vaughan 1995). The underlying assumption is that individuals seek harmony and consistency between their beliefs and their behaviour, as well as between other people's beliefs and behaviour. The four mechanisms that Festinger indicated individuals possibly employ to handle dissonance are the following (McKenna 1994; Robbins 1998):

- *Seeking new information to support one's beliefs and avoiding information that will increase dissonance.* An individual who believes in supportive and cooperative communications in the workplace may find on entering a new workplace that there is a climate of indifference and aloofness. Rather than elaborating on this impression, he or she looks for factors beyond what is apparent and decides that communications are not sound, because the department consists of individuals of different races and backgrounds and all are under pressure of work schedules. By thinking this way the individual changes a cognitive component of his or her attitude.
- *Misinterpreting information that might increase dissonance.* The individual might misinterpret aloofness in the department by assuming that some members see colleagues of different races and backgrounds as threatening to their future success. By thinking this way the individual also changes a cognitive component of his or her attitude.
- *Finding social support for the attitudes one wishes to maintain by seeking out individuals with similar attitudes.* The individual might befriend colleagues who share his or her beliefs and join them in leisure activities outside work. Here the individual tries to reduce dissonance by changing his or her behaviour.

- *Playing down the importance of factors that contribute to dissonance.* The individual rationalises that racial and cultural differences are not significant, since acceptance of differences is a contemporary value in society. He or she works toward facilitating a climate of cooperation in which grievances, aims and work schedules are openly discussed in, for example, group discussions. This involves handling cognitive dissonance by changing factors in the environment.

The degree of dissonance an individual experiences varies from situation to situation (McKenna 1994; Robbins 1998). The need to reduce it or not depends on the *significance* of the factors causing dissonance, the degree of *influence* the individual has over these factors and the rewards involved in changing or living with the dissonance. If the rewards in the dissonant situation are important to the individual, he or she might tolerate the dissonance.

Handling dissonance involves making choices (McKenna 1994). If the choice the individual makes again causes dissonance, the individual will, rather than regretting the choice, change his or her attitude to accommodate the choice.

9.4.1.2 Self-perception

According to self-perception theory, introduced by Daryl Bem in 1972, individuals' attitudes can change through perception of their own behaviour. Individuals may, for example, decide that although they have grievances about their jobs, they still have a positive attitude to the job because of the many years they have been doing the work. Individuals therefore change negative attitudes or infer their real attitude from their behaviour.

Self-perception is applicable to attitude change if individuals have limited internal cues to account for unjustified behaviour, for example if they do not have feelings that justify why their behaviour is not consistent with their opinions (Stephan & Stephan 1990).

Self-perception thus helps individuals to understand why they do something (Robbins 1998).

9.4.2 The individual as recipient

External factors that can result in attitude change include persuasive communications involving the credibility of the communicator, the organisation of the communication and the situation in which the communication takes place.

9.4.2.1 The credibility of the communicator

An attitude is changed more readily if the source of information is regarded as credible. The credibility of an individual is determined by his or her credibility in the past, trustworthiness, expertise, authority, prestige, power to control the rewards involved in changing recipient's attitudes, as well as his or her physical attractiveness, likeability and similarity to the recipients.

The mass media, including newspapers, radio and television, can influence attitude change through, for example, advertising and political commentary.

If a communicator is not perceived as highly credible, the message he or she or it conveys can influence attitudes after some time. This is called the sleeper effect, in which the message rather than the source of the communication is remembered (Arnold et al. 1995).

9.4.2.2 The organisation of the communications

Attitude change is influenced by messages that only present positive information (one-sided), and messages that present both positive and negative information (two-sided) about issues, a type of job or an organisation. One-sided messages are generally more effective if the recipient is neutral or already agrees with the message.

Two-sided messages are generally more effective if recipients' attitudes differ from those of the communicator, as well as when propaganda or counterinformation is involved.

Fear-arousing messages can have a persuasive effect if they are not too intense and relatively impersonal. Messages that evoke excessive fear tend to be ineffectual in that they have an immunisation effect, with the result that similar messages in the future will not elicit a reaction and may also result in viewing the communicators' motives with suspicion (Maier & Verser 1982). Messages evoking extreme fear can also lead to anxiety, which interferes with perceiving the factual content of the message. On the other hand, messages evoking fear at a very low level may not capture attention and interest (Hogg & Vaughan 1995). Eliciting fear can be effective if the message also indicates how the consequences of a fearsome situation can be avoided, for example advertisements that not only show the drastic consequences of road accidents but also indicate the role of safety belts.

Communications that arouse guilt tend to result in compliance with an individual's request. Research has shown that if a researcher induces feelings of guilt in subjects, they will comply with future requests, for example to participate in future research projects. Individuals who are not induced to feeling guilt hardly ever comply (Hogg & Vaughan 1995).

9.4.2.3 The situation

The situation includes the effects of approaching an individual or a group in attitude change (Arnold et al. 1995).

If a group is largely divided with regard to their attitudes, change will more likely occur by approaching individuals. If the majority of a group are in agreement with the communicator, addressing the group will be effective in swaying the small minority toward changing their attitudes.

Groups tend to form attitudes or opinions that are stronger than those that the individuals in the group originally held. This effect is called group polarisation. It could be due to repeated exposure to an attitude voiced by group members. It could also be due to the escalation of strong views as one individual desires to be more influential than another, therefore positing a more extreme view.

Group effects are also noticeable in the higher commitment to attitudes or opinions that are voiced publicly rather than privately.

Attitudes are not necessarily easily accessible, but are deduced from surveys. Attitude surveys in the workplace can reveal which factors in the work situation require change. Maier and Verser (1982), cite a survey showing that the sounding of a bell to announce rest periods was a source of irritation to workers, because they associated it with the strict regimentation of a school. Substituting the bell with musical sounds changed their attitudes.

9.5 WORK-RELATED ATTITUDES

Attitudes that have been investigated specifically in the work context are job satisfaction, job involvement and organisational commitment (Robbins 1998).

9.5.1 Job satisfaction

Job satisfaction can be defined as a predominantly positive attitude toward the work situation. An individual may be dissatisfied with some aspects of his or her work and satisfied with others, but if he or she feels or thinks positively about relatively more aspects, we can deduce there is a general factor that can be labelled job satisfaction.

The components of attitudes in general, the cognitive, emotional and behavioural components, are also involved in job satisfaction. The behavioural component is not necessarily very strong, as an individual may have feelings or views about an issue without revealing it in his or her behaviour. An employee may, for example, feel that the head of the department does not show enough concern for employees' feelings and have good ideas as to how that superior's attitudes could have a positive effect on the job satisfaction of all employees, but refrain from voicing his or her ideas.

Extensive review of the research on job satisfaction indicates that the following factors are conducive to job satisfaction (Robbins 1998):

- *Mentally challenging work,* involving a fair amount of variety, freedom, utilising one's skills and abilities and receiving feedback on one's work. Generally work should be moderately challenging; if it is too challenging it can cause frustration and feelings of failure, while it can cause boredom if it is not challenging enough.
- *Equitable rewards,* such as pay and promotion policies and practices that workers perceive as fair, based on the demands of a job, the individual's skills and industry pay standards. Fairness is vitally important, not the amount of payment. Many people are prepared to work for less money if their work has other rewards.
- *Working conditions* that are conducive to doing one's job well, including safety and comfort, a clean environment, relatively modern facilities and adequate equipment.
- *Working with co-workers and bosses who are friendly and supportive.* The type of supervisor who facilitates job satisfaction is one who shows an interest in workers, offers praise for good performance and listens to workers' opinions.

9.5.2 Job involvement

Job involvement may be seen as the degree to which the individual identifies psychologically with his or her job and considers his or her performance in the job as important to self-worth. Individuals with high job involvement care about their work and strongly identify with it.

9.5.3 Organisational commitment

Organisational commitment refers to the degree to which the individual identifies with his or her employing organisation and its goals. An employee may not experience job satisfaction or job involvement, yet be relatively satisfied with the organisation and therefore wish to continue working for it.

Work-related attitudes are not necessarily good predictors of an employee's subsequent behaviour. A particular attitude may manifest in various behaviours, while a specific behaviour could be based on a range of attitudes. Other factors may also act as intervening variables that come between attitudes and behaviour (Furnham 1997). The individual's personal value system or cultural affinity with regard to religion, for example, can have an influence on the relation between attitudes and behaviour. If the individual's attitude has the same goal as his or her behaviour, attitudes can be used to predict work behaviour.

9.6 THE NATURE OF VALUES

Two generally accepted definitions of values are those of Rokeach and Kluckhorn (Joubert 1986).

Rokeach defines a value as an *enduring* belief that a certain mode of conduct is personally or socially preferable to a converse mode. Kluckhorn defines a value as an *implicit* or *explicit* conception of the desirable, which influences behavioural choices. Rokeach indicates that values are characterised by constancy, while Kluckhorn believes that values can be inherent in the individual or group, and not necessarily perceivable, but become perceivable when expressed in explicit behaviour. An individual may, for example, inherently value the

aesthetic, that is, appreciate beauty and form, which becomes explicit as the individual expresses it in various life activities.

Values are functional in one of the most characteristic activities of humans, that of creating symbolic worlds (Von Bertalanffy 1959).

Values develop through the same mechanisms that influence attitude development, including personal experiences that have a psychological effect on the individual, and external socio-cultural factors. According to Rokeach (1979) socio-cultural norms and requirements become personal aims of the individual, which are transformed to values. Values are thus *cognitive conceptions* of individuals that are based on what is social-culturally sanctioned and acceptable.

Parsons (quoted by Joubert 1986) maintains that the deterministic influence of culture results in institutional values of the culture to which an individual feels committed, being internalised as value-orientations in the individual's personality. Two such patterns which can be distinguished universally are the pragmatic and the idealistic orientation. We can interpret a pragmatic value orientation as being focused on utility, which may influence the individual's occupational choice toward business and finance. An idealistic orientation can be seen as not concerned with utility or practicality, and may influence the individual's occupational choice toward education or religion.

The determining role of culture in the individual's values can make values commanding or compelling forces of which the individual is not always aware (Badenhorst 1992). Thus, although culture forms values, culture can have a limiting effect on the individual, in that values may merely be prescriptive laws by which the individual abides (Tillich 1959). In this sense, individuals' behaviour can become alienated from their personal inner natures. It is,

The theoretical person

The power person

The economic person

The religious person

The social person

The aesthetic person

Dominant value orientations

however, humans' nature to know intuitively what they intrinsically are, and they show this by actualising their inner selves in explicit behavioural forms that symbolise that inner self (Weisskopf 1959).

To understand the individual's values, they should rather be understood as subjective structures. They are not always directly related to the individual's behaviour, they can be not obvious, and they can be used as reasons for rationalising behaviour (Du Preez, quoted by Joubert 1986). This means, for example, that an individual who will not conform to certain norms in a work situation, can rationalise that his or her values do not allow it.

9.7 VALUES AS PART OF PERSONALITY

Spranger (1950) distinguished six value-orientations that are intrinsic in every individual's personality: theoretical, economic, social, power, religious and aesthetic. These orientations are all present in the personality of an individual and function in interrelation to each other. Generally, however, one value-orientation is dominant in an individual's personality, which makes him or her, for example, a social type of person, or an economic type of person, and this orientation influences his or her preferences, motivations, aims and ways of life.

Spranger maintains that these orientations have been universally recognisable in humans from antiquity, but the way they are expressed changes as humans' cultural history changes. A modern value-orientation is the *technical orientation*, which can be seen as an emergent form derived from the combination of a theoretical and economic orientation.

9.7.1 The theoretical person

The theoretical person is the intellectual person who values knowledge, seeking eternal truths rather than the deeper meaning of things. He or she tends to generalise, not noticing the particular in the general, which makes him or her wise, rather than clever, where the particular is concerned. He or she values objectivity, which makes true or false the real criteria for truth. Criteria such as beautiful or ugly, holy or unholy, useful or useless, are seen as irrelevant in that they are subjective. He or she sees general knowledge as personal knowledge and can become too involved in his or her own ideas, and too theoretical. The practical aspects of life become of no interest. The theoretical person is the individual who "looks" at life in a controlled and "correct" way, but does not become part of life. He or she is drawn to natural science or technical subjects, but is not necessarily a skilled person.

9.7.2 The economic person

The economic person is driven by a utility motive which is seldom satisfied because he or she is constantly in a state of striving to produce something visible. He or she sees work and income as synonymous. Both involve utility and sustained yields or products, which are the factors by which the economic person renews himself or herself psychologically. His or her being is analogous to nature, which constantly maintains and renews itself by yielding forces and matter. The economic person uses matter and forces in his or her life, as well as time and space, with thrift, so as to gain the maximum benefit from them. He or she always has to be involved in economic activities, be it at work, in the home, the environment, country or the world, and all the activities must have visible utility value.

The economic person is more in contact with reality than the theoretical person, in that knowledge is only valued if it has a practical purpose. Beauty is seen in terms of utility value and may be valued only in terms of luxury or in terms of economic necessity. Art, for example, is valued for its credit value.

The economic person's basic motive is to maintain himself or herself, which means that his or her ego is the most important aspect of life. Other people are seen as akin to producers and consumers, and their value as worthwhile or "good" people is seen in terms of their diligence, thriftiness, skill, reliability and orderliness. As such, they deserve "credit".

Spranger maintains that in modern economic life the economic person can be so immersed in economic matters that he or she becomes mechanistic to the extent of losing the purpose of his or her real nature, which is striving for utility. Economic striving may be exaggerated to a degree of personal meaningfulness in which he or she lives on a blissful level of superficiality at which he or she is not always aware of his or her real needs or motives.

The economic person in general values work in commerce, manufacturing, banking, manual work, handicraft or farming, because they all involve doing something useful that produces something.

9.7.3 The social person
The social person is the selfless person who lives through other people. He or she only becomes a person in own right by giving and receiving love, and when the need to receive love becomes a need to give love, his or her genuine social nature evolves. This can manifest in a philanthropic love for people in general, or commitment to an individual, be it a friend, lover or family member.

The social person is not interested in theoretical or objective knowledge of people, but is focused on sympathy, empathy and acceptance of the positive and the negative. He or she can cope with the ugly, the sickly, the formless, and bring transformation with his or her warmth and inner light.

If involved in economic activity, the social person has no concern with acquisitiveness, but only with service to others.

Spranger maintains this value-orientation can develop into a one-sided moralistic approach in which everything is condoned in the name of love, even if it is contrary to social norms. If disappointed or hurt, the social person can become hard to the extent of hating and withdrawing into himself or herself. In essence, he or she will always, however, believe in love.

The social person is drawn to life activities in which the focus is on the needs of others. He or she is not necessarily fulfilled in occupations that are generally associated with concern for human needs, such as theology, politics, economics, research or artistic occupations. Individuals who are drawn to these occupations are not necessarily social persons, because love may not be their primary motive – it becomes fused with their particular dominant value-orientations.

9.7.4 The power person
The power person finds meaning in life by experiencing himself or herself as a power. His or her strongest motive is to confirm this life power by being superior to other people.

The power orientation can also be seen as a political orientation, as it manifests in the context of organised collective life. In this context the power person plays a leading role, because he or she has to be above others.

The power orientation is an inner compulsion that the individual has to express. It can be expressed in terms of other value-orientations; using theoretical knowledge, economic utility, aesthetic beauty or religious piety as personal characteristics to rise above other people.

The power orientation can be closely related to the economic orientation, because consumer goods are utility goods with which one can influence people. The power person is, however, not concerned with utility as such, or with thrift, or producing something – he or she rather employs diplomacy or coercion to gain control over material things, and therefore over people. He or she is not concerned with understanding people, but in getting them to "get going". He or she may be interested in art to give external form to himself or herself, since it suggests cultural refinement. By becoming, for example, an art collector, he or she enters a fantasy world in which the power motive manifests in a more subtle way. The power orientation can also manifest in social play, by which one conquers people.

Spranger maintains the power person feels attuned to a standing in which he or she has glory and honour. He or she is, however, not found only on the lustrous high levels of society, but on all levels, including the basic everyday human relations levels, where he or she can emerge as an organiser, a campaigner, an ambitious leader.

9.7.5 The religious person

All the facets of the religious person's life have a spiritual foundation. He or she sees nothing as existing in itself, because everything is part of the spiritual, of which God is the objective correlate. Belief is seen as the highest form of knowledge.

The religious person can forsake things and needs, but may see economic activities as service to God and acquisition of earthly things as gifts from God. Art, music, dance or other aesthetic forms are not appreciated as forms in themselves, but as embodiments of an ideal of something eternal.

The religious value-orientation is closest to the social value-orientation because it involves love, but God, not a person, is the ultimate loved person. Unity with God prevents the religious person from experiencing loneliness.

If the religious person feels that he or she has power, it is seen as God-given. Another religious person may feel a need to acquire power, to get closer to God – the highest in the hierarchy of power.

Spranger sees the religious value-orientation as the most individualistic of the six value-orientations. It is akin to having a sense of fate, and fate is something different for every person.

9.7.6 The aesthetic person

The aesthetic person gives form to his or her inner being by aesthetic experience. He or she can transform something from any sphere of life, be it intellectual, spiritual, physical or emotional, to an experience of beauty. Through this way of experiencing he or she extends his or her inner being and actualises his or her essential nature. This nature is to create form and harmony according to an inherent will-to-form.

The generally valid knowledge that the theoretical person values does not concern the aesthetic person. He or she does not *look* at life, but *experiences* life. The aesthetic person does not seek objective truth, but rather experiences reality intuitively, is open to experience and enjoys the unfamiliar if it is seen as meaningful, and does not rely on the conventional, but rather sees life as a spectacle of colour, rhythm and movement. The diverse is preferable to the generally given, and the particular is enjoyed or appreciated for its own sake.

His or her religious experience is influenced by the orientation to valuing beauty. He or she does not seek a religion of denial, of dualities or chaos, but a religion in which God is seen as the highest giver of the harmony of life.

The aesthetic person does not have a power motive, in that he or she must be above other people. Such a person may, however, have a *feeling* of power, in the sense that his or her individuality and way of experiencing is an inner power with which he or she can influence people. Depending on his or her abilities, such a feeling of power can be expressed by, for example, the art of rhetoric or aesthetic display in his or her home or work environment. His or

Large power distance	Small power distance
Inequalities among people are expected and desired. Less powerful people should be dependent on the more powerful.	Inequalities among people should be minimised. There should be, and there is partly interdependence between less powerful and more powerful people.
As parents teach children obediency and respect centralisation is the norm – initiative is taken at the top and subordinates expect to be told what to do.	As parents treat children as equals, decentralisation is the norm and subordinates expect to be consulted.
The hierarchy in organisations reflects the existential inequality between the higher and lower.	Hierarchy in an organisation means inequality of roles, established for convenience.
The ideal boss is a benevolent aristocrat or a good father.	The ideal boss is a resourceful democrat.
Privileges and status symbols for managers are expected and often implemented.	Privileges and status symbols are frowned upon.
The salary gap between the higher and lower is wide.	The salary gap between the higher and lower is narrow.

Table 9.1 Power distance in organisations
Source: Adapted from Hofstede (1994)

her aim is not, however, that of the power person, who uses aesthetic ostentation to give form to himself or herself. The aesthetic person has inner form which he or she has to express.

In social relations the aesthetic person also seeks form and harmony. He or she values spiritual unity with people, rather than looking at them with sympathy or as utility objects.

Economic striving is diametrically opposed to the aesthetic person's orientation toward harmony. His or her whole orientation is disturbed when forced to be one-sidedly concerned about the useful. In everyday life the practical aspects can be a burden. He or she easily feels anxiety about the heaviness of life, but has the tendency to transform it to an experience that is enriching. Then he or she is akin to an actor who can "feel" himself or herself into things and thus share in the meaning of life.

Besides the tendency to see the ugly as beautiful, the aesthetic person can also see beauty in things that mean nothing to other people, for he or she is the virtuoso of life that can make an artwork of life. He or she is not necessarily an artist working in artistic occupations, but is drawn to situations where something extraordinary can be made of the ordinary, and be in harmony with himself or herself, others and the environment.

Individualism	Collectivism
The employee's independence of the organisation is important.	The employee is dependent on the organisation and of importance is what the organisation does for the employee.
The employee should have considerable freedom to develop his or her own approach to the job.	The employee should have training opportunities to learn new skills.
Work should be challenging to facilitate a personal sense of accomplishment.	The employee should be able to fully use his or her skills and abilities on the job.
Management is management of individuals.	Management is management of groups.
The task is more important than relationships.	Relationships are more important than the task.
The employer-employee relationship is a contract involving both parties.	The employer-employee relationship has moral dimensions, akin to a family link.

Table 9.2 Individualism and collectivism in organisations
Source: Adapted from Hofstede (1994)

Spranger's conception of these six value-orientations has found application in a psychological test, the Allport-Vernon-Lindzey Study of Values (Allport et al. 1960), which is used in research on values.

9.8 CULTURAL VALUES IN ORGANISATIONAL CONTEXT

Hofstede (1994) relates values in the work situation, including values in the organisation, to value systems in cultures. In a study of 50 countries, including South Africa, Hofstede found that three types of value systems affect the thinking of individuals and the thinking in organisations in predictable ways. These three value systems are power distance, individualism versus collectivism, and masculinity versus femininity.

9.8.1 Power distance

Power distance concerns the distribution of power in organisations, which is inevitably unequal because organisations are mostly organised in hierarchies of supervisor-subordinate relationships. Cultural influences determine how these relationships are handled in organisations. Cultural influences include values instilled by parent-child and teacher-child relationships, for example the degree of dependence of the child on authority figures or the degree of equality granted children by authority figures that is acceptable.

Power distance can be understood in terms of the values of the less powerful members of the organisation. This involves the extent to which they expect and accept that power is unequally distributed.

In most work situations power distance varies between the two extremes of a large

Masculinity	Femininity
Dominant values are material success and progress.	Dominant values are caring for others and preservation.
Money and material things are important.	People and warm relationships are important.
One lives in order to work.	One works in order to live.
Equity, competition and performance are important.	Equality, solidarity and the quality of worklife are important.
Managers are expected to be assertive and decisive.	Managers use intuition and aim at consensus and are not so obvious.
Conflicts are resolved by fighting them out.	Conflicts are resolved by compromise and negotiation.
Security in working for the organisation as long as one wishes is important.	Opportunities for advancement and challenge through job enrichment is necessary.

Table 9.3 Masculinity and femininity in organisations
Source: Adapted from Hofstede (1994)

power distance situation and a small power distance situation. The former is characterised by many inequalities and the latter by fewer. Table 9.1 shows differences between organisations influenced by large and small power distance in society.

Hofstede's research revealed large power distance in, among others, Latin countries including Latin America, France and Spain, as well as in Asian and African countries. In South Africa, Great Britain and the United States of America, power distance was relatively smaller, while it was smallest in New Zealand, Denmark, Israel and Austria.

9.8.2 Individualism versus collectivism

These value systems concern the role of the individual versus the role of the group.

Individualism characterises societies in which the ties between individuals are loose. Everyone is expected to look after himself or herself and his or her immediate family. Families in these societies mostly consist of two parents and children, or one parent and children. This is called the nuclear family. Individuals see themselves as "I", that is, having a personal identity distinct from others' identities, and association with other people is based on their individual characteristics rather than their group membership.

Collectivism characterises societies in which people are integrated into strong in-groups, which throughout their lifetime protect them in return for loyalty. The majority of people live in collectivist societies. Collectivism here does not refer to the influence of the state over individuals in a political sense, but to the influence of the group. Families in these societies include parents, children, grandparents, other relatives and servants. This is called an extended family. The individual's identity is seen in terms of "we" rather than "I".

Characteristics of individualism and collectivism that apply in the work situation are shown in table 9.2.

Hofstede's research showed that individualism characterises wealthy countries, with the United States of America, Australia, Great Britain and Canada showing the highest degree, and South Africa showing a relatively high degree. Collectivism characterises poor countries, including East African and West African countries, Thailand and Indonesia.

9.8.3 Masculinity versus femininity

In *masculine* societies children are socialised towards assertiveness, ambition and competition and in the work situation results are considered important. Men are not seen as tender and taking care of relationships, but as being tough. In *feminine* societies children are socialised toward modesty and solidarity and in the work situation social relationships are considered important. Both men and women are seen as concerned with relationships, akin to the role that women are generally associated with, that of taking care and being tender.

Table 9.3 illustrates characteristics of masculinity and femininity in the organisational context.

Hofstede's research showed that masculinity is highest in Japan, Austria, Italy and Switzerland, while it is relatively high in Great Britain, the United States of America and South Africa. Femininity is characteristic of Denmark, the Netherlands, Norway and Sweden. Masculinity is not related to economic development – there are both rich and poor masculine and rich and poor feminine countries.

The distribution of men and women who work is also not related to the masculinity or femininity of a country. Hofstede indicates that in all countries there are ambitious and unambitious men and women.

In a South African study of human resources management students, incorporating Hofstede's value systems (Hugo & Van Vuuren 1996), no differences were found between black and white respondents with regard to power distance. Both groups indicated acceptance of power distance. Collectivism was found to be higher in black than in white respondents, which reflects the African focus on community values. The greater emphasis by black respondents on development and growth, and on participation and involvement, suggested that both masculinity and femininity are stronger among black than white respondents. The researchers interpret the emphasis on development as related to affirmative action, and therefore a desire to become personally equipped to utilise job opportunities. The emphasis on participation is interpreted as an awareness of democratic and consensus decision-making generated by the previous exclusion of blacks in these spheres.

9.9 VALUES AND THE MEANING OF WORK

The meaning of work embraces the values that individuals attach to work or to working.

A significant factor in the meaning of work is the value that working as such has for the individual at any given time (MOW 1987). This involves the centrality of work as a life interest, that is, the value outcomes or rewards associated with working relative to the outcomes of other life roles (Roberson 1990). In a study of over 15 000 individuals in eight industrialised countries, it was found that seeing work as a central life interest decreases as the importance of leisure time increases. The majority of individuals, however, valued working, and would continue working even if they had the means to live comfortably without working for the rest of their lives (MOW 1987).

Work or leisure? Less work, more play?

Research conducted in 11 countries, ranging from moderately developed to industrially most advanced (Sverko & Super 1995), showed that particular values attached to work are all inner-oriented values. In all the countries the majority of respondents indicated that personal development, utilising ability and achievement, which are all related to self-fulfilment, are most important. The desire for authority and prestige and a willingness to take risks were the two least important.

As part of this study, Langley (1995) found that among South African high school pupils of all population groups, the most important values were: utilising ability (which had the highest value in all the population groups), personal development, achievement, economic security and advancement.

By comparison, the least important values were: social relations, variety, desire for authority, physical prowess and taking risks.

The importance of specific values can change as society and the workplace change. Change as such becomes a meaning attached to work. In post-modern society value is placed on heterogeneity, openness and inclusiveness, and acceptance of difference and otherness (Jencks 1989). The study of values can therefore not be based on an ethnocentric approach involving a one-sided cultural focus (Hofstede 1984).

9.10 CONCLUSION

Attitudes and values are part of the individual's intentional behaviour, that is, they determine his or her preferences, interests and choices. Attitudes can be relatively constant or merely temporary, and accordingly susceptible to lesser or greater change. Values tend to be more constant, as they are intrinsic to the individual, but can change as cultural influences change.

Both attitudes and values manifest in observable behaviour and can be inferred from behaviour, but attitudes are more readily observable in behaviour. Attitudes can be changed by changing behaviour. Values have relatively varied relationships to behaviour and are best seen as subjective factors that should be interpreted as influencing behaviour.

Both attitudes and values involve the personal meaning that individuals derive from social and work situations, as well as the meaning that the individual can give to the situations.

Self-evaluating questions

1. Describe concepts associated with the nature of attitudes and explain how attitudes are functional.
2. Discuss the statement: Both the individual and external factors can be agents of attitude change.

3. Explain how attitudes function in the workplace.
4. Explain how values become internalised and how they function as implicit and explicit aspects of personality.
5. Explain and differentiate Spranger's value-orientations and suggest applicable work situations for each orientation.
6. Discuss the statement: Organisational values are culturally determined.
7. Explain how values influence the meaning of work.

Interpersonal attraction and affiliation
10

Ziel Bergh

CONTENTS

Learning outcomes

After studying this chapter you should be able to:

- relate interpersonal attraction and affiliation to behaviour in work organisations
- define interpersonal attraction and affiliation as processes in relationships
- discuss various explanations for affiliation behaviours
- explain personal and situational determinants of interpersonal attraction
- critically discuss the importance of physical attractiveness for interpersonal attraction
- explain possible problems related to interpersonal attraction and affiliation

Key concepts

social structure, relationships, social needs, interpersonal attraction, affiliation, social exchanges, comparison, rewards and costs, dependence, instrumentality, stimulation, learning, physical attractiveness stereotype, self-esteem anxiety, appearance anxiety, similarity, emotions, proximity, reciprocity, complementarity, social support, cultural differences

10.1 INTRODUCTION

Interpersonal attraction and affiliation refer to people's attitudes and feelings about other individuals or groups of people and their need to have social relationships. Individuals and organisations choose each other in an employer-employee relationship because they are attracted to each other. If dissimilar, or if mutual dislike develops, the relationship will or can be terminated.

Work organisations are complex *open social* systems, operating through various interdependent subsystems such as management structures, technology and materials and people. Of these the people interactions or the *social structure* of organisations is the most important component, as this is how people interact and communicate to achieve business objectives. The social structure in an organisation determines communication patterns between groups and individuals; the social norms relevant in an organisation; social roles allocated to people; and the cohesion, climate and culture (Dipboye et al. 1994). These aspects determine how and if employees work and stay together. If an organisation's internal social relationships are under pressure, other structures and processes, such as task completion, finances and customer relations, will also fail, rendering the organisation powerless to relate to the outside world and serve its own and customer needs.

Interpersonal relationships and social skills are based on people's fundamental social needs and interests to belong, to affiliate with others and to bond in close and enduring relationships. People's attempts to belong are also determined by acquired secure or insecure attachment behaviour styles, that is, their way of being attracted to or to attract others. These fundamental social skills form the basis of their daily interactions in personal and work life; whether they act in a way which will make others accept them, and also help and benefit others, or whether they demonstrate antisocial behaviours which create interpersonal distance and cause discomfort to themselves and others.

Personality is often defined in terms of interpersonal traits, such as empathy, dominance, independence, sociability, self-acceptance and social presence.

Interpersonal attraction and affiliation are social skills, and are criteria for success in many areas: relating well with other employees; being accepted in friendships and intimate relationships; being selected for a job; influencing and controlling people in management and in business. Psychologists require these skills in counselling, to facilitate change in intrapersonal and interpersonal behaviours by modelling these behaviours in the counselling relationship.

10.2 DEFINITIONS OF ATTRACTION AND AFFILIATION

Attraction and affiliation are related and complementary and even inclusive concepts, to explain why people are attracted to one another, and why people want to belong in a relationship.

Attraction refers to the mutual positive, physical, social and psychological attributes of people, which make them approach other people and to have positive feelings towards others. Ask yourself why you like or are attracted to your wife, best friend, work colleague or lover. Attraction may range from feelings of friendliness and liking, leading to more serious commitments in friendships, to intense feelings of physical and psychological intimacy and love. The various forms of intimacy are differentiated from attraction in that intimacy is associated with a depth quality or intensity of feelings in relationships; such relationships are fewer, but are close, warm and trusting. Various forms of love, which also include aspects of intimacy, mostly refer to romantic and passionate relationships, including sexual associations, in which the parties want to share a special close physical and social presence with one another. Attraction in relationships may, of course, also be negative, in the forms of dislike and hatred. Think, in this regard, why you dislike a certain person.

Organisational attributes also "attract" employees by presenting the characteristics of the organisation as attractive to possible applicants. Persons who find a match between themselves and a specific organisation will apply and, if selected, accept the job offer.

Affiliation denotes the human need to establish and maintain many social relationships, with an individual or in a group, in order to enjoy empathy and affection and to belong somewhere. Affiliation (either friendliness or hostility) is one of the basic dimensions of interpersonal behaviour, the other being control (either dominance or submission). The way affiliations are defined between two people will determine the type of control in the interaction, that is, who will determine the interaction and communication patterns in the relationship. If you think about your relationships, how are affiliations defined and who is controlling the relationships?

The literature indicates that affiliative behaviours are closely related to, and determined by, the formation of attachment behaviours in early life. The type of bonding (close emotional and nurturing relationship), between mother and child especially, but also with other important people in early life, will have a lasting effect on friendships, romantic attachments and other types of relationships, and even on the quality of adjustment and performance in later life. These aspects of affiliation are referred to by important theorists and researchers in the field of child development, such as Freud, Erikson, Bowlby and Ainsworth (Buss 1995; Craig 1996).

From this it follows that if people are attracted toward a situation or one another, affiliative behaviours will be enhanced. On the other hand, strong *needs* to affiliate might facilitate or be the cause of the process of interpersonal attraction.

10.3 EXPLANATIONS FOR INTERPERSONAL ATTRACTION

Scientific explanations for attraction and affiliation are, among others, based on certain assumptions and concepts from social psychological theories. A general principle in social or interpersonal interaction is perception. *Perception* involves assessments of persons and situations. These perceptions may contain many emotional and cognitive considerations, from an own frame of reference, such as personality traits, knowledge, physical features, skills, socioeconomic status, preferences, attitudes and values. Another principle involved in the forming and maintaining of relationships is the *need to feel in control*, that is, to have balance or homeostasis in relationships, to enjoy our associations with other people rather than be uneasy about them.

10.3.1 Social exchange or cost and reward ratios

According to the social exchange theories of, among others, Homans, Heider, Foa and Foa, Thibaut and Kelley, Festinger and Kelly (Hogg & Vaughan 1995), interpersonal relationships are based on cost and reward ratios. People may have many reasons to find relationships rewarding, such as information, goods, services, money, status and love. People will establish close ties when the benefits of their involvement, such as emotional happiness, minimum stress, pleasure, acceptance and even physical and economic rewards, exceed the costs or possible negative consequences, such as unhappiness and financial losses. People may select individuals, groups and situations in which they will be best rewarded. In the same manner, people terminate relationships in which the costs exceed the rewards. The power of interpersonal rewards is often expressed in statements such as "I like to work with Dennis, he makes me feel good about myself", or negative types of exclamations, "I hate to do something together with Dennis, he ignores my opinions" and "Please, do not say anything, but Dennis is really a bore".

The rewards-ratio concept may even explain why people remain in unsatisfactory associations, such as an unhappy marriage or friendship, or an unfulfilling job, because no better option is available. We may also, according to social exchange assumptions, understand why people apply for employment in a specific organisation and explain high personnel turnover in an organisation. If job leavers are dissatisfied with the rewards for their efforts, they may choose to find another employer offering more rewarding relationships. In essence, the behaviours between two parties (for example employer and labour union) negotiating on employee benefits will be based on the principle of minimising costs and maximising rewards. The same principle applies in business deals and bargaining between business groups. In the case of people in a training or therapy group interacting with each other, such exchanges may be more subtle, but they still involve the trade-off of behaviours. A group member may decide to be nice to other group members if they will recognise him or her, and therefore smiles more and greets them in a friendly manner. In response the other group members return the greetings and welcome and thank him or her for being there.

In essence, this type of relationship is a process of "socially exchanging behaviours", strategies or manoeuvres for interaction, based on the homeostasis or hedonistic principle, which states that people want to have balance and control in their lives, maximise pleasure and avoid pain as far as possible.

Think about one of your relationships and try to establish on what exchanges it works. What manoeuvres are being used? What are the costs and rewards?

Social exchange also implies equity and *distributive justice* (Hogg & Vaughan 1995). This means that people want things to be fair or fairly distributed and to be able to say, "if you are good to me, and treat me like you treat other employees, I will be friendly to you". People in relationships will be most unhappy if they feel that they are victims of inequitable behaviours. You will, however, seldom see people complaining when the inequitable relationship is in their favour and they are treated better than others.

10.3.2 Social comparison

The idea of social comparison, as postulated by Festinger (1954), states that we evaluate or assess our perceptions, opinions, attitudes, characteristics and actions by comparing them to those of people similar to us or who are in similar situations. If we find a favourable comparison, liking and affiliation might follow, or the person might accept a situation or decision as fair. This could explain why employees will be unhappy when they feel that dismissals are unfair, an application for a job or promotion is unsuccessful, or dissatisfied after salary increases to some employees. Employees who did not receive an increase may feel that they are similar or comparable to the employees who did. Social comparison may also serve to control possible uncertainties or anxieties which people experience about themselves or situations. Social comparison may serve to justify possible actions, for instance, choosing a job, or be the reason to demand a promotion or to complain about matters, as in negotiations about working conditions or criticising supervisory behaviour. Social comparison is also related to the concept of equity expressed in "if I compare, and feel that I am treated as my colleague is, I may support you in your decisions".

We may experience situations where people seemingly want imbalance: preferring to be alone to have some privacy or to think about issues; wanting to be treated differently (uniquely) from everyone else by being allowed to arrive late at work. Such behaviours, seemingly in imbalance, may serve to create balance again, because the reasons for behaving in such a manner may be the result of unhappiness or dissatisfaction.

10.3.3 Biological and social dependence

A classical explanation for social attraction is that people, through social learning, are dependent on interaction with other people for their physical and psychological needs. This holds true in childhood, when children must depend on or learn to be dependent on their parents and other adults for basic needs such as food, safety and love. One of the most authoritative research on human *bonding or attachment behaviours* is the work of Bowlby (Ainsworth & Bowlby 1991). According to Bowlby, infants are helpless and psychologically and biologically dependent on the mother, who "must" provide the necessary physical needs (food, security), psychological care and stimulation. In his theory of self-identity development, Erikson (1968) asserted that the trust or mistrust which mothers instil in infants through their bonding behaviours may well lay the foundation for bonding or attachment behaviours in the child's later relationships.

Think about relationships in your personal or work life that impact on you. Why is someone at work suspicious or aggressive about almost everything? Why is another person too dependent on other employees? Why is someone you know overly obsessed with another person? Do you know someone who is very distant and avoids intimate or close relationships?

Dependency may continue into adulthood. Young adults today are often forced to be dependent on parents for far longer than in the past, due to studies or lack of employment. Financial dependency and fear of unemployment may explain why employees stay in work situations even if they dislike the employer and the working conditions. People with immature or insecure forms of interpersonal reactions, such as overdependence, jealousy and aggressiveness, may still be depending on forms of behaviour which worked as infants or with mothers, but in an adult world such behaviours are unacceptable and may cause opposition from many quarters.

Another form of dependency is apparent in people who always need to be with others. This is explained by the belief that people, in some respects, are *instinctively* inclined (genetically determined) toward affiliative behaviours. Baumeister and Leary (1995) assert that research thus far clearly indicates that the need to belong is a powerful fundamental human motive. This can be illustrated by the crying of children, which automatically elicits a response from parents, and the fact that children are afraid of being far from parents, or a long time away from them. The term "separation anxiety" is used to explain a child's or adult's fear of the breaking of a close relationship, especially if there have been previous forced separations from loved ones. Research by Spitz in 1945 on infant orphans showed low social and mental development in those who had not had nurture from and affiliation with others, and a higher mortality rate. Bowlby's research on attachment behaviours supported these findings and further asserted that childhood attachment behaviours continue in adult life and determine the quality of adjustment in relationships (Franzoi 1996; Hogg & Vaughan 1995). Larson et al. (1982) found that adolescents spend most of their time with other people and are much happier and energetic when doing so.

We might ask whether adults show similar behaviour in other situations. Why do we tend to be sorry for someone crying and hate to be away from loved ones? Why do parents still worry about their children in adverse circumstances? Anxiety studies in the late 1950s by Schachter showed that when people are fearful or anxious, or uncertain in situations, they want to affiliate with others, especially with those whom they assess to be experiencing similar feelings (Schachter 1959). Is this only to experience similarity of circumstances or is it a natural reaction, because they can't do

otherwise? In the well-known experiments by Harlow and associates on rhesus monkeys, also during the 1950s, many commonalities were found between attachment behaviours in these animals and human behaviour, commonalities also verified by Bowlby (Hogg & Vaughan 1995).

The serious effects of *social isolation*, especially the ill-effects of deprivation of maternal care during infanthood, are illustrated by the findings on so-called feral children. Such children were found to be deprived of all human or motherly contact for many years, and in some ways raised like animals. Serious maladjustment and underdevelopment occurred in almost all spheres of functioning. In one case, however, the powerful influence of social learning was illustrated: a young girl (Isabelle) had spent a few years as an infant with her mother, even though the mother was deaf and blind, and this young girl recovered quite well (Hogg & Vaughan 1995).

10.3.4 Instrumentality and needs

According to this view, also related to the concepts of social exchange and comparison, people may associate with others and in situations as a *means to an end*. A person may join a club for the status to be enjoyed, befriend someone to obtain commercial privileges, or take a highly paid job just for the financial status and benefits. According to Maslow, human behaviour is motivated by a hierarchy of needs, from the basic biological needs for food and safety to the highest need to achieve self-actualisation. Hill (1987) proposes that people have four motives for affiliation:

- social comparison (the need to reduce uncertainty)
- positive stimulation (the need to experience interesting relations with others)
- emotional support (friendship when experiencing problems)
- to get attention (to be praised and admired)

Franzoi (1996) and Buss (1995), in summarising research, indicate that, in terms of personality, people may differ with respect to their needs for affiliation, intimacy and attachment, which are aspects to be considered when selecting people for jobs or when organising work groups. People with a high *need for affiliation* try to have as many social contacts as possible and want such affiliations to be successful. They want to be praised and, in work situations, put the emphasis on working with a close friend or on the cohesion in the work group, rather than on being competitive or on task completion. Males with a high need for affiliation tend to associate more with attractive females than with men and don't like to be alone. In contrast, people with a low need for affiliation handle less rewarding relationships better and will possibly be more task oriented. People with a high need and capacity for *intimacy* tend to have genuine concern for others, preferring to have fewer, but more close, friendships. In contrast to people with high affiliation needs, people with high needs for intimacy are judged by others to be loving, reliable, warm and with a genuine interest and regard for other's feelings. People with a high need for affiliation are regarded as superficial or not genuine in their empathy and care for other persons. Bowlby's research and subsequent findings on attachment behaviours also indicate clearly that people with secure attachment styles are less threatened in relationships than persons with insecure attachment patterns of behaviour. However, as long as the two styles are similar, for instance two secure persons or two insecure styles, relationships should be quite amicable. Relationships will be poorer when two people with opposite affiliation styles associate. However, this could sometimes work if the secure person has sufficient resolve and resiliency to put an insecure person at ease. The situation will, however, be more serious when two people with the same insecure attachment style affiliate, for instance two people who are avoidant or ambivalent in relationships (Buss 1995).

In terms of general adjustment, it seems that people with a high need for affiliation are people who ask for special attention and who possibly have low self-esteem, may not be sensitive to other people's feelings because of the strong emphasis on their own social needs. Research by McAdams and Vaillant (1982) over a 17-year period indicates that men with a high capacity for intimacy are better adjusted and more stable and happier in marriage than men with a high need for affiliation. It is possible that persons with negative or insecure attachment styles have characteristics found in many psychological disorders, and such people put relationships under pressure, because they are so demanding.

10.3.5 Social learning

Through various means of learning, people associate their behaviours with the physical and social *rewards* (stimuli) they receive when involved in social interactions. The process of learning may include exchanging and comparing in the forming and maintaining of relationships. At work employees are often rated during performance appraisals on their social skills and whether they keep good relations with other employees and customers. Reward systems condition people in one way or the other to exchange acceptable work and social behaviours for similar treatment from their employer. This principle is also applied when parents reward or discipline their children for being friendly or rude to family and friends. People generally like or dislike others for their affiliative behaviours, because they, or aspects related to them, evoke either positive or negative feelings. This arousal of positive or negative emotions and associated affiliation behaviours is referred to as *reinforcement of affect* or feelings (Byrne & Clore 1970).

Cultural influences are a strong determinant of social behaviour and often the reason for similarities and differences between individuals and groups. Culture refers to all the perceptions, attitudes, values, beliefs, traditions and ways of doing things shared by certain groups of people. It is possible that cultural norms restrict and even prohibit contact, especially intimate associations between persons of different cultures. You may be aware of religious or other groups that place a taboo on marriage with certain other groups.

In this regard Buss (1995) reported research indicating more infants to be avoidant in attachment behaviours in Germany than in America; quite a high frequency of attachment ambivalent (anxious in maintaining contact) infants in Israeli kibbutzim and in Japan. In Japan mothers are nearly always present, which makes separation from children quite difficult. In Israel, especially in the kibbutz system, children often see mothers infrequently, also making separation traumatic.

Even within a specific group, you may find that people of certain status tend to be selective in their associations, and want to prescribe, for instance, their children's friends. Different cultures form associations differently. Western and industrialised societies, such as American and white South African, are often viewed as individualistic, in the sense that people form many relationships easily, but because many relationships are not intimate, people are prepared to leave them just as easily (Franzoi 1996). In contrast, in so-called collectivist societies, such as Russian, Japanese and most black South African communities, people tend to, or are expected to, have more intimate and long-lasting relationships with friends and family (Triandis et al.1988).

With respect to formal versus less formal styles of behaviour, you may observe how peoples of different cultures greet and how they dress. In some white and black cultures, for instance those in America and South Africa, women may consciously dress to attract males or to focus attention, whereas women in Islamic societies are still expected to dress very modestly by modern Western standards. With regard to the importance of physical beauty in affiliation, research indicates that standards for beauty differ between groups and across time, although more agreement may exist within a specific group (Franzoi 1996; Franzoi & Hertzog 1987).

10.3.6 Stimulation

It is generally accepted that humans continuously need a certain level of *stimulation*, often complex and novel, or certain *stress levels*, to function optimally. Social interaction can function as a stimulus for improved performance or other forms of behaviour. Studies indicate that reduced intellectual and work performance can be increased with improved social circumstances and improved social skills (Buss 1995; Argyle 1992). Calvin (Lindgren 1973) found females most frequently wore the colours on which they were complimented, while Grusec and Mischel (Lindgren 1973) reported children to prefer those teachers who gave them personal attention. In therapy and counselling, healing is primarily attributed to the social or interpersonal conditions of the therapeutic relationship, such as acceptance, empathy and warmth (Truax & Carkhuff 1967). Employees, depending on whether they have extroverted or introverted personality traits, may prefer jobs with more or less direct contact with people. First impressions or presences, which often play a crucial part in the selection of applicants or choice of partner in dating, may be based on social stimulation between people.

Social stimulation may also contain or create tension, anxiety and other ill-effects when one or both parties can't cope with the conditions of a relationship, such as not finding positive rewards any more, not fitting into a situation or not being accepted because of different social or other standards. Lack of social support from family, friends and co-workers is often found to be an important moderating or contributing factor in the relationship between illness and health (Ganster & Victor 1988). Some symptoms of psychological disorders are also related to disturbed interpersonal relations (Carson, Butcher & Mineka 1996).

10.4 PERSONAL AND SITUATIONAL DETERMINANTS OF ATTRACTION

Related to the concepts to explain social attraction and affiliation are the following specific factors which could be causes for affiliative behaviours, either separately or interactionally.

10.4.1 Personal characteristics

Despite differences of opinion, there is a vast body of research evidence to indicate that people are attracted to *physical beauty and appearance* in people, such as a pretty face, an attractive body, voice, hair, manner of walking and talking, body weight and length, clothing and the use of cosmetics. This fascination with human beauty may be based on real qualities, but could also be imagined, or an artifact of images and conditioning from "beauty industries" such as Hollywood and glamour, fashion and related media on beautiful people, clothing and cosmetics. These "appearance perceptions" are responsible for correct person perceptions, but often also for inaccurate, positive and negative social stereotypes, vividly expressed by the cliché "beauty is in the eye of the beholder".

Perceived beauty is often translated into a "physical-attractiveness stereotype" stating that "what is beautiful is also good". In terms of traits and competencies, it is a fallacy that beautiful people possess better personality traits and competencies than less attractive people. Attractive people, in some instances, may acquire better social and other skills because of more social contact and exposure to better opportunities and the rewards (praise and compliments, for instance) that arise from such contact (Feingold 1992). However, real or imagined beautiful people are often judged favourably and perceived to have good characteristics and qualities; less beautiful people are seen in a negative or less favourable light. Some research indicates that physically attractive newborn babies (Karraker & Stern 1990), children (Vaughan & Langlois 1983), students (Dion 1972) and adults (Feingold 1992), are stereotyped as having good or better qualities than less attractive persons, such as being sociably more competent and desirable, more intelligent, sexually more warm and able (in the case of adults), and psychologically happier and healthier. Physically attractive people are even forgiven more easily for mistakes, or not easily associated with negative types of behaviours, as Dion (1972) illustrated in a study of teacher ratings of students. Research on legal issues, cited in Baron and Byrne (1994), even indicates that factors such as physical attractiveness, as well as race and intelligence, influence legal processes such as the type and magnitude of judgements.

Beauty is in the eye of the beholder

In personnel assessment, perception errors, such as the "halo effect", might be based on our favourable first impression of an applicant; his or her physical attractiveness. This favourable impression then influences the assessments of all other qualities. Evidence exists that physical attractiveness is an advantage in appointments to jobs, setting of salaries and allocations of salary increases. It even favourably influences the assessment of work performance (Roszell et al. 1990; Mack & Raney 1990; Frieze et al. 1991). Obviously, attractiveness is also related to negative stereotypes, such as blonde women being unintelligent, red-haired females being moody or difficult, pretty women being more vain and materialistic and the notion that achievements are due to looks only.

Research indicates that even if people imagine someone to be physically attractive, for instance from talking telephonically, such imagined impressions elicit charming behaviours from the persons concerned (Snyder, Tanke & Berscheid 1977). Miller et al. (1990) found that despite not knowing the weight or attractiveness of women spoken to on the telephone, obese women were rated less attractive, less likable and less sociable than the prettier and slimmer ladies. In consumer advertisements, human physical attractiveness is arguably commercialised, sometimes even when the product is irrelevant to the human body. In the labour market, physically attractive people are deliberately selected for certain types of jobs, such as in public relations, modelling and marketing of products. During the late 1960s and early 1970s, a certain commercial bank in South Africa had a "perceived" policy to use young and attractive women to interest clients in doing business with it.

Favourable or unfavourable impressions, based on physical beauty only, often serve as a stimulus for initial and further affiliations in the personal or work context

(Baron & Byrne 1994; Franzoi 1996). Married couples and other romantically attached or dating couples have selected partners by matching their similarity in physical attractiveness (Zajonc, Murphy & Niedenthal 1987). In general people will be judged as more attractive, or feel more attractive, if in the company of another very attractive person of the same or opposite sex. People rate their own beauty higher after having been, or been seen, with an unattractive individual (Brown et al. 1992). However, Geiselman et al. (1984) and Kenrick et al. (1989) report the opposite or contrast effect in that people, particularly men, could be assessed as unattractive if the assessors had previously seen a very attractive person, or seen as attractive after the observers had seen an unattractive person earlier.

Inaccurate negative stereotyping based on physical appearance is part of everyday life. In South Africa, in earlier days, a type of woman's hat, a "kappie", was associated in a derogatory manner with either being loyal to the early Afrikaner pioneers, the Voortrekkers, or being a farmer's wife. Actually, the hat provided very good protection while working in the hot South African sun. You may be aware of aggressive connotations with regard to certain types and colours of clothing, for instance the white clothing of the Ku Klux Klan and the khaki outfits of certain Afrikaner political groups, although many South African farmers, geologists and suveyors wear similar khaki garments for their durability.

Perceptions of beauty in men and women and an emphasis on body image are influenced by the cultural and commercial emphasis on physical attractiveness. In many societies people are conditioned to believe that body image is a part of self-identity development, hence the overemphasis, especially by women, on dress, cosmetics, diets and being thin. In general, men are less worried about physical attractiveness in themselves than about being physically strong, but in many women, from childhood into adulthood, an unsatisfactory body image may have lasting effects, such as anxiety about how others assess their physical attractiveness (Hart et al. 1989); they may even experience appearance anxiety (Dion et al. 1990).

Perceptual differences of physical attractiveness also relate to standards, for which little agreement exists among individuals and in groups. Such criteria are often determined by cultural norms and situations. In general, female beauty is emphasised more than male attractiveness, and men are attracted more by female beauty than women are responsive to male attractiveness (Feingold 1992). White women, more so in affluent societies, emphasise beauty and thinness more than most black women. In the latter, cultural norms attribute more value to less thin women, who are seen as better suited for work and to having babies. Lesbians emphasise physical attractiveness and thinness less than heterosexual women. Heterosexual men and homosexuals put less emphasis on their own attractiveness than women do, but use beauty as a selection criteria for romantic associations more often than lesbians or straight women do with regard to partners (Davis 1990; Sprecher et al. 1994). In males, mature facial features, and in women youthfulness, are also generally regarded as a standard for attractiveness (Cunningham et al.1990). This aspect may well be a problem for women, especially older women, when competing with males or younger females in the labour market.

Physical attractiveness is a factor in interpersonal attraction and affiliation. However, we must be careful not to be guilty of "cognitive disregard" (Rodin 1987), judging, assessing and excluding people on an irrelevant feature of their visible appearance.

10.4.2 Similarity

Most research, in Africa and other countries, as summarised in Baron and Byrne (1994) and Myers (1996), supports the fact that real or imagined *similarity*, not only in appearance but also in personality traits, values, attitudes, interests and abilities, is a forceful factor in attraction and affiliation, much more so than dissimilarity ("birds of a feather flock together"). According to what Byrne (in Hogg & Vaughan 1995) named the "law of attraction", liking between people will be in "proportion to the similarity" between them in terms of attitudes and other aspects. The higher the matching or similarity, the stronger the attraction. Dissimilarity will mostly decrease affiliation or liking or at the most not contribute to more satisfactory relationships (Singh & Tan 1992; Smeaton et al. 1989). When dissimilar people associate, they often agree to disagree and keep up a "working" relationship. However (just as more money or a higher salary does not make up for work dissatisfaction), such forced affiliation does not necessarily improve mutual liking. The aspect of similarity is widely applied in practical psychology: in selecting people to match similar characteristics in a job description, and in career and marriage counselling. It is also not impossible that in work teams, people would relate more easily to each other if they are closely similar (Carli et al. 1991).

Similarity of *personality traits* as a basis for initial attraction and longer associations is indicated by findings that close friends and married couples reveal close parallels in personality traits (Caspi & Herbener 1990). When people are attracted to one another because of similarities in physical attractiveness, they may associate positive personal qualities to such similarity in order to affiliate (Anderson & Bem 1981; Sprecher & Duck 1994).

Similar *attitudes* about issues are seen as a very powerful determinant for affiliation and attraction. When people agree on things based on similar attitudes, attraction and affiliation is enhanced (Chapdelaine et al. 1994). Some researchers maintain that similarity in attitudes and values about, for instance, ethnic and political issues, religion, education, recreation, marriage, sport, work and money are stronger determinants for lasting relationships than physical attractiveness, which is often the first impression when new associations are made. Research also indicates that racial prejudice between groups all over the world is diminishing (Argyle 1992); recognition of similarities, which can be facilitated by affiliation, for instance working together and staying in similar environments, is one factor which can change attitudes across cultural and social boundaries (Insko et al. 1985; Baron & Byrne 1994). Demographic similarity, in aspects such as age, race, socioeconomic status, sex and religion, is also a determinant for friendship and romantic associations (Whitbeck & Hoyt 1994).

Similarity in *interests and abilities* is utilised in personnel selection and career counselling to try to achieve a close fit between applicant and occupational situation, for instance, as measured by Holland's typology of personality types and associated occupational types (Holland 1985). Shared interests or activities have been shown to be a binding factor in men's selection of male friends. Women may prefer a female companion of similar values to talk to about intimate issues (Hays 1985). Duck and Wright (1993), however, found that both males and females often associate just to talk, and are not that different with respect to the type of relationships chosen. Regarding abilities, it seems as if women and men may readily associate with others whom they consider intelligent.

Similarity may be influenced by factors such as people's own personalities and needs, cultural factors, proximity (the physical distance between people), age, gender, sex and social status. Rushton (1989) even suggested that people are unconsciously or instinctively attracted to certain others because they have the same type of genes. Such people will manifest similarity cues in the form of similar attitudes and behaviour which might mutually attract them to friendships and romantic associations. Through association and learning, such "affiliation genes" will be internalised, become part of their cultural heritage, and be transferred to feature generations. Bornstein (1989) asserts that this type of biological determination might cause certain people to be attracted to each other, because behaviours seem familiar to them.

10.4.3 Reciprocity

Reciprocity refers to *mutual liking*; if the experience, feeling and perception of attraction in one person is confirmed or returned by the other party. Negative feedback will influence interaction more than feedback of positive aspects. This tendency emphasises the necessity in performance management of employees to emphasise positive aspects, rather than to only offer criticism. Positive feedback must, however, be genuine and reflect the true situation. A false sense of esteem will be created, for example, if a supervisor, out of loyalty only, compliments a colleague whose unacceptable behaviour is observed by others. People may react positively to flattery, if they assess that such gestures are not threatening or not intended to achieve some disguised or dishonourable motive.

As with physical attractiveness, behaviours associated with mutual liking (reciprocity) can be influenced by *perceptions* even more than by the facts about someone. Curtis and Miller (1986) found in an experiment that participants, after meeting for only five minutes and then being fed false information about their mutual liking, reacted favourably toward each other only because of a belief or perception that they

Reciprocity and complimentarity

were liked, a type of "self-fulfilling pro-phecy". The opposite can also apply. If we think that someone does not like us, our interaction towards such persons could be negative too. Some people are better at handling negative feedback and may still react positively afterwards. Our efforts to create new relationships, after painful and ego-shattering experiences, such as losing a job, divorce or the break-up of a long friendship, may be because we need a trusting and meaningful association to rebuild confidence. People's likes or dis-likes toward others may also be a function of self-esteem and attachment needs, for instance being insecure or strong needs for power and control.

10.4.4 Complementarity

Complementarity refers to the possibility of attraction because of *opposites* or different features in people, for instance a very tall woman marrying a very short man; a very outspoken and assertive male choosing a

very quiet and reserved wife; a highly productive company appointing a man-ager who, according to his or her style and work record, primarily emphasises the happiness of people in their work. At first glance it seems as if opposites will repulse each other and lead to negative or unhappy associations. Complementarity, however, can be a source of attraction if such opposing features in people fulfil the other's needs, and if people can find a fit between their differences (Franzoi 1996). Kerckhoff (in Wrightsman 1972) maintains that lasting interpersonal relationships are characterised by three stages. First, the parties must assimilate sociological and demographical disparities (status, religion, race, age, etc.); second, they must then reach agreement on value orientations; finally, they must come to terms with their differences in various areas. Kerckhoff asserts that in the final analysis comple-mentary needs are a cardinal requirement for binding relationships.

Only a few studies confirm complemen-tarity (except for gender, which is a natural opposite) as a reason for affiliation. For instance, heterosexual men all over the world prefer younger partners, while females prefer men older than themselves (Buss 1989; Feingold 1992). In both these instances, the complementarity exchange satisfies status needs; in men their empha-sis on beauty and in women their emphasis on higher social status, which older men are supposed to provide (Davis 1990). To satisfy status needs, women will even choose less attractive, but older and more mature men, but it seems men will not easily select a less attractive and older woman for status only. This type of finding may well fit in with a socio-cultural approach (Howard et al. 1987) which relates women's preference for higher status males to women's exclusion from power and achievement in many areas. By selecting men with status, they can improve their low status role and share power and status through men. If this view is true, the recent empowerment of women in many walks of life may also cause a change in complementary preferences – men may well start to prefer older, less attractive women with more power and status, whereas women may start to prefer men younger than themselves, more attractive and with less status. A socio-biological view (Kenrick & Trost, cited in Franzoi 1996) holds that men select younger women to genetically preserve the attractive features in their offspring, while women's preference for older, more established men is to ensure sufficient resources for themselves and their offspring.

Most research indicates similarity as a reason for attraction to be a much more persuasive and logical explanation than complementarity. Many similarity variables have been positively related to attraction, while few complementary factors have been verified. Complementarity also implies dissimilarity and many studies found dissimilarity to cause dislike. Some of these studies even maintain that some differences will always exist, such as cultural differences and racial prejudices, because these are facts of life (Franzoi 1996).

People may initially even have opposite features and needs, but the effects of close proximity in relationships will often create similarity, even if these are based on consensus or compromise – these often being the trademarks of relationships during negotiations in labour and political disputes.

10.4.5 Emotions and attraction

Emotions or affect are human expressions which communicate our *inner feelings* and attitudes about experiences in our daily lives and toward our functioning in many life spheres, as well as how we relate to others (Forgas 1993). People tend, or have learned, to like things which make them feel good and dislike things which cause discomfort and unhappiness. In general, positive and controlled emotions, such as happiness, love, laughing and even crying, are associated with empathy and nurture, being in touch with our own feelings and good for health and relationships. Empathy, for instance, can be viewed as a relationship competency, denoting the ability to really understand another person's feelings and the meanings of his or her communication and, in turn, to communicate such understanding to such a person. On the other hand, negative emotions like anxiety, anger, fear, hostility and aggression are often related to antisocial behaviour, creating stress and damaging to relationships.

Many researchers have verified the fact that emotions have reciprocal effects; positive emotions will arouse and facilitate positive emotions and reactions from other people, while negative emotions often evoke negative reactions (Clark & Watson 1988; Cunningham 1988). People will often react to how they feel; if happy, other people may be treated well, and if they are unhappy, people may be treated badly. In this sense negative or positive emotions can be contagious and influence others to react likewise (Provine 1992). The "frustration-aggression hypothesis" (Berkowitz 1989) asserts that aggression against someone or something is mostly the result of frustration, which in turn evokes emotions such as anger and hostility. In this respect racial prejudice and stereotyping, as well as conflict between certain groups, may be the emotional expressions of frustrations experienced by people.

Most congenial interactions between people will arouse positive feelings, depending on the type of introduction and the type of verbal and non-verbal behaviours between people. If both parties, on first meeting, experience the interaction positively, in that both experience mutual positive regard (respect), and the meaning of what is said and done is clear and not threatening or demeaning, attraction may follow. Kleinke and Dean (1990) illustrated how opening lines in a first meeting can influence first impressions and attraction. It is important to remember that what we say is often given meaning or qualified by how we say it, and by the accompanying non-verbal behaviours. Consider how you would feel entering an office to start a job and encounter a manager welcoming you, but not smiling, not looking at you and then continuing to read the mail of the previous day, or reading your job application for the first time! People react to what they perceive and interpret, not what they hear. In many work applications, the importance of verbal and nonverbal communications is elaborated on, for instance in customer care training programmes, training for employees in receptionist and public relations jobs, as well as in training programmes for therapists and counsellors. In many jobs and situations *impression management* (the efforts to make a favourable impression on others and in situations) is very important. People doing this effectively may relate well to others and enjoy an advantage in many social situations. Being able to convey the right messages correctly to certain people will enhance the right perceptions and interpretations, which in turn might evoke the appropriate emotions and favourable social responses.

10.4.6 Situational factors

10.4.6.1 Proximity, exposure and familiarity

Physical proximity is one of the most powerful determinants of interpersonal attraction (Myers 1996; Baron & Byrne 1994). Proximity, or propinquity, refers to when people are exposed to each other, and their closeness to each other, such as staying together or near to each other, working and studying together or sharing facilities. This is especially the case if such proximity is functional, that is, people have regular interaction (Arkin & Burger 1980; Moreland & Beach 1992), and not only accidental. Proximity mostly enforces exposure and familiarity. The interpersonal liking effects of proximity, such as becoming friends and getting married, have been proved by many studies (cited in Franzoi 1996; Myers 1996) of people living in the same housing scheme or neighbourhood, working or studying together or using the same facilities. Nearness or proximity creates familiarity and availability, so that in time people become at ease with each other, compare each other to identify commonalities and start to support each other in times of need and in daily hassles, and in this way exchanging rewards.

The principle of exposure is often used in advertisements and political campaigning; if a person does not know enough or is uncertain, he or she will probably choose the most seen, best known or most heard of commodity or person. After certain music had been played in advertisements, people selected that music from among similar tunes, because they had heard it previously, even though they were busy doing something else at the time (Bornstein & D'Agostina 1992). In an incident in America, an unknown attorney named Johnson was elected unexpectedly as a judge, defeating a respected Supreme Court judge named Callow, only because voters had more associated knowledge of the name Johnson. The surname Johnson is more frequently encountered and more Johnsons in various positions were known to voters (Myers 1996). The effect of political candidate exposure on voting behaviours and results is widely recognised. It is possible that if you are told that someone you will meet on a first date, or who is going to join you in your work group, is exceptionally nice, you will like the person even before meeting (Klein & Kunda 1992).

Sometimes exposure may bring discord. After a time people can find that their differences are accentuated by being together. This can be the case when two people, groups with dissimilar attitudes, or parties with "unfinished business" from previous encounters, are forced to stay or work together. Gaertner et al. (1990) found that proximity will increase ethnic prejudice if policies of segregation of opportunities and resources inhibit the development of positive relationships. However, in a study by Van Dyk (1990), it was found that the close proximity relationship between white housewives and their black workers facilitated better ethnic attitudes. Bradnum, Nieuwoudt and Tredoux (1993), on the other hand, found that at the time of their research contact between races in integrated schools in South Africa and Zimbabwe did little to change ethnic attitudes, although they did assert that racial dislike in general was changing in at least parts of South Africa. Dislike as a result of exposure can also occur when people feel that their privacy is threatened or that people are exploiting them by "overstaying their welcome". In counselling, it can sometimes be a good strategy to create physical distance between people to solve problems. The influence of proximity and exposure, especially on long-lasting affiliations, can obviously be effected by factors such as attitudes, values, education levels, socioeconomic status and historical and cultural issues.

Bornstein (1989) explains affiliation resulting from proximity as an evolutionary or biological adaptive response. If confronted with unfamiliar stimuli that threaten our survival, we will, through exposure, change the unknown to a situation which is familiar to us.

10.4.6.2 External events

Similarity in circumstances may also facilitate affiliation. A bonding factor in such affiliations and attraction may be feelings of being "in the same boat" and being thankful for empathy and support. This may happen when people experience fear, feelings of loss and bereavement, isolation, trauma or threat. Married couples or close friends may have met during imprisonment, as prisoners in war camps, during an aeroplane hijack or natural catastrophes like fires, floods and droughts. Chance meetings at social events ("love at first sight") often also lead to friendships and intimate associations.

External events can also be associated with the individual's macro influencing systems, such as historical heritage, ethnic and race group, economic, moral, religious and political policies, which often create a legacy of social stratification, which will facilitate certain relations and inhibit or even prohibit other types of relationships.

10.5 AFFILIATION AND WELLBEING

Social and interpersonal behaviours, like attachment styles, are related to psychological adjustment (Argyle 1992; Craig 1996; Carson et al. 1996). Haley (1963:2), for instance, asserts that "the ills of the individual are not really separable from the ills of the social context he creates and inhabits, and one cannot with good conscience pull the individual from his cultural milieu and label him as sick or well". Many people's emotional problems are really relationship problems, communicating not only about themselves but also about their communication and relationships with others and the world at large. In this sense the "sick" individual may be a symptom-bearer of one or more of his or her social systems (Byang-Hall 1980).

Frustration of infant and childhood attachment behaviours, according to Ainsworth, Freud and Erikson (in Craig 1996), may result in adult insecure attachment behaviours, not only in personal or intimate relationships, but also in various occupational relationships. Examples of insecure adult attachment behaviours are overdependence (Buss 1995; Craig 1996), less competence in work context (Hazan & Shaver 1990), avoidant behaviours (Mikulincer, Florian & Weller 1993), jealousy and difficulties in trusting partners in romantic relationships (Feeney & Noller 1990). When relationships are terminated, feelings of trust, loyalty, closeness, commitment and love can easily be replaced by intense opposites such as loneliness, personal loss, guilt, jealousy, aggression, hatred, pain and despair and even serious consequences such as suicide and family tragedies.

Disturbed relationships may also mean a loss of opportunities for recreation, practising and maintaining social skills and social support. Social support refers to how people are nurtured and helped by affiliation with individuals and groups. *Social support* includes emotional concern (liking, loving, understanding, sympathising); material or instrumental assistance (providing for services, goods, finances); information (advice, knowledge, training); and appraisal (feedback, praise about self-esteem). Social support is viewed as having an important buffering effect on the relationship between illness and health. Close relationships and social support by family, friends, co-workers and the community are positively related to improved work performance, coping better with life's problems, general adjustment and physical and psychological wellbeing (Cohen 1988).

The positive effects of close relations is shown in married people or persons living together, who take better care of themselves and others and are involved less in risky behaviours, habits and lifestyles which may be detrimental to their health (Argyle 1992). From interview surveys Cohen (1988) and House et al. (1988) reported that people with many and good relationships with family, friends and in their communities are less likely to die prematurely, while losing such ties increases the

possibility of illness and premature death. Increased vulnerability for death and diseases was also reported for men and women after losing marital partners (Kaprio 1987).

General happiness with life is also related to various types of satisfactory affiliations, such as having a good marriage, having a good love life, having many friends, enjoying good social support and being happy at home and at work (Myers 1996; Argyle 1992).

Franzoi (1996:328) defined *social anxiety* as "the unpleasant emotion people experience due to their concern with interpersonal evaluation" and discussed various aspects of it. Some people may experience social anxiety as a chronic fear of being rejected even before social contact or when in actual relationships. Such behaviour may result in withdrawal or increasingly awkward and unassertive social behaviours.

Social isolation (Franzoi 1996) is another form of problematic social interaction and manifests when an individual establishes and maintains fewer, or less satisfactory, social relationships than the person really desires. Due to personal and situational factors and the lack of social skills, individuals may have a lonely style of living in which they harbour negative attitudes towards themselves and others and often indulge in destructive types of behaviours, such as excessive substance use.

Langston and Cantor (1989) described a pattern for success or failure depending on competency in social skills. They characterise persons with effective social skills as being positive about social situations, themselves and other people and therefore open and successful in social interactions. Socially incompetent or anxious persons may be negative about social situations and other people, not open about themselves and may therefore be unsuccessful in their affiliative behaviours. Imagine the feelings of a socially anxious person expected to work as a training officer, conducting interviews, addressing people at a public forum, reading a scientific paper at a conference or expected to chair a meeting or arbitration hearing.

Perceived *physical unattractiveness*, too, may have consequences: low self-esteem and even "appearance anxiety" in the presence of certain people. This type of self-esteem anxiety may cause people to avoid contact with people, resulting in a lack of exposure, lost opportunities and inadequate social skills, because avoiding people decreases the opportunities to model others' social skills. A lack of social skills might be evident in indirect contact, as in a telephonic conversation, and possibly even more obvious in direct associations, such as job interviews and efforts to attract someone of the opposite sex for romantic reasons.

In terms of the place and meaning of work in human life, we cannot underestimate the *social meaning of work*. The organisation, work group and co-employees present the individual with opportunities for social contact, social and other competencies. In these environments the individual is protected in many ways and obtains support to perform and enhance his or her self-esteem and feeling of belonging. In job loss, and especially long-term unemployment, one of the most serious complaints of people is being excluded and isolated from friends and other social contacts (O'Brien 1986). However, in unemployment, as in other traumatic experiences and events, like depressions, war and personal losses through death and divorce, those who were able, or lucky enough, to maintain the family unit or other close social support systems were the ones who showed the best resilience in terms of readjustment and health (Craig 1996; Carson et al. 1996).

With reference to work performance Hazan and Shaver (1990) identified a correlation between adult attachment be-

haviours and work attitudes. Persons with secure affiliation behaviours have aspirations to succeed and also enjoy work, while succeeding in keeping work and off-work relationships apart. In contrast, employees with ambivalent interactional patterns have a fear of doing poorly in their jobs and also allow off-work relationships to interfere with their jobs. Persons who wish to avoid relationships try to use work as an excuse not to get involved.

In the phenomenon of *ethnic and racial conflicts* all over the world, and in specific group differences, determinants of affiliation and attraction provide a powerful approach to explain conflict, prejudice and aggression. However, these behaviours may also have other determinants.

A critical determinant to explain social diversity in affiliation behaviours is *cultural differences*. Cultural values, attitudes and behaviours over many generations can be as ingrained and dominant as innate behaviour patterns, as is evident from the many traditions upheld in different societies. Thompson (1991) explains African-American racial identification in terms of physical attributes; psychological aspects, which include a concern for and commitment to the specific racial group; a socio-cultural component, which refers to cultural ways of doing things; and sentiments concerning economic and political empowerment. Although many factors may influence how these components contribute to a person's racial identification, experiencing racial discrimination will really determine the commitment to and support for the specific group and relationships with dissimilar individuals and groups. In this respect a strong racial identification may be a strong factor in conflicts between groups about jobs, money, education facilities, land, housing, medical care and other resources in short supply, which will contribute to negative attitudes about each other, and thus disturb relationships. Political, racial, religious and other attitudes influence actions and thinking, and such actions and thinking indicate beliefs, attitudes and values. In South Africa polarisation and poor relations between certain groups may be even stronger than under the white-domination regimes, as various processes of integration and redistribution of power and resources are still taking place. Racial conflicts are characterised by mutual misperceptions, stereotypes and stigmas. In South Africa, stereotypes about blacks and whites, for instance on cruelty and dominance, will take long to be perceived more realistically.

Such racist attitudes will only change in a completely egalitarian society, not only in South Africa, but also in the wider world order. It seems as if such a state in our world might only be a dream. Franzoi (1996) and Meyers (1996) cite research on racism, which indicates some positive changes, but also that equality might only be partially achieved and that racism in changing times may have new names or different role players. We should also remember that forms of racism and prejudice also occur in the midst of, and between, similar individuals and groups. Baron and Byrne (1994), for instance, cite research indicating Americans associate with other employees of similar status, whereas Japanese will associate with persons of higher status. A possible explanation for this is that of "group" and "individual" inclusiveness, which may be recognised by aspects such as specific conditions for membership and other psychological and physical boundaries. Groups often see themselves as superior to others in many respects and therefore find it difficult to associate with a dissimilar group on many issues or to share certain traditional values. For every collection of groups there is one that tries to be the dominant one, resulting in possible mutual negative attitudes.

The aspect of "uniqueness", imprinted in individuals and groups, may also inhibit social attraction between groups, in that we sometimes tend to believe that strangers will disagree with us on issues that we think they know nothing of. McFarland and Miller (1990) find this to be a "false uniqueness effect", as our own knowledge of things is often not unique. Related to this concept is the "effect of false consensus" (Marks & Miller 1987), the belief that others share our beliefs and opinions, or that others like us or think good about us; if we learn the opposite, such an experience may decrease attraction. If we have consensus with others about ourselves or about issues, we tend to like such persons. In both instances, whether we think others do or do not share our knowledge or opinions, the obtaining of knowledge, for ourselves or to inform other people, may improve social attraction if such knowledge contributes to more realistic perceptions and attitudes about ourselves and others.

Affiliation problems, such as apathy, repulsion, dislike and other negative emotions that characterise relationship difficulties, may also feature in ethnic, race and religious conflicts. Often such problems, notwithstanding continuous negotiation and counselling efforts, seem to be unsolvable. In this regard we should take note of Rosenbaum's repulsion hypothesis (Rosenbaum 1986), which asserts that in social attraction dissimilar attitudes have a stronger influence than similar ones. It is possible that in these times of humanitarianism and emphasis on "oneness" and "sameness", especially in culturally diverse societies, people tend to ignore or minimise the facts of similarity, and therefore efforts to force associations between certain individuals and groups may facilitate repulsion rather than reconciliation.

10.6 CONCLUSION

It may be that one of the greatest human tragedies in life happens daily – our incorrect assumptions that we know how we are affected by the presence of others, or how we influence others, and that when we communicate, others understand and accept our messages just because we have the ability to talk and do. Why, may we ask, is there no end to conflicts all over the world between and in groups? Why are relationship casualties between individuals, in families and among groups so high and why do these and other forms of relationship conflicts often result in tragic events?

Can new socio-political initiatives bring empowerment, development and better relations to people if previous efforts were less successful? In South Africa the new empowering policies, with a renewed emphasis on humanistic principles, human rights, equality, redistribution of resources, reconciliation and healing of disturbed relationships, are supposed to facilitate attraction and affiliation between diverse groups and individuals. The outcomes of these processes are not known yet and renders in-depth research and scrutiny in the short, intermediate and long term.

Perhaps it is time that social psychologists are used more to help solve relationship problems in all spheres of life. In South Africa, as in other developing countries with social diversity, it is important that we do more to create mutual understanding and facilitate mutual attraction and affiliation. It is a priority to really understand how diverse peoples can affiliate and unite, but it is also part of social reality to know that social diversity and cultural differences will always create and uphold own identities, which laws do not change easily.

Self-evaluating questions

1. Explain possible reasons why people establish and maintain affiliations.
2. Use examples from your own social environment and give reasons why physical attraction is overemphasised.
3. Explain personal factors which may influence interpersonal attraction.
4. Explain how in the world of business the principles of attraction and affiliation are used to achieve objectives.
5. Use examples to explain the possible ill-effects of interpersonal attraction and affiliation.
6. Discuss situational factors which may facilitate or inhibit affiliation and attraction behaviours.
7. Identify those factors which you think will facilitate, and those which will inhibit, affiliative behaviours between people in South Africa.

Leadership

11

François Badenhorst

CONTENTS

Learning outcomes

After studying this chapter you should be able to:

- define leadership
- discuss the trait theory of leadership
- discuss situational theories of leadership
- discuss transformational leadership
- describe the difference between transactional and transformational leadership
- explain the various styles of leadership
- explain the difference between leadership and management

Key concepts

traits, behaviour, influence, power, communication, contingency, styles, charisma, transformation, followers, management, roles, definition

11.1 INTRODUCTION

Leadership refers to the process whereby one individual influences other group members towards the attainment of defined group or organisational goals (Greenberg & Baron 1993). Leadership can be viewed as the process of influencing the activities of a group towards goal setting and goal achievement.

It is important to note that there are various approaches to the concept of leadership, including the trait, behavioural, situational and cognitive approaches.

The *trait approach* emphasises the personality, abilities and personal dispositions of a leader as primary determinants of effectiveness. The *behavioural approach* is based on the assumption that effective

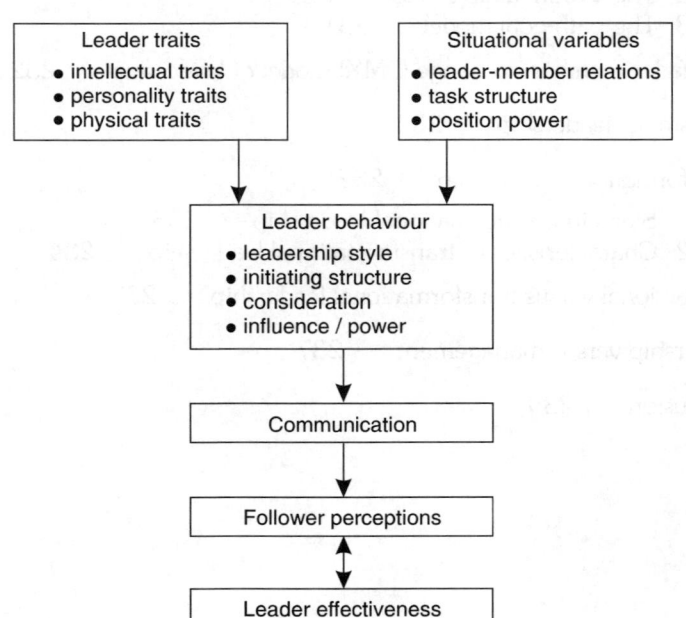

Figure 11.1 A model of the leadership process
Source: Adapted from Dipboye et al. (1994)

leaders differ according to what they do in performing their roles. The *situational approach* stresses factors outside the leader as critical determinants, for example the organisation, task and role. According to the *cognitive approach* the beliefs and perceptions of the leader and followers determine whether a person will be an effective or ineffective leader (Dipboye et al. 1994).

In order to grasp the concept of leadership, a working model of leadership is presented in figure 11.1.

11.2 LEADERSHIP TRAITS

At its most extreme the trait theory proposes that leaders are born with innate characteristics allowing them to wield influence over others (Dipboye et al. 1994). This approach assumes that there are a finite number of individual traits in effective leaders. According to Ivancevich and Matteson (1993) they are: intellectual traits, personality traits and physical traits.

Intellectual traits refer to the dimensions of intelligence associated with effective leadership, for example decisiveness, judgemental ability, knowledge and verbal abilities.

Personality traits have the following five dimensions (Dipboye et al. 1994), which correlate with the five-factor theory of personality:

- extraversion – a personality dimension describing someone who is sociable, talkative and assertive
- agreeableness – good-natured, cooperative and trusting
- emotional stability – calm, enthusiastic, secure (positive); not nervous, depressed or insecure (negative)
- conscientiousness – extent to which the individual is careful, thorough, responsible, achievement-oriented and persevering
- openness – extent to which the individual is imaginative, cultured, curious, original, broad-minded and artistically sensitive

The two traits which seem to be the most strongly related to leadership effectiveness are extraversion and conscientiousness.

In addition to the above traits, research suggests (Ivancevich & Matteson 1990) that the following personality traits are also linked with effective leadership: alertness, originality, personal integrity, self-confidence, creativity, emotional balance, nonconformity and diplomacy.

A critical problem surrounding this approach is finding a valid way to measure personality traits, and much research is still needed in this regard.

Physical traits may also have an influence on effective leadership. They include age, height, weight and appearance, but research in this respect has been contradictory (Ivancevich & Matteson 1993).

Although some popular beliefs are that a physically large person can secure compliance from followers – a notion relying heavily on the coercive or fear basis of power – contradictory evidence seems to exist in, for instance, the example of Napoleon Bonaparte, the French leader from a previous century, who was of small stature.

It is also important for a successful leader to have a need for power and high power inhibition. Power inhibition refers to psychological constraints against exercising power in a coercive or bullying manner (Dipboye et al. 1994). Power as such is discussed later in this chapter.

11.3 LEADERSHIP BEHAVIOUR

According to the behavioural approach to leadership a successful leader depends mainly on adopting the right behaviour, and such behaviour can be learned (Dipboye et al. 1994).

Regarding leader behaviour, a distinction can be made between two specific leadership styles, that is, job-centred and employee-centred, which results from studies conducted at the University of

Michigan during the 1940s (Ivancevich & Matteson 1993). The difference between these two styles can be found in the level of supervision and participation. A job-centred leader practices close supervision (more autocratic) and uses specified procedures so that subordinates can perform their tasks, while delegating is exercised regarding decision-making in the case of the employee-centred (democratic) leader. The latter also tends to aid followers in satisfying their needs by creating a supportive work environment and a climate that is conducive to motivation. The behavioural approach discussed so far can be viewed as a one-dimensional model, as a leader can choose to be autocratic or democratic (Dipboye et al. 1994).

During the late 1940s, research was conducted at the Ohio State University in the USA to develop a more complex two-dimensional model. People occupying different types of jobs generated a list of attributes to describe the behaviour of their leaders, and these were then subjected to what is known as factor-analysis (Dipboye et al. 1994). This programme

resulted in a two-factor theory of leadership, separated into initiating structure and consideration.

Initiating structure can be defined as behaviour in which the supervisor organises and defines group activities and his or her relation to the group, for example emphasising the meeting of deadlines and letting group members know exactly what is expected from them. This involves organising work, inducing subordinates to follow rules, setting goals and making leader and subordinate roles explicit (Greenberg & Baron 1993).

Consideration is that part of behaviour indicating mutual trust, respect, a certain warmth and rapport between supervisor and group (Dipboye *et al.* 1994). The leader tends to be friendly and approachable, puts group suggestions into operation and treats all group members as equals. Such leaders may engage in actions such as doing favours for subordinates, explaining things to them and ensuring their welfare. Consideration is thus concerned with establishing good relationships with subordinates and being liked by them.

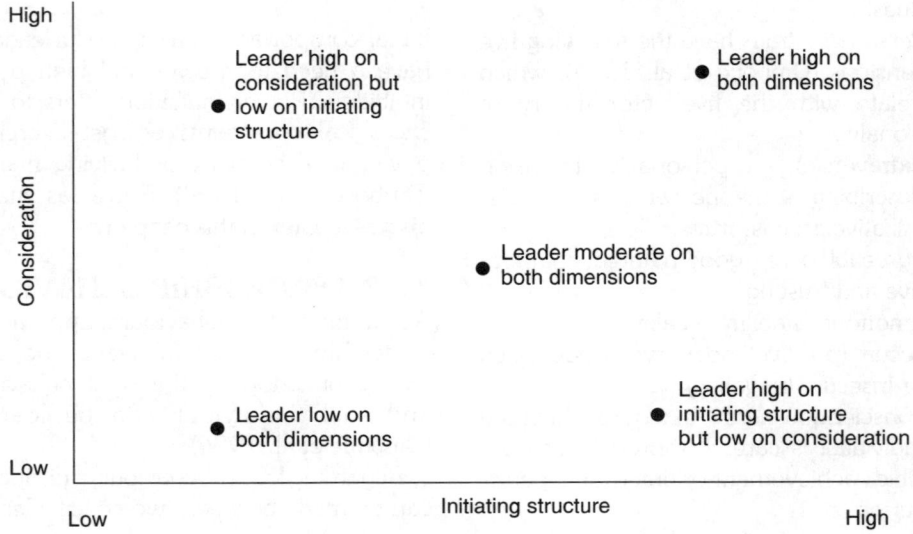

Figure 11.2 Key dimensions of leadership behaviour
Source: Greenberg & Baron (1993:452)

At first glance it may seem that initiating structure and consideration are closely linked, but in fact they are largely independent, and, as illustrated in figure 11.2, a leader high on one dimension is not necessarily low on the other (Greenberg & Baron 1993).

11.4 INFLUENCE AND POWER

Due to the very nature of leadership, a leader will possess a certain influence and power over others. In order to explain this, it is important to distinguish between authority and power, both aspects linked to a certain extent to leadership.

Authority is closely related to leadership in the sense that every manager, on occasion, is a leader who has to see to it that subordinates cooperate in attaining organisational goals, and therefore, no manager can manage without authority.

Power, unlike authority, is not awarded to a manager, but can be seen as a reward from subordinates to the leader.

Five types of power can be distinguished: legitimate, reward, coercive, referent and expert.

In the case of *legitimate* power, authority is allocated to a certain position within the organisation and in this instance power is synonymous with authority. When exercising *reward* power, rewards are given or withheld. Such rewards may include salary increases, bonuses, recognition or interesting tasks. Power can also be exercised through psychological fear, for example by unionists propagating violence. In this case power is *coercive.* Certain unique individual characteristics may lead to social power, a form of personal power an individual may possess over others, also known as *referent* power. In other words, it is personal traits that make a leader attractive to others, for example a manager's personal commitment to his work and consideration for employees' feelings. *Expert* power is based on knowledge and expertise, that

is, a leader has a certain power over others due to their need for his or her knowledge or information.

Leadership

In the context of leadership, power and authority the question can be asked: what is influence?

Whereas power refers to whether a person can wield influence, *influence* itself refers to what the individual actually does that leads to a change in others (Dipboye et al. 1994).

In an attempt to change others, people in leadership roles may apply pressure, appeal to those above them, promise rewards in exchange for compliance, form coalitions, use rational arguments, inspire through appealing to values and ideas, allow others to participate in decision-making and use their legitimate authority.

It is important at this stage to distinguish between position power and personal power. *Position* power constitutes formal leadership in all organisations from top to bottom, whereas *personal* power constitutes the informal leadership allocated to a leader, due to either personal characteristics or qualities, by subordinates or followers.

It seems that more is achieved by using personal power than by using position power, as overreliance on position power may have negative consequences. Position power can be abused, as in the case when supervisors are given power to give pay increases, deduct pay, etc. They tend to use these influencing tactics more frequently than personal persuasion.

For leaders to be successful, leadership must be exercised so that a healthy balance exists between their power and that of their subordinates.

11.5 COMMUNICATION

Communication is one of the basics of all leadership behaviours, with verbal communication probably the most important. The success or failure of leadership depends largely on the communication skills of the leader.

Effective communicators are, according to Dipboye et al. (1994):

- careful in transmitting the message
- open and two-way regarding other points of view (communication is not one-sided and others must be given the opportunity to participate)
- frank in saying what they think
- careful listeners in attention given to the response of the recipient of the message
- informal, in that they are natural and relaxed when communicating.

Management style influences the credibility of the communicator, as indicated by perceptions of others, for example of trustworthiness. The perceived credibility of the communicator influences role clarity, satisfaction and the effectiveness of the recipients of communication.

Another factor influencing communication is the power of people in leadership roles (Dipboye et al. 1994). The greater the power, the more careful a leader should be in choosing his or her words, for example extreme care in the case of the president of an international banking concern, or a communications manager in an import/ export concern. Their communications can have far-reaching implications.

11.6 SITUATIONAL THEORIES OF LEADERSHIP

Any approach to leadership focusing on identifying a style of behaviour or mix of traits to be effective in all situations may be thought of as a "universalist" theory. Such theories suggest that effective leadership depends on the nature of the leadership situation.

The most prominent situation-oriented approaches are the Fiedler contingency model, the Vroom-Jago model and the path-goal model (Ivancevich & Matteson 1993).

11.6.1 Fiedler's contingency model

According to this model a leader's contribution to successful performance by his or her group is determined by the leader's traits and by various features of the particular situation. It postulates that group performance depends largely on the interaction between leadership style and situational favourableness.

A distinction is made between a *task-oriented* leadership style and a *relationship-oriented* leadership style. A task-oriented leader will portray a controlling and structuring leadership style, whereas a more passive and considerate style will be adopted by a leader who is relationship-oriented (Ivancevich & Matteson 1993).

Fiedler proposes three factors which determine the degree of situational favourableness: leader-member relations, task structure and position power.

The most important factor is *leader-member relations,* which refer to the degree of confidence, trust and respect followers have in their leader. The extent to which the tasks the followers are engaged in are *structured* forms the second most important factor, with *position power* the

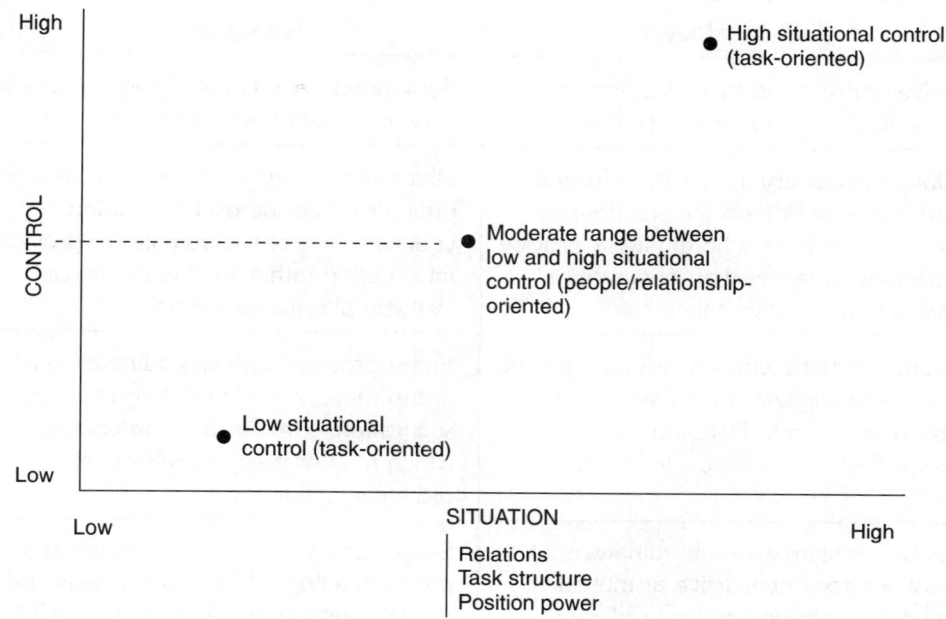

Figure 11.3 Situational control of a leader

final factor. It refers to that power inherent in the leadership position.

By combining these factors, the situational control of the leader can range on a continuum from very high in positive relations, high in structure and position power to very low, resulting in negative relations, unstructured tasks and low position power (Greenberg & Baron 1993). This continuum is presented in figure 11.3.

When considering which leadership style is the most effective, Fiedler states clearly that no absolute style exists and that the particular situation will determine the best possible style to be adopted by the leader.

In cases where situational control is either very low or very high, the task-oriented leader should fare better but in the case of a moderate range between low and high situational control, the people- or relationship-oriented leader would be more effective. Sometimes conditions can be mixed, in which instances good interpersonal relations are often required (Greenberg & Baron 1993).

11.6.2 The Vroom-Jago model

This model was originally developed by Vroom and Yetton (Ivancevich & Matteson 1993) with the aim of having a model for leadership decision-making indicating situations in which various degrees of participative decision-making would be appropriate.

According to Vroom and Yetton (Greenberg & Baron 1993), leaders adopt one of a few basic strategies when making decisions.

Sometimes a leader may choose to adopt an *autocratic* style by solving the problem by himself or herself, or by making decisions unilaterally, using available information. Sometimes a leader obtains the necessary information from subordinates but makes the decision *unilaterally*, which is still an autocratic form of leadership. A leader may, however, decide to *consult* with subordinates, which can be done in one of two ways. Either the leader shares the problem with subordinates individually, making the decision unilaterally, or may elect to share the problem in a group meeting, then

Individual level	Group level
Solve problem and make decision yourself – use information available at that time	Solve problem and make decision yourself – use information available at that time
Obtain necessary information from subordinate – decide on the solution yourself – role of subordinate to provide information rather than generate or evaluate alternative solutions	Obtain necessary information from subordinates – decide on the solution yourself – role of subordinates to provide information rather than generate or evaluate alternative solutions
Share problem with subordinate, getting ideas and suggestions – then make decision yourself. Decision may or may not reflect subordinate's influence	Share problem with subordinates in a group meeting – obtain their ideas and suggestions – make decision yourself which may or may not reflect subordinates' influence
Share problem with subordinate, analyse problem together, arrive at mutual solution, both you and subordinate contribute to solution	Share problem with subordinates in a group meeting – obtain their ideas and suggestions – make decision yourself which may or may not reflect subordinates' influence
Delegate problem to subordinate, providing him or her with relevant information – give him or her responsibility of solving the problem – any solution reached will have your support but you still have to be informed and consulted	Share problem with subordinates in a group – generate and evaluate alternatives together and attempt to reach consensus on the solution. Your role is that of chairperson and not of influencing the group – accept and implement group's decision

Table 11.1 Decision-making styles for leadership: individuals and groups

making the decision unilaterally. In *group* decision-making, the leader shares the problem with subordinates in a group meeting and then, in contrast to the group meeting mentioned earlier, a decision is reached through discussion and consensus.

The original model was, however, revised by Vroom and Jago (Ivancevich & Matteson 1993) a number of years later in an attempt to improve its accuracy and predictability, which involves three critical elements: decision effectiveness, decision styles and diagnostic variables describing the aspects of the leadership situation.

11.6.2.1 Decision effectiveness

It is important when selecting an appropriate decision-making process to consider two criteria of decision-making effectiveness: decision quality and subordinate commitment.

Decision quality refers to the extent to which the decision impacts on job performance, for example a decision on whether the floors should be swept daily or not does not require such a high quality decision as whether or not the organisation should expand.

In order for a decision to be successfully

implemented, subordinates need to *commit* themselves to or accept the decision. Once again, using the example, a greater commitment is required when deciding that the organisation will expand than deciding that the floors need to be swept on a daily basis.

Time considerations play a crucial part here. Regardless of quality or commitment, a decision that takes too long to make becomes ineffective.

11.6.2.2 Decision styles

According to the Vroom-Jago model a distinction can be made between individual and group decision-making situations.

Individual decision-making situations occur where the outcome will have an effect on one individual, and group situations where several followers will be affected by the decision reached.

As in the case of the Vroom-Yetton model, five leadership decision-making styles to fit individual and group styles can be distinguished – see table 11.1 (Ivancevich & Matteson 1993).

11.6.2.3 Diagnostic variables

In order to decide on an appropriate decision-making style, it is important for leaders to perform a situational diagnosis (Ivancevich & Matteson 1993). This can be done by asking a number of questions which correspond with those indicated by Vroom and Yetton (Greenberg & Baron 1993; Ivancevich & Matteson 1993). The questions are:

- Is high-quality decision-making required?
- Do I have enough information to make such a decision?
- Is the problem structured?
- How important is subordinate commitment to the decision?
- If I make the decision alone, is it likely to be accepted by subordinates?
- Is conflict among subordinates over preferred solutions likely?
- Do subordinates have sufficient information to make a high-quality decision?

11.6.3 The path-goal model

The path-goal model attempts, like the previous situational theories, to predict leadership effectiveness in different situations (Ivancevich & Matteson 1993).

Subordinates will react favourably to a leader only to the extent that they perceive this person as helping them progress towards various *goals* by clarifying actual *paths* to such rewards (Greenberg & Baron 1993). It means that actions by a leader to clarify the nature of tasks and reduce or eliminate obstacles will increase perceptions that working hard will lead to good performance, and that such performance will be recognised and rewarded.

The path-goal theory suggests that a leader can adopt one of four basic leadership styles: instrumental or directive, supportive, participative or achievement-oriented (Greenberg & Baron 1993).

By being *instrumental*, a leader can focus on providing specific guidance, establishing

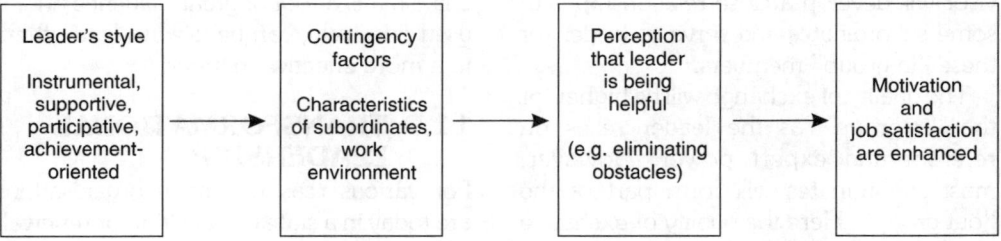

Figure 11.4 Path-goal theory: an overview
Source: Adapted from Greenberg & Baron (1993:467)

work schedules and rules. A leader can also focus on establishing good relations with subordinates, satisfying their needs and thus be *supportive*. A *participative* approach can be followed by consulting with subordinates, permitting them to participate in the process of decision-making. Another alternative is to set challenging goals and seek improvement in performance, making the style *achievement-oriented*.

What is important is that none of these styles are mutually exclusive; the same leader can adopt them at different times and in different situations. Showing such flexibility is an important aspect of an effective leader.

According to Greenberg & Baron (1993) the type of style depends on the contingency factor and is influenced by the characteristics of subordinates and several aspects of the work environment.

An overview of the path-goal theory is presented in figure 11.4.

11.7 THE LEADER-MEMBER-EXCHANGE (LMX) MODEL OF LEADERSHIP

Most work on leader behaviour assumes that leaders act the same toward all subordinates; leaders who apply a high level of structuring are assumed to apply this toward all whom they are leading. An alternative to this is the "leader-member-exchange (LMX) model" (Dipboye et al. 1994).

The initial assumption is that the immediate supervision forms the primary influence in defining the social role of organisational members, and it proposes that the supervisor will develop a close relationship with some subordinates and serve as leader for these "in-group" members.

The quality of exchange will be higher for the "in-group" as the leader relies on referent and expert power. However, most subordinates will form part of the "out-group". Here the quality of exchange is much lower than in the case of the "in-group" and the leader relies more on formal authority, rules and policies.

11.8 CHARISMATIC LEADERSHIP

Another form of leadership is charismatic leadership, and there are numerous individuals who, through charisma, reached high positions in organisations or society and led vast numbers of people, for example some influential political and religious leaders.

Charismatic leaders possess certain characteristics which make them unique and successful, no matter what their purpose might be, whether it be to lead a country or to lead campaigns on certain crucial issues in society.

An important characteristic is vision, and the ability to articulate the vision (Robbins 1993). It would be almost impossible to be a successful leader or to be any kind of leader for that matter without a vision. Charismatic leaders normally have very strong convictions regarding their vision. What makes charismatic leaders stand out, however, is that they portray behaviour that is out of the ordinary. They engage in behaviour that is perceived as being novel, unconventional and counter to norms. They are also perceived as being change agents, in the sense of agents of radical change rather than being supportive of the *status quo*. In their aim to bring about change, charismatic leaders are able to make realistic assessments of environmental constraints and resources needed to bring about change and are thus sensitive to the environment (Robbins 1993).

In order to be a successful leader it may help to possess charismatic qualities, since charisma is a tool of great influence and, if used positively, can be used to lead others in a more effective manner.

11.9 TRANSFORMATIONAL LEADERSHIP

For various reasons, many organisations are today in a state of transition or renewal, adapting to environmental changes brought about by socio-political or socio-economic factors.

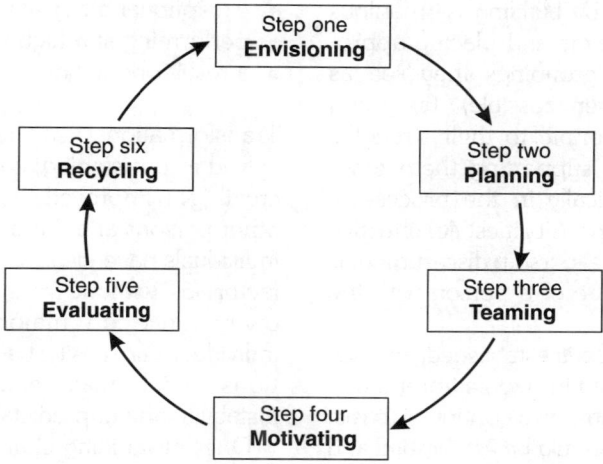

Figure 11.5 Steps in the transformational leadership process
Source: Anderson (1992:66)

The following aspects are important theoretical and practical bases that can be considered for forming a more integrative and comprehensive model dealing with transformational leadership (Anderson 1992):

- interpersonal communication
- counselling
- human development
- human resources development
- organisational development
- transformation of leadership theory and principles
- effective personnel practices

Transformational leadership can be seen as a model of leadership based on research and philosophy. The concepts of transformational leadership are based on validated theory in communication, counselling and consultation, as applied in organisational development and human resources development (Anderson 1992).

11.9.1 Steps in transformational leadership

Transformational leadership is a process involving the following steps (Anderson 1992): envisioning, planning, teaming,

motivating, evaluating, recycling the process through evaluation. These steps are presented in figure 11.5.

Envisioning requires imagination, creativity and an understanding of the history of the group or organisation, in order for the future to be more accurately and realistically specified and articulated. This can be a difficult step as habits are strong and new ideas are accepted slowly, and sometimes there seems to be more risks than people are willing to take. It is critical for a vision to be based on specifying and meeting the needs of both individual and organisation.

Once a vision is captured it can be built up through a process of *planning,* carefully specifying how, where and when something can best be done. It may involve practices such as brainstorming, team development sessions, conflict resolutions and negotiations. For the plan to be successful it needs to be accepted with enthusiasm for both the plan and the vision. The planning process must include specific and concrete goals, objectives and programmes for the timely accomplishment of worthy and realistic aims.

Teaming is of primary importance. Responsibilities should be selectively given to those involved by building harmonious and productive teams and placing appropriate people in groupings they see as desirable (whenever possible), by giving them tasks appropriate to their strengths and interests and supporting them emotionally and physically in the process of taking on their responsibilities. An effective way of exercising leadership discernment is matching the nature of a person with the nature of the job.

Once acceptance is established, *motivation* must be infused in people (for internal and external reasons) on a continuing basis. A reward system should be established and valued with regard to motivation. Motivation leads to action, and higher levels of motivation and achievement can be accomplished by meeting the deeper needs of people.

An important aspect in any planned process is *evaluation*. When designing a plan, evaluation criteria should form part of it and should be realistic, desirable, concretely defined in terms of accomplishments and be measurable.

Due to the complex nature of the process, all steps need to be repeated on a periodic basis: this is termed *recycling the process through evaluation*. During this process the vision needs to be rethought, plans may need to be reformulated and renegotiated, new motivators must be found and regrouping should occur for greater harmony and productivity.

11.9.2 Characteristics of transformational leaders

Various characteristics can be attached to transformational leaders, including the following (Anderson 1992):

- envisioning, communicating and creating a new future
- clear personal beliefs
- sense of mission
- arousing a sense of excitement
- having working knowledge and skills

- exceptional physical health
- performing at a high level
- a result orientation

Transformational leaders are critically involved in *envisioning*, communicating and creating an improved future for themselves, other persons and the organisation. These individuals have *clear beliefs*, an important factor, as without clarity regarding one's own stance on major life issues, an individual can easily be swayed by situations which may lead to complexity, instability and unpredictability.

One outstanding characteristic of transformational leadership is a well-defined *sense of mission*, purpose, values, goals and strategies which are based on a deep understanding of people and the aims which are served and a clear understanding of the cultural, political and economic environment surrounding the change endeavour (Anderson 1992).

A transformational leader is also capable of *arousing a sense of excitement* regarding the significance of the organisation's contribution to society or the contribution of the group to the organisation.

Working knowledge and skills are also required in areas such as human development, interpersonal communication, organisational development, counselling, consulting, problem management and problem-solving.

Physical health is important. Mental and physical health can go hand in hand. Should a leader not possess good physical health, his or her mental health could be negatively affected. Transforming leaders, as should be the case with all leaders, need to be in good physical health and therefore engage in frequent exercise, have healthy sleeping and eating habits and ensure healthy relaxation (Schafer 1987). As a result they are able to deal with mental demands. It is important to be able to handle stress and difficult situations with some degree of resilience.

Transformational leaders *perform* at a *high level*. Motivated by a personal sense of mission, they possess twin capacities of self-management and team mastery and have the ability to correct course and manage change. Research has been conducted in this regard (Anderson 1992).

Important aspects in the exercising of self-management through self-mastery are self-confidence, bimodal thinking and mental rehearsal. *Self-confidence* in this regard refers to going out and if getting "no" for an answer, to move the focus to the next opportunity. Macro and micro forms of attention are combined in *bimodal thinking,* where a problem situation within the company requires a broader perspective. It is also of importance to prepare for action so that both mind and emotions are conditioned positively for upcoming events, a process referred to as *mental rehearsal.*

A peak performer will also utilise course correction through mental agility, concentration and learning from his or her mistakes. It is important to be flexible and to seek alternatives and to do the creative thinking necessary to deal with challenges, a process known as *mental agility. Concentration* includes having stamina to work long hours; adaptability refers to change; and hardiness means resilience under stress. *Learning from mistakes* is crucial in the sense that appropriate action can be taken based on updated information.

One may *have a result orientation* in four spheres: as an individual, as a collaborator, as an innovator and as a facilitator.

As *individual,* the following can be highlighted: envisioning and communicating a clear mission; following up with an appropriate plan of action, including specific goals, complete with bench-marks or standards necessary for assessing timing, quality and quantity of results.

As *collaborator* a "magnet mentality" should be used to draw what is needed from other people. An *innovator* understands that no guaranteed path exists from A-Z, and is prepared to create new paths to obtain results. The role of a leader as a *facilitator* is closely linked to the socio-technical approach in organisational psychology.

Socio-technical design is a way of designing high-performance organisations and establishing a novel way of viewing work and the organising of work. According to Ivancevich and Matteson (1993) this approach is analytical and entails self-design in the sense that people can analyse and improve their own operation. A socio-technical analysis may lead people to establish a work-group form of organisation, resulting in greater worker involvement in long-range issues, which may lead to higher productivity and employee commitment.

Regarding non-routine work, the technical and social aspects of office work are seen in terms of deliberations and discretionary coalitions (Ivancevich & Matteson 1993). Deliberations occur in many forums (arenas in which a topic is deliberated either with one's self or with others – holding a meeting where the topic is discussed) and may be structured, semi-structured or unstructured. Discretionary coalitions are alliances struck of necessity, in which intelligent trade-offs are made for the sake of general objectives. Such situations may arise because of the continuing equivocality of non-routine office issues. As a definitive solution is unobtainable, a process of continuing trade-offs becomes essential. For example, when a new product needs to be designed and manufactured, every function and speciality will tend to seek optimisation of its own narrow subunit's agenda. Such functions and specialities include marketing, production, finances and sales.

Within this context the role of the leader is that of facilitator. During group discussions the leader facilitates the skills and

Transactional	Transformational
1. Contingent reward – exchanges rewards for effort, good performance, recognises accomplishments	1. Charisma – provides vision and sense of mission – instils pride – gains respect and trust
2. Management by exception (active) – watches, searches for deviations from rules and standards – takes corrective measures or action	2. Inspirational – communicates high expectations – uses symbols to focus efforts – expresses important purposes in simple ways
3. Management by exception (passive) – intervenes if standards are not met	3. Intellectually stimulating – promotes intelligence – promotes rationality – careful problem-solving
4. *Laissez-faire* – abdicates responsibility – avoids making decisions	4. Individualised consideration – gives personal attention – treats each employee individually – coaches – advises

Table 11.2 Transactional versus transformational leadership

specialities of the various functions relevant to the matter under discussion with the aim of reaching the best possible decision. In this way the leader does not impose any specific decision on group members.

A transformational leader should also cultivate necessary skills, by developing new skills and by using leverage. It is important to assess what new skills are required and then develop these skills through reading, courses, workshops, tapes, audiovisual recordings and by asking for and getting feedback. Opportunities should also be maximised to use the skills already present in order to stay in a zone of "peak performance".

Teams can also be developed to accomplish results through delegation, by stretching others' abilities and encouraging educated risk-taking. By delegating to others tasks and assignments they do best,

they are empowered. People should be challenged to develop their potential and stretch their abilities by offering them opportunities and projects and giving the necessary support for them to succeed. It is always important to encourage others to take risks for a higher payoff should there be a reasonable chance of success.

The environment has changed so drastically that even excellent leaders have not been able to find solutions for all their problems, and hence the concept of the "learning organisation" was created. A learning organisation is that organisation which continually expands its capacity to create its future. Important concepts in this regard are "survival learning" or "adaptive learning". Adaptive learning must be joined by "generative learning", that is, learning that enhances the capacity to create (Senge 1990).

Within this context the successful organisation will be the one that discovers how to tap people's commitment and capacity to learn at all levels in an organisation.

To be a successful transformational leader and thus a peak performer, the process to gain future success should be managed, which can be accomplished by remaining a student forever, by expecting to succeed, by mapping alternative futures and updating the mission.

11.10 TRANSACTIONAL VERSUS TRANSFORMATIONAL LEADERSHIP

A *transactional* leader guides his or her followers or motivates them in the direction of established goals by clarifying role and task requirements, whereas the *transformational* leader provides individualised consideration and intellectual stimulation. He or she also possesses charisma (Robbins 1993).

There are noticeable differences in the characteristics of transactional and transformational leaders, which are presented in table 11.2.

A transactional leader follows a contingent reward system, whereby rewards are exchanged for effort, rewards are promised for good performance, and accomplishments are recognised. Active management or management by exception is another characteristic; the leader watches or searches for deviations from rules and standards and then takes corrective action. Another form of management by exception is passive management. In this instance the leader only intervenes if standards are not met. It may be that the transactional leader abdicates responsibilities and also avoids making decisions; this is known as *laissez-faire* leadership (Robbins 1993).

Transformational leadership, on the other hand, involves charisma, inspiration, intellectual stimulation and individualised consideration. By using charisma, characterised by vision and a sense of mission, the leader instils pride and gains respect and trust. He or she also communicates high expectations, uses symbols to focus efforts and expresses important purposes in simple ways, and is an inspiration to followers. Intellectual stimulation is used to promote intelligence, rationality and careful problem-solving. The transformational leader gives personal attention, treats each employee individually, coaches and advises and thus gives individualised consideration to employees.

It is important to note that transformational leadership is more than mere charisma, and is built on transactional leadership to produce levels of subordinate effort and performance that go beyond what would be achieved with a transactional approach only (Robbins 1993).

11.11 LEADERSHIP VERSUS MANAGEMENT

According to Kroon (1990) management entails the following four main functions:

- *Planning.* The process of planning can be divided into two phases. The first phase deals with environmental scanning of future circumstances as well as goal formulation (long term) and formulating objectives (short term) in all areas where performance or results are expected. The second phase entails the drafting of realistic, feasible plans spelling out activities to be executed and the resources required to reach the stated objectives and goals.
- *Organising.* Organising refers to the grouping and allocation of activities into main functional divisions and subdivisions. It also deals with creating posts within such divisions and determining the duties, authority and responsibilities of those in such posts.

Category	Management	Leadership
Goals	Impersonal (if not passive) attitude towards goals	Personal and active attitude towards goals
View regarding work	Views work as an enabling process involving some combination of people and ideas interacting to establish strategies and make decisions	Views work from high-risk positions Often temperamentally disposed to seek out risk and danger, especially when opportunity and reward appear high
People	Prefers to work with people Avoids solitary activity as it makes them anxious Relates to people according to the role they play in a sequence of events or in a decision-making process	Concerned with ideas Relates to people in more intuitive and empathic ways
In general	About coping with complexity Brings out order and consistency by drawing up: • formal plans • designing rigid organisational structures • monitors results against plans	About coping with change Establishes direction by developing a vision of the future Aligns people by communicating this vision and inspiring them to overcome hurdles

Table 11.3 Leadership versus management

- *Activating*. In order to achieve stated organisational goals as efficiently as possible, people need to be influenced so that they enthusiastically contribute towards work activities. This process is called activating, which encompasses effective leadership, effective motivation and effective communication.
- *Monitoring*. Monitoring refers to the process by which the execution of plans and instructions can be recorded

as well as controlled through a management information system. Actual feedback regarding performance is measured against standards and objectives set during the process of planning. It is a continual comparison between what is and what should be.

Although many managers enjoy positions of leadership, there is a *difference* between management and leadership. The main difference is that a manager holds a formal position of authority within the hierarchy of the organisation, whereas a leader (who also holds authority) gets results without force and does not necessarily occupy a formal position of authority in the organisation (Robbins 1996).

Leadership can be seen as a process of social influence in which the leader tries to obtain the voluntary participation of employees in an effort to reach stated organisational goals (Kreitner & Kinicki 1995). It involves more than having authority and power.

In order to explain the differences between a leader and a manager, it is best to divide crucial aspects into categories (Robbins 1996) as presented in table 11.3.

These differences do not imply that a manager cannot be a leader. A leader can emerge from within a group or be formally appointed to lead a group (Robbins 1996).

What is, however, important, is that good managers are not necessarily good leaders. The ideal would be to have an individual who is both a good leader and a good manager.

Managerial and leadership potential can be measured by means of assessment centres. An assessment centre is not a particular place but a process. It is a meaningful, standardised procedure using multiple techniques such as situational exercises and task simulations, for example business games, discussion groups, reports and presentations.

11.12 CONCLUSION

Leadership refers to the process whereby one individual influences another towards the attainment of certain organisational and individual goals.

Several aspects influence leader behaviour, for example leader traits and situational variables.

Due to the very nature of leadership, a leader will possess a certain influence and power over others. Where power depends on whether a person can wield influence, influence itself refers to what the individual actually does that leads to a change in others.

One of the most critical aspects in leadership is leadership style. Although a variety of styles may be applied by an effective leader, it must be noted that the style practised at a particular moment should be highly influenced by the situation. In order to be an effective leader it is important to possess a certain degree of charisma and to be a transformational leader.

For various reasons many organisations are today in a state of transition or renewal adapting to environmental changes, an aspect which requires transformational leadership.

As effective management is also required, it is necessary for successful leaders to also be successful managers. Assessment centres may be the ideal process of ascertaining which individuals within an organisation have management and leadership potential.

Although much research has been done on leadership, it remains a major field of investigation which yields ongoing research findings.

Self-evaluating questions

1. Define leadership.
2. Discuss the trait theory of leadership.
3. Use examples to explain how the situation in which the leader functions plays a crucial part in leadership style.
4. Explain the differences between a leader and a manager.
5. Discuss transformational leadership with reference to leader characteristics and style.
6. Evaluate leadership as perceived in your organisation against the content of this chapter.
7. You are the supervisor in a manufacturing department. A high-quality decision is required and conflict among subordinates over preferred solutions is likely. Select an appropriate decision-making style.

Aggression and conflict $\quad$ **12**

Dirk Geldenhuys

CONTENTS

Learning outcomes

After studying this chapter you should be able to:

- define aggression
- distinguish between different forms of aggression
- differentiate between the causes of aggression
- explain the factors that influence aggression
- describe the handling of aggression
- define conflict
- describe different types of conflict
- differentiate between the traditional, human relations and interactionist views of conflict
- distinguish between functional and dysfunctional conflict
- explain the different causes of conflict
- describe the different phases and stages in the escalation of conflict
- explain the five different styles of resolving conflict
- explain the necessity for conflict in organisations

Key concepts

forms of aggression, measuring aggression, instincts, imitate, displacing, anger, frustration-aggression, contagious violence, deindividuation, deprivation, punishment, catharsis, conflict, incompatibility, interactionist, functional conflict, escalation, competing, collaborating, avoidance, accommodating, compromising, industrial relations, managing conflict

12.1 INTRODUCTION

Aggression and conflict form part of our daily lives. We see hijacks, armed robberies, vandalism, assaults and violent arguments almost every day on television, hear of them over the radio, and read about them in virtually every newspaper. Some of us are victims of aggressive acts, physically or verbally, or at least know somebody who is a victim.

We must also acknowledge that we are not only victims of aggression and conflict, but we also act aggressively ourselves from time to time. Our own conduct also causes conflict in certain instances. Some of us find pleasure in playing aggressive games, or get involved in aggressive sport activities.

If aggression and conflict affect our lives to such a large extent, it is not surprising then that they are also an integral part of our lives at work. Just think of aggressive behaviour during strike actions, or damage caused to the property of organisations. We can also think of all the conflict between organisations, between groups at work, between supervisors and subordinates, and even between colleagues. Because of the tremendous influence of aggression and conflict in the workplace, it is important to study them in more detail.

12.2 WHAT IS AGGRESSION?

Although most of us have a reasonably clear idea of what we mean when we talk about aggression in everyday speech, there is no consensus within or across the sciences about its components. To an extent, what is considered to be aggressive is determined by the social and cultural standards of the perceiver (Hogg & Vaughan 1995).

The conceptual differences in the literature are apparent when comparing the following definitions of aggression (Hogg & Vaughan 1995):

- behaviour that results in personal injury or destruction
- behaviour intended to harm another of the same species
- behaviour directed towards the goal of harming or injuring another living being who is motivated to avoid such treatment
- the intentional infliction of some type of harm on others

From a theoretical perspective, it is therefore not easy to give a clear definition of aggression. One of the reasons is that different criteria can be taken into account. Should we, for instance, take the aggressive act as criterion, or rather the intention of the person? If the act is our criterion, aggression can be defined as any behaviour that harms another person. Although this definition links aggression directly to perceivable behaviour, it ignores the intention of the person performing the act. If, for example, an artisan injures an assistant with a tool, can we define the act as aggression? Although the artisan actually performed the act, it was probably not at all intentional. It is therefore important to take the *intention* of the act into account (Worchel et al. 1991). Aggression can then be defined as any behaviour which has the intention of harming another person.

12.2.1 Forms of aggression

To describe aggression more precisely, we have to differentiate between forms of aggression. One way of differentiation is on the basis of the motive or the intent of the behaviour. In the case of *hostile aggression*, the only intent of the aggression is to harm someone. It can therefore be ascribed to a motive of rage, such as an impulsive emotional reaction. In contrast, if harming another person is only a secondary objective carried out to gain another primary objective, it is called *instrumental aggression*. Instrumental aggression can be

"cold-blooded" and motivated by remuneration, for example damaging the property of employers to force them into negotiations.

A distinction can also be made on the basis of the legitimacy of the behaviour. *Antisocial aggression* occurs when the objective of aggressive behaviour is to harm other persons or their property with malicious intent. Prosocial behaviour may be regarded as a reaction to antisocial aggression, for instance in the case of a person who tries to apprehend a burglar. *Sanctioned aggression* involves acceptable behaviour, for instance an act against another person in self-defence. The difference between antisocial aggression, sanctioned aggression and prosocial behaviour depends largely on cultural norms. The individual's or group's concept of aggression must be judged in terms of the context in which it occurs.

A distinction is also made between aggressive behaviour and aggressive feelings. As in the case of intentions, it is difficult to determine the nature of emotions. For instance, what happens if a person feels extremely annoyed (aggressive)? Nothing may be said or done, but his or her expression speaks volumes.

Although aggression has been defined as any behaviour which has the intention of hurting another, it is clear that making use of other criteria will suggest further definitions.

12.2.2 Measuring aggression

Because of the lack of agreement among researchers on the definition of aggression, different measures are used in the measurement of the concept.

Early research studies measuring aggression tended to use *verbal measures* (Lippa 1990). After some sort of provocation, subjects were asked to rate another person on some characteristics, and if the ratings were negative, the subjects were presumed to be showing "aggressive" behaviour. A problem with verbal ratings is that they may have no real consequences for the target of aggression. To remedy this, experimenters sometimes lead subjects to believe that their ratings may actually hurt another person.

More recent research tends to use *behavioural measures*. The so-called "aggression machine" was developed by Arnold Buss as a laboratory device. Under the guise of studying the effects of punishment on learning, subjects were given the opportunity to deliver electric shocks to a "learner". The number, intensity and duration of shocks served as measures of aggression (Lippa 1990). Other behaviour measures of aggression include observed violence and simulated aggression, such as playing war games.

A problem that was experienced in measuring aggression was that the measures used were substitutes for real aggression, or applied to animals. This was done for ethical reasons. How can you justify inducing an actual physical assault against a person in an experimental setting? Consequently, the extent to which findings can be generalised is problematic (Hogg & Vaughan 1995).

Today there are different *psychological tests* that are used for measuring aggressiveness. Tests commonly used include the Thematic Apperception test and the Rorschach test. These are projective tests where the persons tested project their own unconscious motivation into ambiguous pictures or inkblots. Questionnaires, for instance the 16PF, are very popular for selection purposes in organisations. They also give an indication of persons' aggression levels.

12.3 CAUSES OF AGGRESSION

Why would someone intentionally harm another person? There are more than one possible answers to this question. The causes of aggression can be classified into three main groups (Banyard & Hays 1994):

aggression as an inherent part of human nature; aggression as a learned behaviour; aggression as a response to frustration. The different explanations are now discussed in more detail.

12.3.1 Aggression as an inherent part of human nature

People such as Freud and Lorenz explain aggression as the result of inherent and biological drives or *instincts*. They see aggression as a basic human need, such as hunger, thirst and affiliation. Freud believes that aggression is based in one of humans' two basic motives, namely Thanatos (the death drive), which forms the basis of destructive and aggressive human behaviour. Destructive behaviour, of which the death drive is a manifestation, can be directed towards the self (masochism) or towards the external environment, in which case aggressive behaviour will be manifested. Given these realities, our efforts could best be directed toward lessening aggression by redirecting it toward less objectionable targets.

K.A. Meninger argued that the destructive instincts are redirected by the life instincts of the individual. His idea was that these have to be fused in industrial societies, otherwise such societies cannot survive. One method by which aggressive instincts are sublimated is through work. Work itself is therefore regarded as an expression of aggression.

According to advocates of this view, work requires an individual to act aggressively on materials, problems and people in order to change them and direct them in desired ways. However, it also requires them to act with enough care so that materials and people are not destroyed. The dilemma of managers is to manage the amount of aggression, and the unconscious dilemma of the workers is how aggressively they must act to be competent, without feeling guilty or anxiously awaiting reprisal.

Although it is difficult to make instinct theory scientifically acceptable, the concepts are still used to a certain extent to explain aggression at the workplace. If it is accepted that aggression is an inherent part of human nature, then there will inevitably be aggression and conflict in organisations. The effort applied by people to control their aggression, hostility and anger in the workplace is also explained. From this point of view, a trade union is seen as a closely knit alliance and the organisation as an enemy on which they can project all their aggression. The task of the shop steward is then to act out the aggression on behalf of the workers. Does this perspective not assist us in explaining the nature of industrial relations in South Africa?

Acting out aggressive instincts?

12.3.2 Aggression as learned behaviour

Another major explanation for the causes of aggression is that it is learned in the same way other behaviours are learned. The infant expresses "aggression" uninhibitedly and instinctively, but as a toddler learns to express it in specific ways in relationships with other people and in his or her environment. Children therefore learn through a series of experiences when it is appropriate to act aggressively, what forms of aggression are permissible and to whom they can express aggression without disapproval or punishment. Aggressive behaviour patterns can become firmly established in the individual through the well-known learning principles of imitation and reinforcement.

"Do I really base my punishment on my own experience?"

In the process of learning aggressive behaviour and learning to deal with it, people observe and *imitate* the behaviour of others. Primary models for learning are the individual's parents and media violence. Mass media, for example newspapers, magazines, radio, films and especially television, make increasing use of aggressive and sexual contents to achieve their commercial objectives. Children and adults are inevitably exposed to a tremendous amount of media violence. Individuals can either become so insensitive to violence that they accept it as a model for their own behaviour, or develop reactions of fear which cause self-assertive behaviour to suffer.

In a work situation managers and supervisors may also act as models for their subordinates. When persons are promoted to a managerial level, it is most likely that they will act out the aggressive behaviour that they experienced and learned from their own aggressive manager or supervisor.

In many organisations in South Africa workers are purposefully involved in self-assertiveness training. *Self-assertiveness* and aggression are two different concepts that must not be confused. *Self-assertiveness* is any behaviour whereby individuals in their environment assert themselves, communicate directly and openly, and take responsibility for their behaviour and decisions without affecting the self-esteem of others or harming them.

The other principle that applies to the learning of aggression is *reinforcement*. When aggressive responses are rewarded, they tend to occur more frequently. People thus learn that aggression does pay. Aggressive acts of trade unions can successfully intimidate employers to negotiate a better deal. It may then happen that other trade unions follow this example (imitation).

12.3.3 Aggression as a response to frustration

Aggressive behaviour or its acquisition can also be explained in terms of the frustration-aggression hypothesis. According to Dollard et al. (in Franzoi 1996) frustration always leads to some form of aggression, and whenever aggression occurs, some form of frustration is responsible. An individual experiences frustration when either internal or external obstacles in his or her environment block the achievement of objectives, especially when the goal that is blocked is extremely important, when gratification is expected and when goal attainment is completely blocked.

The expression of aggression is not always directly against its source, especially when others might disapprove or punish. People rather learn to express their aggression in a modified way, either when it is safe to do so or indirectly by displacing it to other, nonpunishing objects. We are all familiar with the situation in which a supervisor acts out his or her aggression towards subordinates because of a reprimand from his or her own supervisor.

Is aggression necessarily preceded by frustration, and does frustration always leads to aggression? Knowing that the frustration-aggression connection is overstated, Berkowitz (1989) theorised that frustration produces anger, an emotional readiness to aggress. A frustrated person is especially likely to act aggressively if the environment produces aggressive cues. Aggression cues are defined as stimuli associated with the source of frustration and with aggressive behaviour in general, for example guns, films of violence, disliked persons or a name associated with a frustrater. A cue assumes its quality to elicit aggression when an individual associates certain instruments, persons or situations with aggression. The intensity of the frustration which is experienced and the person's perception of it are the two factors that will determine the relationship between frustration and aggression.

Although it is clear that the presence of aggression cues will increase the likelihood of aggression following anger, we now know that aggression is not necessarily preceded by frustration. The latter can also give rise to other types of behaviour, such as despair and depression, or more positive behaviour such as being spurred on by frustration to work harder in order to achieve goals.

Which explanation for the causes of aggression is the correct one? As with most other human characteristics, aggression cannot be explained by any single factor. It is rather more likely that each of these factors may contribute to a specific instance of aggression or even have a cumulative effect. If one for instance assumes that aggression comes naturally to humans, their level of aggression can still be meaningfully affected by learning, by the relative frustration in the work environment and by the pressures toward or against aggression exerted in the settings in which persons function.

12.4 FACTORS INFLUENCING AGGRESSION

Following the theory that aggression may be the result of conditioned cues, various factors have been identified that influence the possibility of aggressive behaviour. One viewpoint is that environmental factors such as crowding, heat and noise serve to heighten physiological arousal, which makes the individual more sensitive to stimuli that are potentially irritating. Other factors are more related to the individual, for instance deindividuation, which is a psychological state of diminished self-awareness (Wiggens et al. 1994) and deprivation.

12.4.1 Environmental factors

Crowd violence is something that we are familiar with in South Africa. Think about the number of so-called necklace murders that took place in black townships before the elections of 1994, or the mine manager who was killed during a strike in Witbank in Mpumalanga in 1997. Aggression in one community can also be imitated by another community. This form of imitative aggression that occurs in crowds is called contagious violence.

The most-studied environmental factor that has a pervasive impact on aggression is *heat*. Correlational as well as experimental studies suggest that people become more aggressive as temperatures increase, until the heat becomes so oppressive that people don't have the energy to be aggressive (Lippa 1990). Other environmental factors that have been linked with aggressive behaviour are noise, offensive odours, cigarette smoke and air pollution. It is important to take cognisance of these findings when designing workplaces.

Frustrated expectations or mob behaviour?

12.4.2 Individual factors

One factor that makes individuals susceptible to aggressive behaviour in crowd settings is *deindividuation*. Deindividuation is a psychological state of diminished self-awareness and can also be related to mob behaviour. A crowd is anonymous and in a crowd the sense of personal responsibility is lessened, thus making aggression more likely. The following conditions may lead to diminished self-awareness and shifts in perception, causing a sense of deindividuation (Banyard & Hays 1994):

- a sense of personal anonymity
- a high level of arousal, possibly induced by being in a crowd
- an increased focus on external events rather than personal feelings or interpersonal events
- when the group forms a close unit

It is often assumed that *deprivation*, for instance social injustice, causes frustration that eventually leads to aggressive behaviour. Although deprivation may be a root of frustration, advancement may even increase frustration and escalate aggression. The major cause of the frustration is therefore not so much the deprivation as such, but the gap between the expectations and attainments of deprived people (Myers 1996). When there is a rapid raising of expectations, frustrations may escalate, even while conditions are improving. A possible implication is that if the expectations created by the new labour laws in South Africa are not met, then this may contribute to aggression in the workplace. Think about the expectations that are often created by the implementation of affirmative action.

12.5 HANDLING AGGRESSION

The question that we still need an answer for is: How do we deal with aggression? People find themselves in a somewhat paradoxical situation. On the one hand they are taught (and pressure is brought to bear) that aggressive behaviour is taboo and must be inhibited; on the other hand the community "propagates" aggressive behaviour as acceptable, for instance in domestic fights, street violence, some sport activities and as portrayed by the mass media.

12.5.1 Punishment

Punishment is one of the most common means that society and individuals use to control aggression. Violent people are punished by throwing them into jail. Aggressive rugby players are punished by suspending them. At work, disciplinary action is taken against employees involved in aggressive conduct. Punishment, or the threat of punishment, can be effective and is sometimes necessary in reducing violence (Lippa 1990; Myers 1996). Punishment is more effective in controlling instrumental than hostile aggression.

The use of punishment as a method of controlling aggression will, however, not necessarily have the expected positive effect. Although fear of punishment and actual punitive measures may inhibit and even prevent aggression, these factors may also elicit worse aggressive behaviour. Punishment is itself a kind of aggression. Aggression often instigates counter-aggression, thus reinforcing it. Furthermore, an aggressive punisher may serve as a model of aggression.

It can be said that the extent to which aggression is inhibited is a function of the intensity of the aggressive impulses and concomitant feelings, the way in which the individual has learned to handle aggression, the situation in which people find themselves and the person confronting them.

12.5.2 Catharsis

In a therapeutic context, aggression is frequently used to counteract aggression, the assumption being that it leads to catharsis if the individual is allowed to give expression to his or her aggressive behaviour in the therapeutic situation. In other words, he or she learns to be less aggressive and to express aggression in more acceptable ways. The person is given the opportunity to "blow off steam" or to "get it out of his or her system". Several studies corroborate this assumption, but this therapeutic principle also has limitations. The expression of aggression in the therapeutic situation may be based on role-playing, with the result that the person does not experience aggression as intensely as when he or she truly acts aggressively. Furthermore, catharsis may cause the person merely to transfer the aggression to another person or object towards whom or which he or she may feel even more aggressive. Catharsis may also lead to temporary inhibition or fantasies about aggression, which may subsequently be manifested in real aggressive behaviour.

What should we then do with our aggression? Should we bottle up our anger or sulk in silence? These actions are hardly more effective, because they allow us to continue reciting our grievances as we conduct conversations with ourselves. Fortunately, there is, across cultures, an unaggressive way to communicate feelings that better enables the other person to make a positive response (Myers 1996). This is done by reframing accusatory "you" messages as "I" messages, and informing others how their behaviour effects us. An example may be, "When you answer the phone while I am busy talking to you, I feel that I am not being respected."

12.6 WHAT IS CONFLICT?
Conflict is closely related to the concept of aggression. Although the different definitions of conflict emphasise only certain aspects of the concept, several common themes underlie most of the definitions. First of all, conflict must be *perceived*. If no one is aware of a conflict, it is generally agreed that no conflict exists. Whether the differences are real or not, does not matter, it is a matter of perception. Other common themes that underlie most definitions are opposition or *incompatibility* and some form of *interaction*. Wiggens et al. (1994) describe conflict as reciprocal aggression. Broadly speaking, conflict can be described as a process that begins when one party experiences or perceives that another party has negatively affected, or is about to negatively affect, something that the first party cares about (Robbins 1998).

12.7 TYPES OF CONFLICT
The following distinctions can be made between various types of conflict:
- *Intrapersonal* conflict is within the individual. It points to the existence of simultaneous, opposing and conflicting thoughts, feelings and activities. Characteristics of intrapersonal conflict are uncertainty, hesitation, stress, anxiety, depression and sleeplessness.
- *Interpersonal* conflict refers to the existence of simultaneous, opposing and conflicting thoughts, feelings and activities between persons in the same environment. Negative feelings such as anger, a lack of trust and a fear of rejection may be causes for interpersonal conflict.
- Conflict *between individuals and groups* often relates to the manner in which individuals handle pressure to conform, meaning pressure by the group of what is expected from its members.
- *Organisational* conflict occurs when there are differences between two or more personnel or groups in the organisation. The conflict is caused by having to share scarce resources or work activities, or because their status, objectives, values and perceptions of each other differ. The inherent conflict of interest between *employees and employers* is the most well known conflict in organisations. It arises out of the clash of

economic interests between the two parties. While this conflict is usually limited and not all-encompassing, it is nevertheless a permanent feature of industrial relations (Tustin 1994).

- Another type of conflict within organisations that often occurs is conflict between *line personnel* (e.g. production workers) and *staff personnel* (e.g. personnel department). Line personnel often regard staff personnel as watchdogs and withhold information from them. On the other hand, line personnel are often blamed for not following the correct procedures, for example during recruitment of employees.
- Conflict *between organisations* is characteristic of the free market system, and stimulates the development of new products, technology and services, which can lead to lower prices.

12.8 DIFFERENT VIEWS OF CONFLICT

There is no agreement among scholars on the role of conflict. Is conflict detrimental to the functioning of groups, is it necessary, or must it be seen as a given that has to be handled in the best possible manner? Robbins (1998) distinguishes between the traditional view, the human relations view and the most recent perspective, the interactionist view, as follows:

- *Traditional view.* According to the traditional view of conflict, it is assumed that conflict is bad and must be avoided. Conflict is seen as a dysfunctional outcome resulting from poor communication, a lack of openness and trust between people, and the failure of managers to be responsive to the needs of their employees. It is also assumed that conflict results in negative physiological and psychological symptoms. In the working environment, employees involved in conflict make poor decisions as a result of their bias and their disturbed view of reality.

- *Human relations view.* This view accepts conflict as natural, inevitable and part of human nature. It advocates the acceptance of conflict and proposes that there are even possible benefits from conflict for group performance.
- *Interactionist view.* The third and most recent perspective on conflict is called the interactionist approach. While the human relations approach accepts that conflict can be a positive force in a group, the interactionist approach argues that some conflict is absolutely necessary for a group to perform effectively. Conflict is encouraged on the grounds that a harmonious, peaceful and cooperative group is prone to become static, apathetic and unresponsive to needs for change and innovation. The major contribution of this approach is to encourage group leaders to maintain an ongoing minimum level of conflict, in order to keep the group viable, self-critical and creative.

It is therefore evident that to say conflict is all good or all bad is inappropriate. Whether conflict is good or bad depends on the type of conflict. It is therefore necessary to differentiate between functional and dysfunctional conflict.

12.9 FUNCTIONAL AND DYSFUNCTIONAL CONFLICT

According to Robbins (1998) the interactionist view does not propose that all conflicts are good. Some forms of conflict can be destructive and hinder performance and the achievements of goals. These are called dysfunctional conflicts. Conflict that is constructive and leads to innovation and creative problem-solving is called functional conflict, because it contributes to the enhancement of effectiveness.

In the practical work environment it is, however, not so easy to determine whether conflict is functional or dysfunctional.

Conflict that may be functional today, may at another time, between the same people, or at the same time between different people, be highly dysfunctional. There is therefore not a level of conflict that can be acceptable or unacceptable under all conditions and at all times.

12.10 CAUSES OF CONFLICT

Many causes or sources of conflict have been identified. According to Robbins (1998) these causes of conflict, or necessary conditions for conflict to arise, can be condensed into three general categories: communication problems, structural variables and personal variables. These are now discussed in more detail.

12.10.1 Communication problems

Communication problems are regarded as one of the main sources of conflict because communication is the method of human contact. Semantic difficulties, insufficient exchange of information and noise in the communication channel are all barriers to communication, and potential sources of conflict. Semantic difficulties arise as a result of differences in training, selective perception and inadequate information about others.

Robbins (1998) points to the fact that not only too little communication, but also too much communication, may increase the potential for conflict. Apparently an increase in communication is functional up to a point, whereafter it is possible to overcommunicate. The channel of communication can also stimulate conflict. The filtering process that occurs as information is exchanged and the divergence of communications from formal or previously established channels offer potential opportunities for conflict to arise.

12.10.2 Structural variables

Structural variables include size, degree of specialisation in the tasks assigned to group members, jurisdictional clarity, member-goal compatibility, leadership styles, reward systems and the degree of dependence between groups (Robbins 1998).

Conflict tends to be more likely in larger groups with more specialised tasks. Tenure and conflict have been found to be inversely related. The potential for conflict tends to be greatest where group members are younger and where turnover is high. The potential for conflict also increases if there is ambiguity in defining the responsibility for action. When groups within an organisation have different goals, the possibility of conflict also rises, for instance the different goals of a purchasing department (timely acquisition of inputs at low prices) and a marketing department (deposing of outputs and increasing revenues). Although the evidence is not strong, a rigid style of leadership increases the potential for conflict. On the other hand, too much reliance on participation may also stimulate conflict. Research tends to confirm that participation and conflict have a high correlation, apparently because participation encourages the promotion of differences (Robbins 1998). Reward systems, too, are found to create conflict when one member gains at the expense of another. Finally, if a group is dependent on another group or if interdependence allows one group to gain at the expense of another group, conflict is stimulated.

12.10.3 Personal variables

Personal variables include individual value systems and personality characteristics that account for individual idiosyncrasies and differences. Certain personality types, for example individuals who are highly authoritarian and dogmatic, and with low esteem, have high potential for conflict. Robbins (1998) indicates that probably the most overlooked variable in the study of social conflict is different value systems. Value differences, for example, offer the best explanation for prejudice and other common disagreements that are based on value judgements.

Although conflict is most often blamed on the characteristics of the individuals involved, Dipboye et al. (1994) indicate that the combination of personalities in a situation may be even more important than the personality of a single individual. For instance, if two domineering people are assigned to a group and both attempt to control the meeting, conflict seems more likely than if a domineering individual is paired with a submissive person.

12.11 THE ESCALATION OF CONFLICT

When conflict is not dealt with appropriately and timeously, it might be expected to grow in intensity and size. According to Glasl (1982), conflict escalates in three main phases, each separated by thresholds or "points of no return". Each phase also has three stages.

12.11.1 Main phase one

- *Stage 1*. At this stage the parties are aware of obstacles in their interaction but they are still *attempting to co-operate*. Incidental slips into tension and friction occur.
- *Stage 2*. Although the parties are still cooperating, this stage is characterised by *polarisation and debating*. Irrational tactics such as personal attacks, emotional pressure, exaggerated demands and illogical reasoning are now used.
- *Stage 3*. The focus now moves from verbal combat to *deeds*. Negotiation teams will, for example, walk out of a meeting.

12.11.2 Main phase two

- *Stage 4*. The attitudes of the parties harden into *"win/lose"* positions. In order to accomplish their aims, parties look to other groups for support and coalitions are formed. Parties develop

extremely stereotyped images of themselves that contrast completely with the images of the opposite party.
- *Stage 5*. The parties start attacking each other in *public* in order to prove that the other party is fighting on immoral grounds. This usually results in a dramatic loss of face for one or for all parties. Compromises are no longer considered as a way of settling differences.
- *Stage 6*. The conflict process accelerates and causes intense feelings of stress. *Threats of violence* predominate and determine everything that happens. The aim of the threats is to force the other party into compliance. To show credibility and to emphasise commitment to more serious deeds, some acts of violence are demonstrated. This provokes violence by the other side and leads to an escalation of threats, and the threshold is crossed to the final phase of violence and potential destruction.

12.11.3 Main phase three

- *Stage 7*. The *intention to cause damage* to each other predominates. It is no longer possible to achieve anything positive. The parties are only concerned with the other party's damage being greater than that suffered by themselves. The power base of the other party is attacked to prevent it from introducing sanctions of its own.
- *Stage 8*. The parties concentrate on the essentially *destructive* effects of their attacks. The core attributes of the other party are attacked irrespective of the implications for the relationship and the financial costs. The conflict reaches a completely irrational stage.
- *Stage 9*. In the final stage the parties *lose all control* and it is possible that their behaviour can culminate in destruction.

The escalation of conflict is illustrated in figure 12.1.

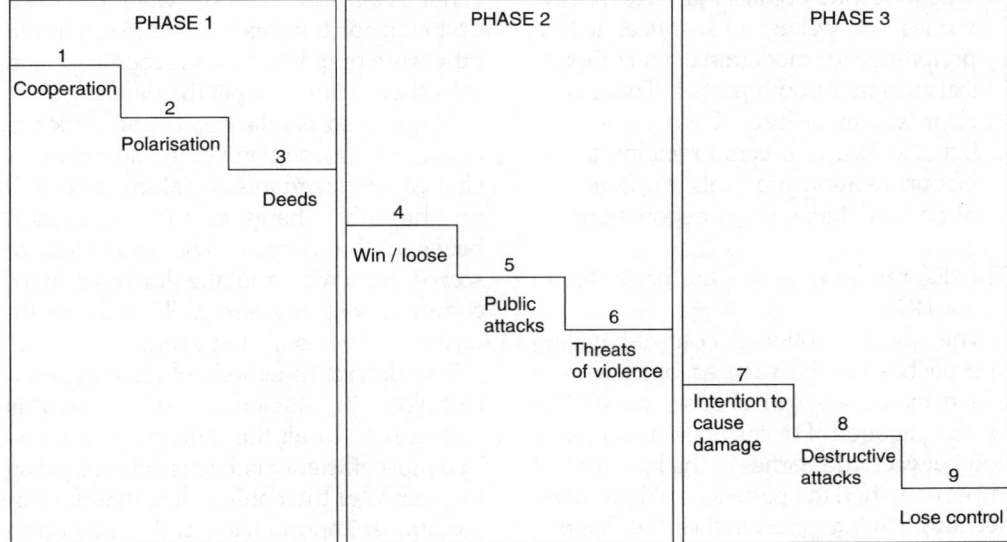

Figure 12.1 The escalation of conflict
Source: Adapted from Glasl (1982)

12.12 HANDLING CONFLICT

Based on two underlying dimensions, the degree to which a party would like to satisfy his or her own concern (assertiveness), and the degree to which the party would like to satisfy the concern of the other party (cooperativeness), the following five approaches to handling and resolving conflict have been identified (Thomas 1983):

- *Competing* (assertive, uncooperative) refers to a situation in which a person seeks to satisfy his or her own interests at the expense of the other party, namely to dominate. In the management-labour relationship, both parties will exercise whatever legal bargaining they have in a given situation. Such a relationship is characterised by win-lose power struggles.
- In *collaborating* (assertive, cooperative) the intention is to fully satisfy the concerns of both parties by means of integrating the concerns. This approach can also be seen as a problem-solving approach to handle conflict, in which conflicting parties meet face to face to identify the problem and resolve it through open discussion. In the management-labour relationship, both parties will give their cooperation in order to reach mutually beneficial agreements. Attempts are therefore made to find a win-win solution that incorporates the valid interests of both parties.
- *Avoidance* (unassertive, uncooperative) is an approach whereby the conflict is ignored or suppressed, for example when you avoid parties with whom you disagree. Although conflict is not permanently resolved by this approach, it is a popular short-term solution.
- *Accommodating* (unassertive, cooperative) occurs when one party places the opponent's interests above his or her own. The party willingly sacrifices the attainment of own goals, to the advantage of the opponent. This normally happens when it is important that the relationship between the two parties must be maintained.
- *Compromising* (intermediate in both assertiveness and cooperativeness) as a

style to resolve conflict indicates that the parties are willing to sacrifice. It is a preference for moderate but incomplete satisfaction for both parties. There is no clear winner or loser. Both parties win but also lose to a certain extent. In the labour relationship, this approach is often used during wage negotiations.

The different approaches are presented in figure 12.2.

The above-mentioned conflict-handling approaches can be seen as *options* from which individuals can choose, depending on the situation. For instance, if cooperation between the parties in the long term is important, then the parties would prefer an accommodating style. On the other hand, a situation can be of such a nature that a competing style is preferred. Some trade unions currently find it more beneficial to win at all costs during specific negotiations.

Research (Robbins 1998) indicates that people rely quite consistently on one of the above-mentioned ways when handling conflicts. It may also be appropriate, then, to view the five styles as *relatively fixed* and not only as a set of options. When confronting a conflict situation, some want to

win it all at any cost, some want to find an optimum solution, some want to run away, others are prepared to make sacrifices, and still others want to "split the difference".

Methods to handle conflict at work are aimed on the one hand at the adapting, or change, of the organisational structure, and on the other hand at the negotiation between the parties. The extension of scarce resources and the formulation of common goals are also well-known methods to resolve conflict at work.

The different methods of handling conflict vary in efficiency. No method is appropriate to all the different situations. The most efficient method is determined by the source of the conflict. It is therefore of the utmost importance that the method to resolve conflict is chosen with care.

12.13 CONFLICT AND INDUSTRIAL RELATIONS

As already mentioned, conflict is an inherent part of industrial relations, mainly because of the clash of economic interests between management and the employees, the latter often represented by trade unions. In South Africa, the Labour Relations Act of 1995 therefore makes provision for a

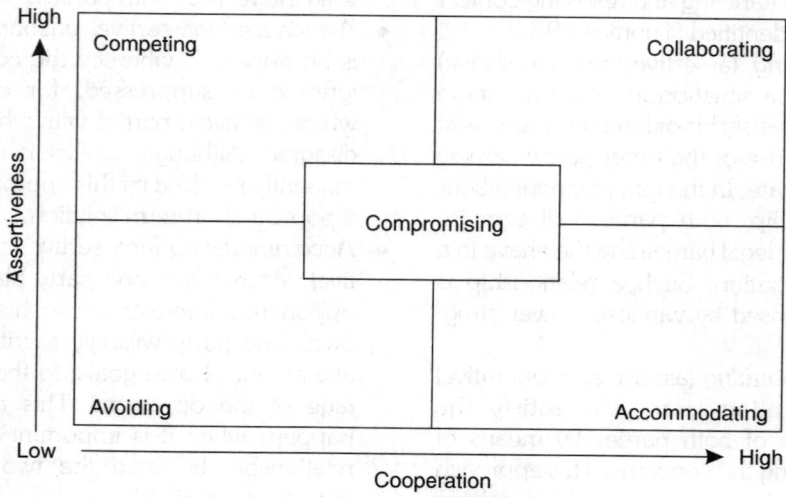

Figure 12.2 Five conflict-handling approaches
Source: Adapted from Thomas (1983)

formal way of handling conflict between employers or employer organisations and trade unions. Not only does it make provision for collective bargaining, but brought about the Commission for Conciliation, Mediation and Arbitration, a Labour Court as well as a Labour Appeal Court, to settle disputes arising out of the workplace (Bendix 1996).

Internal formal structures in organisations are also used to handle conflict. These include the establishment of workplace forums and the use of grievance and disciplinary procedures.

Most of the time efforts are made to resolve conflict in an informal manner, by means of communication, training, problem-solving and other problem-solving approaches discussed earlier. Formal structures and procedures are usually only resorted to when informal methods fail.

Negotiating

12.14 STIMULATING CONFLICT

We have already seen that conflict can be a positive force in a group, or that some conflict is even necessary for a group to perform effectively. Most people, however, have learned from their childhood to avoid conflict. The social environment expects an individual rather to suppress his or her thoughts, feelings or behaviour.

In the organisational context, it is the task of management to manage conflict. If the conflict level is so high that it is dysfunc-

tional, the conflict must be resolved. On the other hand, if the conflict level is so low that the organisation tends to stagnate, or if more creativity is needed, the conflict must be stimulated. The following guidelines will assist managers to stimulate conflict in constructive ways (Cilliers 1986; Robbins 1998):

- *Restructure* the organisation, work groups, departments and divisions. This normally creates uncertainty that may lead to better cooperation, a relaxed atmosphere and open discussion where everybody can give his or her ideas.
- *Act against communication rules.* This can be done by cutting out individuals or groups from communication, or by including new persons in the communication network.
- *Bring in outsiders.* Add employees with different backgrounds, attitudes or cultures to an existing group.
- *Appoint a devil's advocate.* Designate a critic to purposely argue against the majority positions held by the group.
- *Encourage competition.* Introduce bonuses and other incentive schemes.
- *Choose managers* according to the situation and the characteristics of the group.

12.15 CONCLUSION

As discussed in this chapter, conflict is to a certain extent regarded as necessary in the functioning of organisations, whereas it was seen as unacceptable in the past. The emphasis is now on the management of conflict. This implies that conflict at times has to be stimulated. Ascribing "aggressiveness" to a person in the workplace is, however, seldom regarded as a virtue. If aggression is, however, seen as energy, people would not be able to do a day's work without possessing a certain amount of it. This would assume that aggression is an inherent part of human nature. This does not deny the importance of the influence of learning, frustration or other environmental factors. Because of the important contribution that can still be made by the view that aggression is an inherent part of human nature, it is hoped that more research will be done in future, especially on ways to make this view scientifically more acceptable.

Self-evaluating questions

1. Discuss the contributions of the different theories to the understanding of the causes of aggression.
2. Compare the different ways of handling aggression.
3. Differentiate between the types of conflict.
4. Compare the traditional, the human relations and the interactionist views of conflict.
5. Relate the management of conflict with the concepts of "functional" and "dysfunctional" conflict.
6. By means of practical examples, describe the causes of conflict and suggest ways of handling the different situations.
7. Describe the different phases of the escalation of conflict and identify the stages, using a practical example from the workplace.

Group behaviour

Frans Cilliers

13

CONTENTS

Learning outcomes

After studying this chapter you should be able to:

- define groups and describe types of groups
- discuss reasons for and stages of group development
- explain various aspects of group structure
- evaluate the importance of group norms
- compare process to dynamics in group functioning
- describe group tasks and group cohesion
- explain group decision-making by comparing advantages and disadvantages
- explain effectiveness and efficiency in group decision-making
- evaluate the role of groupthink and groupshift in group decision-making
- discuss various techniques used in group decision-making
- explain group facilitation by emphasising the role and training of the facilitator
- provide some explanations of how prejudice and discrimination develop
- indicate how prejudice and discrimination can be reduced

Key concepts

group, development, structure, process, dynamics, cohesion, group decision-making, group facilitation

13.1 INTRODUCTION

Group behaviour can be studied from different viewpoints, for example the psychodynamic, humanistic and systems thinking approaches. For the purpose of this chapter, a more practical and integrated approach is used.

13.2 BACKGROUND TO GROUP BEHAVIOUR

The following general knowledge is necessary to understand the working of groups in a work situation.

13.2.1 The unavoidability of groups

Participation in group activities is unavoidable and part of everyday activities, as found in family, sport, recreational, church and work groups. In modern work organisations employees are mostly grouped in various types of groups for formal work, informal activities and recreational activities. Individuals, in addition to the contribution made through their own jobs, collectively contribute to the group dynamics, corporate culture and climate in determining individual and organisational effectiveness. Work groups are powerful sources for employees' identification, need satisfaction and support, but may also contribute to employee stress and frustrations.

13.2.2 The field of study

The literature on group behaviour stems from social psychology, and more specifically from group psychology, defined as the study of the influence of a group on the behaviour of the individual, or the study of the behaviour of groups (Plug et al. 1986:129). This field of study focuses particularly on group characteristics and processes on the one hand, and group dynamics on the other hand.

Group processes are the cause-and-effect relationships that exist in the group and the study of their development (Robbins 1996). The idea here is that "a group is more than the sum total of the behaviour of each individual member".

Group dynamics refer to the psychodynamics of groups (De Board 1978) and the unconscious elements that influence the individual as micro-system, the group as meso-system and the organisation as macro-system. Unconscious behaviour refers to the manifestation of dependency; fight or flight; pairing in the group; the level of anxiety in the group; defence mechanisms against anxiety, such as projections onto someone or something else; and the containment of this energy (Bion 1989; Hirschhorn 1993; Miller 1993; Obholzer & Roberts 1994). In a broader sense group dynamics refer to all group characteristics and group factors, as discussed in this chapter, that determine a group's effectiveness. In organisations, groups and their powerful forces must be understood and managed well, so that the supportive properties of groups can be used to obtain desirable consequences for the individual and organisation.

This field of study also focuses on the application in organisations, which are themselves examples of complex groups. The role played by groups is increasingly being recognised in this field of study (Gibson et al. 1991; Muchinsky 1983; Randolph & Blackburn 1989; Robbins 1996; Steers 1991). Groups are even being called the building blocks of the organisation. Research by Organ and Bateman (1986:459) indicates that the average manager devotes approximately 80% of his or her time to group activities. An organisation is a living, open system of groups, individuals and other components and all their interrelated relationships.

13.3 DEFINITION OF GROUPS

A group is defined as two or more persons who are united by a common interest, characteristic or bond, and whose activities

Group interaction

influence each other (Plug et al. 1986:129). The members of a group may be together or separate. Schein (1980:145) defines a group as any number of people who are in *interaction* with one another, are psychologically aware of one another and who experience one another as a group. Robbins' (1996:294) definition corresponds largely with the last mentioned, although he puts more emphasis on the interaction of the members with one another and the interdependence in an effort to achieve a specific goal: a group is defined as two or more individuals, interacting and interdependent, who have come together to achieve particular objectives. Furnham (1997:429) integrates all these views in his definition of a group as "persons (more than two, which is a dyad) who communicate regularly, share goals and interact with each other over time, so building up affective (or emotional) bonds". All these definitions emphasise one or more of the following defining characteristics of groups:

- social interaction which allows people to communicate and to exert influence on each other
- agreed on or common goals and targets in order to achieve certain objectives
- group structure such as tasks, roles and rules to enable interaction over and across time and situations
- group members acknowledge or perceive themselves as a group

13.4 TYPES OF GROUPS

Groups can either be formal or informal, but other classifications can also be made:

- *Formal groups* refer to those defined by the organisation's structure, with designated work assignments and established tasks. All activities that one should engage in are stipulated by and directed towards organisational goals.
- *Informal groups,* in contrast, are alliances that are neither formally structured nor organisationally determined.

These groups are natural formations in the work environment that appear in response to the need for social contact. Informal groups provide a very important service by satisfying their members' social needs. Sometimes they also act as a support group to members in times of difficulty and could have a profound effect on members' behaviour.

- A *command group* is determined by the organisation's structure. It is composed of subordinates and the manager to whom they directly report. A director and his or her managers form a command group.
- A *task group,* which is also organisationally determined, represents those working together to complete a job task. However, a task group's boundaries are not limited to its immediate hierarchical superior. Reprimanding a worker, for instance, may require communication and coordination between a director, a manager, an industrial psychologist and a union representative. Such a formation would constitute a task group. Robbins (1996) mentions that all command groups are task groups as well, but because task groups can cut across the organisation, the reverse need not be true.
- An *interest group* exists when people, who may or may not be aligned into common command or task groups, affiliate to attain a specific objective with which each is concerned. Employees who stand together to improve fringe benefits can be classified as an interest group.
- A *friendship group* exists when individual group members have one or more common characteristics. Social alliances, which frequently extend outside the work situation, can be based on similar age, living in the same neighbourhood or taking part in the same after-hours activities.

13.5 REASONS FOR GROUP DEVELOPMENT

Individuals may be encouraged to join groups for various reasons. Because most people belong to a number of groups, it is obvious that different groups provide different benefits to their members. Important reasons for joining a group are related to need satisfaction, such as the need for security, status, self-esteem, affiliation, power and goal achievement (Maslow 1971).

The reasons for group forming may also be responsible for intergroup behaviours, such as cooperation, competition and conflict. The latter, especially, can be destructive in organisations if not managed correctly. Intergroup conflict may be caused when different groups have to work together on tasks; when one group is dependent on tasks from another group; when groups differ in the speed, quantity and quality of their work; when they are dependent on the same resources, such as processes, environments and customers.

13.5.1 Stages of group development

There seems to be no standardised pattern of group development. The most popular views are that groups develop in five stages or according to the punctuated-equilibrium model. To create effective work groups, it is necessary that the dynamics of group development be managed well in order to get synergy, that is, attitudes of cooperation or combined action, among group members. Group members must experience the characteristics of a group, know their goals and tasks and have the necessary equipment and ongoing support in order to be effective in task completion.

13.5.2 The five-stage model of group development

The five stages of group development are called forming, storming, norming, performing and adjourning:

- *Forming* is characterised by a great deal of uncertainty, as an emotional undertone, about the group's purpose, structure and leadership. Group members are aware of a vacuum and dependency manifests. Members "test the waters" to determine what types of behaviour are acceptable. The group defends against the discomfort by making use of defence mechanisms such as suppression, denial and projection – especially toward a leader who does not help to remove the discomfort. This stage is complete when members start to think of themselves as part of a group.

- *Storming* is a phase of intragroup conflict. Members accept the existence of the group, but there is resistance to the constraints that the group imposes on individuality. Furthermore, there is conflict over who will control the group. Aggression also manifests in the form of fight (against authority or peers) or flight (leaving the group or talking about irrelevant issues to escape from a difficult current situation). Another way to cope with the uncertainty is to form pairings (such as management/others, males/females, blacks/whites, members with long/short tenure). When this stage is complete, there will be a relatively clear hierarchy of leadership within the group.

- *Norming* happens when close relationships develop and the group demonstrates cohesiveness. There is now a strong sense of group identity and camaraderie. Rules are laid down in explicit or implicit ways. This stage is completed when the group structure solidifies and the group has assimilated a common set of expectations of what defines correct member behaviour.

- *Performing* manifests in a fully functioning and accepting group. Group energy moves from getting to know and understand each other to performing the task at hand. For permanent working groups this is the last stage of development.

- *Adjourning* or *mourning* happens when the task is completed, for example in a temporary group such as a committee. The group prepares for its disbandment. There is a sense of leaving, "dying" and preparing for what follows. High task performance is no longer the group's top priority. Instead, attention is directed toward wrapping up activities. Responses of group members vary in this stage. Some are optimistic, basking in the group's accomplishments. Others may be depressed over the loss of camaraderie and friendships gained during the work group's life.

Many interpreters of the five-stage model have assumed that a group becomes more effective as it progresses through the first four stages. While this assumption may be generally true, what makes a group effective is more complex than this model acknowledges. Under some conditions, high levels of conflict are conducive to high group performance. This means that situations may occur where groups in the storming phase outperform those in the norming or performing phases. Similarly, groups do not always proceed clearly from one stage to the next. Sometimes several stages go on simultaneously, as when groups are storming and performing at the same time. Groups even occasionally regress to previous stages. Therefore, even the strongest proponents of this model do not assume that all groups follow its five-stage process precisely, or that the performance phase is always the most important.

13.5.3 The punctuated-equilibrium model

This model suggests that groups do not develop in a universal sequence of stages. What is important is the consistency of the timing when groups form and change the way they work. More specifically, the following has been found:

- The first meeting sets the group's direction.
- The first phase of group existence is one of inertia (inactivity).
- A transition takes place at the end of the first phase, which occurs exactly when the group has used up half its allotted time.
- Major changes are initiated with the transition.
- A second phase of inertia follows the transition.
- The group's last meeting is characterised by markedly accelerated activity.

The first meeting sets the group's *direction*. A framework of behavioural patterns and assumptions, through which the group will approach its project, emerges in this first meeting. These are lasting patterns that can appear as early as the first few seconds of the group's life. Once set, the group's direction becomes "written in stone" and is unlikely to be re-examined throughout the first half of the group's life. This is a period of inertia, that is, the group tends to stand still or become locked in a fixed course of action. Even if it gains new insights that challenge initial patterns and assumptions, the group is incapable of acting on these new insights in phase one.

One of the more interesting discoveries about this model was that each group experienced its transition at the same point in its life – precisely halfway between its first meeting and its official deadline – despite the fact that some groups may spend as little as an hour on their project, while others may spend six months. It is as if the groups universally experience a midlife crisis at this point. The midpoint is like an alarm clock, heightening members' awareness that their time is limited and that they need to "get moving".

This transition ends phase one and is characterised by a concentrated burst of changes, the dropping of old patterns and the adoption of new perspectives. The transition sets a revised direction for phase two.

Phase two represents a new equilibrium or period of *inertia*. In this phase, the group executes plans created during the transition period. The group's last meeting is characterised by a final burst of activity to finish its work.

A typical example is the following: A project team meets for the first time and a basic timetable is established. Members size up one another. They agree that they have nine weeks to complete their project. The project manager's requirements are discussed and debated. From that point, the group meets regularly to carry out its activities. About four or five weeks into the project, however, problems are confronted. Criticism is taken seriously. Discussion becomes more open. The group reassesses its position and aggressively moves to make the necessary changes. If the right changes are made, the group will develop a first-rate project within the next four or five weeks. The group's last meeting, which will take place just before the project is due for completion, will last longer than the others. During this meeting all final issues will be discussed and details resolved.

In summary, the punctuated-equilibrium model characterises groups as exhibiting long periods of inertia interspersed with brief revolutionary changes, triggered primarily by their members' awareness of time and deadlines. Or, to use the terminology of the five-stage group development model, the group begins by combining the forming and norming stages, then goes through a period of low performing, and finally, adjourning.

13.6 GROUP STRUCTURE

A working group is not an unorganised mob. It has a clear structure that shapes the behaviour of members and explains and predicts individual and group behaviour. Structural variables include formal leadership, roles, norms, conformity, group status, group size and composition.

13.6.1 Formal leadership

Almost every work group has a formal leader. He or she is typically identified by titles such as unit or department manager, supervisor, foreman, project leader, task force head or committee chair. This leader can play an important role in the group's success.

Research into the effects of leader traits on group performance is inconclusive. Situational variables, such as the task structure in the jobs and the characteristics of followers, are definite moderators of group leadership. For high group satisfaction, participative leadership seems to be more effective than an autocratic style. However, participation does not necessarily lead to higher performance. In some situations, the group guided by a directive, autocratic leader will outperform its participative counterpart.

13.6.2 Roles

Group members have distinctive roles in their groups. Roles refers to a set of expected behaviour patterns attributed to someone occupying a given position in the group. The understanding of the role is often complicated by the individual playing different roles in an inconsistent way. A number of diverse roles, both on and off the job, are filled (or played) in this way. The task in understanding and managing group behaviour is to grasp the role that the individual is currently filling. An example is that of an individual with various, often conflicting, roles at work, home and in society. These different roles demand various behaviours, which are difficult to integrate into the normal flow of life.

13.6.2.1 Role identity

The attitudes and actual behaviours consistent with a role create the individual's role identity. The individual has the ability to shift roles rapidly when recognising that the situation and its demands require changes. This could happen if a pro-union attitude changes to a pro-management attitude when the individual is promoted to a senior management position.

13.6.2.2 Role perception
People's view of how they are supposed to act in a given situation is described as their role perception. The interpretation of how to behave will lead to specific behaviour. These perceptions are formed from stimuli around people: friends, books, movies, television and many more. Even a television series about medical doctors or lawyers may influence perceptions of how to behave.

13.6.2.3 Role expectation
Role expectation is defined as how others believe the individual should act in a given situation. Thus behaviour is determined by the role as it is defined in the context (for example family and society) in which people act. The expectations about how a cabinet minister should act (possibly dignified) and how a rugby player should act (possibly aggressive, inspiring) are quite different. When role expectations are concentrated into generalised categories, role stereotypes evolve. An example is the role stereotype of females at home and in careers. Today, roles at home are often shared by males and females; women are found at all levels of the labour market, and many aspire to professional and managerial positions, rather than to "traditional" female tasks and jobs. Because of this, many people have changed their role expectations of women, and similarly, many women carry new role perceptions.

Expectations are embodied in the *psychological contract* between employees and their employer, an unwritten contract about mutual expectations that defines the behavioural expectations in roles. Problems may occur when role expectations, implied in the psychological contract, are

not met. If management does not keep its part of the bargain, negative repercussions on employee performance and satisfaction can be expected. When employees fail to live up to expectations, the result is usually some form of disciplinary action up to and including discharge. The psychological contract should be recognised as a "powerful determiner of behaviour in organisations" (Robbins 1996:306). It points out the importance of accurately communicating role expectations.

13.6.2.4 Role conflict
Role conflict occurs when an individual is confronted by divergent role expectations. It exists when an individual finds that compliance with one role requirement may result in greater difficulty in complying with another. The extreme case would be a situation in which two or more role expectations are mutually contradictory. For instance, the difficulty in reconciling the expectations placed on the individual as manager, colleague and friend on the one hand, and husband or wife, father or mother and caretaker on the other hand, may lead to conflict in choosing between work and home.

The critical issue is how role conflicts, imposed by divergent expectations within the organisation, impact on behaviour. They tend to increase internal tension and frustration, resulting in different behavioural responses in, and outside of, the work situation, such as:

- giving formalised bureaucratic responses. An example is where a worker is faced with the conflicting requirements imposed by head office on the one hand and a dissatisfied customer on the other. This conflict can be resolved by relying on the rules, regulations and procedures that govern organisational activities.
- withdrawal, stalling, negotiating or redefining the facts or the situation to make them appear congruent, that is, not conflicting.

13.6.3 Norms

Norms exist in every life situation: not talking loudly in a cinema; employees not criticising their bosses in public; families supporting one another. All groups have established norms, meaning standards of behaviour that are shared by the group's members, and which provide guidance of what to do or not to do in certain circumstances. When agreed on and accepted by the group, norms act as a means of influencing the behaviour of group members with a minimum of external controls. In an organisational context the rules and regulations can be seen as the formalised "written down" norms, setting out rules and procedures for employees to follow. However, most norms are informal. It will generally be unacceptable to stand around and make a noise when the managing director visits the office. In a job interview an individual will not speak about conflicts with his or her boss, but rather about the inadequate opportunities for advancement or un-important and meaningless work – giving the socially desirable responses.

A work group's norms are like an individual's fingerprints – each is unique. However, the following common classes of norms appear in most work groups:

- *Performance-related processes.* Work groups typically provide their members with explicit cues on what to do, how to work, and related expectations and processes. These norms are extremely powerful in affecting an individual employee's performance and are capable of significantly modifying a performance prediction that was based solely on the employee's ability and level of personal motivation.
- *Appearance factors.* These include appropriate dress, when to dress formally, loyalty to the work group or organisation, when to look busy and when it is acceptable to relax slightly. However, even when not explicit, norms frequently

develop to even dictate the kind of clothing that should be worn to work. Presenting an appearance of loyalty is important in many work groups and organisations. For instance, in many organisations, especially among professional employees and those in the executive ranks, it is considered inappropriate to be openly looking for another job. This concern for demonstrating loyalty, incidentally, often explains why ambitious aspirants to top management positions in an organisation willingly take work home at night, go in on weekends and accept transfers to places they would prefer not to live in.

- *Informal social arrangements.* These norms come from informal work groups and primarily regulate social interactions within the group – with whom group members have lunch or friendships on and off the job.
- *Allocation of resources.* These norms can originate in the group or in the organisation and cover aspects such as pay, assignment of difficult jobs and allocation of new tools and equipment. In some organisations, for example, new personal computers are distributed equally to all groups. Every department might get five, regardless of the number of people in the department or their need for the computers. In another organisation, equipment is allocated to those groups who can make the best use of it. Some departments might get 20 computers and some none. These resource allocation norms can have a direct impact on employee satisfaction and an indirect effect on group performance.

Norms typically develop gradually as group members learn what behaviours are necessary for the group to function effectively. Critical events in the group might short-circuit the process and quickly solidify new norms. Most norms develop in one or more of the following four ways:

- *Explicit statements made by a group member.* This is often the group's supervisor or a powerful member. The group leader might, for instance, specifically say that no personal phone calls are allowed during working hours or that coffee breaks are to be kept to 10 minutes.
- *Critical events in the group's history.* These set important precedents. A bystander, for example, is injured while standing too close to a machine and, from that point on, members of the work group regularly monitor each other to ensure that no one other than the operator gets within 2 m of any machine.
- *Primacy.* The first behaviour pattern that emerges in a group frequently sets group expectations. Groups of student friends, for example, often stake out seats near each other on the first day of class and become perturbed if an outsider takes "their" seats in classes.
- *Carry-over behaviours from past situations.* Group members bring expectations with them from other groups of which they have been members. This explains why work groups typically prefer to add new members who are similar to current ones in background and experience. This is likely to increase the probability that the expectations they bring are consistent with those already held by the group.

Groups do not establish or enforce norms for *every* conceivable situation. The norms that the group will enforce tend to be those that are important to it. The following factors can make norms important:
- *Facilitating the group's survival.* Groups do not like to fail. Therefore, they enforce those norms that increase their chances for success. This means that they will try to protect themselves from interference from other groups or individuals.
- *Increasing the predictability of group members' behaviours.* Norms that increase predictability enable group members to anticipate each other's actions and to prepare appropriate responses.
- *Reducing embarrassing interpersonal problems for group members.* Norms are important if they ensure the satisfaction of members and prevent as much interpersonal discomfort as possible.
- *Allowing members to express the central values of the group and clarifying what is distinctive about the group's identity.* Norms that encourage expression of the group's values and distinctive identity help to solidify and maintain the group.

13.6.4 Conformity

Members of groups normally desire acceptance by the group. Because of the desire for acceptance, the individual is susceptible to conforming to the group's norms. There is considerable evidence that groups place strong pressures on individual members to change their attitudes and behaviours to conform to the group's standard.

Individuals do not conform to all the pressures of all the groups they belong to, because people belong to many groups whose norms vary. They may even have contradictory norms. It seems that people conform to the important groups to which they belong or hope to belong. These are referred to as reference groups, which have the following characteristics:
- The individual is aware of others.
- The individual defines himself or herself as a member, or would like to be a member.
- The individual experiences that the group members are significant to him or her. The implication is that all groups do not impose equal conformity pressures on their members.

Group norms press group members toward conformity. Members desire to be one of the group and to avoid being visibly different. It can be generalised further that when an individual's opinion of objective data differs significantly from that of others in the group, he or she is likely to experience extensive pressure to align his or her opinion with that of others.

13.6.5 Status

Status is a socially defined position or rank given to groups or group members by others. Many aspects of life and organisational life are ruled by status – there seems to be no such thing as a statusless or classless society. Even the smallest group will develop roles, rights and rituals to differentiate its members. Status is an important variable in understanding human behaviour, because it is a significant motivator and there are major behavioural consequences when individuals perceive a disparity between what they believe their status to be and what others perceive it to be.

Status can be formal or informal, and is awarded as follows:

- *Formal status* is awarded through titles or amenities. This is the status that goes with being recognised as someone special, or receiving an award. In the organisational context it refers to status symbols such as a large office, an impressive view, titles, high pay, fringe benefits and preferred work schedules. Whether or not management acknowledges the existence of a status hierarchy, organisations are filled with amenities that are not uniformly available and, hence, carry status value.
- *Informal status* is awarded through attributes such as education, age, sex, skill and experience. Anything can have status value if others in the group evaluate it as status-conferring. This kind of status is not necessarily less important than the formal variety.

Status equity refers to the belief that the status hierarchy is equitable. When inequity is perceived, it creates disequilibrium that results in various types of corrective behaviour. The trappings that go with formal positions are also important elements in maintaining equity. When it is believed that there is inequity between the perceived ranking of an individual and what that person is given by the organisation, status incongruence can be expected. Examples of this kind of incongruence would be more desirable office space held by a lower-ranking individual, and paid country club membership provided by the company for clerks, but not for directors. Employees expect the things an individual has and receives to be congruent with his or her status.

Groups generally agree within themselves on status criteria and, hence, there is usually high concurrence in group rankings of individuals. However, individuals can find themselves in a conflict situation when they move among groups whose status criteria are different, or when they join groups whose members have heterogeneous backgrounds. For instance, business executives may use income, wealth or size of the companies they run as determinants of status. Academics may use the number of grants received or articles published. Blue-collar workers may use years of seniority, job assignments or bowling scores. In groups made up of heterogeneous individuals or when heterogeneous groups are forced to be interdependent, status differences may initiate conflict as the group attempts to reconcile and align the differing hierarchies.

13.6.6 Size

Group size affects the group's overall behaviour and depends on what variables play a role.

Smaller groups tend to be faster at completing tasks than larger ones. However, if the group is engaged in problem-solving, large groups consistently get better results than their smaller counterparts.

Deciding on the ideal size for a group is not easy, but the following parameters can be considered:

- Large groups – 12 or more members – are good for gaining diverse input. If the goal of the group is fact-finding, larger groups should be more effective.
- Smaller groups are better at doing something productive with that input. Groups of approximately seven members tend to be more effective for taking action.

The research on group size leads to two additional conclusions:

- Groups with an odd number of members tend to be preferable to those with an even number.
- Groups made up of five or seven members combine well the best elements of both small and large groups. Having an odd number of members eliminates the possibility of ties when votes are taken. Groups made up of five or seven members are large enough to form a majority and allow for diverse input, yet small enough to avoid the negative outcomes often associated with large groups, such as domination by a few members, development of subgroups, inhibited participation by some members and excessive time taken to reach a decision.

One of the most important findings related to the size of a group has been labelled *social loafing*. This is the tendency of group members to do less than they are capable of as individuals. It directly challenges the logic that the productivity of the group as a whole should at least equal the sum of the productivity of each individual in that group.

It seems untrue that the sense of team spirit spurs individual effort and enhances the group's overall productivity. Social loafing may be due to a belief that others in the group are not pulling their weight. If the individual sees others as lazy or inept, he or she re-establishes equity by reducing his or her own effort. Another explanation for social loafing is the dispersion of responsibility. Because the results of the group cannot be attributed to any single person, the relationship between an individual's input and the group's output is clouded. In such situations, individuals may be tempted to become free riders and coast on the group's efforts. In other words, there will be a reduction in efficiency when individuals think that their contribution cannot be measured.

The implications of this effect on work groups for organisational behaviour is significant. Where managers utilise collective work to enhance morale and teamwork, they must also provide means by which individual efforts can be identified. If this is not done, management must weigh the potential losses in productivity by using groups against any possible gains in individual worker satisfaction.

13.6.7 Composition

Most group activities require a variety of skills and knowledge. Given this requirement, it would be reasonable to conclude that heterogeneous groups (those composed of dissimilar individuals) would be more likely to have diverse abilities and information and should be more effective.

When a group is *heterogeneous* in terms of personalities, opinions, abilities, skills and perspectives, there is an increased probability that the group will possess the needed characteristics and creativity to complete its tasks effectively. The group may be more conflict-laden and less expedient as diverse positions are introduced and assimilated, but the conclusion is that heterogeneous groups perform more effectively than those that are homogeneous.

Another variable to consider is *group demography* – the degree to which members of a group share a common demographic attribute, such as age, sex, race, educational level or length of service in the organisation, and the impact of this attribute on turnover. This refers not to whether a person is male or female or has been employed by the organisation for a year rather than for 10 years, but rather to the individual's attributes in relationship to the attributes of others with whom he or she works.

Group demography has a certain logic which can be reviewed and considered as follows: groups and organisations are composed of cohorts, which can be defined as individuals who hold common attributes, for instance everyone is of the same age and shares common experiences. Group demography, therefore, suggests that such attributes as age, or the date that someone joins a specific work group or organisation, should help to predict turnover. According to Robbins (1996:316), the conclusion is that turnover will be greater among those with dissimilar experiences, because communication is more difficult. Conflict and power struggles are more likely and more severe when they occur. The increased conflict makes group membership less attractive, so employees are more likely to leave. Similarly, the losers in a power struggle are more apt to leave voluntarily or be forced out.

In working groups where a large proportion of members entered at the same time, there is considerably more turnover among those outside this cohort. Where there are large gaps between cohorts, turnover is also higher. Discontinuities or bulges in the group's date-of-entry distribution is likely to result in a higher turnover rate within that group.

The implication of this evidence is that the *composition* of a group may be an important predictor of turnover. Differences *per se* may not predict turnover, but large differences within a single group will lead to turnover. If everyone is moderately

dissimilar from everyone else in a group, the feelings of being an outsider are reduced. It is the degree of dispersion on an attribute, rather than the level, that matters most! It can be speculated that variance within a group in respect of attributes other than date of entry, such as social background, sex differences and levels of education, might similarly create discontinuities or bulges in the distribution that will encourage some members to leave. To extend this idea further, the fact that a group member is a female may mean little in predicting turnover. In fact, if the work group is made up of nine women and one man, it is easier to predict that the lone male would leave. In the executive ranks of organisations, however, where females are in the minority, it could be predicted that this minority status would increase the likelihood that female managers would leave.

13.7 GROUP PROCESSES

Group processes is the term used to refer to group phenomena such as the communication patterns used by group members for information exchanges, group decision processes, leader behaviour, power dynamics and conflict interactions.

One way to understand the importance of group processes in understanding work group behaviour is to return to the topic of social loafing. It is evident that one plus one plus one does not necessarily add up to three. In group tasks, where each member's contribution is not clearly visible, there is a tendency for individuals to decrease their efforts. Social loafing, in other words, illustrates a process loss as a result of using groups. But group processes can also produce positive results. That means that groups can create outputs greater than the sum of their inputs.

Synergy is a term used in biology to refer to an action of two or more substances, resulting in an effect that differs from the individual summation of the substances. This concept is also used to understand group processes. Social loafing, for instance, represents negative synergy. The whole is less than the sum of its parts. On the other hand, research teams are often used in laboratories, because the diverse skills of various individuals combined in a group produce more meaningful research than could be generated by all of the researchers working independently. That is, they produce positive synergy. Their process gains exceed their process losses.

13.7.1 Group dynamics

Group dynamics is the term used to describe the psychodynamic phenomena in groups. This represents the original views of Freud and his colleagues applied to systems: the individual as micro-system, the group as meso-system and the organisation as macro-system. The assumption is that these systems are in constant conscious and unconscious interaction and reflect one another's dynamic behaviour.

In order to understand the group's behaviour, group development is used as point of reference. Group development manifests in different behaviour patterns:

- *Dependency.* The group as a system will experience anxiety because it cannot cope with the demands of its existence. To cope with this anxiety, the group will become dependent on the authority figure (manager or management). Because this is a painful process, the dependency will be avoided through denial or projection (or other defence mechanisms). Thus, the expectancy is that the authority must carry the pain or do the work for the group. When the authority does not do this (because it is not its job), the group becomes angry and aggressive. A state of counter-dependency results where the group says, "then we will do it ourselves". If the group can keep working at its task with the authority figure facilitating the growth

process, the group can move towards interdependency, using authority when needed in a mature working way.

- *Fight or flight.* The aggression described above, is part of fighting or experiencing aggression toward the authority figure who does not take up the leadership role in a way the group wants him or her to do. Flight occurs when the group gets involved in non-task activities. It manifests in members leaving the group, talking about non-issues or avoiding becoming engaged in the primary task of the group in a constructive way.

- *Pairing.* In order to cope with the anxiety and lack of direction, the group divides itself into various combinations, for example males and females or blacks and whites. This helps the individual in finding a place where he or she feels less threatened by the overwhelming chaos and newness of what is happening.

- *Oneness.* Groups can function as a whole and survive because individual members in certain respects surrender themselves to the collective powers of the group. The group as a system in this way becomes more than the sum of the individual members, a living organism in its own right with pooled energies, competencies and other resources which can be used to ensure its survival. In this way individuals and groups are often better assured of their needs and goals being achieved.

13.7.2 Group tasks

Management should take cognisance of the size of the group in assigning tasks. Large groups facilitate pooling of information. The addition of diverse perspectives to a problem-solving committee typically results in a process gain. But when a group's task is coordinating and implementing a decision, the process loss created by each additional member's presence is likely to be greater than the process gain he or she makes. The size-performance relationship, therefore, is moderated by the group's task requirements.

The preceding conclusions can be extended to the following:

- The impact of group processes on the group's performance and member satisfaction is also moderated by the tasks that the group is performing.
- The complexity and interdependence of tasks influence the group's effectiveness.
- Tasks can be generalised as either simple or complex. Complex tasks are those that tend to be novel or nonroutine. Simple ones are routine and standardised. The more complex the task, the more the group will benefit from discussion among members on alternative work methods. If the task is simple, group members do not need to discuss such alternatives. They can rely on standardised operating procedures for doing the job. Similarly, if there is a high degree of interdependence among the tasks that group members must perform, they will need to interact more. Effective communication and minimal levels of conflict, therefore, should be more relevant to group performance when tasks are interdependent.

Tasks that have higher uncertainty – those that are complex and interdependent – require more information processing. This, in turn, puts more importance on group processes. However, it does not necessarily mean that a group will be low-performing just because it is characterised by poor communication, weak leadership and high levels of conflict. If the group's tasks are simple and require little interdependence among members, the group may still be effective.

13.7.3 Group cohesion

It is often implied that effective work groups are cohesive. Intuitively, it would appear that groups in which there is a lot of internal disagreement, and a lack of cooperative spirit, would be relatively less effective at completing their tasks than groups in which individuals generally agree and cooperate, and where members like each other. This refers to group cohesiveness, defined as the degree to which members are attracted to one another and are motivated to stay in the group.

The determinants of cohesiveness include the following factors:

- *Time spent together.* Group members who spend long and productive time together will increase their cohesiveness and synergy, as attitudes, knowledge, interest, attraction and general responsiveness will improve among them. The opportunity to spend time together is dependent on their physical proximity. People who live on the same block, belong to the same car pool or share a common office, are more likely to become a cohesive group, because the physical distance between them is minimal.
- *Severity of initiation.* The more difficult it is to get into a group, the more cohesive that group becomes. The initiation rites through which fraternities typically put newcomers is meant to screen out those who do not want to commit and to intensify the desire of those who do to become fraternity active.
- *Group size.* As a group's size expands, interaction with all members becomes more difficult, as does the ability to maintain a common goal. As the group's size increases, the likelihood of cliques and subgroups also increases, thus also decreasing overall cohesiveness.
- *Gender of members.* Women report greater cohesion than men. A reasonable hypothesis, however, is that women are less competitive and more cooperative than men with people they see as friends, colleagues or teammates, and this results in greater group bonding.

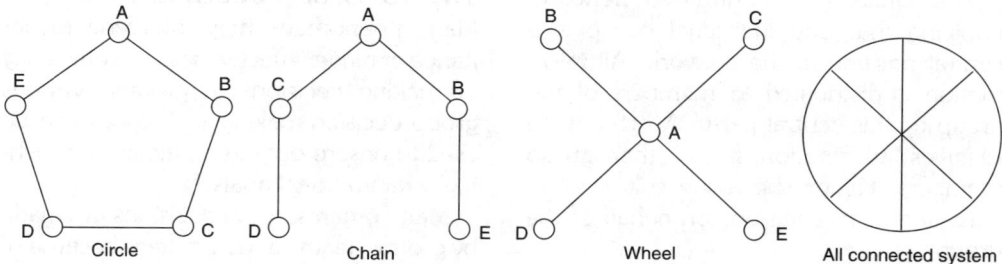

Figure 13.1 Communication patterns in groups

- *External threats.* Cohesiveness will increase if the group comes under attack from external sources. This is illustrated by support for group members against management in cases of dismissals, other disciplinary actions or downsizing in organisations. This type of support against an outside threat does not occur under all conditions, especially if members perceive the group might disband or if personal security could be at stake.
- *Previous successes.* If a group has a history of successes, it builds an *esprit de corps* that attracts and unites members. Successful firms find it easier to attract and hire new employees than unsuccessful ones. The same holds true for successful research teams, well-known and prestigious organisations and winning sports teams.

Cohesiveness affects group productivity. Highly cohesive groups are more effective than those with less cohesiveness, but the relationship is more complex than merely allowing us to say high cohesiveness is good: high cohesiveness is both a cause and an outcome of high productivity and the relationship is moderated by performance-related norms.

Cohesiveness influences productivity and productivity influences cohesiveness. Camaraderie reduces tension and provides a supportive environment for the successful attainment of group goals. As already noted, the successful attainment of group goals, and the members' feelings of having been part of a successful unit, can serve to enhance the commitment of members.

The relationship of cohesiveness and productivity also depends on the performance-related norms established by the group. If performance-related norms are high (for example high output, quality work, cooperation with individuals outside the group) a cohesive group will be more productive than a less cohesive group. But if cohesiveness is high and performance norms are low, productivity will be low. If cohesiveness is low and performance norms are high, productivity increases, but less than in the high cohesiveness – high norms situation. Where cohesiveness and performance-related norms are both low, productivity will tend to fall into the low-to-moderate range.

13.7.4 Communication in groups

Group effectiveness is also dependent on the type of communication structure. This will determine the channels of communication available for group members, how group members communicate and to whom, and the type of feedback from management on aspects such as performance, roles and decision-making.

Possible communication patterns in groups are depicted in figure 13.1. as wheel, chain, circle and system (completely connected).

The *wheel* is a centralised network, implying that one individual occupies a central position in the network. All information is distributed to members of the group by this central party, A, who alone receives information from other group members. He or she alone solves problems and takes decisions on behalf of the group.

As a rule such a network conveys information speedily and accurately, but group morale, as determined by the satisfaction of members, is low. Members B, C, D and E are dissatisfied because their communication with each other is limited and they are prevented from joint participation in decision-making. The central figure, A, enjoys most satisfaction because of the greater influence and leadership bestowed on him or her in this position.

Wheel patterns are associated with autocratic leadership.

The *chain* is another centralised network, though to a lesser extent than the wheel. The central person, A, communicates directly with two other people, C and B, before distributing information to D and E. Feedback between A and B and between A and C influences A's decisions.

Communication is fairly rapid and accurate in such a communication network, but again morale is low since not all group members have an equal say.

The *circle* is a decentralised network in which all members receive all available information and are in an "each-to-all" relationship. Information is disseminated rather slowly in such a network and may be conveyed inaccurately owing to distortion by group members. On the other hand, morale is high since all group members are equally involved in decision-making.

In the *all connected* system, cohesion may be high and everyone communicates. However, due to possibly too much communication, time loss and lapses in production may result, while leadership roles could be obscured.

13.7.5 Group decision-making

Many phenomena may intervene to enhance or hinder effectiveness and efficiency in making decisions in groups. Various group decision-making techniques can be used to ensure optimum efficacy in reaching organisational goals.

Many organisational decisions are made by groups, teams or committees because of their collective resources. This does not imply that group decisions are necessarily preferable to those made by an individual. A number of factors may play a role in this issue and it is helpful to study the advantages and disadvantages that group decisions hold.

13.7.5.1 *Advantages of group decision-making*

The advantages of groups over individuals are the following:

- By aggregating the resources of several individuals, more input is brought into the process.
- In addition to more input, groups can bring heterogeneity, or diversity, and more alternatives to be considered.
- There is increased acceptance of solutions, because more people will feel part of, and support, decisions, the resulting actions and consequences.
- Increased legitimacy. The group decision-making process is consistent with democratic ideals and may be perceived as being more legitimate than decisions made by a single person. The latter may be viewed as autocratic and nonconsultive.

13.7.5.2 *Disadvantages of group decision-making*

The disadvantages of groups over individuals are the following:

- Time-consuming. Assembling groups, the interaction that takes place, and slow decision-making, take time and may limit management's ability to act quickly and decisively when necessary.

- Pressures to conform. Social pressures in groups, and the desire by group members to be accepted and considered an asset to the group, can result in discouraging overt disagreement, thus facilitating conformity and possible poor decisions.
- Domination by the few. Group discussion can be dominated by one or a few members. If this dominant coalition is composed of members of low and medium ability, the group's overall effectiveness will suffer.
- Ambiguous responsibility. With an individual decision, it is clear who is responsible and accountable, while in group decisions the responsibility is often undecided or obscured.

13.7.5.3 *Effectiveness and efficiency*

The effectiveness of group decision-making, as opposed to individual decision-making, depends on the criteria used for defining effectiveness. Groups are more *effective,* because they are more accurate, creative and enjoy more acceptance than individuals. However, individuals work faster. This criterion indicates that individuals are more *efficient,* because they use less time and are possibly also less costly.

Groups are an excellent vehicle for good management and decision-making processes if the problems of time, internal conflicts and group conformity can be managed.

13.7.6 **Groupthink and groupshift**

Two by-products of group decision-making that have the potential to affect a group's ability to appraise alternatives objectively, and arrive at quality decision solutions, are groupthink and groupshift.

13.7.6.1 *Groupthink*

Groupthink relates to norms. It describes situations in which group pressures force conformity, which deters the group from critically appraising unusual, minority or unpopular views. Important pointers to the groupthink phenomenon are:

- Group members rationalise any resistance to the assumptions they have made.
- Members apply direct pressure on those who momentarily express doubts about any of the group's shared views or who question the validity of arguments supporting the alternative favoured by the majority.
- Those members who have doubts or hold differing points of view seek to avoid deviating from what appears to be group consensus by keeping silent about misgivings and even minimising to themselves the importance of their doubts.
- There appears to be an illusion of unanimity. If someone does not speak, it is assumed that he or she is in full accord. In other words, abstention is viewed as a "yes" vote.
- Groups act as if they are invulnerable, ignoring other influences or danger signals.

Not all groups are equally vulnerable to groupthink. Three moderating variables seem to manifest here – the group's cohesiveness, the leader's behaviour and insulation from outsiders.

13.7.6.2 *Groupshift*

Groupshift can be viewed as a special case of groupthink. The decision of the group reflects the dominant decision-making norm that develops during the group's discussion.

Groupshift indicates that in discussing a given set of alternatives and arriving at a solution, group members tend to exaggerate the initial positions they hold or shift the issue, sometimes in a conservative manner. However, the evidence indicates that members and groups tend toward a *risky shift.* What appears to happen in groups is that the discussion leads to a significant shift by members towards a more extreme expression of the position to which they were already leaning before the discussion. Thus, conservative types become more cautious and the more aggressive types take riskier positions. The group discussion tends to exaggerate the initial position of the group.

The greater occurrence of the shift towards risk has generated several explanations for the phenomenon. It has been argued that the discussion creates familiarity among members. As they become more comfortable with each other, they also become more bold and daring. Another argument is that society values risk and admires individuals who are willing to take risks, and group discussion motivates members to show they are at least as willing as their peers to take risks. The most plausible explanation of the shift towards risk, however, seems to be that the group diffuses responsibility among individual members.

13.8 GROUP DECISION-MAKING TECHNIQUES

The most common form of group decision-making takes place in face-to-face interacting groups. But as the discussion of group-think demonstrated, interacting groups often censor themselves and pressurise individual members towards conformity of opinion. Brainstorming, nominal group technique, the Delphi technique, SWOT analysis and electronic meetings have been proposed as ways to reduce many of the problems inherent in the traditional interacting group. Brainstorming is a process for generating ideas. The other four techniques go further by offering methods of actually arriving at a preferred solution.

13.8.1 Brainstorming

Brainstorming is meant to overcome the pressures for conformity in the interacting group that retard the development of creative alternatives. It does this by utilising an idea generation process that specifically encourages any and all alternatives, while withholding any criticism of those alternatives.

In a typical brainstorming session, half a dozen to a dozen people sit around a table. The group leader states the problem in a manner understood by all participants. Members then freely offer whatever ideas or solutions occur to them in a given length of time. No criticism is allowed, and all the alternatives are recorded for later discussion and analysis. The fact that one idea stimulates others, and that judgement of even the most bizarre suggestions is withheld until later, encourages group members to think the unusual.

13.8.2 The nominal group technique

The nominal group technique restricts discussion during the decision-making process, hence the term "nominal". Group members are all physically present, as in common meetings, but members operate independently. More specifically, a problem is presented and then the following steps take place:

- Members meet as a group but, before any discussion takes place, each member independently writes down his or her ideas on the problem.
- The silent period is followed by each member presenting one idea to the group. Each member takes his or her turn, going around the table, presenting a single idea until all ideas have been presented and recorded (usually on a flip chart or chalkboard). No discussion takes place until all ideas have been recorded.
- The group discusses the ideas for clarity and evaluates them.
- Each group member silently and independently puts ideas in rank order. The final decision is determined by the idea with the highest aggregate ranking.

The chief advantage of the nominal group technique is that it permits the group to meet formally, but does not restrict independent thinking, as does the interacting group.

13.8.3 The Delphi technique

A more complex and time-consuming alternative is the Delphi technique. It is similar to the nominal group technique, except that it does not require the physical presence of the group's members. In fact, the Delphi technique never allows the group's members to meet face to face. The following steps characterise the Delphi technique:

- The problem is identified and members are asked to provide potential solutions through a series of carefully designed questionnaires.
- Each member anonymously and independently completes the first questionnaire.
- Results of the first questionnaire are compiled at a central location, transcribed and reproduced.
- Each member receives a copy of the results.
- After viewing the results, members are again asked for their solutions. The results typically trigger new solutions or cause changes in the original position.
- Steps four and five are repeated as often as necessary for consensus to be reached.

Like the nominal group technique, the Delphi technique insulates group members from the undue influence of others. The Delphi technique can be used for decision-making among geographically scattered groups, because it does not require the physical presence of the participants.

13.8.4 The SWOT analysis

SWOT is an acronym for strength, weakness, opportunity and threat. The first two dimensions are internal to the organisation and the last two are external. The analysis of these dimensions is used for strategy evaluation purposes. The idea is not to list specific strengths, weaknesses, opportunities and threats but rather to ask questions about the existence of them and then to formulate strategies related to them. Examples of questions about the four dimensions are:

- *Strengths.* Is there distinctive competence, are there adequate financial resources, are there competitive skills, is the company well thought of by consumers, are there cost advantages, is management competent?
- *Weaknesses.* Are facilities obsolete, is there a lack of management depth and talent, what key skills or competencies are missing, is the market image weak, what competitive disadvantages are there?
- *Opportunities.* Can additional customer groups be served, can new markets or segments be entered, can the product line be expanded, can faster market growth be attained, can complementary products be added?
- *Threats.* Is it likely that new competitors will enter, is a slower market growth possible, are there growing competitive pressures, are there adverse demographic changes?

The SWOT analysis is more than just a set of four lists, therefore the listing must be evaluated in terms of what the implications are for strategy and what adjustments in strategy need to be explored.

13.8.5 Electronic meetings

The most recent approach to group decision-making blends the nominal group technique with sophisticated computer technology. It is called the electronic meeting.

Once the technology is in place, the concept is simple. Up to 50 people sit around a horseshoe-shaped table – empty, except for a series of computer terminals. Issues are presented to participants and they type their responses onto their computer screen. Individual comments, as well as aggregate votes, are displayed on a projection screen in the room.

The major advantages of electronic meetings are anonymity, honesty and speed. Participants can anonymously type any message they want to and it flashes on the screen for all to see. It also allows people to be brutally honest without penalty. It is fast, because "chitchat" is eliminated, discussions do not digress and many participants can "talk" at once without stepping on one another's toes.

Experts claim that electronic meetings are as much as 55% faster than traditional face-to-face meetings. Yet there are draw-backs to this technique. Those who can type fast can outshine those who are verbally eloquent but with poor typing skills; those with the best ideas do not get credit for them; the process lacks the richness of information given in face-to-face oral communication. Although this technology is currently in its infancy, the future of group decision-making is very likely to include extensive use of electronic meetings.

Other techniques to facilitate group deci-sion-making and creativity are focus groups and the techniques of devil's advocate and expert system. Used a lot in business, especially in marketing, *focus groups* consist of selected persons who give feed-back and discuss products, services and ideas. In the *devil's advocate* technique two groups present their ideas on a selected issue and exchange or present their recommendations to the other group. Each group criticises the other group's ideas, after which they both revise their initial ideas. This process of presentation and criticism is followed until final solutions are reached. The *expert systems* technique in organisations means that management

uses whatever technology or human re-sources it has to increase innovation and change. In this technique computer tech-nology is of great help, but management must also have employees who are leaders, idea generators and good project man-agers.

The choice of one technique over another will depend on what criteria you want to emphasise. The interacting group is good for building group cohesiveness, brainstorming keeps social pressures to a minimum, the Delphi technique minimises interpersonal conflict and electronic meet-ings process ideas fast. The criteria used to evaluate the group will help in choosing the best technique.

13.9 THE FACILITATION OF LEARNING IN GROUPS

Facilitating as concept, activity and role is becoming more generally known and used in human resources practices. The impor-tance of understanding facilitation and a high skill level for the facilitator in the facilitating relationship is illustrated by Carkhuff's research (1983), indicating that this form of "helping" can be used "for better", meaning learning and growth in the persons being facilitated. If not, "helping" can be "for worse", meaning pain will be caused and development inhibited.

13.9.1 Description of facilitating

In human resources activities facilitating refers to making available a process of learning and growth in a second person within a one-to-one relationship or in a group. More specifically, facilitating can be defined as creating a climate and providing opportunities for a second person to *learn how to learn* about, and experience, himself or herself, with the goal of enhan-cing his or her quality of life, as manifested in psychological optimal functioning. This refers to the process whereby the individual grows further to become more fully functioning, characterised by the taking of responsibility for himself or herself in decision-making, the experiencing of emotions and feelings and in actions (Cilliers 1984; Rogers 1983a).

In more popular terms this means that instead of giving the person a fish to eat every day (as in the traditional way of teaching, training and instructing), the facilitator will teach him or her how to catch fish, so that he or she will be able to help himself or herself in future problem-solving and need satisfaction. The song "Let it be", by the Beatles, could be considered a theme song for facilitating, referring to the facilitator allowing the second person to be free to explore himself or herself, irrespective of what the facilitator sees as the possible solution or only way of conduct.

13.9.2 What facilitating is not
In order to understand this process more fully, facilitating can be contrasted to the following:
- traditional classroom teaching, in which the teacher or trainer accepts responsibility for the students by structuring, deciding and even acting for them
- a meeting in which the chairperson acts within a structure of an agenda, rules, regulations and minutes
- being a leader or manager who takes responsibility for another person and his or her performance
- being autocratic, deciding for another person and implying that *every* problem has a right answer
- instructing, prescribing and giving solutions, or telling someone what to do, which creates dependency
- examinations to test knowledge

13.9.3 The facilitator
According to literature (in Cilliers 1984, 1995, 1995a) the facilitator and his or her personality are the most important variables for effectiveness. More specifically, this refers to the following:

- *Intrapersonal characteristics.* The facilitator possesses a high level of physical fitness, which stimulates stamina to handle stress optimally. Psychological optimal behaviour can be described as the basis for the personality profile of the facilitator. The intellectual level is characterised by objective and realistic thinking, understanding the contents of the group's task, having the technical know-how to work on the task at hand, understanding the technicalities of the task, the skills to distinguish between effective and less effective decisions and the ability to make sound judgements. On the feeling level the profile is characterised by sensitivity towards his or her own feelings and the acceptance of responsibility for them, a realistic self-image, self-respect and self-acceptance. On the motivational level the facilitator has an internal locus of control and values of growth toward increasing personality integration.
- *Interpersonal skills.* The facilitator functions at high levels of reality, respect, empathy and concreteness as the core dimensions of growth stimulating communication (Rogers 1973). This is supported by the micro skills of listening to, looking at and integrating the second person's behaviour. In a group facilitation situation this includes feedback on group dynamics, meaning, communication, leadership, roles, status, norms and conflict as well as the summarising, paraphrasing and reflection of these in the group.
- *Modelling.* The facilitator is a *model* for optimal functioning as well as for the skills required to "be there" for the second person.

All these required competencies emphasise the need for care in the selection of facilitators.

13.9.4 Theoretical background

Facilitating, as used in industry, originates from client-centred psychotherapy (Rogers 1973), as well as theory on helping and helping skills (Carkhuff 1983; Egan 1975). The facilitator, however, is not a therapist, but acts as a mirror, reflecting what he or she sees and hears without putting meaning or an evaluation to it from an abstract, or from his or her own, frame of reference.

13.9.5 Training of the facilitator

Literature (in Cilliers 1984, 1995, 1995a) shows the following integrated training model for facilitating as being effective:

- the stimulation of the characteristics of psychological optimal functioning by means of laboratory training, which refers to an unstructured, experiential learning input such as sensitivity training, encounter groups, growth groups or T-groups
- didactic, systematic training in the core dimensions and micro skills by means of role playing, with objective feedback, for example by video, according to a facilitating model

Facilitating as activity has to do with, firstly, *attending* (looking and listening) to the second person's behaviour in terms of mechanics and dynamics, content and process, intellect (concept) and feeling (experience), left and right brain activities and verbal and non-verbal behaviour. This leads to the second person becoming *involved* in his or her own problem, because someone is caring and listening. In the next activity, the facilitator *responds* to the information by paraphrasing, summarising and reflecting back to the speaker, which helps him or her *explore* himself or herself and the problem. These last two activities can continue for a long while, until the second person reaches the point of understanding (the "aha-experience"), which means the facilitator has helped him or her to *personalise* (own and take

responsibility for) the problem. As a final step the facilitator *initiates* action ("what do you think will be the solution for your problem"), which is then discussed in terms of responsible *action* taking.

Research with this model has shown significant enhancements of psychological optimal functioning as well as the mentioned skills (Cilliers 1984, 1995, 1995a).

Facilitating is a necessary skill for *every* group leader. Too often group leaders are too active, thus forcing group members into comfortable, inactive roles. In this regard, Rogers (1983a) quotes the Chinese philosopher Lao-Tse, who 2 500 years ago said:

A leader is best when people barely know he exists, not so good when people obey and acclaim him, worst when they despise him. But of a good leader who talks little when his work is done, his aim fulfilled, they will all say "we did it ourselves".

In many groups, however, it must be remembered that more structured facilitation or work is also necessary.

13.10 CONCLUSION

Knowledge of group behaviour can be applied in any group activity in the work situation – including meetings, training, development and drinking tea. It applies to working with teams and improving their performance to attain higher productivity. A new concept in this field is "self-directed work teams". This refers to the facilitation of learning within the group so that the group can move itself along the path toward higher maturity, self-management and productivity. In this way the group becomes aware of its own processes and dynamics and uses them to work effectively.

Self-evaluating questions

1. Explain what a group is and what types of groups occur in the work situation.
2. Using your work group or organisation as an example, explain which structural factors you think are enhancing or inhibiting performance.

3. Distinguish between group process and dynamics.
4. Explain group cohesion and the importance of group norms.
5. Using your experience in a meeting, work group or your organisation, do the following:
(a) Explain how decisions are made.
(b) Explain signs of disruptive conformity such as groupthink and groupshift.
6. Compare five group decision-making techniques.
7. Using your own experiences in groups, describe the processes in group formation.

Social processes in organisations

14

François Badenhorst _____

CONTENTS

Learning outcomes

After studying this chapter you should be able to:

- define social processes within organisations
- identify the various components of social processes
- describe organisational structure, organisational and individual development, roles and socialisation in organisational context
- discuss the importance of social processes in organisations
- explain the influence of workforce diversity on social processes

Key concepts

diversity, culture, structure, division of labour, span of control, participation, role, development, socialisation definitions

14.1 INTRODUCTION

How well people work together is a crucial factor in the success of any organisation or group. Employers have traditionally viewed their employees as collections of individuals held together through self-interest, policies, rules, procedures and authority. Slowly, however, employers are coming to grips with the inherently social nature of organisations, as presented in figure 14.1.

Due to the diversity in the workforce, handling aspects such as socio-cultural diversity and instilling mutual trust are key factors in successful social processes. Should people not trust one another, successful integration is not possible.

All employees fulfil various roles in both work and private life. Sometimes it may lead to role conflict and other problems, all of which have an influence on social processes.

Individual development, organisational structure, organisational development and

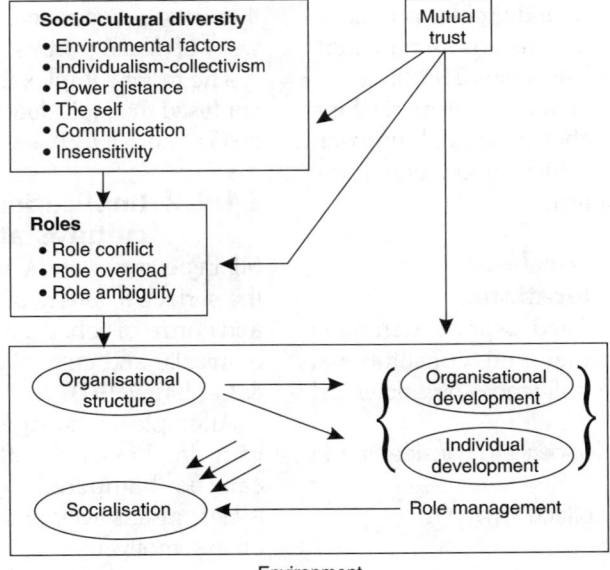

Figure 14.1 Social processes in organisations

the process of socialisation discussed in this chapter form integrated parts of psychology in the work context.

14.2 SOCIO-CULTURAL DIVERSITY IN THE WORKFORCE

Understanding cultural variables is critical to the success of an organisation's operations.

Organisations are becoming more heterogeneous in terms of gender, race and ethnicity. When employees come to work they don't set aside their cultural values and life style preferences. Systematic differences between cultures exist with regard to the value placed on aspects such as conformity and independence and these values can have an effect on individual behaviour (Taylor et al. 1994). The challenge to organisations is to become more accommodating to diverse groups of people by addressing their differences in life style, family needs and work style.

Managers need to change their approach of treating everyone alike to recognising differences and responding to such differences in ways that ensure employee retention and greater productivity, and at the same time ensure nondiscriminatory practices (Robbins 1993).

If diversity is not managed properly there is potential for higher personnel turnover, more difficult communication and more interpersonal conflict.

14.2.1 Culture-related considerations

Several culture-related aspects stemming from environmental and constitutional factors have an influence on individual behaviour.

Culture-related aspects to consider in the workforce are:

- individualism-collectivism
- power distance
- the self
- cultural patterns

Individualism refers to the social framework within which people take care of their own interests (Robbins 1996). Due to the nature of the workforce as a group, people expect others in the group of which they are a part to look after them and protect them, an aspect referred to as *collectivism*.

Power distance is the extent to which the less powerful members of institutions and organisations expect and accept that power is equally or unequally distributed (Kaplan 1995).

The most important factor is *the self,* which can be defined as all aspects of social motivation linked to the self of an individual, and is presented in all statements made by an individual, overtly or covertly, including words like "I", "me", "mine" and "myself" (Triandis 1989).

In every society *cultural patterns* exist which portray cultural complexity and is reflected in language; technology; economic, political and educational systems; religious and aesthetic patterns and within social structures (Triandis 1989).

Culture is to society what memory is to the individual. It specifies designs for living that have proven effective in the past, and ways of dealing with social situations.

The more complex the culture, the more confused the individual's identity is likely to be (Triandis 1989).

14.2.2 Implications of mixing cultures at work

Mixing cultures at the workplace brings to the surface a variety of values, work ethics and norms of behaviour, all aspects that are ethnically and culturally rooted (Jamieson & O'Mara 1991).

Attempts by managers to work together with employees of different backgrounds can be hampered by communication issues, insensitivity and ignorance of each others' motivation.

In order to successfully mix cultures at work it is important for all groups and individuals to know their own cultures in order to be sensitive to others.

One way of effectively supervising people from different cultures is by studying those cultures and adjusting management practices accordingly.

The challenge is not to assimilate but to integrate. In order to successfully do this, various steps can be taken, including the following (Jamieson & O'Mara 1991):

- *learn* how to handle frustrations when differences are encountered
- *increase* cultural awareness training
- *rethink* communication techniques to accommodate differences in language
- *provide* remedial education to those groups that were previously disadvantaged
- *rethink* participative management and what the participation tendency for each culture is
- *create* special career development programmes to better match people to jobs that fit their skills, needs and values
- *reward* managers for successfully blending a diverse workforce

14.2.3 Mutual trust in mixing cultures at work

To achieve high performance in the workplace, it is important for mutual trust to be present among members. Trust can be defined as a characteristic present in a high-performance team where members believe in the character, integrity and ability of one another (Robbins 1996).

According to Robbins (1996:356), the following five dimensions underlying trust can be distinguished:

- *integrity:* characterised by honesty and truthfulness
- *competence:* technical and interpersonal knowledge and skills
- *consistency:* reliability, predictability and good judgement in the handling of situations

- *loyalty:* in the sense of having the willingness to protect and save face for a person
- *openness:* characterised by a willingness to share ideas and information freely

14.2.4 Adjustment in cross-cultural interaction

Adjustment can be described as the experience of learning to live within a new and different cultural environment.

Cross-cultural adjustment should not be viewed as a unitary process but as being multifaceted, involving psychological and behavioural adjustment.

Psychological adjustment can be evaluated in terms of maintaining good mental health or psychological wellbeing and is generally marked by the following:

- positive mood state
- feelings of contentment
- acceptance of one's new environment

This component is represented in the impressions or feelings of the individuals themselves (Moghaddam et al. 1993).

Behavioural adjustment refers to individual behaviour or "cultural learning". It involves the acquisition of appropriate social skills and behaviours to carry out day-to-day activities successfully (Moghaddam et al. 1993). Behavioural adjustment can be divided into:

- the development of social skills
- demonstrations of behaviour that result in the effective accomplishment of one's required tasks

Successful *cross-cultural adjustment* involves the following elements:

- positive feelings and satisfaction with one's own situation
- development of positive interpersonal relations
- some level of effectiveness in carrying out necessary tasks at hand

The underlying social psychological rationale for multiculturalism is that members of

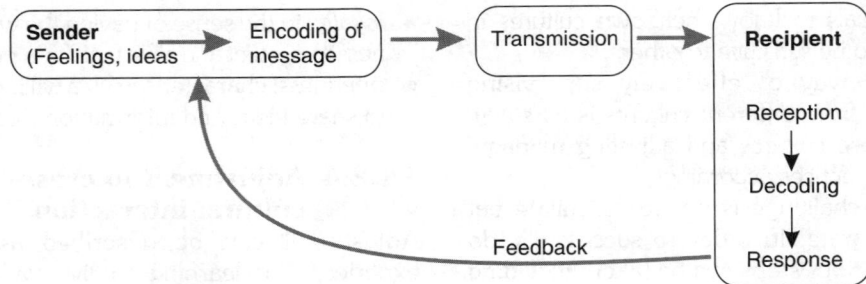

Figure 14.2 The communication process

a cultural group can feel open and charitable towards other cultural groups only if they feel secure in their own identity (Moghaddam et al. 1993).

14.3 COMMUNICATION IN ORGANISATIONS

Communication is one of the basic social processes and can be defined as the exchange of information and meaning by two or more people (see figure 14.2).

Communication begins with the feelings and ideas of the sender, with the intent often being to focus on the ideas and suppress the feelings, but feelings frequently leak into communications. When feelings and ideas are communicated, not only the *content* of the message is conveyed but also the nature of the relationship between the sender and the receiver. The content of a message could be "I like your work!", but depending on facial expression, tone of voice and posture, a different message could have been communicated, for example, "You are competent!"

The second step in the communication process is the *encoding* of the sender's thoughts and feelings, which means that they are put into words. At this point a breakdown in communication could occur if the sender and receiver speak different languages. Communication problems could also occur as a result of differences in the backgrounds of sender and receiver.

Once encoded, the message is transmitted through a medium. Breakdowns in transmission are likely to occur in the form of distortion and filtering. Filtering refers to the omission of parts of the message as it is transmitted from the sender to a second person and on to a third person or even more persons. The more people involved in this transmission chain, the more omission of parts of the message will occur. In distortion the various parts of the message may be retained but the transmitted message still deviates from the original as a result of rephrasing of the message by various persons. Again distortion increases as the number of persons involved increases. Filtering and distortion also appear to increase as the size of a group or organisation increases. With large groups, communications can fail not only because there are more people through whom the message must pass, but also because there is less overall participation and more dominance by a few members.

An especially important step in the communication process is the *reception* of the message. Misunderstanding can occur if a message does not reach the receiver. A written message about an important meeting could be buried among other letters, memoranda and documents, or be forgotten in the in-tray. Failures in reception also occur because the volume of information exceeds the processing capacity of the receiver. Filtering and distortion could therefore also occur when there is an overload of information. The psychological state of the receiver is another source of breakdown in reception. If the relationship between a supervisor and subordinate is not positive, the message of the supervisor may be clearly transmitted but the subordinate may only hear the supervisor's negative comments and may fail to hear the positive comments. Intense emotions, such as stress, can also be a source of incomplete reception, as people are only able to focus their attention on a much smaller range of information.

Even if the words of a message are received, communication can fail if the receiver decodes or interprets the message differently to what the sender intended. People do not always interpret concepts in similar ways. Different interpretations by superiors and their subordinates are seen as one of the most consistent and important sources of breakdowns in communication.

The next step in the process is how the receiver *behaves* in response to the message. The failure to respond as intended may or may not represent a communication problem. Lack of ability, knowledge or motivation could be the causes. The solution to the problem would then be to implement incentives or training.

The final step is *feedback*, which is crucial to improving communications and avoiding breakdowns. Feedback provides information on the consequences of the message to the sender. This could be acknowledgement by the receiver that the message was interpreted correctly or evidence that the receiver behaved as requested. To ensure effective feedback in the communication process, the receiver should feel free to ask questions and give comments. Without feedback a sender can never be sure if the message was received and interpreted correctly.

14.4 INFLUENCE AND POWER

Two basic social processes in groups are exerting influence and power. Examples of this are two members in a group meeting who both want to lead the group; a group member who has such clout that others allow his or her views to prevail even though they privately disagree with them; in a group meeting, conforming with the majority view to avoid criticism from group members.

Communication is closely interwoven with these two processes in that it not only serves as the primary vehicle for exerting influence and power, but the power that individuals possess in a relationship can shape the nature of communications. Influence can be defined as the actual change of one person's perceptions, attitudes, or behaviour by another person or persons. The amount of influence that is achieved depends on social power, which is the ability to influence others.

There are five types of power, each originating from a different type of relationship between the agent of power and the recipient of the influence attempts.

14.4.1 Reward power

The amount of reward power that person A has over person B is a function of how much B can be rewarded and the perception that A controls these rewards. Monetary incentives administered at the discretion of a manager is a good example of reward power.

14.4.2 Coercive power

The extent of coercive power is a function of the amount of punishment that can be administered and the perceptions of the person that compliance will lead to an avoidance of these punishments. Coercive power also occurs as a consequence of believing that rewards can be withheld. An example of coercive power would be the ability of a group to get individual members to go along with work practices through threats of isolation and rejection.

14.4.3 Legitimate power

Individuals have this type of power to the extent that others perceive them as having the lawful authority to influence them. Who is granted this authority depends on the values of the organisation. Legitimate power normally derives from the pyramidal structure of a typical hierarchical organisation. A department head who has the right to direct first-line supervisors exercises legitimate power.

14.4.4 Referent power

Referent power is the ability to influence others as a result of their attraction to the agent of influence. An example of referent power would be when a group member accedes to the demands of peers because he or she wants to be accepted by them. The motivational source of referent power is the ability of the leader to affect the followers' feelings of personal acceptance, approval and self-esteem.

14.4.5 Expert power

Expert power is the ability to influence others as the result of being perceived as having special knowledge and expertise. An employee in an organisation who has access to information that others do not have has expert power. The range of influence is likely to be restricted to topics on which the person is considered knowledgeable.

The bases of power are the consequence of how others perceive that individual, regardless of whether these perceptions have any basis in reality. A person may have no actual expertise but may still be seen as an expert. Power is the end result of a combination of forces, for example past attempts of the person to influence, the characteristics of the person and the situational context. These bases of power are interrelated. For example, an individual who possesses expertise may acquire legitimate power as the result of others seeing him or her as having the right to issue directives.

Whereas power is defined by the potential to influence others, influence tactics are what an individual actually does to influence others. The most frequently used tactics are consultation, rational persuasion, inspirational appeals and ingratiation. The least frequently used are exchange tactics.

14.5 COMPETITION, CONFLICT AND COOPERATION

Conflict can emerge because of the organisational context, task interdependence, goal and reward structure, competition for scarce resources and communication obstacles. Perhaps the most fundamental factor in causing conflict is the extent to which the successful performance of one person or unit depends on the performance of another. When people depend on each other, breakdowns in cooperation can easily escalate into conflict, but when task interdependence is low, conflict is much less likely.

Whether conflict occurs in a group or organisation depends to a large extent on the formal goals defining task achievement and the rewards given to people for their performances. A cooperative goal structure positively links the goals of group members, so that one person's goal achievements are beneficial to the achievement of other members' goals. In an individualistic goal structure, there is no such correlation. In a competitive goal structure, individual members cannot attain their goals unless other members fail in theirs.

As in goal structures, people can be rewarded individually for their collective efforts (cooperative rewards), their individual performance (individualistic rewards) or on a winner-take-all basis (competitive rewards).

Competition is not the best approach if the parties involved must cooperate to get the job done. Competitive reward systems can have harmful effects on the performance of a group's tasks. Research has supported the contention that cooperative reward systems achieve better results than rewarding people competitively. Imposing cooperative goal structures is also more effective than imposing individualistic goal structures. In a situation in which cooperation is important to performance, competitive or individualistic bases may encourage competition that detracts from effective performance. On the other hand, if the task does not require cooperation, competitive and individualistic rewards might serve as a boost to performance.

Closely related to the effects of reward and goal structures is conflict. Conflict emerges when different units within an organisation use limited or scarce resources.

It is important for organisations to restrain communication to some extent through physical separation and organisational arrangements. Because different functional units occur within an organisation and employees usually have access to these units through communication channels, any inability of those involved to openly communicate their intentions can serve as a source of conflict.

Another aspect that may serve as a source of conflict is status incongruence. Status refers to the rank or worth attributed to an employee by other employees, and is achieved as a results of the efforts of the employee. A particularly common source of conflict occurs when an employee with low status initiates work for an employee with a higher status. Such conflict is found among waitresses and cooks in restaurants, where the latter receive instructions from the former regarding customers' orders.

Further causes of conflict are ambiguity in work responsibilities and organisational differentiation. Conflict will occur where uncertainty exists regarding who should do what, how tasks should be performed and the relative responsibilities of employees.

One of the most common sources of conflict is organisational differentiation as a result of division and specialisation of labour.

14.6 ROLES

A role can be defined as a *set of expectations* regarding behaviour of an individual occupying a certain position (Reitz 1987). These expectations are usually communicated to members in an organisation through a role set. Most individuals occupy several roles. A role set can be described as those individuals who interact with the particular individual.

Role expectations play a major part in regulating employee behaviour. A job description is a powerful tool to define expectations of how a particular role should be played (Robbins 1990).

According to Muchinsky (1987) the following aspects regarding roles should be highlighted:

- roles are impersonal, as the position, rather than the individual, determines role expectations
- roles are related to task behaviour in the sense that organisational roles consist of behaviour expected in a particular job
- roles can be difficult to determine as "other" people define the rules and have opinions of what the roles should be
- roles are learned quickly, which may produce major behavioural changes in the individual
- roles and jobs are not the same concepts – an individual occupying a certain job might play several roles

An individual learns a new role or roles through a role episode (Muchinsky 1987) as presented in figure 14.3.

During stage one expectations are formed among members of a group regarding a given position, and then these expectations are communicated to a new incumbent. As a result the incumbent's actual role, behaviour will be determined by

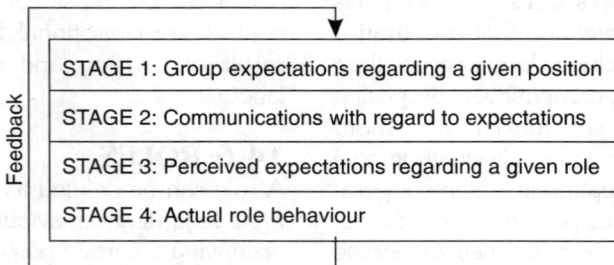

Figure 14.3 A role episode
Source: Adapted from Muchinsky (1987)

his or her perception of such expectations in respect of the given role.

An important aspect is that of *a boundary role*. A boundary role is present where an individual interacts with people outside the organisation and spends most time outside the organisation (Reitz 1987). The success of his or her role depends largely on the extent to which he or she can satisfy people outside the organisation. An example is the role of marketing personnel of a large retailer. Success in the role depends on how well the individual is able to satisfy the needs of potential and existing customers.

14.6.1 Role conflict
Role conflict is present the moment expectations regarding how an individual should perform a particular role are in conflict (Reitz 1987).

It occurs, for example, when the owner of a large corporation must keep costs as low as possible to ensure organisational growth and expansion, while at the same time employees are demanding higher wages and shareholders a higher pay-out of dividends.

Role conflict can occur in the following three forms:
- intraperson role conflict
- intra-role conflict
- inter-role conflict

Intraperson conflict occurs when an individual's values and attitudes clash with his or her role (Reitz 1987). An individual who

values creativity will experience conflict if required to adhere strictly to prescribed standards and procedures.

Intra-role conflict is present where two or more members of an individual's work group express different expectations for that individual's behaviour and he or she cannot satisfy everyone's expectations.

Inter-role conflict occurs when an individual occupies multiple roles and there are conflicting expectations of each role. For example, it can occur in the case of a working mother, or where someone is a member of an organisation but at the same time serves on the local tender board.

No matter what the source, role conflict is a potential and pervasive cause of stress within organisations. The consequences of role conflict for organisations range from mild or slight tension in members to complete indecision, frustration and dissatisfaction among them.

14.6.2 Role loading
Role overload occurs where more is expected from an individual than time permits (Reitz 1987).

Role overload could manifest:
- as a result of role conflict
- from having too much work to do
- because of too many things to be done at the same time

In contrast, role underutilisation occurs when the job (or lack of one) prevents the individual from being interested, aroused, challenged and feeling worthwhile.

Common stress symptoms associated with underutilisation are:

- physical or mental weariness
- headaches
- nervous complaints
- high frequency of absenteeism

14.6.3 Role ambiguity

It can happen that uncertainty exists regarding how a role should be performed due to unclear or insufficient information. The term used to describe this situation is role ambiguity (Reitz 1987).

According to Muchinsky (1987), the differences between what other people expect of individuals on the job and what the individuals themselves feel should be done are caused by one or more of the following:

- not understanding what is expected
- not knowing how these expectations should be met
- feeling the job should be performed in a different manner

As a result, role ambiguity may arise. Problems that could result from role ambiguity include stress, tension and decreased job satisfaction.

14.7 ORGANISATIONAL STRUCTURE

The organisational structure defines how tasks are allocated, who reports to whom, and the formal coordinating mechanisms and patterns of interaction to be followed (Robbins 1990). Organisational structure is the result of division of labour, delegation of authority, departmentalisation, span of control (Ivancevich & Matteson 1993) and has four dimensions.

14.7.1 Division of labour

Division of labour refers to the extent to which jobs are specialised (Ivancevich & Matteson 1993). Specialisation in this context refers to the particular grouping of activities performed by an individual which can be achieved by one of the following:

- *Functional specialisation.* This refers to the breaking down of jobs into simple and repetitive tasks. For example, an administrative worker's task can be defined in terms of the methods and procedures required for him or her to perform the task over a given period.
- *Social specialisation.* This occurs where an individual is specialised, rather than the job. For example, an organisation can hire professionals, such as civil or electrical engineers, who possess skills to perform a task that cannot be readily routinised.

14.7.2 Delegation of authority

It is of great importance to decide on the degree of authority to be delegated to each task performed, as well as on the individual to perform the task.

Authority can be defined as the right of an individual to take decisions without prior approval from higher management (Ivancevich & Matteson 1993). It is important to note that delegation here does not refer to doing the task, but to making decisions.

Authority is delegated from top management to lower management. A high level of delegation has the following advantages:

- it encourages the development of professional managers
- it can lead to a competitive climate in the organisation
- it grants the opportunity to individuals to satisfy the need to participate in finding solutions to problems

What is important is that there are various ways of delegating authority.

14.7.3 Departmentalisation

After the total task of the organisation is broken down into successively smaller

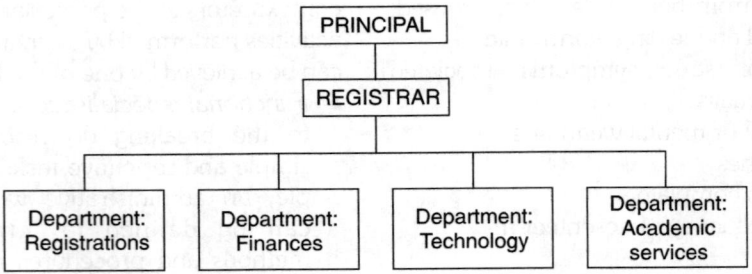

Figure 14.4 Functional departmentalisation

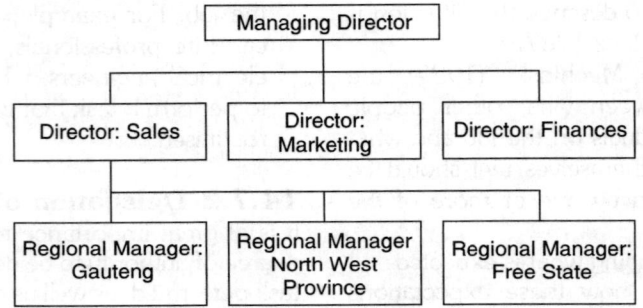

Figure 14.5 Territorial departmentalisation

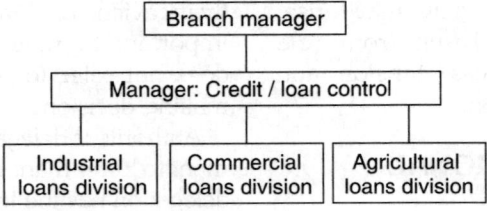

Figure 14.6 Customer departmentalisation

tasks, departmentalisation takes place. Departmentalisation refers to the placing of such smaller tasks in groups or departments. Specialised tasks can be seen as separate, interrelated components which form the task. The crucial consideration when creating departments is to determine the bases of grouping jobs. Such bases are termed departmentalisation bases (Ivancevich & Matteson 1993).

Forms of departmentalisation include functional, territorial and customer departmentalisation bases, which are now discussed.

14.7.3.1 Functional departmentalisation

Functional departmentalisation refers to combining tasks in correlation with the various functions of the organisation. A great advantage of functional departmentalisation is efficiency.

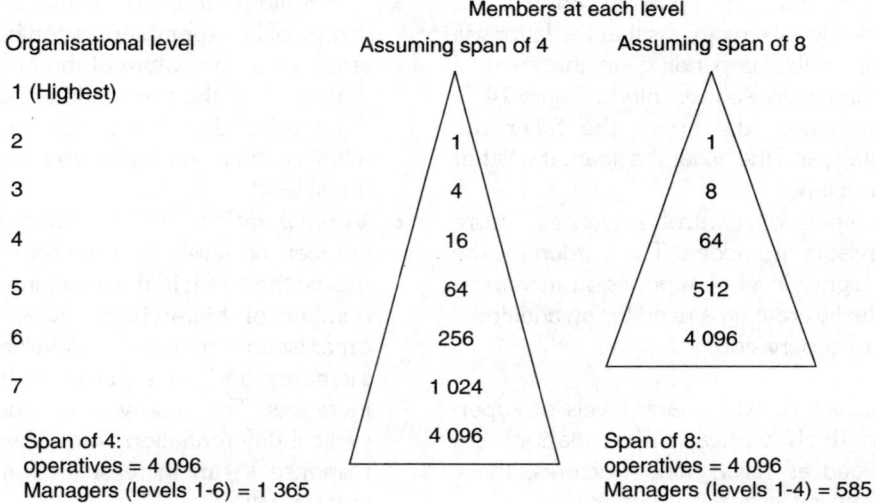

Figure 14.7 Contrasting spans of control

In an educational institution the following form parts of critical functions:
- registration of students
- taking of fees
- teaching
- technology

They are shown departmentalised in figure 14.4.

14.7.3.2 Territorial departmentalisation

Territorial departmentalisation, as presented in figure 14.5, is conducted by using geographical bases, where all activities in a given geographical area are assigned to one manager.

14.7.3.3 Customer departmentalisation

In the same manner, activities can be grouped in terms of various products or specific categories of customers. An example of customer departmentalisation, as presented in figure 14.6, is the loan department in a commercial bank, which has three divisions – industrial, commercial and agricultural – offering loans. Depending on the customer's needs, one of these divisions will serve him or her.

Within an organisation, the bases for departments do not remain unchanged. Over time, an organisation may use a mix of functional, territorial and customer bases.

14.7.4 Span of control

Span of control is defined as the number of subordinates that an individual manager can and should supervise (Robbins 1990).

With a wide span of control a number of subordinates report to the manager, in contrast to only a few with a narrow span of control. The question to be answered is whether the organisation will be more effective with a wide or narrow span of control. What is important is not to limit span of control to the number of subordinates only but to all interpersonal relations of the manager. Not only does a manager have interaction with subordinates, but he or she most probably serves on various committees and work groups, an aspect to consider in deciding on the span of control.

The impact of span of control on organisational structure is that the latter will be tall or flat, depending on the span of control chosen. As presented in figure 14.7, the narrower the span, the taller the structure, and the wider the span, the flatter the structure.

As span of control increases, more supervisors are added. The burden on the next higher level of supervision increases, eventually creating a need for an additional level of supervision.

Organisations with many levels of supervision (high vertical differentiation) are described as having tall structures, those with few levels as flat structures.

Vertical differentiation refers to the division and allocation of supervisory responsibilities among levels of management (Reitz 1987). In an attempt to improve coordination and control, a manager creates more levels of supervisors between himself or herself and employees at operative level.

14.7.5 Dimensions of organisational structure

In order to understand organisational structure it is important to distinguish between the following dimensions involved:
- complexity
- formalisation
- centralisation
- decentralisation

14.7.5.1 Complexity

Complexity refers to:
- the number of occupational specialities
- the professional activity
- the professional training of employees

Complexity is the direct result of work division and the creation of departments. The more complex the tasks and the more variety, the more complex the organisation will be (Ivancevich & Matteson 1993).

Complexity comprises the following three subcomponents:

- *Horizontal differentiation* indicates the degree of horizontal separation between employees, the nature of the tasks they perform and their education and training. It refers therefore to the number of different units on the same organisational level.
- *Vertical differentiation* refers to the number of levels in an organisation, that is, the depth in the structure. As the number of hierarchical levels in the organisation increases, differentiation increases and as a result complexity increases. The best way to understand vertical differentiation is to view it as a response to an increase in horizontal differentiation.
- *Spatial differentiation* refers to the degree to which the location of an organisation's offices, plants and personnel are geographically dispersed.

14.7.5.2 Formalisation

Formalisation refers to the degree to which jobs within an organisation are standardised (Robbins 1990).

In a job that is highly formalised, the job incumbent has minimum discretion over what needs to be done, when it's done and how it should be done.

Where high formalisation is applied, the following will be present:
- explicit job descriptions
- organisational rules
- clearly defined procedures covering work processes

Where formalisation is low, employees' behaviour is relatively unregulated and a great deal of freedom is allowed to such employees in the carrying out of the job.

Standardisation defines the range of variation tolerated in the rules that apply to the jobs (Robbins 1990).

14.7.5.3 Centralisation

Centralisation is the most complicated dimension of organisational structure. It refers to the degree to which decision-making is concentrated at a single point in the organisation.

The concept of centralisation refers to the delegation of authority between tasks or jobs within an organisation and therefore in terms of decision-making and control (Ivancevich & Matteson 1993).

It is important to note that although centralisation of decision-making encompasses those with formal authority in the organisation, it also takes into consideration those people who have informal influence over decisions (Robbins 1990).

Robbins (1990:106) describes centralisation as:

> the degree to which the formal authority to make discretionary choices is concentrated in an individual, unit or level (usually high in the organisation), thus permitting employees (usually low in the organisation) minimum input into their work.

14.7.5.4 Decentralisation

Decentralisation can be viewed as the opposite of centralisation.

The old concept that a manager manages everything is slowly disappearing and the modern organisation, in a state of transition, will experience the following (Kaestle 1990):

- the need for increased decentralisation in order to secure lower costs and shared resources
- the need to enhance reaction to the market by means of greater decentralisation

The successful organisation will be the one that can handle these opposing requirements best (Kaestle 1990).

14.8 ORGANISATIONAL DEVELOPMENT

Organisational development refers to the process, and management, of change (Ivancevich & Matteson 1993). A dynamic

and changing environment requires organisations to adapt in order to survive.

Organisations are social-technical systems

Characteristics of organisational change are the following:

- it is a planned process
- it is problem-oriented
- it uses a systemic and systematic approach
- it forms part of the management process

As a *planned process*, organisational development is a data-based approach to change which includes all aspects of management: setting goals, plans of action, implementing, monitoring and taking corrective actions where applicable.

Organisational development is *problem-oriented*. In order to find solutions to problems within organisations, information must be obtained from a variety of disciplines.

Using a *systems and systematic approach*, attempts are made to link human resources as well as the potential of the particular organisation with the organisation's technology, structure and management processes.

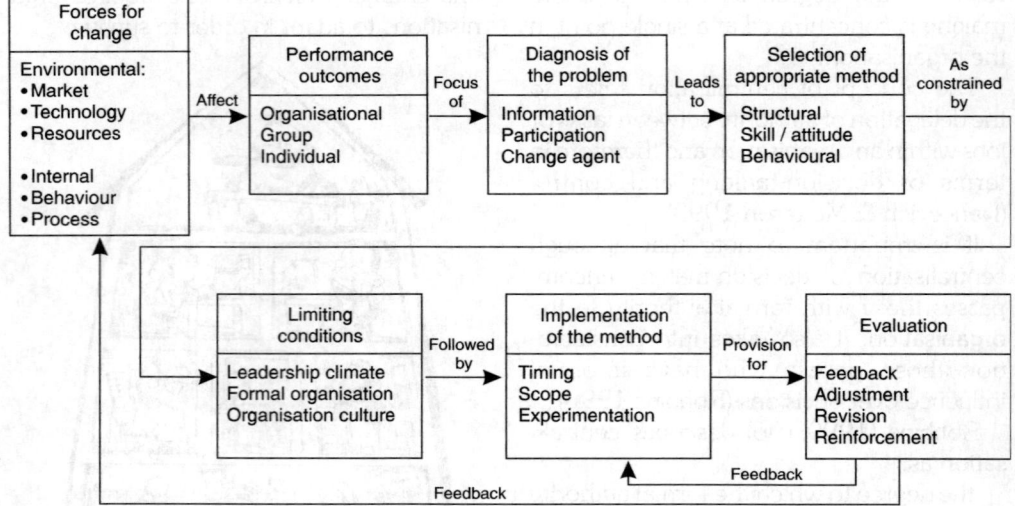

Figure 14.8 The process of organisational development
Source: Ivancevich and Matteson (1993:472)

It is important for organisational development to be an *integrated part of management*. In other words, action cannot be initiated by outsiders, but must be done by the organisation itself by means of change management.

Organisation development is not a crisis strategy, but should become part of the everyday activities of an organisation.

14.8.1 Organisational development: the process

The process of organisational development must be conducted systematically.

The following aspects are suggested as a framework for the process by Ivancevich and Matteson (1993):

- forces for change
- diagnosis of the problem
- selection of an appropriate method of change
- resistance to change
- recognition of limiting conditions
- implementation of the method
- evaluation

These aspects are presented in figure 14.8.

It is important for managers, prior to the second phase of diagnosing the problem, to decide the following:

- the degree of participation by subordinates
- whether a change agent will be used or not

There are three types of employee participation in organisational development: unilateral, delegated and shared. These are presented in figure 14.9.

Employee participation in the process of organisational development cannot be overemphasised. It is of prime importance for individual and organisational development efforts to be combined (Pasmore & Fagans 1992). It can be easily accomplished because people, given the opportunity, will opt for participation rather than non-participation.

It seems from the above that the most effective participation is in shared decision-making, where the emphasis is on interaction and the sharing of authority between manager and subordinates.

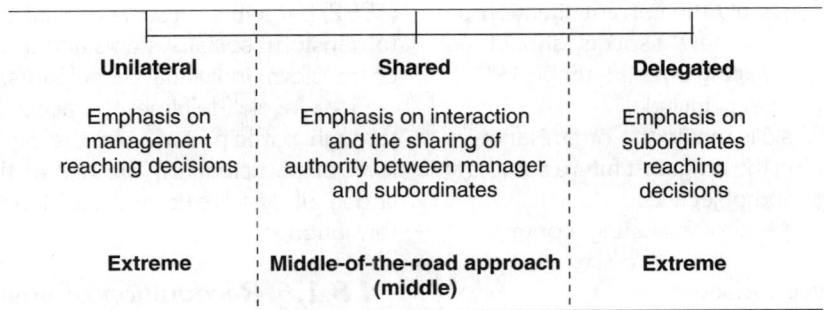

Figure 14.9 Degrees of employer participation in the process of organisational development

14.8.1.1 Forces for change

Forces for change can be divided into external and internal forces (Ivancevich & Matteson 1993).

External forces include social developments, political changes, economic conditions and clients. Pressure may be placed on organisations to restructure the workforce, for example, and in this case there will be major changes in workforce demographics (Hattingh 1993).

Internal forces for change involve behavioural and process-related aspects. A source in the environment that has an influence on organisational change is technology. Changes in worker attitudes, organisational structures and government regulations occur because workers now have access to information, as a result of technological advances, previously only available to chief executives.

Process-related aspects include problems with decision-making and communications. For example, decisions are either not made, or made too late or are of poor quality. Problems can also occur in the communication networks in organisations when information is withheld or insufficiently provided.

Problems regarding interpersonal and interdepartmental relations can have a negative effect on the change process. Symptoms of behavioural problems are low levels of morale, high levels of absenteeism and a high personnel turnover (Ivancevich & Matteson 1993).

14.8.1.2 Diagnosis of the problem

It is important for problems to be properly *diagnosed*. Management must ask which problems need to be focused on during the change process and what the end result could be, and then take appropriate action.

Answers to the above questions can be sought from an organisation's information system and by obtaining information through committees and work groups on an *ad hoc* basis.

14.8.1.3 Intervention by a change agent

In the search for solutions to problems it may be deemed necessary to involve a third party, known as a change agent, of which there are three forms.

An *external* agent is a total outsider, while an *internal* agent is an individual in the service of the organisation who therefore has knowledge of the organisation and its particular problems. The best option would be a *combination* of external and internal agents (Ivancevich & Matteson 1993).

14.8.1.4 Selection of an appropriate method

The choice of an appropriate method depends on the problem as diagnosed by management. It is important that the method chosen makes provision for interrelationships between skills, attitudes, behaviour and the structure of the organisation.

Not only should the current situation be reassessed, but new aspects should be added to the existing ones (Hattingh 1993).

Existing aspects include:

- the total skills mix in the organisation
- measuring these against future company strategy and objectives
- retraining and re-educating workers

New aspects include:

- newly-shared values among employees
- the agreed, desired work ethic
- revitalised spirits of the people
- the strength of the diversity
- performance ethos
- the capacity of humans to grow and develop in nurturing, caring hands

14.8.1.5 Resistance to change

Everyone expects a certain degree of stability and predictability in his or her life and experiences negative feelings towards anything that threatens them (Ivancevich & Matteson 1993).

The strength of resistance from people to change will be determined by the degree to which the process of change meets the following criteria:

- Change must be a pre-planned process.
- The availability and amount of information regarding the process must be adequate.
- The change must satisfy all relevant needs.
- The expectation must be created that the change will be a positive experience.
- It must be the choice of the individual to experience change.

In most instances it will be necessary to remove or modify group resistance to change. This can be done by, among other things, the use of group meetings, in which management effectively communicates the need for change and stimulates group participation in the planning of the change process.

According to Pasmore and Fagans

(1992) participation serves a dual purpose: to transform social systems and to develop or transform individual participants.

Goal- or self-fulfilment is accomplished through participation, and the higher the level of participation, the higher the likelihood of systematic and individual transformation.

14.8.1.6 Recognition of limiting conditions

Over and above resistance, factors such as leadership, the formal organisation and organisational culture may place a damper on organisational development (Ivancevich & Matteson 1993).

Leadership and other processes of the organisation must be such that they ensure maximum probability that each member, in the light of his or her background, values, desires and expectations, will view the experience as supportive and one which builds and maintains his or her sense of personal worth and importance.

14.8.1.7 Implementation of the method

When implementing an appropriate method of organisational change, the timing and scope of the change are important factors.

It is crucially important that the *appropriate time* be selected for implementing the change. Timing depends on the work cycle of the organisation and the groundwork conducted by the organisation prior to the process of development.

The *scope* of change is important. For example, should change need to occur in a university, it must occur simultaneously in all departments, as change in one department only will have a negative effect on the links of the departmental chain.

14.8.1.8 Evaluation

What actually takes place during organisational development is that organisational resources are exchanged for desired outcomes.

According to Ivancevich and Matteson (1993) the results of successful organisational development are:

- *Short term:* organisation effectiveness, efficiency and job satisfaction
- *Medium term:* adaptability and development
- *Long term:* survival

It is important for the programme of change to be evaluated against the above outcomes.

Evaluation involves feedback, adapting the programme (where applicable), revision and strengthening (Ivancevich & Matteson 1993).

14.8.2 Types of change

The following types of change can be distinguished (Armstrong 1995):

- *Strategic change* is concerned with broad, long-term and organisation-wide issues. It is concerned about moving to a future state which has been generally defined in terms of strategic vision and scope. It includes the purpose and mission of the organisation, corporate philosophy regarding matters such as growth, quality and innovation, as well as values concerning people, clients and technology.
- *Operational change* involves aspects that will have an effect on working arrangements, for example new systems, procedures, structures and technology.

14.8.3 Basic mechanisms to manage change

In simple terms the basic mechanisms to manage change are unfreezing, changing and refreezing (Armstrong 1995). These are presented in figure 14.10.

During the process of *unfreezing,* the state of equilibrium that supports existing behaviours and attitudes needs to be altered with due consideration of the inherent threat that change poses to people.

Changing involves the development of new responses based on new information.

For the process of change to be successful it is crucial that new responses are introduced into the personalities of the individuals concerned and thus stabilise the change. This stage of the process is known as *refreezing* (Armstrong 1995).

14.9 INDIVIDUAL DEVELOPMENT

Individual development and organisational development should go hand in hand.

Although the individual will ultimately be responsible for his or her own well-being, the need for organisations to create an environment for individual development is of equal importance. Development should be an interaction between the individual and the organisation. The essential process to achieve this mission is through organisational development (Roodt 1992).

Especially because of affirmative action, it is important for organisations to mobilise actions to unleash critical mass momentum in the development of women and other disadvantaged groups.

14.9.1 Participation and individual development

An individual can easily become alienated and therefore needs to be able to express his or her thoughts on issues that are significant and that make life worth living.

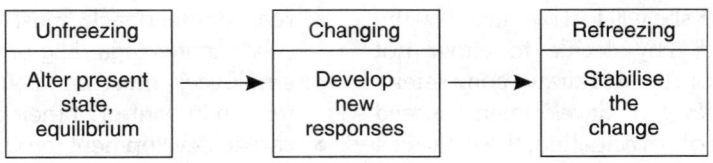

Figure 14.10 Basic mechanisms to manage change

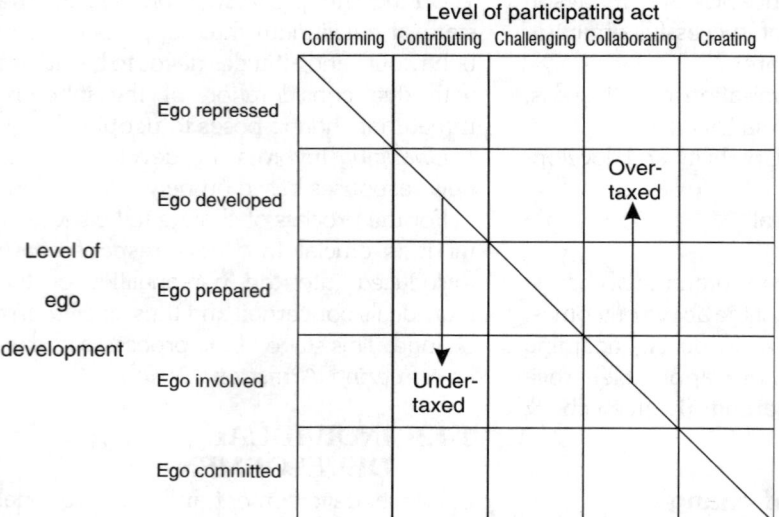

Figure 14.11 Participation and ego development
Source: Pasmore and Fagans (1992)

Especially because of changing work environments, it is important to prepare to participate in the process of change.

Organisational development is sustained by individual development, which in turn depends on the creation of an organisation in which people can experience, reflect, experiment and learn. There must be opportunities for genuine participation and individuals must be permitted to achieve distinction and personal excellence through courageous action (Pasmore & Fagans 1992).

According to Pasmore and Fagans (1992) the level of individual participation correlates with models of adult ego development, as presented in figure 14.11.

As can be seen in figure 14.11, should participation involve more risk and complexity than the individual is prepared to assume, he or she will feel overtaxed by the situation and may decide to either not participate or to withdraw completely. Should the level of development exceed the demands of participation, the individual might feel undertaxed and perhaps alienated.

14.9.2 Career development interventions

Career development interventions can be defined as an attempt by an organisation to support individual employees in the management of their careers and, as a result, fulfil organisation goals such as greater efficiency.

Where previously the aim of such interventions was to satisfy the needs of the organisation, changes within the workplace have resulted in programmes that satisfy both the needs of the organisation and the individual worker (Russell 1991).

Russell (1991) suggests the following criteria for successful career interventions:
- career expectations of the individual must be realistic
- skills must be periodically assessed
- realistic feedback must be given to subordinates regarding progress
- employees must be assured they will remain in control of their own careers
- career development programmes must be integrated with other systems of human resources within the organisation

14.10 SOCIALISATION

Socialisation refers to those processes by which an individual acquires attitudes, values and norms necessary to function as a member of a social unit (Reitz 1987). In the context of an organisation, it is a process of obtaining knowledge with regard to values, norms and expected behaviour patterns required by the job, as well as the organisation of which the individual will be a part.

14.10.1 Process of organisa- tional socialisation

Socialisation can be viewed as the process by which organisations bring new employees into the culture of the organisation (Ivancevich & Matteson 1993). Although socialisation takes place throughout an individual's career within an organisation, it is most pronounced when a new employee enters the organisation.

At this early stage the organisation seeks to mould the new employee into someone who will eventually display "acceptable behaviour". What is important here is that a "fit" or congruence evolves between individual and organisational goals.

The socialisation process is presented in figure 14.12.

As the needs of the organisation change, it is important for employees to adapt to these new needs through the process of socialisation.

14.10.2 Stages of socialisation

Socialisation stages coincide with the stages of a career. Generally the following three stages can be identified:

- anticipatory socialisation
- accommodation
- role management

14.10.2.1 Anticipatory socialisation

Anticipatory socialisation involves those activities the individual undertakes prior to assuming a different job within the same organisation; or on entering a new organisation, the activities needed to acquire information regarding the new organisation or job.

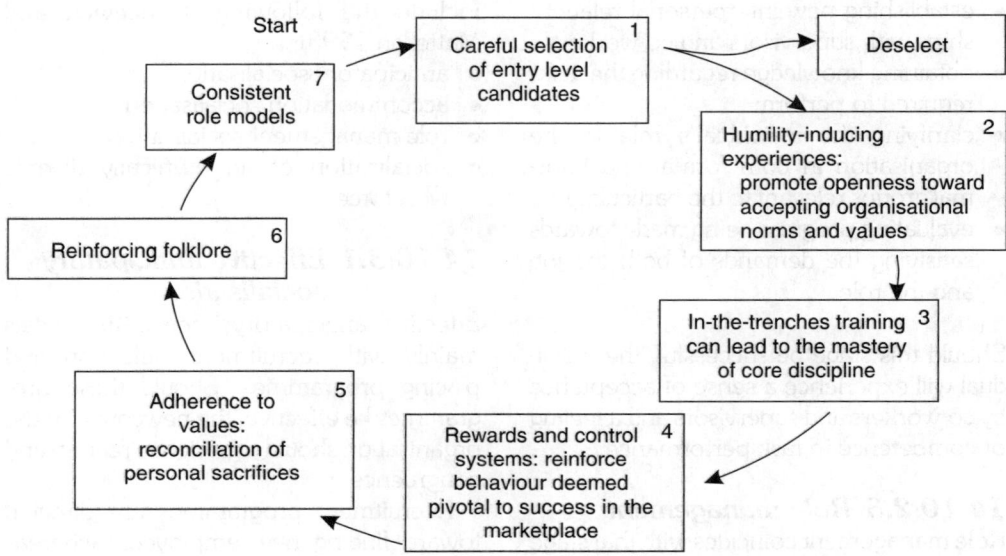

Figure 14.12 The process of organisational socialisation
Source: Ivancevich and Matteson (1993:684)

Before entering an organisation individuals are interested in the following:
- what working for the organisation is really like
- whether they are suitable for jobs available in the organisation

For fit between individual and organisational goals, the following two conditions are necessary:
- both the individual and the organisation must portray themselves realistically
- the skills, talents and abilities of the individual must be congruent with, and fully utilised in, the job

14.10.2.2 Accommodation

Accommodation occurs after the individual has become a member of the organisation or after entering a new job (Ivancevich & Matteson 1993). It is the stage where the individual views the organisation, or job, for what it really is and attempts to become a competent performer of the job and an active participant in the organisation.

The accommodation stage comprises the following activities:
- establishing new interpersonal relationships with supervisors and co-workers
- obtaining knowledge regarding the tasks required to perform
- clarifying the individual's role in the organisation in both formal and informal groups relevant to the particular role
- evaluating progress being made towards satisfying the demands of both the job and the role

Should this stage be successful, the individual will experience a sense of acceptance by co-workers and supervisors and a feeling of competence in task performance.

14.10.2.3 Role management

Role management coincides with that stage in the career of the individual characterised by stability. This stage is in contrast to the accommodation stage.

During the accommodation stage the individual has to adjust to the demands and expectations of the work group. Role management involves a broader set of issues and problems.

An aspect that arises during this stage is conflict in the work and home environment. Energy needs to be expended on, and split between, job and family and, because the amounts of time and energy are fixed and the demands of work and family seem insatiable, conflict cannot be avoided.

Those individuals unable to resolve such conflicts often choose to terminate their services with the organisation or to perform at an ineffective level.

In both instances, neither the individual nor the organisation is served well.

14.10.3 Characteristics of effective socialisation

The processes of organisational socialisation vary in form and content from one organisation to another, and even within the same organisation individuals experience different processes.

Effective organisational socialisation can include the following (Ivancevich and Matteson 1993):
- anticipatory socialisation
- accommodation socialisation
- role management socialisation
- socialisation of an ethnically diverse workforce

14.10.3.1 Effective anticipatory socialisation

Effective anticipatory socialisation deals mainly with recruitment, selection and placing programmes. Should these programmes be effective, the newcomer in the organisation should experience realism and congruence.

Recruitment programmes are directed toward finding new employees, whereas selection and placement programmes convey information to those employees who are to join the organisation.

14.10.3.2 Effective accommodation socialisation

Effective accommodation socialisation comprises the following activities:

- designing orientation programmes
- structuring training programmes
- providing information for performance evaluation
- assigning challenging work
- assigning demanding superiors

Orientation programmes should be designed to enable new employees to meet the rest of the workforce as soon as possible. As training programmes frequently provide feedback regarding progress in acquiring the necessary skills, new employees should undergo initial training, followed up by performance evaluation, which provides important feedback about how well the individual is progressing in the organisation.

One of the principle features of effective socialising programmes is assigning challenging work to new employees. It is important for an employee to demonstrate his or her full capability and this should therefore not be stifled.

A practice that seems to hold considerable promise for increasing the retention rate of employees is assigning demanding superiors. It is important not to confuse demanding with autocratic. New employees are set in the right direction with the understanding that high performance is expected and rewarded and that their superior fulfils a role as coach and counsellor throughout the process.

14.10.3.3 Effective role management socialisation

Effective role management is important in the sense that organisations dealing with conflicts associated with role management recognise the impact of such conflicts on job satisfaction and turnover. Roles should be effectively managed because organisations can ill afford to lose capable employees.

14.10.4. Socialisation of an ethnically diverse workforce

Socialising an ethnically diverse workforce has become one of the biggest challenges today. More members of more ethnic groups are attempting to become part of the workforce than ever before.

Although cultural and ethnical aspects were discussed earlier, the following aspects are relevant to the organisation because of the proliferation of diverse ethnic backgrounds:

- differences in work ethic
- ethnically rooted norms of behaviour
- the fit of the individual with the culture of the organisation

It is by no means a simple process to comfortably integrate and welcome culturally diverse workers with established histories, rituals and ceremonies into organisations.

14.10.5 Socialisation as an integrated strategy

Organisational integration is achieved primarily by aligning and integrating individual goals with those of the organisation (Ivancevich & Matteson 1993). The greater the correlation between individual goals and organisational objectives, the more successful the integration. What actually takes place is that the previously held goals of the individual are *undone* and new ones are formulated that are more aligned to those of the organisation.

14.11 CONCLUSION

The workforce of the modern organisation is becoming more and more heterogeneous, which brings with it complex problems.

Apart from role conflict, role overload and role ambiguity, mutual trust forms one of the most complex issues. As a result of the diversity of the workforce, people may not trust one another. If this issue is not addressed it may lead to even more complex problems. It is of great importance, especially for socialisation to be successful, that workers in the new era enter and operate in an organisation without the hindering element of mistrust.

In order to deal with all these issues it is important for organisational structures to be adequate and for the process of organisational development to be on-going. All organisations form part of a larger, ever changing environment and must adapt to survive. Organisational development goes hand in hand with individual development. It is important to view both individual and organisation as one entity.

Self-evaluating questions

1. Explain the impact of cultural and ethnic diversity in the workplace.
2. Define the term "role" and discuss the problems that may arise from role conflict.
3. You are requested to design an appropriate structure for your department. Discuss all the aspects to be considered.
4. Discuss the dimensions of organisational structure.
5. Explain the process of communication with reference to a situation.
6. Explain individual and organisational development.
7. Evaluate the process of socialisation in your organisation or department.

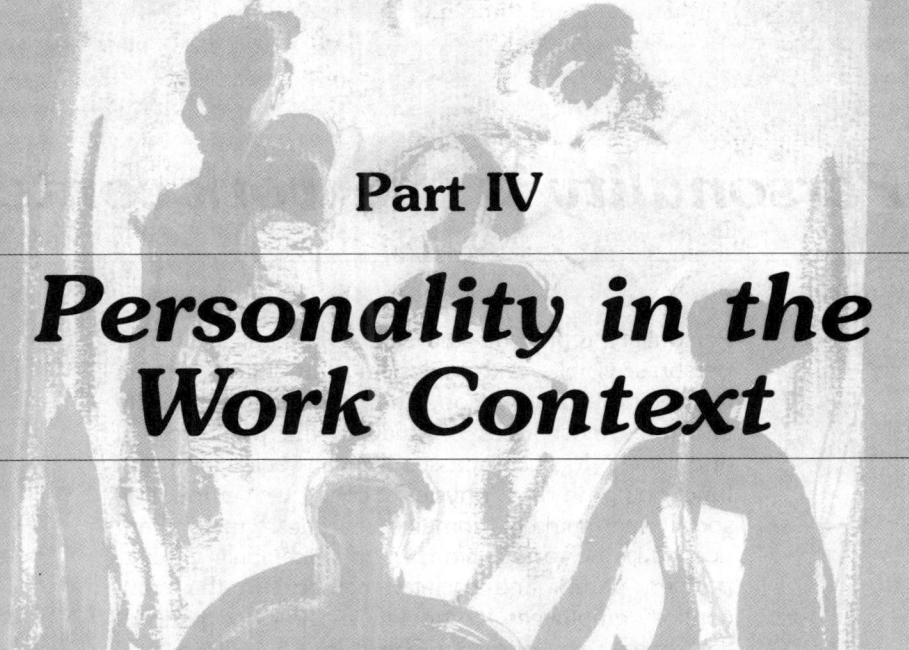

Part IV
Personality in the Work Context

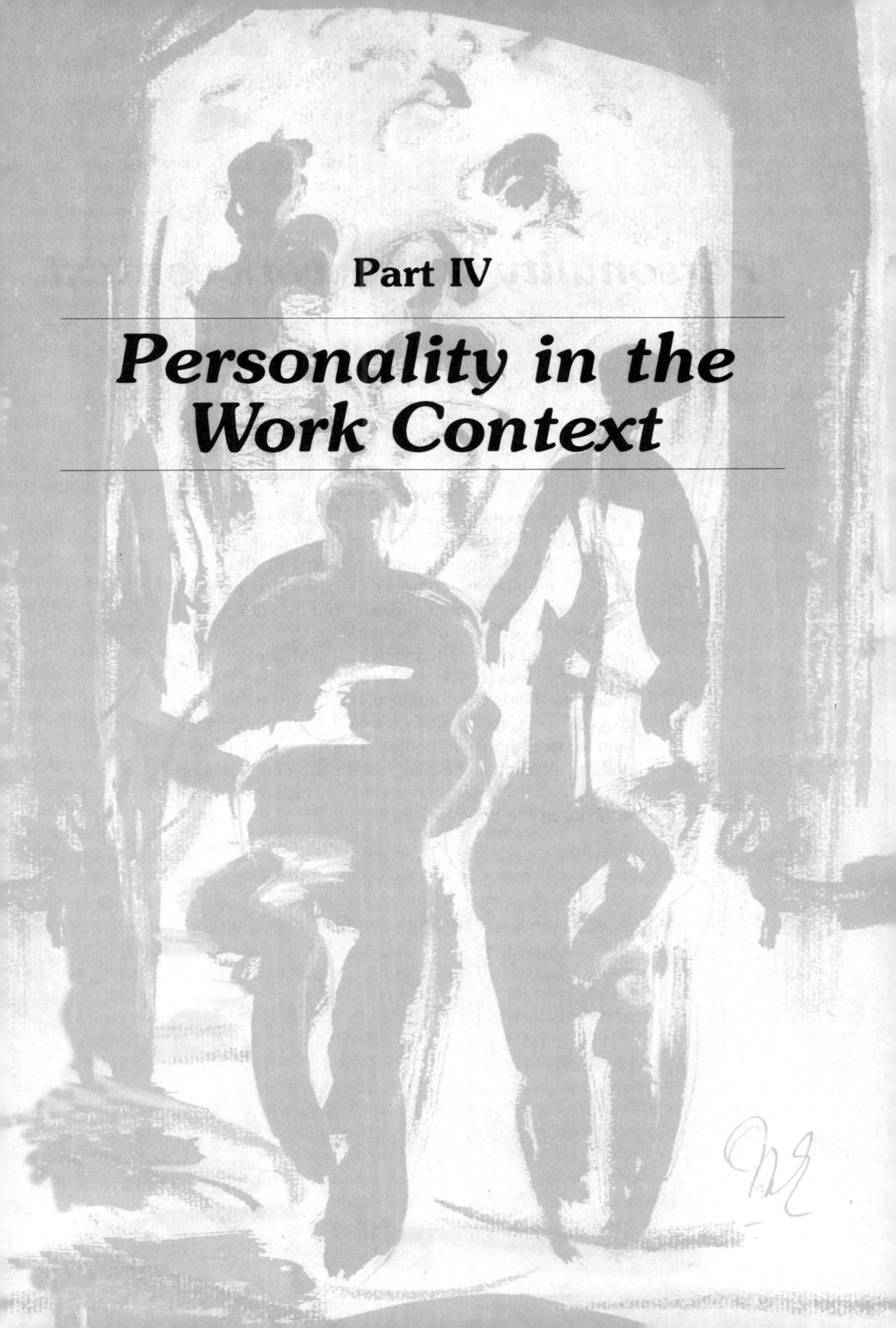

Personality in the work context

Personality represents the self, it integrates all of a person's visible and underlying attributes. As an integrating phenomenon, the study of personality integrates most areas of study in the psychological disciplines. It encompasses human behaviour and functioning in the physical, cognitive, emotional, social and spiritual domains, as these factors are needed in the various life roles of child, adult, worker, partner, parent and societal member. In the work context, employees' competencies and occupational adjustment are primarily based on the direct and moderating effects of personality variables. The scientific and optimal management and development of human resources in organisations depend on the ability to determine individual differences in employees' personality attributes and their congruence with organisational attributes. Organisational culture and organisational effectiveness are also dependent on the collective "personality profile" which employees attribute to the organisation.

The foundations of personality

Ziel Bergh

CONTENTS

Learning outcomes

After studying this chapter you should be able to:

- describe the nature of personality study
- construct and explain a definition of personality
- use examples to explain the dimensions of personality study
- briefly explain the various approaches to personality study
- give examples of how various factors influence personality
- explain the underlying assumptions in personality study
- demonstrate the cultural context of personality study
- use examples to indicate the practical use of personality concepts in the work context
- explain research approaches in the study of work-related personality factors

Key concepts

personology, criteria, individual differences, culture, African, approaches, occupational, fundamental view, structure, motivation, development, adjustment, assessment, physical, cognitive, social, psychological, idiographic, nomothetic, assumptions, determinants, heredity, environment, research

15.1 INTRODUCTION

In the midst of transformations such as socio-political change, which also influence interactions in the workplace, understanding differences and similarities between individuals and groups forms the basis of managing conflict and diversity. Recently, when the interest in personality psychology decreased somewhat, it was in the fields of industrial and organisational psychology and human resources development that the research on, and application of, personality concepts emerged with renewed vigour.

The applications of personality psychology or personology (the study of individual characteristics and differences) in occupational behaviour and processes are many. Personology is applied in assessments for selection and career development and occupational choice, work motivation, occupational health, education and training,

management and leadership, work satisfaction and productivity (Furnham 1992). In future the changing nature of work may increasingly necessitate the use of personality measures, as human resources competencies will be sought not only in technical fields, but even more in the area of personality variables such as interpersonal and communication skills, self-control, emotional stability and integrity.

15.2 PERSONOLOGY: A SCIENTIFIC FIELD OF STUDY AND APPLICATION

In human resources development, competency models in personnel assessment for selection, promotion, training and performance appraisal are based on various aspects of personality, such as knowledge, abilities, skills and other attributes necessary for successful occupational performance. Recent research and meta-analysis of previous research now recognises the usefulness in the work context of personality concepts and assessment (Schneider & Hough 1995; Furnham 1992, 1997; Barrick & Mount 1991; Hough 1997; Hough & Schneider 1996). This is in contrast to earlier findings (Guion 1965).

The study of personality or personology in general is about the consistent and repetitive patterns of behaviour, in both unique and universal aspects, which affect people's functioning in the context of their environment. Personality study includes nearly all domains of human behaviour, such as physical, biological, intellectual or cognitive, psychological, social and spiritual aspects. More specifically the study of personality is about the principles and processes which underlie and affect people's personalities and behaviour patterns. Personality is primarily explained by the concepts and assumptions of the various personality theories, but also by personality research and personality assessment of these concepts and assumptions. Personality theories provide conceptual and integrative systems or paradigms for logically and consistently explaining, describing and predicting human behaviour.

The science of personology is not much different from our own personal or "implicit" theories about people, except that personology has a *scientific* basis, which allows researchers to substantiate assumptions and concepts about behaviour. Personality psychology has grown from mere philosophical speculations to verified psychological knowledge based on systematic and controlled empirical research on human behaviour. It must, however, be added that many of the concepts and assumptions of existing personality theory are still only speculation or hypotheses, because these have not been verified satisfactorily by scientific research. In contrast, our personal theories about people and human behaviour are often the result of a few observations, often invalidated by our own values, prejudices and other subjective judgements.

Effective personality theories must not only have a systematic and logical framework, with complete, clear and usable concepts, but the concepts must be capable of being tested, in order to establish a scientific base of knowledge from which to explain personality, predict future behaviours and allow for the application of theories. In this regard Hall and Lindzey (1957) give the following three criteria against which personality theories and concepts can be compared and evaluated:

- *Comprehensiveness.* The theory must be capable of explaining the many significant facets of human behaviour in the most clear and specific manner.
- *Simplicity.* The theory must be understandable, with usable concepts, not vague, confusing or too abstract, and well structured in presenting the various aspects of personality.
- *Empirical support.* This relates to a theory's concepts facilitating further research questions and hypotheses, thus contributing to the expansion of knowledge and the applications of concepts and methods.

The criterion that personality theory must be useful through empirical verification coincides with the aim of any scientific activity – to establish valid or satisfying explanations for phenomena in order to expand and improve on the current state of existing knowledge (Popper 1959, 1969). However, the premises of objective science are also questioned, the reasoning being that precise mathematical, mechanical and reductionistic models cannot always be applied to psychology and nuances in human behaviour. For this reason the more intuitive approaches which are often used in psychology, such as Freud's, also have value, especially to explain certain aspects of behaviour. These two approaches, objective and subjective, also apply in the practices of research and assessment, and one of the main controversies in psychology surrounds them.

15.3 THE CULTURAL CONTEXT OF PERSONALITY

Culture is a rich source of information on personality, and with genetic factors, can explain uniqueness and similarities, as well as how different life roles are expressed and executed by people through their personalities and behaviour. In an organisational and also in a more general context, culture can be defined as those *collective norms*, values, beliefs, thinking and behaviours, based on past events especially, which characterise the unique or distinctive ways in which people do things and which may influence personality and behaviours. Insensitivity to cultural influences may be one of the main factors in prejudice in the human sciences, for instance racial and gender discrimination in practices such as personnel assessment, selection, financial remuneration, promotion and training. However, cultural heritage must not be used as an excuse to exclude any existing psychological idea or practice which best explains individual differences and similarities within a certain context. It is, however, essential to grasp the difference between considering and applying individual differences optimally and to being prejudiced and discriminating because of those differences. This is borne out by the South African Employment Equity Bill (Notice 1840 of 1997:23) regulating that:

> no person may unfairly discriminate, directly or indirectly, against an employee, in any employment policy or practice, on one or more grounds, including race, gender, sex, pregnancy, marital status, family responsibility, ethnic or social origin, colour, culture, language and birth.

From this, even affirmative action strategies or other policies and practices for empowering people must be based on principles of justice and equality.

The application of psychology in the work context is often heavily based on American and European schools of thought, even in Africa. Only a few of these assumptions have been influenced by African or Asian cultures. Nobles (1991) and Ho (1988) argue that psychologists too often only use Western models and standards in researching and explaining African and Asian people's behaviour, thus perpetuating the misunderstanding of blacks and Asians in Western society. We argue that emphasis on cultural stereotypes should not be allowed to perpetuate discrimination against any individual or group, especially in the "global world society" of today, in which economics and technology cause increasing cross-cultural contact, or in those societies where culturally diverse peoples are forced to co-exist. It is only in recent times that more knowledge of African culture, psychology and personality has started to surface to differentiate them from Western and Asian thinking (Sow 1980; Jones 1991; Azibo 1996; Steyn & Motshabi 1996). Earlier assumptions were often based on speculation or, at best, on sociological, philosophical, theological and anthropological research and writings and research on specific psychological concepts.

The valuable truths on human behaviour as established by Western psychology must be acknowledged. However, such knowledge and practices cannot be universally true without also considering viewpoints from other cultures, especially in countries where people of diverse cultures must co-exist. At the same time researchers also have the task of finding commonalities between cultures, as well as understanding commonalities and uniqueness from existing psychological knowledge.

Personality and culture are reciprocal

Views on people and personality in Western, Eastern and African cultures will be influenced by basic epistemological and ontological points of departure, that is, fundamental views about knowledge, science and people's existence in the world. It is important, however, to realise that Western, Asian (Eastern) and African culture and psychology are only umbrella concepts to describe general trends. Each of these consists of many subcultures and subdisciplines, influenced by many factors (gender, ethnicity, race, social roles, geography, traditions, etc.) in societies which will cause differences in cultures and even in subgroups such as families.

In Western society, psychology derives from a philosophical and scientific history, which in modern psychology emphasises a positivistic and empirical paradigm of human behaviour. Western psychology is characterised as scientific, analytical and reductionistic, and tries to assess, analyse, control, change and predict human behaviour in its various environments. In contrast Asian (Eastern) and African psychology originates from a metaphysical and spiritual (religious) tradition, resulting in a more intuitive and integrated discipline. Eastern psychology emphasises knowledge of the soul and freedom of the individual through self-realisation, especially through self-experiencing. In this process the emphasis is not so much on the individual, the self or the ego, but on the person or "personage" (Roland 1988; Hsu 1971) as an interpersonal being connected to his or her culture, society, family and spiritual values. Eastern culture emphasises the unity and mutual interaction of all things and the intrinsically dynamic and changing nature of the cosmos or universe (Atwood & Maltin 1991; Ho 1988). Although African cultures share similarities, many different African subcultures exist, both in white and black traditions. Black African cultures, especially, are in a state of transition and adjustment between Western, African and Eastern cultures.

According to Sow (1980) and Azibo (1996), it is possible to isolate an overall African school of thought or perspective which characterises African realities and values and which reflects African views on life and people. Viljoen (1997:617) summarises this African worldview and view on people as follows:

founded on a holistic and anthropocentric ontology, whereby humans form an indivisible whole with the cosmos (and therefore a unity with God and nature), and whereby humans are the point of departure and the centre of the universe, from which everything is understood and explained.

In more specific terms, Nobles (1991:299) differentiates the African worldview and view of mankind from Western views as shown in table 15.1.

It is obvious that these basic orientations will facilitate differences in how people explain human behaviour, people's management styles, work orientations and how to solve conflict.

In their perspective of time, black Africans' emphasis is more in terms of the past (history) and the present, the future not being that important because the future cannot be experienced and therefore does not actually exist. In contrast, Western civilisation is very time driven (time is money!) with the present and past being very important for future events. In many instances, therefore, time management according to Western norms, for purposes such as planning for present and future actions, might be a strange experience for Africans, because in their view time is awaited and created by each person for his or her own needs (Mbiti 1989). The same could be true for existing practices in leadership, management and other organisational and human resources activities.

We also know that although many general patterns exist, and there are controversies about this, the explanation

	African	Western
Ethos	Survival of the tribe Unity with nature	Survival of the best and fittest Controlling nature
Values and customs	Cooperation Collective group responsibility Interdependence through cooperation	Competition Individual rights Independence and separateness
Psychological modalities	Group orientation Sameness/equality Commonality	Individuality Uniqueness Differences

Table 15.1 African and Western views of the world and mankind
Source: Nobles 1991

and expression of personality maladjustment and the treatment of such problems is influenced by socio-cultural factors (Carson et al. 1996; Gobodo 1990; Prince & Tcheng-Laroche 1987).

It seems as if there is more congruence between Asian and African values than between them and Western values. This is especially evident from the African and Asian emphasis on the metaphysical and religious aspects, and their views of the unity of man with the universe and the stress on family and group relatedness. Further commonalities are their emphasis on intuition and self-experience, rather than on rational reasoning only.

15.4 APPROACHES TO PERSONALITY IN THE WORK CONTEXT

Many factors have influenced the emergence of different schools of thought in psychology and relevant personality theories.

Important influencing factors are events in the history and times of mankind and the world, events in theoreticians' own lives, different parts of the world, cultures and levels of civilisation, the emergence of the scientific method as opposed to philosophical speculation and the arrival of the computer age and information-processing technologies.

The new South African socio-political order, for example, is encouraging social scientists to rethink their theories, concepts and methodologies in explaining and assessing human behaviour. This is already visible in organisational restructuring, management strategies and the composition of workforces. The effects of globalisation (interaction between peoples of the world) will also increasingly influence South African ways of thinking and doing. Increasing contact with other cultures, such as those in Asia, will further influence existing South African perceptions.

The many influences are responsible for the fact that not one generally accepted approach exists on how to study personality or what personality in all its manifestations is. This lack of integration may be criticised; however, the richness of various types of theories, assumptions, concepts and methods provide for creative thinking about human behaviour and interventions in it. One theory or method may be more suited for describing or explaining personality and behaviour in a specific situation than the next. The various approaches to personality have caused controversy and even irreconcilable differences, but many have commonalities in concepts and processes; it is often a case of saying the same things differently. The concepts of traits, ego or self, responses and constructs, for example, although from different perspectives, more or less all indicate the consistent structure or characteristics in personality. Most approaches also agree on personality as having some structure, an enduring pattern in personality, motivating forces, personality as a developing phenomenon and the aspect of uniqueness and similarities in and between personalities.

Personality theories are classified in various ways, as indicated in books on personality (Meyer et al. 1997; Möller 1995; Carver & Scheier 1996; Pervin & John 1997; Caprara & Van Heck 1992; Schultz & Schultz 1994; Allen 1994). Some theories, for instance those of Allport and Kelly, are sometimes classified in more than one group.

Many or most theories in these classifications can be referred to as mega or grand theories on personality. They are the more complex and complete theories on personality by certain theorists in which all or most aspects of personality are covered, including structure, motivation and development. Others are single area theories, covering only a specific aspect of personality, for example motivation, development aspects, cognitive development, communication, self-concept, self-efficacy, perception, affiliation, emotions, stress, leadership, values, intelligence and career choice. Recent approaches in books on personality may be described as meta-perspectives, that is, they explain a concept from various

perspectives and apply concepts and methods from various perspectives in certain situations (Cloninger 1996; Buss 1995; Furnham 1992).

We have grouped together the following theories and perspectives which are relevant in the work and a South African context.

15.4.1 Psychodynamic or psychoanalytic theories (depth psychology)

The main emphasis is on people's experience of conflicts because of internal biological drives, *unconscious* motives, past events and the norms of society. The main theories are those of the classical psychoanalysts, Freud and Jung; neo-Freudians such as Melanie Klein, Sandor Ferenczi, Anna Freud and Otto Rank; ego psychologists such as Erikson and the socially-oriented psychoanalysts of whom Adler, Fromm, Sullivan and Horney are examples. Although heavily influenced by Freud, most writers after him have a more positive view, and emphasise a "stronger" self-concept, people being more in control of their lives and the influence of social factors. In more recent times, Lacan and Hillman have based their ideas on the work of Freud and Jung (in Meyer et al. 1997).

15.4.2 Behaviouristic or learning theories

The main idea is that personality is characterised by *responses* (behaviours), expectations and thoughts as learned and rewarded in the various types of environments in which humans function. People's environments and circumstances are dominant influences on what they become and may even override basic natural or genetic potentials. Important contributions to behaviourism theories are Darwin's ideas on evolution, research on conditioning by the Russian psychologist Pavlov (the forerunners of behaviourism); the work of John B.

Watson, Edward Lee Thorndike, Clark L. Hull and Edward C. Tolman; the radical and objective behaviourism of Skinner; the more subjective behaviourism of Dollard and Miller and the cognitive-learning approaches of Bandura, Mischel and Rotter.

15.4.3 Humanistic, phenomenological, existential approaches

According to these more person-oriented approaches, human personality and self-image are best understood by their *subjective existing* in, and unique experiences of, reality and the striving toward self-actualisation. The person is recognised as an active, unique and free being and not necessarily controlled by unconscious motives and environmental factors. Approaches which can be classified here are the self theories of Rogers and Maslow, Victor Frankl's existentialism and phenomenology by authors such as Buhler and May, while even theorists like Allport and Kelly are sometimes classified here.

15.4.4 Factor or trait theories

Human behaviour is characterised by enduring and consistent patterns of behaviour described as *dimensions*, traits, factors and types. This approach is predominantly emphasised in workplace applications, especially in the area of assessment of work competencies. Many factor theories have been proposed and many factors identified in various spheres, such as abilities, motivational states, interpersonal behaviours, emotions, beliefs, goals, attitudes, interests, values, managerial behaviours, entrepreneurial traits and "organisational effectiveness criteria", the latter often an attempt to give work organisations personality type characteristics. Important theorists are Allport, Cattell, Eysenck and Wiggins. Goldberg, Costa and McCrae, Hough and many other authors are researching new trait approaches on the so-called five-factor model of person-

ality, which arguably can be viewed as the most integrative trait approach on personality and possibly a meta-perspective.

15.4.5 Cognitive theories

According to these theories people are rational and thinking and form their own personality and destiny by using cognitive powers to create and change *cognitive constructs*, processes and schemas about reality. Many of these ideas originated in earlier or other theories, such as the Gestalt ideas of Wertheimer, Koffka, Köhler, Heider and Lewin. With the emphasis today on technology and information-processing, the cognitive perspectives may be more relevant than in earlier days, with many contributors, including Miller, Neisser, Kelly, Piaget, Mischel and Cantor.

15.4.6 Occupational-oriented personality theories

Some traditional personality theories explain aspects of occupational development. However, it is primarily theories about human development and career development and adjustment which explain how the "work personality" develops as part of personality development. In this regard Neff (1977) described the development of a so-called work personality as the acquisition of a productive role. Many sources emphasise the importance of various clusters of work-related personality concepts, such as introversion and extroversion, type A behaviours, hardiness, locus of control, self-efficacy, commitment.

Specific career development theories can be classified as so-called trait or factor approaches, as they mostly relate certain personality traits or types with similar dimensions from the work environment. The idea of *person-environment-fit* asserts that for optimal occupational performance employee characteristics must be congruent with the characteristics of the work environment. An example of this is the theory of Holland, which explicitly makes a connection between six personality types and corresponding work environments. The theory of Dawis and Lofquist (1984) describes career development and work adjustment as the efforts of both individual and organisation to achieve and maintain congruence between them. The individual's work personality involves skills and needs which are determined by values and will facilitate certain behaviours when interacting in the workplace. The degree of congruence will determine the satisfaction of both the employee and the employer, which will be a factor in the individual's staying in the organisation.

Some theories, such as those of Super and Ginzberg (in Schreuder & Theron 1997; Möller 1995), emphasise career development as a *continuous* process and part of human development or as *phases* in the stages of general human development. Super, for instance, sees personality and self-concept as finding expression in many focal points, of which an occupation is an important one. In the field of "organisational health", Kets de Vries and Miller (1984) assert that the possible "neurotic styles" of managers may relate to organisational pathology. Using the same classifications as for individual pathology, these authors describe five types of neurotic styles in organisations.

15.4.7 Biological perspectives

In people, like other animals, behaviour is foremost determined by *genetic* or biological processes and evolutionary history. In this approach many contributions come from other traditional personality theories, for instance the role of inheritance and evolution. Specific theories which emphasise the relationship between biology and personality are the approaches by Sheldon and Kretschmer, whilst theorists such as Eysenck, Cattell, Gray, Cloninger and Zuckerman also did important work in relating various personality and behavioural characteristics to human biology.

15.4.8 AFRICAN AND OTHER PERSPECTIVES

In Asian (Eastern) cultures there is less emphasis on the individual (and concepts like ego and self) and more emphasis on the interconnectedness of things, the interpersonal nature of personality, the influence of culture, society and family as well as spiritual values (Roland 1988). Personality formation is best acquired by knowledge of the soul gained through meditation and self-experiences. This emphasis is congruent with the more religious and metaphysical cultural traditions which point to an emphasis on subjective experience (intuition) and direct experience.

African views on personality are few and no single coherent personality theory exists. Akbar (in Azibo 1996) asserts that Western personality theories in the different schools are too deterministic, mechanistic, reductionistic and rational and do not really explain human functioning adequately. African psychology explains personality and personality development as purposeful behaviour, a unitary concept of interdependent physical, mental and spiritual dimensions in harmony with the values of its history, ecology, nature and the laws of life. The basic natural ingredient of the human personality is *spiritual* and from before birth a guiding spirit is developed and preserved through all other physical and mental experiences in interaction with nature. The physical dimension of personality is to survive, the mental or intellectual domain is to obtain knowledge about the world and the self, to create order in knowledge and events and especially to communicate knowledge meaningfully; both the physical and mental domains serve the spiritual survival of humans. The most important motivation for spiritual growth in human functioning is to realise transcendence away from an egoistic self to a meaningful relationship with God, which will also indicate a strong sense of morality and some form of immortality and *oneness* (unity and peace), the highest form of human yearning. All other aspects of existence should be secondary to this spiritual desire. According to an African perspective, dealings with people in the human sciences, such as psychology and the medical sciences, are often one-dimensional, without consideration for the intricate nature of the physical, intellectual and spiritual nature of human functioning.

However, personality is neither only shaped by its environment or circumstances, nor is it something "godly", with endless and goalless freedom as presented in some Western theories. When personality distortions occur in the physical, mental and spiritual domains, they are often created from humans' own norm-based values or from destructive unnatural environments.

While the influence of culture is recognised, it is unscientific to repeat old mistakes, such as trying to create new theories, concepts and applications for specific groups based on emotional and ideological reasons only. Many concepts and applications from existing personality theories can be used adequately to interpret other cultures. From ecosystemic theory, for instance, the assumption is made that all aspects of a system are in some way related to each other. In therapeutic and organisational psychology the implications of systems theory have long been utilised to understand the complex interactions between various subsystems. This assumption of oneness and interaction in nature and between humans and systems is also important in Asian and African cultures. The ideas of interactionism and transactionism in behaviouristic theories can adequately explain the interconnectedness between peoples and their environments and with cultural aspects. Some of the traditional personality theories not only adequately explain the individual as a

person, but also in relation to other people, the physical environment and to spiritual aspects such as religion; the latter, for instance, is addressed in the theories of Jung, Maslow and Allport. The notion of Ubuntu in black cultures, which indicates humaneness, is arguably congruent with concepts in humanistic psychology such as Rogerian theory, and concepts such as positive regard, empathy, transparency and acceptance which relate to how people should interact or be treated.

15.4.9 Personality psychology – an integrated science?

A few theories on personality, for instance Freud's psychoanalysis and Allport's trait theory, cover personality quite extensively. However, it cannot be said that the complete theory exists!

Examples of meta or integrative views appear in systems theory and in the recent attempts to explain personality according to the *five-factor* and related models (Goldberg 1990; Block 1995; Eysenck 1992; Hough 1997). There are a few variants of these models, and they have their critics, but generally all agree that personality in many areas can be explained by using at least five bi-polar trait dimensions, each with various subfacets (extroversion vs introversion, agreeableness vs antagonism, conscientiousness vs lack of direction, neuroticism vs emotional stability and openness to experience vs closeness).

The principles of an *ecosystemic* approach (Keeney 1979) (cybernetics and general systems theory) can also be utilised to explain the complex interactions and interdependence of the various aspects of personality functioning, or to explain specific psychological concepts and other aspects in human sciences, for instance family and group functioning, psychotherapy and work organisations. In general such an approach considers the interrelatedness of all things, including people as consisting of various interacting and changing systems and subsystems (e.g. physical, psychological, social, intellectual and spiritual aspects) and interacting in various systems and subsystems (e.g. person, marriage, family, work, culture, nation). Another important assumption is that all behaviour has meaning for people in terms of the *context* in which it occurs and in terms of the meaning or reality which each person attributes through language and communication. Human systems are also open systems and operate according to their own structures, rules, roles and feedback, which determine how stable, healthy or unhealthy the system will be. Personality, a work group, family, an organisation and a nation are examples of human systems. Optimal health will exist if there is balance and integration between all systems and their characteristics, rather than them being unstable and changing. Systems theory can be used to explain organisations as consisting of interdependent socio-technical systems (people, technologies and structures).

Modern theoretical and applied psychology in its various applications is evidence of a wider and more creative utilisation of psychological and personality constructs. It seems as if there is a shift in the criteria for effective personality theory – a shift to complexity from simplicity, diversity rather than similarity, specificity over generality and an emphasis on uniqueness more than on common characteristics. This also coincides with integrative views, such as systems theories, in which the complexity of interactions is emphasised, and the consensus that, except for intellectual and cognitive aspects, individuals show much fewer similarities over time and between situations than was previously accepted (Caprara & Van Heck 1992). The time has gone when we could use one theory, some factors only or one method to assess, explain and comprehend personality satisfactorily.

Although it is sometimes doubted whether personality psychology has really accumulated much knowledge or has expanded on existing knowledge or even has its own paradigms, many would agree that remarkable advances have been made. This is evident when original schools of thought and earlier assumptions on behaviour are compared to current assumptions and practices. It must, however, be emphasised that although the study of personality integrates many concepts and findings of psychology, is a factor in many spheres of human functioning and is used in many applied fields, personality psychology does not include all aspects of psychology. However, more than other psychological disciplines, it should have an "integrator function" in the study of various aspects of human behaviour. Students of psychological disciplines should study the creative contributions of the great theorists, but also take cognisance of the modern tendency to study personality according to relevant concepts, as well as integrative approaches to the study and use of personality concepts.

15.5 DEFINITION OF PERSONALITY AND RELATED CONCEPTS

Definitions of personality try to explain what people are, that combination and interaction of all possible personality characteristics. In this respect, it can be said that when we say "I am" or "I do", we try to define or identify who we are.

The variety of approaches and theories on personality is reflected in the different definitions, as no universally accepted definition exists. Some agreement, however, exists on some aspects which should be included in a personality definition and aspects which influence personality. In the latter case it seems that most psychologists now agree that personality can only be adequately explained if the interaction between characteristics or traits of the person and the situation or environment is considered (interactionism and transactionism). Definitions of personality may also reflect the theoretical and assessment preferences of theorists.

To define personality in all its dimensions, the following criteria or aspects must be emphasised:

- the external, visible and observable physical appearances, behaviour and traits, often referred to as "mask", the original meaning of personality
- possible invisible or covert behaviours, emotions, attitudes, values, thoughts and feelings
- enduring patterns and consistencies, but also the dynamic nature of behaviour, indicating motivation and change
- uniqueness
- organisation or wholeness and differentiation in personality, a person being body and mind with all its separate and integrated functions
- the necessity to accept that personality refers to a living human able to adapt to situations.

The following definitions from the literature all succeed to a degree in integrating some or most of these aspects and can be viewed as being systemic, interactional or integrated in nature:

- Allport's widely accepted definition describes personality as "the dynamic organisation within the individual of those psychophysical systems that determine his characteristic behavior and thought" (Allport 1961:28).
- Mischel (1976:2) refers to personality as "the distinctive patterns of behavior (including thoughts and emotions) that characterise each individual's adaptation to the situations of his or her life".
- Schultz and Schultz (1994:10) view personality as "the unique, relatively enduring internal and external aspects of a person's character that influence behavior in different situations".

- Cattell (1965:25) takes a broad view of personality and views it as "that which people will do, think or say when placed in a specific or given situation".
- Child (1968:83) offers an integrative definition of personality as "more or less stable, internal factors that make one person's behavior consistent across, and different from, the behavior other people would manifest in comparable situations".
- From an interpersonal perspective personality is about interactions between people. Sullivan (1953:111) asserted that personality is the "relatively enduring pattern of recurrent interpersonal situations which characterize a human life". This view is echoed by descriptions of what self-concept means: it is mostly people's self-identity as perceived by themselves, others or as the people think others see them.
- Meyer (Meyer et al. 1997:12) defines personality as "the constantly changing, but nevertheless relatively stable, organisation of all physical, psychological and spiritual characteristics of the individual which determine his or her behaviour in interaction with the context in which the individual finds himself or herself". The inclusion of the physical, psychological and spiritual characteristics recognises the concept of the human as a "person" having these characteristics, and being independent with free decision-making powers.

From a work perspective personality might be seen as those attributes which fit the demands of the working environment. Neff (1977), for instance, defines the work personality as semi-autonomous from other aspects of personality, and includes acquired work styles, behaviours, abilities, feelings and attitudes necessary to fulfil a productive role as demanded in work situations.

Related to personality are the concepts of temperament, character and self.

Character here has a more specific meaning, with emphasis on a person's values and moral and ethical principles. *Temperament* or nature denotes a person's emotional orientation and has genetic, physiological or biological connotations, for instance when we say "he is moody, overreacts or has a high frustration or pain tolerance". The "self" may have many personality-related connotations, as defined by various authors (Epstein, in Staub 1980). In general the self denotes anything which people themselves, or through others, perceive as belonging to their sense of being a person and describes the "I", "me" and "mine". The self may also refer to something which unifies various aspects of personality or which motivates or energises personality.

15.6 DIMENSIONS AND DOMAINS OF PERSONALITY AND HUMAN BEHAVIOUR

Most theories of personality have a *fundamental view of mankind*, which usually describes a theorist's central ideas and overriding assumptions on those things which are common to all human behaviour and human existence. Allport describes people as unique individuals with unique personality traits and purposeful behaviours; Freud views people as motivated by internal biological and unconscious forces which are often in conflict with societal norms; Kelly describes how people exist in the world by cognitively forming and adapting their own personal constructs; Rogers describes people as basically good and positive and able to realise their potential to be fully functioning persons.

Personality theories use a number of dimensions to explain personality and personality functioning. Personality is described in terms of interdependent dimensions, the most important being structure of personality, motivation or dynamics of behaviour and growth or development of personality. Some theories also emphasise personality adjustment (psychological health) and preferences for methods of research and assessment.

15.6.1 Structure of personality

Structure of personality refers to the basic building blocks that constitute personality and how they are organised. Various concepts are used, some complex and abstract and difficult to assess or observe, others more clear, concrete, easily observable and measurable. Allport, Cattell and Eysenck used traits as examples of structural concepts; Freud proposed dimensions in three mental structures referred to as id, ego and superego; Kelly preferred a structure in terms of cognitive constructs; Rogers utilised the self-concept; and learning theorists take the concept of behavioural responses as an integrative structural concept.

Structural concepts partly determine concepts for the dimensions of motivation, development, assessment and research.

15.6.2 Motivation of behaviour

Motivation, or dynamics, of behaviour describes why people behave in particular ways and what activates or energises behaviour. Hence, some theories emphasise internal drives, motives or needs that consciously or unconsciously create tension and direct behaviour. Others propose that people are or must be drawn by external forces or goals. Still others believe people want stimulation, that is, to grow towards and to achieve self-fulfilment, while others emphasise behaviour to become competent through cognitive abilities and skills in order to satisfy needs. All these approaches may explain motivation by emphasising the past, present or future, or conscious and unconscious states or in terms of biological and social determinants.

15.6.3 Personality development

Personality development refers to growth, maturation and expansion of, and in, personality in the physical, cognitive and psychosocial domains, development over time and influencing factors such as heredity and socio-environmental conditions. In this regard some theorists emphasise maturation as a result of predetermined biological processes, while others accentuate learning and experience. Some theorists stress development through progressive, often critical stages, while others describe it as a continuous process, often similar for all people. Others again see the uniqueness of personality development for every individual. General and career development theories also describe the formation of work-related knowledge, tasks and attitudes necessary for occupational maturity and adjustment.

15.6.4 Personality adjustment

Most theories, in addressing the concepts of structure, motivation and development, also explain personality adjustment (psychological or mental health), as well as ways to treat adjustment and psychological health problems. Normal behaviour, as described in personality handbooks, and abnormal behaviour or psychological disorders, as described in sources on psychopathology, are considered by most theorists as two separate types of behaviours. Many other theorists and researchers, such as Cattell, emphasise the importance of understanding normal behaviour in the diagnosis and understanding of abnormal behaviours (Strack & Lorr 1994). Helmes and Jackson, and Morey and Glutting (in Strack & Lorr 1994), provide evidence that the same taxonomy of personality constructs can be used to study normal and abnormal behaviours. Helmes and Jackson also advocate the possibility of normal "personality pathology", that is, the existence of personality behaviour deviations

in normal individuals, which should be differentiated from behaviour which can be classified as a personality disorder. Different theorists emphasise different aspects in explaining psychological health.

Rogers associates psychological health with a positive self-concept in relation to a person's environment and his or her success in achieving self-actualisation; Freud again coupled psychopathology to traumatic past experiences, conflicts between the id, ego and superego as well as overuse of defence mechanisms, while a person with a behaviouristic approach will explain adjustment problems as stemming from faulty learning and negative environmental influences.

In respect of personality adjustment, many theorists also address those aspects of personality that are possible to change, that could be influenced by change and how to facilitate change, for instance in psychotherapy.

15.6.5 Assessment and research methods

Personality theories often also have preferences for assessment and research methods. In this respect mention is often made of the so-called two sciences in psychology – clinical and statistical.

The *clinical* approach typically emphasises an intensive analysis of the individual and the uniqueness of behaviour, often using subjective means of assessment and relying strongly on *qualitative* sources of information, for instance test results and the psychologist's interpretation and judgement of events. Psychoanalysts would use a person's own verbalisations and experiences of events as well as dream analyses, to assess behaviour. Rogers, who could be viewed as an existentialist or phenomenologist, also preferred to rely on an individual's personal experiences as the most reliable source for analysis.

In contrast the *statistical* approach emphasises the use of more objective and *quantitative* sources of analysis, such as scientifically constructed tests and questionnaires, controlled experiments and other observations, as well as statistical methods to present and interpret data. Cattell's and Eysenck's approaches are an example of the statistical approach. They utilised factor analysis to isolate traits to explain most aspects of personality, and assumed that all people to some degree possess such traits. Behaviourists believe in exact measurements, observation and experimentation to test hypotheses about behaviours, and to establish cause and effect relationships between them.

In practice today, a combination of approaches and techniques is often used for personality assessment, depending on the application. In selection, for instance, a combination of methods might be used: job and situational analysis, biographical and other background information, previous performance analysis, personality and aptitude testing. Any number of methods could be used, including questionnaires, projective techniques, interviews and interests and values testing.

In all the dimensions of personality functioning the three domains of human behaviour used to explain personality are the physical, cognitive (intellectual) and psychological domains. The latter may also include social and emotional functioning. Especially in the description of personality development and growth, the separate and interdependent progression and integration of these domains towards maturity is emphasised. Magnusson and Törestad (1993), for instance, emphasise this complexity and integration when they reiterate the necessity of personality study to include all possible levels of study, especially physical, biological, psychological and social determinants of a person's functioning. It is in the unique combinations of all these influences in individuals that personality will develop and manifest.

The concepts we use to assess people in research and in practical applications derive from the multitude of concepts of structure, motivation and development as proposed in the various theories. Personality assessment is about how people think, behave and feel.

15.7 ASSUMPTIONS AND CONTROVERSIES ON PERSONALITY

Theories and research postulate assumptions or presuppositions about human nature and personality; some of these are facts because they are verified by research, others are only philosophical ideas or speculation. It is on the following issues that many controversies exist and over which theorists differ.

15.7.1 Knowability vs unknowability

Some theories postulate that human behaviour can be fully explained and known, while others contend that our knowledge of human personality and behaviour can never be complete. This coincides with various perspectives on time, because some theorists believe that human behaviour exists and develops within certain time limits and constraints, such as past, present and future influences and stages of development, whereas others hold that every human has his or her own time "clock", and that human behaviour can never be fully developed, as it is an ongoing process.

15.7.2 Holism (Gestalt) vs elementalism

Most theories assume personality to be more than the sum of its separate "parts". Personality is seen as a unified system of body, soul and mind; physical, intellectual, psychological, social and other elements are all integrated, or a synthesis, and function together to result in a fully functioning person. The interaction between heredity and social-environmental factors eventually determines personality. Many theorists use the concept of self or ego to indicate the pattern, organisation or integration of various behavioural elements into a recognisable self-identity as a person. Such theorists believe that you can only study personality in context or in interaction with its other subsystems and surrounding systems, such as family and work. Other approaches, such as behaviourism and dimensional or trait theories, also use elements of behaviour to do assessments and explain personality.

15.7.3 Determinism vs responsibility (free will)

Determinism refers to a compelling aspect of causality, postulating that things occur because of a dominant determinant. In this respect some theories assume that personality is determined or caused by past events such as traditions and traumatic experiences; others also emphasise present or future influences; some stress the dominant influence of brain processes, heredity or the environment; still others highlight factors beyond our control, such as unconscious drives and ancestors. The issue of consciousness or unconsciousness as states of awareness or as causes of behaviour remains one of psychology's most interesting controversies and research areas. There are thinkers who reject unconscious concepts and believe people are consciously in control of their own destiny, rational and with a free will to choose what they want and what is going to happen in life. Determinism also assumes that if we know all the causes or influences on personality and behaviour, we will be able to predict future actions by people and groups accurately, something that in the practice of psychological assessment is still only possible to a certain degree. We already know that we can control and change certain things and

events in our lives, while others, such as physical growth, happen no matter what we try.

Another aspect of determinism on which theorists differ is the belief that behaviour is only influenced by the *person* (personism); some hold that the *situation* in which the person operates predominantly influences behaviour (situationism), while others assert that behaviour is always the result of the *interaction* between personality and the situation (interactionism).

Most psychologists today agree that behaviour is a function of the interaction between the person and the situation. This, however, does not mean that all authors agree on what personality is and how personality develops.

15.7.4 Causality vs relationships

It is assumed in most personality theories that factors inside and outside the individual are responsible for personality development and behaviour. Causation or etiology implies that we should be able to find evidence that certain factors are really deterministic, forcing or compelling the consequences or effects. Much research in the behavioural sciences is about relationships between behaviours. The causes of behaviour should enable us to predict future events or actions better, but they are not easy to establish. If they were, human resource practitioners would have it easy in selecting or placing applicants in jobs, training the most successful workers and advising young people more accurately on career or marriage choices! In research terms it is a fact that we are able to indicate causal relationships or predictions of future behaviours only with limited degrees of certainty, mostly by controlled observations, as in experiments. A problem in much research may be that researchers assume causation, while actually they only refer to a relationship between variables, for instance that high scores on one test of intelligence have a positive, significant relationship with high scores on a work-performance measure.

An aspect of causality is the *consistency* of behaviour over time and across situations, for instance the continuity between childhood and adult behaviours. In some theories and research, personality consistency across situations is stressed; others again emphasise the variation in personality as a result of the context or situation. Some agreement exists as to personality consistency in traits and across time and situations, although Caprara and Van Heck (1992) and Pervin and John (1997) cite research indicating that the magnitude of agreement could be less than generally assumed.

15.7.5 Heredity vs environment (nature vs nurture)

One of the oldest arguments in psychology is about the influence of hereditary, congenital, inborn or natural factors in human behaviour and the formative influence of the various environmental factors the individual is exposed to. This is often referred to as nature versus nurture. Many theorists believe, and researchers in certain instances have verified it, that certain characteristics and behaviours are determined by genetic endowment. In addition to physical attributes, many behaviours, such as instinctive reactions, three-dimensional perception, people's tendency for social belonging and caring (attachment behaviours), even personality traits such as intelligence, and a talent for music, may be based on genetic causes.

Supporters of the environmental viewpoint, on the other hand, reason that behaviour is learned and that personality is formed and transformed by stimulation or inhibition from physical, social and psychological environmental influences. Thus an individual or group and even a society could manifest aggressive or any other type of behaviour if such behaviours were conditioned and approved or rewarded by

dominant environmental agents such as parents, peer groups and other forces. Intelligence and other intellectual capacities can only be realised from the influence of environmental stimulation, the reasoning often being that even a born genius would end up a "dummy" if not developed by stimulating environmental forces.

Theories also differ in the extent to which they emphasise the place of and interaction between behaviour, emotions and intellectual or cognitive aspects.

Which body, temperament?

An integrating view on this issue assumes that many human characteristics are genetically determined by the interaction (interactionism) of parental dominant and recessive genes, or even abnormalities in these combinations (genotype). However, how these characteristics manifest or develop (phenotype) will often be a result of, or at least co-determined by, environmental influences.

15.7.6 Idiographic vs nomothetic understanding

In theory and assessment practices and in interventions, some theories stress an idiographic view. This view asserts that people are unique or "individual", rather than merely different. The individual and his or her experiences must be considered as unique, even if responses seem the same as those of others in situations, on questionnaires or in tests. The individual and the context in which he or she functions must be considered as a whole. Psychologists or practitioners holding this view do not emphasise norms and standards or other statistical indices to compare individuals and groups, and sometimes may disregard such indicators altogether. Instead they make use of their own clinical and subjective judgements or impressions of people.

In contrast the *nomothetic* approach uses objective measures, such as psychometric tests, ratings and statistical manipulations of data to emphasise individual differences, and general laws of comparison, such as norms and correlations, for individuals and groups. This view holds that all persons are more similar than different, all possess certain traits to a lesser or greater degree and these similarities and differences can be, and must be, accurately and objectively assessed.

Recent personality literature (Day & Bedian, in Howard 1995) has promoted the concept of "fit". Scores of applicants on personality measures must be compared to those of others in the organisation or job, for instance co-workers and supervisors, and not to those of the population on which the test was standardised.

15.8 DETERMINANTS OF PERSONALITY DEVELOPMENT

The influences on an individual's personality, its formation, development, functioning, motivation and adjustment, can be ascribed to many individual and combined factors. All these factors can be classified into four main categories: hereditary or biological, psychological, social and external. On closer analysis these four categories are all about either hereditary (genetic) or environmental factors, these two determinants being responsible for an ongoing controversy about their importance in personality formation. In general a con-

sensus view prevails. Genetic and environmental factors are important, and depending on the development stage and domains of behaviour (cognitive, physical, socio-psychological) may have more or less influence in personality development and well-adjusted or maladjusted behaviours. Perhaps it is more important to realise that we must create the conditions to complement genetics and environment in order for human potential to develop optimally over the life span.

15.8.1 Hereditary and biological factors

Genetic influences are related to biological maturation, growth and changes that takes place, notwithstanding environmental factors, although these may delay or distort certain processes.

The uniqueness of each person with respect to some aspects can be sought in genetic endowment, especially in physical traits, intellectual capabilities and emotional or temperamental traits (Plomin et al. 1990; McGue, Bacon & Lykken 1993; Kagan 1994). Definite genetic influences are reported for aspects such as activity level and emotions such as fearfulness, negative emotionality and aggression.

As well as genetic similarity between people with respect to certain physical features, findings also indicate general similarities in certain social and emotional behaviours due to genetic influences. Examples are certain attraction behaviours between male and female, affiliative behaviours and emotional expressions such as anger, fear, surprise, joy, sadness and disgust.

15.8.2 Environmental factors

Environmental influences may be physical, social or psychological. They are important in how genetic potential develops and affects psychological and social behaviours, and the values, attitudes and beliefs that characterise individuals and groups. One of the important functions of environmental influences is to socialise the developing person for adult responsibilities and roles such as marriage, family life and work. The most important environmental agents are now discussed in some detail.

15.8.2.1 Family influences

The developing child's parents, especially its mother (although the father's role is often underemphasised), provide the type of psychological and social examples, models and rewards that will either enhance or inhibit healthy personality and career development. Immediate and extended family interactions are the basis for the growing child's attachment behaviours, self-concept and identity development — who and what the person is! The parents' own behaviours and how children's behaviours are rewarded will elicit certain types of behaviours, either positive and constructive or negative and destructive. These could and most probably will be modelled on the parents' behaviours. The child's experience of family life will lay the groundwork for many roles, future relationships, gender identity, and identity as a student, worker, parent and member of society. Every child in a family may have different experiences of the same family interactions and of the outside environment, which together with genetic differences may also explain personality and behaviour differences.

15.8.2.2 Social affiliations outside the family

Important people outside the family, such as peer groups and friends, often serve as an extension of the family, a place in which the child can explore and extend the perceptions of himself or herself and the world, and often also test the behaviours relevant in the family. Harris (1995) asserts that experiences outside the home are really responsible for differences between family members. In a world with different values and attitudes, especially with regard to being responsible and independent, peer involvement may lay the basis for a culture of healthy competition, learning and work.

15.8.2.3 Cultural membership

Cultural membership is important in that it often provides the historical and immediate mega-environment which prescribes certain behaviours or creates opportunities. The group in which a person belongs at a certain time in life may create a legacy of socioeconomic status and other identities and roles, with related ways of behaving, which are not easy to change. Culture will determine in many ways how people think, feel and what they do. In this sense cultural differences between individuals and groups may be much more important than is often recognised, for instance by political and labour systems wanting to force integration among various peoples.

15.9 RESEARCHING PERSONALITY IN THE WORK CONTEXT

The goals of personality research are to obtain valid and reliable research support for theories and related assumptions, concepts and methods in order to expand knowledge and applications on personality and to build or form and revise personality theories. In the work context there is interest in the reciprocal relationship between personality (behaviours, feelings and abilities) and occupational behaviours, in order to facilitate the best fit between an employee and the work environment.

Despite earlier contrasting opinions (Guion 1965), recent research and meta-analysis of previous research emphasises the value of personality assessment in work-related applications (Muchinsky 1993; Hogan 1991; Schneider & Hough 1995; Barrick & Mount 1991; Tett et al. 1997; Hough 1992; Hough 1997; Furnham 1992, 1997). Longitudinal research (over longer periods) cited in Cloninger (1996) and Craig (1996), indicate the reciprocal effects between personality and work variables. Personality, value patterns and work attitudes formed in early life may have enduring influences in adult occupational behaviours, although later influences and changes, such as work involvement and autonomy, may also be instrumental in creating or maintaining work attitudes and may even influence the expression of personality. Results also indicate that employees who are poorly adjusted in early life may in later occupational life show less career advancement.

Findings also suggest that overall career success and happiness are aided by personality factors, such as being optimistic, serious minded, energetic, contented, open, spontaneous, self-confident, self-sufficient, ambitious and free from negative feelings, hostility, aggression, anxiety, irritability, unhappiness and dissatisfaction.

A special application of correlational research in the work context is *criterion research*, in which problems of validity, reliability and restrictedness are special issues. Researchers and practitioners try to find work performance criteria that are specific to certain jobs and situations but also have universal applications. An example of a cluster of work-related personality criteria is the eight-factor performance taxonomy for high-level jobs by Campbell et al. (1990). They suggested an eight-factor performance taxonomy for high-level jobs as follows:

- job-specific task proficiency
- non-job-specific task proficiency
- written and oral communication tasks
- demonstrating effort
- maintaining personal discipline
- facilitating team and peer performance
- supervision
- management and administration

A problem in criterion research is the use of too broad an approach, in which too many predictors are correlated with too many criteria. Researchers will have to be more specific in isolating, defining and measuring those personality and work performance variables that belong together. Another problem in work performance criteria is that task or technical performance is not clearly differentiated from contextual activities, sometimes referred to as prosocial and organisational citizenship behaviours, such as support, offering extra help, volunteering and being loyal, the latter referring to job outputs that are not technical, but support the technical task performance (Brief & Montewidlo 1986).

In general all types of personality information can be classified as one or more of the following (Pervin & John 1997):

- *L- or life data.* Information from a person's personal history, such as in archival studies.
- *O- or observer data.* Information obtained by observations and ratings of people who are involved with or knowledgeable about participants, such as family, friends and colleagues.
- *S- or self-report data.* Information obtained from what the respondent verbally tells the researcher, such as during interviews and when answering questionnaires.
- *T- or test data.* Information gathered from standardised tests and questionnaires and during experiments.

In a related approach Furnham (1997) analysed the following six different approaches that are used to research personality in the work context:

- *biographical or case history research*, which is aimed at analysing personal life details and experiences
- *classic personality theory*, in which many different traits are measured and related to work-related personality variables
- *specific personality measures* for very specific work applications, such as using a measure of locus of control or hardiness to predict success in fighter pilots

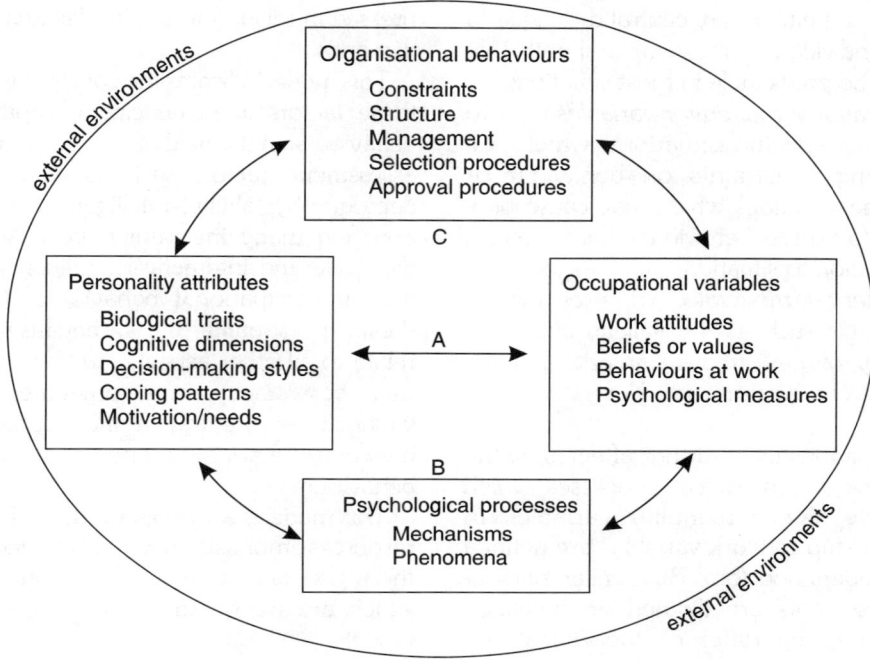

Figure 15.1 A research model of the relationship between personality and work
Source: Adapted from Furnham (1997:143)

- *analysing the attributes of work environments and employees* to find the best fit (or misfit) in order to take decisions in occupational choice or selection
- *classical organisational and occupational psychology,* in which work-related variables are researched for their relationship with personality
- *longitudinal studies* of people at work on how various personal and personality factors stay consistent or change over time.

Furnham (1992, 1997) asserts that many of these approaches and much research on work-related personality variables are theoretically and methodologically poor. He suggests a research model to illustrate the relationships between personality and work, of which figure 15.1 is an adapted version.

This model illustrates the complex possibilities in the relationship between personality and work-related variables.

The relationship between personality factors and work variables (line A) is not direct and can be influenced by many other factors. This relationship may be bi-directional, that is, personality and work factors may have mutual or interactional influence; personality may influence work behaviours, but work variables may also influence the expression of personality. In many instances we must assume that personality is an indirect influence on work behaviours. In a model proposed by Schneider and Hough (1995), they emphasised three types of moderator variables (intervening factors) that may influence the relationship between personality and work performance. These moderators may be related to each of the boxes in the model:

- *Personal moderator variables* are traits that are either very central or unique to an individual or more general traits that will be predictable in most situations.
- *Situational moderator variables* refer to either specific situations which are strong constraints on behaviour or some situations which may cause people to express behaviour differently from situation to situation.
- *Criterion moderator variables* include aspects such as the validity and reliability of performance criteria and the time of measurement.

The relationship is further affected by the way the psychological processes which underlie the personality variables in relationship to work variables are defined and understood (box B). Similar personality concepts are defined or explained differently by different theoretical approaches: some emphasise biological and situational influences; others the influence of emotional or cognitive processes in behaviour.

The relationship between personality and work variables is further impacted by formal and informal organisational behaviours and constraints (box C). The way an organisation functions can have a facilitating or inhibiting effect on the work personality and on the fit between the employee and the organisation. In some instances an employee must do a task in one way only, thus inhibiting individual expression, while in other instances an employee will be allowed or forced to act differently in each situation.

The broader environments (circle) in which the organisation and individual exist will also influence the relationship between personality and organisation. In times of change and transformation both employee and organisation must adapt, and these adjustments will be reflected in the expression of personality and work behaviours. Many non-work factors, through "spill-over

effects", influence how personality is expressed in relation to work roles and work demands.

This model indicates the complexity of all these factors in influencing occupational behaviours. In the field of human resources assessment, factors such as personality, demography, ability, intelligence, motivation and many intervening variables, individually and interactively, influence and modify occupational behaviours. Of all these, personality traits, because they relate to all other aspects, and because of their consistency, and sometimes their variance, are central in the relationship between personality and occupational behaviours.

This model is also in line with the human resources emphasis on job competencies in the work context, as it specifies attributes which are measured in job competency models.

15.10 CONCLUSION

Personality study is an *integrative discipline* in the study of human behaviour, although not all psychological topics are covered in the study of personality. Many theories on personality exist, but research is still necessary to find a universally acceptable theory which will be able to stand the tests for completeness and research support. Such a theory must be able to explain and describe the human personality in all its dimensions and domains, its variations across time and its situations and cultures. Cultural diversity in human behaviour, however, raises the question whether such integration will ever be possible. The variation in personality theory and constructs may be necessary to reflect the richness of human individuality and cultural diversity in this world!

Notwithstanding the lack of a unifying paradigm in personality study, that is, an integrating model and set of assumptions, it is necessary to acknowledge the momentous influence of the older traditional theories, especially Freud's psychoanalysis, which, if nothing else, energised the systematic study of personality. The traditional behaviourism and humanistic theories also influenced, and still do, the thinking of many authors, researchers and practitioners of human behaviour. We must also support new, emerging and possibly unifying personality theories, such as the important five-factor model, which could succeed in integrating decades of psychological knowledge and may break ground for revised and new applications in assessment, research and other practical uses of personality constructs. It is also possible that the principles in systems thinking will be translated into an integrated personality theory which could accommodate differences and commonalities in and between cultures. We must also applaud the ongoing research efforts to verify existing personality constructs and to find more valid assessment methods and applications. As psychologists we may sometimes be guilty of not promoting the many well-researched and well-founded assumptions, concepts and methodologies which the science of psychology offers us to make meaningful impact.

We agree with Viljoen's assertions (Meyer et al. 1997) that although differences exist, psychological thinking in personality psychology enables us to explain human behaviour in the four aspects of human existence: people as individuals or persons; in relation to other people; in relation to the physical environment and in relation to a transcendent existence (spiritual and religious functioning). We may add an important life interest, work life! Managing and developing diverse work forces, groups and individual employees in changing work environments may increasingly rest on our abilities to understand expressions of the human personality.

Self-evaluating questions

1. Describe the nature of personality study and indicate which dimensions are usually covered.
2. Critically discuss the issues on which personologists either agree or disagree.
3. How would you evaluate a theory or construct on personality for effectiveness?
4. Taking your own life line (critical points in your development), isolate and describe at least five formative influences and indicate specifically how these factors contributed to your choice of a career direction.
5. Using any work environment, draw up a research plan to study the interaction between employee personalities and the workplace.
6. Explain the role of culture in personality study.
7. Briefly explain the different approaches to personality study.

Psychodynamic perspectives

16

Linda Albertyn

CONTENTS

Learning outcomes

After studying this chapter you should be able to:

- identify the central themes in psychoanalytic theories
- recognise the application value of psychoanalysis to work behaviour
- describe the structure of personality as delineated by the main psychoanalytic theorists
- explain what directs and motivates personality, and from where it has its origin
- explain the development of personality as postulated by the main psychoanalytic theorists
- describe the healthy personality as viewed by the major psychoanalytic theorists
- describe abnormal behaviour as viewed by the major psychoanalytic theorists
- outline the major criticisms against psychoanalysis
- discuss the main contributions of psychoanalysis with reference to future directions to be taken

Key concepts

depth psychology, psychoanalysis, to-pographical, unconscious, instincts, drives, libidinal energy, personality structure, id, ego, superego, psyche, personal unconscious, collective unconscious, anxiety, defences, developmental stages, Oedipal conflict, individuation, self-realisation, sibling rivalry, attitudes, types

depth psychology, which was followed by Adler's individual psychology and Jung's analytical psychology. Depth psychology encompasses the work of orthodox Freudians, neo-Freudians, ego-psychologists, socially-oriented psychoanalysts and a few post-modern psychoanalysts. Most of them were influenced by Freud's classical psychoanalysis, but they also created other concepts and even opposed Freud on some issues.

16.1 INTRODUCTION

Psychology started to gain independence from philosophy in the second half of the 19th century. In accordance with the direction set by Wilhelm Wundt, the founder of the first psychological laboratory and the structural school, the prevailing emphasis was on conscious processes (Hjelle & Ziegler 1992). This was also the era of Victorianism, of a smug, self-satisfied society that emphasised rationality and did not openly recognise human sexuality. It was during this time that Freud developed his theory and view of humankind that stunned the scientific world of his time. His influence was far-reaching, and many of his concepts are still accepted today. Although there were some forerunners, Freud is considered the father of

Sigmund Freud

16.2 BASIC ASSUMPTIONS OF PSYCHOANALYSIS

Freud's basic view of humankind is that behaviour is determined and motivated largely by unconscious forces inside the person which are in conflict with societal norms.

First, in contrast to the prevailing emphasis on conscious mental processes, Freud likened the consciousness to the tip of an iceberg. He believed the larger part of the structure of personality, the *unconscious*, was of most importance to understanding human behaviour. Second, contrasting further with the view of humans as rational beings, Freud stated that people were in a perpetual state of conflict between the expression of unconscious sexual and aggressive instincts (drives or desires) and societal demands. This *conflict* motivates or determines all behaviour. Third, Freud described the mind as a battleground for the factions of instinct and reason. This later gave rise to the term "psychodynamic", referring to this constant conflict for control over the person's behaviour.

Freud developed a unique approach to psychotherapy, called *psychoanalysis,* which was aimed at understanding the unconscious desires motivating his patients' behaviour. As his theory evolved from his therapy, theory and therapy are not easily distinguishable from each other, and often the two terms are used interchangeably. As a result of his emphasis on biological instincts and the influence of early childhood in setting personality, his theory is often classified as biologically deterministic and pessimistic – Freud's person did not have any control over his or her behaviour or the past that so strongly determines current behaviour.

What is important in the history of psychodynamic theories is that Freud's is the core theory from which many new theories developed. Most of the theorists who followed Freud in the psychodynamic movement opposed his excessive emphasis on sexuality and aggression as determinants of human behaviour. Rather, they emphasised the role of social factors in shaping personality, the role of interpersonal relationships in determining behaviour, and developed further Freud's idea of the ego to explain the development of human personality. In doing this, they moved away from biological determinism to social determinism, from the id to the ego, from the study of the child to the adult, and acknowledged the potential for overcoming primitive drives and to lead fulfilling lives.

Despite the differences, certain central ideas can be identified from all psychodynamic theories (Carver & Scheier 1996; Hjelle & Ziegler 1992; Marx & Cronan-Hillix 1987):

- Personality is seen as a *dynamic set of processes* – processes that are always in motion. These processes include instincts, interpersonal and social processes on the one hand, and rationality and conscience on the other.
- The processes sometimes work in harmony with one another and sometimes against one another, but are *rarely, or never, passive.* Personality is a dynamo from which forces emerge that can be set free, channelled, modified or transformed. In this view, the work context serves as an important outlet for these energies. For example, aggressive instincts may be transformed in a socially acceptable way by choosing the career of a surgeon or becoming a professional boxer.
- Competing pressures within the personality, primarily life and death instincts, *conflict* with each other. The processes of personality sometimes compete or wrestle with each other for control over the person's behaviour. A career in professional sports could constitute a good balance between these two forces: first, the aggressive need to compete and overpower others, and second, the gratification derived from being loved and admired.

- The conflicts, and many of the motivations, that take place among the elements of personality are often *unconscious*. Psychoanalytic thinking therefore strongly emphasises the role of the unconscious in determining people's behaviour. The surgeon or boxer in the example above would probably not be aware of acting out in the chosen career a desire experienced as a young child to kill his or her siblings; the rebellious employee would be unaware that he or she is unconsciously acting out against his or her own father.
- The basic drive is *sexual* (life instinct), supplemented by *aggression* (death instinct), and has its foundations in the biology of the individual. These drives serve as a reminder that humans are "animals" whose purpose in life is reproduction. Work serves as an excellent outlet for satisfying sexual and aggressive impulses through intimate contact, competition, discussion, meetings or sadistic pranks against colleagues (Czander 1993).
- The history of the individual, in particular *early childhood*, is of extreme importance in determining contemporary behaviour. Parental relationships with the child account for neurosis. (The contemporary term is "anxiety-based disorders"; however, since this chapter describes the original depth psychological concepts, the term "neurosis" is used throughout.) Freud argued more specifically that human sexuality must be taken into account at all stages of development – even infancy. A person displaying inappropriate consumption of alcohol at work may have had needs for oral gratification that were not satisfied during childhood.
- The *defence mechanisms* of the ego protect the individual from psychological harm. Every person has psychological processes to keep those elements of self-knowledge that is most threatening from

becoming overpowering. Work offers good opportunities for acting out defences. For example, an individual who fears that his or her personal anxieties will become known to other people may work toward a position of authority and control over others, in order to hide his or her own insecurities (Czander 1993).
- Mental health depends on a *balance of forces* in one's life. It's good to express your deep desires, but not to let them control your life. It is good to act morally, but a constant effort to be perfect can cripple your personality. It is good to have self-control, but it's not good to be overcontrolled. Moderation and balance of these forces provide the healthiest experience of life.

As mentioned earlier, the unconscious plays an important role in psychodynamic thinking. The unconscious provides a setting for the conflicts that motivate behaviour which ultimately leads to the development of a healthy or abnormal personality. We now take a closer look at the unconscious and the conscious as perceived by the major proponents.

16.3 THE ROLE OF THE UNCONSCIOUS AND CONSCIOUS IN PERSONALITY

Due to the centrality of the unconscious in Freud's theory, and the fact that many psychodynamists differed from him in this respect, a short explanation of Freud's view of the unconscious and conscious follows.

Freud believed that the human mind was organised into three levels of awareness – this is often referred to as the *topographical* model of the mind. The three levels are the conscious, preconscious and unconscious. Freud's notion of the *conscious* corresponds with our everyday notion of the conscious, in other words, it includes all the sensations and experiences of which we are aware at any given moment. For example, you might be aware of a car passing as you are reading this text. Since we can only be aware of a small portion of our thoughts, sensations and memories at any given time, the conscious must be a small and limited aspect of our personality. The *preconscious* refers to "available memory", in other words, experiences that are not readily available to our awareness, but that can easily be retrieved into awareness. Examples are what your favourite foods are and where you spent your last holiday. Freud placed the unconscious central in his theory, of greater magnitude and importance than the conscious and the preconscious. The *unconscious* refers to those experiences that are not easily accessible to awareness. It contains memories, emotions and instincts that are so threatening to the conscious mind that they have been pushed into the unconscious mind. An example of material that could be found in the unconscious mind is a forgotten trauma experienced in childhood.

The concept of unconscious factors motivating behaviour has been applied in the work situation through the Johari-window. The Johari-window provides a model for feedback on self-knowledge and personal and interpersonal behaviour. The Johari-window works with two dimensions, feedback to self and exposure to others. Within the feedback dimension are elements that are known to the self and elements that are unknown to the self and the same applies to the exposure dimension. The ideal situation to strive for in the work situation is one in which few elements are unknown to the self and to others.

Freud used the analogy of the iceberg to describe all three levels of personality (see figure 16.1). The conscious is the portion above the surface of the water. The part underneath the surface, the unconscious, occupies nine-tenths of the mind. The preconscious is the bridge between the conscious and the unconscious mind.

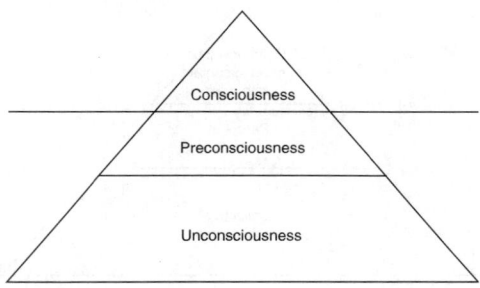

Figure 16.1 Freud's three levels of consciousness

The unconscious contains the major driving power behind our behaviour and is the basis for explaining all behaviour. It exerts a continuing influence on later actions and conscious experience. Freud believed that even the simplest, most accidental aspects of human behaviour could not be ascribed to chance. Slips of the tongue, slips of the pen, misplacing objects and forgetting appointments and names can all be ascribed to unconscious material. Unconsciously, people often forget the name of a person who has angered them, or the details of a frightening experience. The purpose of dreams, jokes and work is to permit the indirect expression of socially unacceptable impulses. For example, an individual with a fascination for the human body may choose to become an art photographer. In this way, his or her desires can be channelled in both a socially acceptable way and in a manner which satisfies his or her own need to attain pleasure.

Although Jung agreed with Freud's notion of the unconscious, he added another important dimension, the collective unconscious. He distinguished between a *personal unconscious*, which is a blend between Freud's unconscious and preconscious, and the *collective unconscious*, which refers to certain culturally inherited predispositions and experiences common to all mankind (see figure 16.2).

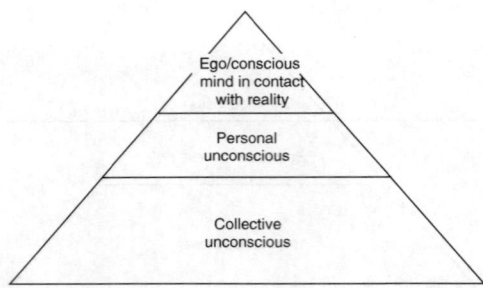

Figure 16.2 Jung's three levels of consciousness

Jung's ideas on the unconscious have had a significant impact on assessment and research in personality. He developed the word-association test, which provided the first experimental data on unconscious processes and is still widely used today.

Because the social psychodynamists, such as Adler, emphasised the influence of social and cultural factors rather than biologically driven instincts, they regarded humans as largely conscious and able to soar above their past experiences. They did, however, still regard the uncovering of the unconscious an important part of understanding human behaviour. The image of a jade tree has been used to describe Adler's view of the conscious and unconscious (Aiken 1993). The jade tree has a small underground root system (the unconscious) and extensive growth above the ground (consciousness). Adler believed that people were able to overcome their instincts and the effects of the past and strive for more fulfilling lives, shaping their own destinies and improving themselves through growth (Hjelle & Ziegler 1992).

16.4 THE STRUCTURE OF PERSONALITY

In addition to his topographical model of the mind, Freud developed a structural model of personality. According to this model personality is made up of three components: the id, ego and superego (see figure 16.3).

The *id* is found in the unconscious and contains the energy to drive behaviour or personality. The energy is the result of the conflicts described earlier between biological instincts, rationality and conscience. Instincts are divided into two groups: life instincts, of which the most important is the libido (or sexual instincts) and death instincts, of which the most important is aggression. All the instincts reside in the id, each has its source in biological tensions, aims at discharging this energy in a certain activity (behaviour) and needs an object to discharge this release. Freud believed that there is always a certain amount of instinctive tension or pressure that we must constantly try to reduce. In reducing its tension, the id operates according to the *pleasure principle.* Its function is to obtain maximum pleasure through striving for immediate satisfaction of all needs.

The second substructure of personality, the *ego,* is an evaluative agent which intelligently selects the behaviour which

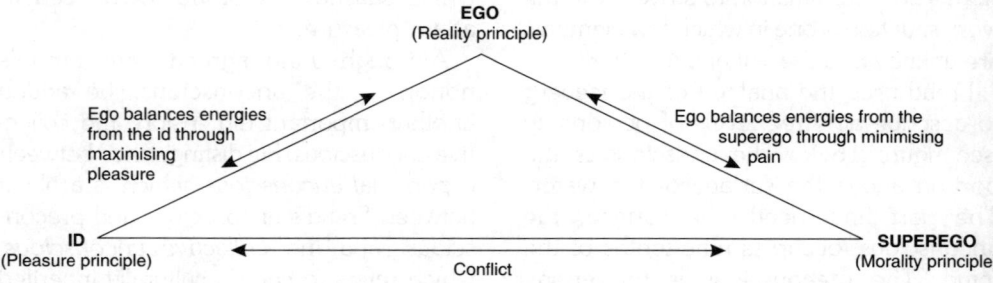

Figure 16.3 Freud's structure of personality

The relation between the id, ego and superego

minimises pain while maximising pleasure (in contrast with the id, which strives to attain pleasure at all costs). The ego is also known as reason or rationality – it determines appropriate and socially acceptable times, places and objects that will satisfy the id impulses. Although the ego still strives to attain pleasure, it is modified by the *reality principle*. This implies that the ego has the ability to sometimes temporarily turn aside the gratification of certain desires to increase overall gratification. Freud compared the relation of the ego to the id with that of a rider to a horse. The raw, brute power of the horse must be guided, checked and reined in by the rider, otherwise the horse may bolt and run, throwing the rider to the ground (Schultz 1990). Work satisfaction can only be attained if the "reality principle" modifies the individual's "pleasure principle" according to the accepted social perception at work (Czander 1993).

As a result of contact with cultural realities, especially as embodied in the parents, a third mental agent, the *super-ego,* develops. It functions as a suppressor of pleasurable activity in the same way as parents do during a child's formative years. This is also referred to as an internal morality, or a "conscience", governing ideas on what is right and what is wrong. It operates according to a *morality principle*. The superego has two subsystems: a conscience that punishes behaviour and an ego ideal that rewards it. The conscience brings about feelings of guilt, and the ego ideal brings about feelings of pride. The superego is relentless, even cruel, in its constant quest for moral perfection. Its purpose is not to postpone the pleasure-seeking demands of the id (like the ego) but rather to inhibit them – particularly, in Western society, those concerned with sex and aggression. As with the id, the operation of the superego is largely unconscious.

The ego then, is the balancing agent, although it is mostly driven by the id (as it derives its energy from the id) in its quest for eventual needs or wish-fulfilment (as a substitute for the real thing). The ego is caught in the middle of three dangers: the id, reality and the superego. This leads to a continual conflict within the human personality. Freud's human has been described as "basically a battlefield. He is a dark cellar in which a well-bred spinster lady (the superego) and a sex-crazed monkey (the id) are forever engaged in mortal combat, the struggle being refereed by a rather nervous bank clerk (the ego)" (see illustration on previous page) (Bannister in Schultz 1990). The inevitable result of this friction, when the ego is too severely pressed, is the development of anxiety.

Berne used the concept of the id, ego and superego in his theory of *transactional analysis*. He identified three states corresponding to the three constituents of personality: the child ("id"), adult ("ego") and parent ("superego"). These three states are often used in industrial training to explain interpersonal behaviour patterns. The ideal state is adult to adult communication. If a supervisor acts as the "parent" (superego) in communication to his or her subordinates it can be expected that they will react in the "child" (id) mode and results to the satisfaction of both the employer and the employee (as achieved by the "ego" or "adult" state) would not be achieved.

Jung stated that personality or the *psyche* consisted of the ego, the personal unconscious and the collective unconscious. His concept of the *ego* is similar to Freud's – it is the conscious mind in contact with reality. Jung's *personal unconscious* resembles a blend of Freud's unconscious and preconscious. The *collective unconscious* was an extension of Freud's unconscious. Jung believed that the collective unconscious contained ar-

chetypes: inherited predispositions to perceive, act or think in a certain way. The archetypes are formed as a result of the experiences of our forefathers and are universal.

The five most important *archetypes* are the persona, anima, animus, shadow and self.

- The *persona* is the mask presented by an individual to society – it is feminine in women and masculine in men.
- The *anima* is the feminine part of men.
- The *animus* is the masculine part of women. The anima and animus are the balancing agents of the persona. Both develop in interaction with the opposite sex.
- The *shadow* corresponds with Freud's id, in that it consists of inherited biological instincts. Immoral and passionate impulses emanate largely from the shadow, as with Freud's id.
- The *self* is the most important archetype, as it holds all the others together. The self represents the striving to wholeness and an integrated personality and is represented in various cultures in the mandala or magic circle (see illustration below).

The mandala: symbol for the self

Like Freud, Jung saw human personality as the result of an internal struggle. But Jung's conception of the self reveals a more optimistic viewpoint than Freud's, as he considered the future and potentialities of the individual as well (Aiken 1993).

Although most early psychodynamists agreed with the structural model of personality, later psychodynamic theorists shifted the focus from the id (and unconsciousness) to the ego (and thus consciousness) and to the role of social influences.

For Adler, humans have a *creative self*, which is their central concept for personality structure. People give meaning to life through their creative powers, a basic social interest in people, the development of social skills and the overcoming of a basic sense of inferiority.

In Adler's theory the important conflicts often occur between the individual and the environment, rather than within the individual, as Freud had held.

16.5 THE MOTIVATION FOR PERSONALITY

Due to the energy released from the constant tensions between instincts and societal or superego demands, the *instincts* are considered the basic motivating force of all human behaviour, especially in terms of unconscious behaviours. The instincts drive behaviour in its striving to attain satisfaction. Because the id operates according to the pleasure principle, the striving to attain pleasurable sensations is a strong motivational factor. According to Jung's view the archetypes, or the universal inherited predispositions towards certain behaviours, direct behaviour. The basic motivating force is therefore biological in nature. As both the instincts and archetypes reside in the *unconscious*, the unconscious plays an important role in personality. In other words, people are mostly not aware of what motivates their behaviour.

Freud believed that the most important instinct in the development of personality was the libido or *sexual instinct*. He believed that infants had to satisfy certain sexual instincts in order to develop normally and that any frustration in doing so would lead to later behavioural and adjustment problems. In fact, Freud believed that the human personality was set by the age of six. The motivation for personality is therefore also found in *past events*. In contrast to Freud's insistence that childhood events determine personality, Jung adhered to the teleological principle. The *teleological principle* links the present with the future through a future goal that guides and directs behaviour. Jung had a more future-directed view of the motivation for personality, stating that the individual strives toward the future goal of self-fulfilment.

Adler stated that human infants begin life with a *sense of inferiority*, a feeling that is never outgrown, no matter how long one's life may be. Adler considered the lifelong struggle to overcome feelings of inferiority to be the principal motive behind human behaviour. Adler's views on sexuality differed from Freud's. He saw the overcoming of femininity by both males and females ("masculine protest"), rather than sexuality in itself, as the important thing. The *will to power* (through overcoming inferiority) was thought to be the greatest motivating force in people's lives, and sex at times was a manifestation of that will. The sex act represented domination of the female, rather than simply satisfying sexual impulses.Fromm's ideas on the basic motivation for behaviour are a mixture of Freudian and Adlerian ideas. He distinguished between *organic and nonorganic drives* as the motivation for behaviour. Organic drives refer to animal-like instincts such as hunger, thirst, sex and defence through flight or fight. Nonorganic drives distinguish humans from animals and include needs for others, for transcendence and for identity. To Fromm, humans can escape isolation or loneliness toward greater security and freedom through creative powers.

Cross-cultural research found that employees from individualistic countries (i.e. where individuals are expected to look after their own self-interests) are more inner-directed, whereas in collectivist countries (i.e. where societies place strong emphasis on the ties between people), individuals are more traditional and outer-directed (Cooper & Robertson 1990). South African research in particular has found a greater collectivist attitude among black respondents (Hugo & van Vuuren 1996). The implication of this is that the application of psychoanalytic theories could be of more value in individualistic communities and societies.

Another important motivating factor in personality is the development of *defence mechanisms* in order to cope with anxiety. Defence mechanisms have two features: they operate on an unconscious level (we are unaware of them) and they distort reality so as to make it less threatening (Engler 1995). Examples of defences described by Freud are projection, regression, and displacement. Freud used displacement to explain a range of socio-psychological phenomena. For instance, racial prejudice and wars can be attributed to the displacement of the aggression drive. He even maintained that art, music and literature are the products of the displacement of sexual and aggressive energy (Hjelle & Ziegler 1992). Regression may be found in the work environment when anxiety-producing events occur, for example technological change. Employees may long for the "good old days", a previous and more comfortable stage of development.

Traditional psychoanalysis views defences as maladaptive. Freud's daughter, Anna, believed that it was important in therapy to make the person aware of these defences. Hartman maintained that the ego was able to use defence mechanisms to its benefit. For example, a student may be able to concentrate and study better after a weekend of play. Here regression serves the ego.

Freud's concepts of anxiety and defences have been applied with great success in the work situation (Hirschhorn 1993). Feelings of anxiety can be at the root of dysfunctional relationships at work – these can be caused by the task structure of the organisation. A work group manages its anxiety by developing and deploying a set of social defences. Every social defence depersonalises relationships at work and distorts the group's capacity to accomplish its primary task. The social defences can even distort relationships between the group and its wider environment, that is, customers, clients and competitors. This happens when the group retreats into its own fantasies and blames the "outside" to preserve the "inside". Group development takes place when group members stop looking for scapegoats or project their own unacceptable shortcomings onto others (Holway 1991). The common occurrence of depression among the long-term unemployed is an example of aggressive instincts turned against the self, as the person no longer has an outward outlet in work for these destructive forces (Czander 1993).

16.6 THE DEVELOPMENT AND GROWTH OF PERSONALITY

The psychoanalytic theory of development is based on two premises: the genetic approach, which emphasises that *early childhood* experiences play a critical role in shaping adult personality, and the premise that a certain amount of *sexual energy* is present at birth, and continues to progress through a range of psychosexual stages. Adler, however, differed from this position in that he did not view the infant as a small sexual animal whose incestuous desires must be repressed, but as a small and helpless organism whose every need must be administered to by relatively powerful adults. These feelings of helplessness and inferiority motivate the individual to strive for independence and to overcome the inferiority complex.

Freud defined four sequential stages of personality development, referred to as *psychosexual stages*: the oral, anal, phallic and genital phases. A period of latency, normally between the ages of six to seven and the onset of puberty, was included by Freud, but not considered a stage of psychosexual development. The term "psychosexual" emphasises that the major factor underlying human development is the sexual instinct as it progresses from one erogenous zone (body part that experiences sexual pleasure) to another throughout a person's development. Psychosexual development is biologically determined and occurs in the same sequence in all cultures. But, the individual's social experiences at each stage leave their mark in the form of attitudes, traits and values acquired at that stage. Each psychosexual stage has certain *development tasks* that need to be resolved before progression to the next stage is possible. If development does not take place *fixation* results, which refers to being "stranded" in the tasks of a previous stage. The weaker the resolution of those tasks, the easier it is for an individual to regress to

an earlier stage of psychosexual development later in his or her life. This happens because libidinal energy is not successfully transferred from the unresolved stage to the next, thus leaving too little energy for attaining the mature genital stage. A variety of adult character types are connected to each stage of psychosexual development. Table 16.1 provides a summary of the psychosexual development stages and the character types associated with each.

A concept that attracted a lot of attention is that of the *Oedipal conflict*. The Oedipal conflict refers to the unconscious desire to possess the opposite-sexed parent and simultaneously dispose of the same-sexed parent. From a work perspective all struggles between subordinates and superiors can be viewed as Oedipal struggles, as the hierarchical structure of work closely resembles that of a family system. Psychodynamically all employees want to be the favoured child of the idealised leader and all want the leader's power and perks (Czander 1993).

Horney in particular challenged Freud's ideas on the Oedipal conflict and the Electra complex (penis envy). She believed that both sexes are envious of each

Psycho-sexual stage	Age	Erogenous zone	Development task	Personality type
Oral stage	± 0-1,5 years	Mouth *Pleasurable activities:* • sucking • chewing • biting	Weaning from breast or bottle	1. *Oral-dependent type:* cheerful, optimistic, expect "mothering" from the world, continually seeks approval 2. *Oral-aggressive type:* argumentative, pessimistic, "bitingly" sarcastic, cynical

Table 16.1 Freud's psychosexual stages and personality types

Psycho-sexual stage	Age	Erogenous zone	Development task	Personality type
Anal stage	± 1-3 years	Anus *Pleasurable activities*: retention and expulsion of faeces	Toilet training (learn self-control through distinguishing between immediate id satisfaction and social con-straints)	1. *Anal-retentive type*: obstinate, stingy, orderly, punctual, intolerant of ambiguity 2. *Anal-expulsive type*: destructive, impulsive, cruel, disorderly, sees others as objects to be possessed
Phallic stage	± 2-6 years	Genitals *Pleasurable activities*: mastur-bation	Identify with same-sex adult role model **Boys**: Overcome Oedipal conflict **Girls**: Overcome Electra complex	1. *Phallic male*: boastful, Don Juan, tries to win others over 2. *Phallic female*: flirtatious, seductive, naïve
Latency period	± 5-12 years	Non-sexual activities *Pleasurable activities*: peer relations, sports		
Genital stage	Puberty onwards	Genitals *Pleasurable activities*: Hetero-sexual activities	Establishment of intimate relationships. Contributing to society through work	*Genital type*: This is the ideal character type – the person who has developed mature social-sexual relationships

Table 16.1 Freud's psychosexual stages and personality types (continued)

other, men being envious of women for their breasts and ability to produce children (Aiken 1993). She referred to this envy as "womb envy". In line with her social focus, Horney ascribed the psychological differences between the sexes to social and cultural conditioning. Personality thus develops in line with the social relationship between the child and his or her parents. Childhood is characterised by two needs: the need to *satisfy basic needs* and the *need for safety*. Parental mistreatment can lead to an attitude of basic hostility, which places the child between dependence on its parents and resentment towards them. This in turn can be manifested in relationships with other people which lead to a feeling of *basic anxiety*. A child with excessive basic anxiety could develop into a neurotic adult (Hjelle & Ziegler 1992).

Chodorow expanded on the relationship between gender identity and the organisation of work. She believes that the early relationship between mothers and their children explains why boys' nurturing capabilities are limited and why they are prepared to work outside the family. Mothers and daughters see each other as extensions of themselves during infancy. However, they view their sons as dissimilar and do not experience the same feeling of "oneness" as they have with their daughters (Engler 1995). This prepares the two sexes for different roles: nonrelationship activities for men, which would explain why they often choose occupations in the natural and engineering sciences, and relational activities for women, which would explain why women often choose occupations in the helping professions.

Although Freud's theories are often viewed in the light of 19th-century biological determinism, empirical child development research argues against complete rejection of Freud's ideas on psychosexual development (Neubauer & Neubauer in Engler 1995). Research findings seem to support the existence of the oral, anal and phallic character types, but not the existence of the psychosexual stages *per se* (Tribich & Messer, Fisher & Greenberg, Kline in Aiken 1993).

Unlike Freud's conception of psychosexual developmental stages and their critical influences on adult character and personality, Jung's theory does not place much emphasis on stages in personality development nor on the influence of childhood experiences on personality development. Research indicated that the middle childhood years may be considerably more important in forming adult personality patterns than the early childhood years. Although this does not mean that the first five years of life have no impact on personality development, it is apparent that personality continues to develop beyond the age of five, the time at which Freud said no further development occurred (Schultz 1990).

Jung emphasised the notion of *individuation*, in which, over time, people develop different degrees of introversion and extroversion (*attitudes*) and varying tendencies towards the four *functions* of sensing, intuition, thinking and feeling. The process of individuation is only thought to occur by middle age. Jung was the first theorist to define the *introversion/extroversion typology*. It is used to measure traits (e.g. the Myers-Briggs Type Indicator) and is one of the main factors in the trait factor models on personality, such as the three-, five- and 16-factor models. Jung's concepts were also heavily relied on in the development of projective tests to measure personality, such as the Thematic Apperception Test (TAT) and the Rorschach Inkblot Test.

Although a mixture of the two attitudes and four functions are present in all individuals, one attitude and two functions normally dominate the personality. Jung identified eight personality *types* resulting from the various combinations of the two attitudes and the four functions. The types constitute the theoretical basis of the Myers-Briggs Type Indicator (MBTI), a personality inventory extremely useful in determining a career suited to a certain personality. Research into this inventory is consistent with Jung's types. For example, introverted types tend to enter technical and scientific fields, sensing types tend to enter practical fields and feeling types tend to enter the helping professions (Aiken 1993). An extroverted-thinking type can be suited for a career in the physical sciences, an extroverted-intuitive type would undoubtedly prefer an entrepreneurial profession, whereas a career as a salesperson would not be recommended to an introvert. Successful adjustment in work, as in other areas of life, requires that one follows the innate predispositions of the collective unconscious (Ewen 1993).

The MBTI also has great potential for helping people to understand learning styles, leadership styles and how to motivate workers (Keirsey & Bates in Engler 1995; Engelbrecht 1994). Research comparing a black South African sample and Australian sample, however, found no evidence for the introversion or extroversion dimension among black South Africans (Heaven et al. 1994).

Erikson asserts that personality develops over the entire lifespan, in contrast to Freud, who emphasised that it was developed and set in the first six years (and remained fairly set thereafter). Erikson is best known for his eight stages of psychosocial development and the conflicts and goals of each stage. Corresponding to the ideas of Freud, Erikson proposed that the manner in which the person resolves each crisis affects the direction that personality development takes and how further crises are resolved. Each stage is characterised by a crisis, which has both a negative and a positive component. If the conflict is resolved satisfactorily, the positive component is absorbed in the ego and further healthy development is

assured. Conversely, if the conflict remains, the negative component is incorporated into the ego, which hampers further healthy development.

A South African study conducted by Ochse and Plug (1986) found some evidence for the validity of Erikson's stages, but in general, few studies on his ideas were conducted, as he did not set a theory that could easily be verified by research. Erikson's theory can be applied with great effect in the work situation. In terms of his theory, adults would need to define their identity before an occupational choice can be made. In other words, they must know themselves well enough to know where they would "fit" best. Vocational indecision would then reflect a more fundamental indecisiveness about personal identity (Hjelle & Ziegler 1992).

Like Freud, Adler believed that the first five years of life set the stage for later psychological development. If the child is pampered and overindulged he or she will become spoiled, or cold and unsympathetic if neglected. Overindulged children are likely to become demanding neurotics who take without giving, whereas rejected children, who are dominated by the need for revenge, often become delinquents and criminals. Adler believed that a child's *birth order* in the family determines how he or she will be treated. Parents tend to pamper both an only and a youngest child. The oldest child may feel neglected as he or she has to stand back for siblings. In fact, he referred to the oldest child as a "dethroned monarch", who as an adult tends to be conservative, power-oriented and predisposed towards leadership. Adler viewed the middle child as achievement-oriented, because he or she has to compete with an older sibling. Some research findings support Adler's proposition of the relationship between birth order and personality. For example, compared to later-borns, first-borns are more likely to become alcoholic and to seek psychotherapeutic help (Barry & Blane in Aiken 1993), which is consistent with Adlerian thinking that first-borns are more anxious and more likely to see social contact as a means of coping with their anxieties. Wagner and Schubert (in Hjelle & Ziegler 1992) found that oldest sons were overrepresented among United States presidents. Melillo (in Hjelle & Ziegler 1992) found that first-borns were overrepresented among women earning doctorates.

Hartman believed that the ego could function seperately from the id and be conflict free in certain areas. In work, we could function purely for the sake of the ego and not to satisfy id impulses as modified by the ego (Czander 1993). In the development of personality, Mahler focused on the relationship between the child and early caregiver. She described the process by which the ego unfolds in the child through a process of separation and individuation. The process is composed of four stages:

- *differentiation:* the development of a body image separate from that of the mother;
- *practising:* perfecting motor abilities;
- *rapprochement:* the time during which a child experiences conflict between the urge to separate and the fear of loss;
- *consolidation:* an image of the mother as a separate entity in the external world and the beginnings of the child's separate personhood.

16.7 PERSONALITY ADJUSTMENT

16.7.1 The healthy personality

For Freud, the components of the healthy personality work together in relative harmony, under the influence of the ego, to achieve pleasurable yet safe discharges of tension. The majority of the libido reaches the genital stage, enabling the ego for the demands it has to face. It either blocks or sublimates dangerous id impulses, but not those that are healthy. It helps the superego to function in a moral way without allowing the conscience to speak too loudly or the ego ideal to become too perfectionist. Though life has its frustrations, the well-adjusted person is able to do two things: love and work (Ewen 1993).

Adler held a more optimistic view of the individual. He did not view the person as a collection of segments at war with itself, but as an integrated, striving individual. Adler's theory was popularised by practical applications to educational and social problems. This is evident in the ease with which terms such as inferiority complex and sibling rivalry were assimilated into lay language. For Adler, the healthy individual is measured by his or her success in fulfilling the three major challenges of life: society, occupation, and love and marriage (Ewen 1993).

Fromm described the healthy personality in terms of the *productive* frame of orientation. This personality type corresponds roughly to the Freudian genital character, but results from social and environmental influences (such as parental behaviour) rather than from libidinal instincts.

For Jung, the mature (and thus healthy) individual was characterised by the emergence of the self. It strives for oneness of the individual with the world through religious experience, as well as for oneness of the psychic systems within the individual. The self can appear only as the other psychic systems become separate enough to require integration, which does not occur until middle age. Jung thought that Freud might be essentially correct about the importance of sexual motivation before middle age, but he believed Freud had simply ignored what happened after this point had been passed, when the self developed and sex became a subsidiary consideration (Marx & Cronan-Hillix 1987). Jung did not single out any of his personality types as the ideal one, as he believed that all attitudes and functions are possessed in varying degrees by everyone. All functions and attitudes are necessary for successful living. The integrated individual has all these factors acting in harmony; people who are nearly pure types are seen as pathological (Marx & Cronan-Hillix 1987).

16.7.2 Psychopathology (abnormal behaviour)

Psychoanalytic theories have certain implications for the development of neurotic or abnormal behaviour. For Freud there were no clearly defined boundaries between illness and health. Both neurotic and healthy people struggle with the same conflicts and complexes. The difference between the two lies in the extent of the negative impact of these conflicts on functioning. Neurosis emerges from fixated libidinal development. This occurs when the realistic satisfaction of erotic needs is denied and the person turns to neurosis as a surrogate satisfaction. In psychodynamic thinking anxiety develops as a result of pressures on the ego to balance the demands of the id and the superego. Freud distinguished between three forms of anxiety:

- *Reality anxiety* refers to the anxiety experienced in the face of real dangers such as fleeing a burning building.
- *Neurotic anxiety* is the anxiety experienced when id impulses are in conflict with the ego and generally develops in childhood, when children are punished for impulsive sexual and aggressive behaviour.
- *Moral anxiety* represents a conflict between the ego and the superego and is experienced due to a fear of the guilt feelings provoked by a person's conscience when expressing instinctual wishes.

In order to cope with anxiety, the ego develops defence mechanisms.

Freud believed that the past strongly influences the present and that libido frustration in an earlier stage of development can influence a current stage. This means that libido becomes fixated at a particular stage, which creates excessive needs characteristic of an earlier stage. The fixated libido expresses itself in adult life according to character types or traits that reflect the earlier level of development (see table 16.1). Hence, an orally fixated person is likely to be dependent on and easily influenced by others. Oral personalities are optimistic and trusting to the point of being gullible. Most people do not reflect a pure type, but the personality traits and their opposites do have their origin in the various psychosexual stages. It is important to note that prototypes of behaviour considered maladjusted in adulthood are acceptable in childhood, as the child needs to work through these conflicts in his or her development. For example, sadistic and masochistic forms of behaviour, in which a person obtains sexual pleasure by inflicting pain (sadism) or receiving pain (masochism), are apparent during the toddler years. Voyeurism, obtaining pleasure from seeing sexual organs or sexual acts, is present in the curiosity of the pre-school child. Homosexuality, primary attraction to the same sex, is apparent during the latency period and early adolescence, when one's primary association is with same-sexed peers (Engler 1995).

Freud viewed *transference* as an important therapeutic tool in curing neurosis. Transference occurs when the patient transfers to the therapist emotional attitudes that he or she felt as a child toward important persons. Freud distinguished between positive transference, friendly affectionate feelings towards the therapist, and negative transference, the expression of angry, hostile feelings. By displaying the behaviour, the therapist is better able to understand the patient's characteristic way of perceiving and reacting, and to assist him or her in finding better ways of handling conflict. It is important during the therapeutic relationship that the therapist does not reject or disapprove of the patient as others might. Freud's solution is therefore one of applying insight and working through the conflict. Therapy is a lengthy process, normally requiring a 50-minute session five times a week for several years in order to gain a full understanding of the personality structure. Freud wrote in 1917 that neurotics who have been cured will really become different people ... they become their best selves, what they would have been under the most favourable conditions (Engler 1995). Transference can also be utilised with success in the industrial consulting environment. In positive transference change may occur because the consultant is seen as a symbol of hope that things will improve. Conversely, in negative transference change may be resisted because the consultant is viewed as an extension of the "evil leader" (Czander 1993).

Jung was also interested in the future, and the potential of the individual, in order to gain a complete understanding of him or her. Jung considered neurosis as a difference in degree rather than a difference in kind. The ideal of normality is rarely reached and virtually every personality is somewhat one-sided, but complete dependence on one function or attitude does constitute abnormal behaviour. Jung and his followers turned to the study of mythology and art as more useful methods of revealing the form of the unconscious. In contrast to this, Freud made use of hypnosis and free association. Jung saw self-realisation as the overall goal of psychotherapy. He agreed with Freud that sexuality was the main cause of neurosis in young adults, but in contrast, felt that a denial of religious needs in older adults led to neurosis (Ewen 1993).

Adler saw neurosis as the result of feelings of inferiority leading to self-absorption and neurosis. One way of overcoming feelings of inferiority is to compensate by overemphasising another form of behaviour. For example, a sickly child may overcome his or her inferiority by working hard and becoming a great athlete. Normal and healthy persons are genuinely concerned about others and their goal of superiority is social, encompassing the wellbeing of all people. In this context, superiority involves the desire to be competent and effective in whatever one strives to do. The concept is similar to Jung's idea of self-realisation.

Maladjusted people, by contrast, are those who lack *social interest*. They are self-centred and strive for personal superiority and superiority over others. Adler held an interesting notion on how psychopathology expresses itself through work. Pathology is indicated when a person tries to escape an unhappy marriage or social life by becoming a "workaholic", or when a pampered individual is unable to accept a subordinate position. The inability of children and adolescents to select a prospective occupation is also indicative of an underlying inferiority complex (Ewen 1993).

In accordance with Adler's views, Erikson believed that the inability to choose a vocation during adolescence is indicative of psychopathology. The best way to avoid the pain of identity confusion is to feed the ego through a satisfying career. Erikson's view of psychopathology differs from Freud's in that he maintained that pathological symptoms often represent a desperate attempt to develop and retain a sense of identity, rather than resulting from some instinctual force (Ewen 1993).

Rank saw neuroses as originating in birth trauma, when the child experiences a forcible and painful expulsion from the comfort of the womb into the unfriendly world. The *separation anxiety* that results from the birth trauma remains with the individual as he or she grows up and experiences a clash of will with his or her parents. The task of the therapist then is to alleviate the guilt of the patient over this clash and his or her anxiety over separation.

Both Rank and Ferenczi advocated shorter therapies, setting definite dates for the separation of patient and therapist. Both believed that it was not necessary to get to the historic origins of symptoms and that it was therefore possible to conclude therapy in a shorter time span. Ferenczi thought that a warm, nurturing relationship with the mother was missing in the lives of his patients and that the therapist should supply this element. Accordingly, he cuddled patients, holding them on his lap and kissing them sometimes (this is not recommended for the industrial psychologist though!).

Horney viewed neurosis as any deviation from normal behaviour, and not necessarily pathological. Pathological behaviour occurs only if our innate tendency toward positive growth is blocked by external social forces, such as pathogenic parenting. The idealised self becomes a crutch for neurotic persons. They come to believe that they are the idealised picture. This solution brings a temporary reduction of anxiety but in the long run increases it. The attempts by neurotics to live up to the idealised, unrealistic picture of themselves result in new conflicts and consequently greater tension. This leads to a vicious circle of neurotic behaviour in which inappropriate behaviour is elicited to cope with anxiety, which in turn leads to more anxiety. Horney was optimistic about avoiding neurotic reactions; a secure and loving home would be insurance against the development of neurosis (Schultz 1990). Horney felt that Freud had neglected sociocultural influences in the development of the individual. More specifically, her clinical observations of the differences in personality dynamics between patients seen in Europe and those seen in the United States confirmed the importance of cultural

factors. These observations led her to conclude that the interpersonal conditions of a person's life are at the core of disturbed personality functioning (Hjelle & Ziegler 1992).

Horney's theory of pathology is also based on the concept of *basic anxiety*. The predominant reason that basic anxiety develops from parent-child relationships is the absence of genuine love and affection. The child responds to basic anxiety by developing a neurotic trend. Neurosis is then not, as Freud had claimed, the result of frustration of the sexual instinct. Horney maintained that sexual difficulty is the result, and not the cause, of conflicts. Horney identified three neurotic trends which are present in all people, but over-accentuated in the neurotic. They are *moving toward people* (the compliant type who has a strong need for approval and affection from others); *moving against people* (the hostile type who has a constant need to feel superior to others and to exploit other people); *moving away from people* (the detached type who copes with anxiety by becoming distant and independent of others). The exclusive use of a single type of behaviour, regardless of the situation, is indicative of a neurosis. This view corresponds with that of Jung, who asserted that persons who are pure types display pathology.

Research on parenting styles confirms that children can endure considerable stress provided they have a warm and affectionate relationship with at least one caring adult (Engler 1995).

Fromm described four non-productive orientations:

- The person with a *receptive orientation* is similar to the oral-dependent character in Freudian theory and to Horney's conception of "moving toward people". This type believes that the sources of everything desirable are external and consistently seeks to be loved and nurtured by others.

- The person with an *exploitative orientation* resembles the Freudian oral-sadistic character and Horney's "moving against people". This person also views the source of all good as external, but obtains it through force or cunning.
- The person with a *hoarding orientation* is denoted by miserliness, compulsive orderliness and obstinacy and resembles the Freudian anal character and Horney's "moving away from people".
- The person with a *marketing orientation* does not correspond to any of the Freudian character types, but does resemble Jung's overdeveloped persona. These people tend to repress their own needs for identity and self-realisation in order to become what others want them to be (oversell themselves) (Ewen 1993).

According to general psychoanalytic theory people need to fuse work and play in their chosen occupation in order to obtain work satisfaction. This is consistent with Super's findings (Cooper & Robertson 1990) that individuals who were most satisfied with their jobs and their lives in general tended to have hobbies similar to their jobs.

16.8 CONCLUSION

Psychoanalytic theories have been described in terms of a *conflict model* in which each person is caught in a clash between two great forces, which continues throughout life. The best that can be achieved in terms of life style is a compromise. The ideal life style involves a dynamic balancing of the two opposing forces, with both getting more or less equal expression. In terms of development, the conflict model also emphasises compromise as an ideal. Parents must be careful neither to reward nor punish too many behaviours of their developing child, because youngsters need to learn to express all aspects of their inborn nature, however full of conflict they may be

(Maddi 1996). The same applies in the work context to supervisors and their subordinates.

The psychodynamic perspective has made a fundamental contribution to personality theory by presenting the following ideas to the psychological fraternity: unconscious processes; overdetermination, conflict and compromise; the bodily and the animal (psychoanalysis dares to ask what one would prefer not to think about); defensive processes; concept of a personality structure; viewing the present in the context of the past and the interpretation of meaning (the intuitive approach) (Pervin 1990). In fact, the emphasis on the dynamics of the unconscious and on the importance of powerful, primitive forces is unique to psychoanalysis – no other theory of personality has the power to capture the uniqueness of our individual experiences in quite the same way (Carver & Scheier 1996; Lester 1995). This also provides an extremely useful tool to understand behaviour in the work context apart from "hard" scientific data.

The impact of Freud's accomplishments has been favourably compared with the impacts of Copernicus, Darwin and Einstein (Engler 1995). In addition, Freud is a household name – many people wonder what the unconscious motivation for certain utterances (the so-called "Freudian slips") is. Jung's optimistic conception of human nature and destiny, and in particular his concepts of the self and self-actualisation, influenced humanistic theorists of a later generation (Aiken 1993). The concept of complexes and introverted and extroverted personality types is well accepted in psychology today and the personality scales that measure introversion/extroversion are frequently used as diagnostic and selection devices. Jung's notion of individuation or self-actualisation anticipated the work of Maslow. He was the first theorist to emphasise the role of the future in determining behaviour, an idea adopted by Adler. Jung's suggestion that middle age is a time of crucial personality change is widely accepted today and was extended further by Maslow, Erikson and Cattell.

Jung's importance has grown in recent years. His ideas are in part based on Oriental religion and philosophy, in which there has been a surge of Western interest. His view of humans is a refreshing antidote to Freud's pessimism. His views seem more acceptable to women, and women played a crucial role in the development of Jungian theory. Jung's position affords a comfortable resting place for those who have had a surfeit of the scientific approach and its results. Jungian psychology fits well with modern existentialism and even with mysticism (Marx & Cronan-Hillix 1987) and should have meaning for Asian and African psychology. Horney's writings served to promote greater interest in the role of socio-cultural factors in neuroses and inspired feminists in later generations. Her belief that people possess an inborn drive for self-realisation is consistent with the humanistic psychology movement. Horney's writings on female sexual development constitute the most influential and far-reaching of her contributions.

Freud's ideas that have applications in the counselling situation are defence mechanisms, influences of childhood experiences on adult behaviour, unconscious and sexual motivation and the nature of intrapersonal conflicts (Drapela 1995).

Paradoxically, the greatest criticism against the psychodynamic perspective was levelled at what was also considered its greatest strength – its intuitive orientation – which was attacked for a lack of research orientation, vague concepts and reliance on mysticism. Freud was criticised, as were many other psychodynamic theorists, for not integrating his models and theories fully. His primary interest

was in psychopathology and the data source for his theories was what patients told him during clinical sessions (Pervin 1990).

The only theory with sufficiently clearly defined concepts in a systematised theory to be investigated properly by research is that of Erikson. Researchers tend to focus on personality constructs that are easier to translate into operational terms. As societal needs change and the median age of our population increases, gerontologists turn to Erikson's work for insight into the needs of our senior citizens. Further progress may be made by linking psychodynamics with neurology, cognitive and developmental psychology, evolutionary theory and information and systems theory (Engler 1995).

Other criticisms of psychodynamic thinking include the pessimistic and deterministic view of behaviour originating in biology and its historical approach in its focus on past events. Freud has also been severely criticised for what is viewed as a degrading view of women (Schultz 1990).

Although psychoanalytic theories have been criticised for a lack of systematic theory to be researched (as have most other personality theories), some critical aspects of contemporary psychoanalytic thinking have not only been examined empirically, but appear to be accurate in the light of available evidence. This includes the notions that:

- much mental activity is unconscious and that this has an impact on emotion and motivational processes;
- patterns of relatedness developed early in life may be expressed in later relationships and form the basis for behaviour in later relationships;
- multiple unconscious mental processes may produce behaviour; and
- individuals differ in the extent to which they are able to regulate their impulses and feelings in socially acceptable ways (Pervin 1990).

Due to the lack of emphasis on scientific validation, psychoanalysis can be seen as in an intermediate stage of scientific development, which might lead to a general theory. It is part of the holistic method, which begins with concrete data, discovers themes in the data, then constructs typologies and finally develops a general theory which accounts for all the types (Marx & Cronan-Hillix 1987).

In future, it can be expected that the concepts of the ego and social and interpersonal influences on behaviour will be further expanded (Schultz 1990). A number of new theorists believe that the ego has an energy of its own and is able to function on its own. Other recent developments in psychodynamics include the setting of a time limit on the duration of therapy (which used to continue for years), approaching group or family therapy from an analytical perspective and prescribing medicine in addition to administering therapy (Hjelle & Ziegler 1992).

In conclusion, Freud and some of his followers as yet have not convincingly persuaded the professional scientific psychologist, but Freud did conquer the popular mind. In his determinism Freud tried to persuade us not to surrender to the joys of the id, but rather to substitute rational self-control for unconscious repression. He asked us to face the unconscious in order to conquer it in the name of reason (Leahey 1992).

Self-evaluation questions

1. Describe the nature and function of the three basic structures of personality, the id, ego and superego. In what ways do the interactions among these structures create conflict within the individual?

2. Describe, and illustrate with examples, three motivating factors in personality according to the psychodynamic perspective.

3. Compare and contrast the views of Freud, Jung, Adler and Horney on the development of personality.

4. Explain psychological health and psychopathology according to psychoanalytic thinking.

5. Observe work behaviours in your organisation or people's behaviour at home and explain some of them by using psychoanalytic concepts and thinking.

6. List the contributions of psychoanalytic thinking to the work context and to society at large.

7. For a week, on awakening each morning, and before you do anything else, write down as many of the details of your dreams of the night before as you can remember. At the end of the week, read through the dreams and try to identify common themes in them. Apply free association to each of the elements of the dream to ascertain their particular meaning to you. Then try to determine:
   (a) the needs they try to fulfil
   (b) what the symbols in the dream might mean
   (c) what significance the characters might have for you
   (d) how the dreams end (e.g. happily, sadly, undecided, etc.)

Learning perspectives

17

Ziel Bergh

Learning outcomes

After studying this chapter you should be able to:

- explain the behaviouristic view of humankind
- describe the main assumptions of behaviourism and learning perspectives
- explain personality structure according to learned responses
- discuss learning principles in human motivation
- explain how the person and environment contribute to personality development
- use concepts and examples to explain the role of self-control in human behaviour
- illustrate how faulty learning influences psychological health

Key concepts

behaviour, environmental determinism, stimulus-response (S-R), person-situation interaction (S-O-R), learned responses, respondent behaviour, operant behaviour, habituation, conditioning, reinforcement, drives, modelling, shaping, cognitive control, expectancies, self-efficacy, locus of control, learned helplessness, self-handicapping, behaviour modification

17.1 INTRODUCTION

In contrast to psychoanalytic emphasis on the unconscious and past events, and Wilhelm Wundt's assertions of consciousness and introspection as the primary influences on personality and behaviour, the behaviourist or learning theories, especially the classical theories, emphasise behaviourism as the objective and experimental study of observable and external behaviour. Only if behaviour can be accurately observed can it also be effectively assessed, controlled and predicted. The behaviourists' *view of humankind* is related to their scientific orientation and beliefs that human behaviour can be controlled, manipulated and accurately assessed. They believe that humans' existence is dependent on their abilities to repeat those behaviours that are needed in their environments. Personality is characterised by *patterns of responses* or behaviours that are learned and reinforced

(conditioned) by influences in the environment, because animals and humans are conditioned to react to certain stimuli. The behaviouristic view, as is Freud's, is somewhat pessimistic and mechanistic in its emphasis on human behaviour being controlled by certain stimuli and external reinforcers. The strong emphasis on *environmental influences* in the shaping of personality is as deterministic as is a psychoanalyst's emphasis on unconscious factors. In this respect, however, Skinner, for one, also emphasises people's ability to be responsible and to influence and change their environments and society. In general, behaviourists do not find a place, or the necessity, to explain behaviour by concepts such as unconscious or other unobservable behaviours. More recent behaviouristic theories (neo-behaviourists, social learning theories) deviate somewhat from the strict beliefs of John B. Watson, the father of behaviourism, and include aspects such as social and cognitive aspects in their explanation of personality, while others, such as those of Dollard and Miller, even transferred some psychoanalytic concepts into behaviouristic explanations (Pervin & John 1997).

Contrary to many misperceptions about the control of human behaviour by learning approaches ("brainwashing") and jokes about people being conditioned mechanically, like animals (mice and Pavlov's dogs), behaviouristic assumptions and techniques contribute much to the better understanding of human behaviour. In the work context learning principles are essential in the fields of assessment of behaviour (especially through accurate observation), training and in motivating work performance. Behaviouristic principles and methods are applied with much success in the field of therapy and counselling, for instance, to teach people to be less sensitive toward fearful situations (stimuli). As is the case with traits, it is common knowledge that events in a person's environment have definite forming influences on personality, both positive and negative. Important contributions to behaviourism theories are Darwin's ideas on evolution, British empiricism, research on conditioning by the Russian psychologist Pavlov (the forerunners of behaviourism); the work of John B. Watson, Edward Lee Thorndike, Clark L. Hull and Edward C. Tolman; the radical and objective behaviourism of Skinner; the more subjective behaviourism of Dollard and Miller and the cognitive-learning approaches of Bandura, Mischel and Rotter (Pervin & John 1997; Schultz & Schultz 1996).

Behaviouristic theories can basically be classified in two types.

The *classical or radical behaviouristic perspectives* as promoted by Pavlov, J.B. Watson and in some respects Skinner, in which personality and behaviour are viewed rather mechanically. Personality, like animal behaviours, is determined by learning or *conditioning* processes. People learn to react to stimuli because certain behaviours are rewarded or punished. Personality can only be studied by observable behaviours; it is an association between stimuli (S) and responses (R).

The *social learning or social-cognitive theories* are represented by authors such as Woodworth, Tolman, Guthrie, Hull, Skinner, Bandura, Walters, Rotter, and Dollard and Miller. The important difference to the classical behaviourists is the recognition that the person or organism and his or her

characteristics mediate between the stimuli (S) and responses (R), thus giving a more interactive relationship between people and environments (S-O-R) (interactionism). People will react to stimuli not only involuntarily but also because of the motivational value of certain stimuli and behaviours. In this respect people are more in control of events, through internal motivation, perception or observing of others, personal competencies, expectancies, self-control and other cognitive processes. Although some behaviourists recognise processes inside people or try to interpret such phenomena, they believe that such factors are not observable enough and too obscure for scientific study and assessment.

Skinner

17.2 MAIN ASSUMPTIONS OF BEHAVIOURISTIC THEORIES

Although differences between some of the behaviouristic or learning theories exist, the main assumptions of behaviouristic theories can be summarised as follows.

17.2.1 Observable behaviour

Human personality can best be studied by means of the objective observation of external and observable behaviours. The best methods are observational, such as controlled experiments and observations in natural settings (field studies), physical measurements of behavioural responses and checking behaviour on checklists and questionnaires. From this it follows that behaviourists see personality study as an empirical science, characterised by careful research designs, objectivity, accurate measurements and the testing and verifying of hypotheses. However, some behaviourists agree that human behaviour may be the result of factors other than only external environmental determinants, for instance information beyond awareness levels and biological drives.

17.2.2 Environment shapes behaviour

Human behaviour is directed, controlled and formed by environmental and situational influences. People are conditioned to react in certain ways to various types of environmental stimuli. Stimuli from the environment may be fairly simple or more complex; some may be well known to people and others not. In this respect some behaviourists acknowledge intrinsic factors in the person, such as inherited factors or unconscious motives to determine at least some behaviour. For instance, Hull, and Dollard and Miller (in Pervin & John 1997) describe biological or innate drives as stimuli which could be sufficiently strong to trigger responses from people.

The behaviourists' lesser emphasis on genetic or biological influences (nature), and past experiences is clear from Watson's statement in this regard (Schultz & Schultz 1996:274):

> Give me a dozen healthy infants, well-formed, and my own specified world to bring them up in and I'll guarantee to take any one at random and train him to become any type of specialist I might select – doctor, lawyer, artist, merchant-chief, and yes, even beggar-man and thief, regardless of his talents, penchants, tendencies, abilities, vocations, and the race of his ancestors.

Although behaviourists did not deny genetic or biological influences, these were not emphasised, because genes are not directly observable, except for their affects on physical appearance. However, in their emphasis of drives as internal tension states, it is clear that they recognise the activation of behaviour by biological factors. The influence of human history and the past is acknowledged in the sense that they recognise that response patterns and acquired social drives are accumulated from all learning experiences.

17.2.3 Personality is learned responses

All human behaviour or personality is nothing but learned responses. Learning is an association or conditioning process of controlling stimuli from the environment, people's responses and the rewards or punishments they get as a result of certain responses. This relationship is referred to as S-R, that is, stimuli causing or controlling the organism (person) to react with certain responses. The S-O-R-principle, however, recognises that people (organisms) and their characteristics have an intervening effect between the stimulus and response. In this way patterns of behaviour or learned responses characterise a person's personality. People will react in certain ways to certain stimuli or in certain situations because they have learned to do so. In this sense "past learning experiences" do influence present and future behaviour. Personality structure, or what personality is, therefore consists of various types of controlled responses as determined by certain stimuli and the rewards the person associates with these stimulus-response interactions. Learning explains simple behaviours and more complex behaviours. As people develop, learned responses accumulate, which allows people to function on higher and more complex levels. It is also possible for certain behaviours to be "unlearned" or extinguished under certain conditions, for example if the person wants to cease giving certain types of responses or if such behaviours are not rewarded. This principle is utilised in training and therapy in which people are taught not to react in certain ways, usually by substituting one form of behaviour for another. Positive and negative behaviours, emotions, as well as social and work performance, are the result of learning, be it correct or incorrect learning.

17.2.4 Self-control
By way of cognitive processes and structures people are able to apply self-reinforcement and are able to regulate or be in control of their environment.

17.2.5 Learning and unconscious factors
In general it is correct to say that learning approaches, especially those of classical behaviourism, do not recognise unconscious factors in personality functioning. However, the fact that authors such as Dollard and Miller took the trouble to explain psychoanalytic concepts may indicate a recognition that "unobservable" stimuli, like unconscious processes and other psychological contents, are more important than some behaviourists would like to acknowledge. Their explanation of people's tendencies not to think about, or to avoid, unpleasant stimuli, is in essence similar to Freud's concept of repression, although they explained learning not to think about certain stimuli as a conditioned response, and not an unconscious motive. In later developments on cognitive influences in learning, some writers also referred to unconscious cognition or *non-consciousness*, to indicate that much of people's thinking happens at a level of "unawareness" of information. An example is research on subliminal perception, in which it has been shown that people learn although stimuli might be below their conscious levels of awareness, that is, even

if people do not see or hear stimuli (Greenwald 1992). You may have had the experience of "sleeping on a problem", after which you solved the problem!

17.3 RESPONSE PATTERNS IN PERSONALITY STRUCTURE
Although behaviourists in general do not describe personality structure in depth, they utilise various response or behaviour concepts to indicate the consistent characteristics of personality. Responses can be defined as learned or recurrent patterns of behaviour which characterise personality and which people utilise to act on stimuli and in situations. In this respect response patterns also provide consistency in personality and behaviour. Because they render people's behaviour predictable, we tend to learn what to expect from certain people in certain environments or what demands or challenges certain stimuli will provide. Response patterns are described in various ways.

Skinner refers to the consistency in behaviour as response tendencies. *Respondent behaviour* is behaviour that follows on from certain known stimuli from the environment, for instance a simple, automatic or involuntary response, such as a reflex eye blink, or when startled by a red light flashing on your machine. Respondent behaviours can also be complex as a result of more complex stimuli, such as solving a mathematical problem. However, the stimuli or operants that really force responses from people are those internal to people, because of their biological nature. Certain behaviours in people occur without stimuli necessarily eliciting such responses. According to Skinner, many human behaviours occur spontaneously or involuntarily because of environmental stimuli, and such behaviours will be shaped or modified if the environment reinforces such behaviours. Positive reinforcers or rewards are mostly used to structure people's behaviours, but

Stimulus of arriving for a job interview	Possible hierarchy of responses
	1. Not honour the appointment at all
	2. Leave a message, will possibly be late
	3. Phone and cancel or postpone the appointment
	4. Keep the appointment but with reservations
	5. Keep the appointment with much self-confidence

Figure 17.1 A hierarchy of response tendencies

negative rewards, such as punishment, can also be used to make people avoid or perform certain types of behaviour.

In contrast to respondent behaviour, *operant behaviour* has an influence on the environment. These response tendencies are the result of many learning experiences and can be related to many types of stimuli or situations. Stimuli may be associated with a hierarchy of possible response tendencies. For instance, when a person goes for a new job interview, they may typically react in various ways, based on previous learning experiences or through trial and error (see figure 17.1).

You may test this on yourself by listing typical behaviours which you might manifest in certain situations. Now recall what really happened in one of the situations. If you did react differently, consider what factors caused you to alter your behaviour.

Responses are conditioned by *reinforcers* (stimuli). If such reinforcement follows a response it will increase the chances that such response will repeatedly occur.

A variation of the response idea, to indicate the consistent conditioned or acquired behaviours in personality, is the concept of *habit* proposed by Dollard and Miller, and also by Hull, which refers to the association between stimuli and responses. Adult behaviours are no more than learned habits which are activated by primary (biological needs) and secondary drives (needs formed from the satisfaction of primary drives, such as achievement). Habits are formed, maintained and discarded by reinforcement. Habits are discarded when they no longer serve a purpose either as responses or as reinforcers, thus not satisfying human drives. Habits in themselves may become secondary drives

Response tendencies in certain situations

and represent response patterns or hierarchies of responses.

Later learning theorists, such as the social and cognitive learning theorists Mischel, Bandura and Rotter, do not clearly designate structural concepts, because they primarily emphasise the motivation of behaviour. According to Meyer (Meyer et al. 1997), however, their emphasis on personality as a function of the interaction between person and situation may render person and situation as structural personality concepts. A better option is to view as structural concepts their concepts for motivation or personal control of the environment and behaviour, such as previous experiences, incentives or reinforcement values, expectancies, competencies or efficacies, cognitive abilities such as thinking, symbolising, planning and encoding strategies.

In terms of personality structure, consistency is one of the "ideals" of personality researchers. If specific or general personality attributes and behaviour can be verified as enduring across cultures, time and situations, then it is possible to predict behaviour. In this regard Mischel's work on situationism (Mischel 1984) emphasises that personality and behaviours can be situation-specific. This sparked an ongoing controversy, with an acceptance that similarities between people and consistency of behaviour over longer periods may not be as consistent as has been asserted by some theorists and researchers (Kenrick & Funder in Derlega et al. 1991; Schmitt & Borkenau in Caprara & Van Heck 1992).

Structural concepts in learning, such as responses and control patterns denoting the characteristic and consistent behaviour of people, have much the same meaning as psychoanalytic and phenomenological concepts of ego or self, the cognitive theories' concepts of constructs and the idea of traits as proposed by trait psychologists.

17.4 MOTIVATION

17.4.1 Reinforcement

There are variations in learning approaches to the dynamics or motivation of behaviour. The older or classic theories emphasise learning through conditioning, reinforcement, consequences of behaviour and environmental influences. The later social and cognitive learning theorists do not emphasise learning by reinforcement only, but strongly emphasise the interaction between people and their environments, that people can use their own social and cognitive competencies to influence events and the consequences of behaviour, and that observational learning is more important than conditioning and reinforcement only.

In general behaviourists agree that behaviour is motivated and directed by *conditioning or reinforcement processes* in the learning of responses. Responses or behaviour are activated by certain internal stimuli in people (drives) or external stimuli from the environment. Reinforcement of behaviours in people is shaped and maintained through positive reinforcement, such as praising an employee, which the person finds pleasant. Positive reinforcement stimuli will cause such behaviours to be repeated. However, expected behaviours can also be reinforced by negative reinforcement stimuli or aversive stimuli, such as disciplining the employee or threats of dismissal. If certain behaviours do not serve a purpose anymore or are continually discouraged, responses could be extinguished. In human resources practices it is important that practitioners and professionals are aware of how employees differ in respect to reinforcement and related factors and how different personalities react. This awareness will influence how management facilitates in the work environment and in performance outcomes to improve work performance and work productivity. In these areas, however, relatively little research on personality variables and research has been done, the exception being locus of control. A reason for this neglect may be that motivational interventions in organisations are often generalised to groups or organisations as a whole and not differentiated in terms of each employee's reinforcement preferences.

In work practices, however, schedules of reinforcement are applied, for instance regular rest periods and salary increases. In training and work design the principle of reinforcement *shaping* is applied when employees are trained to execute tasks in stages or smaller elements.

17.4.2 Habituation

Perhaps the simplest form of learning and motivated behaviour is the forming of habits. If an incoming stimulus is infrequent or unimportant we tend to forget or ignore it; for instance, you may not be bothered by the noise of your neighbour's barking dogs anymore or the noise from typists next door to your office. In these cases the stimuli never become learned and a habit. On the other hand habits can become ingrained or learned when initial stimuli are frequent, important or coupled to emotions. In violent societies crime, aggression and violent acts might become habits, because people's emotions are blunted and they become used to such acts through seeing them repeatedly. Raping, stealing and murdering for no apparent reason might become negative habits in violent societies. Habituation may also motivate social behaviours, for instance shyness, because people cannot get used to strangers, or becoming blasé about pleasant activities such as watching TV shows, or married couples becoming bored with each other because they know each other so well.

17.4.3 Drives as activators

According to learning theories drives are stimuli that activate certain responses from people. Drive concepts appear in many otherwise unrelated theories, such as behaviourism and psychoanalysis, while concepts from other theories, such as needs (for instance Maslow's need hierarchy, Murray's manifested needs and Rogers' self-actualisation), instincts and motives, tend to convey the same meaning of internal or external forces eliciting and maintaining motivated behaviours in people.

According to drive theorists, such as Hull, drives are internal biological, but also acquired, social states, which cause tension or stress that motivates people to act in ways to reduce, dismiss or change the tension. In this sense drive theories emphasise homeostasis (creating balance or stability in behaviour), for instance eating only when hungry or completing an assignment to be approved by parents or supervisors. This also illustrates the idea of reducing tension. Drives, however, do not sufficiently explain heterostasis, or the tendency in people to grow and to continually develop themselves. Drive concepts also assume that motivated behaviour will follow from a state of drive or tension, such as being hungry, while we know that we often eat without necessarily being hungry or do extra work without necessarily having to do it. Why, for example, do creative people write, model, draw, design and invent?

17.4.4 Conditioning processes

Classical or respondent conditioning takes place when a response is caused by a specific identifiable stimulus. Such responses are mostly automatic or involuntary, such as blinking an eye in sudden bright light, and may not explain new behaviours in people. It is possible to use other stimuli to obtain the same response, for instance to get an eye to blink by sounding a hooter, without the light being bright at all! Classical conditioning also has a role in more complex human behaviours such as phobias and fear. Examples of this are the mining operator who has developed claustrophobia (fear of confined spaces) underground, and generalises this to other small spaces, or the motorist, traumatised after being mugged or robbed at gunpoint, who develops intense fears for driving or visiting shopping centres. In all these cases the stimuli (sharp light, hooter, confined spaces) serve as reinforcers for certain responses to occur again with the same, a similar or a substitute stimulus. In these cases the behaviours become stimuli which might be triggered in certain situations. In this way certain environments or situations or persons even serve as conditioned stimuli to certain people. Why, for instance, are some employees always aggressive or dependent in the workplace and why do certain people always irritate you at work?

Classical or operant conditioning?

Operant or instrumental conditioning can be viewed as reward or consequences learning. In Skinner's opinion, operant conditioning describes responses or behaviour which may be spontaneous or voluntary without clear, identifiable, eliciting stimuli. People do not react only passively to stimuli or their environment. Responses or behaviour may be shaped and maintained because of the consequences or effects, rewards or value of the association between stimuli and re-

sponses (law of effect). Completing a task might bring recognition and financial rewards. For this reason an employee may make it a habit to complete all tasks well in the expectation that certain outcomes will result. In contrast, if behaviour in response to certain stimuli leads to unpleasant or less satisfying outcomes, such behaviours may cease or decrease. Operant or instrumental responses are performed by people to obtain certain results and to influence and change environments. We might ask the question whether employees who procrastinate obtain rewards through it, such as avoiding responsibility, getting help or creating an image of suffering work overload. It is possible to explain most work performance through instrumental reinforcement, in that employees' behaviour is modified if they experience rewards or reinforcement continually. If the employee's rewards and reinforcement are based on his or her performance, the possibility exists that work performance may increase, for instance higher pay for more units produced per day. However, this relationship is dependent on each individual's preferences, values and expectancies.

17.4.5 Person-environment interaction, cognitive control and behaviour regulation

Possibly the strongest argument of learning theorists for motivation (and personality development) is the influence of various types of environmental factors and the person's interaction in and with the environment. The interaction between people and the environment, and especially their freedom and powers to influence the environment and regulate their own behaviours, is strongly emphasised by social and cognitive learning theorists such as Bandura, Rotter and Mischel (Pervin & John 1997; Carver & Scheier 1996, Meyer et al. 1997).

Although many environmental factors directly elicit responses from people (situationism), the interaction between people and all their characteristics (interactionism) is more important, because interaction determines the control people exert in their behaviour through their thinking, imagination, feelings, attitudes, perceptions and expectations. Bandura coined the term *reciprocal determinism* for this process of interactional influence between the person's characteristics, situation and observable behaviours.

Rotter refers to *psychological situations* (Allen 1994) as situations very important to an individual, which may be classified together with other situations and which may be rewarding to such an individual, but not to others. For one employee work may be seen as relaxation and enjoyed together with many other forms of relaxation, while for another work is nothing less than monotonous, as are other uninteresting activities.

An important idea in this interaction between individual and environment, in addition to the idea of reinforcement, is the notion of the mediating effect of *cognitive control,* emphasised by Rotter, Mischel and Bandura: that people perceive, interpret and think about stimuli, rewards and how they want to react. Cognitive control enables people to expect and predict outcomes, and which behaviours to use in situations. Mischel & Ebbesen (1973), for instance, describes *self-regulatory plans,* which denote a person's repertoire of behaviours for specific and different situations, and if and when such situations change and demand adjustment in behaviour.

Central to the idea of being in control of the consequences of behaviour is the concept of *expectancies,* recognised by many learning theorists such as Rotter, Walter, Mischel and Bandura. Expectancies are people's beliefs that certain reinforcement or consequences will result

from certain behaviours in certain situations. Expectancies and related learning concepts may be the same as what others call positive thinking, goal-setting behaviours or self-actualisation, and are related to a type of response pattern, which we often refer to as self-image or self-evaluation.

Expectancies may be influenced by certain incentives, that is, the values people allocate to certain behaviours or outcomes (reinforcement value), or how much people want certain consequences in particular situations. For some people it might be important to achieve in all situations, while for others only certain situations matter. When people believe that their behaviour or the expected outcomes apply to many, all or new situations, they may generalise their expectancies to all these situations. This idea of generalised expectancy is similar to Kelly's idea that people's personal constructs have "construct validity", that is, the meaning of certain behaviours may be applicable in specific and related situations.

Rotter (1966, 1975, 1990), for instance, coined the term *locus of control* to explain people's expectancies that outcomes of their behaviour (reinforcement) can be or are controlled. People who strongly believe that they have control of what they accomplish because of their personal behaviour and competencies are referred to as having an *internal* locus of control (they are internals). On the other hand, people whose behaviour is reinforced by expectancies that their accomplishments are ruled by luck, fate, other people and circumstances, have a high *external* locus of control (they are externals). This concept of locus of control is an area of much research and assessment in psychological disciplines (for instance Rotter's own internal-external (I-E) scale), and has been influential in the development of many other related measurement scales and the creating of many other concepts which relate to personal control. Examples of related concepts are personal hardiness (Kobasa 1979), which refers to people's belief that they can control or influence events, feeling committed to activities and anticipation of change as a challenge.

Locus of control is very much integrated and applied in occupational behaviours (Furnham 1992) such as motivation, job performance, job satisfaction, leadership and management, job perceptions, retirement, unemployment, career choice, leisure and turnover. Most research on internals and externals suggests that they react differently in most situations. Internals are more successful in several work performance variables (cited in Furnham 1992 and Cloninger 1996) because they are more self-sufficient in planning and executing tasks, are easier to motivate and take responsibility for decisions and outcomes. It is also possible that internals may be more prone to stress or substance abuse; on the other hand, they may be more successful in solving such problems. Research on psychological adjustment indicates externals are more vulnerable to psychological maladjustment (Ormel & Schaufel 1991). In an analysis and criticism of research on locus of control O'Brien (1986) asserted that locus of control expectancies are influenced by many factors: each situation, the value of outcomes, ability, demographic factors

such as ethnicity and the type of performance ratings used. This variance in research on personal control indicates that locus of control is not a generalised behavioural pattern or trait only, but also person- and situation-specific.

Self-efficacy, a concept coined by Bandura (1977), refers to people's convictions that they are competent or can successfully carry out the behaviours needed to achieve or produce the expected outcomes. Self-efficacy then is coupled to outcome expectancy, in other words, that certain behaviours will lead to certain or desirable outcomes. Self-efficacy may be a general tendency, but is more a unique type of behaviour different for each person, depending on the situation (situation-specific). Ethnic differences may also be found. Self-efficacy is related to many areas, such as academic and educational behaviour (Multon, Brown & Lent 1991), career choice (Lent & Hackett 1987), and health behaviours (O'Leary 1991; Carlisle-Frank 1991). Scales for the measurement of self-efficacy as a general construct or for situation-specific applications, such as particular careers and specific occupational activities, have been constructed (Schunk 1989; Bores-Rangel 1990).

Self-efficacy may be one of the most powerful self-regulatory mechanisms to improve performance behaviours. Self-efficacy touches on people's self-evalua-

Beliefs in what can be achieved!

tion and intrinsic motivation to be in control and to realise potential. In the work context this may be brought about in low achievers by inducing and rewarding a sense of performance accomplishment, so that the employee experiences what success is. Some ways of doing this are to show someone (a role model) working successfully, decreasing the fear of failure or success by exposing the employee to a successful performance event, teaching the employee to relax, to think positively and to use self-instruction, such as setting obtainable goals.

The emphasis on self-control is also evident in the social-cognitive learning theories' emphasis on learning through *vicarious or observational reinforcement* (Carver & Scheier 1996). Vicarious learning means social learning from observing others (models) while they perform certain behaviours, for instance experiencing strong emotions, assisting someone in a friendly manner or completing a task adequately. In principle, observational learning is similar to the person-centred approaches in humanistic psychology in which experiential learning is emphasised. Both imply self-reinforcement or feedback from the person to himself or herself by talking and thinking positively or giving self-praise, or negative self-reinforcement and punishment, when people correct themselves by self-criticism.

In contrast to self-efficacy and a positive locus of control, the concept of *learned helplessness* (Pervin & John 1997) indicates people's real or perceived inabilities to be in control of their lives in general or in specific events, as a result of negative reinforcement of self-control or perception of helplessness. In the same way, many fears of physical objects may also be learned by reinforcement processes. The fear of success and failure is described as a *self-handicapping* psychological fear. Due to early learning experiences, such as too much emphasis on excellence and high

expectations or criticism in successful or unsuccessful situations, people might perform in ways to avoid either success or failure (Lay, Knish & Zanatta 1992; Cloninger 1996).

The principles of reinforcement and learning are often applied in the work and organisational context, as when management either manipulates the stimuli in the work environment, such as design of jobs, reward structures, management and organisational changes, or tries to influence employee outputs by training, performance appraisals and possibly by threats of dismissals. In the latter case it seems as if punishment or negative reinforcement is seldom effective. It might be better to reward desired behaviours and initially ignore undesired performances. It is also more effective in many cases to try to change or influence smaller tasks first (shaping of behaviour) in a sequence for the progressive improvement of total work performance. It might, for instance, be wise to first support a typist to type well before expecting her to be effective also in filing, reception and general clerical tasks. It is also advisable to reward good performances as soon as possible and to be aware of factors in the work environment which might influence individuals differently. Rewards based on consequences of behaviour must be clear to all employees.

17.5 LEARNING IN PERSONALITY DEVELOPMENT

Many human behaviours, such as physical growth, movement, talking and sexual maturity, are regulated by genetic and biological processes over which we do not have much control, except if illness and other traumatic factors impair these developments. Even amid serious impairment some of these developments still take place. Our "built-in time clock" will make for certain physiological changes over time, as people age and as they develop and grow.

This process of physical maturation goes hand in hand with the development of psychological and social behaviours amid environmental influences.

In general, learning theories view personality development as a gradual or continuing learning through *reinforcement* processes and predominantly determined by many physical and psychosocial environmental factors. People will repeat certain behaviours in certain situations if they experience or observe positive reinforcement, that is, consequences are pleasant, but avoid negative reinforcement or certain behaviours in situations if the consequences are unpleasant. In this way over time people develop *contingencies* or certain types of responses that apply to certain situations. Specific behaviours, patterns or hierarchies of reinforced behaviours become a person's enduring, consistent and core characteristics or personality. These may change as people's experiences of the consequences change, as the environments or situations change and when existing behaviours no longer

serve any purpose. Personality development can therefore be recognised in the existence of response patterns which will be suited to each individual at a certain time in life. As people mature behaviour patterns become more differentiated, but also more integrated and complex, to give the person a wider repertoire of responses in various situations.

Personality is shaped by various forms of learning, such as formal education in schooling systems and at home, but also by informal life experiences. Much research on infants and children (Craig 1996) indicates that positive and negative behaviours through various forms of learning take place from a very early age. Development according to learning theories does not take place in stages, but is a continuous and lifelong process of learning, changing and unlearning, as situations and the effects of behaviour also change. Learning can also happen through very simple and passive processes, such as by trial and error and classical conditioning, or can be more active and complex, in which

Various environmental influences on personality

the person rationally and actively intervenes to determine the consequences of behaviours and situations.

It is possible that habituation plays a part in many simple forms of human behaviour. We can experience certain stimuli, become accustomed to such stimuli and either not react to them again or automatically respond. In this regard habituation serves the role of self-control or self-regulation and adjustment. It is believed that the human foetus (before birth) learns to respond to sounds inside and outside the mother's womb by the simple learning process of habituation. In the same way many behaviours of babies and infants may be the result of habituation. Experiments by Armitage and Hepper indicated that foetuses are startled by new sounds, but calm down when used to such sounds. Newborn babies reacted calmly to sounds similar to the mother's heartbeat and stopped crying in response to music which mothers had listened to while pregnant. Babies of mothers who did not listen to such music did not react at all to the playing of it. Cohen and Gelber found that infants as young as two months can recognise visual images by learning through habituation (Craig 1996).

Most human behaviours, however, are learned through the processes of classical and operant conditioning.

Classical conditioning is often associated more with involuntary or autonomous behaviour such as control of blood pressure and skin temperature regulation. Many negative responses, such as fear, can be unlearned by classical conditioning. If people react with fear to certain stimuli, for example having a phobia for dark places, such people can unlearn these fears by counter-conditioning or the process of systematic desensitisation. In these processes a person is progressively given more neutral, less threatening and relaxing stimuli. In this way the old fear or anxiety stimulus and response associations are

replaced by new responses to cope with the original stimuli.

Operant or instrumental conditioning is widely recognised in practices such as psychological and medical treatment, child rearing and educational and training applications. Most human behaviours are learned because of the effect, reward or reinforcement value of the behaviours themselves. If people experience that their behaviours elicit the expected consequences and are rewarded, such behaviours will occur repeatedly. Operant conditioning is a form of behaviour modification through progressive and controlled rewards if certain behaviours occur. For example, if employees experience that their suggestions are implemented, such rewards will enhance their feelings of self-efficacy and more suggestions may follow voluntarily. In medical-related treatment, it is possible to learn to control heartbeat, blood pressure or tension once people have experienced less pain or less tension, because these outcomes are rewarding. At home, school, work and in institutions such as prisons, performance can be facilitated by a system of *token economy,* that is, certain rewards will be allocated only if certain behaviours occur. Examples are getting leisure time if no mistakes are made, being allowed to train for being punctual and being treated to a special meal. In training and work situations the operant principles of shaping and partial reinforcement are also often used to establish expected work behaviours. Employees are taught to master small parts of tasks or to work for short periods and are then rewarded. In the process they learn to do whole tasks successfully or to work for longer periods. Operant conditioning is also applied in cases of negative or avoidance learning and punishment. If unwanted behaviour needs to be modified, the rewards for such behaviour can be removed or changed, in which case the behaviour will not occur again because it will not have the expected results for the person. Examples are to stop overtime payment if production does not increase, to decrease the amount of bonuses if sales drop and to stop "time off from work" if relationships in the work group do not improve. Consequence learning is also emphasised by learning from own responses, which Bandura (1977) referred to as *response consequences,* which may be similar to what people often referred to as experiential learning in a humanistic sense.

Learning theories, for instance those of Dollard and Miller, also strongly emphasise the various types of environmental determinants or influences on personality. Environmental stimuli may be of a physical, psychological and socioeconomic nature or a combination of all these. This leads to their emphasis that learning is influenced by the type of situation and circumstances. Infants have primarily innate behaviour and few acquired responses, which in time, through social experiences, develops into more advanced social and psychological behaviours. According to Bandura children, especially, develop through *imitation,* or modelling of parents and many other models in their social environment, an idea which coincides with Freud's view of identification. Rewards from models, such as parents being supportive and loving, will do much to establish behaviour patterns.

The social-cognitive theorists also emphasise lifelong change and development in people as a result of the *interaction* between people and their environments. They refer to specific types of behaviour in people developing as a result of certain interactions in situations. In this respect they stress social learning through observational or vicarious reinforcement. Empathy, or in their terms, *vicarious emotional arousal* (Eisenberg et al. 1994), refers to experiencing the same feelings as another by observing that person experiencing

certain feelings. Is this not what we experience when we see or hear people grieve or worry? Even when only reading about the problems of others, some people experience emotional arousal such as tearfulness and sadness! *Observational reinforcement* is a factor in how many other behaviours develop in people, for instance aggression, cruelty, dependence, loyalty, sex roles (Carver & Scheier 1996). In many cultures traditional gender or sex roles are learned and internalised by observing how parents and other models perform their roles and what types of work men and women do. Therefore, change of these roles in modern society will also require "unlearning" of old roles and the learning of new roles by experiencing and observing the roles by other models. Research cited in Weiten (1995) clearly indicates the role of reinforcement through role models, such as parents and the media, in altruistic (helping) behaviours and aggression.

In the language of the social-cognitive theorists much learning takes place, as a result of *cognitive* processes such as thinking, perception, interpretation and anticipation, in the forming of cognitive structures by which meaning is given to the world and events. In this respect, Mischel (1968) describes competency as the *developed cognitive ability* of people to assess situations and the ability to perform behaviours that will suit the demands of situations.

17.6 LEARNING AND MENTAL HEALTH

Generally, learning theories do not explain mental health as adequately as some of the other theories and they also differ somewhat in their explanations. In fact, most of these theories do not see the need to describe symptoms or classify people in categories of maladjustment. They especially reject the medical model of explaining mental disorders and prefer to refer to psychological health. In general, though, psychological maladjustment is viewed as unadapted habits or response patterns and lack of life skills and knowledge as a result of *faulty learning* and inappropriate reinforcement, or the negative influence of environmental stimuli and models and not from unconscious or other unobservable influences. Psychologically healthy people, on the other hand, have correctly learned to react so as to receive positive reinforcements and avoid negative ones. The same principles of conditioning and reinforcement which explain adaptive behaviours also apply to maladaptive behaviours. In general, positive rewarding or reinforcement of desirable or proper behaviours is associated with positive psychological health. In certain cases, however, when desirable behaviours are rewarded without really giving attention to the person, subsequent misbehaviour may follow because that person wants attention from people. On the other hand, negative or aversive reinforcers and punishment are mostly associated with psychological maladjustment, except if it is intended to extinguish undesirable behaviours. A problem with punishment and other forms of negative reinforcers, such as fear and social disapproval, is that undesirable behaviours may reappear once people get used to the stimuli or when such stimuli have been removed. This may have been the case in societies in which oppression occurred and rules were enforced by negative reinforcement and punishment.

Classical conditioning can be responsible for many fears, anxieties and stress reactions. People's fears of various objects and ideas in life are nothing less than the association of stimuli and responses. Once afraid of an object or situation, the fear can be generalised to many other situations, even if the original stimulus is not present. The employee stuck in the cabin of a high crane might not be able to work in a crane again and could have fears of any enclosed space. This type of problem may even extend to other areas of life. For instance, the same employee may have difficulty in driving a car.

Operant conditioning can also be responsible for behaviour deficiencies. Skinner explains behaviour deficiencies as the result of *incorrect reinforcement*. People will behave in deficient ways if they are rewarded for it or if their deficient behaviours are reinforced by their environments. The underachieving employee, sloppy in his or her tasks, never submitting work on time, may have these behaviours because they were allowed or he or she succeeded in avoiding negative punishment. In this way the deficient behaviours were reinforced. The same principle may apply for many maladaptive forms of behaviour, such as verbal aggressiveness, tantrums in children and even behaviours such as obsessiveness and compulsiveness. In some organisations, people with deficient work behaviours may even be promoted, perhaps because of favouritism, which could be an indication of how maladaptive work behaviours can be reinforced and become a norm in organisations. According to Hull's two-factor theory (Möller 1995) even physical reactions can be conditioned, as these often go hand in hand with emotional reactions. Orleman's three-factor theory of emotions (1976) expands Hull's idea of emotional arousal by describing cognition or thinking as a third factor contributing to the conditioning of maladaptive emotional behaviours. The social-cognitive learning theories especially emphasise the effect of cognitive interpretation of events. People might overemphasise one or two negative events to the extent that they influence their lives for long periods. This might also explain why some people react differently to work and life stressors; it depends largely on how they perceive and interpret events. It can be said that stress does not exist until people decide that something causes stress.

An interesting explanation for depression is given by learning theorists (Möller 1995). Depressive people's behaviours are caused by *insufficient reinforcement* from their environment and other people. This low level of reinforcement results in low levels of activity, accompanied by increased complaints of illness and other less effective behaviours, such as pessimistic thinking and emotional outbursts. In this way, people may learn to act in a negative or self-defeating manner which prevents them from getting positive reinforcement. In terms of cognitive learning theories depressed people might also believe that they are helpless and not in control of their lives. This form of learned helplessness and other *self-defeating* or self-handicapping behaviours, such as fear of failure and success, is in contrast to the idea that people might also learn to take control, as illustrated by concepts of learned resourcefulness and self-efficacy.

To change behaviours by means of training, therapy and counselling, learning approaches also utilise learning principles. Through various techniques, such as conditioning, reinforcing and rewarding of other stimuli and behaviours, people learn new behaviours, or faulty behaviours are modified, extinguished or unlearned. In social cognitive therapies people are taught to use their thinking skills to assess the causes and consequences of undesirable behaviours and to find new ways to obtain more desirable consequences. In many instances people are progressively *desensitised* from threatening stimuli or behaviours by offering them less threatening stimuli until the consequences of the old or new stimuli can be coped with by the person. Various techniques of behaviour modification are used: aversive therapy, implosive therapy, assertiveness training, systematic desensitisation, modelling and role play, token economies, various forms of self-control programmes such as systematic relaxation and bio-feedback and the cognitive learning techniques of rational-emotive therapy and

thought stopping (Rimm & Masters 1979; Carson et al. 1996).

17.7 CONCLUSION

Learning principles are a part of historic and modern psychological theory and practices and will have an important place in the future. Behaviouristic and learning assumptions are simple, understandable and have face validity in their statements on behaviour that is observable and is measurable. "Seeing is believing" might be an appropriate motto! The norm and practice of precise measurement also complies with the requirements of scientific thinking. Their main idea is based on observable human behaviour, and in order to be classified as such, it must be possible to study behaviour scientifically through accurate controls and observation. Behaviourism has contributed much to the development of objective methods to observe and assess personality.

In the work context, practitioners use behaviouristic principles in techniques such as behaviour-anchored rating scales, behaviour-based interviewing and observation of behaviour dimensions in real or simulated work activities (e.g. in assessment centre activities). In work motivation, leadership behaviour, training, advertising practices and in behaviour-modification practices, learning principles offer economic and quick ways to impact on human behaviour.

Learning principles contributed much to research and stimulating differences in psychological disciplines, thus contributing to a better understanding and explanation of human development and motivation and the causes of behavioural disorders. Criticism can be levelled at the possible oversimplification of personality and the ignoring of less observable influences in human behaviour. The fact that the results of experimental observations cannot be generalised to real-life situations, due to small research samples and unnatural situations, is often a problem. However, experimentation is one of the few methods which really can explain the underlying causes in behaviour.

Self-evaluating questions

1. Discuss the main assumptions of behaviourism and learning theory and try to determine whether these are applied in your workplace.
2. Recalling your own or your parents' behaviours at home, explain how reinforcement has a role in human motivation and development.
3. A person tells you of a fear of being among people. How will you explain this condition using learning principles? How will a psychoanalyst's explanation differ from yours?
4. What do you think of the behaviouristic idea that human behaviour is, and can be, controlled by conditioning and manipulating environments?
5. You are a behaviourist psychologist and working as a counsellor in an organisation. An employee is reported as having a serious substance abuse problem. How will you go about understanding and treating this problem?
6. Using examples, discuss how reinforcement principles operate in societies such as in South Africa.
7. Using examples from your daily newspaper or other media, explain how behaviouristic principles are used in business.

Dimensional or trait perspectives

18

Ziel Bergh

CONTENTS

Learning outcomes

After studying this chapter you should be able to:

- define the concept of trait and cite examples
- use Allport's definition to explain assumptions of the trait approaches
- describe personality structure by using one or more trait approaches
- list many traits and fit them into a model of personality traits
- list traits in people and classify them as different types of traits
- explain someone's achievements by using trait concepts
- explain personality development using the trait concept
- give evidence of why you believe traits to be consistent in people, across time and in situations
- explain psychological adjustment according to trait approaches
- practically demonstrate the trait concept's utility in human resources practices

Key concepts

elements, factor analysis, individual differences, psychophysical systems, trait models, work related traits, types, surface traits, source traits, dynamic traits, common traits, personal disposition, cardinal traits, central traits, ability traits, proprium, proprium stages, functional autonomy, needs, consistency, mature personality

18.1 INTRODUCTION

The trait-factor approach encompasses perspectives also referred to as dimensional, dispositional or type theories. Trait concepts are used to describe personality structure, motivation and adjustment and even personality development in terms of specific and combined *elements* or dimensions. In the sense that most or all theories of personality use constructs to describe the various aspects of personality, they can all be regarded as dimensional, such as the psychoanalytical descriptions of id, ego, superego, conscious and unconscious. However, only certain theories formed their trait and type descriptions through rigorous research, such as factor analysis and other types of correlational research. *Objective trait research,* which had its beginnings in research on intellectual abilities, is, together with behaviourism's research through experimental observation, one of the dominant factors in qualifying psychology as a science. This is especially due to its contributions in objective or psychometric test development. An important contribution of trait research was to establish general laws on human behaviour by which similarities and differences between people can be explained. Trait psychology also contributed vastly to assessment methodology in psychological disciplines, especially the use of psychological questionnaires on various personality domains in the occupational context and other applications.

Trait approaches to personality may well be the most explicit exponents of personality description emphasising *individual differences.* Traits, however, may also be the most neglected approach, especially in explaining human behaviour, for instance in the clinical field. Other, but often more unsubstantiated and subjective, personality theories and research approaches are favoured.

Because traits are phenomena that people have in varying quantities and qualities, and these elements can be measured, people can be differentiated and compared and these measurements used to predict a person's behaviour across time and in situations. Traits may be in terms of abilities, motives, interests, values, emotions, attitudes and interpersonal behaviours. Most psychological assessments of people and related situations are based on measuring the frequency or quantity of incidence of certain personality or behaviour traits, whether for selection or promotion in jobs, career counselling, training or therapeutic purposes. In recent times "competencies" has become the buzz word in human resources applications to describe the profile of abilities, knowledge and skills and other attributes which render an individual suited for a position, or which may be used to predict success in work performance. The objectives of all these applications are to fit a person's disposition to the characteristics, demands and conditions of a work situation. In daily life and in lay use "trait language" has become common, for instance in what factors caused an accident, in persuading one to buy a certain car or vote for a candidate, and the reasons for liking or disliking someone. The idea is also illustrated by the trait or type language used when a person is praised or criticised in the media or in verbal discussions.

The concept of *factor* is often used to describe combinations of traits, because most trait descriptions of personality are derived from empirical research in which factors were isolated from masses of data by using variations of the statistical techniques of factor analysis. In this way various types of factor models for personality or aspects of personality have been isolated. The trait type of approaches are sometimes referred to as psychometric, because of the emphasis on objective measurement and the quantitative analysis of the elements of personality.

The best exponents of trait or dimensional approaches in personality are Cattell, Eysenck, Allport and Wiggins, although there are many others. The structural theories on intelligence, such as those of Spearman, Thurstone and Guilford, all depict intellectual abilities in terms of different elements. The same applies to the conceptual approaches on interests, values, attitudes, motivation, emotion, career development, consumer behaviours and aspects such as leadership and management. Of recent writers, Goldberg and Costa and McCrae can be viewed as modern exponents of revised or newer trait models, such as the five-factor model (Pervin & John 1997). Efforts to propose a new personality theory according to the five-factor model may signal the beginning of not only a new trait approach, but also a more integrated view on personality (Wiggins 1996).

18.2 MAIN ASSUMPTIONS

An important assumption of trait theorists on their *view of humankind* is that personality consists of certain *elements* which people may have, which direct and organise behaviour and also provide each individual with a more or less identifiable personality profile. Cattell, for instance, does this by a process of "inductive-hypothetico-deductive spiral" (Allen 1994:423), which means that by first doing scientific empirical research on traits, Cattell put five hypotheses to be tested. He followed a process of reasoning from the specific to the general (inductive), which made it possible to then reason from general statements to specific aspects (deductive). This approach is in contrast to many other theories which start out as pure speculation or subjective observations.

A further assumption of trait psychology is that traits, or a pattern of traits, types or a person's disposition, are quite *consistent and enduring,* that is, they will not change much over time and across situations. Traits are tendencies or predispositions to act in certain ways and people who have similar traits may behave similarly. You may agree that many people you have known for a long time have remained the same in respect of their "basic" personality characteristics and ways of doing things. Often physical changes will be more noticeable than changes in underlying behaviour. A person's traits may also be quite observable in behaviour, although many assert that much of our behaviour may be from unconscious causes; in fact many trait descriptions may suggest the existence of unconscious causes in behaviour.

According to trait approaches people may be *similar* in some respects, but every individual also has a *unique* disposition, because traits may manifest differently in different people as a result of different genetic, learning and situational experiences. Cattell, for one, recognises that certain traits have a genetic origin, but environmental factors also influence the formation and expression of personality. Cattell explains personality interactionally (an aconitic model), defining personality as "that which predicts what a person will do when placed in a particular situation" (Cattell 1966:25). Allport, who is classified as an eclectic psychologist because he fits in with various schools of thought such as person-centered and traits approaches, also emphasises studying the whole person as a unique and independent being.

18.3 PERSONALITY DEFINED AS TRAITS

Trait descriptions of personality fall into two categories. To some, such as Allport, traits are *real and observable* in a person; to most, among them Cattell, traits are primarily viewed as *abstractions* or fictions used to describe observed behaviours. In the latter case, known as an implicit personality theory, personality is viewed as something created in the mind of the researcher or observer. This criticism of trait theory serves to make us aware of our ethical responsibility to be objective and not to allow our own preferences to distort our observations of a person's behaviour. However, in scientific trait research the formulation of

theory and concepts rests on widely accepted empirical evidence.

In general, traits denote the characteristic and consistent ways in which people respond across time and in various situations (Pervin & John 1997).

Gordon Allport

One of the most recognised definitions of personality as a dispositional phenomenon is by Gordon Allport (1961:28). He defines personality as "the dynamic organisation within the individual of those psychophysical systems that determine his characteristic behaviour and thought". Traits are seen as *psychophysical systems,* made up of physical and chemical or neurological processes as well as psychological functions; both are ways in which personality attributes and behaviour are expressed. Traits determine or elicit certain types of behaviour, and various types of traits ensure that the individual's behaviour is more or less consistent. Traits can be general (the same for many people, or many behaviours can be explained by such traits) or unique to each individual, or every individual may have unique traits, which will explain individualistic types of behaviours.

Allport's definition of personality is, on analysis, quite complex and complete. It recognises that personality is determined by the interaction of biological and psychological processes; personality is an organised whole consisting of interdependent physical, cognitive and psychosocial aspects; personality is dynamic, in other words, it develops, grows and changes as the individual matures and learns; changes or variations in how personality is expressed may also occur from time to time or across situations; personality, through the psychophysical systems, motivates and directs behaviour; personality provides recognisable or characteristic unique attributes, thoughts and behaviours, which enable the individual to adapt in his or her environment.

For Allport traits are psychophysical systems that really exist, that give structure to personality and direct and motivate behaviour. Traits, especially as a result of underlying neurological processes, provide stability to behaviour and personality. The same trait, for instance trusting, should elicit the same type of response from various stimuli or situations. Other authors view traits not as concrete or directly observable, as does Allport, but as images or abstractions to represent certain types of behaviour and that can only be observed indirectly.

Cattell (1965:25) defines personality as "that which predicts what a person will do when placed in a particular situation". In this definition, Cattell refers to traits which must provide personality with characteristic behaviour and consistency in behaviour to allow us to predict or to know what to expect of people. He also recognises that personality, expressed in behavioural traits, is a function of people and all their attributes in interaction with their environments.

18.4 TRAITS AND TYPES IN PERSONALITY STRUCTURE

18.4.1 Traits

Trait descriptions of personality have specific dimensions to describe and explain characteristic ways of behaving, thinking, feeling and doing. Traits are inherited and represent learned potential or *predispositions*, which direct and motivate our behaviour and which give structure to personality, because they also characterise personality. A combination of traits can lead to a profile or a type or style description. In many instances scores on questionnaires are manipulated through statistical techniques to present types, for instance team roles, leadership style, conflict and stress management style and occupational type. Traits can thus be used to indicate possible sources or causes of behaviour, descriptions of characteristic and consistent behaviour and methods to explain the structure of personality. Many trait descriptions of personality can be found. Allport and Odbert, for instance, recorded almost 18 000 different descriptive words, which they arranged into more than 4 000 trait names. These trait names, as were many others, were mostly described in terms or words common to everyday language use (lexical approach). Many later theorists and researchers produced their own lists, especially through the statistical process of factor analysis. In this way personality traits or profiles are coupled to many applications, such as various types of jobs, professions and to leadership.

Timmons (cited in Furnham 1992) describes 13 general characteristics for entrepreneurial success: drive and energy, self-confidence, long-term involvement, valuing money as a measure of success, persistence in problem-solving, ability to set goals and to commit to them, moderate risk-taking behaviours, ability to learn from failures, concern for feedback on performance, initiative and taking responsibility, actively using available resources, competing against own standards and tolerance for ambiguity and uncertainty.

Apart from layman's knowledge or our own private "theories", the scientific and more objective measurement and trait descriptions of personality will be based on one or other theoretical model.

18.4.1.1 Personality as three factors

One of the most sophisticated and influential trait approaches, in theory, research, personality assessment and other applications, is Eysenck's *three-factor model* of personality (Eysenck 1992). According to Eysenck, who was influenced by, among others, the work of Galen and Jung, personality consists of three major factors: extroversion-introversion, neuroticism-stability and psychoticism (tender-mindedness) -super-ego functioning (tough-mindedness); each one of the main factors is described by subfactors or specific traits. This model influenced the construction of various personality questionnaires, such as the Eysenck Personality Inventory to assess the three-factor model (Gregory 1996). Digman (in Wiggins 1996) asserts that if we also include Eysenck's concept of intelligence, his model really has four factors.

The three main factors and their sub-factors are described in table 18.1

This model is widely backed by factor analytical research and is used in the assessment and description of behaviours in various applications, such as smoking, health, sex, criminality, and cross-culturally, but to a lesser degree, in occupational behaviours. Two of the factors, extroversion and neuroticism, have similarities to two factors in the five-factor model of personality. Some would have it that Eysenck's model even closely resembles the five-factor model (Digman 1990).

18.4.1.2 Personality as sixteen factors

Cattell proposed that personality be represented by 16 relatively independent factors, which are measured by the well-known 16-Personality Factor Questionnaire (16-PF), various versions of which are available and used in many clinical, educational and occupational applications (see table 18.2). Cattell's theory on personality is one of a few that emerged as a result of extensive factorial research over many years on personality traits, utilising various types of data on personality, such as people's self-reports, personal history, observations and scores in psychological tests (Cattell 1965, Pervin & John 1997).

Table 18.1 Eysenck's personality factors and subfactors

Extroversion vs introversion	Emotional stability vs neuroticism	Tough-mindedness vs psychotism
Activity	Low self-esteem	Aggressiveness
Sociability	Unhappiness	Assertiveness
Risk-taking	Anxiety	Achievement orientation
Impulsiveness	Obsessiveness	Manipulation
Expressiveness	Lack of autonomy	Sensation seeking
Lack of reflection	Hypochondrias	Dogmatism
Lack of responsibility	Guilt	Masculinity

Source: Gregory 1996

Table 18.2 Personality as sixteen primary factors

Reserved	Outgoing
Concrete reasoning	Abstract reasoning
Affected by feelings	Emotionally stable
Submissive	Dominant
Serious	Happy-go-lucky
Expedient	Rule-conscientious
Timid or shy	Venturesome or socially bold
Tough-minded	Sensitive
Trusting	Suspicious or vigilant
Practical	Imaginative
Forthright	Shrewd or private
Self-assured	Apprehensive
Traditional	Open to change
Group-oriented	Self-reliant
Tolerate disorder	Controlled or perfectionist
Relaxed	Tense

Source: Carver & Scheier 1996

Cattell's approach played a dominant role in the further development of trait psychology and objective personality assessment, including the most recent development of an integrated personality theory based on an integrated research and assessment trait or factor model, the so-called Big Five-Factor model, of which Cattell must be the "intellectual father".

When using the 16-factor approach according to the 16-PF, personality (see table 18.2) is analysed into 16 so-called first-order factors, or these factors can be calculated and reduced to six (or nine) second-order factors including anxiety, extroversion, independence, tough-poise, control and intelligence. Cattell's model encouraged an enormous amount of research and applications, but also caused controversy. His model and questionnaires are used all over the world in many applications, including occupational settings. Cattell provided many profiles for various types of jobs based on the 16-Personality Factor Questionnaire.

Although Cattell emphasises still more factors for an adequate understanding of personality (as much as 35 if abnormal personality traits are included), his second-order factors integrate personality into five factors, if intelligence is excluded (Strack & Lorr 1994). In this sense Cattell's 16-factor approach is comparable with the five-factor model.

18.4.1.3 Personality as five factors
The so-called "Big Five" or five-factor model of personality has developed into an approach that arguably now enjoys the

most support as an integrative trait description of personality (Digman 1990; Goldberg 1993; McCrae & John 1992), despite criticism (Block 1995). Wiggins (1996) and Wiggins and Trapnell (in press) give an excellent account of the progressive development of the five-factor model, from its modest conception by Thurstone in the 1930s, through the many contributions by, among others, Tupes and Christal, Norman, Eysenck, Guilford and Cattell, its rediscovery in the 1980s, through to the present where it is asserted that the five-factor model really represents a new, integrative way of

describing, assessing and studying personality. It was the vigorous writings and research of Costa and McCrae in particular that revived interest in the five-factor model and also showed that some or all of the five factors are measured by some of the well-known personality questionnaires. Concepts in the five-factor model represent psychological knowledge from many personality theories and decades of personality and other psychological research.

Although quite a number of five-factor models are proposed, there is much agreement on the lexical basis (everyday

Table 18.3 Factors and trait descriptions from the five-factor model

Factor	Factor
1. **Extroversion (surgency)** warmth, assertiveness, activity-seeking excitement, gregariousness, positive emotions	**Introversion** silent, unadventurous, timid, unenergetic, unassertive
2. **Agreeableness (friendliness)** trust, tender-mindedness, straightforwardness, altruism, compliance, modesty	**Antagonism** stingy, unkind, selfish, distrustful, unhelpful
3. **Conscientiousness (dependability)** order, competence, achievement, striving, deliberation, self-disciplined, dutifulness	**Lack of direction** impractical, lazy, disorganised, irresponsible, careless
4. **Neuroticism (emotional instability)** hostility, anger, anxiety, impulsiveness, depression, self-consciousness	**Emotional stability** relaxed, calm, contented, unemotional, stable
5. **Openness to experience (intellect)** values, fantasy, aesthetics, actions, feelings, ideas	**Closedness** uncreative, uninquisitive, unreflective, unsophisticated, unimaginative

Source: Pervin & John 1997

meanings of factor names) and the contents of the five factors.

To summarise the various five-factor models (see Carver & Scheier 1996) the five factors with some of the characteristic traits or subfacets are illustrated in table 18.3.

Each one of the five factors is described by specific traits, which represent a finer analysis of personality, much like Cattell's idea of the six second-order factors and the 16 primary factors. Costa's and McCrae's neo-personality questionnaires (NEO-PIR and the NEO-FFI) are designed to measure the big five personality factors (Costa, McCrae & Dye 1995). Every one of the complex five factors has roots in the knowledge or conceptual base of psychology, that is, from theory and research. All subtraits belonging to each factor have been scrutinised, leading eventually to the description of each factor with all its characteristics. These trait names have stood the test of time in general lexical use, in personality research and in assessment practices and enjoy general acceptance in many circles, as well as cross-culturally.

The five-factor model has been verified by assessments on a broad range of personality questionnaires in various fields, as well as applications in fields such as psychopathology and work-related assessment (Barrick & Mount 1991, 1993; Strack & Lorr 1994; Schneider & Hough 1995). Barrick and Mount (1991), for instance, found positive relationships between the big five factors and three types of work performance measures: job proficiency, training proficiency and personnel data. These authors found that conscientiousness, especially, is a consistent predictor of work performance, extroversion is closely related to job factors such as social interaction and training proficiency, and autonomy is an intervening variable in the relationship of personality and work performance. It seems evident that future classifications, such as for abnormal psychological syndromes, and especially descriptions of personality disorders, will have to include or integrate research based on the five-factor model. In efforts to predict occupational performance, the value of the five-factor model of personality cannot be ignored.

The five-factor model does a lot to organise data on personality variables, which makes it easier to use other existing theories to explain such variables. Some researchers assert that a complete description of personality will have to be based on more factors, and also that five-factor models do not explain personality efficiently in all its manifestations (Block 1995). Block (1995), for instance, criticises the easy acceptance of the five-factor approach, the acceptance of layman's language for trait descriptions, and too heavy an emphasis on objective assessment by questionnaires only. Hough (1997) asserted that the five-factor model is too broad and does not accommodate some existing personality scales. She therefore described four more factors: achievement, affiliation, locus of control and masculinity/femininity, or rugged individualism. It is also obvious that the five-factor model will have to be integrated with assumptions on personality structure, motivation and development as proposed by older, and other, types of personality theories. In the practice of measurement to predict behaviour it might always be better to use more factors and associated traits. For now the five-factor model does well in describing personality, but not as well in explaining behaviour, especially with regard to underlying causes, internal personality dynamics and underlying motivation (Saucier & Goldberg, in Wiggins 1996). The Big Five-Factor Model as yet is not a complete theory of personality and much must still be done. However, there are some efforts to postulate a five-factor theory of personality (Costa & McCrae, in Wiggins 1996).

We can no longer disregard this trait paradigm in our modern way of thinking about and assessing personality. We will have to adapt existing theories and methods to also reflect the five-factor model.

18.4.2 Other applications of trait descriptions

We have already referred to the trait approach of Jung, as applied by the Meyers-Briggs and Jung questionnaires.

If we think about specific aspects of personality, such as motivation, leadership, self-concept and adjustment, it is possible to find trait descriptions for these in every context. For instance, profile analysis describes and compares job profiles, people, situations and even organisations in terms of traits. The same applies when we analyse diagnostic models, such as the APA's Diagnostic and Statistical Manual of Mental Disorders (DSM) (1994). Mental disorders are classified according to certain dimensions or axes, to which behaviour must be compared according to certain minimum criteria before a person can be diagnosed as suffering from a specific psychological disorder.

An approach which is used increasingly in work-related personality testing is the Occupational Personality Questionnaire by Saville and Holdsworth (OPQ) (Matthews et al. 1994). Based on a sound theoretical rationale, personality is described comprehensively in as many as 31 subfacets, if a social desirability scale is also included. These subfacets are classified into three main personality domains: relating, thinking and feeling. Many studies indicate that the OPQ-personality factors are really work-related (Robertson & Kinder 1993).

An interesting factor or trait approach to classify interpersonal behaviours is the so-called interpersonal circumplex model proposed by Wiggins (Wiggins & Broughton 1991; McCrae & Costa 1989). Wiggins developed the interpersonal trait model from a broader model of trait categories,

which he termed interpersonal, temperamental, material, character, social and mental traits. The interpersonal model is based on the assumption that personality is best expressed in interpersonal situations, so vividly defined by Sullivan (1953:110-111) in his interpersonal approach to personality: "the relatively enduring pattern of recurrent interpersonal situations which characterise a human life". Together with writers such as Freud, Erikson, Bowlby and Ainsworth (Craig 1996), he also emphasised the need for tenderness which infants especially need from a mothering person.

How people react in social situations is really determined by interpersonal traits. Wiggins distinguished eight interpersonal trait categories, which he represents as opposites on a circle. Such opposites should be negatively related, while traits at right angles to each other should be independent of each other. The eight interpersonal trait categories are illustrated on the circle in figure 18.1.

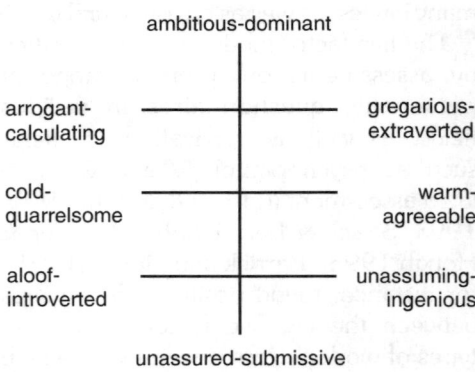

Figure 18.1 Interpersonal circle of personality traits

Source: Cloninger 1996

Note that some of the trait descriptions in figure 18.1 closely resemble those of some of the three-, five- and 16-factor approaches. Correlations with many other questionnaires, based on other models, were found and this type of approach is used in many applications. Kiesler (1979), for instance, produced the Interpersonal Impact Message Inventory to assess the impact of interpersonal contact in, for example, therapy.

A special application, and also a difficulty, of correlational research on personality research in the work context is *criterion research*. This entails finding the work-related variables which have a positive and significant relationship with personality. This is necessary to predict work performance if certain personality measures are used as predictors. Researchers try to find clusters or taxonomies of work-related personality traits for specific situations and for general use, and even to describe organisational characteristics.

McLellan's and Paajanen's (1995) measure, the Customer Service Orientation Inventory (CSI), is an example of a work-related personality traits measure which could be used universally. The dimensions in this questionnaire are: sociable, communicative, courteous, positive body language, perceptive, responsive, tactful, cooperative, flexible, open, even-tempered, optimistic, accepting of authority, externally rewarded, competent and reliable.

These authors found good evidence of criterion validity between customer service orientations and four criteria related to customer service, while Costa and McCrae (1995) and Ones et al. (1993), also report a positive relationship between customer service orientation and personality factors such as emotional stability, agreeableness and conscientiousness. McDaniel and Frei (in Hough & Schneider 1996) reported employees with good customer orientation to be resilient, cautious, cooperative, adhering to strict standards of conduct, helpful, cool headed, planful and thoughtful.

Another measure of work criterion clusters or taxonomies is the 18-factor model, reduced to four main factors by Borman and Brush (1993), on manage-

rial performance. The four main factors are: interpersonal dealings and communication, leadership and supervision, technical activities and mechanics of management, useful personal behaviour and skills. The specific criteria applicable to management performance are the following 18 traits:

- planning and organising
- guiding, directing, motivating subordinates
- giving feedback, training, coaching and developing subordinates
- communicating effectively and keeping others informed
- representing the organisation to others and the public
- technical proficiency
- administration and paperwork
- maintaining good working relationships
- coordinating subordinates and other resources to get the work done
- decision-making and problem-solving
- staffing
- persisting to reach goals
- handling crises and stress
- organisational commitment
- monitoring and controlling resources
- delegating
- selling and influencing
- collecting and interpreting data

The above criteria should also fit well with personality variables as measured on many recognised personality tests. It is, however, possible that technical task criteria will be better predicted by measures of ability, while the more contextual activities of job performance will be better predicted by personality measures. In this regard, Brief and Montewidlo (1986) described the so-called prosocial organisational behaviours and *organisational citizenship behaviours* in contrast to pure task behaviours. The former two refer to the extra supportive behaviours, which are not always in a job description, but that are very necessary in successful job performance. Some of these are:

- volunteering to carry out task activities that are not formally a part of the job
- showing extra enthusiasm or effort and doing more than the expected, if necessary, to complete own and other tasks
- cooperating and helping others
- following organisational rules and policies even if it is personally inconvenient
- supporting, defending and endorsing organisational objectives

A similar work-related trait that received much attention is *organisational trust and integrity*, by which is assessed a range of dishonest, illegal and counterproductive attitudes and behaviours. These were found to correlate with measures of job performance and counterproductive behaviours (Ones et al. 1993).

In conclusion, we should note examples of classifying organisations according to certain traits or types (Davies 1992; Kennedy & Everest 1991; Cox & Blake 1991). All these authors described the organisation that manages diversity successfully, according to certain traits such as:

- understanding of own culture and how employees are influenced
- strong positive values
- practising and accepting cultural differences
- open, trusting climate
- good structural integration and flexible (not rigid)
- mutual feedback with good communication and encouragement
- absence of prejudice and discrimination
- low levels of conflict
- concern for interpersonal relationships
- creative problem-solving
- long-range goals

The so-called "learning" or adapting organisation is another classification, in which traits such as systems thinking, having a shared vision, team learning, participating management systems, a climate of learning

and sharing information, efficient communication and flexible structures describe the way an organisation copes with transformation and changes and deals with its human resources demands (Pedler et al. 1992).

By observing and writing down behaviours and processes in individuals, groups or organisations over time, you should be able to identify certain characteristic traits and even repeated patterns.

18.4.3 Types and styles

The concept of traits and types is similar, in that it denotes a disposition of a person to act in a specific way if he or she has certain traits or if he or she is of a certain type. In many instances styles are used to describe behaviour in the same way as type is used.

Types or styles are mostly seen as a *combination of traits* which result in a person having a distinct type or style, for instance either introvert or extrovert. However, you can't be both; like male and female, these terms represent a discontinuous description. Although type theories and concepts are still used to classify and describe people, type descriptions of personality are less used than trait concepts. In occupational practice, however, type and style concepts are utilised to describe personality or behaviours such as communication, leadership, management, conflict resolution, thinking and learning styles, group roles, and stress management or coping styles. A problem with the use of type descriptions is the tendency to be labelled with a certain type, and in much the same way as we get used to a certain actor in certain roles, we can create the impression that such a person can perform in no other role. The Meyers-Briggs Type Indicator (MBTI) (Briggs Meyers 1993), like the Jung Personality Questionnaire (Du Toit 1983), is a questionnaire based on Jung's theory of psychological type, especially his descriptions of two attitudes (extroversion and introversion) and four functions (thinking, feeling, sensing and intuition). Depending on the test scores a person is allocated one of eight possible codes, which denotes the person's psychological type. Such a psychological type is then interpreted in terms of certain behaviours or how a person will react in certain circumstances. In research some aspects of the MBTI assumptions were verified, for instance the relationship between these Jungian types and job interests, different types of occupations, different ways of thinking, and other personality traits (Schultz & Schultz 1994, Furnham 1992).

Many other examples of personality typologies exist. The Greek physician, Galen (about AD 150), in accordance with the ideas of Hippocrates (about 400 BC), identified four personality types (Carver & Scheier 1996). Each personality type was associated with internal body fluids. The types were sanguine (associated with blood), optimistic in temperament; choleric (associated with yellow bile), with a tendency to be irritable and angry; melancholic (associated with an excess of black bile), depressed; phlegmatic (associated with an excess of phlegm), calm and controlled. This reasoning about the possible relationship between personality and biological processes was, much later, taken further by Kretchmer in the 1920s and Sheldon in the 1940s who associated physique and personality, which resulted in Sheldon describing three personality types made up of the interactions between body types (somatotypes) and temperament. These were the endomorphs (associated with the heavier, soft and round body types, temperamentally the more sociable and easy-going person); the mesomorphs (associated with the more muscular body type and being more energetic and assertive in nature); and the ectomorph (associated with thinner body types and reflecting a more sensitive, shy and intellectual temperament) (Carver & Scheier 1996; Cloninger 1996). More recently Eysenck proposed three dimensions: neu-

roticism-stability, extroversion-introversion and psychotism-impulse control, which integrates the description of the types by Galen, Kretchmer and Sheldon.

Other typologies were also identified and applied. For instance, to differentiate patterns of work commitment or patterns of stress management, people are often classified as either an A- or B-type personality (Matthews 1988). A-type behaviour is characterised by, among others, impatience, high standards for achievement, tight time schedules and competitiveness; the B-type presents a more calm orientation with less emphasis on achievement and time constraints. In many research findings the A-type personality is indicated as at high risk of cardiovascular diseases (CHD) (Matthews 1988). In career development literature Holland differentiated between six occupational types: realistic, investigative, conventional, artistic, enterprising and social. The occupational type which a person will become or may change into is dependent on the interaction between personality and work environmental characteristics (Holland 1985). Schein (1990) identified eight so-called career anchors, which comprise an employee's self-image, a vocational self-concept of preferences, values, needs, work experiences and abilities at a certain stage in life which will motivate him or her to prefer certain types of jobs or job tasks.

There are various typologies in leadership and managerial theory and research that are applied in human resources management. Examples of typologies which describe *leadership types* or roles are administrative, bureaucratic, expert, ideological, charismatic, symbolic, democratic, autocratic and transformational (Kreitner & Kinicki 1989). In conflict management, certain styles are closely related to the type concept. An example is the description by Blake and Mouton of conflict-management styles along the two dimensions of concern for people versus concern for task completion. The conflict-management styles are withdrawal (low concern for people and task); smoothing (high concern for people, but low for task); forcing (high concern for task, low concern for people); compromise (balance between task and people concern); and problem-solving (solutions satisfy people and task concerns). Power and conflict management in organisations and between groups can also be described by certain styles, for instance nine styles by Yukl and Fable (1993) and Rahim's five conflict-management styles in complex organisations (Rahim 1985): integrating, obliging, dominating, avoiding and compromising. A person's or group's style will be indicated on a continuum (see figure 18.2) depending on concern for others or self and which conflict-management styles are used.

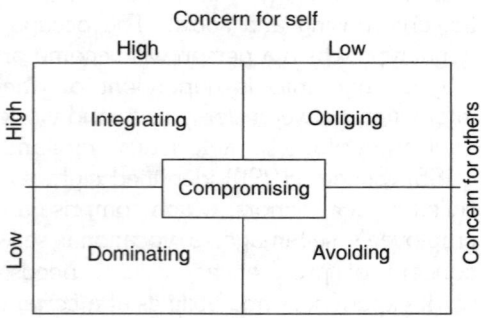

Figure 18.2 Five conflict-management styles
Source: Kreitner & Kinicki 1989

Eight types of roles which persons may assume in a group are described by Belbin (1981), and these are often used in facilitating interaction in work groups. These *team roles* are chairman, shaper, plant, monitor-evaluator, resource investigator, team worker, company worker and completer or finisher. Kolb (Furnham 1997) developed a questionnaire about learning styles designed to identify the type of cognitive attitudes and learning styles people utilise to disseminate infor-

mation and to solve problems. In this way Kolb identified four types of learning styles: accommodator, diverger, assimilator and converger. These styles reflect the person's development in the acquisition of certain skills, as well as whether the person is concrete or abstract (theoretical), and whether the person utilises active (direct) participation, or reflective (indirect) observation, in thinking and learning processes. Honey and Mumford (Furnham 1997) also measured four types of learning styles: activist, theorist, reflector and pragmatist.

Latack's three types of job-related coping styles: control, escape and symptom management (Latack & Havlovic 1992), and the Ways of Coping Checklist (WCCL) of Lazarus and Folkman, in which two styles of coping, problem-focused and emotion-focused, are identified (Lazarus & Folkman 1984) are often used in stress research. These styles indicate the type of behaviours which might be followed in order to manage work or general stressful situations.

18.5 DIFFERENT TRAITS

The discussion on the various models indicates types of trait descriptions. Most trait models try to explain various aspects of personality, for example structure, motivation, development and adjustment of personality by using trait concepts. Traits not only describe personality, but also specific issues such as values, interests, motives, attitudes and abilities. Cattell, for instance, differentiates between source traits (which may include ability traits), temperament traits dynamic traits and surface traits. Allport distinguished between various types of traits, such as common and individual traits, cardinal and central traits and secondary traits, as well as habits and attitudes.

Various theories emphasise these different types of concepts to describe different functions of different types of traits.

18.5.1 General traits

Allport (1961) asserted that in some respects all people are alike, in some respects some people are similar and in some respects every individual is unique.

General traits are traits in all or some groups of people which enable us to compare people across cultures and situations. This is referred to as a *nomothetic principle* to describe or assess personality according to general laws or norms. The assumption is that such traits will be present in all persons, but in varying strength. In this way we use test norms to compare different individuals or groups. Allport and Cattell viewed traits like neuroticism, intelligence, extroversion, introversion, masculinity and gregariousness as *common traits* which all people, as a result of similarities in hereditary potential, possess to a lesser or greater extent and on which they can be compared. The three-, five- and 16-factor models of personality represent general traits on which people can be compared. If some of these traits or specific facets of them frequently and strongly manifest in people's behaviour or in measurements the traits can be classified as unique.

18.5.2 Unique traits

Traits may be unique to a cultural group or a specific individual, a principle referred to as an *idiographic* way of describing, assessing and acting with people. In this respect it often does not make good sense to compare people. Allport, for instance, used the concept personal disposition to describe traits specific to individuals which differentiate them as unique. He utilised the concept of *cardinal trait* to describe a dominant trait, such as authoritative, ambitious or obsessive, that is so dominant or pervasive that it is observable in about every aspect of the person's life. Not everyone necessarily has cardinal traits. In contrast, Allport's concept of *central trait* does not denote a single dominant trait, but rather the five or six characteristic or general traits which in most

ways describe an individual's personality or explain daily behaviour, for instance friendly, aggressive, sociable, empathetic, shy, alert, energetic and self-confident. You may test this by naming the few traits that you think really describe your personality best!

People may also have *secondary traits*, less obvious but very specific in certain situations, such as preferences for food, colour and certain values or attitudes.

Cattell's description of source traits seems to have similarities with Allport's idea of central traits. *Source traits* are the basic factors of personality and provide consistency in behaviour. Allport also describes habits and attitudes which can be traits, but are also specific tendencies toward certain life issues, such as habits of being accurate and clean and an attitude of loyalty toward a specific country or group.

18.6 TRAITS IN PERSONALITY DEVELOPMENT

Trait approaches do not emphasise personality development as vividly as, for instance, Freud did, especially with regard to the stages of development, although both Allport and Cattell give stages noticeable attention in personality development. In contrast, however, to Freud, Allport and Cattell do not believe that the adult personality is absolutely determined by what happens during childhood, and discount the influence of unconscious factors. They rather believe in the individual's own motivation and goals to give the person freedom to develop his or her personality. Allport and Cattell, however, acknowledged the important formative influence of parents in learning experiences, especially the mother during the early childhood years.

Allport views adulthood as separate from previous phases. Children do not have personality and function dependently according to their needs. Adults have more propriate strivings, even in the event of hardships, which enable adults to be independent and autonomous from childhood experiences. He emphasises that positive psychological growth into a mature adult can only be achieved if positive conditions and a healthy biological make-up are present during the gradual development of the person's potential. If development is frustrated, the personal traits or dispositions which will characterise consistent behaviour, and are necessary to function as an autonomous adult, will not develop.

Trait approaches such as Allport's, Cattell's and Eysenck's emphasise the importance of both *biological and environmental* factors in the development of those traits which are the building blocks for all aspects of personality and human behaviour. Allport emphasised that as the person grows the environmental learning processes increasingly come into play; a baby does not have a personality, as bodily functions, intelligence and temperament are all determined and controlled by biological processes. Cattell, through his research, indicated that some traits are more or less influenced by either heredity or environment. Cattell, in fact, differentiates between constitutional and environmental-moulded traits.

Allport's developmental theory has not had much impact on disciplines concerned with human development, in comparison to Erikson's, although his emphasis on the progressive development of a self-identity toward fully fledged adulthood has merits.

According to Allport, personality develops through seven proprium stages, from infancy through adolescence into adulthood. *Proprium* is his term for ego or self. During these developmental stages physical processes, personal dispositions and intelligence progressively mature and become more differentiated and integrated. The seven ego-development stages are bodily self, self-identity, self-esteem, extension of the self, self-image, self as a rational coper and propriate striving.

The first three stages of ego development are characterised by the baby or young child becoming aware of himself or herself, others and the environment through body and biological functions. In this regard Allport's ideas are similar to those of

Like adult like child?

Freud, in that he also sees the young child as reflex driven and also motivated by pleasure from bodily functions. At stages two and three a sense of self-identity starts to develop as the child identifies with its name and takes pride in its achievements while exploring its world, which may be the early development of a learning and work ethic. Conflicts may arise when the child's exploring of itself and its world is frustrated by parents and others.

During stages four and five (about 4-6 years) the child begins to know the what and who of its world and starts to evaluate its own accomplishments, successes and failures; the child now starts to value its own self-image, as well as the role of other people and aspects of its self-perception.

Stage six (6-12 years) is characterised by strong cognitive development and the solving of everyday problems.

During stage seven (adolescence into adulthood) the young person prepares for adulthood, and sets long-term life goals.

Stage seven is followed by adulthood, which is independent of childhood. The adult is an autonomous being, having his or her own self-image and motivation to rationally create his or her own life style. The mature adult is open to all experiences and is not a slave of the past. The mature and healthy adult personality is characterised by unselfishness, warm interpersonal relationships, self-acceptance, realistic perceptions of life, self-insight and has a unifying philosophy of life which directs life and strivings. The mature adult behaves *functionally autonomously*, and his or her behaviour is "appropriate" in terms of himself or herself and the environment. In this regard Allport, Vernon and Lindzey constructed a Study of Values Scale, based on Spranger's work on types of men. Their six value orientations are theoretical, economic, social, political, aesthetic and religious, which singly or interactionally may influence many aspects of a person's life. It is, for instance, possible that the occupa-

tional values a person has and which are used to select a job and an employer may be grounded in such values. A Values Scale by Super and Nevill, used in career counselling, also reflects some of the values which Spranger and Allport described (Gregory 1996).

18.7 TRAITS AND PERSONALITY DYNAMICS (MOTIVATION)

Dynamics refers to processes and factors in the motivation and adjustment of personality. The trait approaches also use trait concepts to explain behaviour motivation, that is, why people behave as they do. In general, trait psychologists explain a person's behaviour in terms of the strength of a trait, and for this reason traits are portrayed in personality test profiles on, for instance, a nine- or 10-point scale. Extremely high (or low) scores on a trait mean that in a specific situation the person's behaviour manifests with a certain magnitude, or that intrinsically the person possesses a strong trait. This may pose problems and the individual will have to learn to behave differently.

Allport emphasised the importance of motivation, but as it applies to the present and how people rationally and consciously create their own opportunities. In this regard he and Cattell both differed from Freud and others who emphasised unconscious and other irrational factors in motivation. Allport insisted that motivation in children is based on immediate and reactive mechanisms, mostly arising from basic needs. In adults, however, motivation is based on *propriate strivings*, that is, behaviour initiated by the individual. Adults are consciously aware of what they do and plan and not dependent on previous motives or environmental forces. To Allport motives are unique to each person and people may have various motives, which cannot easily be explained by one single concept or principle.

Allport's concept of *functional autonomy* is the essence of his ideas on motivation. Functional autonomy implies that behaviour learned for a specific reason is persisted with even when the original motive no longer applies.

When people's motivations are healthy and realistic and they have become self-motivating, when their motives are appropriate for the needs and demands of the situation and no longer based on previous motives or unresolved issues, they have attained functional autonomy. As an example, you may now be studying industrial psychology at university because your parents, for their own reasons, want you to obtain a degree. Hopefully, as time passes, you will study because you enjoy the subject and want to become a professional psychologist, and not because you have to please your parents or are forced to study. The same may apply when you start to work and only work for money. Later, as you become financially independent, you may work because you enjoy work and feel yourself a partner in the business. Allport used the concept of *propriate functional autonomy* to indicate that we select the motives that we like and that suit our self-concept (proprium). This is why we often select activities that we are interested in or have strong abilities and skills in.

A young child or a person suffering anxieties can seldom be functionally autonomous, because their behaviours are based on immediate gratification and tension reduction, which Allport termed *deficiency needs*. It is possible that deviant behaviours or childish selfishness may also become functionally autonomous, which means that such unhealthy behaviours will continue to direct behaviour. In contrast, the mature adult may sometimes be motivated by deficiency needs (such as uncertainty or hunger), but has the ability to put aside such motivations in order to achieve long-term goals and values, which Allport termed *growth needs* or *propriate needs*. A healthy personality has outgrown original motives, accepts itself as part of a bigger world and enjoys healthy life values and goals.

Allport explained behaviours such as habits, addictions and automatic responses, that once had a motive, as *perseverative functional autonomy.* Many of our biological behaviours cannot be explained by the functional autonomy concept, as they clearly always have a biological origin. As adults, however, we mature to a stage where even the initial biological needs are satisfied in other ways, thus they have also become functionally autonomous.

Cattell also used traits, specifically his concept of *dynamic traits,* to describe and explain behaviour motivation and interests. He described two types of dynamic traits, ergs and sentiments. *Ergs* (the term is derived from a unit of work or energy) are described as goal-directed and the basic, permanent, innate energy of all behaviour, much like drives or instincts. Cattell, through factor analysis, identified 11 ergs: curiosity, gregariousness, sex, self-assertion, security, protection, hunger, disgust, appeal, self-submission and anger. *Sentiments* are learned or environmentally moulded traits which direct and motivate behaviour, much like interest can be a tendency to be interested in certain career activities. Sentiments can change and be unlearned. Sentiments are about our central life interests, such as work, family, religion, recreation and nation. Every person, through the combination of sentiments, develops a *self-sentiment,* which really represents the self-concept. The self-concept provides consistency to many aspects in people's behaviour, organises the source traits and attitudes and determines how people express their basic needs (ergs) and interests.

Cattell's view on *attitudes* is broader than the usual meaning and refers to people's interests, emotions and behaviour toward things, situations and persons.

Cattell asserts that *ability traits,* which include intelligence, will determine how we advance in work and toward our goals. He believed that our general intelligence is largely inherited, and termed it fluid general intelligence; learned or crystallised general ability is acquired in our learning processes and is not genetically influenced.

Cattell proposed the principle of subsidisation, meaning that people's motives are mutually subordinate; attitudes to sentiments and sentiments to ergs, the latter being the main motivating drives of all behaviour.

Other important trait contributions towards behaviour motivation are Murray's need theory and McClelland's concept of achievement motivation (Carver & Scheier 1996; Cloninger 1996).

Murray described human motivation through underlying needs, which can be either primary biological needs or secondary psychological needs. Needs are aroused by every person's cognitive and emotional motives (the thought and feeling of wanting something) and influences from the external environment, termed press by Murray.

Murray's need descriptions are really trait descriptions and their associated behaviours. Emphasising psychological needs, Murray proceeded to describe a list of needs which were later used in the Edwards Personal Inventory (Gregory 1996), a questionnaire to assess some of the needs described by Murray.

McClelland built on Murray's description of the need for achievement, a topic that has stimulated wide research and has been widely applied, for instance in analysing achieving patterns in societies, selection of personnel and in management development practices. The *need for achievement* is defined as the desire for excellence, to perform well in tasks, to overcome obstacles and to improve on previous levels of performance. Many questionnaires and other techniques have been developed to assess achievement behaviour.

In a continuation of Murray's work, several other need factors, such as the needs for power, affiliation, intimacy and nurture, have been extensively researched (Carver & Scheier 1996).

Traits can direct behaviour in many ways

18.8 CONSISTENCY OF PERSONALITY

In previous sections we have referred to the agreement among trait approaches that traits provide stability and consistency to personality over time and across situations. In most cases the trait approaches also tend to align this consistency with hereditary or biological factors. The controversial issue is whether traits really are consistent indicators of personality, especially amid some findings that personality measurements are rather poor predictors of actual behaviour. This is borne out by self-reports of people on how they see themselves compared to what is measured by questionnaires, and by personality factors as predictors of work success, where low correlations, often lower than 0,35, are reported. This means that other influences account more for behaviour than personality. This is in contrast to measurements of cognitive or ability factors, which generally have high predictive powers for job and training success criteria. The longitudinal stability of intelligence and achievement behaviours are also well established by research. More recent meta-analytical research, however, indicates personality factors to be better predictors of occupational behaviours than was asumed previously (Barrick & Mount 1991).

18.8.1 Consistency in and across situations

One explanation for the inconsistency in personality measurements is called "situationism", which means that the situation in which a person operates will influence the person more than personality itself. This is also the viewpoint of people who emphasise the influence of environmental factors, such as social psychologists and behaviourists. With respect to situationism, most research, however, indicates that situations generally do not contribute more to the accurate prediction of behaviour than does personality (Funder & Colvin 1991; Funder & Ozer 1983). In terms of consistency of behaviours between situations (cross-situational stability), it is asserted that although they are generally low, correlations will vary depending on the type of personality factors involved. In a study by Funder and Colvin (1991), correlations between situations for different personality domains varied between -0, 0,09 and 0,70. An interesting finding is that certain behaviours have consistency among themselves, such as certain habits and acts. In a study Borkenau and Liebler (1992) found that when different judges rated the same behaviours on either visual or acoustic information their ratings were quite similar.

A fundamental mistake in situationism is the underemphasis on the "human factor" in situations; in fact behaviour in most situations will be influenced more by a person's perception of the situation and not by the situation in itself. In this regard a cognitive view of stress is that a stressor, for instance work overload, will only cause stress reactions once the employee perceives himself or herself as not being able to cope with the demands of the work.

18.8.2 Consistency from interactionism

A second approach towards explaining the consistency of personality is interactionism (Endler & Edwards 1986). Interactionism (of which Cattell's definition of personality is an example) states that personality and the situation in collaboration contribute to personality consistency and both should be taken into account in behaviour predictions. We are all aware of how similar situations can influence some people differently. Different personalities (or types of traits) may react differently in similar situations. Examples are the achievement-oriented person who may be more productive under stressful conditions than the person who cares more for relationships on the job; or a person who is prone to depression committing suicide because of a traumatic event such as loss of work. We may also wonder why people select different types of jobs or marriage partners.

This principle of interactionism is important in human resources development whenever we want to place people in situations, with or without other people, to perform certain tasks.

It is also important to remember that different people with different traits will or may "change" situations, which may cause the results to be different to what we expected, or the situation to be different for some people. In a meeting a dominant person may influence interactions to such an extent that people react negatively on a questionnaire to what has transpired; a person who usually offers creative ideas and solutions withdraws and suddenly seems to be unproductive.

Traits do not apply in all situations to the same extent. You may test this by observing a colleague's assertiveness in the work situation and comparing it to assertiveness at the sports club. You may find him or her assertive in a one-on-one situation, while in a group situation he or she may be described as submissive. If you consider yourself to be outgoing in temperament, are you always outgoing, in all situations and with all people? In general people learn appropriate behaviours for situations and will tend to behave consistently in certain situations, which provides for consistency across situations. In some individuals we also learn to expect consistency of behaviours over time and across situations, while others might always or mostly behave inconsistently. This also illustrates the learning perspectives of people in acquiring contingencies or hierarchies of behaviour.

Consistency over time, especially over longer periods of time (longitudinal consistency), is also a controversial issue with respect to personality traits. Longitudinal research (research over longer periods) on people's own reports about changes, and of questionnaire data, shows that in general personality remains quite consistent, although some changes with regard to certain traits may occur, for instance becoming more responsible and independent (Costa & McCrae 1989; McCrae 1993). We may note fluctuations in a person's behaviour from day to day, which might be ascribed to certain hassles or events on different days. During such brief periods certain behaviours tend to be emphasised, which may lead one to believe that personality traits are inconsistent, but if we compare the same behaviours over longer periods we might find more consistency.

With reference to stability of personality, we must realise that the causes of behaviour are many and complex. People are not all the same and react differently in situations and over time. Many of the findings on consistency of behaviour may also be the result of errors in our measurements and research processes.

Most of the research on the consistency in personality over time and on interactionism tends to verify that personality traits do exist in people. This is demonstrated by certain characteristic patterns of behaviour in individuals and groups as portrayed by trait descriptions, models, such as the three-, five- and 16-factor models, as described by people themselves and as measured by certain personality questionnaires.

There is sufficient evidence of existing trait patterns and on behaviour consistency to use trait measurements on specific aspects of personality to understand, describe and predict behaviour in the field of human resources development and management.

18.9 PSYCHOLOGICAL ADJUSTMENT

Trait approaches do not postulate a specific theory or concept to explain *psychological maladjustment*. Most theorists, such as Allport, are interested in the healthy, mature personality. They empha-sise how personality traits develop as a result of the interplay between genetic endowment and influences in the environment and how these traits give rise to the type of behaviour that can be classified as either adjusted or maladjusted. In general, traits as measured by certain self-report techniques (e.g. questionnaires) are used to explain adjustment or maladjustment. Both Cattell and Allport emphasise genetic, biological or constitutional traits, such as physique, intelligence and temperament, which influence how personality develops. Temperament traits, especially, are coupled to people's emotional or mood expressions and how they react in situations.

Allport emphasises the mature, adult personality, independent from childhood. However, the quality of adult maturity is dependent on how the proprium (self) has developed in all its stages during childhood.If the proprium development is insufficient, for instance the child is insecure, lazy, dependent, aggressive, unreliable and demanding, the adult personality can follow suit; in Allport's term, the proprium cannot become functionally autonomous. This means that behaviour traits are not sufficiently organised, integrated and consistent to give the adult the competence and mastery to manifest appropriate coping behaviours in life situations. Functionally autonomous or *psychologically healthy or mature people* have the following traits or characteristics:

- behaviour is future directed according to a positive life philosophy and certain attainable goals
- psychologically mature people have the ability to extend their sense of self to other people and activities; they are not egocentric or live for themselves only
- mature people have positive relationships with others, and show consideration, empathy and tolerance

- adult, mature people have achieved self-acceptance and manifest emotional security in their behaviours
- psychologically healthy people have self-insight, that is, they are not over-sensitive and also show humour in appropriate situations
- mature people have a realistic perception of realities, and are realistic about their own competencies and the goals they set for themselves and others

18.10 CONCLUSION

Personality traits is an empirical paradigm to describe and predict personality through more objective and accurate assessment. If we apply the rigorous criteria of scientific thinking, it is possible that the trait approach and its psychometric tradition of assessing personality variables represents the only true paradigm in psychology. Evidence of this scientific status includes the following:

- models such as the five-factor model, which provide a well-researched description of the structure of personality traits (Goldberg 1991; McCrae & John 1992)
- advances in thinking about, and methods of, personality assessment (Nicholson & Hogan 1990), especially a richness in personality questionnaires
- research on the existence of personality traits, such as heritability (Loehlin 1992); longitudinal stability (Costa & McCrae 1995); universality of traits across situations and cultures (Yik & Bond 1993) and the use of traits in many applied fields (Barrick & Mount 1991; Miller 1991)
- the research on personality traits also facilitates our better understanding of various concepts and issues about human behaviour, such as the self-concept, sexual behaviour and evolutionary aspects, personality disorders, interpersonal behaviours, unconscious behaviour and hypnosis (in Wiggins 1996)

• Apart from the empirical evidence, trait approaches, with their simple logic of lexicon trait descriptions, are useful in daily life, very "user friendly" in practice and offer the layman understandable and testable psychological concepts.

On finer analysis, for instance by Wiggins and Trapnell (in Wiggins 1996) and McCrae and John (1992), the trait approaches are more then only empirical research. They offer much about the classical issues raised in personality theories: personality structure, motivation, development, adjustment, as well as issues on research and measurement. Trait theories on personality also offer much on the philosophical questions on the nature of humans, constructs to describe human characteristics and differences, as well as clear guidelines on which constructs and phenomena must be researched and studied in personality psychology.

In human resources practices, where much of our information is about the fit between employees and the demands of the business environment, the empirical and objective assumptions of the trait approaches offer a lot. We will do well to try and locate our existing thinking, theories and practices into the trait paradigm, which has come a long way in integrating knowledge on personality.

Self-evaluating questions

1. Using your own behavioural patterns as examples, explain the assumptions underlying trait approaches on personality.
2. Giving examples, describe personality by using any trait theory.
3. Using any existing job description or your own job description, make a list of five to 10 critical performance areas (the main dimensions or areas in which you must perform).
4. Make a list of the personality traits you think a person must have to perform well on these critical performance areas you have identified in question three.
5. Define or describe the personality traits you listed in question four and see whether you can fit these into one of the factor models.
6. Ask your parents or a close relative, and friends, to independently describe you by at least five characteristic traits when you were 16 years of age and as you are now. Try to assess:
   (a) whether your family and friends agree on the trait descriptions
   (b) whether you are still more or less the same person
7. Observe someone in the workplace and analyse the person's work motivation in terms of Allport's and Cattell's concepts of motivation.

The humanistic-phenomenological perspectives

19

Ziel Bergh

CONTENTS

Learning outcomes

After studying this chapter you should be able to:

- illustrate the basic assumptions of the humanistic perspectives by using examples
- explain a person's self-concept by analysing the attributes which determine the self
- illustrate the concept of self-actualisation
- give examples of behaviours which indicate why people do not achieve self-actualisation
- explain how you will use humanistic ideas to motivate people in the work situation
- describe a real-life situation in which you believe you had a peak experience
- describe a traumatic event which you think caused someone to find new meaning in life
- explain personality development and psychological health according to humanistic concepts

Key concepts

phenomenology, existentialism, self, self-experience, wholeness, meaning, self-esteem, self-identity, positive regard, congruence, organism, phenomenological field, self-actualising, peak experience, constructs, self-efficacy, self-control, needs, optimal, salutogenis

19.1 INTRODUCTION

The humanistic approach, like many others, is not based on one single theory but is made up of various theories within the so-called existential-phenomenological and humanistic perspectives. Although similar ideas are shared elsewhere, the humanistic approach is American in origin, spearheaded by Maslow, Rogers, May and Kelly. Existentialism and phenomenology preceded the humanistic approach and originated in Europe; early and modern contributors are philosophers and psychologists such as Kierkegaard, Heidegger, Sartre, Van den Berg, Frankl, May and Jaspers (Shultz & Schultz 1996; Van Niekerk 1996; Meyer et al. 1997). Compared to other personality theories, the older phenomenological and existential approaches are not really personality theories but rather *philosophical ideas* about the meaning of life. The theories of Rogers, Maslow and Kelly, however, are

viewed as theories in their own right. However, the initial ideas had and still have an enormous influence on the thinking and practices of many personologists and are recognised in many applied settings.

Carl Rogers

Humanistic approaches are often referred to as the "Third Force" as opposed to behaviourism and psychoanalysis. The idea of "humanism" in personality psychology derives from a more *optimistic view* on personality, in reaction to Freud's rather pessimistic emphasis on the unconscious; the behaviourists' emphasis on the dominant deterministic influence of environmental factors and the existentialists, who often write about despair in life to illustrate the finding of meaning. The humanists, such as Maslow and Rogers, rather emphasise joy, love and creativity in people's strivings to achieve self-realisation.

The idea of *phenomenology* emphasises the *subjective experiences* (obtaining knowledge about the self and the world) or meaning which individuals attach to things and their experiences in terms of what reality is for each. In this regard the individual as a whole is emphasised instead of only certain dimensions. A central idea is the uniqueness of every person's *context* and frame of reference; how each individual experiences and interprets himself or herself in relationship with mental, physical, religious, social and psychological phenomena in the world. Rogers, for instance, emphasises that reality is whatever an individual experiences it as at a particular moment.

The concept of *existentialism* in personality psychology derives from humans' efforts to transcend or move above or outside themselves, to become persons by being open to all experiences and to rise above the hard realities of life. Reality is only what every person lives through their own subjective experiences and people can't be studied outside their context or as "being" in the world (Schultz & Schultz 1994).

Although not the first, these theories really extend and expand various aspects and concepts of the ego or self to explain how individuals can evolve toward fully functioning or self-actualised people, and to live meaningfully without necessarily being enslaved by circumstances.

19.2 MAIN ASSUMPTIONS

Together with sociologists and social psychologists, who differ with Freud, humanistic-oriented theorists emphasise the strong influence of *social factors* and important people in people's lives on personality. Rogers, for one, emphasised the corruptive and destructive effects which society can have on the otherwise intrinsic goodness of people.

19.2.1 Subjective or phenomenological experiences

People do not only react to physical realities, which are perceived (see, feel, hear and smell), but also to how they subjectively interpret events and phenomena. This is an important principle in understanding why employees, for instance, often react so differently to work stressors, poor employee relationships, supervision and management styles, selection decisions, salary increases or traumatic work experiences such as work loss, accidents and economic decline in business. It is also the reason why many authors and practitioners believe it is dehumanising to assess a person's behaviour and compare it to others according to certain numerical or statistical norms or a general law, because this often ignores the person's subjective and idiographic experiences of the situation. Subjective experience is measurable only when it happens. The moment an event, feeling, action or thought passes, it is gone, a memory, not reality anymore and thus not easily measurable, except through recollection.

The idea of *self-experience* is widely used in training, development and therapy groups, in which the emphasis is learning about oneself and others by experiencing whatever happens in such groups, without undue pressure from the group facilitators.

A person's *self-concept* is formed by progressive subjective experiences during personality development. In this way a person's self-concept or the "integrated pattern of subjective experiences" will have an influence on his or her feelings, reactions and thinking in many areas in life, such as values and attitudes about things, relationships with friends and intimates, family life, occupational choices and work attitudes and the way he or she copes with the demands and changes of work life. Super (1970) maintains that the different self-concepts that develop in the individual's personality influence his or her work life.

19.2.2 Uniqueness of each individual

People's experiences are not only subjective, but uniquely so, and may never be the same as for someone else. Therefore, according to humanistic approaches, the emphasis in measurement and other applications is often idiographic, focusing on the experiences of the individual rather than on comparing numerical scores and norms to those of others.

19.2.3 Personality as a Gestalt or holistic phenomenon

Humanists also emphasise the person and his or her behaviour as a *whole*, totality or "Gestalt", which is in contrast to what some behaviourist (personality as stimuli and responses) or dimensional theories (personality as traits) do, or Freud's description of personality in various structures such as the id, ego and superego. Personality is an integrated whole and more than only the sum of its various parts. The integration of physical, mental, psychological and social characteristics and all their attributes and relationships is what makes us function as a coherent whole person. Perhaps this integration is what people miss and grieve for in the trauma, for instance, of death or divorce after many years, losing a job, or becoming disabled after an accident.

Sometimes, however, using only certain factors to understand some types of behaviour in context does make sense, even working from a humanistic paradigm, as long as we recognise that other factors may have an influence. This is often done when employees are assessed in the work context, such as studying the contents of jobs, selecting in terms of certain critical traits, doing performance appraisals on certain work performance criteria and surveying only some organisational factors. It is often time-consuming and impractical to assess holistically.

On the other hand, we must also be aware of how a single intervention, for instance disciplining one employee only, or obtaining or losing a job, can change or influence a workplace or an individual.

19.2.4 Intrinsic goodness (potential) of people and self-actualisation

In contrast to, for instance, psychoanalysis, according to which a person often has conflict due to internal anxieties and external forces, humanists emphasise people's intrinsic ability to grow toward healthy adjustment, maturity and the achievement of goals. In this respect the concept of self-actualisation is utilised to refer to a person's intrinsic ability to choose and achieve what he or she wants to be. One may ask how any person's goodwill, positiveness or potential can withstand the seemingly insurmountable obstacles of life that millions of disadvantaged people experience. In many instances the tragedy of the world is that many never achieve self-actualisation or never have a choice, except if we assume that self-actualisation for some may be at the most basic level of satisfying daily biological and safety needs. In other instances, again, the resiliency of individuals and groups to continuously withstand overwhelming odds and to eventually succeed is the answer. Did survivors of despair, like prisoners of war or victims of other human atrocities, transcend the realities of their circumstances? Victor Frankl, a renowned existential psychologist and father of logotherapy, based some of his positive ideas on freedom and finding meaning in life, or giving meaning to life, on his personal sufferings in the German concentration camps at Auschwitz and Dachau during World War II (Möller 1995).

19.2.5 Free will or self-determination

Coupled to self-actualisation is people's ability and freedom of choice to be in control of what happens to them, for instance electing to be governed by their own wishes, and not by forces in the past or outside their control. Thus freedom of choice also means taking responsibility. This idea of will to freedom and meaning coincides with cognitive psychology's idea that people can take responsibility for what happens to them (internal locus of control) or they may blame others or attribute all to the outside world (external locus of control).

The humanistic-phenomenological *view of humankind* has an emphasis on people's unique and subjective experiences and meaning in the context of their existence in the world and with others, as well as the more optimistic belief that people are more in control of their own lives and destinies. This approach may make for a greater emphasis on the meaning of "being" human.

19.3 SELF-CONCEPT: INTEGRATING PERSONALITY STRUCTURE

Many of the humanistic theorists, such as Rogers, are referred to as self or ego psychologists, making the concept of *self* the central theme in their exposition of what personality or personality structure is. Humanistic and related theories use the concept of the self differently to Freud's concept of ego in the sense that they view the ego as more autonomous, having its own energy and able to influence personality development throughout the life cycle.

Essentially, Rogers's theory comprises three premises: the organism, which is the total individual; the phenomenological field, which incorporates the totality of experiences and perceptions; the self, constituting a differentiated part of the phenomenological or experiential field, and composed of a pattern of conscious perceptions and values, including "I" and "mine", of the world and other people (Schultz & Schultz 1994; Carver & Scheier 1996).

The *organism* refers to the total psycho-physical individual and possesses the following attributes: it responds to the phenomenological field as an organised entity to satisfy its own needs; its one basic motive is to actualise own potential, to maintain and improve itself; it can symbolise (recognise) its experiences so that they become conscious, deny them and keep them unconscious, or ignore them altogether. These characteristics of the self describe it as an organised and rational entity and in control of what the person wants to experience and wants to retain from all the experiences.

The *phenomenological field* represents all experiences, perceptions and meanings attached to objects and events outside the person or internal experiences and meanings about the person's own self.

Self is Rogers's focal concept and refers to a person's perceptions of himself or herself as a result of the person's (organism) many experiences in the phenomenological field. The self may include many "I", "mine", "me" and "them" perceptions, which may be very personal and may influence, and be related to, other people and other aspects of the world and environment. The individual perceives that objects, people and events of significance to him or her, are related to the "I" and eventually differentiates part of the perceptual field as the self. Thus the self is an organised perceptual pattern, the functioning individual in fact. The self also tends to be quite consistent across time and situations, which is because the self really consists of those "proven" ideas which the individual has experienced "work" for himself or herself. This idea of self-concept consistency or patterned experiential knowledge of the self is similar to the trait and learning psychologists' idea of a pattern or hierarchy of enduring behaviour which is mostly consistent across time and in situations. A person's self-concept at a certain stage also regulates encounters with new experiences, and whether the person, in terms of the values of his or her existing self-concept, feels comfortable in accommodating such experiences.

The self mostly holds positive aspects, but can also integrate negative attributes and even attributes which are not really a part of the self. Markus (1977) described the self as not a unitary phenomenon, but consisting of "self-schemas", which are the various attributes which people attach to their self-concepts, for instance being pretty, intelligent, talkative and gregarious. In this way self-concepts of people can more easily be differentiated, and we may also understand the idea of self-concept better by considering all its various aspects. For instance, we would avoid thinking people have low self-esteem because they have weak points in certain areas. People may have a sense that their self-concepts are unified or integrated, but self-concepts are also flexible, for instance as our environments and experiences (phenomenological field) change or in different situations. We may have as many "social selves" as other people we know or encounter attribute to us.

In a more specific sense the self-concept may denote *self-identity,* that is, who we are, being a person and belonging somewhere. According to Erikson most people develop towards self-identity through various stages in which certain identity crises are overcome. In other individuals, certain identity development tasks develop insufficiently, resulting in certain problems during later stages of life.

Another part of self-concept is our self-assessment or *self-esteem,* that is, whether we regard ourselves as being good or bad or able to do things well. Self-esteem and related concepts are essential concepts in work behaviour. A significant body of research regards self-esteem as a significant contributor to work involvement, work motivation and the quantity and quality of work performance, and that may moderate the effects of events in the workplace and work performance. According to Brockner (in Furnham 1992), people's level of self-esteem will influence how they act, feel and think about themselves and the job. Employees with high self-esteem manifest the following work-related behaviours:

- They try to improve on work performance (work harder) when negative feedback is received. Employees with low self-esteem are more sensitive to negative feedback.
- They are more able to work and decide independently. For instance, they are not likely to imitate a supervisor's managerial style. Employees with low self-esteem are less certain about the value of own behaviours.
- They are less negatively affected by chronic stressors, such as role ambiguity, or acute stressors, such as work loss.
- They are more ambitious and this may be reflected in job-seeking behaviours and in career decisions and job choices.
- They are less likely to conform to group norms or need group support. Workers with low self-esteem, on the other hand, are likely to expect a lot of the work group or colleagues in terms of acceptance and approval.

In general, these research findings indicate that employees with low self-esteem are more adversely affected by many work and organisational issues, such as intergroup relations, performance feedback, managerial practices and other organisational stimuli.

Another concept related to self-esteem is *self-efficacy,* which denotes the "conviction that one can successfully execute the behaviour to produce the (expected) outcomes" (Bandura 1977:193). In later research self-efficacy was specifically related to occupational behaviours (Lent & Hackett 1987).

Our quest to value ourselves will mostly have positive consequences; however, overvaluing may be detrimental. For instance, people who pretend or whose aspirations are too high may overreach themselves, fail and cause reduced self-esteem! Overemphasis on physical attractiveness or bodily self-esteem, especially in Western society and among women, reaps benefits for the media and health and beauty industries, but also creates a lot of physical and psychological pain. This emphasis on attractiveness created a belief that "what is beautiful is also good", and often causes inaccurate perceptions of people, for instance when assessing applicants for jobs and in close or friendly relationships (Brehm & Kassin 1990). In women, especially, low bodily self-esteem may lead to interpersonal and appearance anxiety (Franzoi 1995), while the failure to fulfil expectations and the resultant low self-esteem may even cause serious stress-related diseases such as anorexia and bulimia (Nevid et al. 1997).

People's self-concepts, in other words what their personality or aspects of personality are, grow and develop from their collective or accumulated life experiences, attitudes and thoughts. In this way people use their self-concepts to give meaning to their lives and experiences. People have one personality but many self-concepts. Various forms of the self-concept idea are used by different writers to denote the integrative force in personality, or to indicate specific aspects of personality, as shown in table 19.1.

In most cases self-concepts have one of, or both of the following connotations: self as the *integrative force* in personality (a person's attitudes, feelings and perception of himself or herself) and self as *director and motivator* of behaviour. From table 19.1 it is possible to see that a person's ideas and perceptions about himself or herself derive from many sources: true knowledge of self, the person's understanding of what others may think, his or her wishes to be a certain way and various aspects of himself or herself, other people and the environment. In the following sections the self-concept and other self-concept-related constructs are used to explain aspects of personality functioning such as motivation, development and psychological adjustment.

Proprium (Allport)	A sense of self, all aspects denoting personality unity
Ideal self (Rogers)	What the individual would like to be
Real self (Rogers)	Person's true behaviour or what he or she can become
Spiritual self (James)	Desires and feelings
Material self (James)	Family, body perceptions
Social self (Mead, James)	What we think other people think we are
Looking-glass self (Cooley)	How we think others see or perceive us
"I" and "Me" experiences (Mead)	Perceptions of ourselves through the eyes of others
Bodily self (Allport)	Part of self which denotes perceptions of our body image and physical abilities

Table 19.1 Different meanings of self-concept

An interesting humanistic view on the uniqueness of personality is Kelly's idea of *constructs* to describe personality structure (Pervin & John 1997). The fact that Kelly explains people's representations of reality as personal constructs places him in the ranks of the humanists or existential psychologists, although he is viewed as more of a cognitive psychologist. According to Kelly, people cognitively create their own representations or perceptions of reality by construing or interpreting things and events according to mental constructs. The constructs people have about various things in life, such as their self-concept, relationships, religion and work, represent the meaning they attach to their experiences regarding these aspects. In line with Kelly's idea that the meaning of things can always change (constructive alternativism), people will or can continuously change their constructs or representations of things and experiences as changes necessitate. Kelly described constructs as being *hierarchical,* or often related to each other; as having a *range of convenience,* that is, certain constructs are only valid for certain situations and events, for instance if you perceive a person as dishonest you cannot also relate this to being unintelligent; as being *changeable or permeable,* although constructs will differ in the degree to which we can add new meanings, change meanings or discard meanings.

Kelly also described various types of constructs, such as *core constructs,* which refer to the central and consistent aspects in our character, personality and behaviour. They are the way we see ourselves and how others may characterise us. Core constructs can be changed, but with important consequences for the rest of our construct system and resulting behaviours.

Peripheral constructs refer to the meaning of things in a person's life, which can be more easily changed or accepted, such as accepting a new construct on equal pay for equal work regardless of gender or creed, or not feeling threatened if you are told that you are not as beautiful as the next person.

Pre-emptive and constellatory constructs are rather inclusive and fixed representations of things, people and events, and are difficult to change or to add new elements to. In South Africa transformation has forced many new constructs. However, for many people it may always be difficult to alter certain meanings, especially those associated with race and characteristics of people belonging to different ethnic groupings. The phenomenon of racism, in its many manifestations, is possibly a worldwide construct, which is difficult to change.

Propositional constructs refer to meanings about things and events that can be more easily added to or changed. It is not difficult for us to describe a person as black or white, male or female, homosexual or heterosexual. The problem arises when we typify people on the basis of certain less distinct characteristics.

Although constructs have a convenience range in certain situations and for certain events, all types of constructs are necessary for a meaningful life, or to represent reality accurately. In this regard you may find seemingly less rigid constructs, such as propositional and peripheral constructs, less applicable in certain situations than other seemingly more rigid constructs.

Existentialists, such as Frankl, described personality as being a *wholeness,* consisting of physical, psychological and spiritual levels, though only the spiritual dimension really distinguishes humans from animals. The spiritual is something more than the psychophysical; it refers to people being aware of themselves, of being inside themselves and of being able to move outside themselves, and thus able to relate to phenomena in the unconscious, preconscious and the conscious. Frankl, however, believed that the essence of personality is unconscious, but not in a Freudian sense, because people cannot understand themselves fully. Only God is able to totally understand people.

19.4 DEVELOPMENT AND MAINTENANCE OF THE SELF

According to humanistic and existential-phenomenological theories, personality development, and therefore self-development, is a continuous process throughout life. The ongoing self-concept formation and development centres around the physical, intellectual and psychosocial spheres of human behaviour. If development is "healthy", self-concept development at all stages seems to happen in an integrated way and the individual is able to be congruent with respect to how different aspects of self-expression coincide. Influencing factors on development are mostly coupled to a person's own progressive experiences and perceptions, and also in relation to other people. In this regard, Kelly emphasises the formation of construct systems (meaning systems) because of repeated patterns of events. Construct systems increase, become more complex and less concrete, and also become related to other persons' constructs as the individual matures. Obviously individual constructs will differ as a result of cultural, social and educational circumstances and opportunities. Every individual possesses the ability of cognitive complexity, which denotes the level, number and flexibility of constructs a person has to enable him or her to explain reality.

Allport, who is also viewed as a humanist, sees self-concept development as the integration of every person's unique attitudes, perceptions and other experiences. Self-development is also a progressive process in which people at different stages of life may be more aware of specific aspects of who and what they are.

In his theory of development Rogers postulates the inherent capacity for growth towards self-actualisation. The growth process centres on the self, and comprises differentiation, expansion, autonomy and socialisation, in other words, *self-actualisation* develops into a fully-fledged self-structure. Initially, organismic survival values play a major part, but in time the structure of the self is determined by interaction with others, when the evaluation of these significant others exerts great influence on the self-concept. This progressive development takes place as people's phenomenological fields expand. People, especially children, have an innate ability to value or judge whether or not every new experience belongs to their existing self-perceptions and whether or not it helps them toward self-actualisation. According to Rogers, the self develops from the interaction between organism (individual) and experiences in the environment. The self can introject the values of other people (e.g. the individual changes his or her conduct in the light of what is observed in others, which may cause conflict within himself or herself, or with others) and may distort them. The self strives for stability, that is, the organism seeks to maintain a relation or congruence with the self, and experiences that bear no relation to the self are seen as threatening or incongruent. The self can also change and adapt in the processes of maturation and learning. People tend to look for positive events and will avoid negative influences.

Rogers maintained that optimal self-development requires an atmosphere of positive valuing, acceptance, love and respect from others. In this regard he refers to the need for *positive regard* (love, respect, acceptance, trust and values as building self-worth). Individuals can only develop into fully functioning persons if they experience unconditional positive regard, that is, being regarded and accepted unconditionally as they are in relationships, so that they feel worthy and are able to develop a complete self-image. Many people, however, only experience conditional positive regard, because they are only accepted under certain conditions, for instance if they obtain a degree, if they work long hours or achieve in sport. In many relationships, such as between parents and children, husband and wives, and close friends, interactions may be based on conditional acceptance. According to Rogers, such patterns of acceptance may cause incongruence or conflict in terms of what the person really wants, and may block self-actualisation. Although such behaviours may also be part of the self-concept, it may cause some people to not trust others completely and only commit to relationships under certain conditions.

Many of Rogers's ideas of interpersonal regard and valuing find application in training, counselling, interviewing, therapy and group work in which the emphasis is on *person-centredness*. In these approaches, for example between counsellor and client, the emphasis is on the positive and healing characteristics of the relationship, or empathy, with all its related attributes of warmth, acceptance and honesty or congruence (Rogers 1951; Truax & Carkhuff 1967).

19.5 MOTIVATIONAL FORCES IN BECOMING A PERSON

Humanists' main focus in personality is on motivation and growth toward finding meaning in life and achieving self-actualisation.

19.5.1 Finding meaning in life

Frankl believes people, as spiritual beings, have a free will, and therefore are responsible for the choices they make in daily events and for the meaning they eventually find in life. Because people's ultimate goal in life is to grow toward and find meaning in life, people have an intrinsic *will to meaning* (Frankl 1969). In this respect people will always ask questions about what they are and what they can become, or want reasons for positive and negative events in life. The will to meaning is the strongest motivational force in people; even people who have succeeded in many things may still experience unfulfilment if they feel that their lives have no meaning. Frankl's concept of *self-transcendence,* which is similar to Maslow's self-actualisation and Allport's concept of propriate striving and functional autonomy, indicates people's ability to rise above themselves in order to grow or find meaning in life (Allen 1994). Frankl believes that people must be fully committed in everything they do, because that represents finding meaning in things. Work is one of the main tasks in life to which people can fully commit and find meaning in. This commitment to work should be more in the interests of others than for one's own career goals (Möller 1995). Other spheres of life in which people must learn to transcend, to find meaning, are suffering, love and death. Transcendence in all life's endeavours should not only be for the sake of specific activities, but for the meaningful values and attitudes which people derive from these experiences. Frankl described creative values (doing and making things), attitude values (positive or negative attitudes from experiences) and experiential values (being open to events) as values which can make life or specific situations meaningful (Frankl 1969).

19.5.2 Needs and self-actualisation

Maslow is known as the father of humanistic psychology and, together with Goldstein and Angyal, is classified among "organismic" theoreticians, chiefly because of his insistence that personality is an organised entity, a view shared by Rogers and Frankl.

Maslow asserts that human behaviour is directed by a number of physiological and psychological needs, which are represented in a hierarchy of five levels of needs. Maslow differentiates between deficiency needs and growth needs. *Deficiency or primary* needs are physiological needs (hunger, thirst), safety needs (physical security), love and belonging needs (close bonds with other people) and esteem needs (competence, self-respect and respect from others). *Growth or secondary* needs entail the needs for self-actualisation, that is, to be creative and express potential and to be meaningfully connected to the broader universe. All these needs function according to a hierarchy and the principle of drive-reduction. If the deficiency needs are satisfied, the individual will do better in achieving the higher order growth needs. As the lowest order needs are satisfied, the individual has time and energy to aspire to growth or secondary needs. Maslow's social needs, to be loved and to belong (needs for affection and acceptance) are satisfied in interaction with other people, much the same as is positive regard, as stated by Rogers.

Self-esteem and self-actualisation are higher levels needs and are responsible for the individual's constant striving behaviour, which causes stress to increase. Self-esteem entails the needs for mastery and power and to be appreciated (evaluated) by others for the quality of behaviour, not only because you are a person, the latter being

acceptance only. Self-actualisation, as Rogers also views it, refers to becoming what one's potential allows one to become and explains humans' continuous need to grow, achieve more and explore further. Like Rogers, Maslow also recognises the power of basic needs if they are not satisfied. Although needs for food, water and safety do not motivate people to work harder, they will lead to serious work dissatisfaction if unsatisfied. In this regard even the most highly developed person is very "dependent" on basic needs being satisfied. If not, such basic needs will hamper self-esteem and self-actualisation needs.

Needs are manifested differently in different people and situations. Maslow also defines needs of knowledge and insight.

Maslow's and Rogers's most important idea on motivation, as derived from Angyal, is people's striving for *growth towards self-actualisation*. Maslow and Rogers established sets of criteria and behaviours that characterise self-actualising personalities (Schultz & Schultz 1996; Carver & Scheier 1996). Maslow studied various famous people and other groups and eventually described certain characteristics and behaviours of self-actualisers (Maslow 1967), although his criteria for self-actualisation are often criticised (Allen 1994).

Rogers	Maslow
Self-actualisation	Self-actualisation
Positive regard (affection and acceptance)	Self-esteem
Positive regard (affection and acceptance)	Love and belonging
	Safety and physical security
	Physiological

Table 19.2 Comparison of needs as described by Rogers and Maslow

According to Maslow, self-actualisers have certain meta, growth or "being" self-actualisation needs, which if not satisfied may result in negative feelings and maladjustment. For example, if the growth need for truth is not satisfied it may result in mistrust and skepticism; frustrated needs for wholeness may lead to disintegration, and the need for meaningfulness if frustrated can cause despair and hopelessness.

According to Rogers, self-actualisation derives its energy from biological and physiological sources, because self-actualising also includes enhancement of the body and physical powers. In this sense Rogers's concept of actualisation indicates the maturation of all aspects of people's potential (inherited and psychological attributes) if conditions are favourable. However, in contrast to Maslow, Rogers does not really describe lower order needs, such as physiological needs for food and safety.

Self-actualisation which overrides all other motivational forces may include actualisation, but denotes *fulfilling the self* as the integrating part of personality. In this sense self-actualisation refers to the whole fully functioning person or complete human fulfilment, and not specific endeavours, such as achieving well academically.

Psychologically, self-actualisation manifests in developing and maintaining the self toward greater self-dependence, autonomy, efficiency, creativity and positive psychological health and in the individual feeling congruent and comfortable in his or her environment, fitting in and not being alienated and feeling ill at ease. The tendency to self-actualisation also serves to generate tension, for humans aspire not merely to homeostasis, but also to progress and change. Self-actualisation provides a criterion for measuring expectancies and experiences. Those which are incongruent or do not fit in with self and self-maintenance are avoided. In this sense the individual has an internal valuing capacity, a protecting mechanism, to know when experiences are good or bad. Rogers sees a "good life" not as homeostatic, but as purposefully directed and always striving. It is clear, however, that other people and the need for acceptance or positive regard may be stronger than the need for self-actualisation and may even impede on self-actualisation.

In work behaviours we often refer to a manager, for instance, as being either task or people oriented. The strength of emphasis on either of the two, or in combination, has a bearing on how people work or how they are assessed to be working.

Concepts such as optimality, maturity and fully-functioning person reflect the idea of facilitating human potential, which is a core objective of the humanistic movement in many of its applications. In contemporary, ever changing work environments one tends to think that emotional maturity or integration must be a stronger competency for survival than having all the technical skills (Howard 1995).

Self-actualisation is not necessarily coupled to achievements such as creating works of art. It is not "what" is being done, but rather "how" things are done. In this respect self-actualisation refers to a continuous, intense involvement in living a meaningful life and using potential to realise goals, though not everything we do will represent self-actualisation.

For some people self-actualising is more directed toward how they themselves use their capacities to live and achieve their own goals in the world. Other persons again are more motivated to actualise things outside of themselves (transcendent self-actualisers), a type of sacred involvement in universal goals to make the world a better place! We think of the late Mother Theresa as a transcendent actualiser, or someone who spends a lifetime in nature conservation or trying to achieve peace in the world! It is possible that in our dreams or ideals each of us nurses these needs for self-actualising. It is, however, also possible that the daily efforts to make a living and to survive in many ways (meet primary needs) distract us from the ultimate need to achieve something that is important for reasons other than ourselves. In these circumstances one wonders whether, and when, growth needs becomes deficiency needs for some people.

Self-actualisation may be coupled to so-called peak experiences, according to Maslow. *Peak experiences* or "flow experiences" according to Csikszentmihalyi (1993:xvi) may occur when we are related in a special way to events in ourselves or in our environment, for instance suddenly realising why a problem can't be solved, the passive experience of admiring great beauty, or the ecstasy and happiness of receiving recognition for an important achievement. Tasks or activities that may produce flow experiences have the following characteristics: clear goals with manageable rules; the possibility of adjusting opportunities to suit our abilities; provision of feedback or information about performance; the opportunity to really be involved and concentrate (not be distracted). If we study these criteria they are not different to what a job or task description should be to enable an employee to be motivated and to work creatively and for a supervisor to carry out efficient performance management.

In contrast to Rogers and Maslow and differing from many other authors, Kelly does not find it necessary to use motivational concepts such as traits, needs, motives or drives. He asserted that we are motivated because we are alive, which is akin to the existentialists' idea of the spiritual drive because of "being". According to Kelly, in the work context there should be no need to "pull" or "push" an employee to perform. The individual's will to do things will be determined by how he or she thinks about, anticipates and predicts events through his or her various constructs, and by what constructs are best suited for the event or situation, which Kelly describes and explains through a number of corollaries (Kelly 1955). This resembles Frankl's idea of life values giving meaning to events. In what Kelly referred to as the *C-P-C cycle* (circumspection, pre-emption, control) he describes how people, like a scientist during a research project, plan how to act in certain situations: they observe the problem, analyse possible solutions and

Different ways of self-actualisation

finally choose a plan of action and proceed with it. Kelly also described a creativity cycle in humans' ability to construct new meaning systems. As in brainstorming, the individual allows any type of idea to enter his or her thinking, after which usable constructs or constructs that are congruent with existing constructs are integrated into the existing meaning system. This assumption reminds of the idea of valuing, in which people weigh new experiences before including them into existing self-concepts.

Maslow wrote exhaustively on the role of work in personality functioning. There is a connection between job dissatisfaction and inadequate, or no, self-actualisation. He stresses the role of management in considering the needs of workers at all levels and in creating channels for need satisfaction. His motivational theory had a significant effect on later well-known industrial psychologists, such as Argyris, Likert, McGregor and Porter, although his theory of a need hierarchy no longer enjoys the same esteem as earlier. The most influential idea may still be that if lesser primary needs are unsatisfied, this will inhibit striving for higher order needs such as self-actualisation. The satisfying of basic needs is often seen by employees as a human right. Even if basic needs are satisfactorily met in the workplace, it does not necessarily ensure work satisfaction or improved performance. The absence of working conditions to satisfy basic needs will, however, definitely cause worker dissatisfaction. Intrinsic motivation, that is, if employees experience meaningfulness in their jobs and perform tasks because they really want to, will always be a better motivator for work performance. In this respect the job character-istics model of Hackman and Oldham (1976) integrates the ideas of Maslow and others in stating that if jobs or tasks have certain core dimensions, employees will have certain psychological experiences of work which will result in certain personal

and work outcomes. This model, illu-strated in figure 19.1, was an influential force in much research on how to design and redesign work in organisations. If, for instance, job tasks demand a variety of skills, task identity (that is, the employee completes an identifiable task) and the work has a significant contribution, the employee may experience the job or tasks as meaningful and may feel responsibility, which may lead to high internal states of motivation, work and personal satisfac-tion.

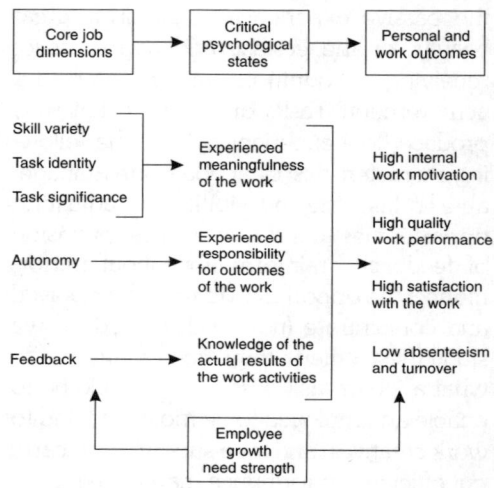

Figure 19.1 Experiencing work meaningfully
Source: Moorhead & Griffin 1989

19.5.3 Free will as perceived self-control

In summary, we argue that the humanistic emphasis on freedom of choice and the internal motive to self-actualise also relate to the learning and cognitive ideas of perceived self-control, internal locus of control, self-determination, self-regulation and self-efficacy. The self as a person is not powerless under the determination of outside events (behaviourism) or the influence of past events or irrational internal and external forces (psychoana-lysis). Various self-concept-related topics indicate this human ability to self-regulate behaviour and to be personally in control of behaviour in relation to events. In humanistic psychology this does not indicate actual physical control, but rather the person's perceptions, values and attitudes of being in control. This would be the case when an employee completes a task successfully because he or she is really committed, is interested or wants to do it, as opposed to being pulled and pushed by the promise of an increase if performance is up to standard. Externally controlled behaviours may inhibit self-actualising behaviours, because they de-flate the person's self-esteem. However, if control, such as a reward, can inflate a person's self-worth, it may facilitate performance, for instance if the employ-ee experiences the reward as a recognition of self-worth and not only a reward for doing a task.

The concepts of learned helplessness (Seligman 1975), self-handicapping beha-viours (Berglas & Jones 1978; Lay, Knish & Zanatta 1992; Wood et al. 1994), and also fears of success and failure, can be viewed as the opposite state of mind or attitude when compared to freedom of choice and will to meaning. People in this frame of mind, through their choices and experiences, believe that they have no control over one or more aspects of their lives, that nothing they do has meaning or are afraid to take responsibility. Their negative behaviours indicate meaninglessness and a fear of taking responsibility or control.

For Kelly (Pervin & John 1997) humans have control because they give meaning to repeated experiences and events by form-ing constructs which are representations of reality. These constructs allow people to know themselves as well as people and events outside themselves, and as they mature, enables them to plan and create, and to anticipate and predict their own behaviour in relation to others and possible events and situations.

19.6 OPTIMALITY AND DEFICIENCIES IN BEING

Humanists, like phenomenologists and existentialists, are more concerned with the healthy personality, in that they emphasise personality evolving into its full potential, the real self and becoming a fully functioning person. In this approach they emphasise more than adjustment only, but *optimality,* which can be viewed as the end result of a movement or process toward self-actualisation. Frankl's concepts of the will to meaning and self-transcendence imply growing into more than the ordin-ary, and searching for something more than has already been achieved. Both Maslow and Rogers describe attributes of psychologically healthy people (self-actua-lisers or fully functioning people). Accord-ing to Rogers fully functioning individuals are those who use, recognise and develop all their abilities and talents to further self-knowledge. In more specific terms Rogers attributes the following characteristics to such people: awareness of all experiences; existential or full and quality living (richness of experience); organismic confidence (confidence in own decision-making powers) and freedom of experience (se-lectivity and creativity); creative and adap-table to changes; having courage to face problems of life (Schultz & Schultz 1994).

Optimality relates to ongoing growth and the realising of potential, and may include aspects such as work and how other tasks and problems in life are handled. In a sense optimality can be viewed as self-actualisa-tion. Figure 19.2 illustrates that optimality is more than the minimum standards for functioning or living. In terms of health this approach does not only emphasise illness versus health, but rather behaviours on a continuum of unwellness, health and optimality. This approach emphasises an orientation to stay healthy. Optimality (or self-actualisation) then is a natural, ongoing and creative process in which the individual takes responsibility to develop (optimalise) his or her physical, psychological and mental capacities, which will be shown in behaviours and attitudes, such as in work, relationships and religious associations (Cilliers 1984).

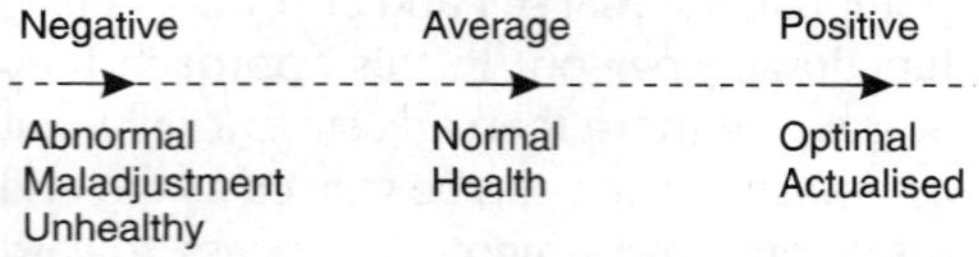

Negative	Average	Positive
Abnormal	Normal	Optimal
Maladjustment	Health	Actualised
Unhealthy		

Figure 19.2 Maladjustment, adjustment and optimality

We have indicated earlier certain positive and negative aspects of self-actualisation and self-control: the overemphasis on physical or bodily image, the phenomena of learned helplessness and self-handicapping, as well as both Rogers's and Maslow's criteria for self-actualising people.

Humanists and existential-phenomenologists do not suggest a "utopia" where people have no problems in life, but believe in the intrinsic goodness and potential of people that can be realised through the positive influences of other people and the environment. These approaches emphasise the following general facilitating or inhibiting influences for optimal growth:

- unconditional acceptance from others as having self-worth and potential as a person
- self-regard, which develops in the person through experiences about himself or herself in relations with other important persons
- self-esteem, as the person gets feedback from others and from the manner in which he or she is accepted and grows toward, and experiences, self-actualisation
- positive societal and environmental opportunities and freedom to develop potential and to self-actualise

If these conditions are present most of the time, people have freedom and choices and

are able to be in control of many influences in themselves and in relation to others and outside events. In contrast, however, this approach views social influences and people's own self-defeating behaviours (defences, avoidance, etc.) as serious inhibiting factors in people's quest to develop the real self and to live a full life. Much research relates high self-esteem to having positive feelings and good mental health, while the opposite is mostly reported for low self-esteem or negative self-evaluations (Sedikides 1993; Greenberg et al. 1993). However, the pains and problems of life are viewed by some of these authors, Frankl for one, as opportunities to overcome, and find meaning in, negative circumstances.

In general, psychological health is seen as dependent on congruency of self, perception and experience. Incongruency in the person, in perceptions of himself or herself or in relationships with others and the environment will cause problems for the individual. Rogers, for instance, defines anxiety as resulting from low self-esteem, because the individual experiences events as threatening. In such cases people may use defence mechanisms, such as avoidance and rationalisation, to reconstrue reality for themselves. The supervisor who gets feedback that staff do not like him or her because he or she treats them unfairly, may reconstrue the situation by asserting that all the employees are incompetent and blame him or her for everything! In the same vein, the incompetent employee may view the supervisor as assessing his or her behaviours unfairly. Rogers terms the defence mechanisms by which the individual copes with threatening situations *perceptual distortion* (incorrect perceiving and interpretation of events) and *denial*. Kelly identifies maladjustment (anxiety and fear) when events or experiences are irreconcilable with a person's constructs or meanings of life, when the person uses existing constructs inappropriately in terms of reality's demands or feels threatened when realising that he or she will have to change existing constructs. Such individuals have no frame of reference to give meaning to existing or new events and experience fear, anxiety and threat because they do not know how to handle experiences in life, nor how to predict events. According to Kelly, to maintain good mental health a person must be able to preserve unity or integration and balance in personal constructs, that is, consistency in the interpreting of events in life. If a personal system of constructs is too rigid (impermeable) or too loose (permeable), the individual will lose contact with reality: be too compulsive (try to use one or a few constructs for every circumstance or event) or experience much confusion as to what reality is, as in schizophrenia.

The humanistic movement was and is a big contributor to the idea of the power of positiveness and positive thinking in human nature and human wellbeing. In contrast, some of the most influential models on the classification and explanation of psychological problems are "pathogenic", that is, explaining emotional problems in humans in a rather negative way, as illness symptoms resulting from certain causes inside and outside the person (APA 1994). The tendency in humanistic thinking is not to ignore psychological problems but to emphasise humans' intrinsic health potential, the powers of positive thinking and self-control and the resilience of humans to cope with stress and the problems of life, even in harsh circumstances. In the literature many concepts, including some from authors not traditionally associated with humanistic approaches, are used to emphasise psychological health, rather than psychological problems. Examples of these are shown in table 19.3.

In this regard the so-called "salutogenetic" paradigm, as postulated by Antonovsky (Strümpfer 1990, 1995), indicating humans' ability to be healthy and resilient even under stressful conditions, and to strive for optimality, may be an integrating concept for most of these. Research indicates that people who have salutogenetic types of personal characteristics tend to strive for optimality and manifest good coping behaviours in stressful experiences. The concepts most often used to describe the salutogenetic resources in human behaviour are a sense of coherence (Antonovsky 1987), hardiness (Kobasa 1979), learned resourcefulness (Rosenbaum & Ben-Ari 1985), internal locus of control (Rotter 1966), potency (Ben-Sira (1985), stamina (Thomas 1981; Colerick 1985) and self-efficacy (Bandura 1977). There are similarities in these concepts. Important commonalities are the emphasis on personal control (a person's feelings that he or she can manage and master events) and experiencing the meaningfulness of events. Strümpfer (1995) coined the term "fortigenesis" for an even stronger form of salutogenesis and he indicated that fortigenesis may have its origins in work behaviours, because employees must repeatedly demonstrate behaviours such as self-dependence, control and responsibility, which are salutogenetic types of behaviours. The employee with a high level of resilient behaviours may manifest an effective and positive work orientation, which also indicates elements of self-actualising or optimality. Authors such as Cilliers (1988) and Viviers (1996) describe and compare the relationships between the salutogenetic personal and optimal work and organisational behaviours in terms of employee intrapersonal (cognitive, emotional and motivational behaviours) and interpersonal attributes.

These optimal or self-actualising behaviours are in contrast to concepts such as alienation, which denotes employee work experiences that are without influence or autonomy (powerless), meaningless, normlessness (unethical ways to achieve goals), isolation from other employees and self-estrangement (working for external re-

Jung	Individualising	Growth of psyche into adulthood
Adler	Striving for superiority	Ultimate goal of reaching perfection
Fromm	Productivity	Ultimate goal to realise potential
Horney	Self-realising	A realistic ideal of self-image and of potential
Erikson	Emotional integration	At older age the achievement of wisdom about life
Allport	Adulthood	Mature, autonomous behaviour
Rogers, Jung, Perls, Maslow	Self-actualisation	Intrinsic tendency to grow and achieve full potential
Antonovsky	Sense of coherence	Feeling of events being comprehensible, manageable and meaningful
Kobasa	Personal hardiness	Behaviour marked by high levels of control, challenge and commitment
Rosenbaum	Learned resourcefulness	Behaviours and skills to control events and behaviour
Ben-Sira	Potency	Confidence in own abilities and environment to cope with stress
Bandura	Self-efficacy	The belief that one can realise expectancies
Thomas, Colerick	Stamina	Physical or moral strength to be resilient to disease and stress
White, Deci	Competency Motivation	Intrinsic motivation, competency and self-determination
Peterson & Seligman (1987)	Optimism	Positive view on events
Harris (1978)	Winners behaviour	Behaviours and efforts to achieve set expectations and objectives

Table 19.3 Concepts emphasising the positive and healthy nature of personality

wards only) and learned helplessness. In all of these the emphasis is on the person's dependence on external events and the feelings of not being in control (Kanungo 1982; Cook, Hepworth et al. 1981).

In general, interventions, such as therapy, are aimed at giving persons with problems "new" experiences or constructs with which to give meaning to events and life. Frankl's logotherapy is meant to make it easier for people to confront meaningless aspects of being and to discover meaning in their lives. Kelly expects people in therapy to reconstruct existing inefficient constructs into constructs which will have personal meaning. Rogers's client-centred therapy is intended to create a climate of security in which the individual's behaviour can change from incongruency to congruency. A therapeutic climate is created by the therapist, who accepts the client unconditionally, shows warmth towards him or her and acts congruently and honestly. In such a climate the client can explore and self-actualise and acquire new ways of relating to himself or herself, others and the world.

19.7 CONCLUSION

The humanistic approach puts "being human" in perspective in its emphasis on people's unique experiences, freedom of choice and internal motivation to develop toward realising potential. Many of the humanistic ideas are viewed as idealistic and vague, which makes scientific verification difficult. Criticisms of humanistic theories and concepts include the oversimplification of humans' existence in this world; not recognising that for many people the actualising of their innate goodness will always be suppressed, not for being, but for being in the wrong place at a wrong time; the vagueness of concepts, which makes them difficult to define and measure.

However, this approach has stimulated much research, while also contributing in practice, for example, in the fields of assessment, therapy, training, work motiva-

tion and career development. In the work context, for instance, self-esteem is very much a part of our perceptions and assessment of occupational behaviours. Rogers's Q-Sort technique and Kelly's Repertory Grid Test are valuable contributions in self-concept assessment (Gregory 1996). Self-actualisation has become a buzz word when we explain employees' intrinsic motivation to achieve potential and to reach life goals. In many training applications much is made of experiential learning, that is, people learning more about themselves and others when they perceive and interpret real-life experiences, rather than being told by others. The *contextual emphasis*, used in so many applications, is of existential-phenomenological origin. Phenomenological research emphasises the determining of people's own here-and-now subjective realities and experiences and incorporates the idiographic and case study methods of research.

Rogers's emphasis on the importance of interpersonal relationships in interaction, for instance in therapy and groups, is probably his greatest contribution. More recently he has tried to apply his theory, especially its emphasis on favourable conditions in interpersonal relations (acceptance, congruence and empathy), to groups and communities to solve conflict. His visits all over the world, including to South Africa in 1979 and 1986, are evidence of his efforts.

The research interest and application of the concepts of self-actualisation in various areas must be one of the humanists' greatest contributions. Self-actualisation as a concept enjoys research support, but measurement in this area is a problem (Allen 1994). Das (1989), for instance, criticises the concept of self-actualisation as being too vague and promoting self-absorption or selfishness. He proposes that the concept of *self-realisation* should rather be used, because it is not dependent on lower need satisfaction and is a more active process.

Notwithstanding criticism, Maslow's hierarchy of needs is fundamental to many measures and interventions with regard to work motivation and work design.

The essence of humanistic theory is to recognise and cultivate the natural, positive potentials of humankind and to encourage people to find commitment and meaning in whatever they do, rather than to emphasise people's dependency on influences outside their control. The emphasis on health, rather than pathology, is also a positive aspect in people's striving for optimal physical and psychological health.

The resilience of people is not a coping resource only for employees, but also for human resources workers, especially in a labour-saving and results-inclined world in which the "human factor" is often ignored in business practices. Like psychoanalysis in understanding unconscious behaviours, the humanistic ideas may be relevant in explaining what "being human" should really mean.

Self-evaluating questions

1. Critically discuss the main assumptions of the humanistic perspectives.
2. Analyse a situation you are familiar with and explain how positive regard or the lack of it influences people's behaviours.
3. Describe how you would change your current work to facilitate employees' perception of meaningful work.
4. You are to facilitate a group discussion between 12 people of different cultures. How will you go about this task using a humanistic approach?
5. Explain the applicability of the concept of self-actualisation to South African transformation processes.
6. With practical examples, explain how the will for meaning can be applied in work design or in school work.
7. Which principles will you use to apply humanism in the transformation of South African society?

Cognitive, information-processing perspectives

20

Linda Albertyn

CONTENTS

Learning outcomes

After studying this chapter you should be able to:

- understand the cognitive view of basic human nature
- compare cognitive concepts with behaviourist/learning concepts and psycho-analytic concepts
- describe Kelly's view of personality in terms of the fundamental postulate and 11 corollaries
- understand the cognitive perspective on mental health
- describe possible applications of these theories and concepts
- critically evaluate cognitive theories and indicate implications for future research

Key concepts

cognitive, information processing, decision-making, self-regulation, cognitive structures, man-as-scientist, personal constructs, constructive alternativism, postulate and corollaries, security vs adventure, cognitive complexity, cognitive simplicity, C-P-C cycle (circumspection, pre-emption, control), emotion

20.1 INTRODUCTION

Cognition refers to the process of knowing (Stuart-Hamilton 1995). Broadly defined, however, the term covers the full range of mental functions.

The cognitive psychologist is concerned with answering certain questions. These are visually represented in figure 20.1. First, there is the question of how knowledge is *acquired*, and two psychological

processes are important here: *perception,* the process by which events are detected and interpreted by the person, and *learning,* the process by which new ideas and behaviours are acquired. The second question is how knowledge is *retained* – this leads to the concept of memory. The third question is how knowledge is *used*, and the various applications are investigated. Some of the prominent uses are thinking, reasoning, problem-solving and decision-making. Fourth, if knowledge is to be retained and used, then in what form is it *represented* internally? Two general categories of representation can be identified. The first is visual or auditory images, also referred to as *episodic memory.* The second is *semantic memory*, which refers to abstract representations of the meanings of things, for example our knowledge of mathematics or grammar (Marx & Cronan-Hillix 1987).

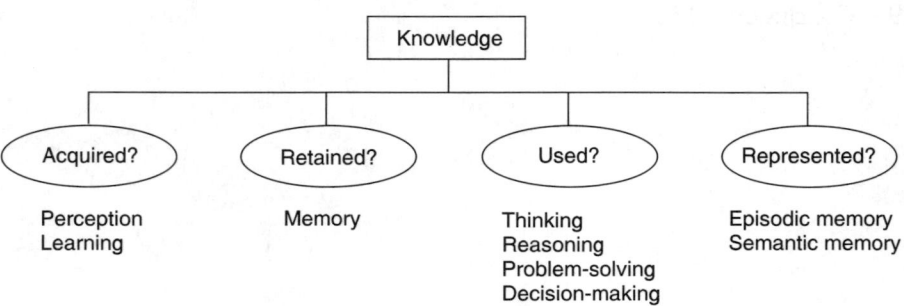

Figure 20.1 The processes that cognitive psychologists are concerned with

It is important to note that although some theorists of other schools of thought did recognise the importance of cognition (e.g. contemporary psychoanalysts, Erikson, Adler, behaviourists, humanists and Gestalt psychologists), none of them brought it into the mainstream of their theory. The difference between these theorists and *cognitive theorists* lies in the fact that cognitists attempt to understand and define all aspects of personality in terms of *cognitive processes*. Therefore the process of knowing is not seen as an element of personality, but *is* the entire personality.

In the discussion of cognitive theories, Kelly is the first theorist who comes to mind, as he is the only cognitive theorist who developed a comprehensive metatheory of cognition. Notwithstanding, Kelly did not view himself as a cognitive psychologist (Engler 1995). It is clear, however, that Kelly's theory has a cognitive ring to it, not only because he explains how people "construe" their worlds but also due to his undisputed influence on the newer cognitive, information-processing theories.

Recent influential cognitive behavioural theorists include Ellis, Beck and Lazarus. Their theories are not comprehensive cognitive metatheories, but developed in their endeavours to help clients with present problems. Others, such as Mischel, Festinger, Lecky, Lundh, McReynolds, Miller, Piaget and Chomsky, elaborated on certain elements of cognition only. For example, Chomsky's theory of language was developed in response to Skinner's interpretation of the acquisition of language. Piaget described the development of intellect in the child. Beck developed a theory of depression based on the belief that negative cognitions influenced the negative affect.

In this chapter we provide an outline of the cognitive view of human nature, the structure of personality, development of personality and motivation. In all the discussions on the cognitive perspective that follow, the focus is on Kelly's standpoint, as

he developed the most comprehensive metatheory of cognition, and unattributed direct quotes in this chapter are by him. Other cognitive theorists are referred to where they elaborate on a particular aspect.

20.2 MAIN ASSUMPTIONS

Partly due to the fragmentation, or lack of metatheories, and partly because it coincided with the shift in focus to information processing or computer programming, cognitive psychology only became a recognised subfield of psychology in the 1960s. All cognitive theorists, though, subscribe to the following main assumptions (Carver & Scheier 1996; Marx & Cronan-Hillix 1987):

- In order to understand human behaviour one needs to understand how *information is processed*. All of us are surrounded by visual and auditory stimulation which we use as sources of information. Although the information reaches us in tiny bits, it is not experienced in that way, as we integrate and organise the bits of information so as to make sense of the world around us.

- Life consists of a continuous process of *making decisions,* most of which are made consciously, although some are made outside of awareness. Personality is expressed in part by how the decision-making process functions.

- We are *active gatherers of information* relevant to making decisions. Information from the environment comes in through the senses and is processed or coded for storage in a systematic, probably hierarchical, arrangement for later use. It is later decoded and combined with other available information so that action can be intelligently guided.

- Human behaviour is intrinsically *goal directed* or *self-regulated* (future oriented). The analogy of a robot is useful in explaining this premise: a robot has a purpose programmed into it that it fulfils through taking certain steps. In a similar fashion, people create goals and take steps to move toward them. In addition, people monitor their progress in the desired direction – this process is called self-regulation.

• Cognitive theorists use concepts to explain how people organise information in their minds in order to make sense of the world. *Cognitive structures are "schemata"* which describe how people perceive, organise and interpret information about themselves, other people, events and objects. For instance, Kelly uses the concept of "construct" in various ways to explain how people categorise their information on knowledge.

In the work environment, cognition is also of great importance. An individual's intelligence and personality, motivation, memory, perception and attention, as well as the way he or she learns, thinks and solves problems, are all factors that determine how work is done (Ribeaux & Poppleton 1978). An implication of the cognitive approach for training is that if we ask trainees to pay attention to some specific aspect of the learning situation, they will learn faster than if they had not received the instruction. Trainees can be instructed using words and symbols (Landy 1989).

20.3 THE PERSON AS SCIENTIST: BASIC VIEW OF HUMAN NATURE

Kelly rebelled against the common perception among psychologists that they acted as scientists, but that their subjects were motivated by unconscious needs and desires over which they had no control. His basic view is that not only psychologists act as scientists, but the people that they study do as well. In our attempts to predict and control our external environment, we constantly develop and test hypotheses. In a similar way to how the scientist uses his or her hypotheses to predict future events, we use our constructs to predict future situations. Constructs are thus our hypotheses or "filters" through which we view the world.

The view of the person as a scientist leads to a number of important consequences for the basic nature of humans (Hjelle & Ziegler 1992; Schultz 1990). First, it suggests that people are *future-oriented* as behaviour is directed by predictions for the future and changes from yesterday to tomorrow as constructs are tested and modified. Second, people have the capacity to *actively react* to their environment, rather than merely passively respond to it (unlike the psychoanalytic and behaviourist views). For Kelly, life is characterised by continuous efforts to make sense of the world – it is this quality of life that enables a person to shape his or her own destiny. Third, a person is not controlled by present events (as Skinner suggested) or past ones (as Freud suggested), but rather *controls* events depending on the questions raised and the answers found. The only way in which we can be enslaved by the past or present is through our interpretation of events (over which we have control). Fourth, Kelly did not postulate any ultimate goal in life, except that we should *define a set of constructs* that best enables us to predict events.

20.4 COGNITIVE INTERPRETATION OF PSYCHOLOGICAL CONCEPTS

The cognitive perspective on the basic nature of personality is further explained through comparison with some of the concepts used by other main schools of thought.

20.4.1 Cognition and the behaviourist/learning perspective

The cognitive movement rejects the behaviourist view that people react passively to stimuli. Whereas the traditional behaviourist/learning theorists are only concerned with stimulus-response (S-R) reactions, cognitive psychologists are also interested in the processing that takes place. Consequently they changed the formula to Stimulus-processing-response (Leahey 1987).

This fundamental difference led to differing views on the understanding of language. Skinner explained language in terms of stimulus-response reinforcement principles only, whereas Chomsky felt that a more innovative approach was required to explain the creativity and flexibility inherent in human language (Leahey 1987). In fact, Chomsky's ideas had an enormous influence on psycholinguistics, the study of the psychological aspects of language (Stuart-Hamilton 1995).

The basic behaviourist concept of learning considers it to be a process of *expansion, and refinement* of the personal construct system. In a similar fashion, Lecky viewed learning as the assimilation of new experiences. In order to assimilate new experiences conflict between two modes of organising must always precede learning – thus it is also a way of resolving conflict (Lester 1995).

Despite the differences between behaviourist/learning theorists and cognitive theorists, many cognitive theorists consider themselves methodologically as behaviourists. As can be seen from the next section, most of them use very little introspection and infer the nature of personality from observing behaviour (Marx & Cronan-Hillix 1987).

20.4.2 Cognition and the psychoanalytic concepts

Although cognitive psychology is largely concerned with the conscious (in its focus on rationality), we do not find the concepts of ego, motivation, reinforcement, drive, unconscious or needs. These aspects are considered to be parts of the personality that are controlled, like all the other parts, by cognitive processes (Schultz 1990).

Some of the fundamental psychological concepts that are discussed in the next section, also pertain to the psychoanalytic school of thought.

20.4.3 The cognitive perspective on some fundamental psychological concepts

20.4.3.1 Self-construct

To Kelly, there is one personal construct found in virtually every system: "self vs others". However, this *self-construct* is often subordinated in different ways. One person may include "self" under "friendly" and "considerate" and act accordingly; while another subsumes "self" under "intelligent" and "others" under "stupid". When "self" is subordinated to constructs that concern essential interactions with other people, the resulting subsystem is referred to as the *core role*. Core roles are the roles people assume on the basis of how they think others perceive their core constructs. As opposed to core constructs *peripheral* constructs are those that have less relevance to a person's sense of self (Ewen 1993).

Kelly viewed vocational development as one of the central ways in which one's life role is given meaning.

20.4.3.2 Basic motivating forces

The basic motivation, except for the mere fact that we are alive, is to *interpret current events* so as to better predict future events. Whereas Freud's basic element of the mind consisted of instincts or wishes, Kelly's are constructs (Lester 1995). In Kelly's own words, "confirmation and disconfirmation of one's predictions [have] greater psychological significance than rewards, punishments or drive reduction" (Ewen 1993).

Festinger viewed the basic motivation as an attempt to reduce *cognitive dissonance*. Cognitive dissonance occurs when one cognitive element (i.e. opinions, beliefs, attitudes and values) implies the opposite of the other. For example, you may believe that humans will reach the stars soon, but also be aware that the journey might take too long. Dissonance increases with the number of cognitive elements that are incompatible with one of your cognitive elements as well as with the importance of the cognitive elements involved in your behaviour. For example, when you have to choose between two relatively unimportant objects, such as which film to see on a given night, the amount of cognitive dissonance is small. However, if the choice is between two careers that are equally attractive, dissonance may be great. Cognitive dissonance leads to a motivation to reduce the dissonance (Lester 1995; Robbins 1996).

The organisational consequence of Festinger's theory is found in equity theory. *Equity theory* is based on the premise that an individual compares his or her perceived input to output ratio with that of others and that this impacts on motivation and worker behaviour. For example, if the individual feels that he or she is being underpaid, this will result in decreased effort, demands for more pay or other attempts to achieve equity in the organisation (Campbell & Pritchard 1983).

Lecky viewed the basic motivation as the *need to maintain unity or self-consistency.* He saw individuals' need to maintain unity as a need to attain harmony, which is manifested in two ways (Lester 1995):

- maintaining "inner harmony" in their minds, that is, an internally consistent set of ideas and interpretations
- maintaining harmony between their minds and the environment, that is, between their experience of the outside world and their interpretations of this experience

20.4.3.3 Unconscious

Kelly acknowledged that some constructs are not readily available to awareness. He identified the following three (Ewen 1993):

- *Preverbal constructs* are difficult to identify, because they are formed before the person has acquired language and therefore a verbal label to attach to it.
- A *submerged construct* is the pole of a personal construct that is less available to awareness due to the intolerable implications it holds for the individual.
- A *suspended construct* excludes certain elements from awareness because certain constructs that would lead to the recall of certain experiences have not been devised. A suspended construct is similar to repression, but the difference is that we remember what is structured and forget what is unstructured, rather than remembering what is pleasant and forgetting what is unpleasant.

Although Kelly used concepts such as preverbal, submerged and suspended constructs, he stated firmly that there was no unconscious in his theory. He identified a *level of awareness* that is highest when construing in socially acceptable symbols, such as your native language (Lester 1995).

20.4.3.4 Defence mechanisms

Although Kelly did not pay direct attention to the notion of defence mechanisms in his theory, it is possible to draw analogies to defence mechanisms using his constructs. For example, a person can be said to display reaction formation when he or she reclassifies elements of a construct from one pole to another pole of the same construct. If a person who was viewed as honest is now considered dishonest, reaction to the person will be diametrically opposite to what it once was. Similarly, identification can be said to occur when an important person in your life becomes one pole of a construct (like my father vs not like my father), you classify yourself at a pole (e.g. I am like my father) and the construct becomes one of your core constructs (i.e. relevant to your sense of self).

Lecky defined identification as the attempt to unify the self-concept with the view of others by assimilating and imitating the opinions of others. Resistance is the response to counter reorganisation (Lester 1995).

20.5 THE STRUCTURE OF PERSONALITY

Kelly's theory is based on the underlying assumption of *constructive alternativism*. This means that every person interprets the world in terms of his or her constructs, which can be changed or replaced at will (alternativism) (Schultz 1990). In Kelly's judgement objective reality is perceived in different ways by different people. The objective truth of a person's interpretations are unimportant because they are unknowable. The implication of constructive alternativism is that our behaviour is never totally determined – we are always free to some extent to revise or replace our interpretation of events (Hjelle & Ziegler 1992).

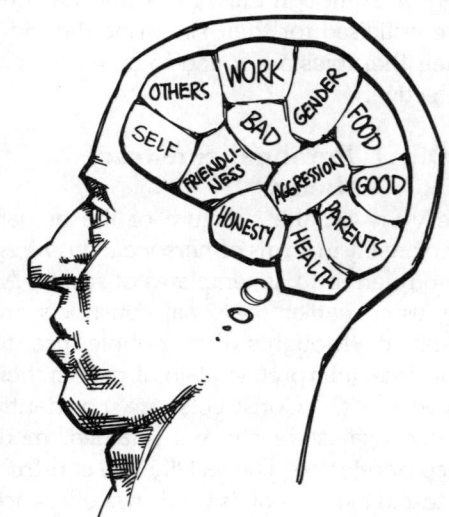

Forming constructs about the world

Kelly never stated a definition of personality, but did indicate that personality could be considered the abstraction made by personologists of the psychological processes they observe or infer in others. These psychological processes are made up of individual constructs to interpret experiences and to anticipate future events. To know a person then, is to know how he or she construes personal experience as well as your own abstraction or perception of these processes in the individual.

Mischel, another cognitive theorist, differed from Kelly in that he was interested in analysing constructs to better understand the structure of personality, rather than simply using them to predict behaviour. Mischel described the person in terms of five person variables (Aiken 1993):

- *Construction competencies* are concerned with the individual's cognitive and behavioural competencies. In other words, what does a person know and what skills does he or she possess?
- *Encoding strategies* are concerned with how people perceive, group and construe events. For example, a situation that is frightening to one person could be boring to another, for example a mathematics class.
- *Expectancies* refer to the individual's expectation of what will occur in a given situation.
- *Goals and subjective values* indicate the influence of goals and subjective values attached to certain situations on the outcome of the person's expectancies.
- *Self-control systems and plans* are the different rules or standards that people adopt to regulate their behaviour. Mischel considered most behaviour to be intrinsically rather than extrinsically reinforced.

Mischel's research focused on how people could learn self-control by concentrating their attention on certain stimuli. This is of particular use in performance management (Aiken 1993).

Lundh viewed the organisation of the mind as a system of *meaning structures*. Meaning structures explain why people perceive the same situations and events differently – every event has a different meaning for each of us. Meaning structures change over time. The implication of this is that we can never recollect past events exactly as they occurred, because we view them in terms of our current meaning structures. If we know another person's meaning structures, we are able to relate to them – this corresponds with Kelly's sociality corollary (see 20.5.3.11) (Lester 1995).

McReynolds called the basic conceptual units *percepts* and not constructs. Human personality consists of two processes: obtaining and receiving percepts, then assimilating or integrating them. The combined process is known as perceptualisation. Percepts are organised into *conceptual schemata* in a similar fashion to Kelly's personal construct system. Some percepts fit easily into existing schemata, others require restructuring. In accordance with Kelly's notion of inconsistency within construct systems and Festinger's notion of cognitive dissonance, McReynolds acknowledged that contradictions can exist among percepts and schemata.

Miller formulated a theory of cognition based on two major concepts: images and plans. For example, you imagine what your holiday is going to be like and make plans to attain this image. The *image* includes all the organised knowledge that an individual has about himself or herself and its world. The *plan* is a hierarchical process that controls the order of operations, much like a computer program does. Plans are normally tested against an image and then executed (Lester 1995).

Piaget termed the basic structures of the mind *schemata*. Schemata form a framework into which incoming information can fit. Every input is compared to the existing schemata and, if assimilated, results in accommodation into the schemata (Lester 1995). Research into Piaget's work continues and his theories are currently being extended (Beilin & Pufall 1992).

Lazarus, a cognitive theorist born and bred in South Africa, was the first theorist to recognise the importance of interpersonal relationships in maintaining maladaptive behaviour. He developed a set of clinical strategies called *multimodal behaviour therapy*, also known as BASIC-ID. B stands for behaviour, A for affect, S for sensation, I for imagery (e.g. memory), C for cognition, I for interpersonal relationships and D for drugs (or neurological and biochemical factors that influence behaviour). These seven modalities make up human personality and any aspect of behaviour, emotion or cognition can be explained in terms of an interaction among these modalities. People tend to favour a specific BASIC-ID modality; thus, we may speak of a "sensory reactor" or a "cognitive reactor". Multimodal therapy focuses on problems in all the modalities, approaching the client from his or her preferred modal (Engler 1995). Although Ellis, Beck and Lazarus are criticised for their simplistic theories, their therapies are found to be extremely effective.

20.5.1 Personal construct theory

Kelly viewed the structure of the human personality in terms of *personal constructs*, also referred to as templates of reality. As discussed earlier, personal constructs are ideas or thoughts that people use to construe, interpret, explain or predict their experiences. Constructs are constantly tested against reality and retained, modified or rejected. The validity of a construct is tested in terms of its predictive efficiency (Hjelle & Ziegler 1992).

Kelly proposed that certain types of constructs can be identified. A *pre-emptive construct* is one that prohibits its elements from belonging to any other range of convenience. Ethnic labelling can be classified as pre-emptive. A *constella-*

tory construct determines the ways in which other constructs apply to its elements. Stereotyped thinking is an example of this type of construct, for example, "if this man is a second-hand car dealer he must be dishonest and manipulative". A construct that leaves its elements open to alternative constructions is called a *propositional construct*. Propositional thinking is flexible thinking, for example the car dealer would not necessarily be viewed as dishonest merely on the basis of his occupation. While it is tempting to "construe" pre-emptive and constellatory constructs as undesirable and propositional constructs as desirable, Kelly proposed that if this was the case, no one would ever be able to reach pressing decisions (Hjelle & Ziegler 1992). On the other hand, propositionality must be achieved for one's construct system to be open to change (Ewen 1993).

A further characteristic of constructs as identified by Kelly is whether they are tight or loose. A tight set of constructs leads to clear and unambiguous predictions about an event. Loose sets of constructs lead to varying predictions (Lester 1995).

The following assumptions can be derived from applying personal construct theory to organisations (Jelinek & Litterer 1994):

- Organisations consist of people who consciously and deliberately coordinate their activities in search of a common goal.
- Individuals within an organisation coordinate their activities through shared cognitions. This could include a shared set of purposes, values and problem-solving procedures.
- Organisation members understand that the organisation is the beneficiary of the outcomes produced by their coordinated efforts.

The formal structure of personal construct theory consists of one fundamental *postu-late* or assumption so crucial that it underlies everything that follows, and 11 *corollaries* designed to clarify and elaborate on the nature of personal constructs (quotes from Engler 1995).

20.5.2 The fundamental postulate

A person's processes are psychologically channelised by the ways in which he anticipates events (p. 399).

All human behaviour (including thoughts and actions) is aimed at predicting events. Predictions are made by forming personal constructs, and the process by which forming takes place is explained in the following corollaries.

20.5.3 Corollaries

20.5.3.1 Construction corollary

A person anticipates events by construing their replications (p. 400).

The construction corollary points to the similarities in repeated events. In order to predict the future, we must construe previous incidents in our lives and identify the similarities and differences among them. On the basis of these similarities, we are able to make predictions or anticipate how an event will be experienced in the future. For example, if an individual needs to deal with two colleagues, he or she will anticipate the nature of their relationship by basing predictions on relevant prior experiences (replications) (Ewen 1993).

20.5.3.2 Individuality corollary

Persons differ from each other in their construction of events (p. 400).

The individuality corollary points to individual differences in interpreting events. Different people construe events differently, because they perceive and interpret events differently. For example, the colleague viewed by one person as friendly might be construed as manipulative by someone else.

20.5.3.3 Organisation corollary

Each person characteristically evolves, for his convenience in anticipating events, a construction system embracing ordinal relationships between constructs (p. 400).

The organisation corollary points to the relationship among constructs. Kelly proposed that constructs were organised in a hierarchical structure, with constructs placed on various levels with varying importance. The more important constructs are referred to as *superordinate*, whereas the less influential are termed *subordinate* (Ewen 1993). For example, a person who feels harmed in some way by people more attractive than himself or herself may switch the construct "attractive" from a subordinate place under the construct "good" to its opposite pole "bad". The hierarchical structure is therefore not fixed – it can be changed according to its predictive efficiency. People then not only differ in the number of constructs they have in their systems, but also in the way in which their construct systems are organised.

20.5.3.4 Dichotomy corollary

A person's construction system is composed of a finite number of dichotomous constructs (p. 400).

All personal constructs are *bipolar* or *dichotomous*. Each one must be specified in terms of two opposite poles, which also differ across individuals. For example, one person may form a construct of "gentle vs aggressive", whereas another person may construe a construct of "passive vs aggressive" (Ewen 1993). Personal constructs are formed through a process of observing

similarities and differences. The dichotomies (opposites) need to be noted in order to have predictive value. If such contrasts did not exist, for example all people were honest, then forming the construct of honesty about a person would serve no predictive purpose. Therefore at least three elements are needed to form a construct; two of the construct elements must be perceived as similar to each other, while the third element must be perceived as different from these two. All constructs have two opposite poles: the way in which two elements are construed to be similar is called the *emergent* or *similarity* pole of the construct dimension; the way in which they are contrasted with the third element is called the *implicit* or *contrast* pole of the construct dimension (Hjelle & Ziegler 1992).

A vocational construct system would consist of a number of bipolar constructs used in anticipating the world of work, for example high vs low salary, limited vs extensive upward mobility, high job security vs insecurity, stimulating vs boring (Niemeyer 1992). In order to understand the individual in the work situation, his or her system of constructs need to be ascertained.

20.5.3.5 Choice corollary

A person chooses for himself that alternative in a dichotomised construct through which he anticipates the greater possibility for extension and elaboration of his system (p. 400).

The choice corollary points to the freedom of choice of individuals. As the only way to anticipate the future is to make use of our personal constructs, we must constantly seek out ways to improve their usefulness. There are two different ways to do so. First, we may choose to clarify the constructs we already have, thus narrowing our world for the sake of *security*. This has a higher predictive efficiency, because similar experiences and events are repeated. Second, we may choose the *adventurous* way of exploring new aspects of life. This has a lower predictive efficiency, because the construct system is expanded by seeking out new experiences. Having chosen either security or safety, we might value that pole of the dichotomous construct that will better enable us to achieve this end. For example, take a look at the "friendly vs hostile" construct. A person who has decided on security may perceive a stranger as "hostile", whereas a person who has decided on adventure may regard the same stranger as "friendly". It is important to choose the adventurous path at times, in order to improve the predictive value of our constructs (Ewen 1993).

20.5.3.6 Range corollary
A construct is convenient for the anticipation of a finite range of events only (p. 400).

The finite range is also known as the *range of convenience*, which includes all of the events to which the construct is relevant or applicable. The predictive efficiency of a construct is jeopardised whenever it is generalised beyond the range of events for which it was intended. For example, the construct "academic vs nonacademic" cannot be used to evaluate the merits of being "married vs single" (Hjelle & Ziegler 1992). Conversely, in understanding an individual, it is just as important to know what is excluded from the range of convenience of a construct as to know what is included.

20.5.3.7 Experience corollary
A person's construction system varies as he successively construes the replication of events (p. 401).

The experience corollary points to exposure to new experiences. Even the best construct system is not perfect and must be frequently revised if we are to cope with an ever-changing reality. This process is also known as the C-P-C cycle, which is discussed under heading 20.8.1.

20.5.3.8 Modulation corollary
The variation in a person's construction system is limited by the permeability of the constructs within whose range of convenience the variants lie (p. 401).

The modulation corollary points to the adaptation to new experiences. A *permeable* construct is open to construing new events, whereas an *impermeable* construct remains closed to the interpretation of new experiences. This corollary implies that the more permeable (open) a person's superordinate constructs, the greater the possible variation (systematic change) within the substructures. This also relates to the range of convenience, as it can only be applied in suitable situations. For example, a racist person may hold an impermeable construct of "competent vs incompetent", whereas a person who is open to new experiences may adjust the same construct as he or she interacts with new cultures (Hjelle & Ziegler 1992).

20.5.3.9 Fragmentation corollary
A person may successively employ a variety of construction subsystems which are inferentially incompatible with each other (p. 401).

The fragmentation corollary describes the competition among constructs. To allow for the illogical aspects of human behaviour, Kelly assumes that contradictory subsystems of constructs may be used at different times by the same individual. Because of this, we are often surprised by people's behaviour. This is more likely to happen when a person's constructs are impermeable or when they are undergoing change (Engler 1995). For the most part, however, our anticipations form a consistent pattern. An example of the employment of contradictory subsystems of con-structs may be that of the person who usually couples "tolerance" with "good", but may nevertheless take exception to an act of cowardice, because "cowardice" happens to be included under "hateful" (Ewen 1993).

20.5.3.10 Commonality corollary

To the extent that one person employs a construction of experience which is similar to that employed by another, his processes are psychologically similar to those of other people (p. 401).

The commonality corollary points to the similarities among people in interpreting events. This is also the way in which a culture is formed – people of a given culture may find certain predictions more often confirmed than others (Ewen 1993). Research has supported the idea that cultural differences are rooted in variations in constructs that people use (Triandis et al. in Hjelle & Ziegler 1992). Although experiences are never identical, our ability to share and communicate with other people is based on the fact that we share similar personal constructs with them (Engler 1995).

20.5.3.11 Sociality corollary

To the extent that one person con-strues the construction process of another, he may play a role in a social process involving the other person (p. 401).

The sociality corollary explains interper-sonal relationships. To anticipate and relate well to other people, it is essential to construe the ways in which they interpret the world. To facilitate this process, Kelly recommends that we play readily understandable *roles* (Ewen 1993). Roles are determined by construing the constructs of people with whom one is socially engaged – you literally have to place yourself in the other person's shoes, although you might not agree with the way in which the person has constructed his or her system. Roles need not be reciprocal in order to have a social relationship, for example the doctor-patient, lawyer-client, employer-employee relationships are one-sided. The optimal relationship, how-ever, involves a mutual understanding of another's views of life, as is the case in a healthy relationship between wife and husband (Hjelle & Ziegler 1992).

Research has indicated that social open-ness will become increasingly important in the age of multiculturalism. For example, it may facilitate success in organisational environments where individuals of various ethnicities must work together effectively (Schneider et al. 1996).

20.6 THE DEVELOPMENT OF PERSONALITY

Kelly did not elaborate on the development process of personal constructs or person-ality. This can be understood in the light of the historical nature of Kelly's theory – constructs are formed throughout life. Critism of his perspective, however, is that it is likely that different histories or life experiences of people may account for the variability among individual construct sys-tems (Hjelle & Ziegler 1992).

Piaget is the only cognitive theorist who attempted to elaborate on the development of personal constructs over a person's life span. According to Piaget, the child enters the world lacking the cognitive competen-cies an adult has, and develops schemata through a process of *assimilation* (incor-poration into existing schemata) and *accommodation* (the forming of new schemata). Four major stages of develop-ment are identified, namely sensomotoric, pre-operational, concrete operational and formal operational.

In order to understand further how a person interprets the world, Kelly devel-oped the Role Construct Repertory Test

(Rep Test). The Rep Test permits a person to reveal constructs by comparing and contrasting a number of significant persons in his or her life. Most of the research into Kelly's theory has been on the Rep Test, which is surprising, given the clear nature of his theory. Research has validated Kelly's ideas about thought disorder in schizophrenia (Bannister in Hjelle & Ziegler 1992). The Rep Test has also been applied in assessing the enduring nature of friendships, indicating that those who share a similar view of the world tend to form stronger relationships (Duck in Hjelle & Ziegler 1992).

Repertory grid methods are used to obtain change in an organisation, for example in job analysis, writing job descriptions and specifications, selection and placement, to prepare task descriptions for training, to appraise performance and to evaluate job families for purposes of remuneration and compensation. In job descriptions, the grid is particularly useful in analysing jobs in which the job content is not self-evident, such as those of supervisors and managers. In employee selection, it is useful to compare applicants' constructs with "constructs" known to be typical of successful managers already employed. In task analysis the respondent is asked to provide constructs that characterise the differences between more and less effective job holders.

Research on cognitive styles derived from the Rep Test has focused on cognitive complexity and cognitive simplicity. *Cognitive complexity* relates to the ability to perceive differences between oneself and others (Schultz 1990). *Cognitive complexity* is the more desirable cognitive style, as it enables a person to predict a greater variety of situations. It increases with development; therefore adults possess a greater degree of cognitive complexity than children (Hjelle & Ziegler 1992).

Cognitive complexity measures have been used with success to determine managerial performance. These measures show how persons think and behave and can be applied to computer-based simulations requiring a number of diverse managerial activities, such as preventive action, use of strategy, planning, responsiveness action and information search (Cascio 1991). Satisfaction or dissatisfaction with a vocational choice can also be explained in terms of cognitive complexity. Left vulnerable by the inadequate structure of constructs, a less complex individual may choose a work environment inconsistent with his or her personality style (Niemeyer 1992). In a 10-year study Kohn and Schooler demonstrated that the level of repetitiveness of work that people performed affected their cognitive flexibility (Adler 1996).

In addition to the Rep Test, various other cognitive tests have also been developed. One that has generated widespread research is the "business game", of which various forms exist. The business game seems to have validity for assessment purposes (for example performance on a manufacturing problem and changes in position level), but they seem less valuable as training devices (Neuhouser in Cascio 1991).

20.7 COGNITION AND MOTIVATION

Motivation is an important part of cognitive theories.

Recent performance interventions suggested by cognitive psychological research are key elements in the development of competitive advantage by organisations. Good performance at any job requires knowledge and motivation. *Knowledge* is the "engine of performance", while *motivation* is the "energy of performance" (Clark 1992; Ribeaux & Poppleton 1978; Robbins 1996). All motivation results from a drive to increase personal self-efficacy, or predictive validity.

The incentive value of an outcome is dependent on a number of factors:

- Its *motivational value* is determined by two subprocesses: the assessment of the personal value of a situation (a primary value would be placed on a situation that would establish our self-efficacy); and the amount of challenge involved in the situation. If we are moderately challenged by a situation we will invest maximum effort. Low levels of challenge result in overconfidence and the possibility of failure from too little effort. Excessively high levels of challenge result in anxiety and avoiding tasks through defensive behaviour.
- The *perceived locus of control,* that is whether it is perceived to be under the individual's control (internal) or due to factors beyond his or her control (external), also influences the incentive value of the outcome.
- *Failure* reduces motivation only if we attribute the failure to uncontrollable external causes, outside our range of control.
- *Monetary rewards* have little impact on motivation unless they are perceived as evidence for self-efficacy.

According to Kelly, *creativity* involves the ability to first think loosely and then tighten the constructs. The creative person can switch from loose to tight construing and back at will. Creative people can break the assumptions that people in their field make (loose thinking) and then build a good theory around the alternative assumptions (tight thinking). What if the earth revolved around the sun rather than the sun revolving around the earth? Rather than simply thinking about these possibilities (loose thinking), scientists such as Galileo built formal theories based on these assumptions (tight thinking) (Lester 1995).

There are several implications of motivational theory on an organisational level. First, because all individuals strive toward improving their self-efficacy, organisations must strive to move control and decision-making downward in the hierarchy as much as possible. Second, performance review systems should be sensitive to motivational issues and rather focus on the adjustment of challenge, beliefs about failure, personal values and the amount of perceived versus actual control exercised by employees (Clark 1992).

In the South African context it was found that a lack of intrinsic and extrinsic rewards handicapped the development of performance values in black managers. Motivation theory states that performance depends on the perceived value of the outcome. Operational support for this study is found in the fact that remuneration for black employees was generally based on union agreements, rather than incentives for performance. Traditionally, black employees were denied the opportunity to participate in performance evaluation, which may have led to a situation in which competitiveness, status aspiration and authoritarianism failed to emerge as important values for black managers (Watkins & Mauer 1994).

Cognitive change is an important aspect of organisational consulting. In fact, most consulting is considered to be linked to cognitive change, or the process by which information is imparted to the client in order to clear up distortions and provide more realistic alternatives to previous ways of functioning (Czander 1993). It is furthermore utilised in management development (construing constructs in terms of organisational politics), team building (assessing shared constructs), decision-making (organising hierarchies) and career guidance (matching client constructs to career constructs) (Jankowicz 1990).

The cognitive revolution has had a profound impact on research in personnel and human resources management with its emphasis on decision-making aspects. Personnel managers are decision-makers: they are responsible for decisions pertaining to job selection and placement, performance appraisal decisions, negotiations and personnel planning and forecasting. Personnel selection has evolved into a highly complex cognitive task, focusing on judgement, prediction, choice, evaluation and assessment. Recent stress management research also focuses on the individual's construing of events and anticipation of future outcomes (Brodt 1990).

Recently there has been reference to "managerial cognition", which attempts to comprehend how managers think and then compares them to other managers. For example, it has been found that industry structure is an important influence on management thinking; top managers in multi-business firms have less connected cognitive maps of the dynamics of industry than ones in more focused firms (Sparrow 1994).

Fiedler and Garcia explained the process by which a leader obtains effective group performance through a theory called *cognitive resource theory*. They have shown how intelligent and competent leaders formulate more effective plans, decisions and strategies and communicate them through directive behaviour, than those who are less competent (Robbins 1996).

In the South African context, it has been found that cognitive modifiability is a better predictor of success of disadvantaged black students than traditional intellectual assessment methods (Shochet 1994). Cognitive modifiability refers to the process whereby a person is able to apply cognitive principles to new situations after being coached in them. This corresponds to the finding of Taylor (1994) that competence in numeric and verbal skills is a function of the quality and quantity of training. Rather than assessing potential through traditional verbal or numeric skills tests, abstract-diagrammatic material should be used. Employers would need to place more emphasis on potential than skills if the inequalities of the past in South Africa are to be addressed (Taylor 1994).

20.8 PSYCHOLOGICAL HEALTH: THE COGNITIVE PERSPECTIVE

In this section the cognitive perspective on mental health is considered from three vantage points, namely psychological adjustment, psychological maladjustment and its perspective on emotions.

20.8.1 Psychological adjustment

Well-adjusted individuals test their personal constructs against reality in logical ways, confirm or discount the predictive accuracy of these constructs and revise them appropriately. This sequence often takes the form of the *C-P-C cycle:* considering several constructs that can be used to interpret a particular situation ("circumspection"), deciding upon a single construct for dealing with the issue in question ("pre-emption") and selecting that pole of the construct that promises to improve one's predictions ("control" or "choice") (Ewen 1993). The healthy individual's constructs are more permeable, less pre-emptive and more propositional (Engler 1995).

From Kelly's perspective, the well-functioning person is defined by four distinct characteristics.

- First, healthy persons are willing to evaluate their constructs and to test the *validity* of their perceptions of other people.
- Second, healthy persons are able to *discard* their constructs and *reorientate* their core role systems whenever they appear to be invalid. The implication of this is that their constructs are permeable, and they are able to admit when they are wrong and to update their constructs when necessary.
- Third, healthy persons display a desire to *extend* their construct systems by opting for the "adventurous" choice. They remain open to new possibilities for growth and development.

- Fourth, healthy persons have a well-developed *repertoire of roles* and are able to perform the social roles required of them (Hjelle & Ziegler 1992).

20.8.2 Psychological maladjustment

Psychological disturbances represent the failure of a person's construct system to predict future events. Anxiety is provoked by this inability, which may be dealt with in one of two ways. The person can either frantically attempt to search for new ways of construing the events of his or her world or may choose to rigidly adhere to invalid predictions. Based on the choice corollary, Kelly felt that the tendency to take the secure, no-risk alternative may explain why some people persist in behaving in the wrong way.

Why does a person persist in behaving in a hostile fashion, even if he or she is constantly rebuffed for it? Kelly suggests that this person is taking the secure route of knowing what to expect from the hostile behaviour. Choices are made in terms of what is best for predicting the future, not necessarily for what is best for the individual (Schultz 1990). Whatever the case, the maladjusted person cannot predict events with much accuracy and hence fails to learn about or cope with the world (Hjelle & Ziegler 1992).

Miller stated that abnormal behaviour is the result of two incompatible plans. When the individual discovers this, it might require an adjustment of the image. Neurosis is the result of two incompatible plans, neither of which can be abandoned (for example if one plan comes from the mother and the other from the father) (Lester 1995).

20.8.3 Emotions

In addition to the description of mental health, five *emotions* are detailed in cognitive therapy: guilt, threat, anxiety, hostility and aggression. Lecky later added the emotions of love and pleasure.

Guilt occurs when the self is perceived as dislodged from the core role, or, in other words, if we depart from our sense of who we are. For example, if you consider your core role to be responsible and conscientious as a worker and you violate this role intentionally or unintentionally by being ill often, guilt will follow (Hjelle & Ziegler 1992). Miller viewed anxiety as the result of abandoning or changing plans (Lester 1995).

Threat is aroused by apparent widespread changes in the core constructs. To illustrate, the retired executive will experience threat because he or she cannot maintain his or her core role any more (Ewen 1993).

Whereas threat and guilt result from perceived changes in one's core constructs, *anxiety* results from an inability to construe important events and anticipate the future. Every person would feel a certain amount of anxiety due to the imperfect nature of every construct system (Hjelle & Ziegler 1992). To illustrate the difference between a threatening and an anxiety-provoking situation, consider the following example: missing a promotion would be threatening if it indicated the need to reconstrue one's fundamental abilities and professional goals, but it would be anxiety-provoking if it could not be explained by any construct in the system, leaving the person confused and unable to take corrective action. McReynolds viewed anxiety as the result of unassimilated percepts. For him the difference between normal and pathological anxiety lay in the degree of coping strategies necessary. Trauma would cause anxiety resulting from percepts that cannot readily be assimilated (Lester 1995). Recent research has indicated that a two-way relationship between anxiety and cognitive processes exists; not only does anxiety influence thinking and the interpretative process, but cognitions can also moderate anxiety (Booth-Butterfield 1991).

Hostility, according to Kelly, refers to the attempt to hold onto an invalid construct in the face of contradictory or invalidating evidence. The hostile person refuses to accept that his or her expectations of other people are unrealistic and need revision. Instead, he or she tries to make other people behave in ways that would fit his or her preconceived notions. Many of the tactics that people use to reduce what Festinger identifies as cognitive dissonance resemble what Kelly calls hostility (Lester 1995).

Aggression is used in much the same way as assertiveness is used: it is the deliberate placement of oneself in situations that call for decisions (Engler 1995). For Kelly, the opposite element of aggressiveness is passiveness. The aggressive business person seeks out business opportunities and actively pursues them. Kelly made the interesting clinical hypothesis that people are especially aggressive in areas that cause them anxiety, that is, which they cannot construe well (Lester 1995).

Lecky extended Kelly's ideas to include definitions of love and pleasure. *Love* is defined as the reaction to someone who has already been assimilated and who serves as a strong support to your idea of self (in Kelly's theory, your core constructs). *Pleasure* is found when we master new experiences; for example, as we mature we enjoy more complex music and art. The more difficult the task that was overcome, the greater the pleasure derived from it (Lester 1995).

Some attempt has been made by recent cognitive psychologists to acknowledge the effect of emotion in behaviour. For example, Beck's theory of depression is based on the belief that cognitive processes play a crucial role in affective processes. Depression is the result of persistent cognitive errors. For example, *catastrophising* refers to the error of overstating consequences or defining an anticipated event as catastrophic. Compared to nondepressed individuals, depressed people tend to see themselves as responsible for problems and frustrations and to see situations as unchanging and globally negative (Pervin 1990). Beck's therapy is intended to change the cognitions of depressed persons, in the belief that a more positive cognition would lead to more positive affect (Marx & Cronan-Hillix 1987). Although research indicates that emotions might be changed by altering one's preconscious cognitions, more research into this matter is needed (Beck 1991).

Ellis is a cognitive behavioural theorist who devoted a lot of attention to human emotions. He developed a theory of *rational-emotive therapy* (RET), which states that emotions and cognitions are intricately interrelated. His A-B-C theory of personality that underlies RET holds that when a highly charged emotional consequence (C) (for example an anxiety attack) follows a significant activation event (A) (such as seeing a spider), A may seem to, but does not actually, cause C. Instead, emotional consequences are caused by the individual's belief system (B) (all spiders are dangerous and therefore I should be anxious). This statement helps to explain why two people may react differently to the same statement. For example, if two people are told they are stupid, the one might laugh and the other become depressed. This difference is not caused by the activation event, A (being told that he or she is stupid), but rather by the individual's belief system (B) (for example, I am what other people think of me). Most major personality theories concentrate either on A, the activating events in a person's life (such as psychoanalytic theories), or C, the emotional consequences, and rarely consider B, the belief system. Ellis believes that irrational beliefs are at the centre of maladaptive behaviour (Engler 1995). He believes that we inherit a tendency to raise cultural preferences into musts and social norms into absolute shoulds. Ellis then disputes these irrational beliefs rationally and behaviourally. Through cognitive therapy he attempts to show clients how to reorganise their "should" and "must" thoughts, how to separate rational and irrational beliefs and how to accept reality.

20.9 CONCLUSION

Cognitive theory can be viewed from varying points of view. Maddi (1996) provides a useful model for viewing Kelly's theory by categorising it under the consistency model, because, instead of focusing on forces motivating behaviour, it emphasises the influence of *feedback* from the external world on the individual. As we interact with the world, our experiences confirm or discount external norms. If this feedback is consistent with what we expect, everything is fine. If not, we experience emotional discomfort. The overall goal of living is to minimise experiential inconsistencies.

Kelly's idea of personal construct has proven to be a very useful psychotherapeutic tool, as well as being particularly useful to the industrial psychologist. While allowing for a considerable degree of distinctiveness, his theory still provides a logical framework for the scientific study of personality (Ewen 1993). Kelly has been praised for his lack of rigidness in his theory, and even admits that each theory is the result of one's own personal construct system. Theories are built to be modified and even rejected, so that better theories can be devised (Lester 1995).

Cognitive research has been widely applied in consumer psychology, which is particularly concerned with opinions, values, attitudes and life styles associated with preferences for certain products and services. On the basis of the cognitive attributes assigned to a particular market, products are advertised, packaged and promoted in a manner that would appeal to that market (Aiken 1993).

A criticism of cognitive psychology has been that human behaviour cannot be seen in isolation from its social and physical environment and nonintellectual variables such as emotion (Marx & Cronan-Hillix 1987). It is expected, though, that the influence of cognitive psychology will continue to grow. If it is true that biologically we are what we eat, it may also be true that psychologically we are what we *remember*. Memory is a central function in cognitive psychology, but is not always conscious. More research into conscious and unconscious memory is needed.

Psychoanalytically oriented theorists criticise Kelly's theories for the lack of attention to childhood development and consider as an oversimplification his notion that hostility is the result of a failure to construe behaviour (Ewen 1993).

Despite its distinctiveness, Kelly's theory has not gained wide acceptance. Possible reasons for this include the omission of familiar concepts such as motivation, unconscious influences and needs and that the style of his writing does not allow for human passion and drama as experienced by the psychologist in everyday life. Furthermore, there are a number of questions left unanswered by Kelly's theory. First, why do two people construe the same event in different ways? Second, why, or under what conditions, will a person opt for security or for adventure? Kelly's theory, as with all the other approaches discussed, contains gaps and leaves questions unanswered. Kelly himself viewed his theory as an "interim theory", at best, that needed to be expanded in the light of new evidence. His singular, though controversial, contribution cannot be ignored (Schultz 1990).

Personal construct theory has generated a substantial amount of empirical research, especially on the Rep Test and the therapeutic implications of the theory (Ewen 1993). Epstein identified a number of important directions for research in cognitive psychology. First, research is needed in the course of development of critical thinking over the life span. Second, measures other than self-report inventories need to be developed if development in children is to be measured. Third, remedial procedures for improving constructive thinking need to be developed (Pervin 1990).

Future directions for organisational research point toward new ways of assessing job performance in constantly changing organisations (DeNisi 1996). Research on cognitive processes in personnel management decision-making, especially in the field of human resources planning, is a new area of opportunities for the industrial psychologist (Brodt 1990). Although much of cognitive research on the applications in an organisational setting has focused on decision-making processes, there is a growing concern with the characteristics of high-performing organisations and the restructuring of organisations. This represents a shift from micro-processes (for example decision-making) to macro-level variables such as team decision-making and performance. Consequently research into cognitive appraisal is moving toward the design of appraisal systems based on cognitive processes and not the traditional job analysis techniques (DeNisi 1996).

Further directions for research include determining the effectiveness of personal vs provided (for example through career information) constructs and gender-related differences in construct-system structure (Niemeyer 1992). Likely developments in the business situation are the development of grid manuals, applicability to management training and computerised applications (Jankowicz 1990). The Rep Test has recently been computerised, but more research into subject protocols and statistical methods of analysis is needed.

The effects of computer use have had widespread implications for the work-

force. For example, due to computerisation, professional and managerial-level hierarchies will flatten as more information become available at a central point (some predictions are that middle-level management will fall away in future). The concept of artificial intelligence, designing a computer or robot with the ability to think, and to execute fine motor skills, may mean that a person may provide a job analyst with a description of his or her job, whereafter the analyst would program a mathematical model into a computer to enable it to do the work (Hunt 1995).

Despite the criticisms, Beck (1993) maintains that cognitive therapy has fulfilled the criteria of a system of psychotherapy by providing a coherent, testable theory of personality, psychopathology and therapeutic change; a teachable, testable set of therapeutic principles, strategies and techniques that articulate the theory; and a body of clinical and empirical data that support the theory and its efficacy.

Self-evaluating questions

1. How are fundamental psychological concepts such as learning, the self-construct, basic motivating factors, unconscious and defence mechanisms viewed from the cognitive perspective?

2. Explain the meaning of Kelly's fundamental postulate. What are some of the major corollaries that serve to elaborate on it?

3. Use an example of your own values or of our society to illustrate different types of personal constructs.

4. Evaluate cognitive thinking in your organisation if you consider how the organisation is managed.

5. Give an example from your own life, from the life of someone you know well, or from fiction, to illustrate each of the following:

(a) How the same event can be construed in alternative ways, and the different effects of these constructions

(b) Constructions based on relevant prior experiences

(c) The healthy use of the C-P-C cycle

(d) A construct becoming more permeable as one grows older

(e) The unhealthy use of a pre-emptive or constellatory construct

(f) The beneficial use of roles

6. Do you believe that "personality" is the personologist's construct? If so, might this explain why we have so many different theories of personality? What, then, is the relationship between personologists' constructs and their basic assumptions concerning human nature?

7. What does Kelly mean when he says that all people are scientists, and how does this relate to constructive alternativism?

Psychopathology

21

Ziel Bergh _____

CONTENTS

Learning outcomes

After studying this chapter you should be able to:

- explain the concepts of psychopathology and psychological health
- describe psychological adjustment and maladjustment by using definitions, criteria and models
- explain cultural differences with regard to criteria for adjustment or maladjustment
- explain possible causes of psychological disorders
- identify possible hassles and life changes as stressors
- explain the relationship between stress, illness and health
- explain why people are sometimes resilient to adverse stressful situations
- indicate how people use intrapsychic defence mechanisms to cope with problems in life
- explain and differentiate various psychopathological conditions

Key concepts

psychological disorders, afrocentric paradigm, DSM, criteria, etiology, adjustment, defence mechanisms, stress, hassles, coping, adaptive reactions, general adaptation syndrome, psychophysiological, anxiety, schizophrenia, delusional, substance abuse, violence, personality disorders, dissociative somatoform, manic-depressive, cognitive, sexual, childhood

21.1 INTRODUCTION

Psychopathology or abnormal psychology is the scientific study of the psychological principles, criteria, causes, behavioural characteristics or symptoms and treatment procedures of psychological disorders in individuals and groups. *Psychological disorders* refer to the physical, cognitive, behavioural and emotional (psychological) signs and symptoms in people which impair their functioning in one or more life roles. According to research cited in Louw and Edwards (1997), an average of 15-30%, with a high of 50%, of people in society suffer from some form of psychological disorder.

Although psychological disorders often imply disordered or deviant personality functioning, psychopathology also involves other aspects of human behaviour. For this reason classifications of different types of psychopathological conditions or syndromes exist, including personality disorders. A *syndrome* is a distinct, recognisable group of characteristics and symptoms, which can be used to recognise disorders, for instance anxiety disorder or schizophrenia.

21.2 NORMALITY AND ABNORMALITY

Psychological health as a comprehensive concept refers to certain behaviours, cognitions and feelings in individuals, which, in the context of their social setting or cultural and related norms, characterises their psychological wellbeing or maladjustment in their various life roles. Psychological health can include factors such as the degree of general life and career satisfaction, emotional control, kinds of interpersonal relationships, social behaviour, self-actualisation, stress reactions, substance use and the presence or absence of psychological disorders.

It seems obvious that abnormality and normality in behaviour should be characterised by opposites, or the presence and absence of symptoms respectively. However, for many reasons the distinction is not that simple. The distinction between adjustment and maladjustment in certain cases is very clear, for instance in cases of hereditary deviations and cognitive disorders. In others, and for many reasons, especially dysfunctions of psychological or emotional behaviours, the differences are not always that clear.

General and specific criteria or standards are used to assess behaviour as either "normal" or "abnormal". One major objection to psycho-diagnosis and psychopathological criteria is that they are frequently subjective, vague, ambiguous and overlapping, and that they often fail to describe characteristics in terms of observable behaviour. Some of these criteria may be equally applicable to "normal" people or may be applicable to more than one disorder. Adjustment or maladjustment does not necessarily mean opposites on a continuum of behaviour, nor the absence of symptoms. Helmes and Jackson (Strack & Lorr 1994) discuss findings in which the same set of constructs is used to assess normal and abnormal personality attributes. Criteria for psychological health, for instance those of Rogers, Allport and Maslow, also met with criticism for being vague and subjective (Allen 1994; Schultz & Schultz 1994).

The distinguishing factors between normal and abnormal behaviours are the frequency, duration and intensity of deviant behaviours, the personal distress and impairment of the person, impact on others, the environment and whether intensive psychological, psychiatric and other interventions are necessary.

21.2.1 Characteristics of psychological adjustment and maladjustment

Most personality theorists use concepts or criteria to describe the healthy personality. Maslow and Rogers in particular outlined typical attributes of self-actualising or fully-functioning individuals (Carver & Scheier 1996; Schultz & Schultz 1994). Maslow asserts that if the "being" or metaneeds of people are frustrated certain "metapathologies" may result, as illustrated in table 21.1, which will inhibit healthy development. This approach is similar to Bowlby's, Erikson's and Freud's ideas of possible negative behaviours in adulthood if development in certain critical periods during childhood does not occur.

The classification in Brammer and Schostrom (1982) for a healthy personality basically incorporates therapeutic objectives aimed at development. It is similar to Rogers's ideas on self-actualisation and

Metaneeds	Metapathologies
Truth	Cynism, scepticism, mistrust
Beauty	Loss of taste, vulgarity
Uniqueness	Deindividualising, anonymous
Justice	Lawlessness, selfishness, anger
Meaningfulness	Despair, senselessness, worthless
Self-sufficiency	Not responsible, dependent

Table 21.1 Unsatisfied metaneeds and metapathologies

human potential and also contains elements of the ideas put forward by Maslow:
- spontaneity toward others and an "openness" to personal and other experiences
- living in the present, which implies that the individual has the ability to participate wholeheartedly and joyfully in the activities of life without fixating on the past or entertaining fantasies of the future
- self-confidence, which refers to individuals' confidence in themselves as a person, their self-esteem and the validity of their decisions and actions
- self-knowledge, the awareness that one lives and responds in one's environment and the experiencing and acceptance of every emotion
- honesty or congruency, referring to individuals' ability to be themselves, not to hide behind defence mechanisms and to know themselves so that they can learn to know others
- effectiveness, which relates to the individual's ability to live purposefully because of the aforementioned skills; in other words, to fulfil the requirements of life within the context of the level of development

Phillips (in Azibo 1996) discussed an *Afrocentric paradigm* to understand and manage mental health. As an African value system based on the Nguzo SABA principles by Karenga (1977), it includes the following seven principles for living harmoniously and authentically:
- *unity* (umoja), which refers to solidarity and harmony between persons and groups
- *self-determination* (kujichagalia), which emphasises internal influences and self-knowledge rather than external influences
- *collective responsibility* (ujima) denotes connectedness with other people in terms of, for example, family, meaningful work and a common destiny

- *cooperative economics* (ujaama), meaning that people must share in wealth, thus excluding individual favouritism
- *purpose* (nia), encompassing an individual's goal-directedness, but strongly connected to other people's objectives, even if it means delaying gratification
- *creativity* (kuumba) emphasises the abilities to use intelligence, imagination and ingenuity to improve existing things and the quality of life
- *faith* (imani), denoting empowerment by past, present and future events, means to live now but also to leave something of value behind

These principles place emphasis on the individual's behaviours in his or her specific context, interaction with other people and spiritual values.

Although these criteria may include adjusted and maladjusted behaviour by implication, some authors provide specific criteria for abnormal behaviour. Rosenhan and Seligman (1989) give seven criteria or features for abnormality:
- *Maladaptiveness.* Normal or common life roles and enjoyment are seriously influenced, for instance inability to work and seriously disturbed relationships result.
- *Suffering.* People with psychological disorders have more psychological pain, discomfort, stress and unhappiness than is common in most people.
- *Irrationality and incomprehensibility.* There is no logical explanation for actions that may involve illogical and bizarre behaviour such as incoherent speech, delusions and hallucinations.
- *Observer discomfort.* Psychologically disordered people may ignore or be very uneasy with common habits, such as keeping physical and social distance, eye contact in conversations and dressing appropriately.
- *Unpredictability and loss of control.* Psychologically disturbed behaviours

are often characterised by fluctuations and emotional expressions which do not relate to the circumstances.

- *Unconventionality and vividness.* Behaviours are often strange and uncommon.
- *Deviations from ethical and moral codes of conduct.* Unlawful, aggressive, sexual and social behaviours visible to others which create discomfort for them.

These general criteria must be refined when professionals diagnose and classify people's behaviours, for instance according to the Diagnostic and Statistical Manual of Mental Disorders (DSM-IV) (APA 1994). Despite criticism, the DSM is used widely all over the world, and provides accepted standards of reliability and validity (Wilson et al. 1996). Across cultures there is much agreement on similarities of symptoms and clinical conditions (German 1987; Carson et al. 1996). The DSM assesses disorders and not people and works eclectically, that is, not according to any specific theory. The fourth edition improves on previous editions by using more research findings and also better integrates cultural differences (Wilson et al. 1996; Nevid et al. 1996).

The DSM-diagnostic system is used to group information or characteristics (sometimes referred to as the clinical picture) of specific psychological disorders, or syndromes, or taxonomies, according to the features or criteria specified by the DSM, to allow professionals to recognise or classify psychological disorders. Professionals use the DSM to organise and integrate assessment information on clients (from tests, interviews, bio-data, illness history, etc.) to make a psycho-diagnosis and to classify a person's behaviour as belonging to a specific syndrome. First, the signs (features that the person may be unaware of) and the symptoms (observable behaviours) of a person's behaviours are organised according to the *DSM-operational criteria* for specific disorders to determine a possible classifica-

tion. Second, the clinician must decide how the person's behaviours relate to one or more of five axes: (I) any clinical disorder, (II) personality disorder or mental retardation; (III) possible general medical or physical problems; (IV) psychosocial and environmental problems; and (V) on a rating scale from 1-100, a global assessment of the person's general functioning in various life roles (APA 1994). It is only axis IV, and to a lesser degree axis V, which addresses some aspects of occupational behaviours as possible causal or symptomatic indicators.

21.2.2 Definitions

The American Psychiatric Association (APA) (1994:xxi-xxii) defines a mental disorder as:

> a clinically significant behavioral or psychological syndrome or pattern that occurs in an individual and that is associated with present distress (a painful symptom) or disability (impairment in one or more areas of functioning) or with a significantly increased risk of suffering death, pain, disability, or an important loss of freedom. In addition, this syndrome or pattern must not be merely an expectable and culturally sanctioned response to a particular event, for example the death of a loved one. Whatever its original cause, it must currently be considered a manifestation of a behavioral, psychological, or biological dysfunction in the individual. Neither deviant behavior (e.g. political, religious, or sexual), nor conflicts that are primarily between the individual and society, are mental disorders unless the deviance or conflict is a symptom of a dysfunction in the individual, as described above.

Black African definitions of mental health are derived at from the emphasis on a *shared spiritual essence* which creates an extended self-concept with all blacks in the present, past and feature, as well as the

emphasis on organismic or race maintenance. Azibo (1996:53) proposes an
amended definition of Welsing (1981),
"patterns of perception, logic, thought,
speech, action, and emotional response,
whether consciously or unconsciously determined – that reflect personal and
extended self-respect and personal and
self-affirmation". A definition by Azibo
(1989:177), which incorporates much of
the African thought on mental health, is as
follows: "mental health is that psychological and behavioural functioning that is in
accord with the basic nature of the original
human nature and its attendant cosmology
and survival thrust."

In the work context Neff (1977:172,
192, 247) maintains that work adjustment
is a process of development in which the
individual progressively learns a productive
role or acquires a positive work attitude
which will eventually characterise the work
personality. The work personality is a semi-
autonomous area of the general personality. *Work psychopathology* implies some
area of deficiency or defect in the development of the work personality. People who
are unable to work are unable to tolerate or
accept the demands of work as a social
situation.

Lowman (1993:4) defines *work dysfunctions* "to refer to psychological conditions
in which there is a significant impairment in
the capacity to work caused either by
characteristics of the person or by an
interaction between personal characteristics and working conditions".

All these definitions emphasise: the
psychological impairment in the individual
of cognitive, social, emotional, physical and
also work behaviours; that a psychological
disorder must also be observed in the
individual's present distress; and that a
psychological disorder is not related to
cultural or situational sanctioned behaviours.

The following models explain how causal
factors are related to psychological disorders.

21.3 MODELS OF THE CAUSES OF PSYCHOLOGICAL DISORDERS

Personality and behavioural theories and
research in many instances explain personality and human behaviour in various
dimensions, including determinants of
psychological adjustment and maladjustment, assessment methods and techniques
for change or treatment of maladjustment.
The determinants, causes or *etiology* of
psychological disorders are emphasised in
this section. In this regard similar factors
have been discussed concerning human
and personality development and other
domains of human behaviour. The same
factors that facilitate healthy adjustment
and personality development can be responsible for maladjustment, if experienced
negatively.

A controversy centres on the fact that
most of our knowledge of mental health is
based on a *negative approach* (pathology,
illness), since research is concerned mainly
with psychiatric patients, their symptoms
and biologically related causes which predispose to illness. This is the approach
mostly followed in medical, clinical and
psychiatric theory and practices. It is often
criticised as negative and exclusive of many
other factors. In recent times much emphasis has been on a *positive view* of
physical and psychological health, *salutogenesis* rather than pathogenesis only.
Salutogenesis refers to the health-protect-
ing resources in and available to people,
such as optimism, experiencing meaningfulness, self-actualisation, self-efficacy, personal hardiness, sense of coherence, self-
control and social support in their environments, which facilitate health and make
people *resilient,* even in the midst of severe
stress (Carson et al. 1996; Antonovsky
1984, 1987; Strümpfer 1990, 1995).

Causal factors may be considered in terms
of their roles or functions. *Necessary causal
factors* or etiology must occur for a disorder
to be diagnosed. *Sufficient causes* may

indicate factors which if present (and sufficient) will lead to certain disorders. *Contributory causes* are factors that will increase the possibility of disorders occurring. A related causal explanation is the so-called *diathesis-stress model,* especially followed in psychiatric and medical practice, which proposes that certain people may be predisposed (it will or might happen) to maladjustment if certain biological or other related stressors are present (Carson et al. 1996; Halgin & Whitbourne 1997).

From the preceding definitions and criteria, it is clear that causes (etiology) and problem (cause and effect) are not always clearly distinguishable. Although a single factor or stressor can have a dominant influence, psychological health can best be understood by considering the continual interaction between a complex number of factors.

In this regard a *systems model,* especially, emphasises the individual as a fully-fledged system consisting of a number of subsystems (such as body, mind, intelligence, emotions and motivation) which are influenced by and function within many other systems and subsystems, for instance political, government, nation, culture, work group, religion, family relations and marriage. The interactive and circular influence of factors on the individual and his or her behaviour and the context of a person's behaviour should always be taken into consideration. For instance, an employee's alcohol problem could have a specific functional meaning if he or she achieves sympathy (a secondary gain) in the family, or if the family or work group functions according to it. In a *socio-cultural systems perspective,* Kleinman (1988) emphasises that psychological disorders can only be understood correctly if the interaction between psychological, biological and cultural influences are considered. In this regard the medical model of explaining symptoms according to biological predispositions does not consider the imbedded-ness of psychological symptoms in the values, norms, learning and habits of cultures. For this reason the same symptoms in two people may not necessarily mean the same and should not necessarily be diagnosed as the same disorder. This is also why culture-bound syndromes are increasingly included in classification systems and why traditional healers are recognised alongside modern medicine and psychological treatment.

To the outsider, who does not consider all the implications, it is sometimes easy to say that a person is an alcoholic or behaves strangely because he or she has a problem. Such simple explanations could result in less effective treatment approaches.

In general the etiology or causes of maladjustment can be subdivided into at least four groups of factors (Carson et al. 1996: Wilson et al. 1996; Nevid et al. 1997): biological, psychological, socio-cultural and external, although more specific classifications can be made.

21.3.1 Descriptive models

Several descriptive models are used to explain mental health in terms of external, mostly subjective standards, such as people themselves (subjective model), ideals such as ideologies or important figures (normative model) and statistical standards such as averages and cultural norms.

All of these have obvious flaws, but the cultural view on mental health is being given increasing scientific status.

The *cultural model* illustrates the social meaning of psychological disorders. It requires that the psychologically sound individual conforms to the social meaning, norms or standards of a particular culture and as such provides little or no universally accepted basis for comparison.

Cultural explanations will provide many inconsistencies, because people in different cultures behave differently. Some symptoms of disorders manifest differently in different cultures and in some cultures

Do unnatural and natural forces influence mental health?

specific culture-bound disorders are described (Nevid et al 1996; Halgin & Whitbourne 1997), which are not always reflected in the Western-oriented DSM-diagnostic system. Classifications used by traditional healers in South Africa include culture-bound syndromes. Examples, with DSM close equivalents, are: intloko engxolayo (anxiety); ukuphuthelwa (major depression); isthuthwane (epilepsy) and phambana (psychotic disorder) (Louw & Edwards 1997:702). Many culture-bound syndromes are described, some of which are well explained by the DSM, and others not. A few of these, for instance "amafufunyana" among Zulu and Xhosa (Louw & Edwards 1997), "koro" in Asia and "zar" in North Africa and Asia, concern being possessed by spirits and accompanied by behaviours which do not easily fit into one DSM category (Halgin & Whitbourne 1997; Nevid et al. 1996).

In the time of primitive man, and also during the Middle Ages, *animist explanations* for behaviour disorders were given, that is, in terms of supernatural forces, sorcery, devil possession, ancestral spirits and other mystical phenomena. Hippocrates (460-377 BC) explained mental disorders in terms of natural organic causes and four body fluids: blood, phlegm, yellow bile and black bile. Even some modern cultures still utilise naturalistic

explanations, and retain animistic views (Nevid et al. 1997; Louw & Edwards 1997). In this regard the African definition of mental health has a very strong cultural or traditional application. In black cultures, such as Xhosa, Zulu and Sotho, psychological and physical health is related to contact with the ancestors (representing the unconscious), and training or treatment by traditional healers is given, through which the person can integrate the conscious and unconscious (Van Niekerk 1996). Most white cultures do not share these beliefs and explain psychological disorders according to known scientific, medical and psychological principles and interpret spiritual and mystical factors in other ways.

Most psychological disorders or their symptoms have commonalities across cultures. For instance, a schizophrenic or a depressive psychosis will be recognised as such in many cultures if comparable assessment procedures are used (German 1987; Carson et al. 1996). In a study of teachers in four cultures (in Greece, United States of America, Germany and France) Minsel, Becker & Korchin (1991) reported general agreement that the most important components of *positive mental health* are a positive attitude towards others, optimism, good problem-solving skills, autonomy and responsibility. Although the DSM is used all over the world, including Africa, to classify and diagnose psychological disorders, it is also important to explain and treat symptomatic behaviour in terms of its meaning in the context in which it occurs (Kleinman 1988).

21.3.2 Explanatory models

In explanatory models, psychological health is explained more scientifically in terms of the psychological dynamics or motivation of behaviour, in other words, the underlying behavioural processes and causes in the individual or the interaction between the individual and his or her environments. These models correlate closely with psychological schools of thought and the various perspectives on personality and related research.

21.3.2.1 The organic or biological perspective

The organic or biological perspective of psychological disorders was first postulated in Hippocrates's naturalist-organic view. It was perpetuated and continues to this day in the medical and psychiatric model which defines behaviour disorders as "illnesses" with specific physical and organic symptoms and predispositions. *Biological causes,* which have an organic or biological basis, are the influence of the nervous system, heredity, hormones and neurohormones, physical neurochemistry, nutrition, infections, intoxication, brain injuries and tumours, and degenerative changes in the human body (due to age). Personal factors, such as age, gender, ethnicity and family history of illnesses, are often influential in explaining differences. In many instances psychological disorders, especially stress-related and viral illnesses, are discussed in terms of the effects of stress on the biological immune systems of the body.

In health psychology (Friedman & DiMatteo 1989), and in research on the relationship between stress, psychological factors and many physical and psychophysiological conditions such as cardiovascular diseases, cancer, asthma, headaches and eating diseases, the influence of a biopsychosocial perspective has recently been emphasised (Friedman 1990, 1991).

21.3.2.2 The psychodynamic approach

This approach began with the first use of hypnosis by Hans Mesmer, and was established by Freud's psychoanalysis, the neo-Freudians and social and ego-psychology theorists, who stressed the influence of dynamic processes and conflicts within the individual, such as unconscious drives, defensive behaviours, emotions, fears and memories of traumatic events. According to Freud, for instance, defence mechanisms, some of which are illustrated in table 21.2, are the ego's unconscious defences against anxieties which arise as a result of conflicts between id-impulses, ego-functioning and the demands of the superego and environment. Defence mechanisms can sometimes be normal ways of coping with and handling conflicts and tensions in daily life. However, defence mechanisms bring about maladjustment when they become the only, or a dominant, way in which individuals handle reality, problems, conflicts and tensions. Such people continue to consciously or unconsciously mislead themselves, and their problems are never really solved.

21.3.2.3 The developmental perspective

The developmental perspective emphasises the importance of human development over the life span; the critical aspects within certain stages; the effects of environmental influences, especially dysfunctional family dynamics; prominent influencers such as the mother and parents. Systems and interactional perspectives assert that the person with the disorder is only the "symptom-bearer" for the bigger system, such as the dysfunctional family or parental system, the work group or the political

Defence mechanism	Characteristic	Example
Repression	Unconsciously preventing or denying threatening and painful impulses, thoughts and feelings, buried in the unconscious, to reach consciousness.	An employee traumatised by unemployment experiences, forgets appointments, fails to perform tasks or arrives late at work.
Projection	Ascribing of own, often threatening and undesirable thoughts, feelings, mistakes or motives to others.	An employee believes he or she is not promoted because of the boss's prejudices or dislike of him or her.
Reaction formation	Behaving in a manner exactly the opposite of one's true, possibly undesirable, feelings.	An employee boasts about his or her supervisor's excellence while actually harbouring feelings of rivalry.
Displacement	Directs negative emotions or attitudes away from their original source to a substitute person or object.	Employee insecure at work or reprimanded is very strict and demanding at home.
Fantasy	Fulfilling frustrated needs by imaginary achievements or wishful thinking.	Insecure subordinate imagines being selected as president of the company.
Overcompensation	Protecting self-image or weaknesses by over-emphasising certain aspects.	Entrepreneur achieves to compensate for growing up in very poor family and neighbourhood.
Intellectualisation (isolation)	Isolating or insulating threatening experiences or emotions by speaking rationally or intellectually about it.	Employees are fired but asserting that procedures were followed exactly according to law.
Rationalisation	Finding logical, plausible but false excuses to justify unacceptable or irrational behaviour or disappointments.	Student, after an exam, asserts that he or she did not study more because the paper would have been unreasonable in any case (sour grapes).

Table 21.2 Ego-defence mechanisms and examples

Defence mechanism	Characteristic	Example
Regression	Avoids painful feelings and experiences by reverting to earlier, immature or less stressful patterns of behaviour (a form of fixation).	Supervisor has temper tantrums when he or she doesn't get his or her way with employees.
Identification	Defending against threatening feelings or low self-esteem by relating to someone or an idea.	Young employee is very demanding in work group, emulating the company's manager.
Sublimation	Channeling threatening or socially undesirable thoughts and impulses into acceptable outlets (related to displacement).	The minister transforms aggression into preaching or the artist sublimates sexual frustrations in artistic expressions of women.

Table 21.2 Ego-defence mechanisms and examples *(continued)*

system (Byang-Hall 1980; Keeney 1979). Positive development will resolve conflicts at certain stages and provide the individual with the necessary maturity and coping skills to handle transitions and problems in life. Psychological disorders may result from fixations or unresolved conflicts, defective attachment behaviours and the development of ineffective coping and life skills. In this regard disorders of childhood and adolescence, as well as personality disorders and career development problems, may illustrate this perspective most vividly.

21.3.2.4 The cognitive perspective
According to this perspective psychological disorders are coupled to negative and self-defeating thinking and perceptions, such as emphasising own mistakes and only considering shortcomings, feeling helpless or having fears for failure and success. In many psychological disorders, for example schizophrenia and delusions, disturbances in thinking are also characteristic. In stress-related diseases the nega- tive perception or appraisal of stress is often regarded as the factor causing the disease and not the stressors themselves.

21.3.2.5 The behaviouristic approach
This approach puts the accent on mental health as a function of learning and reinforcement processes in the environment, attributing behaviour disorders to faulty learning and habits or "abnormal" responses. The person with psychological disorders is viewed as having been given reinforcement of his or her condition, or having had poor learning models and inappropriate influences in the physical and social environments. In this manner problems such as alcoholism, gender identity confusion, aggression, crime, personality and conduct disorders are often seen as patterns of behaviour ingrained in personality due to the complexity of society. Influences may also relate to certain health attitudes and behaviours, such as sleep, eating habits,

substance use, health habits and unhealthy life styles and behaviours. Physical environmental influences such as technological factors (for example pollution and safety aspects) and events such as natural disasters, may also be dominant influences.

21.3.2.6 The socio-cultural perspective

The socio-cultural perspective, related to the developmental and behaviouristic approaches, seeks the causes of psychological disorders in the failures of society, such as poor morality, bad socioeconomic conditions and oppressive political systems, and in factors such as ethnicity, prejudice, discrimination and types of health policies and practices. Some have asserted that mental illness is a myth, created by professionals and society to control people. Obviously we have much evidence of the real existence of psychological disorders! Socio-cultural influences, which emanate from culture, relate to family dynamics and the immediate environment, for instance values and habits, socioeconomic factors, urbanisation, religion, ethnic groupings, marital state and educational and social status. Psychological disorders must also be interpreted in terms of the meaning of symptoms in the specific cultural context.

21.3.2.7 The humanistic, phenomenological and existential approaches

These approaches emphasise mental health as a function of people's subjective experiences, how they perceive their world, "exist" and find meaning in life roles. Psychological disorders may arise if people experience incongruency between themselves and their experiences in the world, and cannot find meaning in life or in what they do. Maladjustment may also manifest if people's needs for self-actualisation are frustrated. According to systems and person-centred approaches, psycho-

logical disorders and their symptoms are modes of human communication and interaction about the problems experienced by people in their relationships. The symptoms in question enable people to gain a better understanding of their world and help them to handle others, as such symptoms are only interactional manoeuvres that help people to cope in their environment and to create their own reality and meaning. Therefore some may say that the schizophrenic patient's symptoms are only a response to how they relate to and understand their world.

21.3.2.8 Stress models

Stress models study the physical, cognitive, emotional and behavioural effects of certain stressors or stimuli on people and how people cope with stress demands. Stress refers to the physical and psychological reactions of people to the adjustment or coping demands of stressors. Both positive (eustress) and negative stress (distress) demand adjustive or coping reactions from people. Stress may be *acute*, resulting from the sudden onset of events, such as death in the family and work loss, or *chronic*, of long duration caused by, for instance, a frustrating intimate relationship, an unsatisfactory work situation or daily hassles.

Stressors

Stressors, the causes or stimuli for stress reactions, can arise from a single biological, psychological, social-cultural or external factor, or combinations of these, and they can be classified in various ways.

Kanner et al. (1981) proposed that stress may arise from, in their term, our daily *hassles and uplifts*. Out of 117 possible sources, they identified the 10 most frequently reported hassles and uplifts, and these are shown in table 21.3. These authors consider daily stressors to be a better explanation for psychological and physical wellbeing than life events that only occur from time to time.

Most frequent hassles	Most frequent uplifts
1. Concerns about weight	1. Relating well with spouse or lover
2. Health of a family member	2. Relating well with friends
3. Rising price of common goods	3. Completing a task
4. Home maintenance	4. Feeling healthy
5. Too many things to do	5. Getting enough sleep
6. Misplacing or losing things	6. Eating out
7. Outside home maintenance	7. Meeting own responsibilities
8. Property bonds/investments/taxes	8. Visiting, phoning or writing to someone
9. Crime	9. Spending time with family
10. Physical appearance	10. Home (inside) pleasing to you

Table 21.3 Most frequent hassles and uplifts in life

Obviously, hassles and uplifts differ between people and situations. In this regard, you may find questionnaires on hassles and uplifts for specific situations, such as work or university life, but you may also be able to compile your own list related to your personal or work situation.

Hassles or uplifts?

A very influential approach in assessing and studying the effects of stressors is according to *life changes* or events occurring in people's lives, as indicated in table 21.4. According to Holmes and Rahe (1967), life event changes which are extremely intense, positive or negative, are life stressors which can cause acute or chronic stress reactions. Any change disturbs homeostasis, or balance, in people's lives, thus creating uncertainty and demanding adjustive behaviours.

Holmes and his colleagues (Holmes & Rahe 1967) developed the Social Readjustment Rating Scale (SRRS), an objective method for measuring the cumulative stress an individual has been exposed to over a period of time. This scale measures life stress in terms of "life change units" (LCU) involving stressful events and is shown in table 21.4. For persons who had been

Table 21.4 The Social Readjustment Rating Scale

Event	Impact	Event	Impact
Death of spouse	100	Change in responsibilities at work	29
Divorce	73	Son or daughter leaving home	29
Marital separation	65	Trouble with in-laws	29
Jail term	63	Outstanding personal achievement	28
Death of close family member	63		
Personal injury or illness	53	Wife begins or stops work	26
Marriage	50	Begin or end school	26
Fired at work	47	Change in living conditions	25
Marital reconciliation	45	Revision of personal habits	24
Retirement	45	Trouble with boss	23
Change in health of family member	44	Change in work hours or conditions	20
Pregnancy	40	Change in residence	20
Sex difficulties	39	Change in schools	20
Gain of new family member	39	Change in recreation	19
Business readjustment	39	Change in church activities	19
Change in financial state	38	Change in social activities	18
Death of close friend	37	Small mortgage or loan	17
Change to different line of work	36	Change in sleeping habits	16
Change in number of arguments with spouse	35	Change in number of family get-togethers	15
High mortgage	31	Change in eating habits	15
Foreclosure of mortgage or loan	30	Vacation	13
		Christmas	12
		Minor violations of the law	11

Source: Adapted from Holmes and Rahe (1967)

exposed in recent months to stressful events that added up to an LCU-score of 300 or more, these investigators found the risk of developing a major illness within the next two years to be very high, approximating 80%.

According to Carson et al. (1996), adjustive demands from various internal and external stressors can be classified into three sources: frustrations, conflicts and pressure.

- *Frustration* arises when people are prevented in some way or other from attaining their objectives. According to the frustration-aggression hypothesis, frustration will mostly cause aggression and anger. The type of reaction will be determined by the importance of the objectives, the strength of the needs to be satisfied and the duration of frustration. More important, however, is the individual's *tolerance* of frustration. Tolerance of frustration is, apart from biological determination, largely a function of the individual's learning behaviour, that is, how people have learned to have needs satisfied.
- *Conflict* arises when people want to satisfy several needs at the same time. The problems arise because they then experience choice anxiety, especially if they have strong negative and positive feelings about an objective (approach-avoidance conflict), have to choose between equally attractive objectives (double-approach conflict) or have to choose between equally unattractive objectives (double-avoidance conflict).
- *Pressures* or expectations to perform or conform in various life roles, such as in studying, marriage, sport and a career, may create too much stress for some people to handle. In this regard "burnout" refers to people being emotionally exhausted due to the physical, cognitive, psychological and behavioural overload of relationships or work. Eating disorders in children, such as anorexia and bulimia, are sometimes related to social expectations in families and societies.

Moderating factors in the stress process

Irrespective of whether stress is negative (distress) or positive (eustress), it influences, or is perceived by people to influence, available internal and external adjustment or coping resources. If the individual does not adjust or cope successfully, a process of *biological and psychological decompensation* occurs. This means that in conditions of intense (acute) stress, or protracted (chronic) stress, the individual is not able to react in an integrated way to stressors, with resultant physical illnesses, stress and psychological disorders.

The effects of stressors, and the individual's response to them, will depend on the following factors, which determine the *intensity of stress:*

- The importance, duration, number of demands and the proximity of stressors, for instance the death of a close member of the family, the day before an examination, job loss, cut in salary, threats of downsizing in organisations, and labour unrest.
- People's stress appraisal, or perception of daily hassles and life events as being irrelevant, relevant or threatening, is important for the person's reactions or coping behaviours.
- People's stress tolerance and internal and external sources of adjustment will also determine how they react to stressors. In this connection, it is particularly important to note how people perceive the stress factors (positive or negative), their stress-coping techniques and other coping resources in the environment.

With regard to coping resources, *internal personality dispositions,* for example personal hardiness, optimism, internal locus of control, stamina, self-transcendency, self-efficacy, sense of coherence, learned resourcefulness and self-actualisation, serve as moderating, protection or resiliency factors in the relationship between stress, health and illness. These dispositions have in common whether people perceive themselves as being in or out of control, being meaningfully involved and whether events and change are seen positively as a challenge or as a threat.

In the *disease-prone personality typology*, it seems as if certain underlying personality factors may be related to or predispose to particular illnesses (Friedman & DiMatteo 1989; Friedman & Booth-Kewley 1987; Eysenck 1991). Various meta-analyses were conducted in this regard and asthma, headaches, stomach ulcers, cardiac diseases and arthritis in particular were studied. Although findings indicate that such a personality repertoire still lacks construct validity, research shows that emotions, especially depression, as well as anger, proneness to hostility and negativity, are linked to diseases. The type A personality, in contrast to the type B, is prone to heart attacks as a result of specific emotional, psychological and social behaviour patterns that also find expression in a certain orientation toward time, activity and job involvement (Friedman & Rosenman 1974; Eysenck 1991). A great deal of research supports the relationship between type A behaviour and coronary or cardiovascular diseases, but there are still conflicting findings, and other researchers are unsure of this relationship (Friedman & DiMatteo 1989; Friedman 1990; Cooper & Payne 1994).

Personality may also relate to health and disease in other ways, such as unhealthy life attitudes and health habits; biological idiosyncracies in people, for example metabolic disturbances or an overactive nervous system which leads to chronic anxiety or to the development of a specific behaviour such as introversion or extrover-

sion; patterns of behaviour as learned or acquired through each person's development history in certain physical and psychosocial environments.

Related to personality dispositions are people's *coping mechanisms,* which are ways of managing stress, adjusting to situations, changing situations, controlling emotional distress and controlling or appraising the meaning of stressors (Mallach 1996).

In this regard a distinction is sometimes made between adaptive or adjustment reactions and defence mechanisms.

Adaptive reactions refer to forms of behaviour which individuals use to handle daily problems and crises, to satisfy possible physical and psychological needs and to alleviate anxiety or stress. Examples are attachment behaviours, listening to music that has a calming effect, eating and drinking, crying and scolding, talking things over, praying and meditating, working or taking on more work, playing games and exercising, travelling and taking holidays, expressing feelings, shopping and buying habits, physical habits such as grooming one's hair and nails, withdrawing or isolating oneself from people or situations, purposive relaxation techniques such as progressive relaxation of the body and cognitive adaptive reactions such as reassessment of problems and imaging of problems.

These reactions can also be classified as problem- or emotion-focused coping reactions. In *problem-focused* coping reactions towards internal and external stressors, people will define their problems, generate and weigh up alternatives and plan in order to eventually select the best solution. Obviously this type of reaction demands rational thinking and self-control. *Emotion-focused* coping is based on efforts to prevent negative emotions and to stay in control. This can be achieved by either behaviour or cognitive strategies. Behaviour strategies can be reactions such as exercise, substance use, avoidance, wishful thinking, self-blame, working or seeking emotional or social support from friends, family and colleagues. Cognitive strategies are directed at appraising stressful situations in order to solve problems instead of negative confrontational reactions, denial, daydreaming and other avoidant reactions (Mallach 1996).

Defence mechanisms are more comprehensive patterns of behaviour, usually unplanned (automatic) and intrapsychic or unconscious, which the individual uses to relieve or avoid emotional conflicts and resultant anxiety and stress. This view of defence mechanisms as intrapsychic and unconscious patterns of behaviour to protect the ego or self against threatening impulses (id impulses such as sexual and aggressive needs) is primarily the Freudian or psychoanalytic view (see table 21.2). These defence mechanisms can be a normal way of coping with, and sometimes of handling, conflicts and tensions in daily life. However, defence mechanisms bring about maladjustment when they become the dominant causes for ineffective ways of coping with problems, conflicts and tensions.

Defensive reactions can be mainly direct or conscious or more unobtrusive. With *direct defence reactions* the individual mostly behaves in a conscious and overtly perceptible way to adapt to conflict, frustration, anxiety and stress, such as showing aggression or withdrawing (fight or flight reactions) from a situation. Aggression can be associated with physical attacks, overt rage and violence but can occur in a more inhibited and less demonstrable way. In such cases, aggression is somewhat more internalised and can manifest in displaced forms, such as verbal sarcasm, refusal to work, slips of the tongue, strikes and hunger strikes. Withdrawal can be observable, but in certain cases people may experience apathy, despair and hopelessness to the extent

that they stop trying or living, as may be illustrated in suicides, prisoners of war and the long-term unemployed.

Another form of direct adaptive reaction, but which manifests in a displaced form, is the so-called *symptom-directed* ways of behaviour. Examples are the use of liquor and drugs as well as more acceptable narcotics such as sedatives and medicine.

Social support has been much researched as an important moderator in the stress-illness-health relationship. Social support refers to the quality of physical, social and psychological or emotional support people receive from their family, intimate relationships, friends, social groups and work groups (Cooper & Payne 1994; Ganster & Victor 1988). External support factors are the type of physical environments and socio-cultural factors which people experience. In this respect family and work environments, separately and interactively, have primary inhibiting or facilitating characteristics which are crucial to physical and psychological health (Frone, Russel & Cooper 1992).

21.4 Classification and description of psychological disorders

Classifications of psychopathology syndromes, according to the DSM, are widely accepted all over the world, including South Africa (APA 1994). Although criticisms are levelled against the validity and reliability of the DSM classification and its ways of describing and classifying disorders, it provides a very useful and functional technique for scientific research, the academic and practising psychologist and communicating coherently about psychological disorders.

In this introductory discussion of some psychological disorders, we concentrate on some of the main characteristics, as we think these are more relevant in occupational behaviours. Due to the seriousness of these syndromes, people diagnosed with such disorders are usually not able to work, or if they are, work behaviours can be seriously impaired (Massel et al. 1990). However, many employees may manifest some of these symptoms, in which case the symptoms will also influence occupational behaviours as considered on axes IV and V of the DSM. Employee competencies entail physical, cognitive, emotional and social behaviours which are also the domains influenced by psychological disorders.

According to the American Psychiatric Association's DSM (1994), Nevid et al. (1996) and Halgin & Whitbourne, (1997), we classify psychological disorders in major diagnostic categories as follows:

- stress, psychological factors, adjustment reactions and psychophysiological disorders
- anxiety disorders
- dissociative and somatoform disorders
- affective or mood disorders and suicide
- personality disorders
- schizophrenia and other psychotic disorders
- substance abuse and dependence
- gender-identity disorder, paraphilias and sexual disorders
- cognitive disorders and disorders of age
- psychological disorders in childhood and adolescence
- violence and abuse

21.4.1 Stress, psychological factors, adjustment reactions and psychophysiological disorders

People's reactions to stressors such as daily hassles, changes due to life events, frustration, conflicts of personality, pressures on life style and socio-cultural and external influences, can be depicted in more than one manner. In general it is agreed that negative stress has many physical, physiological, cognitive, emotional and beha-

vioural effects. There is also general agreement on the mutual cause and effect relationship between body and mind, or physical, biological and psychological factors (Carson et al. 1996; Schafer 1987; Auerbach & Gramling 1998).

An important way in which stress affects people's health is by attacking the body's *immune system*. Biological influences include physical stressors such as temperature extremes and food and sleep deprivation, and psychological stressors such as anger, negativity, divorce and unemployment. Too much stress decreases the ability of the endocrine and nervous systems and other immune systems to effectively combat negative influences such as bacteria, injuries and pollution. In this way many physical illnesses have been positively related to stress, for example stomach ulcers, anorexia nervosa, migraine and tension headaches, cancer, skin diseases, obesity, asthma, hypertension and coronary heart diseases (Auerbach & Grambling 1998). Most of these are also examples of psychophysiological disorders, that is, the interaction between psychological stress and physical diseases.

In a sense all human behaviours in people's daily lives are adaptive reactions, even the unconscious defence mechanisms, to fulfil various social and other life roles and to handle possible problems. In fact the "failures to adjust" in many cases may become psychological disorders, just as bodily ills in some cases are the result of the physiological immune system's being unable to cope. The single main goal or function of all positive and negative human adjustment reactions is to maintain or acquire *homeostasis*, or a condition of equilibrium, in both biological or psychological behaviour. In this regard the moderating effect of personality dispositions, coping strategies and defence mechanisms in the relationship between stress, illness and health has already been pointed out.

The *general adaptation syndrome* proposed by Hans Selye explains how an
individual reacts physically and psychologically to acute and chronic stress, in the
short term or over even longer periods of
time. It describes how the human body
reacts by means of the nervous system and
endocrine functions when it experiences
stress from internal or external influences
(Carson et al. 1996; Nevid et al. 1996).

In the *alarm-and-mobilisation* phase the
individual prepares to counteract stress and
its effects. The functions of the central and
autonomous nervous system are especially
important in this phase. At the psychological level the individual will begin to display
emotional reactions, experience more
stress and be more sensitive. Adaptive
behaviour may also follow, for instance
fight, flight or withdrawal. The psychological reactions may not be too serious, for
instance anxiety or physical reactions such
as increased tension and stomach cramps.

The second phase, *resistance,* is characterised by alarm and mobilisation, but the
rate of adaptive reactions increases as the
endocrine system comes into operation.
For instance, the cortex may facilitate the
secretion of adrenaline, or hormones may
be released into the blood to stimulate
blood circulation. At this stage the individual actually experiences the alleviation of
stress at the psychological level through
effective defensive, or genuine problem-
solving, behaviour. On the other hand, the
individual's adaptive behaviour may be less
successful; there may be more serious
physical and psychological problems and
his or her adaptive behaviour may not
progress if he or she clings to unsuccessful
methods of solving problems.

In the third phase of *exhaustion and
disintegration* the sustained stress exceeds
the individual's capacity for physical and
psychological adaptation. Serious physical
and psychological symptoms or conditions
may follow, for instance metabolic changes,
physical diseases and psychosomatic condi-

tions, such as cardiac or stomach diseases
and paralysis. At the psychological level
there may be symptoms which indicate the
serious decompensation caused by stress.
These symptoms include extreme anxiety,
phobia, breaking with reality, delusions and
hallucinations, thought and speech disorders, in other words, symptoms associated
with psychoses, which can even lead to
death.

There are other stress models that
explain stress in general or in a specific
context, such as in the work context. An
interesting model is the *conservation of
resources* model by Hobfoll (1989), who
describes stress as a response to threat of
loss, an actual loss or inability to gain or
regain resources. When threatened by
stressors, people manage stress by minimising loss and maximising gain of
resources. Resources include any personal
attribute (for example self-esteem) or
physical resources from the environment
(such as friends and employment) which are
valued by the person.

21.4.1.1 Adjustment disorders
Adjustment disorders relate to stress reactions to adverse life events, as depicted in
table 21.4 by Holmes and Rahe (1967).
Reactions such as depression, anxiety,
behavioural or conduct disorders, emotional outbursts, loss of work capacity and
withdrawal, can follow acute (severely
traumatic stress) or chronic (protracted)
stress. Examples of life events that can
lead to adjustment disorders are unemployment, divorce or separation, enforced
relocations and loss, such as the death of
a loved one. Obviously, people's psychological resiliency and other coping resources
will also determine how stressful life events
are handled. Although these types of stress
reactions are associated with intense emotions and often destructive behaviours, and
often have progressive phases of reaction
(such as shock, rage, denial, withdrawal and
acceptance), recovery is usually complete

as soon as the stressor has faded or the individual has learned to adapt. According to Carson et al. (1996), post-traumatic stress disorder (PTSD), caused by catastrophic events and traumas such as rape, being held hostage and military combat experiences, is also an adjustment disorder, on the grounds that PTSD is related to specific acute life events, and is usually cured once the event and related memories fade. The DSM actually classifies PTSD as an anxiety disorder, especially if the anxieties associated with the trauma remain as a chronic condition.

21.4.1.2 Psychophysiological disorders

Psychophysiological disorders (previously conceptualised as psychosomatic disorders) refer to the manifestation of physical symptoms as a *result of psychological stress and negative emotions*. There is sufficient evidence to prove that negative stress and emotions are harmful to physical health, while positive emotions create an increased ability to counteract physical illnesses. In this regard Scheier and Carver found that optimism, as opposed to pessimism, is positively related to good health, and subsequent research also relates optimism to various positive health outcomes (Nevid et al 1997). As already indicated, other factors, including personality dispositions, life style and health behaviours, social support and ways of coping with stress, may moderate the effects of the stress-illness-health relationship. Psychophysiological types of diseases are important causes of death and disability and loss of productive work performance. In the United States of America more than 1,5 million deaths are caused by coronary heart diseases annually. It has been calculated that more than 18 million Americans are affected by migraine and headaches and AIDS is becoming the primary killer disease in many countries,

especially in African countries (Lindegger & Wood 1995). It is important to consider the many survivors of these diseases, with their accompanying disability and other forms of physical and psychological suffering.

Stomach ulcers are caused by excessive secretion of acids and digestive juices that damage the stomach or intestinal linings. Although diets and other organic conditions can cause stomach ulcers, they are ascribed particularly to emotions such as worry, anger and anxiety. In addition, physical symptoms are usually followed by further emotional reactions.

Headaches, which may manifest in many illnesses, include migraine and muscle-tension headaches. Migraine, caused by deficient blood flow to the brain, may have correlates in personality dispositions, life habits, neurological causes and stress. A migraine, due to its duration from hours to days, will influence physical, cognitive and emotional behaviours. Muscle tension headaches are caused by muscle contractions and characterised by intense or dull headaches.

Cardiovascular diseases, of which coronary heart disease (CHD) is a major form, is most frequently related to negative stress conditions and is mostly caused by deficient blood flow, due to the process of arteriosclerosis, which is the gradual thickening of the walls of blood vessels and which leads to many heart attacks (myocardial infarction) (Nevid et al. 1996).

Cardiovascular disease is one of the leading causes of death in many countries, including South Africa. Some of the risk factors identified in cardiovascular disease are: age older than 40, being male, having a family history of CHD, a low socio-economic status leading to unhealthy life habits, obesity, hypertension (high blood pressure), high cholesterol levels, heavy and unhealthy drinking and eating habits, high levels of anxiety and emotions such as anger and hostility, little exercise and environmental stressors such as high-strain jobs. The psychological treatment of CHD relates to alleviating the person's stress due to the overemphasis on, or high incidence of, these factors.

The type A behaviour pattern describes people with a high risk of coronary heart disease because of their stressful life styles, characterised by impatience, strict time schedules, competitiveness, being highly driven, hostile nature and overinvolvement with work. We must, however, emphasise that not all achievers are necessarily type A and that not all type A persons are necessarily prone to coronaries. Many factors may mediate stress; for instance, the type A person may be very resilient and able to stay healthy, even amid adverse or very stressful situations. In this regard Kobasa et al. (1982) found that hardy executives resisted illness despite many stressors; such hardy executives had high levels of all three elements of the hardiness personality type, that is, commitment, challenge and control.

AIDS, or acquired immunodeficiency syndrome, is a deadly, incurable viral disease, primarily transmitted by unsafe sex (also forced sexual acts and rape), that is, vaginal, anal and oral-genital contact. Infected mothers can pass it on to babies during pregnancy and by breast feeding. It has also been caused through using contaminated blood in blood transfusions, by accidental transfer of blood, for example to health workers assisting in operations and with injuries, and through needle sharing by substance abusers. AIDS decreases or destroys the human immune system; victims easily contract diseases and are helpless to fight them, while serious psychological anxieties, negative emotions and depression accompany the illnesses. It is sad that one of the main reasons for unsafe sex might be the "maladaptive" perception by many people that "safe sex" is an unaccepted norm among their reference groups!

Other forms of physical diseases related to psychological factors are asthma, obesity (eating disorders) and certain sleep disorders.

21.4.2 Anxiety disorders

Anxiety disorders (previously referred to as neurosis) could be said to be less serious psychological disorders when compared to psychoses. The main characteristics are consciously experiencing *undefined anxiety* and panic, and unsuccessful and misplaced attempts to control the anxiety, which often only exacerbates it and leads to unresolved problems. In contrast to personality disorders, people with anxiety disorders do not see their problem as part of themselves (egodystonic) and therefore most willingly seek help.

Anxiety has many manifestations: physical features include trembling, heavy perspiration, dizziness, dryness of mouth, upset stomach; anxious social behaviours; cognitive symptoms such as worrying, feelings of losing control, threat, repeated negative thoughts and lack of concentration. Anxiety may vary from acute feelings of panic to more chronic (continuous) anxiety, while the intensity of the anxiety can also vary. Secondary symptoms include tension, depression, anguish, insomnia, irritation, stomach ulcers and cardiovascular problems.

The main types of anxiety disorders are generalised anxiety, obsessive-compulsive, post-traumatic stress, panic and phobic:

- *Generalised anxiety disorders* (GAD) are chronic or reasonably protracted conditions characterised by repeated episodes of intense, undefined or free-floating anxiety. Sufferers are in a constant state of tension, worry, discomfort, have sensitive interpersonal relations, feel ineffective and depressed and often manifest physical symptoms such as nervous movements, bodily pains, diarrhoea, nightmares, insomnia and cardiovascular and respiratory problems. In extreme cases this condition is associated with anxiety attacks, also referred to as panic disorders, in which some of the above symptoms are dramatically manifested.

- *Obsessive-compulsive disorders* are characterised by obsessive thoughts or compulsive actions and rituals. Such thoughts, ideas, feelings or actions are usually irrational, undesirable and unpleasant for individuals but they are unable to control them. Examples of *obsessive ideas or recurrent thoughts* are those about hygiene that result in a preoccupation with neatness and chronic hand-washing, guilt feelings, urges to kill and sexual fantasies. *Compulsive actions* or behaviours include rituals (such as prayers), hand-washing, touching objects and avoidance of objects (such as stepladders). All these rituals are attempts to control anxiety.
- *Post-traumatic stress disorder* (PTSD) occurs during, immediately after, or some time after, an intense, traumatically acute (intense) or chronic (long duration) stressor. A distinction is made in post-traumatic stress disorder between *acute* (begin during or within six months of the stressor), *chronic* (lasts longer than six months) and *delayed* reactions (begin at least six months after the stressor).

In general post-traumatic stress disorders are characterised by repeated experiences of anxiety about the initial stressor, a lack of responsiveness to the environment (apathy) and a variety of symptoms such as fright reactions, irritation, fatigue, insomnia, intolerance (for example of noise), nightmares, loss of concentration, memory impairment, depression, heightened aggression and withdrawal. Examples of experiences that can or have evoked post-traumatic stress reactions are catastrophes (such as collisions, floods, earthquakes, fires, explosions, armed robberies and rape). The First and Second World Wars

and events such as the dropping of atomic bombs on Hiroshima and Nagasaki, the mass deaths of Jews in Nazi concentration camps, prisoners of war, loss of limbs, wars such as those in Vietnam and in various places in Africa, and the situation in Israel, drew renewed attention to the intense negative effects of traumatic stressors. Concepts such as "shell shock", "operational fatigue", "war neuroses", "combat exhaustion" and more recently "burnout", are used to refer to post-traumatic stress disorders. Treatment requires intense medical, psychiatric and psychological intervention and the emphasis recently is on early identification and treatment of potential post-traumatic reactions. Much of these endeavours are to desensitise persons to such intense fears and pain.

- *Panic disorder* is characterised by repeated and unexpected panic attacks and anxiety. Such attacks are not related to a specific threatening event or object. Panic attacks can last some minutes, or even a few hours. They are accompanied by sensations of danger and demonstrated by observable physical symptoms such as heart pounding, increased respiration, trembling, choking sensations, chest pains, dizziness and nausea, fear of going crazy and dying and difficulties in breathing. Panic attacks are also characterised by the feeling of not being in control and are very unpleasant experiences that may even result in suicide. Panic disorder may occur as part of other psychopathological conditions and occurs more in women than men.
- *Phobic disorder* differs from other anxiety disorders in that phobic fear is related to a particular object, idea, person or event, even if such objects do not pose any danger. The fear is intense and out of proportion to the actual stimulus value. Although phobias can be generalised, they are often linked to some or other object, for

instance fear of heights (acrophobia), fear of enclosed spaces (claustrophobia), fear of pain (algophobia), fear of animals (zoophobia), fear of being alone (monophobia), fear of fire (pyrophobia), fear of blood and injections, as well as social phobias, which refer to a fear of being judged negatively by others.

Fear of heights

21.4.3 Personality disorders

Personality disorders are sometimes referred to as character or social disorders. In contrast to anxiety and mood disorders (where anxiety, conflict and ineffective defences against anxiety are characteristic) and psychoses (where there is a total disintegration and almost primitive mode of adjustment), personality disorders are characterised by rigid and poorly acquired patterns of behaviour or conduct, unsatisfactory interpersonal relationships and ineffective occupational performance, often with few signs of anxiety and conflict about such inefficiencies. Personality disorders are often observable during childhood and adolescence and will continue

into adulthood, especially in the workplace, where they can be acted out.

In contrast to anxiety and mood disorders, where afflicted persons are worried about their condition and seek help, people with personality disorders often experience their deviance as an integral part of themselves (egosyntonic), and will often only accept help if forced to do so by persons affected by their self-defeating and often destructive behaviour patterns. It seems as if most categories of personality disorders are predominantly in males (Weiten 1995).

There are many difficulties still in the reliable and valid classification of personality disorders (Nevid et al. 1996). According to the DSM, personality disorders comprise of the following three groups and their subtypes:

Personality disorders characterised by *odd or eccentric* behaviour:
• The *paranoid personality* is very egotistical and manifests feelings of hypersensitivity, is very sensitive to criticism, suspicious and jealous. Emotions are superficial and poor interpersonal relationships will be evident. In contrast to paranoic schizophrenia and delusional psychosis, delusions and hallucinations are absent.
• The *schizoid personality* is characterised by an inability to form and maintain close relationships with other persons.
• The *schizotypical personality* is not schizophrenic, but in emotions, thinking, communication and perception shows behaviour that resembles schizophrenic behaviours, though not in frequency and intensity.

Personality disorders characterised by *dramatic, emotional or erratic* behaviour:
• The *narcissistic personality* describes individuals with excessive concern about their own importance and undue demands for attention and admiration. Although they try to appear very self-

assured, they are actually naïve and insecure, and often unable to have binding relationships.

- The *antisocial personality or psychopath* manifests a lack of judgement, transgresses rules and regulations, is often aggressive, manipulates others to his or her own advantage, shows few signs of responsibility, remorse or guilt and has poor interpersonal relationships. Such people often clash with the law, but learn little from being punished and are often habitual criminals. Criminal behaviour, however, is not caused only by antisocial personality types. Antisocial personality disorder may be prevalent throughout life, may already show in childhood conduct disorders and manifests more in men, but increasingly among women.
- The *histrionic personality* shows overdramatic (hysteric) behaviours, seeks attention, is egocentric and tends to be very emotional.
- The *borderline personality* has mixed symptoms, including an unstable emotional life, impulsiveness, poor self-image with regard to various aspects of self-identity, and maintains disturbed relationships.

Personality disorders characterised by *anxious or fearful* behaviour:
- The *obsessive-compulsive personality* manifests excessive and sometimes irrational concern with neatness, detail, rules and regulations, and is preoccupied with own activities and cannot express emotions.
- The *avoidant personality* is characterised by a fear of rejection and social withdrawal, and will not easily form binding social relationships.
- The *dependent personality* displays behaviour indicating a lack of confidence, submission to other persons and inefficiency in being responsible, making decisions and taking initiatives.

Personality greatly influences behaviour at work. As personality disorders often manifest in work settings, they can be severely detrimental to interpersonal and group relationships and work processes. In addition these styles of behaviour can lead to poor decision-making, poor work attitudes and motivation, slow rate of work, increased production losses because of dismissals, absenteeism and accidents. Neff (1977) identified five types of dysfunctional work personality styles or reactions, which strongly resemble the DSM classification of personality disorders: poor motivation and a negative concept of work and work role; a frequent response of fear and anxiety at work; a regular response of open hostility and aggression at work; mainly dependent and immature work behaviours; and reactions that are socially naïve.

21.4.4 Substance abuse and dependence

These disorders are classified as substance use and substance induced disorders. Many drugs and chemicals are *psychoactive*, that is, they cause disturbances in psychological functioning (thinking, behaviours and emotions). Perhaps the most important issue is that substance abuse may then cause physiological and psychological addiction or dependence, as in the case of the alcoholic and alcoholism, where the abuse of, and dependence on, alcohol severely impairs functioning in most life roles. Examples of psychoactive and addictive substances are alcohol, nicotine from smoking, heroin, morphine, cocaine, caffeine, LSD and marijuana, while many forms of sedatives and other medicines have addictive potential if misused.

Substance use disorders involve maladaptive use or behaviours with regard to psychoactive substances and include substance abuse and substance dependence. *Substance induced disorders* refer to types of disorders or symptoms, for instance anxiety, hallucinations, amnesia and depression, which can be caused by the use or abuse of psychoactive substances.

Substance dependence implies physiological dependence, when the person's body changes physiologically and develops a tolerance for increased substance use; if not used, withdrawal symptoms may develop. Substance dependence also implies psychological dependence, a compulsive, uncontrollable and recurrent use of a drug due to dependence needs. Substance dependence will always be the result of substance use, however it develops into compulsive behaviours to obtain and use certain substances.

Dependence and abuse

The effects of psychoactive substances are often observed in various levels of intoxication or drunkenness or being "on a high". This is characterised by impaired movements and judgement, slurred speech, concentration problems and confusion, and in some cases may lead to death or suicide.

The consequences of substance addictions are seen in a great variety of physical ailments, decreased sensory and motor abilities, poor emotional control, poor social judgement and interpersonal relationships, and decreases in motivation, intellectual ability and work performance. The effects of alcohol and drugs in the work situation may include poverty, absen-

teeism, illness, slow reaction times and coordination, uncontrollability, moodiness, inaccuracy, accidents, untrainability, no progress in the job, dependence, insecurity, indecision, aggression and rigid work styles, all of which may result in a loss of production and resources for employer and employee. The problems of these persons at work are aggravated by the fact that they frequently also experience problems outside of work, for instance clashes with the law and financial and marital problems. In cases such as chronic alcoholism, serious disorders, even psychotic conditions and brain damage, may develop, and these can eventually lead to death.

Even the withdrawal symptoms can be life-threatening. In milder forms the symptoms include nausea, vomiting, poor appetite, sleep disorders and general disorientation.

A big societal blunder is the failure to recognise that alcohol and nicotine are deadlier drugs than many classified drugs, yet alcohol use and tobacco smoking is socially acceptable. Tobacco sales are in countries' vested interests and form a legitimate part of national income. Alcohol and tobacco are *legalised drugs,* sold and used in every sphere of life among young and old, even in hospitals and other healthcare institutions.

There are many biological, social and psychological reasons why people may develop substance dependency. Whatever the underlying reasons, substance dependence usually has a sequence of stages (Carson et al. 1996). Weiss and Mirin (in Nevid et al. 1997) suggest the following stages:

- During the *experimentation stage* substances are used occasionally, users feel euphoric and elated, but still in control.
- The *routine use stage* is characterised by recurrent use, compulsive behaviours for obtaining substances emerge, and people start to minimise previously impor-

tant life interests, such as work and family. Addicted persons at this stage will deny their dependence and use and try to conceal the ill-effects of the dependence.

- The *dependence stage* involves loss of control over the substance use, but often also a near total loss of all life interests; all that matters is a compulsive need to experience relief and to avoid possible withdrawal effects.

Various forms of *psychoses* associated with alcoholism and now classified as cognitive or brain disorders include pathological intoxication, delirium tremens, acute hallucinatory condition and Korsakoff's syndrome.

Other forms of psychological dependence, called impulse-control disorders, are obesity (eating disorders), pathological gambling and pyromania (pathological urge to plan and set fires).

21.4.5 Dissociative and somatoform disorders

Dissociative disorders manifest when the afflicted person experiences loss of memory and conscious life, which result in identity loss or diffusion as a whole person.

"Soma" means body and somatic disorders refer to patterns of behaviour in which the individual complains of physical symptoms, such as difficulty in breathing, or paralysis in a body part, without there being any proof of an actual organic cause. This is in contrast to psychophysiological or psychosomatic disorders, in which real physical diseases such as asthma and ulcers may have been caused by psychological factors. Persons with somatoform disorders are overly concerned with their physical health and these types of symptoms should also be distinguished from malingering (faking of illness). Somatoform disorders may be the result of efforts to cope with anxiety.

21.4.5.1 Dissociative disorders

Dissociative amnesia involves loss of memory for shorter or longer periods. Unlike amnesia with an organic basis, dissociative amnesia is the result of severe traumatic events (such as a war trauma) or intense psychological conflict. People suffering from it forget their own identity, yet retain other intellectual functions, such as reading, writing and speaking. Various forms of dissociative amnesia have been identified, including localised, selective, generalised, continuous and systematised (Nevid et al 1997).

In *dissociative fugue*, memory loss is associated with a "flight reaction" to a new environment where a new life is begun; sufferers are unable to recall personal information, even their own identities. Fugue conditions may be the result of severe trauma, but some individuals may also try to fake dissociative fugue, for instance to escape responsibility.

The *dissociative identity* disorder (multiple personality) is characterised by the assuming of several totally different and independent personalities, each with diverse emotional, thought, physical and behavioural processes. The individual can change personalities time and again. Each personality represents a particular type, for instance a serious personality as opposed to an impulsive one.

Depersonalisation disorder is related to multiple personality. People totally lose their perception of themselves, believe that they are someone else, believe that their body has changed and even claim that they have moved outside the body, for instance in a visit to another planet. Somnambulism (sleepwalking) and trance-like states may be experienced.

21.4.5.2 Somatoform disorders

The best-known example of a somatic disorder is *hypochondria*. Hypochondriacs complain of numerous physical diseases and they fear diseases. They firmly believe in their symptoms, even if medical doctors assure them they are not ill. Complaints involve the whole body and hypochondriacs are keen students and diagnosticians of their own illnesses. In addition to coping with anxiety, hypochondriacs probably achieve secondary gains from their complaints, in that people pay them more attention and do not expect as much from them.

Conversion disorders (previously referred to as hysteria) involve a pattern of behaviour that indicates an apparent physical dysfunction, or loss of control over physical functions, without any underlying organic pathology. Symptoms of hysteria involve: *sensory functions,* including loss of sensation, excessive sensitivity, loss of pain sensitivity and hyper-reactive sensations; *motor functions* such as paralysis, muscular tremors, blindness, deafness and dumbness (mutism); *internal symptoms,* for example headaches, a lump in the throat, choking, coughing, difficulty in breathing and nausea. Symptoms of diseases such as malaria and tuberculosis have even been encountered.

Other examples of somatic diseases are the *somatising* disorders, more common in women, which start early in life and are characterised by complaints of, and treatments for, many physical pains and illnesses over long periods of time, which may result in an inability to perform social and work roles. In the so-called *factitious* disorders people deliberately fabricate and lie about diseases. These are, however, not fabricated for ulterior motives, for instance to dodge work in order to enjoy a longer weekend. Such persons cannot be said to malinger or fake illness.

21.4.6 Mood disorders and suicide

Mood disorders, also called affective psychosis, are characterised mainly by disorders of emotions and moods, which disturb physical, social, thought and perceptual functioning. The moods and emotions of sufferers fluctuate between extreme excitement (manic states) and the deepest depression. Unlike schizophrenia, extreme distortion of cognitive processes does not occur. It is rather distinguished by lack of concentration and negative thinking, although hallucinations sometimes occur. Affective psychosis can vary from *unipolar,* that is, experiencing either depression or excitement (manic states) to the *bipolar* form, that is, experiencing alternating emotional extremes of manic states and depression during the same period.

Depressive disorders may be reactive due to certain external events, such as various forms of trauma. In this regard postpartum depression refers to depression of mothers after the birth of children. Endogenous depressive disorders cannot be coupled to external events, and may be related to biologically and genetically-based causes.

Mood disorders are characterised by four types. Major depressive disorder and dysthymic disorder are *unipolar; bipolar* depression manifests as manic-depressive (or the bi-polar mood disorder) and cyclothymic disorder.

- *Major depressive disorder* is characterised by persistent and recurrent episodes of sadness and depression, without any occurrence or history of manic or elated mood states. People may lose interest in all or most activities and pleasures that were enjoyed previously. In addition to very negative emotions, such persons will become socially withdrawn, unmotivated, slow in thinking, ineffective in decision-making and experience a slowing down of motor behaviours, as well as develop a very negative self-image and feelings of self-blame and guilt. Physical energy will be low, and sleeping and eating problems, accompanied by loss of weight, will occur. Major depression may go hand in hand with other problems such as anxiety and substance abuse.

Major depressive episodes may last for months or years, but can be resolved sooner with treatment. Major depressive disorders will often recur in people.

- *Dysthymic depressive disorder* is a mild but persistent form of depression and may last for longer periods of time.
- *Manic-depressive psychosis* or *bipolar affective disorder* is characterised by alternating manic episodes (excitement and activity) and depression. These diverse emotions often fluctuate, and in other cases the person can be either depressive or manic for long periods, sometimes interspersed with "normal" periods. In general manic-depressive disorder is of shorter duration than major depressive disorder and may also be resolved more abruptly, but some persons experience recurrent episodes. The depressive episode may manifest all the characteristics as described for the major depressive disorder. The manic episodes may be characterised by heightened, even uncontrollable, feelings of energy, optimism and euphoria, to the point where intense demands are made on other people in social interactions and sufferers may even become physically destructive. Such people may also experience delusions and hallucinations and show poor judgement in social interactions, decisions and daily activities.

Mood changes

- *Cyclothymic depressive disorder* is characterised by a chronic or continuous mood disturbance with numerous fluctuations between manic and depressive episodes.

21.4.7 Violence and abuse

Violence and abuse are treated as disorders because of the serious negative effects on victims, individuals, groups and societies. Some psychopathological disorders such as personality disorders, mood disorders and schizophrenia may include aggressive patterns. However, these are mostly part of the syndrome and are seldom consciously executed to harm other people or their belongings. In many instances violent behaviours in other disorders are facilitated by the use or misuse of substances.

Violent behaviour and abuse in society and families, such as spouse and child abuse, rape, child sexual abuse and sexual harassment (often a problem in work situations), are worrying and self-defeating phenomena all over the world. In some societies, such as South Africa's, an aggressive culture goes hand in hand with very high levels of criminality, such as rape, armed robbery and murder. This, together with ethnic conflicts, is a self-destructive psychological health problem of the nation that needs to be addressed through research on causes and proactive and reactive remedies.

Spouse or partner abuse, aggressive physical and psychological acts that cause physical injury (even death) and emotional pain, are often part of broader family or intimate relationship problems and interactional patterns. Although women are more abused, reciprocal abuse often occurs and abuse against men is an increasing phenomenon. In many cases partner abuse coincides with poor socioeconomic conditions, but it happens in all levels of society. Partner abuse is often caused by a combination of factors, including personal feelings of inadequacy and substance abuse, and can be triggered by quarrels and personal differences which make the abuser or the parties involved lose control. In addition to the many forms of pain inflicted on the victims and abusers, their children and families, as well as their societies, are also affected.

Child abuse comprises physical aggression, sexual abuse as well as abuse in the forms of neglect and emotional cruelty. In most instances child abuse happens in the intimate and extended family circle, but is also committed by family friends and acquaintances. Child abusers are often repeating their own experiences, having been abused in one or more forms themselves. The consequences of child abuse for the victims are usually long lasting and some people never outlive or overcome some of these effects. Some of these effects are emotional, such as anxiety and fear, depression and low self-esteem; social and interpersonal, in that later attachment behaviours may be unsuccessful or carry a legacy of possible abuse against their own children; and physical, as injuries and even death can result.

Forcible rape involves the use of violence, force or threats in order to have sexual intercourse. *Statutory rape*, with or without the consent of the victim, is sexual intercourse with a child or someone who is unable to defend, or give informed consent, such as a mentally retarded person. It often also involves violence and force or coercion.

Rape may have its origins in many factors: crime, sexual disorders and dysfunctions, distorted sexual identity and feelings about sexual behaviour, distorted male and female attitudes, stereotypes and values and poor socioeconomic factors. As is the case with abuse victims, the consequences of rape are usually traumatic and often long lasting.

Sexual harassment means people are subjected to unwelcome sexual talk and remarks, sexual proposals, gestures, touching and demands for sexual favours, often as a condition for doing business, providing employment, receiving promotion and being retained in a position. Sexual harassment occurs not only in formal work places, but also between professional persons and clients, in places of recreation and sports training.

Sexual harassment is an important work issue and many companies have strict policies on it, while legal action because of sexual harassment is often taken.

21.4.8 Schizophrenia and delusional psychoses

Schizophrenia, paranoia and affective or mood psychoses are referred to as *functional* psychoses, to distinguish them from conditions with organic causes. Psychosis is the gravest degree of psychological disorder and comprises a severe degree of psychological disorganisation. Serious intellectual distortion, emotional disorders, disorientation (of time, place and identity), behavioural disorders (such as language disorders, motor disorders and meaningless activities) as well as perceptual disorders (delusions and hallucinations), are manifested.

A *delusion* is an idea or belief which is in no way related to truth or reality, for instance a paranoid patient believing that he is a certain famous king (delusion of grandeur) or that people want to kill or persecute him (delusion of persecution).

A *hallucination* is an inaccurate observation without the existence of a corresponding stimulus, for instance the person hears voices and noises, sees faces and smells things.

21.4.8.1 Schizophrenia

Schizophrenia refers to a complex clinical condition that can develop in various ways and that has various causes. In general, it is characterised by the following primary behaviours:

- poor everyday functioning in comparison with previous levels of functioning
- disorders of language and communication
- disorders of thinking (delusions)
- disorders of perception (hallucinations)
- emotional disequilibrium and inappropriate emotions
- identity disorientation
- disordered and poor motivation
- unrealistic relationships with others and the world
- disorders of motor behaviour
- disorder of attention

Schizophrenia is classified in four types, as follows:
- *Paranoid schizophrenia* is characterised by absurd and illogical delusions as well as delusions of persecution or grandeur. Because of disordered intellectual processes and poor judgement patients' behaviour can become dangerous to themselves and others.
- *Catatonic schizophrenia* has as its main characteristic a motor behaviour disorder that may involve extreme withdrawal and stupor (periods of total inactivity), or extreme forms of excitement and activity during which the person can also be dangerous.
- *Hebephrenic schizophrenia or disorganised schizophrenia* manifests severe disintegration of the personality, for instance total emotional blunting or inappropriate emotions, infantile and sometimes vulgar and bizarre reactions, as well as incoherent speech and thinking.
- *Simple schizophrenia*, which often manifests at a young age (roughly adolescence), is characterised by diminishing interest in life, decreasing motivation, emotional blunting and social withdrawal. Symptoms such as moodiness, irritation, hypochondria and personal untidiness are also encountered.

Delusions and hallucinations are not common – one finds rather a pattern of inappropriate and inadequate behaviour. If such people function outside institutions it mostly happens under the protection of members of the family. Antisocial and sexual offences also occur.

With regard to the progression of schizophrenia, *process schizophrenia* refers to schizophrenic conditions which develop over a long period, whereas *reactive schizophrenia* may have a sudden onset, for instance due to death in the family, financial losses or pregnancy. *Type I schizophrenia* refers to so-called positive symptoms, for instance a sudden onset, only slight disassociation, delusions and hallucinations, and good reaction to medication and treatment. In contrast *type II schizophrenia* refers to negative symptoms such as a long period of development, social withdrawal, emotional bluntness, intellectual deterioration and poor response to treatment (Wilson et al. 1996: Halgin & Whitbourne 1997).

21.4.8.2 Paranoia or delusional disorder

Although similar to paranoid schizophrenia in some ways, delusional disorder is a separate disorder. Paranoia as a purely clinical condition is rare. When it is encountered, paranoia is characterised by a protracted, complex, logical and well-arranged delusional system, particularly of grandeur and persecution. The sufferer, who appears to think and react emotionally in appropriate ways, firmly believes in certain matters and may even convince others of these beliefs and so acquire followers. In this regard, there are the cases of leaders of religious sects, whose movements ended in chaos, and even in mass murders of members and others, after periods of isolation and bizarre behaviour.

21.4.9 Other disorders

Other disorders are cognitive and old age disorders, childhood disorders, gender identity disorders, paraphilias and sexual dysfunctions (Wilson et al. 1996):

- *Cognitive disorders* differ from anxiety disorders and psychoses, in that the symptoms predominantly involve a marked change in thinking and memory from previous levels, and the causes are not psychologically based. Cognitive disorders are the result of some or other impairment of brain functioning, such as injuries, intoxication and congenital brain dysfunctions and the influence of age deterioration. The type of psychological or behavioural disorder will be determined particularly by the nature and locality of the brain lesions. The main cognitive disorders are delirium, amnesic disorders and dementia. Some of these cognitive and age-related disorders may be the result of previous problems or life styles. In some cases the early onset of decreased competencies due to age may be a problem for many employees in later career stages. Mentally retarded people are part of some work environments, as are physically and emotionally retarded employees.
- The diverse *disorders of childhood and adolescence* are also determined by the stage of development and socioeconomic dispositions. These difficulties involve behavioural disorders in children associated with emotional and behavioural problems and exclude disorders with an organic basis. Some of the best-known disorders are autism, enuresis, encopresis, speech disorders, hyperactivity and certain conduct problems. For employers the unsuccessful resolution of childhood problems may manifest in problematic adult occupational behaviours such as work personality disorders, relationship problems, negative work attitudes and deficient competencies with regard to learning and communication.
- *Paraphilia* involves deriving sexual pleasure from non-human objects, pain, humiliation and children or other non-consenting people. Examples are exhibitionism, fetishism, paedophilia, sexual sadism and sexual masochism.
- *Sexual dysfunction* involves dysfunctions in sexual intercourse and arousal or response in and between males and females. Examples include sexual desire disorders, sexual arousal disorders, orgasm disorders and sexual pain disorders.

The essence of gender-identity and sexually-related psychological problems and disorders in society and in the workplace, is misguided attitudes to acceptance of male and female differences, power and control, which may result in sexual abuse and misconduct such as sexual harassment.

21.5 CONCLUSION

Although psychological wellbeing is the ideal for self-development and the norm for group and societal functioning, psychological disorders in some form are part of our daily lives. We need only assess the costs involved in preventing, treating and managing psychological maladjustment of individuals and society. In general and in the work context, stress management has become an integral part of people's experiences and discussions and even provides occupations for some people. The media prosper from coverage, often sensational, of the ills of individuals and society on subjects such as substance abuse, suicide, murder, rape, theft, aggressive driving, gangsterism, physical and sexual abuse, pornography, divorce and ethnic violence. A sad and "unclassified maladjustment" is found in the people and groups who prosper from some of these individual and societal problems. Worldwide, many of these problems are also evidence of human interaction and how people are governed, allowed or forced to "be and exist" in the world.

However, in many instances, people do not have a choice in their disorders and problems and often cannot help their maladaptive behaviours. Contrary to physical illness, there are still many misconceptions and stigmas attached to psychological health problems. Professional psychologists and other health workers and groups still have the task of educating people on the realities of psychological problems. At the same time the prevention and treatment of psychological health problems should have a higher priority than is the case in many societies.

The efficiency of individuals in various domains, and therefore of groups and nations, is equally dependent on physical and psychological wellbeing.

Self-evaluating questions

1. Explain the difference between psychological adjustment and psychological disorders by using definitions, criteria and models.

2. Analyse your own behaviour and your environments and describe those factors which you think may cause psychological disorders.

3. Use examples of cases or circumstances you know of to describe why such people are still quite healthy despite many stressors.

4. From your own or someone else's circumstances, make a list of daily hassles and changes in life events which may have caused stress and adjustment problems.

5. From your work or other environments give examples of symptoms or behaviours which you think can be classified as belonging to some of the psychological disorders.

6. List the main characteristics of the various psychological disorders in order to distinguish them from one another.

7. Draw information from the daily media (TV, radio, newspapers, etc.) over a period of one to two weeks and describe or list all cases which you think are examples of maladjustment in individuals, groups and society.

Work adjustment 22

Ziel Bergh

CONTENTS

Learning outcomes

After studying this chapter you should be able to:

- describe the relationship between work, organisations and occupational psychological health
- indicate, by using examples, how changing work scenarios can influence occupational health
- indicate how certain criteria can be used to explain possible work adjustment problems
- describe the causal factors which can influence work adjustment
- use certain characteristics to identify and describe various forms of work dysfunctions
- describe work adjustment problems due to anxieties and personality dysfunctions
- use examples to illustrate overcommitment and undercommitment in work
- explain work stress problems
- recognise career development problems in employee behaviours
- explain managerial and organisational psychological adjustment
- describe work and non-work role conflicts
- identify strategies in the management of occupational health

Key concepts

psychological adjustment, occupational psychological health, work, system, self-system, organisation criteria, changes, discontinuity, person-environment fit, work stress, causes, work dysfunction, undercommitment, overcommitment, inter-role conflicts, personality dysfunctions, anxiety and depression, organisational health, AIDS, unemployment, accidents, physical disability, health promotion

22.1 INTRODUCTION

Work adjustment refers to occupational wellbeing, including physical health, but especially the *psychological or emotional adjustment* of employees facilitating or impairing work performance. The field of study includes causes of occupational maladjustment, symptoms and characteristics of the various forms of occupational maladjustment and health promotion of troubled, and other, employees. The study of work adjustment involves how people are shaped by work and working. Although

work adjustment is arguably an applied field of clinical, abnormal, industrial and organisational and career psychology, many other disciplines contribute to understanding the psychological wellbeing of the employee in the work context.

Related concepts are industrial or occupational clinical psychology, workplace counselling, work dysfunctions, occupational mental health, industrial mental health, psychopathology of work, ineffective work behaviour and even "work stress", while concepts such as work alienation and burnout are sometimes equated with occupational maladjustment. In contrast to psychopathology, and strangely so, if the importance of work activities and the time spent on them is considered, few, if any, integrated sources on occupational psychological health or the psychopathology of work exist. Good contributions have been made by McClean (1970); Miner (1966); Baker et al. (1969); Kornhauser (1965); Noland (1973); Neff (1977); Campbell and Cellini (1981); Roseman (1982); Kanungo (1982); Manuso (1983); Davis and Lofquist (1984); Olivier (1989); Bruce (1990); Visser

(1990); Lowman (1993); Auerbach and Gramling (1998) Cooper and Payne (1994); Carroll (1997); Sharf (1997); Bennett and Murphy (1996); O'Brien (1986); Dejoy and Wilson (1995). Many of these sources also focus on health promotion and workplace counselling or address more specific aspects such as stress and stress management, unemployment and career counselling.

22.2 WORK AND PSYCHOLOGICAL WELLBEING

Despite many opinions about work and changes in the work scenario (Howard 1995), work in some form is here to stay and will always be a dominant influence in people's lives. As Ruskin (in Levitan & Johnson 1982:41) puts it, "Distribute the earth as you will, the principle question remains inexorable, who is to dig it? Which of us, in brief word, is to do the hard and dirty work for the rest?" The effects of "bad" work and working for many people is summarised by Carroll (1997) when indicating that one in five working people, or about 20% of any workforce, may suffer from some form of psychological illness, with approximately 90 million lost working days annually, and 30-40% of all work-related illnesses related to emotional disorders and stress. This also reminds us that people give work its social and emotional nature, which underlie the mechanical or rational aspects of work. Therefore, most work-related problems will have emotional causes and symptoms in areas such as feelings, cognition, behaviour and psycho-physical systems.

Work is generally defined as *purposeful and meaningful activities* which people execute in order to meet and fulfil various physical and psychosocial needs. People's self-concept and psychological adjustment is most related to the quality of their work involvement and productive accomplishments. Many findings verify the idea that work contributes to general life satisfaction and human adjustment (Argyle 1992, 1995; O'Brien 1986). Vaillant and Vaillant (1982), in a longitudinal study, found that working from an early stage in life (teenage) is a significant predictor of later career and life satisfaction and good life adjustment.

Many researchers have reported on the effects of work stress on health (Cooper & Payne 1994; Morris 1989; Ross & Altmaier 1994) as well as the interactional effects of work and non-work spheres, such as family life (Eckenrode & Gore 1990; Long & Kahn 1993; Zedeck 1992).

Everyday evidence of the importance of work in people's lives is the prominence given to it in personal introductions, enquiries into people's identities, who people are, what they do for a living and how they do it. The prominence given to the development of concepts and attitudes about work and career development, in theories and practices in psychological disciplines and education, further emphasises how important work is to human wellbeing. Work as a *central life interest* in human existence is also illustrated by issues of job creation, unemployment, automatisation, affirmative action and related aspects, all of which have become emotional matters where power groups, such as governments, employers and unions, are continually involved in negotiations and even disruptive actions to obtain the best advantages where people interact with work. Work has psychological, social, ethical, moral, religious, economical and political meanings, while also providing for many human needs.

Most people work for some of the following advantages or reasons; these are also the factors most severely impacted on during work loss, unemployment (O'Brien 1986; Warr 1987) or when work performance is seriously impaired. If health workers understand the dynamics of work in life, these influences can also be used as healing factors when counselling troubled employees:

- work contributes to finances, so that people can provide for basic physical needs such as housing, security, clothing, food and health care
- to work is to obtain, exercise and develop a variety of knowledge, cognitive and social skills
- social and friendship needs are met in the workplace because people interact with others and work in groups
- work provides for intellectual stimulation and physical activity, as people are faced with challenging tasks and problem-solving situations
- entering and practising work is to express adulthood and fulfil a productive role in society
- the individual obtains self-esteem by providing for his or her loved ones or family through work
- work is a source of personal identity, as it allocates a certain role and place (status) to individuals within society and the family
- some people, at least, may work for the sheer pleasure of working, or for the achievements which work can generate

- work is a way of managing time productively for many people, thereby fighting boredom, filling the long hours of living and giving meaning to being in the world
- work represents a progression or continuation for families in terms of jobs, wealth and status, in that each family tries to ensure a better quality of life for the next generation
- work provides a sense of creativity and mastery in the sense that people use their knowledge and skills to control events and the environment
- work is a religious and moral obligation for those in societies in which the virtues of work are taught, maintained and rewarded. An example is the so-called Protestant Work Ethic (PWE) or Work Ethic, in which work is seen as good and necessary for prosperity, and laziness and idleness are viewed as sinful and wrong. Most theories and research on work values point out that positive work values and strong work ethics contribute toward work motivation, involvement, commitment and good work adjustment (Furnham 1984; 1990)

Two faces of work

The central role of work in human life is best illustrated in non-work situations, such as unemployment, economic recessions and even retirement, when people are deprived of the advantages or values of work, resulting in many physical and psychosocial problems for the individual, families and often whole societies (O'Brien 1986). The sudden cessation of productive work and earning power caused by compulsory retirement often also leads to physical and emotional deterioration and even premature death. Gillet (in Isaacson 1985:26) gives a striking description of the consequences of unemployment:

> The personal loss of these changes is deep and tragic. A rise in alcoholism, mental illness, heart disease, suicide, child abuse or wife beating follows a rise in unemployment rates. When a plant closed in Chicago, eight out of 2 000 workers committed suicide. In Wayne County, Michigan, where unemployment approaches 20%, a community hotline recently reported that calls about spouse abuse jumped over 300% in a year. Mental health clinics report huge rises in case loads within the past two years.

If the situation in South Africa in the past decade is considered, and one takes note of unemployment, tragic family conflicts, suicide, crime, alcohol abuse, political unrest, criminality, bankruptcies and liquidation of businesses, then the above-mentioned picture is also applicable.

Although work generally has positive effects on people, and unemployment negative effects, "bad" employment may have negative influences on people's psychological health. O'Toole (Healy 1982:15) states, "Effective performance of challenging, socially meaningful work enhances self-esteem and overall mental health, while labouring in an unchallenging, undesirable job reduces self-esteem and correlates with many physical and mental disorders." Camus (Levitan & Johnson 1982:63) expresses this unavoidable interaction between man and work as follows, "Without work all life goes rotten. But when work is soulless, life stifles and dies."

22.3 CHANGES IN WORK AND PSYCHOLOGICAL ADJUSTMENT

Humans alone do not shape the quality of work and working, as work is embedded in a *social-political and economical work context*. The demands for technological changes (products, information and services) on the one hand, and the supply of workers from ever-changing environments and societies on the other hand, are key factors in shaping the needs for, and types of, work. The political and economic rules and agendas of governments and organisations, however, are dominant forces determining how technology is utilised and how people interact with it in the workplace. In contrast to the congenial efforts of human resources practices to create a best fit between employees and employer, economic, societal, governmental, union and employer demands often negatively influence the relationships between employer and employees by adversarial legal approaches to employment, in which the law and other norms are used to define or enforce the work relationships.

It is obvious that the changing nature of work and work organisations (Howard 1995; Cascio 1995), including in South Africa (Mastratonis & Nel 1995; Sadie & Marais 1994), will put ever-increasing responsibilities and demands on employees' personal resources and competencies to cope and adjust in their careers and in the workplace.

According to Howard (1995), an important factor in the changing nature of the work scene is *discontinuity* (little stays the same for very long), especially as a result of ever-increasing knowledge demands, caused by new technologies, higher levels of education, more research and development and the globalisation of individual and organisational competitiveness. The way management uses knowledgeable employees in interaction with technologies will keep organisations competitive, rather than education and technology alone.

Some of these changes in organisations, work, employees and working, and their implications, can be summarised as follows (Howard 1995): in essence these changes comprise adaptive or learning organisations with effective technologies and management styles, demanding added value and responsibilities from employees, updated knowledge, specific skills and multi-skills, but also the abilities to empower and involve employees optimally to perform well, while also continuously learning and adapting to changes.

This scenario is already present in many societies and increasingly in South Africa. As well as presenting many challenges and opportunities, these changes also bring stressors or causes for work maladjustment. These may relate to aspects such as anxieties about change, staying abreast of knowledge and skills, the use of new technologies, fewer job opportunities and conflicts between interest groups. Labour forces may in future be characterised by more *differentiation* in availability of jobs, competencies, opportunities to learn and develop and big differences in income levels. It is possible that in many instances, organisations will employ small numbers of core, highly developed and paid, but possibly overburdened, workers. This could lead to "burnout" in these employees. In contrast, greater numbers will be peripheral, do temporary tasks or only work sporadically, and often from home, "invisible" to the physical employer or organisation. In these latter categories, it is easy to visualise the levels of negative attitudes and perceptions about work and towards employers and the advantaged core workers. These working conditions may well cause

apathy, and anxiety about personal identity and self-image, for not being able to provide sufficiently, not finding work, decreasing levels of competencies, being forced into early retirement and even for the taking of ill-afforded leisure time.

Management of organisations may be characterised by *less centralised control* and the empowerment of employees to be self-efficient and to self-manage, especially through self-management groups.

Obviously, these changes and adjustive demands also require effective human resources management and development in, for instance, job availability, work design, job analysis, the selection of employees and the composition of efficient work teams. For psychological adjustment more non-technical competencies will be necessary, such as learning, responsibility, personal mastery, interpersonal skills, stress management skills, communication, influencing, adaptability, group effectiveness, adaptability and negotiating. This is in contrast to the emphasis on cognitive and task skills only, and means the employee will have to acquire competencies quickly to be suited for tasks in specific situations. In this regard, Coovert (Howard 1995) advocates the strategy of "just-in-time-training", using new learning technologies to enable the employee and work organisations to quickly obtain the competencies needed for tasks in certain times and situations.

In terms of these adjustive demands on employees, we must remember that although changes bring opportunities, people like to experience homeostasis, consistency and predictability in situations. Therefore continuous changes might have severe implications for people's self-concept and feelings of coherence, maturity and integration. In their discussion on the high incidence of work-related stress in the United States of America, Auerbach and Gramling (1998), relate these stress problems to the type of changed work scenario described above. We may also wonder whether the assumptions on personality, self-identity and career development still hold for the demands and characteristics of the changing world of work and all the possible ramifications in other spheres of people's lives. In this respect psychologists in the work context have a task to facilitate people's "survival skills" and psychological health; a sense of coherence, personal control, hardiness, self-efficacy and optimism to feel and be in control of their own career development, even in the midst of work and personal uncertainties. This emphasis is evident in contemporary organisational and personality psychology, in which the importance of personality characteristics, values and motivational tendencies which relate to work performance are emphasised (Howard 1995; Barrick & Mount 1991). If workplaces do not create the opportunities for employees to self-actualise or develop all aspects of their work-related personalities, even those who are naturally self-actualisers, despite being achievers, may become problem employees.

In future more emphasis will have to be on the *interdependence* of all organisational and management functions, that is, management, employees, customers, working processes and technologies. Employees will have to learn to often move beyond their individual orientations and traditional task descriptions, to work in teams, and apply networking, group participation and group management techniques. For adaptive organisational management, a big challenge might be to integrate all the organisational processes and move forward as a whole, with the same objectives and values, despite having more decentralised control processes and more empowered employees. To facilitate employee performance and adjustment, psychologists still need to learn much more about employee behaviours in the midst of changing conditions: work often being less observable, with more team work, more empowered employees,

changed labour or employee compositions and new organisational design and management approaches.

It is clear that the changing nature of work, organisations and working needs a *redefinition of careers* and career development. According to Hall (Howard 1995:330), "the new career is about experience, skill, flexibility and personal development. It does not involve predetermined career paths, routine ticket punching, stability, or security". This demands revised and new roles and responsibilities for employee competencies and in managing own careers; organisational design, management, the development of organisational competencies; human resources practices in the assessment and development of employees to enable them to adapt to continuous changes.

22.4 A MODEL FOR UNDER-STANDING WORK ADJUSTMENT IN THE CONTEXT OF ORGANISA-TIONAL FUNCTIONING

One way to view organisations is from a *systems perspective*, that is, to consider all the possible interactions between persons and groups, their relationships and relatedness to other contexts within and outside the organisation (McCaughan & Palmer 1994; Cummings 1980). Another important systemic principle is *context*, meaning that behaviour must be interpreted in terms of its functions or meanings where, when and how it happens in a certain environment or situation.

The systems-interactional model in figure 22.1 (adapted from Beer in Cummings 1980), and integrating ideas from various approaches on occupational adjustment and counselling, illustrates the various and interactional aspects of occupational psychological health (influences and causes, processes and consequences), as a field of study, but also as a field of human resources development and management.

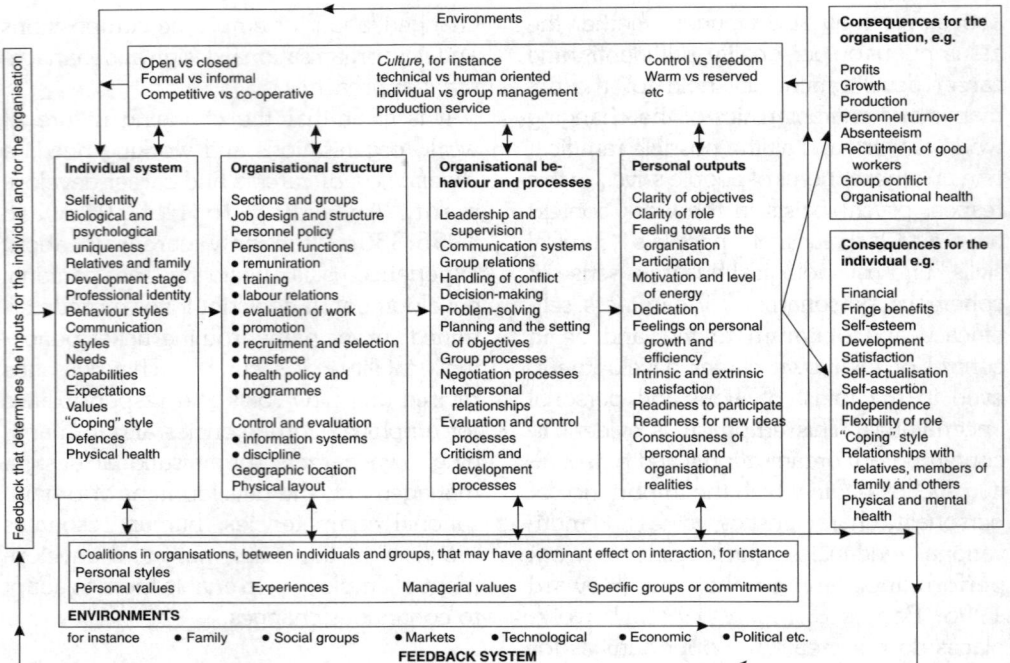

Figure 22.1 A systems-interactional model of occupational mental health
Source: Adapted from Beer (in Cummings 1980).

A premise is that an *organisation*, functioning as a whole or as a unit, is formed to achieve objectives that cannot be achieved by individuals on their own. *Individuals* join an organisation to achieve objectives and to satisfy needs in a work context that would be impossible or difficult to accomplish on their own.

The type of *interaction* between individual and organisation finally contributes to the objectives for organisational and individual success, namely efficiency, effectiveness and "health", the latter including individual physical and psychological health and also organisational health.

The main premise is that individuals, as self-systems in all their domains of behaviour (biological, cognitive, social and psychological), can be best understood by first examining their functioning in the *context* of the wider and hierarchical systems that surround them.

This approach does not endeavour to deal exhaustively with all aspects of organisations. However, because of the interaction, it is impossible to omit certain aspects of organisations from the model. We must bear in mind that the emphasis in the work context is on the individual employee and groups in a specific socio-technical context.

A summarised operational description of the systems-interactional model is discussed below.

The individual as a *self-system* brings a unique frame of reference (individual experiences and characteristics) to the work organisation. The personality of the individual consists of behaviour patterns or relationship styles formed by learning and experiential processes in all his or her hierarchical systems, and this in turn determines his or her behaviour in the relationship with the organisation and fellow employees.

The *organisation* also has specific and characteristic inputs because of its culture and its influential hierarchical systems (environments). Its characteristics, for example structures such as communication, management and decision-making, will determine the type of contact with the individual and also the kind of behaviour and process that can be expected. Through a process of *reciprocal, continuous and circular interaction* determined by specific behaviour and communication styles, structures, rules and transactions, the individual and the organisation define certain types of relationships and a particular climate, for instance being formal or informal, or service or production oriented. It is important to recognise that culture, and especially *organisational culture* or values, has a definite influence on people's health: not only how they think and behave, but also how illness manifests and is treated and managed (Ahia 1991; Prince & Tcheng-Laroche 1987; Varma 1986; Lewis-Fernandez & Kleinman 1994; Carroll 1997; Dejoy & Wilson 1995).

All these inputs lead to certain *outputs* (attitudes, behaviour, feelings, etc.) by the individual, groups and the organisation, which in turn finally result in certain *consequences,* including health, for the individual and the organisation. The consequences reveal the extent to which individual and organisational objectives, needs and expectations have been satisfied. The interaction between individuals, and between individual and organisation, is constantly monitored by means of *feedback or control systems*, which also determine the extent to which the individual accepts or rejects the outputs and consequences. It is important to remember that there are certain *dominant influential factors* in both the individual and the organisation, which stem from their respective behavioural and value systems. These dominant "coalitions" determine the extent to which individuals and organi-

sations are selective in their interactions, observation and acceptance, to gain the maximum benefit from events and situations. As important as the dominant coalitions in organisations are the influences from surrounding *environments* in which organisations exist and function. Often the boundaries, and interaction, between individual, organisation and environment are not clearly defined, because an individual may be a "member" of various systems. We know that in the work context conflicts between family and work roles provide many problems. In many countries, including South Africa, employee and work roles can be determined and facilitated, but also strained, by union interventions and governmental controls. It may be a problem if the boundaries and other characteristics of individual, organisational or environmental systems are so prescriptive or rigid that development inside them becomes strained or restricted, so that growth within and outside the system is either impossible or uncertain. Fortunately organisations can never be absolutely closed, as they are social systems consisting of people, their attributes and interactions. Wherever there are people there can never be "no communication" or "no behaviour".

For purposes of study, diagnosis and interventions, it is necessary to also think in terms of systems, which means that we may have to review former simplistic and linear views and attitudes, or that we may have to conceptualise and apply such ideas differently (Carroll 1997; Keeney 1979). In the diagnosis of, and interventions into, work adjustment problems, management, in its personnel and management functions, has to be aware of what is happening in all aspects of the interaction between employees, organisation and the environments, and what the outcomes of these interactions are. This understanding is crucial in order to make the most efficient intervention at the right place and time. A reported problem may be an idiosyncratic or isolated incident, but could also have wider implications if understood in its specific context or environment. Often a reported problem may only be a "scapegoat", or the "symptom-bearer", for other problems. In this regard, for instance, technological aspects in organisations may be very important, but automatisation may be threatening to many and result in much job alienation and anxiety, among others. We must also remember that, as in the case of culture, the adjustment or maladjustment of the individual and the organisation, in other words the way in which problems are handled, can largely be determined by support or rejection from the environment. For instance, downsizing of organisations, affirmative action, and dismissals are often met with disapproval from other parties.

22.5 CRITERIA FOR ADJUSTMENT AND MALADJUSTMENT IN THE WORK CONTEXT

Most criteria applicable in psychopathology also apply to work maladjustment. However, according to Neff (1977) and Lowman (1993), among others, certain occupational adjustment problems are unique to the "work personality", and the work environment has unique factors contributing to occupational wellbeing.

The human resources practitioner should first establish whether possible psychological disorders (psychopathology) exist according to, for instance, the DSM, then whether these disorders cause work impairment or whether the work dysfunction is caused by the work itself or the work environment (Lowman 1993). Clarkson (1990) describes a model to assess whether the individual employee or the total organisation is dysfunctional or growing. Accurate assessment is important for taking decisions about treatment for the employee and health-promoting interventions in the workplace.

22.5.1 Occupational psychological health defined

Psychological maladjustment at work involves the employee's behaviours, emotions, attitudes and thoughts that impair work performance. Work dysfunctions could include symptoms of, but not necessarily completely diagnosed, psychological disorders or syndromes. Occupational wellbeing may also include group, managerial and organisational phenomena and other work-related problems which cannot be classified as individual psychological or emotional adjustment problems. Neff (1977) and Kutash (Noland 1973), for instance, refer to the separateness of personal and work behaviours, and Kutash asserts that not all people with anxieties and emotional disturbances are problem employees, and not all problem employees are emotionally disturbed. Work-related problems such as absenteeism and accidents may have emotional causes, but are not psychological disorders.

McClean (Noland 1973:25) defines industrial mental health from a very narrow point of view: "in the narrowest sense, it is concerned solely with the psychiatrically ill worker whose symptoms interfere with his effective functioning on the job". In this regard the DSM also considers occupational aspects in diagnosing psychological disorders. This view also reflects the emphasis that still exists on the role of medical science and psychiatry in the diagnosis and treatment of occupational maladjustment. Causality and symptomatic behaviour are attributed purely to the individual, while in many companies the occupational nurse, health worker or human resources practitioner is sometimes also expected to handle employees with emotional problems. Alternatively, only the physical hygiene of employees and work organisations is considered.

In more comprehensive views, McClean (Noland 1973), Kornhauser (1965) and Mickleburg (1986) stress that a worker's psychological health can refer to thoughts, perceptions, feelings, attitudes and behaviours that may affect personal effectiveness and happiness, and impair behaviour.

Neff (1977:80-192, 247) maintains that work adjustment is a process of development in which the individual progressively learns a productive role or acquires a positive work attitude which will eventually characterise the work personality. The attributes of the work personality need not necessarily relate to other areas of personality functioning, such as love, and work maladjustment can also be treated without influencing other areas. According to Neff, the work personality is a semi-autonomous area of the general personality, a set of interrelated motives and coping styles, defensive mechanisms and the like, with which an individual confronts the demands of work. Work psychopathology implies some area of deficiency or defect in the development of the work personality. Neff describes various forms of maladaptive responses in the work context, which in some ways relate to personality disorders. He believes that psychopathological conditions are not by themselves the reason for work maladjustment. In addition to possible emotional problems, people who are unable to work cannot tolerate or accept the demands of work.

Lowman (1993:4) defines work dysfunctions as "psychological conditions in which there is significant impairment in the capacity to work, caused either by characteristics of the person or by an interaction between personal characteristics and working conditions". In his classification of work dysfunctions, he differentiates between various types of emotional problems, which could include aspects of psychopathology, and attitudes and perceptions or involvements with work, as well as problems caused by dysfunctional working conditions.

Occupational adjustment is also explained as work stress, in the sense that too low or too high levels of stress, especially negative stress, generally have detrimental influences on physical and psychological wellbeing, because the demands of distress outstrip the employee's coping resources (Schafer 1987). Keita and Hurrell, as cited in Auerbach and Gramling (1998), describe stress as resulting in "reduced productivity, increased absenteeism due to illness, and decreased sense of personal wellbeing and effectiveness".

If organisations are seen as mirror images or microcosms of their environments, and as composed of all the attributes of their employees and their relationships, it is possible to speak of healthy or unhealthy organisations. Organisations that are ineffective in achieving their business objectives, or experience internal conflicts in their cultural philosophies, values, behaviours and management strategies, can be said to be maladjusted.

22.5.2 Characteristics and specific criteria for occupational adjustment

Criteria applied to psychopathology and psychological adjustment in general are applicable in the work context, but some more specifically work-related standards must also be considered.

From a person-oriented perspective, for instance Rogers's theory, optimal functioning means that the fully functioning, mature and well adjusted employee can allow all experiences into the self-concept. Following from this assumption, Cilliers (1988) describes three areas for optimal functioning in managers:

- In terms of *intrapersonal characteristics*, the employee is physically healthy and fit, uses cognitive abilities and skills as applicable, and is open and sensitive to his or her own, and others', emotions, feelings and needs.
- *Interpersonally*, optimality is characterised by acceptance of the self and of others in a positive and unconditional manner. Relations with others are characterised by respect, warmth, empathy, transparency and honesty.

- In terms of *work characteristics*, the psychologically optimal person is totally involved in his or her work.

All the intrapersonal and interpersonal characteristics mentioned above are therefore preconditions for optimal work performance.

More specifically, optimal work performance requires purposefulness, productivity, responsibility, motivation, leniency, initiative, concentration, creativity and optimal time management. The person who performs work best is focused on the present, is aware of the past without being a victim of his or her history, but is also future-directed. Such a person is cooperative, and shows that he or she is able to transcend opposites (understand differences) and to experience his or her role in the organisation realistically.

Optimally functioning people's mature physical, psychological, cognitive, interpersonal and work attributes leave them with sufficient internal and external resources to manage and cope effectively with occupational stressors.

Kornhauser's (1965) criteria for job satisfaction are:

- observable anxiety and emotional stress
- positive or negative feelings towards the self
- feelings of hostility or confidence in accepting other people
- sociability and friendship as opposed to withdrawal
- contentment with life in general
- good personal morale or self-confidence, in contrast to alienation and despair

Kasl (O'Toole 1974) describes occupational adjustment in four broad categories.

- *functional effectiveness* relates to the employee's ability to perform allotted tasks and to not being absent without good reason

- *general wellbeing* relates to measures of various symptoms such as emotions, stress, self-esteem, job satisfaction and attitudes
- *mastery and efficiency* refer to self-development, self-actualisation, efficient work performance, optimal use of abilities and planned objectives
- *psychiatric symptoms,* as in psychopathology, might indicate an inability to work at all

22.5.3 Models for explaining occupational adjustment

Models or theories explaining psychopathology also have value in explaining work-related psychological health. Many of the personality theories also explain psychological adjustment, which may also relate to occupational behaviours. Most theories try to explain how the structure and contents of work satisfy needs for survival, ego-development and personal growth. In addition to systemic influences (see figure 22.1), theoretical premises in industrial and organisational psychology emphasise the following approaches.

22.5.3.1 Work stress models

Work stress models explain psychological health (adjustment and maladjustment) as a function of the individual's ability to display effective or ineffective adaptive behaviour when internal or external stressors lead to physical or psychological stress, as figure 22.2 illustrates. This stress model can be viewed as a specific model within the systems model in figure 22.1.

Stress is a condition which develops when the demands made on people exceed their adaptive (coping) abilities. Work stress may have its causes in the person, the work situation or external stressors, for instance in employees being overworked or burnt out, underutilised, uncertain of their work responsibilities and decision-making powers, and traumatic work experiences such as work loss. Work

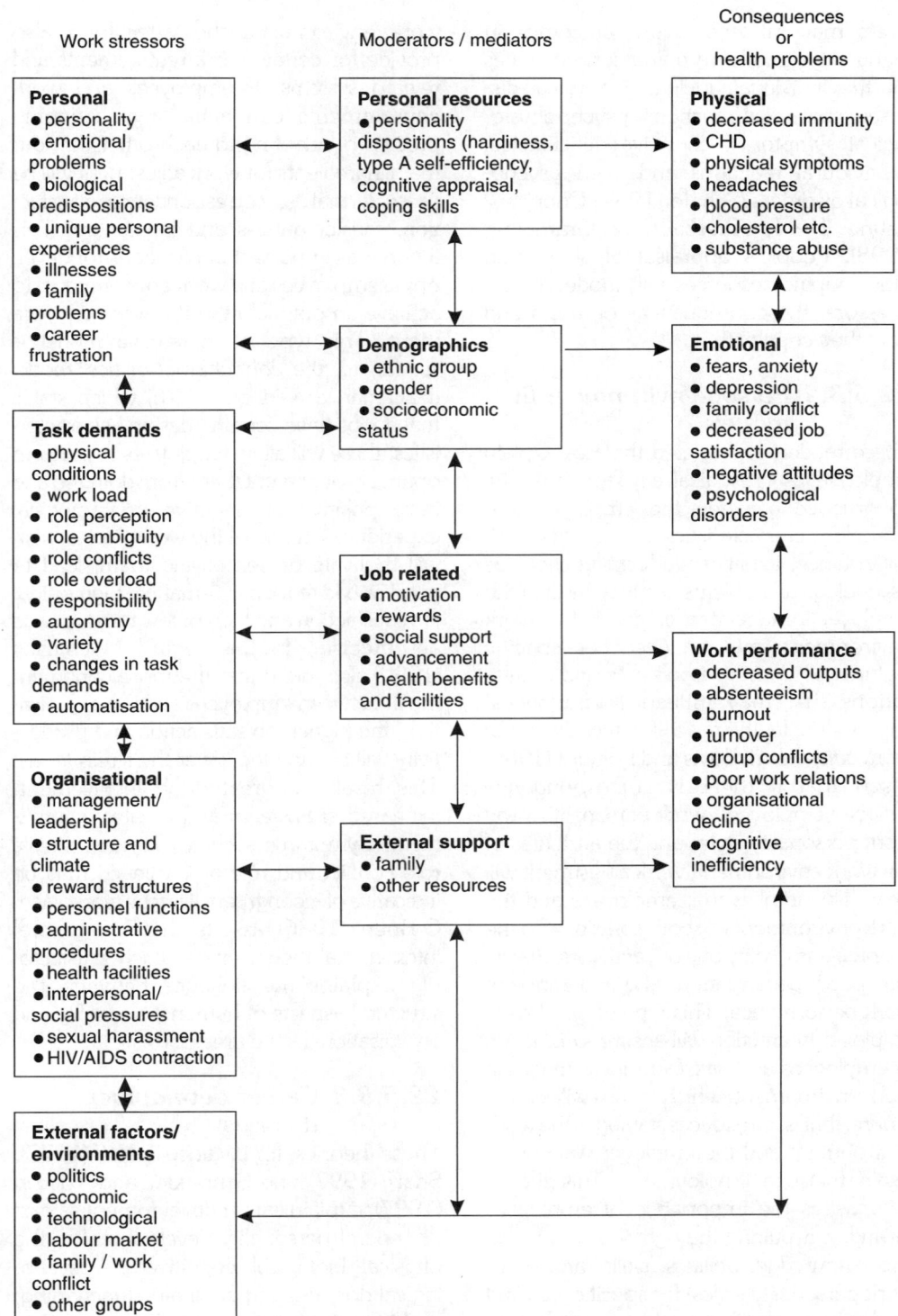

Figure 22.2 Causes, process and consequences of work stress

stress may influence work outcomes in many ways and have many consequences for the individual, including physical diseases, emotional reactions, psychophysiological symptoms, cognitive deficiencies, behavioural reactions and even psychological disorders (Schafer 1987; Cooper & Payne 1994; Auerbach & Grambling 1998). People's appraisal of stress and other coping resources will moderate the stressors, the consequences of stress and how they cope with it.

22.5.3.2 Person-environment fit models

These models and related theories explain employee psychological adjustment as the congruence between the employee and workplace characteristics. Lowman (1993), for instance, explains work dysfunctions as psychological problems due to a misfit of the employee's interaction in his or her work environment, and he describes specific features of work environments and organisations that may influence employees' adjustment. In their well-known *theory of work adjustment*, Davis and Lofquist (1984) assert that if there is *correspondence* between employees' work personalities and work personality styles and the attributes of the work environment, work adjustment will exist. This implies that employees and the work environment will both contribute to the quantity and quality of work activities, that is, the speed, pace, pattern and endurance of work performance. This type of employee-employer interaction will ensure *satisfaction* in employees and *satisfactoriness* from the work environment, which in turn will lead to *tenure*, that is, employees staying in the work environment and the employer wanting to retain them in employment. This theory emphasises the importance of employees having or acquiring the right job competencies (knowledge, abilities, skills, and other work personality styles) for specific jobs and work environments. To achieve work adjustment of employees and the best fit in the

work environment, the latter must also provide for certain work requirements and reward systems. If employees and work environments can achieve an ongoing process of adapting to each other the four main ingredients for work adjustment will be present, that is, correspondence, satisfaction, satisfactoriness and job tenure. This theory has important implications for developing employees and work environments to achieve an optimal fit in the work environment. This type of interactive model is similar to the *job characteristics model* (Hackman & Oldham 1976) which states that if jobs have certain "design" characteristics, these will allow employees to perform optimally or prevent them from doing so and have positive or negative psychological experiences in and of the workplace, which will motivate or demotivate them, lead to good or bad work performance, high or low job satisfaction and high or low turnover and absenteeism. In this regard Muchinsky (1990) also found that the more congruent the fit between employees and the organisation, the higher job satisfaction and productivity will be, and the lower the stress levels. This results in greater job involvement, increased self-esteem and greater commitment. Symptoms such as burnout, stress, role conflict and role ambivalence may be indicative of incongruent fit in the workplace. O'Brien (1986) asserts that no general interactional theory exists which satisfactorily explains the linkages between the structural aspects of human personality and organisational structures.

22.5.3.3 Career development theories

These theories, for instance in Neff (1977), Sharf (1997) and Schreuder and Theron (1997), explain career development as part of general personality development in the physical, biological, cognitive and psychological domains of personality functioning. In this respect, we have earlier referred to Erikson's and Freud's views that critical periods, if not resolved successfully, may result in problematic adult behaviours. Career development involves the progressive acquiring of knowledge, skills, abilities and other attributes (competencies) toward career maturity, in order to obtain and maintain jobs or careers, to progress satisfactorily and finally to retire from them. This means that people must be able to fulfil certain tasks and responsibilities at certain stages in their career development in order to function optimally in work life. If people develop deficiencies in their personal attributes and in interaction with the work environment, work maladjustment in some aspect of occupational behaviour may exist or develop.

22.6 CAUSES (ETIOLOGY) OF OCCUPATIONAL MALADJUSTMENT

Work and working, and the characteristics and principles involved, can be either psychologically "good" or "bad" for the employee. Although unemployment must be detrimental in most cases, for some people it may be preferable, for example for health reasons, to working in a "bad" employment situation. From a broad spectrum of literature on work and human behaviour (including Warr 1987; Argyle 1992; Leatz & Stolar 1993; Lowman 1993; Morris 1989; Cooper & Payne 1994) the majority of complaints about work revolve around the following factors:

- constant supervision, control and constraint
- lack of diversity and variety
- lack of autonomy and decision-making
- unchallenging and boring work
- repetitive tasks
- meaningless work
- isolation in the workplace
- lack of participation and own decision-making
- lack of the necessary support to execute tasks

- unnecessary change (automation, computers, processes) which may lead to deskilling, boredom and unemployment

The things that employees most wish to experience, not necessarily in order of preference, are the following:
- interesting work
- significant work, having impact on others
- adequate help and equipment to do the work
- sufficient information to be able to do the work
- adequate authority to plan and execute work tasks (control and autonomy)
- adequate compensation
- opportunities to develop specific skills and use a variety of skills
- work and physical security
- task identity, to be able to see the results in and of the work (feedback)
- opportunities for interpersonal and social contact
- recognition of personal value and position

Etiology (stressors) in psychopathology, that is, individual biological, psychological, socio-cultural and external factors, and stressful daily hassles and life changes, also apply in occupational health. These factors could relate to the manifestation of possible psychological disorders in the workplace. However, as is obvious from figures 22.1 and 22.2, some additional causal factors of work maladjustment may be very specific to the work environment and not related to personality and psychopathology. These causes may trigger emotional reactions and other forms of work performance impairment. There are, therefore, specific classifications of work-related factors, such as those by Schuler (1982), Miner and Brewer (Dunnette 1990), Neff (1985), Warr (1987), Lowman (1993), Cooper and Payne (1994), Ross and Altmaier (1994). Cited

Extremely stressful	Very stressful	Above average stressful
Pilots, policemen, prison warders, journalism, acting, advertising, mining jobs, building construction, dentistry	Firemen, ambulance workers, broadcasting, musician, film production, personnel workers, social workers, teaching, medical doctor, nursing	Publishing, professional sport, management, marketing and export, public relations, sales and retailing, secretary, printing, psychologist, business endeavours, public transport, stockbroker, barrister

Table 22.1 Stressfulness of certain jobs

in Cooper and Payne (1994), as many as 22 subjective and 26 person-environment variables for work stress were identified by French, and 29 work stressors were found by Fletcher. The influential transactional model of stress of Lazarus and Folkman (1984) also considers most of these causal factors. This approach, and also that illustrated in figure 22.2, emphasises the interaction between the causal factors and the person's cognitive perception or *appraisal* of the stressors as threatening or not. Employees' appraisal of stressors may help to modify the stressors, the affects of the stressors on themselves as well as the ways of reacting to the stressors. Related to this is the finding that the amount of *control or autonomy* an employee experiences in relation to the work demands or the work load also mediates in the relationship between stress and illness. Low levels of control or autonomy and support, coupled to work overload, will cause excessive stress (in Bennett & Murphy 1997).

22.6.1 Factors unique to jobs and people

Various types of jobs have different demand levels on employees. In a classification by Cooper (in Auerbach & Gramling 1998), six experienced stress researchers assessed more than 100 occupations on a 10-point scale for stressfulness, and a summary of these results is shown in table 22.1.

Each type of job, and even the same types of jobs in different circumstances, will have different types of stressful events. In addition, job incumbents in the same job under similar or different circumstances or in different jobs in similar circumstances may experience work stress differently. Individual differences in people, because of biological and psychological attributes, according to the diathesis-stress-model, may predispose people to contract health problems under certain conditions or to react differently. Other individual differences in stress reactions in certain circumstances are related to gender, age and personality traits associated with, for instance, anxiety, locus of control and type A behaviours (Auerbach & Gramling 1998).

22.6.2 Factors in the work situation or task demands

In addition to *factors unique to employees* in terms of their biological and acquired attributes and unique life experiences, the following causal factors are generally viewed as applicable in most work situations.

These relate to employees' perceptions of their roles in the organisation and in relationship to other employees. This especially involves *role conflicts* in various roles or with other employees and the organisation, role overload or underload (too much or too little involvement), role ambiguity (unclear task descriptions) and low levels of responsibility, autonomy, participation and decision-making powers. Role stressors, in perceptions and role execution, may lead to intense feelings of dissatisfaction, frustration and even more serious conditions resulting from stress, such as burnout and psychophysiological illnesses (Auerbach & Gramling 1998).

Role stress may also lead to *work alienation*, or work estrangement, which refers to the worker's emotional and cognitive experiences of aimlessness, hopelessness and work that has lost its positive meaning, because he or she is no longer part of the work process and work results (Kanungo 1982; Kakabadse 1982; Kohn & Schooler 1983).

22.6.3 Organisational and management processes

These are all the formal and informal processes in an organisation which control and manage the activities of employees. They concern management, leadership, administrative processes, reward and development systems, health policies and facilities, social support and communication systems which could facilitate or inhibit the employees' feelings of being important and taken care of. The crucial element in psychological health is probably the extent to which the individual's needs for care, independence, interpersonal relationships and achievement are satisfied. Employees must feel, and experience, that they have a fair chance of achieving and are as equally rewarded as colleagues. High morale and cohesion in the workplace is a powerful positive health factor. Changes in organisational processes and the way these changes are managed can

also be a powerful acute, or chronic, stressor on employee wellbeing.

If the organisation is also viewed as a developing system it is easy to grasp that the *organisational cycles of development* are related to organisational and individual effectiveness and adjustment (Parker & De Cotiis 1983; Krantz 1985; Schuler 1982; Quinn & Cameron 1983). In developing countries such as South Africa, socio-political changes, including those in the workplace, are a primary source of tension for all involved, especially to those suddenly fulfilling new roles in demanding job situations, because of fewer job opportunities for others and in the midst of changed interpersonal and worker relationships.

22.6.4 Social and interpersonal relationships

Work relationships with co-workers, supervisors and clients that have high group cohesion are linked to positive mental health. Relationship stress with, for instance, symptoms of burnout, are highest in the ranks of so-called people-oriented professionals such as psychologists, nurses, hospice workers, teachers and medical doctors (Paradis 1987; Leiter & Maslach 1988). Much research also suggests *social support* at work from colleagues and supervisors to be related to job satisfaction and various indicators of wellbeing. These forms of support include emotional, instrumental (physical support in the workplace), informational and appraisal or feedback support (Cohen 1988; House et al. 1988; Bennett & Murphy 1996).

22.6.5 Physical factors in work and in the work situation

Inadequate physical hygiene factors are often closely equated with work stress. In this respect a discipline such as ergonomics makes a study of the interaction between man and the physical place of work. Concepts such as industrial or occupational hygiene (Schoeman & Shröder 1994), occupational safety and occupational diseases are closely linked to the influence of the physical work environment and in particular to the physical and physiological wellbeing of the worker. The following are some physical factors that could be taken into consideration:

- sustained concentration and physical exhaustion
- work rate that is too fast or too slow
- physical dangers in the workplace
- extreme temperatures
- toxic conditions, pollution and radiation
- poor ventilation
- badly designed workplace and equipment

In addition to the negative influence on physical health, poor physical working conditions often also impact on psychological health, such as negative emotions (for example irritability) and decreased motivation. It is known that individual biological differences may make certain people more or less susceptible to the influence of not only psychological stress, but also physical and chemical work stressors. It is interesting to note that Lowman (1993) views *dysfunctional working conditions* (physical and social) as a work dysfunction in itself, due to the detrimental effect on work motivation, work attitudes and general wellbeing.

22.6.6 External influential factors

This refers to people's dependence on, and interaction with, their environment and other systems, which may directly or indirectly affect employee adjustment behaviour and hence the interaction between themselves and the organisation. For many employees an important non-work stressor is the conflict between *work and family roles*. This is especially evident in dual career couples and single parents, when task and time demands in and between work and family roles may have spillover

effects and provide stress at home and in the work situation. Many writers are of the opinion that a working mother has the most stressful occupation (Auerbach and Gramling 1998).

As discussed previously, many changes in the modern world and work scene, global interactions, the communications media and in the socioeconomic, political and technological spheres have made life uncertain and unpredictable, and this may be too much for some people. Organisations are also affected, through their internal and external environmental systems, for instance the technological, marketing, labour and production demands they constantly have to face.

22.7 OCCUPATIONAL DYSFUNCTIONS

Work dysfunctions are discussed according to a broad spectrum of problems referred to in the literature. The classifications of Lowman (1993) and Campbell and Cellini (1981) are used as central frames of references.

Lowman endeavours to establish a "psychopathology of work", in which he indicates the interaction between psychological or emotional disturbance and work dysfunctions, the latter being an impairment in work performance due to emotional factors in the individual or the interaction between the person and the work environment. Some work dysfunctions in Lowman's classification resemble in some ways psychological disorders according to the DSM classification. However, the DSM classification does not really provide for psychological work dysfunctions; in some of its axes occupational aspects are only vaguely indicated as possible causes or symptoms of psychopathology.

In the first part of his classification Lowman emphasises the necessity for the health worker to determine and assess correctly the relationship between psychopathology and work functioning, and equally important, to assess the influence of work dysfunctions on psychopathology. Such assessment is important to decide on the type of intervention. It is, for instance, unproductive to use career counselling or performance feedback for employees with severe emotional problems such as depression, schizophrenia, paranoia, personality disorders and severe anxiety if these emotional and behavioural problems are not addressed first. Campbell and Cellini (1981) explain possible psychological problems in career development in the various career stages and during work performance in organisations and there are some similarities to Lowman's classification.

22.7.1 Disturbances in the capacity to work

These dysfunctions refer to employees' work motivation, attitudes and *willingness to be involved in work*. The type of work orientation people have can be traced back to the socialisation and reinforcement of work and productive roles, that is, the work ethics, values and attitudes people have acquired in their environments. The capacity to work may also refer to people's career maturity, that is, whether they have acquired the necessary knowledge, skills, abilities and other attributes to fulfil work responsibilities. The capacity to work, however, may also be influenced by the characteristics of jobs and the demands of work environments.

22.7.2 Patterns of undercommitment

All these work behaviours are recognised by *underinvolvement* in the job, in comparison to what could be expected from the employee (Lowman 1993). Some of the causes of work underinvolvement are psychological conflicts in people's developmental experiences in the home, school and even at work, which leave people afraid of rejection and reluctant to perform.

According to Lowman (1993), these conflicts may be misdirected anger at authority, self-esteem problems and fear or reluctance to compete.

Although divergent criteria make it difficult to define *underachievement*, it can be regarded as any behaviour by an individual that does not satisfy job requirements and expected standards in terms of skills and actual potential to perform. Steinmetz (1969) identifies underachievers in terms of resistance to change, moodiness, disorganisation, feelings of being indispensable (contentedness), isolation, inability to communicate, poor sense of responsibility, intolerance, an apologetic attitude, a highly strung nature, unimaginativeness and defensive behaviours.

Temporary *production impediments and procrastination* also refer to inability to perform to standards. In procrastination, employees often postpone the initiation or timeous completion of tasks.

Uninvolved employees may also be *misfits* in terms of occupational and organisational characteristics, which could lead to boredom, dissatisfaction and underachievement.

Undercommitment is often also recognised by fear of success and fear of failure, conditions which could also be interactive. *Fear of success* (FOS) relates to an avoidance and anxiety of being successful or a tendency to diminish achievements. This phenomenon has attracted much research that indicates many possible causes and may manifest differently in terms of factors such as personality profiles, culture, age, gender and occupational groups. In contrast, *fear of failure* (FOF), or hostile press, refers to people feeling threatened and afraid of being rejected if they fail to achieve goals. Such fears may lead to unhealthy work schedules and efforts to impress others instead of working effectively.

Absenteeism could also be a manifestation of undercommitment, especially if this type of behaviour points to anti-organisational behaviour such as dishonesty, laziness and disloyalty. Absence from work could be a main indicator of organisational stress, and it involves great costs, especially with regard to the loss of productivity. *Illness*, especially respiratory problems, stomach disorders, gynaecological problems (menstruation, menopause, spontaneous abortions) and stress conditions such as headaches, insomnia, fatigue, heart problems and endocrinal disorders are responsible for most absences. Other factors that contribute to absence include dissatisfaction with organisational and work factors, for instance insufficient training and supervision, disturbed work relationships, poor work group cohesion and morale and physical job design. Follman (1978) refers to the psychological determinants of absence by describing the following characteristics of persons with an extensive record of absences: uncertainty, stress, self-pity, anxiety, the incidence of compulsive tendencies and phobia, paranoid and schizophrenic qualities, conversion hysteria, alcoholism, broken marriages, behaviour that indicates defence, suspicion, unhappiness, the inability to make friends easily, dissatisfaction, hostility and resistance to change.

According to Miner and Brewer (1990), *personnel turnover* relates to general job dissatisfaction with regard to organisational and industrial variables. The variables include work attitudes towards managerial practices, the quality and nature of working conditions, remuneration, the workers' feelings on whether management is treating them fairly, and work group attitudes. *Emotional conditions* such as anxiety, depression, neuroses, personality problems, alcohol and drug addiction, physical diseases and age can contribute to personnel turnover.

There should be a clear distinction between types of personnel turnover and different forms of absenteeism in order to plan a more effective course of action. *Functional personnel turnover* means that the organisation summarily allows the individual with a negative evaluation to leave. *Dysfunctional turnover* occurs when the organisation allows people to go without trying to retain them, although it would like to. Dalton et al. (1980) point out that these categories, together with voluntary, involuntary, unavoidable and controllable desertion, have to be taken into account to establish the true effect of personnel turnover.

22.7.3 Patterns of overcommitment

In contrast to undercommitment, overcommitment seems to be an intense *overinvolvement* and very strong identification with work, which in many cases results in physical and health problems. A problem with overcommitment is that such behaviours are often rewarded in organisations, which may even reinforce the existing stressful work patterns, resulting in health problems which people will not attend to until it is too late. The reasons for overcommitment are many, such as anxieties as a result of low self-esteem, strong abilities and creative powers, too high aspirations, obsessive-compulsive personality, efforts to compensate for failures or childhood trauma, avoidance of intimate relationships or other social and non-work roles (Lowman 1993).

Workaholism, an obsessive *compulsive addiction* to work roles, is the description applied to employees who are always working, without necessarily achieving. Both Kahn (1981) and Oates (1971), for instance, associate workaholism with work addiction, a compulsion, or irrepressible need, to work continually. Kahn, however, distinguishes between workaholism and work addiction in the sense that the work addict enjoys work, while the workaholic is totally unable to manage work time effectively. Gherman (1981) describes workaholism as a stress reaction to the pressure of time, and as a defence mechanism which is employed in an attempt to associate work overload with success, when it is in fact a withdrawal reaction, say, to unpleasant domestic problems or an inability to relax. Gherman portrays the workaholic's actions as aimless toil and labour, as the work is never really mastered. Machlowitz (1978) differs from viewpoints which overemphasise the time factor. According to her the nature of the workaholic's actions is such that time, and more specifically uninterrupted time, is hard to determine. The workaholic should rather be recognised by his or her relationship with work, namely by the fact that he or she works more than is in any way necessary. The workaholic's work load never decreases. Machlowitz (1978) outlines the following characteristics of workaholics:

- They are intense, energetic, competitive and drive themselves; the motivation for this is not necessarily to receive financial gain, it can be to obtain knowledge or purely to be competitive.
- They seriously doubt their own abilities, often in spite of an attitude of apparent self-confidence and arrogance, and hard work can be an attempt to compensate for inabilities.
- They prefer work to relaxation, hate being away from work, find weekends and holidays depressing and fear the day of retirement. Workaholics will use any place to work.
- They use their time efficiently, sleep no more than six hours, often combine meals with work, try to save time (for instance by not waiting for elevators) and use note books and computers to organise their work and time.
- They draw no clear distinction between their work and recreation activities; if they do have hobbies or take part in activities such as jogging, they do them with the same intensity as they do their work.

The so-called A and B personality types represent two different ways in which people react in the work situation, perform tasks and cope with stress. *Type A* is associated with a high risk factor for coronary diseases and other stress-related problems and the following behaviour patterns (Friedman & Rosenman 1974; Eysenck 1991; Lowman 1993):

- *Intense aspirational behaviour* and conscientiousness. This style of behaviour is characterised by traits such as high ambition, strict performance criteria, willingness to work hard, suppression of tension, working long hours, displaying very responsible behaviour and linking production to self-esteem, competing even during recreation.
- An irrepressible *tendency towards urgency*, characterised by virtually impossible time limits for the completion of tasks, impatience, restlessness, a feeling and sensation of constantly working under pressure, doing everything quickly (for instance eating, walking and talking fast), quick emotional reactions, attempting to do several things at once and even attempting to project occurrences.
- Interpersonal relationships display a *lack of caring* for other people. Characteristics of this style of behaviour include hostility, sometimes aggression and anger, egotism, difficulty in following someone else and accepting others' point of view and often displaying frustrated reactions towards others with less insight, should they receive negative feedback on their interactions.

The type A personality continually wants to be in control. Sometimes, however, in the midst of unrealistic aspirations, he or she simply does not command the physical, emotional, cognitive and social adjustment mechanisms, with a resultant loss of control which may lead, among others, to total helplessness and stress reactions in the form of coronary heart diseases in particular. Roseman (1982) points out, however, that the behaviour problems of the type A person should never be likened to those of the person with anxiety. Sir Peter Medawar (Nobel Prize winner) describes the type A person as follows: "Type A's are without doubt the great doers of the world. Even if Type A's lead shorter lives they live more life while they are living it" (Friedman & Rosenman 1974:iv).

The *type B personality* represents behaviour on the opposite behaviour continuum to that of the type A. Behaviour is characterised by greater work satisfaction, shorter work hours, satisfaction with less compensation, a more relaxed attitude, less competitiveness, more patience, hard work, but without an intense drive and constraint and less critical time limits. Type B's like to relax and maintain sound interpersonal relationships.

Burnout, as initially defined by Freudenberger (1974) and confirmed by later research, refers to work overload and patterns of overcommitment which influence the work behaviour and physical and mental health of workers. Burnout was found particularly in the case of people-oriented groups such as medical practitioners, nurses, psychologists and attorneys (Evans & Fischer 1993). Maslach's definition (Muldary 1983:1) of this phenomenon shows that a combination of symptoms, behaviour and attitudes can be involved. "The loss of concern for the people with whom one is working includes physical exhaustion and is characterised by an emotional exhaustion in which the professional no longer has any positive feelings, sympathy, or respect for clients or patients."

In the field of clinical psychology the term "burnt child syndrome", for instance, refers to previous intense emotional experiences, with the result that the child, and later the adult, reacts with great difficulty to emotional stimuli, such as affection (Klopfer et al. 1954:275, 293).

The definitions of Muldary (1983), Veninga and Spradley, Edelwich, Brodsky and Cherniss (Muldary 1983; Odendaal & Van Wyk 1988) all contain elements of the above-mentioned definition, namely physical, psychological and social exhaustion or burnout, which influence physical wellbeing and health.

Table 22.2 illustrates the wide range of physical, psychological and behaviour problems that can be associated with burnout.

Gherman (1981) also discussed burnout as a more general condition, when management and the organisation are no

Type of commitment?

Physical	Psychological	Behavioural
Fatigue	Feelings	Dehumanisation of clients
Sleep disturbances:	• Anger	Victimisation of clients
difficulty in sleeping	• Boredom	Critical, blaming
and getting up	• Frustration	Defensiveness
Stomach ailments	• Depression, anxiety	Impersonal
Migraine headaches	• Apathy	Poor communication
Frequent colds, flu	• Guilt	Derogatory perceptions
Lingering colds	• Suspicion	Physical distancing
Backaches	• Helplessness	Withdrawal, isolation
Nausea	• Pessimism	Postponing behaviours
Muscle tension	• Irritability	Stick to rigid rules
Shortness of breath	• Resentment	Clock watching
Frequent injuries	• Hopelessness	Absenteeism
Weight problems	Attitudes	Making mistakes
Weakness	• Cynicism	Unnecessary risks
Change of eating habits	• Indifference	Substance use
	• Self-doubt	Marital and family conflict
	• Loss of empathy	Conflict with co-workers
	• Poor concentration	Workaholism and
	• Discouraged	obsessiveness
	• Moodiness	Humour as a buffer from
	• Low self-esteem	emotions
		Decreased job efficiency
		Suicide
		Overcommitment or
		undercommitment

Table 22.2 Indications of burnout
Source: Adapted from Muldary (1983:6)

longer effective. Gherman (1981:41) provides a description of organisational burnout, which resembles Krantz's (1985) and Herman's (1963) views of organisations in conflict, and is characterised by the following symptoms in particular:
• high personnel turnover

• increased absenteeism
• scapegoats are sought
• a style of dependence which manifests as anger towards supervision and feelings of helplessness and despair
• group conflicts and group coalitions
• critical attitudes towards co-workers

- lack of cooperation between workers
- a lack of initiative
- increased job dissatisfaction
- negativism in respect of the role of work groups

22.7.4 Work-related anxiety, fears and depression

Anxiety, fears and depression may be interrelated and factors in many work-related problems or even specific aspects of jobs. The feelings and emotions involved in these conditions may relate to generalised feelings of anxiety and depression, such as feelings of not being able to do things, or as performance anxiety, for instance a manager afraid to write annual reports or to address groups. Anxieties and depression, whether viewed as personality traits or a state of mind, may impair work performance, at varying times and to different degrees, from only slightly to incapacitating. The fact that anxiety is characterised by physiological symptoms, worry and strong emotions will influence the physical, cognitive and interpersonal performance areas in work. In many studies depression is related to problems in work experiences, in women more so than in men and more in younger and older workers (Firth & Hardy 1992; Warr 1992; Heim 1991).

Although much research is still needed on work-specific anxiety and depression, because many factors in the employee and work may modify the manifestation and consequences, it is clear that jobs and also specific aspects of jobs in interaction with some individuals provoke anxiety (Broadbent, in Argyle 1995; Lowman 1993). Changes in personal life situations, such as divorce, and also in the work situation, for example mergers and changes in labour composition, may create many "adjustment dysfunctions" in employees with accompanying fears, anxieties and physiological illnesses (Nevid et al. 1996). Fears for specific situations will impair work

seriously, as in phobias, where employees are fearful of being with other people, working in high, narrow or deep locations or fear contamination.

22.7.5 Personality dysfunctions and work

Personality is increasingly associated with psychological and physical health behaviours, in addition to its association with personality disorders (Nevid et al. 1996; Friedman & Booth-Kewley 1987; Matthews 1988; Friedman 1990; Lowman 1993). The effects of personality disorders are embedded in characteristic *personal and interpersonal* behaviours and habits, thinking patterns, expressive behaviours and inability to cope effectively with problems of life. People with personality maladjustments may be aware of their behaviours, but find it difficult to change or to consistently apply more acceptable behaviours.

Work may be influenced by aspects of all personality disorders, such as narcissism, rigidness, paranoia, avoidance, interpersonal difficulties, obsessive-compulsiveness, antisocial behaviours and passiveness and aggression. Many dismissals and disciplinary actions at work are related to personality clashes. Examples are insubordination, tardiness, difficult interpersonal behaviours, rebelliousness, disobedience of rules, chronic lateness, unacceptable acts towards co-workers (such as sexual harassment), dishonest behaviours (for example theft and fraud), substance abuse, gambling and inability accepting, and working under, authority.

Neff (1977) identified five types of behavioural styles or reactions in the work situation which may prevent correct work attitudes from developing, and which are the consequences of the ineffective development of a work personality and a productive role:

- poor motivation and a negative concept of work and work role

- a usual response of fear and anxiety at work
- a usual response of open hostility and aggression at work
- behaviour in the work situation that is mainly dependent and immature
- reactions at work that are socially naive

Neff also describes two additional types: the reserved (apathetic) type, who evidence a lack of vitality, indifference, emotional unresponsiveness and non-involvement; the self-deprecatory type, characterised by much self-criticism and lack of belief in their own capabilities.

Wheeler (1994) and Martin (1989), in practical approaches, typify difficult behaviours in problem employees along lines that coincide with aspects of personality malfunction:

- passive-aggressive behaviour (silent judges, avoiders, information-keepers)
- hostile-aggressive behaviour (explosives, insulting attackers, hidden sarcasm)
- procrastination (untruthful, idlers, perfectionists)
- negative-complaining behaviour (whiners, idea destroyers, guilt givers)
- arrogant behaviours (credit stealers, know-alls, show-offs)

22.7.6 Work and non-work conflicts

The influence of non-work life roles, such as marriage, parenting, family roles, religion, leisure and societal responsibilities may have *spillover effects* at work, while work roles also influence non-work roles. From all these it is possible that family life and work defines people's identities (who they are, self-concept) most and are supportive of each other. Families are responsible for providing family members with a legacy of progression and life qualities (careers, work, housing, finances, education, culture), while one of the main ego-values for adults is to provide sufficiently for dependents through some form of work. These supportive roles are traditionally defined in a way which generally associates males with the working and providing function, while females provide in the caring function; they are "home makers" and raise children. These traditional roles are changing and are sometimes reversed. As the labour market changes, women are increasingly entering work at all levels, often both parents (dual career couples), or more members of households, are working and more children are alone at home for longer periods. It seems evident that the accumulation of more roles in the life of a working couple will bring more opportunities, but also more stress. *Inter-role conflict* causes the responsibilities of work and family to be incompatible, while *role overload* may cause couples to feel overburdened, which will adversely affect the family. If the work-family interaction or the family context is negative and disruptive for an individual or group, it can, by itself, be viewed as a psychological health problem (Lowman 1993; Greenhaus & Parasurman 1989). Research (Cooper & Payne 1994; Eckenrode & Gore 1990; Loscocco & Rochelle 1991) shows that non-work roles may have positive and negative influences in work satisfaction and other work experiences. Working couples often experience higher levels of work satisfaction than single working parents. Such outcomes are obviously determined by the types of relationships at home and work, as well as the work climate experienced, for instance possible role conflicts, work overload and role ambiguity. Other factors which will influence the stress between work and family are the family members' attitudes towards their own and others' jobs, division of work and social roles at home, children and child-raising practices and other responsibilities. Greenhaus & Parasurman (1989) concluded that the influence of stress on family and work roles among career couples will very much be determined by task characteristics in the work, work and time schedules and the importance of the work for every person. Work overload, for instance, may contribute to the mother's perception and guilt feelings of having to fulfil various life roles. Work role stressors may have spillover effects at home in reactions such as frustration, anger, irritability, anxiety, fatigue, sexual disinterest, complaints of illness, excessive substance use and an increase in other stress-related diseases. On the other hand, if roles at home are distributed more equally between parents and couples, and spouses support each other in recognising the importance of their jobs, multiple roles can facilitate job and general life satisfaction.

22.7.7 Career development problems

In many cultures people have to face extremely high expectations as far as their careers are concerned. Any inability to develop careers, for example failure to be promoted, indecision and uncertainty in making choices, is regarded as a problem and as a weakness that must be rectified.

Career maturity refers to the level of people's vocational development, vocational attitudes and decision-making skills at different stages of life. Career maturity is a function of people's developmental history, age, sex, behaviour styles and socioeconomic factors. Their inability to make choices or to perform developmental tasks at specific points in their career development may lead to stress and emotional problems.

Vocational uncertainty has many causes, including adjustment problems, indecision, incongruence between one's personal attributes and the requirements of the job, behavioural traits (such as dependence, choice-anxiety), a lack of information and intrapersonal and interpersonal conflicts. These factors may determine people's career concepts, their attitudes to work or

work ethic, attitudes to learning, attitudes toward employers and the positive or negative view held about their roles, all of which will determine their attitude and expectations on entering a job, adapting to it and developing in it.

People's job satisfaction and adjustment will also be determined by the emphasis they and employers put on career development, and what happens to the employees in terms of work role fulfilment, task performance, job changes, promotion and status, and by events such as the organisation's life cycle, retirement, unemployment and economic recessions (Isabella 1988).

Apart from choosing an occupation, entering a career and later retiring, the so-called *midlife crisis*, at the age of approximately 30-40 years, is regarded as the most important period of adjustment for some people. This mid-career crisis is brought about particularly by people's uncertainty about future career development, fear of ageing and questioning of their self-esteem and the purpose of life. Manifestations of this stage include changing jobs, substance abuse, poor interpersonal relations, anxiety, depression, hypochondria, marital problems, adopting a new and sometimes strange lifestyle, problems with physical health and appearance and a decrease in sexual energy (Levinson 1978; Warshaw 1979; McClean 1979). It is therefore not surprising that some refer to this period in the lives of men as "the male menopause". In women this phase is likely to coincide with menopause and the resultant physical and emotional problems (Mercer 1989). The approach of retirement and retirement itself also bring stress from uncertainty, fears of not being cared for, boredom and feelings of worthlessness. Much dispute still exists as to generalising of the mid-career crisis phenomenon.

Although Campbell and Cellini's taxonomy (1981) for adult career problems may overlap in some instances with some of the other work dysfunctions, it is more specifically directed at problems during the various *career transitions* and work performance in organisations. This taxonomy (see table 22.3) is based on many career development theories and research of adult career development problems, to identify career development tasks and subtasks and possible problems during four career development stages (Campbell & Cellini 1981:175-190; Lowman 1993).

22.7.8 Managerial stress and "organisational pathology"

The manager of a present-day large industrial organisation probably experiences the same, or more, stressors than other workers. In addition to the generic sources of stress, managers in contemporary industrial settings and ever-changing work environments experience stress from other challenges, such as merging and acquisitions of companies, retrenchments and downsizing of workforces, uncertainty of managerial jobs due to structural changes in organisations, economic declines and affirmative action and personnel policies. These may limit the scope of career development for certain groups and put greater demands on managers to achieve better results, sometimes with even more restrictions on resources and more pressure from employees and unions on managers to negotiate better working conditions, remuneration and other benefits.

Intense stress effects are attributed to the manager's position, his or her roles and the expectations linked to all these responsibilities. Managers are decision-makers, innovators, coordinators, conflict solvers and risk takers, and many stressors may effect their behaviour. If stress affects are noticeable, this will lead to further stress. Moreover, most managers' work behaviour is expected to be achievement-oriented, type A behaviour, which can lead to stress-related problems, including cardiac dis-

eases. In today's competitive business world managers may often be the symptom-bearers for possible problems inside and often outside the organisational system. Managers spend much energy as representatives of employers and as negotiators between employees and employers, which may leave them devoid of sufficient resources to cope with personal stress. Managers often find themselves in positions where the climate for emotional and physical health problems is optimal. Because of managers' qualities, their coping mechanisms operate well initially, but they are inclined to overtax these mechanisms. Consequently any warnings and interventions may be too late!

Organisational health can be explained from different perspectives, all of which are interrelated. Organisations often experience problems because of the demands of their interaction with internal subsystems and external environmental systems. The complex structures and processes in the organisation are frequently the reason why it cannot adjust rapidly enough to change. In other words, its regulating and retentive functions may be the cause of its downfall.

One approach is to assess organisational health according to the effectiveness of an organisation, the extent to which criteria for profitability or success are satisfied, or the successful attainment of business, service, societal responsibilities and research goals.

Another approach is to explain organisational health in the context of the corporate paradigm, for example culture, values, climate and management philosophy. Schein (Cox 1991:1) defines *organisational culture* as the pattern of basic assumptions that a given group has established, discovered or developed in learning to cope with its problems of external adaptation and internal integration, and that have worked well enough to be considered valid, and therefore to be taught to new members as the correct way

Table 22.3 Career and work performance problems

---

1 Problems in making career decisions

1.1 Getting started in a job

a. Lack of awareness of the need for a decision

b. Lack of knowledge of the decision-making process

c. Awareness of the need to make a decision but avoiding taking personal responsibility for decisions

1.2 Gathering of information

a. Inadequate, contradictory or insufficient information

b. Information overload (e.g., excessive information that confuses the decision-maker)

c. Lack of knowledge of how to gather information (i.e. where to obtain, organise and evaluate information)

d. Unwillingness to accept the correctness of the information because it does not agree with the person's self-concept

1.3 Generating, evaluating and selecting alternatives

a. Difficulty in deciding, because of conflicts between multiple career options (i.e. too many equally attractive career choices)

b. Failure to generate sufficient career options because of personal limitations such as health, resources, ability and education

c. Inability to decide because of the threatening effects of anxiety, such as fear of failure to accomplish the task chosen, fear of social disapproval, or fear of commitment to a course of action

d. Unrealistic choice (i.e., aspiring to goals either too low or too high) based on criteria such as aptitudes, interests, values, resources and personal circumstances

e. Interfering personal constraints that impair choices (e.g. interpersonal influences and conflicts, circumstances, resources, health)

f. Inability to assess alternatives because of lack of knowledge of the evaluation criteria (e.g. criteria could include values, interests, aptitudes, skills, resources, health, age and personal circumstances)

1.4 The formulation of plans to implement decisions

a. Lack of knowledge of the necessary process and steps to formulate plans

b. Inability to use a future time perspective in planning

c. Unwillingness or inability to acquire the necessary information to formulate a plan

2 Problems in implementing career plans

2.1 Personal attributes of the individual

a. Failure to undertake the steps necessary to implement plan

b. Failure or inability to successfully complete the steps necessary for goal attainment

c. Adverse conditions, or changes, in family situation

2.2   Characteristics external to the individual

a. Unfavourable economic, social and cultural conditions

b. Unfavourable conditions in the organisation, central to the implementation of career plans

c. Adverse conditions, or changes, in the individual's family situation

3 Problems in organisation/institutional performance

3.1 Deficiencies in skills, abilities or knowledge

a. Insufficient skills, abilities or knowledge on position of entry (i.e. underqualified to perform satisfactorily)

b. Deterioration of skills, abilities or knowledge over time in the position because of temporary assignment to another position, leave, lack of continual practice or development of the skill

c. Failure to modify or update skills, abilities or knowledge to stay abreast of job changes (i.e. job obsolescence following new technology, tools and knowledge)

3.2 Personal factors

a. Personality characteristics incongruent with the job (e.g. values, interests, work habits)

b. Debilitating physical or emotional disorders

c. Adverse off-the-job personal circumstances or stressors (e.g. family pressure, financial problems, personal conflicts)

d. Occurrence of interpersonal conflicts on the job specific to performance requirements (e.g. getting along with supervisor, co-workers, customers)

3.3 Conditions of the organisational environment

a. Ambiguous or inappropriate job requirements (e.g. lack of clarity of assignments, work overload, conflicting assignments)

b. Deficiencies in the operational structure of the organisation or institution

c. Inadequate support facilities, supplies or resources (e.g. insufficient lighting, ventilation, tools, support personnel, materials)

d. Insufficient reward system (e.g. compensation, fringe benefits, status recognition, opportunities for advancement)

4 Problems in adjusting in and to the organisation

4.1 Initial entry into the job

a. Lack of knowledge of organisational rules and procedures

b. Failure to accept or adhere to organisational rules and procedures

c. Inability to assimilate large quantities of new information (information overload)

d. Discomfort in a new geographic location, such as housing and lack of support

e. Discrepancies between individual's expectations and the realities of the organisational environment

4.2 Changes over time

a. Changes over the life span in one's attitudes, values, life style, career plans or commitment to the organisation that lead to incongruence between the individual and the environment (e.g. physical and administrative structure, policies, procedures)

b. Change in the organisational environment which leads to incongruence between the individual and the environment (e.g. changes in structure, policies and procedures)

4.3 Interpersonal relationships

a. Interpersonal conflicts arising from differences of opinion, style, values, mannerisms, etc.

b. Occurrence of verbal or physical abuse or sexual harassment

to perceive, think and feel in relation to those problems.

The assumption here is that all functional and structural processes in the organisation according to which employees function have their foundation in basic organisational values. An organisation's "personality" and individual behaviour patterns are formed and maintained through the selection and promotion of certain types of personalities ("organisational men and women"). Phenomena such as "groupthink" and "dominant coalitions" that can influence decision-making in organisations can also be explained in terms of this.

Many authors emphasise maladjusted organisational behaviour (Ashforth & Lee 1990; Kets de Vries & Miller 1984; Dejoy & Wilson 1995; Carroll 1997). In this respect Hampden-Turner (Carroll 1997) explains corporate culture as a "hologram", in that all parts of the organisation are represented in each smaller segment. This implies that behavioural and relationship patterns will be repeated, especially from the top down, in organisations. It is,

for instance, possible that the same negative attitudes and behaviours between personnel and management will be repeated when personnel negotiate with clients or other parties.

Kets de Vries's and Miller's theory (1984) on *neurotic styles and organisational pathology* relates to the influence of corporate values. These authors see a similarity between organisational pathology and individual pathology as defined in clinical psychology and psychopathology, and as explained by psychoanalytical and psychiatric literature. According to Kets de Vries and Miller, top and company managers have specific fantasies and neurotic tendencies that can lead to organisational disorientation. Because top management, especially in centralised organisations, directly determines and influences organisational culture and climate, structure and processes, these negative tendencies will usually have negative effects, although such orientations can also have positive effects. Specific types of managers will, for example, be appointed and this could lead to an undesirable uniformity and conformity. It stands to reason that individual employee behaviour can also be detrimentally influenced. These authors identify five "neurotic styles" that manifest themselves in five organisation types: paranoic, compulsive, histrionic, depressive and schizoid. In each of these the management style will determine the types of behaviours in the organisation and toward other people, the controls, decision-making and other business activities.

A systemic study of organisations that integrates many of the above approaches also provides a useful framework for understanding and classifying organisational health and pathology. However, when analysing organisational health a few systemic principles must be considered.

- Organisational pathology will be determined largely by the context in which the organisation functions as well as organisational paradigms such as corporate culture.
- There is a systemic or circular correlation between workers' and groups' pathology (parts) and those of the organisation (Gestalt). Therefore, excessive control and rigid structures in organisations which, according to Kets de Vries (Gardner 1987:301), suffer from "bureaupathology", compel employees to attain goals in secretive and "unacceptable" ways, hence deviant ways becomes the norm. This pattern may ultimately influence the corporate culture and goals and damage the image of the organisation in the outside world.
- In organisations with negative feedback patterns, and in which maladjustment is the norm, secretiveness and isolation from others and external systems can become characteristic, with consequent degeneration and ultimate destruction of such a business.
- In terms of Gestalt laws and group dynamics, corporate culture or organisational personality, and therefore also organisational pathology, can be dominant without this necessarily being reflected in the individual's situation.
- In history, groupthink is associated with erroneous actions and decisions (e.g. Nazi Germany and the events leading to the Japanese attack on Pearl Harbour during World War II).

According to Krantz (1985) and Herman (1963), the organisation in conflict, and its management, experiences the following organisational and individual problems, which calls to mind organisational burnout as described by Gherman (1981):

- an increase in withdrawal behaviour (dissatisfaction, low production, absence and personnel turnover)
- an increase in and an intensification of conflict situations
- fewer communication channels
- an increase in authority structures, so that only a few people take part in decision-making
- greater stress for authority figures as authority becomes more centralised
- authority figures evade responsibilities as the stress increases
- a decline in standards because of the stress effects on authority figures
- the further reduction of communication channels
- increasing conflict between management and other units in the organisation
- more people withdraw from tasks and activities because of the increasing conflict
- fewer communication channels for the collection and distribution of information as the conflict and problems increase
- the further increase of conflicts and withdrawal behaviour as organisational standards become even lower
- the reduction of specific communications leads to further withdrawal and less available information

These sequential crises illustrate that *organisational and individual problems are interrelated* and that diagnosis and intervention have to take both into account.

22.7.9 Other work-related problems

Other conditions which may impair work performance due to physical and psychological problems are AIDS, industrial accidents, physical handicaps and unemployment. These may concern the employee, work interaction, the environment or the society at large.

AIDS is not just a medical problem, but an economic, educational and work problem that also influences behaviour patterns, values and attitudes and whose effect is felt in the individual, family, community, society and nations worldwide. AIDS has become an economic problem, as its costs (due to illness and death) are and will become astronomical in respect of decreased workforces, productivity, unemployment and medical care. AIDS is also an educational problem, because in all spheres people's behaviour patterns, knowledge, thinking and attitudes will have to be influenced in respect of the prevention of AIDS. AIDS has also become a legal issue, with regard to, among others, liability for spreading the virus and the rights of AIDS sufferers, for example in obtaining and maintaining work, insurance and legal protection. AIDS is a work problem. As in everyday life, there is also a stigma attached to AIDS sufferers in the workplace. The incidence of AIDS in the workplace affects the formulation of policies regarding employment and work benefits, as well as interaction with other employees. Health workers must help to research the causes and dynamics of AIDS while also educating and counselling all parties. Possibly most important is assistance to AIDS victims with regard to their needs and emotions amidst many personal anxieties and social perceptions. An important counselling aspect is to "empower" male and female persons in the adoption of more responsible attitudes to their own sexuality and safe sexual behaviours. AIDS is also a socioeconomic problem, in that improvements in living standards and a better quality of social life styles can prevent the spreading of the AIDS virus.

Physical handicaps, including blindness, deafness, epilepsy and paralysis, caused by factors such as organic brain damage, accidents, toxic and nutritional influences, may make people's work adjustment extremely difficult, even if they are cognitively and psychologically well adjusted. The problems are related to the type of impairment, but also due to societal or "traditional" attitudes towards the "differentness" of a handicapped person. These prejudices and stereotypes often create a type of job reservation that excludes handicapped people which means they do not have a free choice of vocation. However, there are many examples of handicapped individuals who have been very successful as people and as employees. The work adjustment of physically handicapped people with sensory handicaps such as blindness and deafness, or physical handicaps such as orthopaedic, cerebral and even epileptic conditions, is often better than that of the emotionally and psychologically handicapped (Anglin, in Dunnette 1990). Their work motivation is usually high, while absenteeism, staff turnover and accidents may even be lower among them than in the case of even the ordinary worker (Miner 1966).

Industrial accidents refer to occurrences in the workplace and in work behaviour which may give rise to unsafe working conditions, injuries, death and loss to the worker, colleagues and the organisation. Research has revealed a strong connection between personality factors, physical work conditions and the interaction between these in accidents or safe behaviours. The well-known *accident proneness theory* (much like illness prone behaviour and the stress-diathesis model), emphasises that particular human characteristics will lead to accidents, no matter how safe the working conditions are. This idea of predisposition to accidents is supported by some findings, for instance repetition of accidents takes place mainly in the 17-28 years age group, after which the number of accidents progressively decreases. Older employees may, especially in the light of decline in memory, perceptual and motor activities, pose a risk as far as work safety is concerned. Miner and Brewer (1990) maintain that "accident proneness" should preferably be interpreted on the basis of temporary personality disorders, particularly at the age of about 30 years. This period is perhaps the start of the mid-career crisis for some people, and may be accompanied by emotional instability and risky behaviour. Hirschfield and Behan (1963) as well as Hill and Trist (1962) argue that accidents may be motivated behaviour, for instance self-destructive needs and an attempt to withdraw from the work situation. According to McCormick and Ilgen (1981), the combination of specific personality traits and situations which repeatedly lead to accidents could rather be described as *accident repetitive behaviour*. Other personality traits which may be associated with industrial accidents are expressed by Miner and Brewer (1990) and Miner (1966) as follows: physical handicaps and inefficient task skills; inadequate training; emotions such as hate and aggression, negative attitudes towards management; depressive and self-destructive tendencies; negative work attitudes; characteristics such as impulsiveness, tenseness, immaturity, social irresponsibility and lack of intimate interpersonal relationships. Selzer et al. (1968) found that stress effects and psychopathology occur frequently among drivers who have caused fatal accidents. Their problems include paranoic characteristics, inclinations to-

ward suicide, depression, violent action, social stress (e.g. personal problems and finances), upsetting experiences some time before the accident and a history of accidents.

Authors such as Muchinsky (1983) view the accident proneness theory as invalid, especially in the light of factors such as intrinsically dangerous work, poor workplace design and safety management and the influence of factors such as fatigue and substance abuse. Workers are often also inclined to ignore their safety requirements in order to satisfy other needs. Training of workers, particularly in respect of perception and motor skills, may also not keep track with the technology in modern work environments, especially if the influences of physical fatigue and mental load work are taken into account.

A theory of so-called *biorhythms* explains industrial accidents on the basis of the interaction between the individual's physical, emotional and cognitive functions. When one of these functions, for instance poor cognitive judgement or emotional tension, reaches a low point, accidents can occur. Investigations by Carvey and Nibler (1977) and Wolcott et al. (1977) could not confirm this theory.

Unemployed people are those who want to work but who lack a job, are denied a job or can't find a job. Unemployment, which starts with job loss due to involuntary withdrawal from work through layoffs, downsizing of companies and personnel and firing, is a state of worklessness, exclusion and non-involvement in a working society. In our times it can be said that unemployment is a "social illness", because it is socioeconomic and political conditions in countries (societies) that create workless status for millions of individuals, their families and societies, with serious impact on their quality of life, health and mental wellbeing. Unemployment results in people being deprived of all the advantages and positive values of work, especially income and survival, spending life and time meaningfully, developing and maintaining self-worth and personal growth, being physically and mentally healthy and fostering positive attitudes on work (O'Brien 1986; Warr 1987; Feather & O'Brien 1986; Hayes & Nutman 1981; Leana & Feldman 1988; Smith 1987). Even retirement, which is not unemployment but compulsory non-employment, can have severe consequences, such as intense boredom, a loss of interest in life, reduced income, physical and emotional deterioration and premature death (O'Meara 1977). The consequences of unemployment can be classified in many ways, for instance people's subjective experiences of loss, physical and psychological health, the pathological effects on societies and the consequences of unemployment on people's occupational behaviours. Re-employment does not necessarily reset the "psychological equation", but may leave a legacy of perceived worthlessness, stigma, cautiousness, self-doubt, weariness, anxiety and depression.

22.8 MANAGING HEALTH AT WORK

In much of the literature on work adjustment (Cooper & Payne 1994; Ross & Altmaier 1994; Carroll 1997; Leatz & Stolar 1993; Dejoy & Wilson 1995; Lowman 1993; Warr 1987), the emphasis is on the *interactive roles* of management and the worker in coping with, fighting and managing stress problems. The role of management and corporate responsibility in workplace counselling is emphasised in works such as those of De Board (1983), Manuso (1983), Roseman (1982) Roberson (1986), Carroll (1997) and Lowman (1993). Although it may often be "lip service", most organisations acknowledge human resources are their most valuable asset. Therefore health promotion and workplace counselling should not only be a means of managing stress, but also a

service of caring and assisting employees to adapt to change (Carroll 1997). In contrast, it is possible that the motive for profit may outweigh considerations of care for employees.

D'Alonzo and Belinson (Noland 1973) and Carroll (1997) define the task of industrial psychological health services and the workplace counsellor as follows:

• diagnosing and treating the symptoms of workers with emotional conflicts in both serious and less serious cases
• research on the factors that cause or support emotional maladjustment and monitoring the effectiveness of interventions
• training medical and human resources workers to manage workers with emotional problems, in how to act towards rehabilitated workers, and to conduct general health programmes for workers
• consulting with medical services on problem workers
• advising departments on the selection, placement and rehabilitation of workers with emotional problems or workers who have received treatment
• consulting with management and advising them on matters such as the policy on occupational health and methods to cope with individual cases or groups with emotional or behaviour problems
• facilitating organisational change in culture and attitudes towards health promotion
• mediating between employees, employers and external sources related to health matters

Broadly speaking, these tasks of the industrial psychologist can be described as diagnostic, preventive, remedial and as having a research function. All these actions should be directed at the well-adjusted employee, but more must be done in diagnosing and managing the problem employee at, and outside, work. The programmes and interventions that can be offered at the various levels are many and should be in the context of organisational, environmental and individual needs.

Organisational effectiveness and employee physical and psychological wellbeing should be equally important and are interrelated. Even amid efforts to ensure profitability and maintain the existence of organisations, two of the most important (and expensive) priorities of companies should be the promotion of employee health and combatting the destructive consequences of occupational diseases and psychological maladjustment. These are necessary priorities even if only the enormous incidence, and direct and indirect costs, of health issues for companies, society and individuals are considered (e.g. insurance claims, medical benefits, retraining).

The management and promotion of occupational health requires a *holistic approach*, as many factors and role players are involved (Dejoy & Wilson 1995; Carroll 1997). In comprehensive programmes this relates to health promotion on three levels: *organisational health promotion* (getting management involvement and support); *environmental health promotion* (the physical hygiene factors in workplaces, such as health messages, healthy working conditions and good workplace design); *individual health promotion* in aspects such as healthy working and life attitudes, life styles and behaviours and assisting employees in various ways to cope with work stress and other problems.

Many interventions can be levelled at *individual behaviour change* (Bandura 1986; Bennett & Murphy 1996). These include many stress management techniques to prevent stress, to cope with ongoing stress or to deal with the consequences of stress (Auerbach & Gramling 1998). In South Africa the management of change, crisis and trauma at work is an important health promotion intervention. Individual strategies can also be directed at

health attitudes, behavioural control (e.g. self-efficacy), various forms of counselling and therapy and self-management techniques (Kanfer & Gaelick-Buys 1991). Individual employees can also be helped by group level strategies, in which health is facilitated by various aspects of *social support* from colleagues, work groups, support groups, mentors and other forms of social interaction. In many instances, preventive, remedial or follow-up services from external professionals and institutions are also used.

All the mentioned programmes or specific interventions and techniques at various levels may also be directed at various outcomes, such as creation of awareness, motivation of employees, change of behaviours, improvement of environmental support or a changed culture in organisations with respect to occupational performance and health. In the latter case, various models are used to facilitate *cultural change in organisations* with respect to occupational health promotion, for instance the normative systems model by Allen (in Dejoy & Wilson 1995). Drum (1987) describes seven levels of client needs, from little need to very dysfunctional problems, which must be assessed and addressed in programmes. These need levels will determine whether interventions are preventive, developmental or psychotherapeutic in nature.

In many organisations *integrated health promotion interventions* are offered under so-called Employment Assistance Programmes (EAPs) or Health Promotion Programmes (Dickman et al. 1988; Dejoy & Wilson 1995). In general these programmes offer a broad range of services and refer to job-based programmes and interventions provided in work organisations for identifying problem employees, motivating them, resolving problems and providing counselling (or giving access to counselling) and treatment for troubled

employees. Some elements of these programmes also include physical health promotion, for instance improving on aspects of
life style such as exercising, eating, smoking
and drinking, as well as counselling and
advisory services on aspects such as legal,
financial and family matters. In some
organisations psychological health criteria
are also included in standard *human resource
development and training programmes*, for
instance interpersonal communication and
skills, assertiveness and self-efficacy, stress
and time management, coping skills, creativity and problem-solving skills and change
management. Many will assert that all
organisational functions are supposed to be
health facilitating and not "dehumanising"
or illness-inducing processes. It is sad that
many labour policies, and labour relations,
are sometimes detrimental to health, despite
liberal labour laws. In South Africa labour
disputes and conflicts and the influence of
labour unions often lead to occupational
hardships for many, and numerous organisations are characterised by symptoms of
conflict in employee relations.

Although the government and various
institutions and employers in South Africa
are involved in the field of employee
wellbeing, the emphasis is primarily on
physical aspects of occupational health, as
illustrated by government acts on labour and
various aspects of workplaces. Although
some attempts are made at psychological
care of employees, these are usually isolated
cases and seen as merely a part of
occupational health, a part of the usual
personnel practices or as the personal
responsibility of employees to seek outside
help. At present there is little systematic and
integrated policy and action with regard to
psychological work adjustment.

22.9 CONCLUSION
Although bad working conditions, meaningless work and states of unemployment
influence physical and psychological
health negatively, it is interesting to note

that most people (50-85%) are satisfied or
fairly satisfied with their work and only
10% definitely dislike their work (Argyle
1989). In general, healthy employees will
be happy and productive. The degree of
work satisfaction and adjustment, however, is influenced by many other factors,
which also vary among people. The task
of employers and the human resources
and health worker is to create and sustain
jobs, job environments and health-promo-
tion efforts, which will not only provide for
basic needs, but facilitate optimal growth
and health. This will have to be achieved in
ever-changing work environments, employee compositions, working processes
and changing perceptions, attitudes and
values about work.

Human resources professionals and
researchers will have to update their
theories and assumptions on the role of
work. They must instil a stronger sense of
taking responsibility for oneself and encourage entrepreneurs to create their own
work and to be less dependent on others.
"Joblessness" need not mean to be workless and worthless!

It seems that stress, which can be a
positive factor and an integral part of
personal and business success, might
increase even more in the work context,
thereby putting further demands on the
coping resources of workers, managers
and societies.

Self-evaluating questions
1. Read various definitions of occupational health and write a definition in
   your own words.
2. Read one week's media information,
   then give your view on the incidence
   and types of occupational adjustment
   problems in your society or environment.
3. List your own or another's work
   behaviours and compare them to
   criteria for occupational psychological
   health or maladjustment.

4. Analyse your employment situation or context and describe factors which you think may cause occupational adjustment problems.

5. Consider your work environment and describe cases or examples of what you regard as work dysfunctions.

6. Describe the characteristics or symptoms of any specific dysfunctional situation, or troubled employee, you know.

7. Analyse your organisation and describe its policy and strategies for the management of occupational psychological health.

Personality assessment

23

Ziel Bergh _____

CONTENTS

Key concepts

individual differences, competencies, job analysis, fit, factor analysis, domains, behaviours, emotions, cognition, personality, interest, anchors, values, abilities, intelligence, attitudes, questionnaire, projective, observation, ratings, behaviour-anchored, assessment centre, situational, biographical, interview, physiological measurement, ergonomic

23.1 INTRODUCTION

In the work context personal competencies, that is, knowledge, skills, abilities and other attributes, are assessed to ensure the best *fit* between employees and work environments and to predict the probability of employee success in occupational behaviours. *Assessment,* as used here, denotes measurement (the allocation of numerical values), and evaluation, the process of obtaining and interpreting information.

Assessment of work-related personality attributes is based on *individual differences* and similarities between people in order to explain, describe and predict occupational adjustment and performance. The measuring of personality attributes is based on psychological knowledge that each individual or group is unique in specific aspects, similar to others in some respects and that all people are alike in certain aspects (Allport 1961).

Personality assessment practices also utilise the knowledge that people's expressions of personality attributes may sometimes vary, but that there is a core or enduring pattern which is consistent across time and situations.

Assessing the relationships between personality and occupational behaviours is primarily aimed at making decisions, for instance to select or promote applicants to positions. This application of personality assessment is based on the assumption that there is significant *relationship* between the predictor (personality tests) and external criteria (standards or measures for successful occupational performance) (SIP 1998). Prominent applications of personality assessment in the work context are in career counselling, assessing training needs, allocation of jobs, performance appraisals, teamwork and cooperation, diagnosis of and dealing with problem employees, and in research projects. In the latter application, surveys for organisational diagnosis, that is, to establish employee attitudes, values and perceptions on various organisational aspects, and to assess managerial and leadership profiles, may also include measures of personality variables.

Personality measurement, and finding individual differences, correlations between personality attributes and relationships with other variables, is mostly done according to *psychometrics,* that is, standardised and objective observations, psychological tests and ratings in field studies and real life applications, and less so by experimental methods. Modern psychological testing originated in the work on sensory and motor testing by Francis Galton (1822-1911). Wood-

Francis Galton

worth's Personal Data Sheet constructed in 1920 seems to have been the first personality test to identify men unsuited by personality for service (Walsh & Betz 1985). The development of psychology in South Africa, and aspects related to psychological assessment, are described by Louw and Edwards (1997).

23.2 PERSONALITY MEASUREMENT CONCEPTS AND APPLICATIONS

When assessing personality in the work context scientifically, most assessment approaches derive from the study of personality according to the various theories and research on personality concepts. There is a close relationship between personality theory, research and assessment, the latter used as a research tool to scientifically verify theoretical concepts. Theory and research again provide the measurement approaches and concepts for assessment, while this interactional process also refines theory, concepts and methods.

In psychological assessment you will, therefore, encounter applications of unconscious processes, traits and types, behaviours and social learning, interpersonal behaviours, cognitions, biological behaviours, self-experiences and other measurement issues (such as cultural and gender differences), consistency of behaviours, relationships between and causes of behaviours, and the interaction between personality variables, situations and environments. In respect of these phenomena, in South Africa and worldwide, there is a need to apply assessment approaches which will indicate differences and similarities in cultures ("emic" assessment approach) and across cultures ("etic" approach) (Cloninger 1996).

All assessments of the person or personality are about behaviours, feelings and thinking, or specific aspects of these domains, which can be described as follows:

- *Behaviours* include all states of aware-ness, conscious or overt and directly observable physical, psychological and social behaviours and traits, as well as unconscious or covert and less directly observable behaviours, as in underlying motives, attitudes, traits, values and even thinking and perceptual processes.
- *Emotions* entail expressing feelings such as anxiety, fear, worry, irritation, frus-tration and aggression, all of which may be part of observed behaviours or may be suppressed or expressed in subli-mated ways. Emotions may also be expressed in thinking, perceptions, attitudes and motivations.
- *Cognitions* consist of thought processes, including intelligence, memory, reason-ing, problem-solving, analysing and learning, as well as cognitive styles. Some mental processes are expressed in unconscious ways, that is, while people are not aware that they are reacting on information.

All these variables relate to personality in one or more of the interdependent dimen-sions of structure, motivation, development and psychological adjustment. Assessment is directed at not only determining the *quantity and quality* of existing attributes, but also the *function or role of behaviour* in personality. The latter refers to attributes in relation to others, causes of behaviour or modifying the relationship between per-sonality variables or between personality variables and situations. Demographic or biographical attributes of people are related to personality as a moderator or interven-ing variable. Factors such as previous experiences, age, gender, education level and health can in themselves be important differentiating factors and are important in explaining findings or assessment results about other personality variables or their types of relatedness.

Other ways of classifying measurement concepts in personality are in terms of internal or *intrapersonality functioning* (characteristics or behaviours, emotions and abilities in the person), *interpersonal-ity functioning* (interpersonal traits, the individual in relation to other people) and *external personality relatedness* (how the person's characteristics relate to and fit with situations and environments such as the workplace).

23.3 WORK-RELATED PERSONALITY ATTRIBUTES AND PROCESSES

The characteristics necessary for any task or job are usually established by job analysis techniques, and psychological testing is used to establish applicable personality-related attributes. *Job analy-sis* is the study of jobs to isolate the spe-cific elements, tasks, functions, roles and responsibilities involved in them. Through a further process known as job or person specification the specific characteristics or competencies needed to execute job tasks are specified. *Competencies* may include knowledge, skills, abilities and any other behaviour which job analysis and psycho-logical assessment have shown to be important for successful work perfor-mance in a specific job. Knowledge, skills, abilities and other work behaviours also relate to various interdependent aspects of personality, such as the physi-cal, biological, cognitive, social and psy-chological spheres of human functioning. Competencies may also relate to various aspects of being competent in a job. They may refer to the genetic or acquired characteristics the employee has (input characteristics); how the employee carries out the necessary work tasks (process cha-racteristics) and what results are achieved (output characteristics). Although per-sonality as an assessment variable relates mostly to internal personality character-istics, that is, input characteristics, it is obvious that the personal characteristics

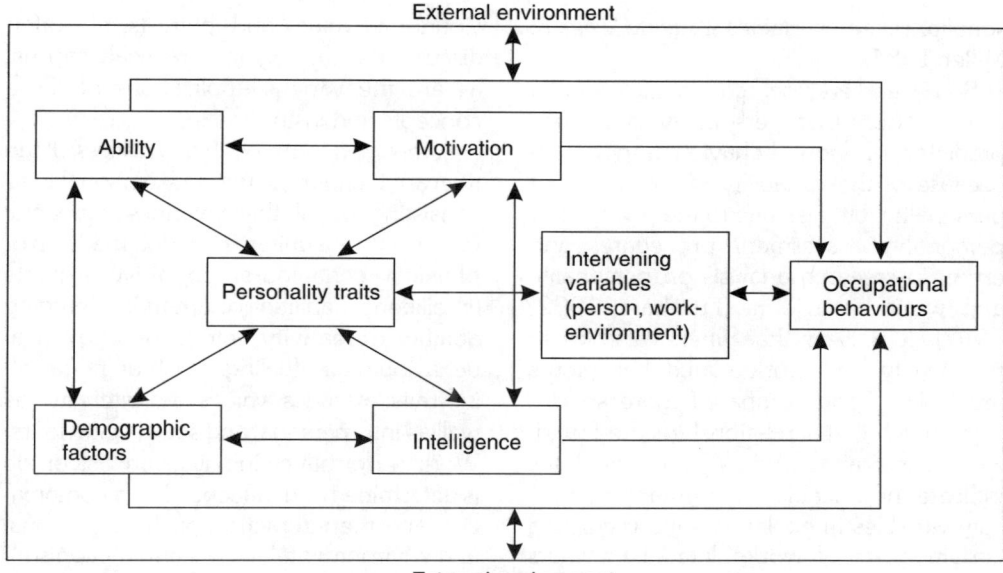

Figure 23.1 Main personal variables predicting work behaviours
Source: Adapted from Furnham (1997:145)

of employees will influence how they perform job tasks and what levels of work success they achieve. A complication in assessing personality is that it may be measured in terms of how people appear to others, or by obvious *visible behaviours,* whereas much of personality relates to people's *internal behaviours* (or their inner sense of self) which are not always overtly visible and may lie hidden below the surface.

Personality assessment is either done by others or by people themselves, as they "tell" or self-report.

Whatever the approach, assessment of work behaviours relates in some way to personality functioning as shown in figure 23.1.

Figure 23.1 indicates that personality is the central and integrating factor that the employee brings to work. All these factors, separately and in combination, and influenced by many other intervening variables in the person, the situation and the greater environment, can affect each individual's

occupational performance differently. The same is true when these variables are assessed in selection. The nature of the assessment instruments, the applicants, the job behaviours and the work situation will all combine to provide information on which employment decisions must be based.

Although personality, arguably, does not include all aspects of human behaviour, many work-related behaviours are linked to a greater or lesser degree to the personality characteristics of employees. If personality is defined inclusively, it refers to the physical-biological, cognitive, emotional or psychological and social aspects of behaviour, and more specific subfacets of these factors, on which individual employees can be measured and compared. Groups in organisations and "organisational personality" or behaviour are characterised by the collective influence of employee characteristics and behaviours in the workplace. Many trait descriptions of organisations include personality-related variables (Kets de Vries & Miller 1984).

Some earlier research findings (Guion 1965) assert that personality is a poor predictor of work behaviours, not only because of the variability in the nature of personality, but also due to the poor use of personality assessment procedures and errors in research analysis on personality and work behaviours (Furnham 1992, 1997). It is clear that when variables in personality and work-related behaviours are isolated and compared more specifically, much better relationships are found. Recent research and research analyses indicate the valuable role of many personality variables in explaining and predicting certain types of work-related behaviours (Tett et al. 1991; Barrick & Mount 1991; Furnham 1992 1997). In *criterion research* on work-related personality factors, various clusters or taxonomies for specific and more general applications were identified (Schneider & Hough 1995), for instance customer service orientations, managerial competency and high level job performance and integrity in the workplace. Many personality concepts, as measured by well-known personality questionnaires and based on the trait models of personality by Eysenck, Cattell and the five-factor models, are shown to have predictive validity for work-related behaviours with regard to various cultures (Pervin & John 1997; Cloninger 1996; Furnham 1997; Barrick & Mount 1991).

23.4 METHODS AND APPLICATIONS OF PERSONALITY ASSESSMENT

In standard textbooks on psychological assessment (Gregory 1996; Aiken 1994; Murphy & Davidshofer 1994) various domains of personality assessments, such as intelligence, and cognitive aspects including aptitudes, achievement and learning, personality, neuropsychological beha-

viours and values and interests, are often discussed separately for practical reasons, as are the various applications of these concepts and instruments.

Although it is impossible to discuss all the relevant techniques, we view personality as consisting of all these various elements. Personality is a unitary concept, made up of physical behaviours, cognitive aspects (intelligence, abilities or aptitudes, learning abilities, creativity, etc.), psychological behaviours and feelings (such as personality traits, attitudes, values and interests), as well as interpersonal and social behaviours. Work performance in any given task or job is determined and influenced by a combination and the interaction of these personal and environmental factors (interactionism). In general, personality tests and techniques are classified as belonging to one or more of the following *content areas:*

- Personality tests (mostly questionnaires) of conscious psychological behaviours, cognitions and feelings, including abilities, personality traits and types, interests or preferences, values and attitudes.
- Personality assessment of unconscious and underlying structures and processes using, among other things, projective techniques.
- Personality and behaviour assessment by observations, interviews and rating scales.
- Personality assessment of psychophysiological and psychoneurological behaviours.

Personality assessment techniques can be classified in other ways as well: objective (standardised and quantitative methods), subjective (personal judgements), self-reporting (in questionnaires, inventories and interviews) and by observers (in observations, experiments, groups, simulations and interviews).

In previous chapters some measurement principles, concepts and assessment methods were discussed. To reiterate, *standards for effective assessment* (standardisation, reliability and validity) are as important in psychology as in any other assessment, or more so, because of the variability of personality and related concepts. Therefore we must be alert for possible perceptual, judgement and rating errors which can decrease the effectiveness of personality measurement and findings. Most registered psychological tests can only be used by professionally qualified people, while the ethical codes for psychologists are especially relevant in personality assessment.

23.4.1 Assessing cognitive personality traits and processes

The classifications of cognitive traits and processes are based on various structural, process and information-processing approaches, including Spearman's G-factor, Thurstone's seven primary or group factors of ability, Piaget's theory of cognitive development and Sternberg's theory of cognitive or information-processing. Some concepts derive from social-cognitive learning and cognitive theories. Examples are locus of control and self-efficacy, which are not forms of intelligence, but ways of cognitive control.

Mental or *cognitive abilities* refer to the cognitive aspects of personality, such as intelligence, memory, reasoning, problem-solving and creativity. Ability tests usually include testing of intelligence, aptitudes, achievement, creativity and cognitive development. This is done by using various verbal and non-verbal ability tests (questionnaires) as well as practical or performance tests.

Intelligence tests, or tests of *mental alertness*, include individual and group tests designed to assess general intelligence, and more specific and in-depth analyses for diagnostic purposes in clinical and psychiatric use. One of the most useful individual tests for assessing adult intelligence is the Wechsler Adult Intelligence Scale, a revised edition of which has been adapted for South African use, though this test is not often used in the work context. Due to cultural differences in the work context, practitioners often prefer to use culture-free and non-verbal (performance) tests of mental alertness, such as the Cattell Culture Fair Intelligence Test (CFIT) or the Raven Progressive Matrices (RPM) (Gregory 1996).

Aptitude testing is mostly directed at assessing an individual's natural potential and acquired learning, which might enable him or her to develop certain proficiencies and skills for certain intellectual tasks. Most aptitude measurements, by various aptitude test batteries or tests, are based on the following general and group abilities, as classified by Spearman and Thurstone (Gregory 1996):

- *Intelligence:* the general mental ability (G-factor) to understand, learn, reason and adapt.
- *Reasoning:* to think logically and find rules for solutions on given information.
- *Remembering/memory:* to reproduce meaningful information such as words, symbols and numbers obtained or retained from previous learning and experiences.
- *Numerical ability:* to reason quickly and accurately by way of addition, subtraction, multiplication and division.
- *Spatial ability:* to perceive form and space, visualising forms and distance in two and three dimensions.
- *Verbal (language) comprehension:* to understand and reason about problems containing language, such as words and verbal analogies.
- *Word fluency:* the ability to be fluent in words and language.
- *Perceptual speed:* the ability to perceive detail and differences quickly and accurately

Of these, verbal, spatial, reasoning and numerical abilities are found to be the best predictors of work performance (Furnham 1992; Hunter 1986).

Sensory, perceptual, psychomotor, computer and mechanical skills, as well as artistic, musical and other creative abilities, are also assessed through aptitude testing.

Achievement tests are meant to assess the amount of knowledge or learning, or to diagnose the nature of such knowledge and learning, after a period of experience, development or training. Performance appraisals and examinations, although not psychological tests, are forms of achievement testing.

In addition to standardised psychological tests, the following may give valuable information on people's cognitive capabilities: analysis by a knowledgeable assessor of people's academic achievements, the level of such achievements, work achievements, general alertness in understanding relevant tasks, creative contributions, logical (common sense) reasoning about problems, speed and accuracy in learning new tasks and even the ease of adapting in new situations.

Job analysis identifies the intellectual demands of jobs. However, intellectual performance is determined not only by intelligence, but also by motivation, commitment, interest and experience.

So-called *cognitive styles* lie somewhere between intelligence and personality. A cognitive style is how people think, based on certain attitudes, perceptions and personality orientations. A cognitive style may have implications for ways of learning, problem-solving, management and leadership styles, conflict management and stress management or coping styles. In this regard Jung's four cognitive styles are often utilised in assessments by either Jung Personality Scales or the Myers-Briggs Type Indicator (MBTI). According to Jung, people's perceptions of things are influenced by sensation or intuition, while their judgements are influenced by thinking or feeling. Jung asserts that people's way of thinking (cognitive style), in their jobs or in management, is determined by combinations of perception and judgement, that is, either sensation/thinking, intuition/thinking, sensation/feeling or intuition/feeling (Briggs Meyers 1993; Du Toit 1983).

Other cognitive styles measured are *cognitive complexity* and *cognitive simplicity,* as coined by Kelly (Schultz & Schultz 1996), denoting the amount, intricacy and variety of information people use to differentiate between people or other aspects. This concept was derived from research on personality by using Kelly's Role Construct Repertory Test (REP-Test). In another application, Niemeyer (1992) uses this concept to indicate how people who have a complex cognitive style will use more information (constructs) on careers and also integrate such constructs better in order to make informed and better career choices.

Creativity is a complex behaviour based on intelligence (not necessarily high), conscious and unconscious mind states, personality factors as well as training and experience in specific fields. Techniques for the assessment of creativity are based on the generation of new or original ideas that are also realistic and useful. This process demands *divergent thinking,* that is, to get as many ideas, alternatives and applications as possible. When you calculate that $20 + 20 = 40$, you think convergently, because you only find one answer from your available memory. However, if you have to find ways to get an answer of 20 by only working with figures between 1-20, you will think more creatively or divergently.

In clinical (psychological-medical) and forensic (legal-psychological) assessments neuropsychological tests are performed in cases of psychological disorders and brain-disabled persons, primarily to assess the relationship between brain functions and personality. For some years now, industrial psychologists, in conjunction with clinical psychologists and medical and legal experts, have contributed in assessing the occupational implications of brain damage and related psychological trauma caused by industrial and traffic accidents, and have appeared as expert witnesses in legal proceedings.

23.4.2 Personality assessment by questionnaires

Questionnaires or self-report inventories usually comprise various statements or questions, prepared in advance and often in multi-choice format, which subjects must answer in certain ways, such as yes or no, agree or disagree, or rate on weighted scales, for example on three-, four- or six-point scales. The rationale for a personality questionnaire is that individuals *know themselves* and are best able to judge and report on themselves. The responses on items are combined to furnish a score for a particular attribute or a number of attributes. Scores are interpreted in accordance with various norms and guidelines based on the test's theoretical rationale. Questionnaires, like many other techniques, can be administered individually or in groups. Many questionnaires can be scored by hand or by computer, and in the latter case computer-generated reports and profiles are valuable aids in the interpretation of scores.

23.4.2.1 Personality traits

Personality questionnaires come in many forms and according to many models and approaches, but many are based on the trait models of Eysenck, Cattell and the five-factor models.

Some personality tests are based on *personality theory* or aspects of these theories. The Edwards Personality Schedule (EPPS) (Gregory 1996), for instance, measures 15 so-called manifest needs which underlie all behaviour, as stated in Murray's theory on personality. Some of these needs, which are most frequently researched, are achievement, dominance,

affiliation, nurturance and aggression. The EPPS was found to have good validity and correlated well with the "big five" personality factors (Piedmont, McCrae & Costa 1992). It is interesting to note that Murray also constructed a projective technique, the TAT, which in a totally different and unstructured way also elicits some of these needs. McClelland and Koestner (in Smith 1992) based his theory, assessment and research of, among others, achievement and affiliation motives, on Murray's need theory. McClelland and Koestner also used TAT and related types of projective cards to elicit stories which they scored in a structured way to measure needs. Many questionnaire measures for job satisfaction are related to needs theory, as illustrated by Maslow's and Herzberg's theories on work motivation.

The assessment of *self-concept*, and especially self-actualisation, and the need to find meaning in life and in the work context, received some attention in questionnaires such as the Personal Orientation Inventory (POI) (Shostrom 1976) and the Purpose In Life Test (PIL) (in Allen 1994). These concepts relate to personality attributes including extroversion, open-mindedness and non-conformity (Tosi & Hoffman 1972). In general, however, it is not easy to identify self-actualisers, except if coupled to very specific events or criteria (Allen 1994).

Other theory-related personality questionnaires that are often used in the work context are the Myers-Briggs Type Indicator (MBTI), Holland's Self-Directed Search (SDS) for assessing the congruence between personality and occupational types based on interest assessment and inventories for assessing type A behaviours.

The MBTI, mentioned previously, is based on Jung's psychoanalytic theory and is used as a type indicator of personality and to indicate people's ways of perceiving or thinking. Furnham and

Stringfield (1993) found some differences on the MBTI between managers in Japan and Europe. Japanese managers, for instance, are more introverted.

There are well-known scales for the measurement of *stress-related conditions*, particularly the so-called type A behavioural pattern (Friedman & Rosenman 1974; Matthews 1988) and burnout (Maslach & Jackson 1984; Ganster et al. 1991; Arthur 1990), while many scales assess so-called coping styles (Leiter 1991; Folkman 1982) and other adjustment problems. The General Health Questionnaire (Goldberg & Hiller 1979; Cook et al. 1981) is often used, in various formats, to assess *general health* related to psychophysical behaviours. To assess personality disorders and other forms of psychopathology professionals utilise diagnostic systems, such as the DSM-classification system, to classify psychological disorders in terms of various types of information, such as from personality assessments. In the work context, assessment of observable behaviours may also provide information on an employee's general wellbeing. Records of, for instance, illness, absences, late arrivals, complaints, disciplinary actions, accidents, errors (waste), interpersonal conflicts at work, underachievement and criminal actions (dishonesty) may say much about employee health, and also organisational health.

Type A behaviours are recognised by time urgency, achievement-driven actions, competitiveness, doing things quickly, aggressiveness and impatience, hostility at times, being easily upset, poor interpersonal relationships, and a life style predisposing to heart diseases (Matthews 1988).

Do you recognise some of the behaviours in figure 23.2? They are examples of items used to assess type A behaviour, taken from questionnaires and interviews. Answer yes or no and rate yourself on a six-point scale from 1 = never to 6 = always.

In type A working women (sometimes called type E), there is an additional dimension, in that career women must handle the pressures and conflicts of work and home or family.

Questionnaires such as the Jenkins Activity Survey (Jenkins et al. 1971) and the Time Urgency and Perceptual Activation Scale (TUPA) (Wright, McCurdy & Rogoll 1992) were specifically constructed to assess various aspects of type A behaviours.

Other personality inventories are based on *factor-analytic* research, indicating personality to be made up of a varying number of factors.

---

1. Strongly emphasise words or phrases in your speech
2. Generally or always do things at a quick pace
3. Tend to want to start things or initiate new efforts
4. Get irritated if others are slow in doing things
5. Tend to do many things at a time
6. Find it difficult to relax even while on holiday
7. Whatever you do, winning is important for you
8. People may think that you are a difficult person to relate to
9. Tend to be physically tense
10. Think that you are getting too little done in the available time

Figure 23.2 Examples of items for assessing type A behaviours

Questionnaires based on Eysenck's two-factor theory, such as the Eysenck Personality Questionnaire (EPQ), are used to measure personality in terms of three bipolar dimensions: psychotism, extroversion and neuroticism. Although the Eysenck questionnaire has very good psychometric qualities (validity and reliability), and is used in clinical practice and research in many cultures (Cloninger 1996), it is used less often in the work context. The concepts of introversion and extroversion, also used in the Myers-Briggs Type Indicator, are however used in many applications, including work-related measures.

Cattell describes personality in terms of 16 so-called source or primary traits, which he believes to be the underlying and consistent sources of behaviour. The primary traits described by Cattell, and assessed by various forms of the 16-Personality Factors Questionnaire (16-PF), are shown in figure 23.3.

Each factor on a scale such as the 16-PF is measured by a number of items. An example of one of the items on the 16-PF for the assessment of factor C (emotional stability), which respondents must answer by selecting one alternative from three, is as follows:

During the day at work, I find myself worrying, which makes it difficult to concentrate on my tasks.

Various forms of Cattell's 16-PF questionnaire are used extensively. When using the 16-PF, personality is analysed into the so-called 16 first-order factors, or these factors can be calculated and reduced to six or nine second-order factors, including anxiety, extroversion, independence, tough-poise,

	Low scores 1 2 3 4 5 6 7 8 9 10 High scores
Factors	
	A Reserved
	B Concrete reasoning
	C Affected by feelings
	E Submissive
	F Serious
	G Expedient
	H Timid
	I Tough-minded
	L Trusting
	M Practical
	N Forthright
	O Self-assured
	Q1 Traditional
	Q2 Group-oriented
	Q3 Tolerates disorder
	Q4 Relaxed

Factors	High scores
A Reserved	Outgoing
B Concrete reasoning	Abstract reasoning
C Affected by feelings	Emotionally stable
E Submissive	Dominant
F Serious	Happy-go-lucky
G Expedient	Rule-conscientious
H Timid	Venturesome
I Tough-minded	Sensitive
L Trusting	Vigilant
M Practical	Imaginative
N Forthright	Shrewd/private
O Self-assured	Apprehensive
Q1 Traditional	Open to change
Q2 Group-oriented	Self-sufficient
Q3 Tolerates disorder	Perfectionist
Q4 Relaxed	Tense

Figure 23.3 Personality as 16 primary factors

control and intelligence. Cattell's model encouraged an enormous amount of research and applications, but also created controversy. His model and questionnaires are used all over the world in many applications (Cloninger 1996), including occupational settings. Cattell provided many profiles for various types of jobs based on the 16-Personality Factor Questionnaire.

Cattell's approach played a dominant role in the further development of trait psychology, including the most recent development of an integrated personality theory based on an integrated research and assessment trait or factor model, the so-called Big Five-Factor Model.

The variants of the five-factor model of personality are the most recent and are recognised and used as models to integrate much research on personality and human behaviour. This is reflected in many questionnaires on personality and cannot be ignored when we describe or assess personality. Although many versions of this model exist, most generally agree on the five multifaceted trait dimensions and specific descriptive subfacets. Costa's and McCrae's Neo-Personality Questionnaires (NEO-PIR and NEO-FFI) are designed to measure the big five personality factors (Costa & McCrae 1995). Most of the recognised personality questionnaires include all or some of these five factors.

The five factors measured by the NEO-Personality Inventory are extroversion, agreeableness, conscientiousness, neuroticism and openness (Carver & Scheier 1996; Cloninger 1996). Each one of the five factors is described by specific facets or traits, which represent a finer analysis of personality, much like Cattell's idea of the six second-order factors and the 16 primary factors.

The trait model used by Saville's and Holdsworth's Occupational Personality Questionnaire (OPQ) also utilises a three domain model (Furnham 1992 & 1997;

SHL Occupational Personality Questionnaires 1993) The domains are feelings, relationships and thinking, while a fourth domain, energies, is implied in the other three. Each of the three main domains are described in detail by specific traits, bringing the total scales of the OPQ to 30 (or 31 if the social-desirability scale is also counted). The OPQ's items are written in work-related terms for occupational use and these questionnaires are being used and validated in many countries (Saville, Sik, Nyfield, Hackston & MacIver 1996), including South Africa (Kriek 1996 unpublished document). This model attempts to assess most of the "Big Five" factors and to predict job success across time and in various situations and cultures (Robertson & Kinder 1993). The QPO may easily be the best personality questionnaire to use in the work context, as evidenced by its multicultural data base on thousands of employees all over the world.

23.4.2.2 Interpersonal traits

The assessment of interpersonal and *prosocial behaviours*, such as interpersonal attraction and affiliation, are important in the social applications of psychology, for instance dating behaviours, counselling, marketing behaviours and in groups and organisations.

Perhaps the most influential works on interpersonal traits are those of Leary 1957; Carson 1969; Anchin and Kiesler 1982 and Kiesler 1996. Various models that refine Leary's work have emerged, such as the 1982 Interpersonal Circle for assessing and describing interpersonal traits. Interpersonal traits are also measured by scales in most of the well-known personality tests or questionnaires, such as the 16-Personality Questionnaire (16-PF), Myers-Briggs Type Indicator (MBTI), NEO and the Occupational Personality Questionnaire (OPQ). Other questionnaires that more specifically evaluate interpersonal aspects of behaviour are the Impact

Message Inventory (IMI), the Interpersonal Check List (ICL) and the Interpersonal Behaviour Inventory (IBL) (Kiesler 1996), which specifically assess the interpersonal impact a person experiences when in contact with another person, as in therapy or counselling.

Affiliation or attraction may also be assessed in terms of specific determinants or features, including body image, facial beauty, physical fitness, sexual attractiveness and similarity in aspects such as attitudes and values. This can be done by questionnaires or other survey techniques or by direct observation of behaviour in either real-life situations or in controlled experiments.

Fallon (1990), for instance, used historical records to establish whether universal standards for physical attractiveness existed in earlier societies; Franzoi and Shields (1984) developed a Body Esteem Scale which measures three different body-esteem aspects in women (sexual attractiveness, weight concern and physical condition) and in men (physical attractiveness, body strength and physical condition). On the same lines Russel et al. (1978) developed a scale for measuring loneliness. In South Africa Duckitt (1991, 1993) developed a scale for determining subtle racism.

23.4.2.3 Career development traits

The assessment of interests, values and attitudes, together with aspects of cognitive and personality traits, is especially important in the assessment of *occupational development* and related issues for career counselling and selection procedures. Assessment of career concepts really is about assessing the maturity of work-related development tasks. These may include certain personality characteristics, abilities, interests, values, career development stage, career decision-making and acquired career efficacy. Assessment of these

aspects also implies the assessment of the fit or congruence between the person and attributes of the work or occupational environment. A bad job entry experience for new or young employees may cause disillusion at finding the job and work environment dissimilar to themselves and their expectations.

Interests

Interests refer to specific tendencies, that is, *likes or dislikes*, for certain types of career or job activities, which may lead a person to pursue certain types of jobs. There are many interest questionnaires (Gregory 1996; Owen & Taljaard 1989), of which Holland's Self-Directed Search (SDS) may be one of the most used in recent times.

According to Holland's career development theory, personality and occupational choice are based on reciprocal interaction, or the idea of person-environment fit. A person's career choice (environment) stems in part from his or her personality and motivation. People may have one or more dominant personality types and may tend to be attracted to work environments that resemble these, as measured by interests on the SDS. Holland identifies *six personality types* and *six parallel occupational environments*. When assessing, we try to find congruence between the personality type and a person's career or job choice. An extended list of careers congruent with certain personality types is given in a booklet on occupational titles accompanying the SDS.

There are other methods that can be utilised to obtain information on interests: *life line analysis* is an analysis of activities which individuals do best and like most in their lives; *analysis of work environment attributes* is used to compare these to people's choices; *verbalising interests* involves asking people in interviews what their preferences are. *Personality profiles* on personality questionnaires also provide interest and career choice information by

Realistic	Investigative	Artistic	Social	Enterprising	Conventional
asocial	analytical	complicated	ascendant	acquisitive	careful
conforming	cautious	disorderly	emphatic	adventurous	conforming
frank	critical	emotional	friendly	agreeable	conscientious
genuine	complex	expressive	generous	domineering	defensive
hard-headed	curious	idealistic	helpful	energetic	efficient
inflexible	independant	imaginative	idealistic	exhibition-	inflexible
materialistic	intellectual	impractical	patient	istic	inhibited
natural	introspective	impulsive	kind	excitement-	methodical
normal	pessimistic	independant	persuasive	seeking	obedient
persistent	precise	introspective	responsible	flirtatious	orderly
practical	rational	intuitive	sociable	optimistic	persistent
self-effacing	reserved	noncon-	tactful	self-confident	practical
thrifty	retiring	forming	under-	talkative	prudish
uninsightful	unassuming	open	standing		thrifty
uninvolved	unpopular	original	warm		unimagi-
		sensitive			native

Table 23.1 Characteristic traits of Holland's Personality-Environment Types
Source: Adapted from Gregory (1996)

analysing the type of characteristics, while some personality questionnaires have also been correlated with interest question-naires.

Work values and attitudes

Values include *integrated beliefs* on many aspects in life, including the self, family, other people, religion and work. In assessment practice the issues of values and attitudes are often integrated con-cepts; even interests in work and life are often integrated with values and attitudes. Allport et al. (1951) and others following Sprangers typology identified six basic (general) values: theoretical, economic, aesthetic, social, political and religious. Rokeach (Robbins 1996) describes 18 *terminal values* (values to achieve during a lifetime, such as happiness and wisdom)

and 18 *instrumental values,* which refer to specific behaviours, say, ambition and obedience, to achieve the terminal va-lues. In work specifically, we are inter-ested in people's *work ethic,* that is, whether people have developed a "work personality", a productive orientation which refers to valuing work as necessary and a worthwhile life interest in order to achieve things for themselves, or whether people generally do not like work and must be coerced into doing or achieving anything. Within people's general work ethic they will have many specific values on work issues, which will often deter-mine how employees will behave in the workplace. In the context of work, the following values, for instance, have been identified by Super's Work Values Inven-tory (1970):

- altruism – to help others
- aesthetic – need to have aesthetic ability (valuing beauty)
- creativity – try out new ideas and suggestions
- intellectual stimulation – solving (new) problems
- achievement – doing good and productive work
- independence – enjoying freedom in own area of activity
- prestige – gain prestige and mastery in own field
- management – enjoy authority over others
- economic return – money is important
- security – want tenure in job
- surroundings – physical work environment must be pleasant
- relationships – interactions with colleagues and supervisors are fair
- associates – being part of the work group
- way of life – be own person, good life style
- variety – want change in job and activities

Wollack et al. (1971) developed a Survey of Work Values to measure pride in work, job involvement, activity preference, attitude towards earnings, social status on the job and upward striving. There are many scales for the assessment of attitudes, such as those for work satisfaction (Weiss in Cook et al. 1981), work involvement (Warr et al. 1979) and work commitment (Hrebeniak & Aluto 1972).

A popular and important concept of value is Schein's (1990) career anchors. *Career anchors* are people's "career self-image", formed by their perceptions of their personality, values, interests, attitudes, abilities, competencies and work experience at a certain stage, or as generally held. People may have a dominant career anchor, or a few, that may influence their career choices and decisions, how they want to function in a job or how they want to progress in a future career. Career anchors may influence the type of work people choose and the emphasis they put on aspects such as rewards, promotion and recognition. Career anchors will change as people's careers develop. Schein identifies these career anchors: technical and functional competence, general managerial competence, autonomy, security and stability, entrepreneurial creativity, challenge and life style.

An important issue in contemporary organisational management is *organisational diagnosis*. It is generally done by survey methods (questionnaires and interviews) to ascertain employee and work group attitudes and work values, as these determine organisational climate, that is, the levels of motivation, synergy and trust in organisations and management.

23.4.3 Personality assessment by projective techniques

Projective techniques are basically intended to evaluate the *covert or unconscious* conflicts, motives and needs in personality functioning proposed in some psychoanalytic theories. These aspects are not always evident from questionnaires, observations or people's own verbal reports. In projective techniques subjects must respond to unstructured stimuli, such as incomplete sentences, drawings, inkblots and pictures of situations and animals. Usually, subjects are given basic instructions to the effect that they must complete sentences, draw, interpret inkblots, tell stories from pictures of situations or do role plays, as they see or experience the stimuli. There are no right or wrong answers. The assessor interprets responses subjectively for every person, based on experience and psychological knowledge of projection and symbolism in human behaviour. In many instances, research on these instruments has established guidelines or "norms" which can be used for analysis and drawing conclusions.

Well-known projective techniques are sentence completion (the Rotter Incomplete Sentences Blank), drawings (the Draw-A-Person Test), the Rorschach Inkblot Test and the Thematic Apperception Test (TAT) (Gregory 1996). Figures 23.4 and 23.5 respectively illustrate the types of stimuli used in the Rorschach and TAT techniques.

Figure 23.4 A Rorschach-like inkblot

The responses and interpretations of projective techniques are based on the *projective rationale.* Projection infers that individuals will project their conscious, and especially unconscious, attributes, experiences, needs, motives, values conflicts and defences into their responses to the ambiguous or unstructured stimuli. When analysed, the responses, and sometimes also the way of responding, will permit certain assumptions to be made about personality functioning. Interpreting demands professional training and experience and although the interpretations are based on subjective judgements, they are mostly supported by integrated research and knowledge. Well-researched scoring and interpretation systems are available for some tests, including the Rorschach and TAT techniques. Projective techniques were and are meant for clinical use on

Figure 23.5 A TAT-like card

individuals to understand and explain behaviours which are often not easy to clarify through other techniques. In work-related uses, most research indicates low predictability for occupational behaviours (Gregory 1996), which, in terms of its original purpose and the subjectiveness of scoring and interpretation, is understandable. However, in clinical use the Rorschach and TAT tests may still be among the most used instruments (Gregory 1996).

The main criticism of projective techniques is that they are not sufficiently objective or standardised in terms of application, scoring and interpretation. However, questionnaires are open to equally severe censure on account of such factors as socially desirable responses and transparent items.

23.4.4 Behavioural assessment techniques

Working from primarily a behaviouristic perspective to assess *observable behaviours*, the techniques discussed below are related, in that personality is mostly assessed by others through the observation and rating of behaviour. This is achieved by direct observation in real-life situations, in simulated situations (for example experiments) or indirectly, by judging behaviour on previous or historical incidents and records and even self-observations and self-ratings. Rating scales and questionnaires allowing for monitoring by observer and subjects are often used, much as with psychological questionnaires. A difference, however, is that the items or numerical scale points are behaviour-based, that is, contain statements or examples of behaviours or situations which must be rated on scale points exactly defined in terms of behaviours or situations.

23.4.4.1 Observations

Observations can be controlled in varying degrees, depending on the type of assessment or research. Assessors can be direct participants in the activities being rated, for example working as a colleague or taking part in group discussions, or be indirectly, but visibly (obtrusive), involved as an observer. Observation can be unobtrusive, for example using one way mirrors and remaining unseen. Observation can also be done by various people: an assessor, assessees themselves or fellow employees (such as in peer ratings). The point of behaviour observation is to *gather* evidence or examples of behaviour in order to classify it. In work applications the so-called "critical incident" technique is often used to list recurrent behaviours from previous or recent work performance, which will indicate a certain trait, disposition or pattern of behaviour and also characterise the type of work environment or job. In this regard examples of failures or successes in work performance may be useful in predicting future work performance. Examples of failure for a "client manager" would be more than 10 complaints every week, failure to return calls, arguments with clients, not recruiting new clients in a specified period and loss of client accounts. Critical incidents of success for this person would be positive observations recorded on all these issues.

23.4.4.2 Biographical ratings

Biographical or demographic information (biodata) is used to rate personality on personal historical facts and experiences. Although biographical questionnaires are used in clinical and educational practices, application forms used in the employment context are the most used and best researched. The rationale for using biographical information to assess personality is that *past events and behaviour* can predict future events and behaviours. Furthermore, much about personality can be explained in terms of what people learned and experienced in their past, and what they remember and how they feel about these past experiences. In this sense biodata also has a psychoanalytic rationale! Biodata represents real-life data or critical incidents concerning people's experiences and behaviours and if used correctly can provide valuable information about personality functioning. For example, with biodata, an applicant's mobility in jobs (few or many changes) could be interpreted as either a positive development or unreliability; an old and solitary qualification could be seen as low internal motivation or self-drive; one could determine why a person was never promoted, but stayed in the same job for 20 years.

In biographical questionnaires, or during interviews, people answer questions about their personal history. In many instances weighted application forms are used, in which certain types of biodata items are positively or negatively weighted in terms of the importance attached to such data. If, for instance, you know that for insurance sales positions a certain age group, years of similar experience and gender are important in certain contexts, these data can be given higher numerical values than others, so as to distinguish applicants. To include weighted items in application forms, the weighing of these items for specific jobs or tasks must be based on research, that is, there must be evidence that such items are important, or have negligible value, for success in jobs. It is possible, however, that certain biographical data may have general predictive value for job success, such as age, having similar experience and seniority. Although biographical questionnaires are mostly constructed for specific use or situations, there are examples of standardised biographical questionnaires. Eberhardt and Muchinsky (1982), for instance, reported a good stable factor structure for a biographical questionnaire by Owens and Schoenfeldt, in which most factors are personality-related. Smernou and Lautenschlager (1991) also found relationships between various biodata items and the

personality factors of extroversion and introversion measured by the Maudsley Personality Inventory.

Examples of biodata which can be obtained by asking the right questions on an application form or during an interview are the following:

- personal identifying details: names, ID number, birth date (age), group relationships, gender, marital status, vehicle licences, addresses
- developmental history: where grown up, etc.
- educational and training history, level of performances and when achieved: schools attended and post school qualifications (College, University etc), informal courses (shorter certificates and other work-related training courses)
- work history: types of work, tenure, levels of work (positions), income levels, reasons for changes of jobs
- possible achievements in work life
- health status: health, illnesses, health habits and life styles
- interests: recreation, cultural, etc.
- reference points: persons or addresses at which enquiries about the applicant can be made (necessary for reference checking)

Biographical data are often used as a *screening technique* in selection, that is, to see whether applicants comply with certain minimum requirements, such as qualifications and work experiences, and to establish a short list of the best candidates for the final selection process. Biodata also provide valuable details to be integrated with information from techniques such as interviews and psychological tests.

In most reviews on biodata as a selection device good reliability and validity are reported, which compare favourably to coefficients obtained on cognitive ability measures (Rothstein et al. 1990; Hackel 1986; McDaniel 1989; Childs & Klimoski 1986). Research indicated biodata to be good predictors of various occupational aspects such as job turnover, job tenure, promotion, productivity, job success, training success, supervisory ratings, job achievements, training success, personal feelings of job and career accomplishment and research competence. Biodata are also valid indicators for success in various types of occupations, as well as in professional, sales, clerical, skilled and unskilled jobs (Furnham 1997; Childs & Klimoski 1986). Biodata also seem to be good predictors across time and situations and cultures. Russell (1990) and Szymanski and Churchill (1990) also find evidence of good predictive validity, notwithstanding some criticism. Some of the criticism relates to fairness, in that items in biographical questionnaires do not always give all respondents a fair chance in answering, especially if such items are weighted. If previous experience in managerial positions is taken as a prerequisite for appointment, some South Africans may assess such an item as unfair. Another point of criticism centres on privacy, as certain questions may concern very personal and sensitive matters. When including questions in application forms and using certain data we must not discriminate or be unfair in any way, and be sensitive and consider whether it is pertinent to the criteria for the advertised job, and whether obtaining or using such data is according to civil and labour laws.

When providing biographical data, people may give false information or distort their own history, for instance answer in socially desirable ways.

The bulk of research suggests that biodata in general are better predictors of work behaviours than personality questionnaires and should possibly be used more.

23.4.4.3 Assessment centres

An assessment centre is a group-oriented and standardised number, or variety, of activities which provide the basis for assessment of behaviour on various dimensions and by various methods. Assessees are rated by many or groups of assessors on behaviour and performance dimensions relevant to the work situation or a specific type or level of managerial position. This is usually done in conjunction with other techniques, such as interviews, performance ratings of employees and personality tests. Assessment centres are primarily used in the work context to assess managerial competence or potential. Assessment centres are sometimes used for selection procedures, but mostly to train or develop employees for possible promotion (Jansen & de Jongh 1997; Gaugler et al. 1987; Schippmann et al. 1990; Thornton & Cleveland 1990; Kriek 1991; Kriek et al. 1994; Klimoski & Brickner 1987).

The assessment centre process in practice consists of participants (assessees) performing various types of activities during one or more days, observed by various assessors or observers. A key aspect of the assessment process is that observers must make written notes of examples of observed behaviours in order to classify behaviours according to certain dimensional definitions and scale descriptions. Many of these are personality-work-related dimensions, an important reason why assessment centres should be administered or controlled by professional psychologists, and why assessors must be well-trained in behaviour observation.

At least some of the measurement techniques used in assessment centres simulate aspects of a job or a category of jobs, such as managerial jobs. Techniques or combinations used in assessment centres are psychological questionnaires, sentence completion tests, biodata questionnaires, interviews and *situational exercises*. The latter are constructed to simulate real-life situations (also on video and computer), for instance to assess behaviour while participants are engaged in a meeting or discussion; or to assess managerial competencies after participants have completed simulated managerial tasks such as writing letters, answering complaints, analysing a financial problem or presenting findings to a panel.

Situational tests can also take the form of questionnaires offering various alternative courses of action to be taken in situations. An example is to ask a manager to select the action he or she would take when an employee refuses to carry out an instruction (repeat the instruction; ask whether the employee is worried about something; fire the employee immediately; change the instruction).

Situational tasks and tests may take the form of *in-basket exercises*: here the participant "manages" in a simulated "office" a selection of tasks, gives directions, delegates tasks, structures work and controls the work of others – all in written form (letters, memos, etc.). In-basket exercises are often also used outside assessment centres as a selection instrument.

Other situational tasks are leaderless group discussions on actual work problems; problem-analysing exercises (for example a marketing problem) and verbal presentations (participants having to present a specific problem and possible solutions).

To develop assessment centre processes and technologies is complex and it must be done by well-trained psychologists and human resources professionals. One of the crucial aspects is the personality-related performance dimensions on which the assessments are based. The following list of managerial performance dimensions integrated with personality variables is suggested by Borman and Brush (1993):
- planning and organisation
- guiding, directing, motivating subordinates and giving feedback
- coaching and developing subordinates
- communicating effectively and keeping others informed
- representing the organisation to others and the public
- technical proficiency
- administration and paperwork
- maintaining good working relationships
- coordinating subordinates and resources to get the work done
- decision-making and problem-solving
- staffing
- persisting to reach goals
- handling crises and stress
- commitment to the organisation
- monitoring and controlling resources
- delegating
- selling and influencing
- collecting and interpreting data

Assessment centres are generally rated as very reliable and as having more predictive validity than other assessment instruments, especially for selection, training and promotion. They are also more free of culture bias (Jansen & de Jongh 1997; Gaugler et al. 1987; Kriek et al. 1994; Kriek 1991). In addition, assessment centres enjoy positive acceptance by management, employees and often other interested parties because they are based on work simulation and work performance criteria. However, they are not without critics.

23.4.4.4 Self-observation
An interesting variant of behaviour analysis is self-observation and self-monitoring techniques. Assessees are trained or expected to observe and record their own behaviours. This may be in the form of carefully writing down feelings and thoughts, and keeping diaries or autobiographies on behaviours such as health and life style habits, fears, eating and drinking habits, ways of doing tasks and solving problems, career interests, etc. Content analysis of these self-observations can render valuable information on personality and specific behaviours.

Problems associated with self-observation are the subjectiveness of people about themselves, and the difficulty of classifying data in valid frameworks for interpretation.

23.4.4.5 Interviews and other interactional methods

Interviews and conjunction with questionnaires are often used in surveys. They are also used for assessments in clinical and work settings, frequently in conjunction with rating scales.

> An interview is a purposeful, face-to-face or interpersonal event, a discussion or communication between two or more persons (for instance a selection officer and applicant), with a specific objective in mind (such as obtaining, giving or sharing information) in order to assess, influence or facilitate behaviour.

The effectiveness of interview assessment depends on how well this *purposeful conversation* between people is planned and conducted. Although interviews may differ in their objectives, most interviews are similar as regards the processes involved.

The interview for personality assessment is an interpersonal, interactive or interactional technique, for example when people are observed in dyadic and group discussions. This means that personality will be demonstrated in the interpersonal situation between interviewer and interviewee or between group members. In this respect, some personality theorists, for instance Sullivan and Rogers, emphasise that personality is best expressed in *recurrent* interpersonal situations and is also dependent on the quality of caring in relationships; while authors such as Anchin and Kiesler (1982) and Wiggins (1979) describe personality in terms of interpersonal traits.

Because of the strong interpersonal influences during interviews, a skilled interviewer must plan the interview and create the conditions to facilitate or elicit the behaviours to be assessed. It is, for instance, essential that the behaviour dimensions to be assessed are described and defined in specific terms and are clearly reflected in the interview questions and rating scales.

The training of interviewers is also crucial. We must never assume that merely because we are humans and talk, meaningful communication takes place. To be effective observers and raters of behaviour in interviews, the assessors must learn not only to listen to the expressed, *overt contents* of messages (the report level of meaning), but especially to understand or "hear" the *underlying meaning* of messages (the command level of meaning). The "command" level of messages is often conveyed by *how* people say and do things and by non-verbal behaviours (body language), rather than by *what* is said or done. This finds expression in how the body and features are moved (kinetics), the distance between people (proxemics), the tone of voice, rate or speed of talking (paralinguistics), and so on.

For an inexperienced person it is better to use a structured format of interviewing in which an exact procedure can be followed in terms of questions, answers and method of scoring and interpretation:

- *Structured or patterned interviews* are those in which an exact interview format is followed according to a specific schedule or guide on topics (for example performance areas or aspects important to the job) and related questions. Structured interviews have the advantage that assessees are asked the same questions by a particular interviewer and even by different interviewers.
- *Unstructured interviews* have little or even no structure in terms of the topics and questions to be covered, and sometimes even in how the interview will be started and conducted. However, even

unstructured interviews can be well planned: the skilled interviewer will determine which areas are to be covered, although the questions may be more open-ended and asked in a random manner.

Both structured and unstructured interviewing assessments of human behaviours and personality require skill. We must take care to construct and ask questions in a way that facilitates and does not inhibit communication and information.

Interviews can produce many errors and subjective rating problems if not planned and executed well. Some of the criticisms are:

- Decisions may be made on the basis of first impressions, such as during the first five minutes.
- Decisions may be influenced by the order in which people are interviewed. People's attributes may be rated either better or worse than they should be, depending on the credentials of preceding assessees – the so-called contrast effect.
- Interviewers use their own preferences, prejudices and stereotypes in rating people.
- Decisions are influenced by interviewers being unprepared, untrained and inexperienced.
- Interviewers will take more note of negative than positive information, or of information obtained earlier or later in the interview.
- Gender and race may influence interview decisions. Examples are an attractive member of the opposite sex; belonging to either the same race or a different race (the latter under the pressures of affirmative action, for instance).
- Decisions are often more influenced by non-verbal behaviours than by verbal behaviours; for instance, an applicant with a specific mannerism, or an applicant sitting very still (who may be assessed as passive).
- Interviewers are influenced by the tendency of applicants to exhibit socially desirable behaviours (to put their best foot forward) or to practise "impression management".

Although earlier findings on interview reliability and validity were often disheartening, more recent findings are more supportive. This is because researchers and practitioners design interviews more carefully (for instance to ensure that specific interviews are used in specific applications), the questions asked are based on the relevant behavioural dimensions to be assessed, there is more use of panel and structured interviews and other techniques in conjunction with interviews, well-defined behaviourally anchored rating scales are used to assess interview behaviour, and interviewers are being well trained.

In general interviews have proved to have reasonable reliability and validity coefficients in relation to predicting work performance outcomes (Harris 1989; McDaniel 1989; Arvey & Campion 1982; Raza & Carpenter 1987; Rynes & Gerhart 1990). This is especially true if panel interviews and a structured interview format are used; in these cases a reliability of 0,70 or higher is reported (Campion, Pursell & Brown 1988). Reliability is enhanced if interviewers are well trained and use the same well-defined behavioural dimensions and rating scales when assessing interview information.

Structured interviews also yield acceptable validity correlations of 0,63 (Schmitt & Robertson 1990), especially those specifically designed for particular situations (Latham & Finnegan 1993). Validity in interview assessment is enhanced if interviewers are "valid" (good in what they do) and if all interview information used in the assessment is valid or relevant to the interview purpose. There is no validity in assessing work-related personality dimensions in an interview if the questions deal only with the applicant's leisure time!

Interviews remain less effective than biodata, scores on cognitive tasks, tests, assessment centres and work samples.

23.5 RATING SCALES

Rating scales involve the assessment, by assessors or subjects themselves, of defined behaviour dimensions on specific numerical or descriptive and behaviourally based rating scales. Rating scales are often used on their own, but mostly in conjunction with interviews and other observation procedures.

Various types of rating scales are used. Each has a different format for stating the behaviour dimensions (for example performance criteria or personality traits) and number of scale points on which dimensions must be assessed (Muchinsky 1990; Saal & Knight 1995; Dipboye et al. 1994).

23.5.1 Graphic scales

The simplest is the graphic rating scale, consisting of trait labels or brief descriptions of performance criteria and a scale or continuum for rating, as shown in figure 23.6. These scales can be utilised to assess any behaviour dimension: time management, supervisory ability, interpersonal sensitivity, and so on.

23.5.2 Behaviourally anchored rating scales (BARS)

Behaviourally anchored rating scales (BARS), of which many variations can be constructed, are very often used. This is one

of the best assessment methods as BARS are criterion-referenced (based on critical incident analysis of desirable and undesirable work behaviours) and describe scale points exactly in terms of specific behaviours or criteria (Harvey 1991; Muchinsky 1990; Landy & Farr 1983; Wiersma & Latham 1986; Kingstrom & Bass 1981). The assessor evaluates the employee on a scale from, say, (1) very positive to (9) very negative behaviours, each of the nine scale points being defined exactly. Figure 23.6 shows a simplified BARS for assessing empathy, which is an important performance personality measure for human resources workers involved in interviewing, feedback, negotiations, councelling and client relations.

23.5.3 Other rating scales

Other types of rating scales include behaviour observation scales (BOS) (Latham & Wexley 1981), forced choice (Tenopyr 1988), checklists, semantic differentials and the Q-sort-technique.

• The *semantic differential* (Osgood, Suci & Tannenbaum 1957) is primarily used in research on social, psychological and personality variables, and also in transactional assessments to determine person-environment fit (Pervin 1968), for instance how employees or students see themselves fitting into an organisation or university.

The technique employs a seven-point scale on which the personal or *connotative meanings* of phenomena or constructs (for example mother, health, work, truth, democracy, fairness, trust, love, religion) are rated on several

(a) Excellent				Poor		
(b) Excellent	5	4	3	2	1	Poor
(c) Always on time	Often on time	Occasionally late	Often late	Always late		

Figure 23.6 Various types of graphic scales

descriptive or adjective scales, such as good vs bad, strong vs weak, poor vs excellent. Once the personal meanings for a person or group have been established on the relevant concepts, these are compared to generic or main semantic dimensions (namely evaluation, potency and activity) which had been established by factor analysis. This determines the extent of similarity between the norm and the semantic meanings attached to the concepts by the individuals and groups, which then represents the person's or group's semantic space.

- The so-called *Q-sort technique* was constructed by Stephenson in 1953, but popularised by Carl Rogers in order to assess changes in the self-concept. The assessee must sort a number of

Empathy:	The social/interpersonal/communication ability to understand (attending, listening, hearing, comprehending, responding, keeping to the point) another person's communication/messages as if in that person's place and to communicate (with questions, remarks, summaries, reflexes, etc.) this understanding in an accurate and unbiased way (by showing caring, creating trust and a positive climate).
4 =	Listens attentively with no interruptions; is absolutely accurate when responding, showing understanding of the obvious and underlying meanings of verbal and non-verbal messages (behaviour, feelings and attitudes); gives accurate responses which enable the client also to respond, elaborate and explore more freely; keeps to the point; even when using personal experiences as an example, this is to facilitate communication and for the client's benefit.
3 =	Has minor attention lapses, such as moving around, sometimes losing eye contact; is mostly accurate, but sometimes misses meanings of messages; the client in some instances has to correct the assessor's responses or repeat messages; tends to ask one or two questions out of place/context and deviates from the point occasionally, such as telling the employee some personal matter without any obvious relevance.
2 =	Has regular lapses in concentration; seems uneasy and often does not make eye contact; often repeats questions; the client must often correct the assessor's understanding of what was said or happened; the client seems rather uneasy and may communicate this, which the assessor may ignore; the assessor often deviates from the point and tends to talk about personal matters, often without relevance.
1 =	Seems totally unprepared and not in control; very uneasy and mostly avoids eye contact; only asks question, without responding to what the client says or does; if the assessor responds it is mostly inaccurate and answers must be repeated; the client seems irritated and communicates this strongly but is ignored by the assessor; the assessor changes topic abruptly and talks mainly about personal matters without any relevance.

Figure 23.7 Shortened behaviourally anchored rating scale to assess empathy

statements (usually 100) about personality, self-concept, aspects of behaviour or any other topic into clusters of 10, ranging from the least to the most characteristic or applicable. Q-sort statements are usually written for specific topics, but standardised sets of statements also exist, for instance on personality. The Q-sort can be used to assess people's rating of their true selves as compared to idealised selves, or their perceptions before and after a specific intervention, such as training or psychotherapy. Kelly, in his personal construct theory, utilises a similar technique (the Role Construct Repertory Test or Rep-test) to assess people's personal constructs about themselves, other people and other aspects in terms of their likes and dislikes (Gregory 1996; Schultz & Schultz 1994).

- *Checklists* on behaviours or traits usually consist of lists of positive or negative descriptive statements about performance tasks or personality traits. The assessee or assessor merely indicates whether each item in the checklist is applicable or not. Although checklists are mostly constructed for specific purposes, standardised checklists exist for personality assessment. Of these, the Adjective Check List (ACL) is well known. Assessees must indicate the applicability to themselves of 300 self-descriptive statements, and are then classified in 37 scales on various aspects of personality and self-concept. Another well-known standardised checklist is the Mooney Problem Check List, of which various forms are available. By checking 210 to 330 items, various aspects of life are assessed, such as economy, occupation, social relations, family, marriage and religion (Gregory 1996).

23.6 PSYCHOBIOLOGICAL AND OTHER TECHNIQUES

Many other techniques – some controversial – may be used in personality assess-ment for the purpose of research, selection, promotion, training and so on.

The *polygraph* or lie detector is a physiological measure to assess the relationship between bodily reactions and psychological behaviours, and in this way to test *integrity*. Although it has many critics and is even prohibited in places, this technique is used in police and legal work, especially in criminal offences. The polygraph measures physiological changes in breathing, pulse rate, perspiration and blood pressure as a result of certain stimuli, for instance questions about offences. Although controversial (Honts & Perry 1992), physiological measurements such as by the polygraph have enjoyed much success, largely because measurements are done on real bodily reactions under controlled conditions (El-laad, Ginton & Jungman 1992).

In the work context, *employee health* is an important consideration when assessing the fit between people's characteristics, the demands of the workplace and job satisfaction. Various physical and physiological measurements can form part of personality assessment. You will remember that psychological and physiological personality factors are linked to various forms of illness, such as cancer, heart disease, asthma, and tension and migraine headaches (Nowack 1991; Friedman & Booth-Kewley 1987), as well as to occupational accidents (Dipboye et al. 1994). Over a two-year period, Howard et al. (1977) found in managerial and professional men a positive connection between increased coronary risk factors such as high blood pressure and increased fat deposits in the blood (as a result of type A behaviours) and lower job satisfaction. Biological models for accident proneness, for instance, explain industrial accidents on the basis of biorhythm cycles, maintaining that people's intellectual, physical and emotional cycles influence accident behaviours. Findings in this regard, however, are still controversial (Dipboye et al. 1994).

Genetic screening, a related technique from the field of occupational diseases, is used to detect employees who are susceptible to certain chemical substances or extreme conditions in work environments (Olian 1984).

A specific application of physical and physiological measurements is in *ergonomic work design.* Its purpose is to achieve a comfortable fit between employees' physical characteristics and the physical characteristics and demands of workplaces, not only in general but also in specific occupations in which certain physical and psychological stress factors are abnormally high, such as working in extreme temperatures or noise. Besides undertaking job and situational analysis to determine the fit between the employee and the work environment, ergonomists are also interested in human factors, especially to determine the cognitive and physiological nature of possible errors. They pay particular attention to the following aspects of human behaviour:

- The *margin of error,* which includes aspects such as omission (forgetfulness), commission (incorrect performance), extraneous or deviant acts (behaviour not according to standards), sequential errors (actions performed out of sequence) and time errors (too early, long, late).
- *Human reliability,* which indicates the possibility or probability that an employee will perform a task successfully. For instance, a reliability probability of 0,65 means that the employee is likely to execute the task correctly 65 times out of 100.
- *Human capabilities and limitations* in respect of hearing (auditory), sight (visual) and smell are important to employees for signal detection; for instance, to see lights, displays and controls, to hear alarms and even to smell substances. The human capability of information processing is also very

important in the execution of work, because people have varying capabilities and limitations in respect of receiving information, remembering information and being able to retrieve such information. We are only capable of learning and concentrating optimally for a certain time duration; therefore there is an optimum mental workload that people can absorb while remaining alert and productive. Obviously, these capabilities vary for different people, in different jobs and in different situations.

Many pseudo-psychological assessment techniques, such as handwriting analysis (graphology) and horoscopy, are interesting, but there is mixed or scant scientific evidence for their efficacy (Ben-Shakar et al. 1986).

23.7 CONCLUSION

After many decades of theorising and research on human behaviour in interaction with various environments, enough is known about these phenomena to enable us to assess human behaviours with reasonable accuracy. The following knowledge about human behaviour is relevant:

- There are many individual and group differences.
- Personality is characterised by a core of behaviours which is reasonably consistent over time and situations.
- People and situations have identifiable dimensions or characteristics, which may be common to all people and situations (generic), common to some people or situations, or unique.
- The characteristics of people and situations can be measured and compared.
- Behaviour can be very situation-specific, meaning that various situations influence different people differently.
- The interaction between an employee and the work environment is reciprocal.
- Some behaviours may be the result of unique or individual characteristics,

while others may result from the interaction between the person and the
situation.

- Human behaviour can mostly only be
assessed indirectly and retrospectively;
that is, our scores and results are
merely representations of human behaviours (and not the actual behaviours
themselves). From these we try to
describe, explain and predict actual
behaviours.

The various techniques and different perspectives help us to explain, describe and
predict human behaviour in all its rich
variety and in and across different cultures. They also enable us to select an
applicable technique for specific situations.
We must, however, never cease to find new
techniques and verify existing ones for
specific people in their unique contexts,
so as never to practise unfairness or
discrimination.

In the work context there is still a need for
much refinement in assessing the relationship between personality and occupational
behaviours. Effectively assessing personality in any context, however, will always
largely depend on how competent we are
in using the available scientific methods of
personality assessment.

Self-evaluating questions

1. Use examples to describe why psychological principles or knowledge allows
us to assess personality.
2. Think about your own personality or job
and define the five to 10 personality
attributes that you regard as the most
important.
3. Use your answer to the previous question to illustrate how you can assess
these attributes by writing a few statements on each or using a rating scale.
4. Analyse your job or a job and write down
its main tasks and a few questions on
each, which you will use in an interview in
order to assess the relevant personality
attributes of an applicant for this job.
5. Use your answer to the previous
question and write down items or
questions that you think should be
included in a biographical questionnaire for applicants to complete.
6. Explain the various methods to assess
personality.
7. Use any classification of abilities, interests and values covered in this book or
in this chapter to describe yourself and
your job or another person's job.

Bibliography

Aamodt, M. G. 1991. *Applied industrial/organisational psychology*. Belmont, CA: Wadsworth.

Ackerman, P. L. 1992. Predicting individual differences in complex skill acquisition: Dynamics of ability determinants. *Journal of applied psychology*, 775: 598-614.

Acklin, M. W., Bibb, J. L., Boyer, P. & Jain, V. 1991. Early memories as expressions of relationship paradigms: A preliminary investigation. *Journal of personality assessment*, 57: 177-192.

Acklin, M. W., Sauer, A., Alexander, G. & Dugoni, B. 1989. Predicting depression using earliest childhood memories. *Journal of personality assessment*, 53: 51-59.

Adams, J. S. 1965. Inequity in social exchanges. In L. Berkowitz (Ed.), *Advances in experimental social psychology* (pp 267-300). New York: Academic Press.

Adler, S. 1996. Personality and work behaviour: exploring the linkages. *Applied psychology: an international review*, 453: 207-224.

Ahia, C. E. 1991. Cultural contextualization of diagnostic signs, symptoms and symbols in international mental health: a focus on DSM – III – R. *Journal of college student psychotherapy*, 6(1): 37-51.

Aiken, L. R. 1993. *Personality: theories, research and applications*. Englewood Cliffs: Prentice Hall.

Aiken, L. R. 1994. *Psychological testing and assessment*. 8th ed. Boston: Allyn & Bacon.

Ainsworth, M. D. S., Blehar, M. C., Waters, E. & Wall, S. 1979. *Patterns of attachment*. New York: Halstead Press.

Ainsworth, M. D. S. & Bowlby, J. 1991. An ethnological approach towards personality development. *American psychologist*, 46: 333-341.

Akbar, N. 1996. African metapsychology of human personality. In A. D. ya Azibo. 1996. *African psychology in historical perspective and related commentary*. Trenton, NJ: Africa World Press.

Allen, B. P. 1994. *Personality theories*. Boston: Allyn and Bacon.

Allport, G. W. 1961. *Pattern and growth in personality*. New York: Holt, Rhinehart & Winston.

Allport, G. W. 1970. The transformation of motives. In W. A. Russell (Ed.), *Milestones in motivation* (pp 344-363). New York: Meredith Corporation.

Allport, G. W., Vernon, P. E. & Lindsey, G. 1951, 1960. *Study of values*. Boston: Houghton Mifflin.

Altman, J. 1990. Centripetal and centrifugal trends in psychology. In L. Bickman & H. Ellis (Eds), *Preparing psychologists for the 21st century: procedures of the national conference of graduate education in psychology* (pp 39-64). Hillside, NJ.: Lawrence Erlbaum.

American Psychiatric Association. 1994. *Diagnostic and statistical manual of mental disorders (DSM-IV)*, 4th ed. Washington DC: American Psychiatric Association.

American Psychological Association (APA). 1992. Ethical principles of psychologists and code of conduct. *American psychologist*, 47: 1597-1611.

Anchin, J. C. & Kiesler, D. J.1982. *Handbook of interpersonal psychotherapy*. New York: Pergamon.

Anderson, S. M. & Bem, S. L. 1981. Sex typing and androgyny in dyadic interaction: individual differences in responsiveness to physical attractiveness. *Journal of personality and social psychology*, 41: 74-86.

Anderson, T. D. 1992. *Transforming leadership: new skills for an extraordinary future*. Massachusetts: Human Resource Development Press, Inc.

Ankrah, E. M. 1991. Aids and the social side of health. *Social science and medicine*, 32(9): 967-980.

Antonovsky, A. 1984. A call for a new question-salutogenesis and a proposed answer – the sense of coherence. *Journal of preventive psychiatry*, 2: 1-13.

Antonovsky, A. 1987. *Unravelling the mystery of health*. San Francisco: Jossey-Bass.

Apostal, R. & Marks, C. 1990. Correlations between the Strong-Campbell and Myers-Briggs scales of introversion-extroversion and career interests. *Psychological reports*, 66: 811-816.

Argyle, M. C. 1992. *The social psychology of every day life*. London: Routledge.

Argyle, M. C. 1995. *The social psychology of work*. Harmondsworth: Penguin.

Arkin, R. M. & Burger, J. M. 1980. Effects of unit relation tendencies on interpersonal attraction. *Social psychology quarterly*, 43: 380-391.

Armstrong, M. 1995. *A handbook of personnel*

management practice. 5th ed. London: Kogan Page, Ltd.

Arnheim, R. A. 1947. Perceptual abstraction and art. Psychological review, 54: 66-82.

Arnold, J., Cooper, C. L. & Robertson, I. T. 1995. Work psychology. Understanding human behaviour in the workplace. 2nd ed. London: Pitman.

Arthur, N. M. 1990. The assessment of burnout: a review of three inventories useful in research and counseling. Journal of counseling and development, 69(11): 186-189.

Arvey, R. D. 1986. Sex bias in job evaluation procedures. Personnel psychology, 39: 315-335.

Arvey, R. D. & Campion, J. E. 1982. The employment interview: a summary and review of recent research. Personnel psychology, 35: 281-322.

Ashford, S. J. 1988. Individual strategies for coping with stress during organizational transitions. The journal of applied behavioral science, 24(1):19-36.

Ashforth, B. S. & Lee, R. T. 1990. Defensive behaviour in organisations: a preliminary model. Human relations, 43: 621-648.

Atwood, J. D. & Maltin, L. 1991. Putting Eastern philosophies into Western psychotherapies. American journal of psychotherapy. XLV(3): 368-382.

Auerbach, S. M. & Gramling, S. E. 1998. Stress management: psychological foundations. Upper Saddle River, NJ: Prentice Hall.

Avery, G. & Baker, E. 1990. Psychology at work. New York: Prentice Hall.

Azibo, D. A. 1989. African-centred theses on mental health and nosology of black/African personality disorder. Journal of black psychology, 15(2): 173-214.

Azibo, D. A. 1996. African psychology in historical perspective and related commentary. Trenton, NJ: Africa World Press.

Badenhorst, D. C. 1992. The limitations and possibilities of the South African education system in the inculcation of values. Scriptura. Tydskrif vir Bybel en Teologie in Suider-Afrika, 41: 1-12.

Baker, F. & McEwan, P. J. 1969. Industrial organisations and health. Vol. 1: selected readings. London: Tavistock.

Baltes, P. B. 1987. Theoretical propositions of life-span developmental psychology: on the dynamics of growth and decline. Developmental psychology, 23: 611-626.

Baltes, P. B. 1993. The ageing mind: potential and limits. Gerontologist, 33(5): 580-594.

Bandura, A. 1977. Self-efficacy: toward a unifying theory of behavioural change. Psychological review, 84: 191-215.

Bandura, A. 1986. Social foundations of thought and action. A social cognitive theory. Englewood Cliffs, NJ: Prentice-Hall.

Banyard, P. & Hays, N. 1994. Psychology: theory and application. London: Chapman & Hall.

Barnett, M. & Pleack, M. 1992. Men's multiple roles and their relationship to men's psychological distress. Journal of marriage and the family, 54: 358-367.

Barocas, H., Reichman, W. & Schwebel, A. I. 1983. Personal adjustment and growth: a life span approach. New York: St. Martin's Press.

Baron, R. A. & Byrne, D. 1994. Social psychology: Understanding social interaction. 7th ed. Boston: Allyn and Bacon.

Baron, R. A. 1996. Essentials of psychology. Needham Heights: Allyn & Bacon.

Barrick, M. R. & Mount, M. K. 1991. The big five personality dimensions and job performance: A meta-analysis. Personnel psychology, 44: 1-26.

Barrick, M. R. & Mount, M. K. 1993. Autonomy as a moderator of the relationship between the big five personality dimensions and job performance. Journal of applied psychology, 78: 111-118.

Barrick, M. R., Mount, M. K. & Strauss, J. R. 1993. Conscientiousness and sales performance of sales representatives: test of the mediating effects of goal setting. Journal of applied psychology, 78: 715-722.

Baumeister, R. F. & Leary, M. R. 1995. The need to belong: desire for interpersonal attachments as a fundamental human motivation. Psychological bulletin, 117: 497-529.

Beck, A. T. 1991. Cognitive therapy: A 30-year relationship. The American psychologist, 464: 368-375.

Beck, A. T. 1993. Cognitive therapy: past, present and future. Journal of consulting and child psychology, 61(2): 194-199.

Beilin, H. & Pufall, P. 1992. Piaget's theory: prospects and possibilities. New Jersey: Prentice-Hall.

Belbin, M. 1981. Management teams. London: Heineman.

Bendix, S. 1996. Industrial relations in the new South Africa. 3rd ed. Cape Town: Juta.

Bennett, P. & Murphy, S. 1996. Psychology and health promotion. Buckingham: Open University Press.

Ben-Shakar, G., Bar-Hillel, M., Bilu, Y., Ben-Abba, E. & Flug, A. 1986. Can graphology predict occupational success: two empirical studies and some methodological ruminations. Journal of applied psychology, 71: 645-653.

Ben-Sira, Z. 1985. Potency: a stress-buffering link in the coping-stress-disease relationship. Social sciences medical journal, 21(4): 397-406.

Berglas, S. & Jones, E. E. 1978. Drug choice as a self-handicapping strategy in response to non-contingent success. *Journal of personality and social psychology,* 36: 405-417.

Berkowitz, L. 1989. Frustration-aggression hypothesis: examination and reformation. *Psychological bulletin,* 106: 59-73.

Bion, W. R. 1989. *Experiences in groups.* London: Routledge.

Block, J. 1995. A contrarian view of the five factor approach to personality description. *Psychological bulletin,* 117: 187-215.

Bluen, S. D., Barling, J. & Burns, W. 1990. Predicting sales performance, job satisfaction, and depression by using Achievement Strivings and Impatience-Irritability dimensions of Type A behaviour. *Journal of applied psychology,* 75: 212-216.

Boehm, V. R. 1980. Research in the real world – a conceptual model. *Personnel psychology,* 33: 495-504.

Bolton, B. & Jaques, M. E. 1978. *Rehabilitation counseling: theory and practice.* Baltimore: University Park Press.

Booth-Kewley, S. & Friedman, H. S. 1987. Psychological predictors of heart disease: a quantitative review. *Psychological bulletin,* 101: 343-362.

Booth-Butterfield, M. 1991. *Communication, cognition and anxiety.* Newbury Park: Sage.

Bootzin, R. R., Bower, G. H., Crocker, J. & Hall, E. 1991. *Psychology today.* 7th ed. New York: McGraw-Hill Inc.

Bordin, E. S. 1990. Psychodynamic model of career choice and satisfaction. In D. Brown, L. Brooks & Associates (Eds), *Career choice and development: applying contemporary theories to practice* (pp 102-144), 2 nd ed. San Francisco: Jossey-Bass.

Bores-Rangel, E., Church, A. T., Szendre, D. & Reeves, C. 1990. Self-efficacy in relation to occupational consideration and academic performance in high school equivalency students. *Journal of counseling psychology,* 37: 407-418.

Borkenau, P. & Lieber, A. 1992. Trait inferences: sources of validity at zero acquaintance. *Journal of personality and social psychology,* 62: 645-657.

Borman, D. H. & Brush, D. H. 1993. More progress towards a taxonomy of managerial performance requirements. *Human performance,* 6: 1-21.

Bornman, W. C. & Montewidlo, S. J. 1993. Expanding the criterion space to include elements of contextual performance. In N. Schmitt & W. C. Borman (Eds), *Personnel selection* (pp 71-98). San Francisco: Jossey-Bass.

Bornstein, R. F. 1989. Exposure and affect: Overview and meta-analysis of research, 1968-1987. *Psychological bulletin,* 106: 265-289.

Bornstein, R. F. & D'Agostina, P. R. 1992. Stimulus recognition and the mere exposure effect. *Journal of personality and social psychology,* 63: 545-552.

Bowlby, J. 1988. *A secure base.* New York: Basic Books.

Bradnum, M., Nieuwoudt, J. & Tredoux, C. 1993. Contact and the integration of racial attitudes in South Africa. *South African journal of psychology,* 23(4): 204-211.

Brammer, L. M. & Shostrom, E. L. 1982. *Therapeutic psychology.* Englewood Cliffs, NJ: Prentice-Hall.

Brief, A. P. & Montewidlo, S. J. 1986. Prosocial organisational behaviours. *Academy of management review,* 11: 710-725.

Briggs Meyers, I. 1962. *Manual: The Meyers Briggs Type Indicator.* Princeton: New York Educational Testing Service.

Briggs, I. 1993. *Introduction to type.* Palo Alto, California: Consulting Psychologists Press.

Brodt, S. E. 1990. Cognitive illusions and personnel management decisions. In C. L. Cooper & I. T. Robertson (Eds), *International review of industrial and organisational psychology, Vol. 5.* (pp 229-279). Chichester: Wiley & Sons.

Brooke, P. P. & Price, J. L. C. 1989. The determinants of employee absenteeism: an empirical test of a casual model. *Journal of occupational psychology,* 62: 1-19.

Brousseau, K. R. & Driver, M. J. 1994. Enhancing informed choice: a career concepts approach to career advisement. *The magazine of the graduate management admission council,* Spring: 24-31.

Brown, J. D., Novick, N. J., Lord, K. A. & Richards, J. M. 1992. When Gulliver travels: social context, psychological closeness and self-appraisals. *Journal of personality and social psychology,* 62: 717-727.

Bruce, W. M. 1990. *Problem employee management; proactive strategies for human resource managers.* New York: Quorum Books.

Buss, D. M. 1989. Sex differences in human mate preferences: evolutionary hypothesis tested in 37 cultures. *Behavioural and brain sciences,* 12: 1-49.

Buss, A. H. 1995. *Personality: temperament, social behaviour and the self.* Boston: Allyn and Bacon.

Byang-Hall, J. 1980. Symptom bearer as marital regulator: clinical implications. *Family process,* 19(4): 355-365.

Byrne, D. & Clore, G. L. 1970. A reinforcement model of evaluative responses. *Personality: an international journal,* 1: 103-128.

Caird, S. 1993. What do psychological tests suggest about entrepreneurs? *Journal of managerial psychology*, 8: 11-20.

Camp, R. R., Blanchard, P. N. & Huszczo, G. E. 1986. *Toward a more effective training strategy & practice*. Englewood Cliffs: Prentice-Hall.

Campbell, J. P. & Pritchard, R. D. 1983. Motivation theory in industrial and organisational psychology. In M. D. Dunnette (Ed.), *Handbook of industrial and organisational psychology*. New York: Wiley & Sons.

Campbell, J. P., McHenry, J. J. & Wise, L. L. 1990. Modelling job performance in a population of jobs. *Personnel psychology*, 43: 313-333.

Campbell, R. E. & Cellini, J. V. 1981. A diagnostic taxonomy of adult career problems. *Journal of vocational behaviour*, 19:175-190.

Campion, M. A., Pursell, E. D. & Brown, B. K. 1988. Structured interviewing: raising the psychometric properties of the employment interview. *Personnel psychology*, 41: 25-42.

Caprara, G.-V. & Van Heck, G. L. (Eds). 1992. *Modern personality psychology; critical reviews and new directions*. New York: Harvester & Wheatsheaf.

Carkhuff, R. R. 1983. *The art of helping*. Amherst: Human Resource Development Press.

Carli, I. L., Ganley, R. & Pierce-Otay, A. 1991. Similarity and satisfaction in roommate relationships. *Personality and social psychology bulletin*, 17: 419-426.

Carlisle-Frank, P. 1991. Examining personal control beliefs as a mediating variable in the health damaging behaviour of substance use: An alternative approach. *Journal of psychology*, 25: 381-397.

Carone, P. A. & Kiefer, S. M. (Eds). 1978. *Misfits in industry*. New York: S.P. Medical and Scientific Books.

Carroll, M. 1997. *Workplace counseling: a systematic approach to employee care*. London: Sage.

Carson, R. C. 1969. *Interaction concepts of personality*. Chicago: Aldine

Carson, R. C., Butcher, J. N. & Mineka, S. 1996. *Abnormal psychology and modern life*. 10 th ed. New York: Harper & Collins.

Carver, C. S. & Scheier, M. F. 1996. *Perspectives on personality*. 3rd ed. Boston: Allyn and Bacon.

Carvey, D. W. & Nibler, R. G. 1977. Biorhythmic cycles and the incidence of industrial accidents. *Personnel psychology*, 30: 447-454.

Cascio, W. F. 1991. *Applied psychology in personnel management*. 4th ed. Englewood Cliffs: Prentice Hall.

Cascio, W. F. 1995. Whither industrial and organizational psychology in a changing world of work. *American psychologist*, 50(11): 928-939.

Cascio, W. F. & Ramos, R. A. 1986. Development and application of a new method for assessing job performance in behavioural/economic terms. *Journal of applied psychology*, 71: 20-28.

Cascio, W. F., Alexander, R. A & Barret, G. V. 1988. Setting cut-off scores: legal, psychometric, and professional issues and guidelines. *Personnel psychology*, 41: 1-24.

Cascio, W. F. & Morris, J. R. 1990. A critical re-analysis of Hunter, Schmitt & Coggin's 1988 "Problems and pitfalls in using capital and financial accounting techniques in assessing the utility of personnel programs". *Journal of applied psychology*, 75: 410-417.

Caspi, A. & Herbener, E. S. 1990. Continuity and change: assortative marriage and the consistency of personality in adulthood. *Journal of personality and social psychology*, 58: 250-258.

Cattell, R. B. 1965, 1966. *The scientific analysis of personality*. Baltimore: Penguin.

Chapdelaine, A., Kenny, D. A. & LaFontana, K. M. 1994. Matchmaker, matchmaker, can you make me a match? Predicting a link between two inacquainted persons. *Journal of personality and social psychology*, 67: 83-91.

Child, I. L. 1968. Personality in culture. In E. F. Borgatta & W.W. Lambert (Eds), *Handbook of personality theory and research*. Chicago: Rand McNally.

Childs, A. & Klimoski, R. J. 1986. Successfully predicting career success: an application of the biographical inventory. *Journal of applied psychology*, 71: 3-8.

Chimezie, A. B. & Osigweh, Y. G. 1988. The challenge of responsibilities: confronting the revolution in workplace rights in modern organizations. *Employee responsibilities and rights journal*, 1(1): 5-23.

Cilliers, F. 1984. 'n Ontwikkelingsprogram in sensitiewe relasievorming as bestuursdimensie. Potchefstroom: Thesis D.Phil PU vir CHO.

Cilliers, F.v N. 1986. Ontwikkeling, konflik en kreatiwiteit. In J. Kroon (Ed.), *Algemene Bestuur*. Pretoria: Kagiso Tersiêr.

Cilliers, F.v N. 1988. Die konsep sielkundige optimaliteit in bestuur. *IPB-Joernaal*, 7(5):15-18.

Cilliers, F. 1991. Die veranderende rol van die bedryfsielkunde in Suid-Afrika. Inaugural lecture: University of South Africa.

Cilliers, F. 1995. Die effek van 'n groeigroepervaring op predikante. *NG Teologiese tydskrif*, XXXVI (4): 630-642.

Cilliers, F. 1995a. Fasiliteerderopleiding. *Journal of industrial psychology*. 213: 7-11.

Cilliers, F. & Koortzen, P. 1996. The psychodynamics of organisations. Paper presented at 2nd annual PsySSA congress, Johannesburg.

Clark, L. A. & Watson, D. 1988. Mood and the mundane: relations between daily life events and self-reported mood. *Journal of personality and social psychology*, 54: 296-308.

Clark, R. E. 1992. Human performance interventions for Irish organisations. *The Irish journal of psychology*, 131: 1-16.

Clarkson, P. 1990. The scope of stress counseling in organisations. *Employee counseling today*, 2(4): 3-6.

Clegg, C. W. & Wall, T. D. 1981. A note on some new scales for measuring aspects of psychological well-being at work. *Journal of occupational psychology*, 54: 211-225.

Cloninger, S. C. 1996. *Personality: description, dynamics, and development*. New York: Freeman.

Cohen, S. 1988. Psychosocial models of the role of social support in the etiology of physical disease. *Health psychology*, 7: 269-297.

Coldwell, D. A. L. 1985. A dialectical approach to investigating role conflict, job satisfaction and situational anxiety in an African industrial context. *International journal of psychology*, 10: 179-188.

Coleman, J. C., Butcher, H. N. & Carson, R. C. 1991. *Abnormal psychology and modern life*. Glenview, Ill.: Scott, Foresman & Co.

Cook, J. D., Hepworth, S. J., Wall, T. D. & Warr, P. B. 1981. *The experience of work: a compendium and review of 249 measures and their use*. London: Academic Press.

Cooper, C. L. & Payne, R. (Eds). 1978. *Stress at work*. Chichester: John Wiley.

Cooper, C. L. & Robertson, I. T. (Eds). 1990. *International review of industrial and organizational psychology, Vol. 5*. Chichester: Wiley & Sons.

Cooper, C. L. & Payne, R. (Eds). 1994. *Causes, coping and consequences of stress at work*. Chichester: Wiley & Sons.

Costa, P. T. 1991. Clinical use of the five-factor model: An introduction. *Journal of personality assessment*, 57: 393-398.

Costa, P. T., McCrae, R. R. & Dye, D. A. 1991. Facet scales for agreeableness and conscientiousness: a revision of the NEO personality inventory. *Personality and individual differences*, 12: 887-898.

Costa, P. T. & McCrae, R. R. 1995. Domains and facets: hierarchical personality assessment using the revised NEO personality Inventory. *Journal of personality assessment*, 64: 21-50.

Cox, T. 1991. Organizational culture, stress and stress management. *Work and stress*, 5(1): 1-4.

Cox, T. & Blake, S. 1991. Managing cultural diversity: Implications for organisational competitiveness. *Academy of management executive*, 5: 45-56.

Craig, G. J. 1996. *Human development*. 7th ed. Upper Saddle River, NJ: Prentice Hall.

Cronbach, L. J. 1957. The two disciplines of scientific psychology. *American psychologist*, 12: 671-684.

Cronkite, R. C. & Moos, R. H. 1984. The role of predisposing and moderating factors in the stress-illness relationship. *Journal of health and social behavior*, 25: 372-393.

Csikszentmihalyi, M. 1993. *The evolving self: a psychology for the third millennium*. New York: Harper Collins.

Cull, J. G. & Hardy, R. E. 1973. *Adjustment to work*. Springfield: G. C. Thomas Publishers.

Cummings, T. G. (Ed.). 1980. *Systems theory for organization development*. Chichester: Wiley.

Cunningham, M. R. 1988. Does happiness mean friendliness? Induced mood and heterosexual self-disclosure. *Personality and social psychology bulletin*, 14: 283-297.

Cunningham, M. R., Barbee, A. P. & Pike, C. L. 1990. What do women want: facialmetric assessment of multiple motives in the persception of male physical attractiveness. *Journal of personality and social psychology*, 59: 61-72.

Curtis, R. C. & Miller, K. 1986. Believing another likes or dislikes you: behaviours making the beliefs come true. *Journal of personality and social psychology*, 51: 284-290.

Czander, W. M. 1993. *The psychodynamics of work and organizations: theory and applications*. New York: Guildford Press.

Dalton, D. R., Krackhardt, D. M. & Porter, L. W. 1980. Functional turnover: an empirical assessment. *Journal of applied psychology*, 66(6): 716-21.

Darwin, C. R. 1970. Comparison of the mental powers of man and the lower animals. In W. A. Russell (Ed.), *Milestones in motivation* (pp 8-17). New York: Meredith Corporation.

Das, A. K. 1989. Beyond self-actualisation. *International journal for the advancement of counseling*, 12: 13-17.

Davies, G. 1992. Ganging up: How to build a multinational team. *Human resources*, Spring: 101-104.

Davis, S. 1990. Men as success objects and women as sex objects. A study of personal advertisements. *Sex roles*, 23: 43-50.

Davis, B. O., Holtz, N. & Davis, J. C. 1985.

Conceptual human physiology. Columbus: Charles E. Merrill Publishing Company.

Davis, R. V. & Lofquist, L. H. 1984. *A psychological theory of work adjustment: an individual-differences model and its applications.* Minneapolis: University of Minnesota Press.

De Board, R. 1978. *The psychoanalysis of organizations.* London: Routledge.

De Board, R. C. 1983. *Counseling people at work.* Aldershot: Gower.

Dejoy, D. M. & Wilson, M. G. 1995. *Critical issues in worksite health promotion.* Boston: Allyn & Bacon.

Delongis, A., Coyne, J. C., Dakof, C., Follman, S. & Lazarus, R. S. 1982. Relationship of daily hassles, uplifts, and major life events to health status. *Health psychology,* 1: 119-136.

DeNisi, A. S. 1996. *Cognitive approach to performance appraisal: A program of research.* New York: Routledge.

Derlega, V. J., Winstead, B. A. & Jones, H. J. 1991. *Personality: contemporary theory and research.* Chicago: Nelson-Hall Publishers.

Dickman, F., Challenger, B. R., Emener, W. G. & Hutchison, J. R. 1988. *Employee assistance programs: a basic text.* Springfield: Charles C. Thomas.

Digman, J. M. 1990. Personality structure: emergence of the five-factor model. *Annual review of psychology,* 41: 417-440.

Dion, K. K. 1972. Physical attractiveness and evaluations of children's transgressions. *Journal of personality and social psychology,* 24: 285-290.

Dion, K. L., Dion, K. K. & Keelan, J. P. 1990. Appearance anxiety as a dimension of social-evaluative anxiety; exploring the ugly duckling syndrome. *Contemporary social psychology,* 14(4): 220-224.

Dipboye, R. L., Smith, C. S. & Howell, W. C. 1994. *Understanding industrial and organizational psychology: an integrated approach.* Fort Worth: Harcourt Brace College Publishers.

Dorfman, P. W., Stephan, W. G. & Loveland, J. 1986. Performance appraisal behaviours: supervisor perceptions and subordinate reactions. *Personnel psychology,* 39: 579-597.

Downs, C. W., Smeyak, G. P. & Martin, E. 1980. *Professional interviewing.* Cambridge: Harper & Row.

Drapela, V. J. 1995. *A review of personality theories.* 2nd ed. Illinois: Charles C. Thomas.

Drum, D. J. 1987. Counseling psychologist or Hefflehump. *The counseling psychologist,* 15: 280-286.

Duck, S. & Wright, P. H. 1993. Re-examining gender differences in same gender friendships: a close look at two kinds of data. *Sex roles,* 28: 709-727.

Duckitt, J. 1992. Psychology and prejudice: a historical analysis and integrative framework. *American psychologist,* 47(10):1187-1193.

Duckitt, J. 1994. The relationship and factorial validity of a multidimensional measure of psychological symptomatology in South Africa. *South African journal of psychology,* 24(4): 194-200.

Dunnette, M. D. 1983. *Handbook of industrial and organizational psychology.* New York: John Wiley & Sons.

Dunnette, M. D. 1990. *Handbook of industrial and organizational psychology.* Chicago: Rand McNally.

Du Toit, L. B. H. 1983. *Manual for the Jung personality questionnaire.* Pretoria: Human Sciences Research Council.

Eberhardt, B. & Muchinsky, P. 1982. An empirical investigation of the factor stability of Owens biographical questionnaire. *Journal of applied psychology,* 67: 130-145.

Eckenrode, J. & Gore, S. (Eds). 1990. *Stress between work and family.* New York: Plenum Press.

Edwards, J. E. & Baglioni, A. J. 1993. The measurement of coping with stress: construct validity of the ways of coping checklist and the cybernetic coping scale. *Work and stress,* 7: 17-31.

Edwards, J. R. & Baglion, A. J. 1991. Relationship between Type A behaviour pattern and mental and physical symptoms: a comparison of global and component measures. *Journal of applied psychology,* 76: 276-290.

Egan, G. 1975. *The skilled helper.* Monterey: Brooks/Cole.

Eisenberg, N., Fabes, R. A., Murphy, B., Karbon, M., Maszk, A., Smith, M., O'Boyle, C. & Suh, K. 1994. The relations of emotionality and regulations to dispositional and situational empathy-related responding. *Journal of personality and social psychology,* 66: 776-797.

Eisenstat, R. A. & Felner, R. D. 1984. Toward a differentiated view of burnout: personal and organizational mediators of job satisfaction and stress. *American journal of community psychology,* 12: 411-30.

Ellaad, E., Ginton, A. & Jungman, N. 1992. Detection measures in real-life criminal guilty knowledge tests. *Journal of applied psychology,* 77: 757-767.

Endler, N. S. & Edwards, J. M. 1986. Interactionism in personality in the twentieth century. *Personality and individual differences,* 7: 379-384.

Engelbrecht, A. S. 1994. Die persoonlikheids-eienskappe en bestuurspotensiaal van bestuurs-gemotiveerde werkers. *Journal of industrial psychology*, 212: 1-5.

Engler, B. 1995. *Personality theories: an introduction*. 4th ed. Boston: Houghton Mifflin.

Epstein, S. 1980. The self-concept: a review and proposal of an integrated theory of personality. In E. Staub (Ed.). 1980. *Personality: basic aspects and current research*. Englewood Cliffs: Prentice-Hall.

Erikson, E. H. 1963. *Childhood and society*. Harmondsworth: Penguin.

Erikson, E. H. 1968. *Identity: Youth and crisis*. New York: Norton.

Evans, B. K. & Fischer, D. G. C. 1993. The nature of burnout: a study of the three-factor model of burnout in human service and non-human service samples. *Journal of occupational and organizational psychology*, 66(1): 29-38.

Ewen, R. B. 1993. *An introduction to theories of personality*. 4th ed. Hillsdale: Lawrence Erlbaum.

Eysenck, H. J. 1970. *The structure of human personality*. London: Methuen.

Eysenck, H. J. 1991. Personality as a risk factor in coronary health disease. *European journal of personality*, 5(2): 81-92.

Eysenck, H. J. 1991. Dimensions of personality: 16, 5 or 3? Criteria for a taxonomic paradigm. *Personality and individual differences*, 12(8): 773-790.

Eysenck, H. J. 1992. Four ways, five factors are not basic. *Personality and individual differences*, 13: 667-674.

Faust, D. & Ziskin, J. 1988. The expert witness in psychology and psychiatry. *Science*, 241: 31-35.

Feather, N. T. & O'Brien, G. S. 1986. A longitudinal study of the effects of employment and unemployment on school leavers. *Journal of occupational psychology*, 59: 121-144.

Feeney, J. A. & Noller, P. 1990. Attachment style as a predictor of adult romantic relationships. *Journal of personality and social psychology*, 58: 281-291.

Feingold, A. 1988. Matching for attractiveness in romantic partners and same-sex friends: A meta-analysis and theoretical critique. *Psychological bulletin*, 104: 226-235.

Feingold, A. 1992. Good looking people are not what we think. *Psychological bulletin*, 111: 304-341.

Festinger, L. 1954. A theory of social comparison processes. *Human relations*, 7: 117-140.

Firth, C. J. & Hardy, G. E. 1992. Occupational stress, clinical treatment and changes in job perceptions. *Journal of occupational and organizational psychology*, 65: 81-88.

Fisher, S. & Reason, J. C. (Eds). 1988. *Handbook of life stress, cognition and health*. Chichester: Wiley & Sons.

Fleming, R., Baum, A. & Singer, J. E. 1984. Toward an integrative approach to the study of stress. *Journal of personality and social psychology*, 46(4): 939-949.

Folkman, S. & Lazarus, R. 1980. An analysis of coping in a midlle-aged community sample. *Journal of health and social psychology*, 21: 219-239.

Folkman, S. 1982. An approach to the measurement of coping. *Journal of occupational behaviour*, 3: 95-107.

Folkman, S. 1984. Personal control and stress and coping processes: a theoretical analysis. *Journal of personality and social psychology*, 46(4): 839-852.

Follman, J. F. 1978. *Helping the troubled employee*. New York: AMACOM.

Forbes, R. 1979. *Corporate stress*. Garden City, NY: Doubleday.

Forgas, J. P. 1993. On making sense of odd couples: mood effects on the perception of mismatched relationships. *Personality and social bulletin*, 19: 59-70.

Frankenhaeuser, M. & Johansson, G. 1986. Stress at work: psychobiological and psychosocial aspects. *International review of applied psychology*, 35: 287-299.

Frankl, V. E. 1957. *The doctor and the soul. An introduction to logotherapy*. New York: Alfred A. Knopf.

Frankl, V. E. 1969. *The will to meaning, foundations and applications of logotherapy*. London: Souvenir Press.

Frankl, V. E. 1969. *Man's search for meaning*. New York: Washington Square Press.

Franzoi, S. L. & Hertzog, M. E. 1987. Judging physical attractiveness: what body aspects do we use? *Personality and social psychology bulletin*, 13: 19-33.

Franzoi, S. L. & Shields, S. A. 1984. The body esteem scale: multidimensional structure and sex differences in a college population. *Journal of personality assessment*, 48: 173-178.

Franzoi, S. L. 1996. *Social psychology*. Madison, Dubuque: Brown & Benchmark.

Freud, S. 1970. The unconscious. In W.A. Russell (Ed.), *Milestones in Motivation* (pp 332-343). New York: Meredith Corporation.

Freudenberger, H. J. 1974. Staff burnout. *Journal of social issues*, 30:159-165.

Friedman, H. S. & Booth-Kewley, S. 1987. The disease-prone personality: a meta-analytic view of the construct, *American psychologist,* 42(6): 539-555.

Friedman, H. S. 1990. *Personality and disease.* New York: Wiley.

Friedman, M. & Rosenman, R. H. 1974. *Type A behavior and your heart.* London: Wildworld House.

Friedman, H. S. & DiMatteo, M. R. 1989. *Health psychology.* Englewood Cliffs, NJ: Prentice-Hall.

Frieze, I. H., Olson, J. E. & Russell, J. 1991. Attractiveness and income for men and women in management. *Journal of applied social psychology,* 21: 1039-1057.

Frijda, N. H. 1996. Passions: emotion and socially consequential behavior. In R.D. Kavanaugh, B. Zimmerberg, S. Fein (Eds), *Emotion. Interdisciplinary perspectives* (pp 1-27). Mahwah, NJ: Lawrence Erlbaum Associates.

Frone, M. R., Russell, M. & Cooper, M. L. 1992. Antecedents and outcomes of work-family conflict: testing a model of the work-family interface. *Journal of applied psychology,* 77(1): 65-68.

Funder, D. C. & Colvin, C. R. 1991. Explorations in behaviour consistency: properties of persons, situations, and behaviours. *Journal of personality and social psychology,* 60: 773-794.

Funder, D. C. & Ozer, D. J. 1983. Behaviour as a function of the situation. *Journal of personality and social psychology,* 44: 107-112.

Furnham, A. 1984. The protestant work ethic: A review of the psychological literature. *European journal of social psychology,* 14: 87-109.

Furnham, A. 1990. *The Protestant work ethic: new psychology of work-related beliefs and behaviour.* London: Routledge.

Furnham, A. 1992. *Personality at work: the role of individual differences in the work place.* London: Routledge.

Furnham, A. 1997. *The psychology of behaviour at work: the individual in the organisation.* Hove East Sussex: Psychology Press.

Furnham, A. & Stringfield, P. 1993. Personality and occupational behaviour. *Human relations,* 46: 827-848.

Gaertner, S. L., Mann, J., Murrell, A. & Dovidio, J. F. 1990. Reducing intergroup bias: the benefits of re-categorization. *Journal of personality and social psychology,* 57: 239-249.

Galer, I. A. R. 1987. *Applied ergonomics handbook.* London: Butterworths.

Ganster, D. C. & Victor, B. 1988. The impact of social support on mental and physical health. *British journal of medical psychology,* 61: 17-36.

Ganster, D. C., Shaubroeck, J., Sime, W. E. & Mayes, B. T. 1991. The nomological validity of the Type A personality among employed adults. *Journal of applied psychology,* 76: 143-168.

Gardner, A. W. 1987. *Current approaches to occupational health.* Vol. 3. Bristol: Wright.

Gaugler, B. B., Rosenthal, D. B., Thornton, G. C. & Bentson, C. 1987. Meta-analysis of assessment centre validity. *Journal of applied psychology,* 72: 493-511.

Gavin, J. F. 1977. Occupational mental health focus and trends. *Personnel journal,* 4: 198-201.

Gechman, A. S. 1974. Without work life goes. *Journal of occupational medicine,* 16(11): 749-751.

Geier, P. D. & Hice, J. 1989. Reliabilities of ratings available from the Dictionary of Occupational Titles. *Personnel psychology,* 42: 547-560.

Geiselman, R. E., Haight, N. A. & Kimata, L. G. 1984. Context effects in the perceived physical attractiveness of faces. *Journal of experimental social psychology,* 20: 409-424.

Georgi, L. & March, C. 1990. The Protestant work ethic as a cultural phenomenon. *European journal of social psychology,* 20: 499-519.

Gerdes, L. C., Moore, C., Ochse, R. & Van Ede, D. 1988. *The developing adult.* 2nd ed. Pretoria: Butterworth.

German, G. E. 1987. Mental health in Africa: The nature of mental disorder in Africa today. *British journal of psychiatry,* 151: 440-446.

Gherman, E. M. 1981. *Stress and the bottom line.* New York: Amacom.

Gibson, J. L., Ivancevich, J. M. & Donnelly, J. H. 1991. *Organizations.* Homewood: Irwin.

Ginzberg, E. 1972. Toward a theory of occupational choice: a restatement. *Vocational guidance quarterly,* 20: 169-176.

Glasl, F. 1982. The process of conflict escalation and roles of third parties. In G. Bomers & R. Petersen (Eds), *Conflict management and industrial relations.* Boston: Kluwer.

Glass, D. C. & Carver, G. D. 1980. Helplessness and the coronary-prone personality. In J. Garber and M. E. P. Seligman (Eds), *Human helplessness: theory and applications.* New York: Academic Press.

Gobodo, P. 1990. Notions about culture in understanding black psychopathology: are we trying to raise the dead. *South African journal of psychology,* 20(2): 93-98.

Goldberg, D. P. & Hiller, V. F. 1979. A scaled down version of the general health questionnaire. *Psychological medicine,* 9: 139-145.

Goldberg, L. R. 1990. An alternative description of personality: the big five-factor structure. *Journal of personality and social psychology,* 59: 1216-1229.

Goldberg, L. R. 1993. The structure of phenotypic personality traits. *American psychologist,* 48: 26-34.

Goldstein, E. B. 1994. *Psychology.* Pacific Grove: Brooks/Cole.

Goldstein, I. L. 1993. *Training in organizations.* 3rd ed. Pacific Grove: Brooks/Cole.

Goleman, D. 1995. *Emotional intelligence.* New York: Bantam Books.

Gorman, B. S. & Wessman, A. E. 1977. Images, values, and concepts of time in psychological research. In B.S. Gorman & A. E. Wessman (Eds), *The personal experience of time...* New York: Plenum Press.

Gough, H. C. 1985. A work orientation scale for the California psychological inventory. *Journal of applied psychology,* 70: 505-513.

Government gazette. December 1997. Notice 1840 of 1997, Department of Labour, *Employment Equity Bill.* Pretoria.

Grandjean, E. 1988. *Fitting the task to the man: An ergonomic approach.* London: Taylor & Francis, Ltd.

Gray, P. 1994. *Psychology.* 2nd ed. New York: Worth Publishers.

Green, M. 1974. Counseling for employees. *Personnel practice bulletin,* 30(3): 234-243.

Greenberg, J., Solomon, S., Pyszczynski, T., Rosenblatt, A., Burling, J., Lyon, D., Simon, L., & Pinel, E. 1992. Why do people need self-esteem? Converging evidence that self-esteem serves an anxiety-buffering function. *Journal of personality and social psychology,* 63: 913-922.

Greenberg, J. & Baron, R. A. 1993. *Behaviour in organizations: understanding and managing the human side of work.* 4th ed. Needham Heights: Allyn and Bacon.

Greenhaus, J. H. & Parasurman, S. 1989. Sources of work-family conflict among two-career couples. *Journal of vocational behaviour,* 34: 133-153.

Greenwald, A. G. 1992. New look 3: unconscious cognition reclaimed. *American psychologist,* 47: 766-779.

Greenwood, J. W. & Greenwood, J. W. 1979. *Managing executive stress.* New York: Wiley.

Gregory, R. J. 1996. *Psychological testing: history, principles, and applications.* 2nd ed. Boston: Allyn and Bacon.

Griffiths, R. D. P. 1977. The prediction of psychiatric patients' work adjustment in the community. *British journal of clinical psychology,* 16: 165-173.

Grossman, H. Y. 1991. *The experience and meaning of work in women's lives.* Hillsdale, NJ: Erlbaum.

Grotjahn, M. 1957. *Beyond laughter.* New York: McGraw-Hill.

Guion, R. M. 1965. *Personnel testing.* New York: McGraw-Hill.

Guthrie Ford, J. 1991. Rogerion self-actualization: a clarification of meaning. *Journal of humanistic psychology,* 32(2): 101-111.

Guyton, A. C. 1996. *Textbook of medical physiology.* 9th ed. Philadelphia: W.B. Saunders Company.

Hackel, M. D. 1986. Personnel selection and placement. *Annual review of psychology,* 37: 351-380.

Hackett, G. & Betz, N. E. 1981. A self-efficacy approach to the career development of women. *Journal of vocational behaviour,* 18: 326-339.

Hackett, R. D. 1989. Work attitudes and employee absenteeism: a synthesis of the literature. *Journal of occupational psychology,* 62: 235-248.

Hackman, J. R. & Oldham, G. 1976. Motivation through the design of work: test of theory. *Organizational behaviour and human performance,* 16: 250-279.

Haley, J. 1963. *Strategies of psychotherapy.* New York: Greene & Stratton.

Halgin, R. P. & Whitbourne, S. K. 1997. *Abnormal psychology: the human experience of psychological disorders.* Madison, WI: Brown & Benchmark.

Hall, C. S. & Lindzey, G. 1957. *Theories of personality.* New York: Wiley.

Harris, J. R. 1995. Where is the child's environment? A group socialization theory of development. *Psychological review,* 102: 485-489.

Harris, M. M. & Schaubroeck, J. 1988. A meta-analysis of self-supervisor, self-peer, and peer-supervisor ratings. *Personnel psychology,* 41: 34-62.

Harris, T. W. 1989. Reconsidering the employment interview: a review of the recent literature and suggestions for future research. *Personnel psychology,* 42: 691-726.

Hart, E. A., Leary, M. R. & Rejeski, W. J. 1989. The measurement of social physique anxiety. *Journal of sport and exercise psychology,* 11: 94-104.

Harvey, R. J. 1991. Job analysis. In M. D. Dunnette & L. M. Hough (Eds), *Handbook of industrial and organisational psychology,* Vol. 2. Palo Alto: Consulting Psychological Press

Hatfield, F. & Ranson, R. L. 1992. Similarity and attraction in close relationships. *Communication monographs,* 59: 209-212.

Hattingh, L. 1991. 'n Teorie van waardes. Unpublished D. Ed-dissertation, Randse Afrikaanse Universiteit, Johannesburg.

Hattingh, M. 1993. Mirror, mirror on the wall. *People dynamics*, 11(11): 3-16.

Hayes, J. & Nutman, P. 1981. *Understanding the unemployed: The psychological effects of unemployment*. London: Tavistock.

Hays, R. B. 1985. A longitudinal study of friendship development. *Journal of personality and social psychology*, 48: 909-924.

Hazan, C. & Shaver, P. R. 1994. Attachment as an organisational framework for research on close relationships. *Psychology inquiry*, 5: 1-22.

Healy, C. C. 1982. *Career development: counseling through the life stages*. Boston: Allyn & Bacon.

Heaven, P. L., Connors, J. & Stones, C. R. 1994. Three or five personality dimensions? An analysis of natural language terms in two cultures. *Personality and individual differences*, 172: 181-189.

Heim, E. 1991. Job stressors and coping in health professions. *Psychotherapy and psychomatics*, 65: 90-99.

Hergenhahn, B. R. & Olson, M. H. 1993. *An introduction to theories of learning*. 4th ed. Englewood Cliffs: Prentice-Hall.

Herman, C. F. 1963. Some consequences of crisis which limit the viability of organizations. *Administrative science quarterly*, 8: 61-82.

Hermans, H. J. M. 1988. On the integration of nomothetic and ideographic research methods in the study of personal meaning. *Journal of personality*, 56: 785-812.

Herr, E. L. & Cramer, S. H. 1972. *Vocational guidance and career development in the schools: towards a systems approach*. Boston: Houghton-Mifflin.

Herzberg, F., Mausner, B. & Snyderman, B. 1959. *The motivation to work*. New York: John Wiley.

Higbee, K. 1988. *Your memory – how it works and how to improve it*. New York: Prentice-Hall.

Higginson, S. 1993. *Wake up your memory: a concise & practical guide to improving your memory*. Wincanton: Forge Press.

Hill, C. A. 1987. Affiliation motivation: people who need people but in different ways. *Journal of personality and social psychology*, 52: 1008-1018.

Hill, N. C. 1981. *Counseling at the workplace*. New York: McGrawHill.

Hill, J. M. & Trist, E. L. 1962. A consideration of industrial accidents as a means of withdrawal from the work situation. In F. Baker, P. J. M. McEwan & A. C. Sheldon. 1969. *Industrial organisations and health*. London: Travistock Publications.

Hirschfield, A. H. & Behan, R. C. 1963. The accident process: ethological considerations of industrial injuries. *The journal of the American association*, 186: 193-199.

Hirschhorn, L. 1993. *The workplace within: psycho-dynamics of organizational life*. Cambridge, MA: MIT Press.

Hjelle, L. A. & Ziegler, D. J. 1992. *Personality theories: basic assumptions, research and applications*. 3rd ed. Singapore: McGraw-Hill.

Ho, D. Y. F. 1988. Asian psychology: a dialogue on indigenization and beyond. In A. C. Paranjpe, D. Y. F. Ho & R. W. Rieber, *Asian contributions to psychology*. New York: Praeger.

Hobfoll, S. E. 1989. Conservation of resources: a new attempt at conceptualising stress. *American psychologist*, 44(3): 513-524.

Hockenbury, D. H. & Hockenbury, S. E. 1977. *Psychology*. New York: Worth Publishers.

Hofmann, J. 1984. Psychological separation of late adolescents from their parents. *Journal of counseling psychology*, 31: 170-178.

Hofstede, G. 1984. The cultural relativity of the quality of life concepts. *Academy of management review*, 9(3): 389-398.

Hofstede, G. H. 1994. *Cultures and organizations: software of the mind*. London: Harper Collins.

Hogan, J. & Hogan, R. 1989. How to measure service orientation. *Journal of applied psychology*, 69: 167-173.

Hogan, R. T. 1991. Personality and personality measures. In M. D. Dunnette & L. Hough (Eds), *Handbook of industrial and organisational psychology*. 2nd ed, Vol. 2. Palo Alto: Consulting Psychological Press.

Hogg, M. A. & Vaughan, G. M. 1995. *Social psychology: an introduction*. London: Prentice-Hall.

Holland, J. L. 1985. *Making vocational choices: a theory of personalities and work environments*. 2nd ed. Englewood Cliffs, NJ: Prentice-Hall.

Holmes, T. H. & Rahe, R. H. 1967. Social readjustment scale. *Journal of psychosomatic research*, 11: 143-218.

Holt, R. R. 1986. Clinical and Statistical prediction: A restrospective and would-be integrative perspective. *Journal of personality assessment*, 50: 367-386.

Holway, W. 1991. *Work psychology and organizational behaviour: managing the individual at work*. London: Sage.

Honts, C. R. & Perry, M. V. 1992. Polygraph admissibility: changes and challenges. *Law and human behavior*, 16:357-379.

Hough, L. M. 1992. The "big five" personality variables-construct confusion: description versus prediction. *Human performance*, 5(5): 139-155.

Hough, L. M. 1997. Personality at work; issues &

evidence. In M. Hakel (Ed.), *Beyond multiple choice: evaluating alternatives to traditional testing for selection.* Hillside, NJ: Erlbaum.

Hough, L. M. & Schneider, R. J. 1996. Personality traits, taxonomies, and applications in organisations. In K. R. Murphy (Ed.), *Individual differences and behaviour in organisations* (pp 31-88). San Francisco: Jossey-Bass.

House, J. S., Landis, K. R. & Umberson, D. 1988. Social relationships and health. *Science*, 241: 540-545.

Howard, A. (Ed.). 1995. *The changing nature of work.* San Francisco: Jossey-Bass.

Howard, J. A., Blumstein, P. & Schwartz, P. 1987. Social evolutionary theories? Some observations on preferences in human mate selection. *Journal of personality and social psychology*, 53: 194-200.

Howard, J. H., Cunningham, D. A. & Rechnitzer, P. A. 1977. Work patterns associated with Type A behaviour. *Human relations*, 30: 825-836.

Hrebeniak, L. G. & Aluto, J. A. 1972. Personal and role-related factors in the development of organisational commitment. *Administrative science quarterly*, 17: 555-573.

Hsu, F. L. K. 1971. Psychological homeostasis and conceptual tools for advancing psychological anthropology. *American anthropologist*, 73: 23-44.

Huber, V. L. 1991. Comparison of supervisor-incumbent and male-female multidimensional job evaluation ratings. *Journal of applied psychology*, 76: 115-121.

Hugo, A. & van Vuuren, L. J. 1996. A cross-cultural analysis of work values and moral reasoning. *Journal of industrial psychology*, 221: 12-18.

Hunt, E. 1995. *Will we be smart enough? A cognitive analysis of the coming workforce.* New York: Russell Sage.

Hunter, J. E. 1986. Cognitive ability, cognitive attitudes, job knowledge and job performance. *Journal of vocational behaviour*, 29: 340-362.

Hunter, J. E. & Schmidt, F. L. 1983. Quantifying the effects of psychological interventions on employee job performance and work-force productivity. *American psychologist*, 38: 473-478.

Hurrell, J. J., Murphy, R. L. R., Sauter, S. L. & Cooper, C. L. 1988. *Occupational stress: Issues and developments in research.* New York: Taylor & Francis.

Hurrell, J. J., McLaney, M. A. & Murphy, L. R. 1990. The middle years: career stage differences. *Prevention in human sciences*, 8(1): 179-203.

Huszczo, G. E. & Fried, B. J. 1988. A labour

relations research agenda for health care settings. *Employee responsibilities and rights journal*, 1(1): 69-84.

Insko, C. A., Smith, R. H., Alice, M. D., Wade, J. & Taylor, S. 1985. Conformity and group size: the concern with being right and the concern with being liked. *Personality and social psychology bulletin*, 11: 41-50.

Isaacson. L. E. 1985. *Basics of career counseling.* Boston: Allyn & Bacon.

Isabella, L. A. 1988. The effect of career stage on the meaning of key organizational events. *Journal of organizational behaviour*, 9: 345-358.

Ivancevich, J. 1992. *Human resource management: foundations for personnel.* NJ: Irwin.

Ivancevich, J. M. & Matteson, M. T. 1988. Type A behaviour and the healthy individual. *British journal of medical psychology*, 61:37-56.

Ivancevich, J. M. & Matteson, M. T. 1993. *Organizational behaviour and management.* 3rd ed. Homewood: Irwin.

Ivancevich, J. M. & Matteson, M. T., Freedman, S. M. & Phillips, J. S. 1990. Work site stress management. *American psychologist*, 45(2): 252-261.

Jacobson, T., Edelstein, W. & Hofmann, V. 1994. A longitudinal study of the relation between representations of attachment in childhood and cognitive functioning in childhood and adolescence. *Developmental psychology*, 30: 112-124.

Jamieson, D. & O'Mara, J. 1991. *Managing workforce 2000: gaining the diversity advantage.* San Francisco: Jossey-Bass.

Jankowicz, A. D. 1990. Applications of personal construct psychology in business practice. In G. J. Neimeyer & R. A. Neimeyer (Eds), *Advances in personal construct psychology*, Vol. 1. (pp 257-287). Connecticut: Jai Press.

Jansen, P. & De Jongh, F. 1997. *Assessment centres: a practical handbook.* Chichester: Wiley.

Janz, T., Hellervik, L. & Gilmore, D. C. 1986. *Behaviour description interviewing.* Boston: Allyn & Bacon.

Jelinek, M. & Litterer, J. A. 1994. Toward a cognitive theory of organisations. In C. Stubbart, J. R. Meindl & J. F. Porac. 1994. *Advances in managerial cognition and organisational information processing* (pp 3-41). Connecticut: Jai Press.

Jencks, C. 1989. *What is post-modernism?* London: Academy Editions.

Jenkins, C. D., Zyzanski, S. & Rosenman, R. 1971. Progress toward validation of a computer-scored test for the Type A coronary prone behavior pattern. *Psychosomatic medicine, 33*: 193-201.

Jones, J. W. 1982. *The burnout syndrome: current research, theory, interventions.* Illinois: London House Press.

Jones, R. L. 1991. *Black psychology.* 3rd ed. Berkeley: Cobb & Henry.

Jordaan, W. & Jordaan, J. 1989. *Mens in konteks.* 2nd ed. Isando: Lexicon.

Joubert, D. 1986. *Waardes: navorsing, metodologie en teorie.* RGN-ondersoek reeks: 2. Pretoria: Human Sciences Research Council.

Kaestle, P. 1990. A new rationale for Organizational Structure. *Planning review, 18*: 20-22.

Kagan, J. 1994. *Galaen's prophecy: temperament and human nature.* New York: Basic Books.

Kagan, J., Reznick, J. S. & Snidman, N. 1988. Biological basis of childhood shyness. *Science, 240*: 167-171.

Kahn, R. L. 1981. *Work and health.* New York: Wiley & Son.

Kakabadse, A. 1982. *People and organizations.* Aldershot: Gower.

Kalat, J. W. 1990. *Introduction to psychology.* 2nd ed. Belmont: Wadsworth.

Kalimo, R. & Vuori, J. 1990. Work and sense of coherence – resources for competence and life satisfaction. *Behavioural medicine,* Summer: 77-89.

Kane, K. W. 1975. Corporate responsibility in the area of alcoholism. *Personnel psychology, 54*(7): 380-384.

Kanfer, F. H. & Gaelick-Buys, L. 1991. Self-management tools. In F. H. Kanfer & A. P. Goldstein (Eds)., *Helping people change: a textbook of methods* (pp 305-360). New York: Pergamon Press.

Kanner, A. D., Coyne, J. C., Schaefer, C. & Lazarus, R. S. 1981. Comparison of two modes of stress measurement: daily hassles and uplifts versus major life events. *Journal of behavioural medicine,* 41:1-39.

Kanungo, R. N. 1982. *Work alienation: an integrative approach.* New York: Praeger.

Kaplan, H. B. (Ed.). 1983. *Psychosocial stress: trends in theory and research.* New York: Academic Press.

Kaplan, M. 1995. The culture at work: cultural ergonomics. *Ergonomics, 383*: 606-615.

Kaprio, J., Koskenvuo, M. & Rita, H. 1987. Morality after bereavement: a prospective study of 95 647 widowed persons. *American journal of public health,* 77: 283-287.

Karenga, M. 1977. *Selections from the Husia.* Los Angeles: Kawaida Press.

Karraker, K. H. & Stern, M. 1990. Infancy physical attractiveness and facial expressions: effects on adult perceptions. *Basic and applied social psychology,* 11: 371-385.

Katz, D. 1960. The functional approach to the study of attitudes. *Public opinion quarterly,* 24: 163-204.

Keeley, M. 1988. Individual rights and organizational theory. *Employee responsibilities and rights journal,* 1(1): 25-38.

Keeney, B. P. 1979. Ecosystemic epistemology: an alternative paradigm for diagnosis. *Family process,* 18(2): 117-129.

Kegan, R. 1982. *The evolving self: Problem and process in human development.* Cambridge: Havard University Press.

Kelly, G. A. 1955. *The psychology of personal constructs: a theory of personality.* New York: Norton.

Kennedy, W. A. 1971. *Child psychology.* New York: Prentice Hall.

Kennedy, J. & Everest, A. 1991. Putting diversity into context. *Personnel journal,* September: 50-54.

Kenrick, D. T., Guttieres, S. E. & Goldberg, L. L. 1989. Influence of popular erotica on judgements of strangers and mates. *Journal of experimental social psychology,* 25: 159-167.

Kenrick, D. T. & Funder, D. C. 1991. The person-situation debate: do personality traits really exist? In V. J. Derlega, B. A. Winstead & W. H. Jones, *Personality: contemporary theory and research.* Chicago: Nelson-Hall.

Kerlinger, F. N. 1973. *Foundations of behavioural research.* New York: Holt, Rinehart & Winston.

Kets de Vries, M. F. R & Miller, D. 1986. Personality, culture and organisation. *Academy of management review,* 11: 266-279.

Kets de Vries, M. F. R. & Miller, D. 1984. Neurotic style and organisational pathology. *Strategic management journal,* 5(35): 35-55.

Kiesler, D. J. 1979. An interpersonal communication analysis of relationships in psychotherapy. *Psychiatry,* 42: 299-311.

Kiesler, D. J. 1983. The 1982 interpersonal circle: a taxonomy for complimentarity in human transactions. *Psychological review,* 90: 185-214.

Kiesler, D. J. 1996. *Contemporary interpersonal theory and research: personality, psychopathology and psychotherapy.* New York: Wiley.

Kingstrom, P. O. & Bass, A. R. 1981. A critical analysis of studies comparing behaviourally anchored rating scales BARS and other rating formats. *Personnel psychology,* 34: 263-289.

Kirkpatrick, D. L. 1977. Evaluating training programmes: evidence versus proof. *Training and development journal,* 31: 9-12.

Kirsch, J. & Kroll, J. 1980. Meaningfulness versus effectiveness: paradoxical implications in the evaluation of psychotherapy. *Psychotherapy: theory and practice*, 17(4): 401-413.

Klein, W. M. & Kunda, Z. 1992. Motivated person perception: constructing justifications for desired beliefs. *Journal of experimental social psychology*, 28: 145-168.

Kleinke, C. L. & Dean, G. D. 1990. Evaluation of men and women receiving positive and negative responses with various acquaintance strategies. *Journal of social behaviour and personality*, 5: 369-377.

Kleinman, A. 1988. *Rethinking psychiatry: from cultural category to personal experience*. New York: The Free Press.

Klimoski, R. J. & Brickner, M. 1987. Why do assessment centres work? The puzzle of assessment centre validity. *Personnel psychology*, 40: 243-260.

Klopfer, B., Ainsworth, M., Klopfer, W. & Holt, R. R. 1954. *Developments in the Rorschach Technique: Vol 1. Technique and theory*. Yonkers-on-Hudson, NY: World.

Knowles, M. S. 1984. *Andragogy in action*. California: Jossey-Bass.

Kobasa, S. C. 1979. Stressful life events, personality, and health: an inquiry into hardiness. *Journal of personality and social psychology*, 37(1): 111.

Kobasa, S. C., Maddi, S. R. & Kahn, S. C. 1982. Hardiness and health: a prospective study. *Journal of personality and social psychology*, 42: 168-177.

Koestner, R., Franz, C. & Weinberger, J. 1990. The family origins of emphatic concern: A 26 year old longitudinal study. *Journal of personality and social psychology*, 58: 709-717.

Kohn, M. L. & Schooler, C. 1983. *Work and personality*. New Jersey: Ablex.

Kolasa, B. J. 1969. *Introduction to behavioral science for business*. New York: Wiley.

Kolb, D. 1976. *Learning styles inventory. Technical manual*. Boston: McBer.

Kornhauser, A. 1965. *Mental health of the industrial worker*. New York: Wiley.

Krackhardt, D. 1990. Assessing the political landscape: structure, cognition and power in organisations. *Administrative science quarterly*, 35: 342-369.

Krantz, D. S. & Raisen, S. E. 1988. Environmental stress, reactivity and ischaemic heart disease. *British journal of medical psychology*, 61: 316.

Krantz, J. 1985. Group process under conditions of organizational decline. *Journal of applied behavioural science*, 21(1): 117.

Krebs, D. & Blackman, R. 1988. *Psychology – a first encounter*. Orlando: Harcourt Brace Jovanovich, Inc.

Kreitner, R. & Kinicki, A. 1995. *Organizational behavior*. 3rd ed. Irwin: USA.

Kriek, H. J. 1991. Die bruikbaarheid van die takseersentrum: 'n oorsig van resente literatuur. *Journal of industrial psychology*, 173: 34-37.

Kriek, H. 1995. Personality questionnaires: breaking the 0.3 barrier. Unpublished paper presented at Centre for assessment symposium. Johannesburg.

Kriek, H. J., Hurst, D. N. & Charoux, J. A. 1994. The assessment centre: testing the fairness hypothesis. *Journal of industrial psychology*, 202: 21-25.

Kroemer, K. H. E., Kroemer, H. B. & Kroemer-Elbert, K. E. 1994. *Ergonomics: how to design for ease and efficiency*. Englewood Cliffs: Prentice-Hall.

Kroon, J. (Ed.). 1990. *General Management*. 2nd Ed. Kagiso Tertiary: Pretoria.

Landy, F. J. & Farr, J. L. 1983. *The measurement of work performance: methods, theory and applications*. New York: Academic Press.

Landy, F. J. 1989. *Psychology of work behavior*. 4th ed. California: Brooks/Cole.

Landy, F. J. & Vasey, J. 1991. Job analysis: the composition of SME samples. *Personnel psychology*, 44: 27-50.

Langley, R. 1995. The South African work importance study. In D. E. Super & B. Šverko. *Life roles, values and careers. International findings of the work importance study* (pp 188-203). San Francisco: Jossey-Bass.

Langston, C. A. & Cantor, N. 1989. Anxiety and social constraint: when making friends is hard. *Journal of personality and social psychology*, 56: 649-661.

Larson, R. Csiksentmihalyi, M. & Graef, R. 1982. Time alone in daily experience: loneliness or renewal? In L. A. Peplau & D. Perlman (Eds), *Loneliness: a sourcebook of current theory, research and therapy* (pp 40-53). New York: Wiley-Interscience.

Latack, J. C. & Havlovic, S. J. 1992. Coping with job stress: a conceptual evaluation framework for coping measures. *Journal of organisational behaviour*, 13: 479-508.

Latham, G. P. & Wexley, K. N. 1981. *Increasing productivity through performance appraisal*. Reading, MA: Addison-Wesley.

Latham, G. P. & Finnegan, B. J. 1993. Perceived practicality of instructional, patterned, and situational interviews. In H. Schuler, J. L. Farr & M. Smith (Eds), *Personnel selection and assessment* (pp 41-56). Hillsdale, NJ: Erlbaum.

Lay, C. H., Knish, S. & Zanatta, R. 1992. Self-handicappers and procrastinators: A comparison of their practice behaviour prior to an evaluation. *Journal of research in personality*, 26: 242-257.

Lazarus, R. S. & Folkman, S. 1984. *Stress, appraisal and coping*. New York: Springer.

Leahey, T. H. 1992. *A history of psychology: main currents in psychological thought*. 3rd ed. Englewood Cliffs, NJ: Prentice-Hall.

Leahey, T. H. 1994. *A history of modern psychology*, 2nd ed. Englewood Cliffs, NJ: Prentice-Hall.

Leana, C. R. & Feldman, D. C. 1988. Individual responses to job loss: perceptions, reactions, and coping behaviour. *Journal of management*, 14(3): 375-389.

Leary, T. 1957. Interpersonal diagnosis of personality. New York: Donald Publishers.

Leatz, C. A. & Stolar, M. W. 1993. *Career success/personal stress: how to stay healthy in a high-stress environment*. New York: McGraw-Hill.

Leedy, P. D. 1989, 1993. *Practical research: planning and design*. New York: Macmillan.

Leiter, M. P. & Maslach, C. 1988. The impact of interpersonal environment on burnout and organisational environment. *Journal of organizational behaviour*, 9: 297-308.

Leiter, M. P. 1991. Coping patterns as predictors of burnout: the function of control and escapist coping patterns. *Journal of organisational behaviour*, 12:123-144.

Lent, R. W. & Hackett, G. 1987. Career self-efficacy: empirical status and feature directions. *Journal of vocational behaviour*, 30: 347-382.

Lester, D. 1995. *Theories of personality: A systems approach*. Washington, DC: Taylor & Francis.

Levi, L. 1984. *Stress in Industry: causes, effects and prevention*. Geneva: International Labour Office.

Levinson, D. 1978. *The seasons of a man's life*. New York: Knopf.

Levinson, D. 1986. A conception of adult development. *American psychologist*, 41: 3-13.

Levinson, H. 1975. On executive suicide. *Harvard Business Review*, 53: 118-122.

Levitan, S. A. & Johnson, C. M. 1982. *Second thoughts on work*. Michigan: Upjohn Institute for unemployment research.

Levy, B. S. & Wegman, D. H. 1988. *Occupational health: recognizing and preventing work related disease*. Boston: Little, Brown.

Lewis-Fernandez, R. & Kleinman, A. 1994. Culture, personality and psychopathology. *Journal of abnormal psychology*, 103(1): 67-71.

Lindegger, G. & Wood, G. 1995. The Aids crisis: review of psychological issues and implications, with special reference to the South African situation. *South African journal of psychology*, 25(1): 1-11.

Lindgren, H. C. 1973. *An introduction to social psychology*. New York: Wiley.

Lippa, R. A. 1990. *Introduction to social psychology*. California: Wadsworth.

Littlewood, R. 1990. From categories to contexts: a decade of the new cross-cultural psychiatry. *British journal of psychiatry*, 156: 308-327.

Loehlin, J. C. 1992. *Genes and environment in personality*. Newbury Park: Sage.

London, M. & Wohlers, A. J. 1991. Agreement between subordinate and self-ratings in upward feedback. *Personnel psychology*, 44: 375-390.

Long, B. C. & Kahn, S. E. (Eds). 1993. *Women, work and coping: a multi-disciplinary approach to workplace stress*. Montreal: McGill-Queens University Press.

Loscocco, K. A. & Rochelle, A. R. 1991. Influences on the quality of work- and nonwork life: two decades in review. *Journal of vocational behaviour*, 39: 182-225.

Louw, D. A. & Edwards, D. J. A. (Eds). 1997. *Psychology: an introduction for students in Southern Africa*, 2nd ed. Johannesburg: Heinemann.

Louw, D. A. 1991. *Human development*. Pretoria: Haum.

Lowman, R. L. 1993. *Counseling and psychotherapy of work dysfunctions*. Washington: APA.

Macan, T. H. & Dipboye, R. L. 1990. The relationship between interviewers' pre-interview impressions to selection and recruitment outcomes. *Personnel psychology*, 43: 364-387.

Machlowitz, M. M. 1978. *Determining the effects of workaholism*. Ann Arbor: Dale University.

Mack, D. & Rainey, D. 1990. Female applicants' grooming and personnel selection. *Journal of personality and social behaviour*, 5: 399-407.

Maddi, S. R. 1996. *Personality theories: a comparative analysis*. Pacific Grove: Brooks/Cole.

Magai, C. 1996. Personality theory: birth, death and transfiguration. In R. D. Kavanaugh, B. Zimmerberg, S. Fein (Eds), *Emotion. Interdisciplinary perspectives* (pp 171-201). Mahwah, NJ: Lawrence Erlbaum Associates.

Magnusson, D. 1990. Personality development from an interactional perspective. In L.A. Pervin (Ed.), *Handbook of personality: theory and research* (pp 193-222). New York: The Guilford Press.

Magnusson, D. & Törestad, B. 1993. A holistic view of personality: A model revisited. *Annual review of psychology*, 44: 427-452.

Magwaza, A. S. 1994. Migration and psychological status in South African black migrant children. *The journal of genetic psychology*, 1551: 283-287.

Maier, R. F. & Verser, G. C. 1982. *Psychology in industrial organizations*. Boston: Houghton & Mifflin.

Mallach, C. 1996. Coping with stress in managers. Unpublished Masters dissertation. Pretoria: Unisa.

Manning, M. R., Williams, R. F. & Wolfe, D. M. 1988. Hardiness and the relationship between stressors and outcomes. *Work and stress*, 2(3): 205-216.

Manuso, J. S. T. 1983. *Occupational clinical psychology*. New York: Praeger.

Marieb, E. N. 1989. *Human anatomy and physiology*. 3rd ed. Redwood City: The Benjamin/Cummings Publishing Company, Inc.

Mark, R. 1996. *Research made simple: a handbook for social workers*. Thousand Oaks: Sage.

Marks, G. & Miller, N. 1987. Ten years of research on the false-consensus effect: an empirical and theoretical review. *Psychology bulletin*, 192: 72-92.

Markus, H. 1977. Self-schemata and processing information about the self. *Journal of personality and social psychology*, 35: 63-78.

Martin, C. L. & Nagao, D. H. 1989. Some effects of computerised interviewing on job applicant responses. *Journal of applied psychology*, 74: 72-80.

Martin, W. T. 1989. *Problem employees and their personalities: a guide to behaviours dynamics and intervention strategies for personnel specialists*. New York: Quorum Books.

Marx, M. H. & Cronan-Hillix, W. A. 1987. *Systems and theories in psychology*. McGraw-Hill: New York.

Maslach, C. & Jackson, S. E. 1984. Burnout in organisational settings. *Applied social psychology annual*, 5:133-153.

Maslow, A. H. 1954, 1970. *Motivation and personality*. 3rd ed. New York: Harper & Row.

Maslow, A. H. 1967. A theory of metamotivation: the biological rooting of the value-life. *Journal of humanistic psychology*, 7: 93-127.

Maslow, A. H. 1971. *The further reaches of human nature*. New York: Penguin.

Massel, H. K., Liberman, R. P., Mintz, J., Jacobs, H. E., Rush, T. V., Gianni, C. A. & Zarata, R. 1990. Evaluating the capacity to work of the mentally ill. *Psychiatry*, 53: 31-43.

Matarazzo, J. D. 1990. Psychological assessment versus psychological testing: validation from Binet to the school, clinic and courtroom. *American psychologist*, 45: 999-1017.

Matlin, M. W. 1992. *Psychology*. Orlando: Harcourt Brace Jovanovich.

Matlin, M. W. 1994. *Cognition*. 3rd ed. Philadelphia: Harcourt Brace.

Matthews, K.cA. 1988. Coronary heart disease and Type A behaviours: update and alternative to the Booth-Kewley & Friedman 1987 quantitative review. *Psychological bulletin*, 104: 373-380.

Matthews, G. N., Stanton, N., Graham, C. & Brinelow, C. 1994. A factor analysis of the scales of the occupational personality questionnaire. *Personality and individual differences*, 11: 591-596.

Mbiti, J. S. 1989. *African religions and philosophy*. London: Heinemann.

McAdams, D. P. & Vaillant, G. E. 1982. Intimacy motivation and psychological adaptation: a longitudinal study. *Journal of personality assessment*, 46: 586-593.

McCaughan, N. & Palmer, B. 1994. *Systems thinking for harassed managers*. London: Koonac Books.

McClean, A. 1970. *Mental health and work organizations*. Chicago: Rand McNally.

McClean, A. A. 1979. *Work stress*. Reading, Massachusetts: Addison-Wesley.

McClelland, C., Atkinson, W. J., Clark, R. A. & Lowell, E. L. 1970. Toward a theory of motivation. In W. A. Russell (Ed.), *Milestones in motivation* (pp 544-572). New York: Meredith Corporation.

McClelland, D. C. & Koestner, R. 1992. The achievement motive. In C. P. Smith (Ed.), *Motivation and personality: handbook of thematic content analysis* (pp 143-152). New York: Cambridge University Press.

McCormick, E. J. & Ilgen, D. R. 1981. *Industrial psychology*. London: George Allen.

McCrae, R. R. & Costa, P. T. 1989. The structure of interpersonal traits: Wiggins's circumplex and the five-factor model. *Journal of personality and social psychology*, 56: 586-595.

McCrae, R. R. & John, O. P. 1992. An introduction to the five-factor model and its applications. *Journal of personality*, 60: 175-215.

McCrae, R. R. 1993. Moderated analysis of longitudinal personality stability. *Journal of personality and social psychology*, 65: 577-585.

McDaniel, M. A. 1989. Biographical constructs for predicting employee suitability. *Journal of applied psychology*, 74: 964-970.

McEnery, J. & McEnery, J. M. 1987. Self-rating in management training needs assessment: a neglected opportunity? *Journal of occupational psychology*, 60: 49-60.

McFarland, C. & Miller, D. T. 1990. Judgements of self-other similarity: just like other people, only more so. *Personality and social psychology bulletin,* 6: 475-484.

McGue, M. & Lykken, D. T. 1992. Genetic influence on risk of divorce. *Psychological science,* 3: 368-373.

McHenry J. J., Hough, L. M., Toquam, J. L., Hanson, M. A. & Ashworth, S. 1990. Project A validity results: the relationship between predictor and criterion domains. *Personnel psychology,* 43: 335-354.

McKenna, E. 1994. *Business psychology and organisational behaviour.* Hove: Lawrence Erlbaum Associates.

McLellan, R. A. & Paajanen, G. E. 1995. PDI customer service inventory manual. In C. L. Cooper & I. T. Robertson, *International review of organisational psychology.* Vol. 10. Chichester: New York.

Mercer, R. T. 1989. *Transitions in a woman's life: major life events in developmental context.* New York: Springer.

Meyer, W. F., Moore, C. & Viljoen, H. G. 1989. *Personality theories: from Freud to Frankl.* Johannesburg: Lexicon.

Meyer, W. F., Moore, C. & Viljoen, H. G. 1997. *Personology: from individual to ecosystem.* Johannesburg: Heinemann.

Meyrs, D. W. (Ed.). 1985. *Employee problem prevention and counseling: a guide for professionals.* Westport: Quorum Books.

Mickleberg, W. E. 1986. Occupational mental health: a neglected service. *British journal of psychiatry,* 48: 426-434.

Mikulincer, M., Florian, V. & Weller, A. 1993. Attachment styles, coping strategies, and posttraumatic psychological distress: the impact of the Gulf war in Israel. *Journal of personality and social psychology,* 64: 817-826.

Millar, L. M. 1995. *Beroepseffektiwiteit by vroue.* Unpublished Master's thesis, University of Stellenbosch.

Miller, T. R. 1991. The psychotherapeutic utility of the five factor model of personality: A clinician's experience. *Journal of personality assessment,* 57: 415-433.

Miller, E. J. 1993. *From dependency to autonomy.* London: Free Association Books.

Miller, J. G., Bersoff, D. M. & Harwood, R. L. 1990. Perceptions of social responsibility in India and the United States: moral imperatives or personal decisions? *Journal of personality and social psychology,* 58: 33-47.

Miner, J. B. & Brewer, J. E. 1990. The management of ineffective performance. In M.D. Dunnette (Ed.), *Handbook of industrial and organizational psychology.* Chicago: Rand McNally.

Miner, J. B. 1966. *Introduction to industrial clinical psychology.* New York: McGraw-Hill.

Minsel, B., Becker, P. & Korchin, S. J. 1991. A cross-cultural view of positive mental health: two orthogonal main factors replicable in four countries. *Journal of cross-cultural psychology,* 22(2): 157-181.

Mirels, H. L. & Garret, J. B. 1977. The Protestant ethic as personality variable. *Journal of consulting and clinical psychology,* 36: 40-44.

Mischel, W. 1968. *Personality and assessment.* New York: Wiley.

Mischel, W. 1970. Personality dispositions revisited and revised: a view after three decades. In L. A. Pervin (Ed.), *Handbook of personality, theory and research* (pp 111-134). New York: The Guilford Press.

Mischel, W. & Ebbesen, E. 1973. Selective attention to the self: situational and dispositional determinants. *Journal of personality and social psychology,* 27: 129-142.

Mischel, W. 1976. *Introduction to personality.* 2nd ed. New York: Holt, Rhinehart and Winston.

Mischel, W. 1984. Convergences and challenges in the search for consistency. *American psychologist,* 39: 351-364.

Mittleman, W. 1991. Maslow's study of selfactualization: A reinterpretation. *Journal of humanistic psychology,* 311: 114-135.

Moghaddam, F. M., Taylor, D. M. & Wright, S. C. 1993. *Social psychology in cross-cultural perspective.* New York: W. H. Freeman and Co.

Mohrman, A. M. & Mohrman, S. A. 1995. Performance management is running the business. *Compensation and benefits review,* July/ August: 69-75.

Möller, A. T. 1995. *Perspectives on personality.* Durban: Butterworths.

Montowidlo, S. J., Packard, J. S. & Manning, M. R. 1986. Occupational stress: its causes and consequences for job performance. *Journal of applied psychology,* 71: 618-629.

Moore, C. 1997. The ecosystemic approach. In W. F. Meyer, C. Moore & H. G. Viljoen. *Personology: from individual to ecosystem.* Johannesburg: Heinemann.

Moorhead, G. & Griffin, R. W. 1989. *Organizational behaviour,* 2nd ed. Boston: Houghton Mifflin.

Moreland, R. L. & Beach, S. R. 1992. Exposure effects in the classroom: the development of affinity among students. *Journal of experimental social psychology,* 28: 255 276.

Morris, L. E. 1989. *Industrial stress injuries.* Los Gatos: Bourne & Allerton.

Morrison, E. W. & Bies, R. J. 1991. Impressionmanagement in the feedback-seeking process: a literature review and research agenda. *Academy of management review,* 16: 522-541.

Mortimer, J. T. & Borman, K. M. 1988. *Work experience and psychological development through the life span.* Colorado: Westview Press Inc.

Mouton, J. & Marais, H. C. 1990. *Basic concepts in the methodology of the social sciences.* Pretoria: Human Sciences Research Council.

MOW International Research Team. 1987. *The meaning of working.* London: Academic Press.

Muchinsky, P. M. 1983, 1987. *Psychology applied to work.* Homewood, IL: Dorsey Press.

Muchinsky, P. M. 1990, 1993. *Psychology applied to work.* CA: Brooks/Cole.

Muchinsky, P. M., Kriek, H. J. & Schreuder, A. M. G. 1998. *Personnel psychology.* Johannesburg: International Thomson Publishing SA.

Muldary, T. W. 1983. *Burnout and health professionals: manifestations and management.* Norwalk: Appleton-Century-Crofts.

Multon, K. D., Brown, S. D., & Lent, R. W. 1991. Relation of self-efficacy beliefs to academic outcomes: a meta-analytic investigation. *Journal of counseling psychology,* 38: 30-38.

Murphy, L. C. 1984. Occupational stress management: a review and appraisal. *Journal of occupational psychology,* 57: 1-15.

Murphy, K. R. & Pardaffy, V. A. 1989. Bias in behaviourally anchored rating scales: global or scale specific? *Journal of applied psychology,* 74: 343-346.

Murphy, K. R. & Davidshofer, C. O. 1994. *Psychological testing: applications and principles.* Englewood Cliffs, NJ: Prentice-Hall.

Myers, D. G. 1996. *Social psychology.* 5th ed. New York: McGraw-Hill.

Neff, W. S. 1977, 1985. *Work and human behaviour.* Chicago: Aldine.

Nevid, J. S., Rathus, S. A. & Greene, B. 1996, 1997. *Abnormal psychology in a changing world.* Upper Saddle River, NJ: Prentice-Hall.

Newman, T. E. & Beehr, T. A. C. 1979. Personal and organizational strategies for handling job stress: a review of research and opinion. *Personnel psychology,* 32: 1-43.

Nicholson, R. A. & Hogan, R. 1990. The construct validity of social desirability. *American psychologist,* 45: 290-292.

Niemeyer, G. J. 1992. Personal constructs and vocational structure: A critique of poor reason. In R. A. Niemeyer & G. J. Niemeyer. *Advances in personal construct theory.* Vol. 2. Connecticut: Jai Press.

Nobles, W. W. 1991. Extended self: rethinking the so-called Negro-self-concept. In R. L. Jones (Ed.), *Black Psychology.* 3rd ed. Berkeley: Cobb & Henry.

Noel, R. 1990. Employing the disabled: A how and why approach. *Training and development journal,* 44(8): 26-32.

Noland, R. L. 1973. *Industrial mental health and employee counseling.* New York: Behaviour Publications.

Nowack, K. M. 1991. Psychological predictors of health status. *Work and stress,* 5(2): 98-108

Oates, W. E. 1971. *Confessions of a workaholic.* New York: Abingdon Press.

Oatley, K. & Jenkins, J. M. 1996. *Understanding emotions.* Cambridge, Massachusetts: Blackwell Publishers.

Obholzer, A. & Roberts, V. Z. 1994. *The unconscious at work.* London: Routledge.

O'Brien, G. E. (Ed.). 1986. *Psychology of work and unemployment.* Chichester: Wiley & Sons.

Ochse, R. & Plug, C. 1986. Cross-cultural investigation of the validity of Erikson's theory of personality development. *Journal of personality and social psychology,* 50: 1240-1252.

O'Connell, M. J. 1976. The effects of environmental information and decision unit structure on felt tension. *Journal of applied psychology,* 4: 493-500.

Odendaal, F. J. & Van Wyk, J. D. 1988. Die taksering van die sindroom uitbranding. *Suid-Afrikaanse tydskrif vir sielkunde,* 18(2): 4-49.

O'Leary, A. 1991. Self-efficacy and health: behavioural and stress-physiological mediation. *Cognitive therapy and research,* 16: 229-245.

Olian, J. D. 1984. Genetic screening for employment purposes. *Personnel psychology,* 37: 423-438.

Olivier, L. 1989. The physical and psychological problems of the peoples of South Africa. *HSRC-Report.* Pretoria: HSRC.

O'Meara, J. R. 1977. Retirement. *Across the board,* January: 4-9.

Ones, D. S., Viswesvaran, C. & Schmidt, F. L. 1993. Comprehensive meta-analysis of integrity test validities: findings and implications for selection and theories of job performance (Monograph). *Journal of applied psychology,* 78: 679-703.

Organ, D. W. & Bateman, T. 1986. *Organizational behavior.* Plano: Business publications.

Orlemans, J. W. G. 1976. *Inleiding tot gedragsterapie.* Deventer: Slaterus.

Ormel, J. & Schaufeli, W. B. 1991. Stability and change in psychological distress and their relationship with self-esteem and locus of control: A dynamic equilibrium model. *Journal of personality and social psychology,* 60: 288-299.

Osgood, C. E., Suci, G. J. & Tannenbaum, P. H.

1957. *The measurement of meaning.* Urbana, IL: University of Illinois Press.

O'Reilly, C. A., Chatman, J. & Caldwell, D. F. 1991. People and organisational culture: a profile comparison approach to assessing person-organisation fit. *Academy of management journal,* 34: 487-516.

O'Toole, J. 1974. *Work and the quality of life.* Cambridge: M.I.T. Press.

Owen, K. & Taljaard, J. J. 1989. *Handbook for the use of psychological and scholastic tests of IPER and the NIPR.* Pretoria: Human Sciences Research Council.

Paez, D., Echebarria, A. & Valencia, J. 1991. Aids social representations: contents and processes. *Journal of community and applied social psychology,* 1: 89-104.

Paradis, L. F. (Ed.). 1987. *Stress and burnout among providers caring for the terminally ill and their families.* New York: Haworth Press.

Parker, D. F. & DeCotiis, T. 1983. Organizational determinants of job stress. *Organizational behaviour and human performance,* 32(2): 166-179.

Pasmore, W. A. & Fagans, M. R. 1992. Participation, individual development, and organizational change: a review and synthesis. *Journal of management,* 182, June: 375-397.

Payne, R. L., Jabri, M. M. & Pearson, A. W. 1988. On the importance of knowing the affective meaning of job demands. *Journal of organizational behaviour,* 9: 49-58.

Pedler, M., Burgoune, J. Y. & Boydell, T. 1992. *The learning company.* London: McGraw-Hill.

Perkel, A. K., Strebel, A. & Joubert, G. 1991. The psychology of Aids transmission. *South African journal of psychology,* 2(3):148-153.

Pervin, L. A. 1968. Performance and satisfaction as a function of individual-environment fit. *Journal of personality and social psychology,* 34: 465-474.

Pervin, L. A. 1990. *Handbook of personality theory and research.* New York: Guildford Press.

Pervin, L. A. & John, P. J. 1997. *Personality: theory and research.* 7th ed. New York: Wiley.

Piedmont, R. L., McCrae, R. R. & Costa, P. T. 1992. An assessment of the Edwards Personal Preference Schedule from the perspective of the five factor model. *Journal of personality assessment,* 58: 67-78.

Plomin, R., Coon, H., Carey, G., DeFries, J. C. & Fulker, D. W. 1991. Parent off-spring and sibling adoption analysis of parental ratings of temperament in infancy and childhood. *Journal of personality,* 59: 705-732.

Plug, C., Meyer, W. F., Louw, D. A. & Gouws,

L. A. 1986. *Psigologiewoordeboek.* Johannesburg: McGraw-Hill.

Popper, K. R. 1959. *The logic of scientific discovery.* Londen: Hutchinson.

Popper, K. R. 1969. *Conjectures and refutations.* London: Routledge & Kegan.

Price, V. A. 1982. What is type A? A cognitive social learning model. *Journal of occupational behaviour,* 3: 109-129.

Prince, R. & Tcheng-Laroche, F. 1987. Culture-bound syndromes and international disease classifications. *Culture, medicine and psychiatry,* 11: 3-23.

Provine, R. R. 1992. Contagious laughter: laughter is a sufficient stimulus for laughs and smiles. *Bulletin of the psychonomic society,* 30: 1-4.

Psychological Association of South Africa (PsySSA) 1987. *Ethical code for psychologists.* Pretoria: PsySSA.

Psychological Association of South Africa (PsySSA). 1992. *Guidelines for the validation and use of personnel selection procedures.* Pretoria: PsySSA.

Puryear Keita, G. & Sauter, S. L. 1992. *Work and well-being: an agenda for the 1990s.* Washington, DC: American Psychological Association.

Quinn, R. E. & Cameron, K. 1983. Organizational life cycles and shifting criteria of effectiveness: some preliminary evidence. *Management science,* 29(1): 33-51.

Raelin, J. 1984. An examination of deviant/ adaptive behaviours in the organizational careers of professionals. *Academy of management review,* 9(3): 413-427.

Rahim, M. A. 1983. A measure of styles of handling interpersonal conflict. *Academy of management journal,* 26: 368-376.

Rahim, M. A. 1985. A strategy for managing conflict in complex organisation. *Human relations,* January: 84.

Randolph, W. A. & Blackburn, R. S. 1989. *Managing organizational behavior.* Homewood: Irwin.

Raubenheimer, I. v W. 1987. South Africa. In A. R. Gilgen & C. K. Gilgen (Eds), *International handbook of psychology* (pp 392-415). New York: Greenwood Press.

Raza, S. M. & Carpenter, B. N. 1987. A model of hiring decisions in real employment interviews. *Journal of applied psychology,* 72: 596-603.

Reddin, B. 1991. *Tests for the output-oriented manager. A self-assessment guide.* London: Kegan Page.

Reddy, M. 1987. *The manager's guide to counselling at work.* London: Methuen.

Reeve, J. 1992. *Understanding motivation and emotion.* Fort Worth: Harcourt Brace.

Reitz, H. J. 1987. *Behavior in organizations*. 3rd ed. Homewood, IL: Irwin

Revicki, D. A. & May, H. J. 1989. Organizational characteristics, occupational stress, and mental health in nurses. *Behavioural medicine*, Spring: 30-36.

Ribeaux, P. & Poppleton, S. E. 1978. *Psychology and work: an introduction*. London: Macmillan Press.

Rimm, D. C. & Masters, J. C. 1979. *Behavior therapy: techniques and empirical findings*. New York: Academic Press.

Rinas, J. & Clyne-Jackson, S. 1988. *Professional conduct and legal concerns in mental health practice*. Norwalk: Appleton & Lange.

Ritchie, M. 1994. Cultural and gender biases in definitions of mental and emotional health and illness. *Counselor education and supervision*, 33(4): 344-348.

Robbins, S. P. 1990, 1993, 1996. *Organizational behaviour: concepts, controversies and applications*. Englewood Cliffs, NJ: Prentice-Hall.

Robbins, S. P. 1998. *Organizational behavior: concepts, controversies and applications*. 8th ed. Upper Saddle River, NJ: Prentice-Hall.

Roberson, C. 1986. *Preventing employee misconduct: A self-defense manual for business*. Massachusetts: Lexicon Books.

Roberson, L. 1990. Functions of work meanings in organizations: work meanings and work motivation. In A. P. Brief & W. R. Nord (Eds), *Meanings of occupational work. A collection of essays* (pp 107-134). Massachusetts: Lexicon Books.

Robertson, I. T. & Downs, S. 1989. Work-sample tests of trainability: a meta-analysis. *Journal of applied psychology*, 74: 402-410.

Robertson, I. & Kinder, A. 1993. Personality and job competency. *Journal of occupational and organisational psychology*, 66: 225-244.

Robinson, T. R. & Howard-Hamilton, M. 1994. An Afrocentric paradigm: foundation for a healthy self-image and healthy interpersonal relationships. *Journal of mental health counseling*, 16(3): 327-339.

Rodin, M. J. 1987. Who is memorable to whom? A study of cognitive disregard. *Social cognition*, 5: 144-165.

Rodin, J. & Ickovics, J. R. 1990. Women's health: review and research agenda as we approach the 21st century. *American psychologist*, 34: 1018-1034.

Rodin, J. & Salovey, P. 1989. Health psychology. *Annual review of psychology*, 40: 533-579.

Rogers, C. R. 1951. *Client-centred therapy*. Boston: Houghton.

Rogers, C. R. 1973, 1983a. *Freedom to learn for the 80s*. Columbus, Ohio: Bell & Howell.

Rogers, C. R. 1978. *Carl Rogers on personal power*. London: Constable & Company.

Rogers, C. R. 1983b. *Client-centred therapy*. London: Constable.

Rokeach, M. 1978. From individual to institutional values: with special reference to the values of science. In M. Rockeach. *Understanding human values* (pp 47-69). London: Colliere Macmillan.

Roland, A. 1988. *In search of self in India and Japan: toward a cross-cultural psychology*. New Jersey: Princeton University Press.

Roodt, A. 1992. Black advancement: personal and corporate responsibility. *Human resource management*, 8(7): 4-18.

Roseman, E. 1982. *Managing the problem employee*. New York: AMACOM.

Rosenbaum, M. & Ben-Ari, K. 1985. Learned helplessness and learned resourcefulness: Effects of non-contingent success and failures on individuals differing in self-control skills. *Journal of personality and social psychology*, 48: 198-215.

Rosenbaum, M. E. 1986. The repulsion hypothesis: on the nondevelopment of relationships. *Journal of personality and social psychology*, 51: 1156-1166.

Rosenberg, K. M. & Daly, H. B. 1993. *Foundations of behavioural research: a basic question approach*. Fort Worth: Harcourt Brace.

Ross, E., Powles, W. & Winslow, W. 1965. Secondary prevention of job disruption in industry. *Journal of occupational medicine*, 7: 3-4.

Ross, R. R. & Altmaier, E. M. 1994. *Intervention in occupational stress: a handbook of counselling for stress at work*. London: Sage.

Rossiter, C. M. & Barnette Pearce, W. 1975. *Communicating personally*. Indianapolis: Bobbs-Merrill.

Roszell, P., Kennedy, D. & Grabb, E. 1990. Physical attractiveness and income attainment among Canadians. *Journal of psychology*, 123: 547-559.

Rothstein, H. R., Schmidt, F. L. et al. 1990. Biographical data in employment selection: Can validities be made generalizable? *Journal of applied psychology*, 75:175-184.

Rotter, J. B. 1966. Generalized expectancies for internal versus external control of reinforcement. *Psychological monographs*, 80(1): complete no. 609.

Rotter, J. B. 1975. Some problems and misconceptions related to the construct of internal versus external control of reinforcement, *Journal of consulting and clinical psychology*, 43: 56-67.

Rotter, J. B. 1990. Internal versus external control of reinforcement. *American psychologist*, 45: 489-493.

Rushton, J. P. 1989. Genetic similarities in male friendships. *Ethology and sosiobiology*, 10: 361-373.

Russel, J. E. A. 1991. Career development interventions in organizations. *Journal of vocational behaviour*, 383: 237-287.

Russel, D., Peplau, L. A. & Curtona, C. E. 1980. The revised UCLA loneliness scale: concurrent and discrimination validity evidence. *Journal of personality and social psychology*, 39: 472-480.

Russell, C. 1990. Selecting top corporate leaders: an example of biographical information. *Journal of management*, 16: 73-86.

Ryff, C. D. 1989. Happiness is everything, or is it? Explorations on the meaning of well-being. *Journal of personality and social psychology*, 57: 1069-1081.

Rynes, S. & Gerhardt, B. 1990. Interviewer assessment of applicant "fit": an exploratory investigation. *Personnel psychology*, 43: 13-35.

Saal, F. E. & Knight, P. A. 1995. *Industrial/organisational psychology: science and practice.* Pacific Grove: Brooks/Cole.

Sackett, P. R., Burris, L. R. & Callahan, C. 1989. Integrity testing for personnel selection: an update. *Personnel psychology*, 42: 91-529.

Sackett, P. R., DuBois, C. L. & Noe, A. W. 1991. Tokenism in performance evaluation: the effects of work group representation on male-female and white-black differences in performance ratings. *Journal of applied psychology*, 76: 63-27.

Santer, S. L., Murphy, L. R. & Hurrell, J. J. 1990. Prevention of work-related psychological disorders. *American psychologist*, 45: 1146-1158.

Saucier, G. & Goldberg, L. R. 1996. The language of personality: lexical perspectives on the five-factor model. In J. S. Wiggens. *The five-factor model of personality theoretical perspectives.* New York: Guilford Press.

Saville & Holdsworth. 1993. *Occupational Personality Questionnaires: Manual and user's guide.* Thames Ditton, UK: Saville & Holdsworth

Saville, P., Sik, G., Nylfield, G., Hackson, J. & MacIver, R. 1996. A demonstration of the validity of the occupational personality questionnaire (OPQ) in the measurement of job competencies across time and in separate organisations. *Applied psychology: an international review*, 45(30): 243-262.

Schachter, S. 1959. *The psychology of affiliation.* Stanford, CA: Stanford University Press.

Schafer, W. 1987. *Stress management for wellness.* New York: Holt, Rinehart & Winston.

Schaffner, P. E., Wandersman, A. & Stang, D. 1981. Candidate name exposure and voting: two field studies. *Basic and applied social psychology*, 2: 195-203.

Schein, E. H. 1980. *Organisational psychology.* Englewood Cliffs: Prentice-Hall.

Schein, E. H. 1990. *Career anchors: discovering your real values.* San Diego: University Associates.

Schiffman, H. R. 1990. *Sensation and perception: An integrated approach.* 3rd ed. New York: John Wiley & Sons.

Schippmann, J. S., Prien, E. P. & Katz, J. A. 1990. Reliability and validity of in-basket performance measures. *Personnel psychology*, 43: 837-859.

Schmitt, N. & Cohen, S. A. 1989. Internal analysis of task ratings by job incumbents. *Journal of applied psychology*, 74: 96-104.

Schmitt, N. & Robertson, I.T. 1990. Personnel selection. *Annual review of psychology*, 41: 289-320.

Schmitt, M. & Borkenau, P. 1992. The consistency of personality. In G-V. Caprara & G. L. Van Heck. *Modern personality psychology: critical reviews and new directions.* New York: Harvester/Wheatsheaf.

Schneider, R. J. & Hough, L. M. 1995 Personality and industrial/organisational psychology. In C. L. Cooper & I. V. Robertson (Eds), *International review of industrial and organizational psychology.* Vol. 10. Chichester: Wiley & Sons.

Schneider, R. J., Ackerman, P. L. & Kanfer, L. 1996. To "act wisely in human relations": exploring the dimensions of social competence. *Personality and individual differences*, 214: 469-481.

Schoeman, J. J. & Shröder, H. H. E. 1994. *Occupational hygiene.* Cape Town: Juta.

Schreuder, A. M. G. & Theron, A. L. 1997. *Careers: an organisational perspective.* Kenwyn: Juta.

Schuler, R. 1982. An integrative transactional process model of stress in organizations. *Journal of occupational behaviour*, 3: 5-19.

Schultz, D. P. 1990. *Theories of personality.* 4th ed. Pacific Grove: Brooks/Cole.

Schultz, D. P. & Schultz, S. E. 1994. *Theories of personality.* Pacific Grove, CA: Brooks/Cole.

Schultz, D. P. & Schultz, S. E. 1996. *A history of modern psychology.* Fort Worth: Harcourt Brace College Publishers.

Schunk, D. H. 1989. Self-efficacy and achievement behaviours. *Educational psychological review*, 1: 173-208.

Scroggs, J. R. 1995. *Key ideas in personality theory.* St. Paul: West Publishing Company.

Secord, P. F. & Backman, C. W. 1964. *Social psychology.* 2nd ed. New York: McGraw-Hill.

Sedikides, C. 1993. Assessment, enhancement, and verification determinants of the self-evaluation process. *Journal of personality and social psychology*, 65: 317-338.

Seligman, M. E. P. 1975. *Helplessness: on depression, development and death*. San Francisco: Freeman.

Selzer, M. L., Rogers, I. E. & Kern, S. 1968. Fatal accidents: the role of psychopathology, social stress, and acute disturbance. *American journal of psychiatry*, 124(8): 1028(46)-1036(54).

Senge, P. M. 1990. *The fifth discipline: The art and practice of the learning organization*. New York: Doubleday.

Seymore, G. O., Stahl, J. M., Levine, S. L., Ingram, J. L. & Smith, R. F. 1994. Modifying law enforcement training simulators for use in basic research. *Behaviour research methods, instruments & computers*, 26: 266-268.

Sharf, R. S. 1992, 1997. *Applying career development theory to counseling*. Pacific Grove: Brooks/Cole.

Sharit, J. & Salvendy, G. 1982. Occupational stress: review and reappraisal. *Human factors*, 24(2):129-162.

Sharrat, P. 1987. Thinking. In G.A. Tyson (Ed.), *Introduction to psychology – a South African perspective* (pp 91-137). Johannesburg: Westro Educational Books.

Shirom, A. 1982. What is organizational stress? A facet analytic conceptualization. *Journal of occupational behaviour*, 3: 21-37.

Shochet, I. A. 1994. The moderator effects of cognitive modifiability on a traditional undergraduate admissions test for disadvantaged black students in South Africa. *South African journal of psychology*, 244: 208-215.

Shostrom, E. L. 1976. *Actualizing therapy: foundation for a scientific ethic*. San Diego, CA: Edits Publishers.

Simons, J. A., Irwin, D. B. & Drinnin, B. A. 1987. *Psychology – the search for understanding*. St. Paul: West Publishing Company.

Simonton, D. K. 1986. Presidential personality: biographical use of the Gough Adjective checklist. *Journal of personality and social psychology*, 51: 149-160.

Singh, R. & Tan, L. S. C. 1992. Attitudes and attraction: a test of the similarity-repulsion hypothesis. *British journal of social psychology*, 31: 227-238.

Slaney, R. B. & Russell, J. C. 1987. Perspectives on vocational behaviour, 1986: a review. *Journal of vocational behaviour*, 31: 111-173.

Smeaton, G., Byrne, D. & Murnen, S. K. 1989. The repulsion hypothesis revisited: similarity, irrellevance or dissimilarity bias? *Journal of personality and social psychology*, 56: 54-59.

Smernou, L. & Lautenschlager, G. 1991. Auto-biographical antecedents and correlates of neuroticism and extraverts. *Personality and individual differences*, 12: 49-53.

Smith, R. C. 1987. *Unemployment and health: a disaster and a challenge*. Oxford: Oxford University Press.

Snyder, M., Tanke, E. D. & Berscheid, E. 1977. Social perception and interpersonal behaviour: on the self-fulfilling nature of social stereotypes. *Journal of personality and social psychology*, 35: 656-666.

Snyderman, M. & Rothman, S. 1987. Survey of expert opinion on intelligence and aptitude testing. *American psychologist*, 42: 137-144.

Society for industrial psychology. 1998. *Guidelines for the validation and use of assessment procedures for the work-place*. Auckland Park: Society for Industrial Psychology.

Solomon, M. R. 1996. *Consumer behavior*. 3rd ed. New Jersey: Prentice-Hall, Inc.

Sow, I. 1980. *Anthropological structures of madness in Black Africa*. New York: International Universities Press.

Sparrow, P. R. 1994. The psychology of strategic management: Emerging themes of diversity and cognition. In C. L. Cooper and I. T. Robertson. *International review of industrial and organisational psychology* (pp 147-181). Chichester: Wiley & Sons.

Sperling, M. B. & Berman, M. D. (Eds). 1994. *Attachment in adults: clinical and developmental perspectives*. New York: Guilford.

Sperry, L. 1991. Enhancing corporate health, mental health and productivity. *Individual psychology*, 47(2): 248-254.

Spranger, E. 1950. *Lebensformen*. 8th ed. Tübingen: Neomarius Verlag.

Sprecher, S. & Duck, S. 1994. Sweet talk: the importance of perceived communication for romantic and friendship attraction experienced during a get acquitted date. *Personal and social psychology bulletin*, 20: 391-400.

Sprecher, S., Sullivan, Q. & Hatfield, E. 1994. Mate selection preferences: gender differences examined in a national sample. *Journal of personality and social psychology*, 66: 1074-1080.

Statham, A. & Bravo, E. 1990. The introduction of new technology: health implications for workers. *Women and health*, 16(2): 105-129.

Steers, R. M. & Porter, L. W. 1987. *Motivation and work behaviour*. 4th ed. New York: McGraw-Hill.

Steers, R. M. 1991. *Organizational behavior*. New York: Harper Collins.

Steffy, B. D., Jones, J. W. & Noe, A. W. 1990. The impact of health habits and life style on the stressor-strain relationship: an evaluation of three industries. *Journal of occupational psychology*, 63: 217-229.

Steinmetz, L. L. 1969. *Human relations: people and work*. New York: Harper & Row.

Stephan, C. W. & Stephan, W. G. 1990. *Two social psychologies*. Belmont, CA: Wadsworth.

Sternberg. R. J. 1994. *The psychologist's companion: a guide to scientific writing for students and researchers*. Cambridge: Cambridge University Press.

Sternberg, R. J. 1996. *Cognitive psychology*. Fort Worth: Harcourt & Brace College Publishers.

Sternhagen, C. J. 1969. Medicine's role in reducing absenteeism. *Personnel*, 46(6): 28-38.

Steyn, M. E. & Motshabi, K. B. (Eds). 1996. *Cultural synergy in South Africa: weaving strands of Africa and Europe*. Randburg: Sigma Press.

Stout, S. K., Slocum, J. W. & Cron, W. L. 1988. Dynamics of the career plateauing process. *Journal of vocational behaviour*, 32: 74-91.

Strack, S. & Lorr, M. 1994. *Differentiating normal and abnormal personality*. New York: Springer.

Strümpfer, D. J. W. 1990. Salutogenesis: a new paradigm. *South African journal of psychology*, 120(4): 265-276.

Strümpfer, D. J. W. 1995. The origins of health and strength: from salutogenesis to fortigenesis. *South African journal of psychology*, 25(2): 81-89.

Stuart-Hamilton, I. 1995. *Dictionary of cognitive psychology*. London: Jessica Kingsley.

Stumpf, S. A. & Rabinowitz, S. 1981. Career stage as a moderator of performance relationships with facets of job satisfaction and role perceptions. *Journal of vocational behaviour*, 18: 202-218.

Sullivan, H. S. 1953. *The interpersonal theory of psychiatry*. New York: Norton.

Sullivan, S. E. & Bhagat, R. S. 1992. Organisational stress, job satisfaction and job performance. Where do we go from here? *Journal of management*, 18: 353-374.

Super, D. E. 1970. *Work values inventory*. Boston: Houghton-Mifflin.

Sussal, C. M. & Ojakian, E. 1988. Crisis intervention in the workplace. *Employee assistance quarterly*, 4(1): 71-85.

Šverko, B. & Super, D. E. 1995. Findings of the work importance study. In D. E. Super and B. Šverko. *Life roles, values and careers. International findings of the work importance study* (pp 349-358). San Francisco: Jossey-Bass.

Szymanski, D. & Churchill, G. 1990. Client evaluation cues: a comparison of successful and unsuccessful sales people. *Journal of marketing research*, 27: 163-174.

Tallent, N. 1989. *Psychological report writing*. Englewood Cliffs, NJ: Prentice-Hall.

Tallent, N. 1992. *The practice of psychological assessment*. Englewood Cliffs, NJ: Prentice-Hall.

Taveggia, T. C. & Hedley, R. A. 1976. Job specialization, work values and worker dissatisfaction. *Journal of vocational behaviour*, 9: 293-309.

Taylor, S. E., Peplau, L. & Sears, D. O. 1994. *Social psychology*. 8th ed. Englewood Cliffs, NJ: Prentice-Hall.

Taylor, T. R. 1994. A review of three approaches to cognitive assessment, and a proposed integrated approach based on a unifying theoretical framework. *South African journal of psychology*, 244: 184-192.

Tenopyr, M. L. 1988. Artifactual reliability of forced-choice scales. *Journal of applied psychology*, 73: 749-751.

Tett, R. P., Jackson, D. N. & Rothstein, M. 1991. Personality measures as predictors of job performance: a meta-analytic review. *Personnel psychology*, 44: 703-742.

Thomas, C. B. 1981. Stamina: the thread of human life. *Journal of chronic diseases*, 341: 41-44.

Thomas, K. 1983. Conflict and conflict management. In Dunnett. M.D. (Ed.), *Handbook of industrial and organizational psychology*. New York: Wiley & Sons.

Thompson, A. A. & Stickland, A. J. 1986. *Strategy formulation and implementation*. Plano: Business Publications.

Thompson, L. 1991. Information exchange in negotiation. *Journal of experimental social psychology*, 27: 161-179.

Thornton, G. C. & Cleveland, J. N. 1990. Developing managerial talent through simulation. *American psychologist*, 45: 190-199.

Tillich, P. 1959. Is a science of human values possible? In A. H. Maslow (Ed.), *New knowledge in .human values* (pp 189-196). New York: Harper & Row.

Toda, M. 1975. Time and the structure of human recognition. In J. T. Fraser & N. Lawrence (Eds), *The study of time II* (pp 314-324). New York: Springer-Verlag.

Tosi, D. J. & Hoffman, S. 1972. A factor analysis of the Personal Orientation Inventory. *Journal of humanistic psychology*, 12: 86-93.

Triandis, H. C., Bontempo, R., Villareal, M. J., Asai, M. & Lucca, M. 1988. Individualism and collectivism: cross-cultural perspectives on self-ingroup relationships. *Journal of personality and social psychology*, 54: 323-338.

Triandis, H. C. 1989. The self and social behaviour in differing cultural contexts. *Psychological review*, 96(3): 506-520.

Truax, C. B. & Carkhuff, R. R. 1967. *Toward effective counseling and psychotherapy.* Chicago: Aldine.

Tsui, A. S. & Ohlott, P. 1988. Multiple assessment of managerial effectiveness: interrater agreement and consensus in effectiveness models. *Personnel psychology,* 41: 779-803.

Tustin, C. 1994. *Industrial relations: a psychological approach.* Halfway House: Southern Book Publishers.

Twist, H. 1992. *Effective interviewing.* London: Blackstone.

Tyson, G. A. 1987. Social psychology. In G. A. Tyson (Ed.), *Introduction to psychology – a South African perspective* (pp 321-349). Johannesburg: Westro Educational Books.

Vaillant, G. E. & Valliant, C. O. 1982. Natural history of male psychological health; X; work as predictor of positive mental health. *Annual progress in child psychiatry and child development:* 602-619.

Van Dyk, A. C. C. 1990. Determinants of ethnic attitudes in a close contact situation. *South African journal of psychology,* 20(3): 206-216.

Van Niekerk, E. 1996. *Paradigms of mind: personality perspectives in context.* Johannesburg: International Thomson Publishing SA.

Varma, V. K. 1986. Cultural psycho-dynamics in health and illness. *Indian journal of psychiatry,* 28(1): 13-34.

Vaughan, B. E. & Langlois, J. H. 1983. Physical attractiveness as a correlate of peer status and social competence in pre-school children. *Development psychology,* 19: 561-567.

Viljoen, H. G. 1997. Eastern and African perspectives. In W. F. Meyer, C. Moore & H. G. Viljoen. *Personology: from individual to ecosystem* (pp 590-653). Johannesburg: Heinemann.

Viljoen, H. G. 1997. Historical overview of psychological thinking. In W. F. Meyer, C. Moore & H. G. Viljoen. *Personology: from individual to ecosystem* (pp 27-40). Johannesburg: Heinemann.

Visser, M. (Ed.). 1990. *Health in South Africa.* Pretoria: RGN.

Viviers, A. M. 1996. Salutogenese in organisatoriese konteks. Unpublished dissertation. Pretoria: University of South Africa.

Vlok, A. 1967. *Agtergrond vir personeelsielkunde.* Pretoria: Van Schaik.

Von Bertalanffy, L. 1959. Reply to Professor Weiskoppf. In A. H. Maslow (Ed.), *New knowledge in human values* (pp 240-241). New York: Harper & Row.

Vroom, V. H. 1964. *Work and motivation.* Florida: Robert E. Krieger.

Walsh, W. B. & Betz , N. E. 1995. *Tests and assessment.* Englewood Cliffs, NJ: Prentice-Hall.

Warr, P. 1987. *Work, unemployment and mental health.* Oxford: Clarendon Press.

Warr, P. 1992. Age and occupational well-being. *Psychology and ageing,* 7: 37-45.

Warr, P. B., Cook, J. & Wall, T. D. 1979. Scales for the measurement of some work attitudes and aspects of psychological well-being. *Journal of occupational psychology,* 52: 129-148.

Warshaw, L. J. 1979. *Managing stress.* Reading: Addison-Wesley.

Watkins, M. L. & Mauer, K. F. 1994. The performance values of white and black managers in South Africa. *South African journal of psychology,* 24(2): 78-90.

Wayne, S. J. & Kacmar, K. M. 1991. The effects of impression management on the performance appraisal process. *Organisational behaviour and human decision-processes,* 48: 70-88.

Weiner, B. 1972. *Theories of motivation: from mechanism to cognition.* Chicago: Markham.

Weiner, B. 1980. *Human motivation.* New York: Holt, Rinehart & Winston.

Weiner, B. 1986. *An attributional theory of motivation and emotion.* New York: Springer.

Weisskopf, W.A. 1959. Existence and values. In A.H. Maslow (Ed.) *New knowledge in human values* (pp 107-118). New York: Harper & Row.

Weiten, W.A. 1995. *Psychology – themes and variations.* 3rd ed. Pacific Grove: Brooks/Cole.

Welford, A. T. 1976. Thirty years of psychological research on age and work. *Journal of occupational psychology,* 49: 129-138.

Wheelen, T. L. & Hunger, J. D. 1990. *Strategic management.* Reading: Addison-Wesley.

Wheeler, M. 1994. *Problem people at work and how to deal with them.* London: Century Business Books.

Whitbeck, L. B. & Hoyt, D. R. 1994. Social prestige and assortive mating: a comparison of students from 1956-1988. *Journal of social and personal relationships,* 11: 137-145.

Wiener, Y., Varid, W. & Muczyk, J. 1981. Antecedents of employee's mental health – the role of career and work satisfaction. *Journal of vocational behaviour,* 19: 50-60.

Wiersma, U. & Latham, G. P. 1986. The practicality of behavioral observation scales, behavioral expectation scales, and trait scales. *Personnel psychology,* 39: 619-628.

Wiggens, J. S. 1997. A psychological taxonomy of trait descriptive terms: the interpersonal domain. *Journal of personality and social psychology,* 37: 395-412.

Wiggens, J. S. & Broughton, R. 1991. A

geometric taxonomy of scales. *European journal of personality*, 5: 343-465.

Wiggins, J. A., Wiggins, B. B. & Van der Zanden, J. 1994. *Social psychology*. 5th ed. New York: McGraw-Hill.

Wiggins, J. S. 1996. *The five factor model of personality: theoretical perspectives.* New York: Guilford Press.

Williams, R. M. 1979. Change and stability in values and value systems: a sociological perspective. In M. Rokeach. *Understanding human values* (pp 15-46). London: Collier-Macmillan.

Wilson, G. T., Nathan, P. E., O'Leary, K. D. & Clark, L. A. 1996. *Abnormal psychology: integrating perspectives.* Boston: Allyn & Bacon.

Wolcott, A., McKeeton, R., Burgin, R. & Yarowitch, R. 1977. Correlation of general aviation accidents with biorhythm theory. *Human factors*, 19: 283-284.

Wolfgang, A. P. 1988. *Job stress in the health professions: a study of physicians, nurses and pharmacists*, Spring: 43-47.

Wollack, S., Goodale, J. G. et al. 1971. Development of the survey of work values. *Journal of applied psychology*, 55: 331-338.

Wood, J. V., Giordano-Beech, M., Taylor, K. L., Michela, J. L. & Gaus, V. 1994. Strategies of social comparison among people with low self-esteem: self-protection and self-enhancement. *Journal of personality and social psychology*, 67: 713-731.

Worchel, S., Cooper, J. & Goethals, G. R. 1991. *Understanding social psychology*. 5th ed. Pacific Grove: Brooks/Cole.

Wright, P. H. 1982. Men's friendships, women's friendships and the alleged inferiority of the latter. *Sex roles*, 8: 1-20.

Wright, L., McCurdy, S., & Roggoll, G. 1992. The Tuppa scale: a self-concept measure for the Type A subcomponent of time urgency and perceptual activation. *Psychological assessment*, 4: 352-356.

Wrightsman, L. S. 1972. *Social psychology in the seventies.* California: Brooks/Cole.

Yik, M. S. & Bond, M. H. 1993. Exploring the dimensions of Chinese person perception with indigenous and imported constructs: creating a culturally balanced scale. *International journal of psychology*, 28: 75-95.

Young, F. W. 1984. Scaling. *Annual review of psychology*, 35: 55-81.

Yukl, G. & Fable, C. 1993. Influence tactics in upward, downward, and lateral influence attempts. *Journal of applied psychology*, 75: 132-140.

Zajonc, R. B. P. K., Aldermann, S. T., Murphy, S. T. & Niedenthal, P. M. 1987. Convergence in the physical appearance of spouses. *Motivation and emotion*, 11: 335-346.

Zedeck, S. 1992. *Work, families and organizations.* San Francisco: Jossey-Bass.

Index

Glossary

abscissa (*x*-axis on graphs) – absis (*x*-as op grafieke)

accommodation – akkommodasie, aanpassing by

achievement motive – prestasiebehoefte/-motief

acquire – aanleer, verwerf

acquired immunodeficiency syndrome (AIDS) – verworwe immuniteitsgebreksindroom (VIGS)

acrophobia – akrofobie, hoogtevrees

action potential – aksiepotensiaal, senuwee-impuls

activate – aktiveer

acute stress – akute, intense stres

adaptation (adjustment) – aanpassing

adaptive learning – aanpassingsleer

adjourning – verdaging

adjustive behaviours – aanpassingsgedrag

aesthetic – esteties

affiliation – affiliasie, betrokkenheid

affirmative action – regstellende aksie

afrocentric – afrosentries

aggregate – aggregaat, totaliteit

agoraphobia – agorafobie, ruimtevrees

aha-experience – aha-ervaring (insigmoment)

alertness – waaksaamheid

algophobia – algofobie, pynvrees

algorithm – algoritme (ondubbelsinnige instruksies vir probleemoplossing)

alienation – aliënasie, vervreemding

allele – alleel (gene gesamentlik verantwoordelik vir oorerwing)

ambiguity – dubbelsinnigheid

amnesia – amnesie, geheueverlies

anchor – beginpunt, ankerwaarde

andragogy – andragogie, volwasseneopvoeding

anima – anima (Jung, vroulike in mans)

animism – animisme, bonatuurlike

animus – animus (Jung, manlike in vrouens)

antecedent – antesedent, voorafgaande

anthropocentrism – antroposentrisme, mensgesentreerdheid

anticipatory socialisation – antisiperende, afwagtende sosialisasie

anxiety disorder – angsversteuring

apparent movement – skynbare beweging

appearance factors – voorkomsfaktore

applied fields – toegepaste velde

applied research – toegepaste navorsing

aptitude – aanleg

articulated – geartikuleerd, duidelik

assessment centre – takseersentrum

assessment method – evalueringsmetode

assimilation – assimilasie, inkorporasie

association – assosiasie, verwantskap

association neurons – assosiasie neurone, verbindingsneurone

attachment – gehegtheid

attending – aandag skenk aan

attitude – houding

attitudinal values – houdingswaardes

attributes – attribute, kenmerke

attribution – attribusie, bydrae

authentic self – werklike, ware self

autocratic – outokraties

autonomic nervous system – outonomiese senuweestelsel

autonomy – outonomie, onafhanklikheid

avoidant – vermydend

axolemma – aksolemma

axon – akson, geleidingsenuwee

axoplasm – aksoplasma

behaviour modification – gedragsmodifikasie, gedragsverandering

behaviourally anchored rating scale (BARS) – gedragsgeankerde beoordelingskaal

behaviourism – behaviourisme, gedrags-, leerbenadering

belief – oortuiging, geloof

bench mark – teikenpunt
bimodal thinking – bimodale denke
binocular – binokulêr (beide-oog-waarneming)
bodily self – liggaamlike self
bonding – binding
borderline personality disorder – grensgeval persoonlikheidsversteuring
bottom-up – onder-na-bo
brainstorming – dinkskrum, ideeberaad
burnout – uitbranding
camaraderie – kamaraderie, maatswees
capability – bekwaamheid, vaardigheid
capacity – kapasiteit, vermoë
cardinal trait – kardinale trek
cardiovascular – kardiovaskulêr, hart-, bloedvatverwant
career anchor – loopbaananker
career development – loopbaan-ontwikkeling
career indecision – loopbaanonseker-heid, -besluiteloosheid
career maturity – beroepsrypheid
career psychology – loopbaansielkunde
carpal (overuse) tunnel syndrome – oorgebruiksindroom (bv. van gewrig-spiere)
carry-over behaviour – oordrag-gedrag
catatonic schizophrenia – katatoniese skisofrenie
causality – oorsaaklikheid
cells – selle
central attitude – sentrale houding
central nervous system – sentrale senuweestelsel
central tendency – sentrale geneigdheid
central trait – sentrale trek
central value – sentrale waarde
centralisation – sentralisasie
cerebellum – serebellum, kleinbrein
cerebral cortex – serebrale korteks, breinskors
cerebral hemispheres – serebrale hemi-sfere
cerebrum – serebrum, grootbrein
character – karakter
charisma – charisma, persoonlike impak
checklist – merklys, kontrolelys

chromosomes – chromosome
chronic – chronies, langdurige
chronological age – chronologiese, ouderdom volgens tyd
chunking – stuksgewys (by geheue)
circular interaction – sirkulêre interaksie
circumspection, pre-emption, control (C-P-C) cycle – omsigtige, vooraf-kontrole siklus
classical behaviourism – klassieke (oorspronklike) behaviourisme
client-centred psychotherapy – kliënt-gesentreede psigoterapie
clinical picture – kliniese beeld, siekteprofiel
closure – sluiting
coalition – koalisie, bondgenootskap
cocktail party syndrome – skemerkelk-party-sindroom (aandagfluktuasie)
coercive power – magsafdwinging, oorreding
cognitive – kognitief, intellektueel
cognitive ability – kognitiewe vermoë
cognitive complexity – kognitiewe gekompliseerdheid
cognitive conceptions – kognitiewe opvattings
cognitive control – kognitiewe kontrole
cognitive disorder – kognitiewe versteuring
cognitive disregard – kognitiewe uitsluiting
cognitive dissonance – kognitiewe dissonansie
cognitive learning – kognitiewe leer
cognitive map – kognitiewe kaart, denk-patroon
cognitive psychology – kognitiewe psigologie
cognitive style – kognitiewe styl
coherence – koherensie, samehang
cohesion – kohesie, samehorigheid
collective – kollektief, gesamentlik
collective responsibility – gesamentlike verantwoordelikheid
collective unconscious – kollektiewe onbewuste
collectivism – kollektivisme

combat exhaustion – gevegsuitputting
command group – instruksie-, bevels-groep
command level – bevels- of betekenisvlak (in boodskappe)
common trait – algemene trek
commonality – eendersheid
compensation – kompensering, vergoeding
competence – bevoegdheid, bekwaamheid
compliance – inskiklikheid, toegeeflikheid
conceptual grouping – konseptuele groepering
conditioned reflex – gekondisioneerde refleks
conditioning – kondisionering
confirmation – bevestiging
conflict management – konflikbestuur
conformity – konformiteit
conformity status – konformiteitstatus
congenital – kongenitaal (eienskappe aanwesig vanaf geboorte)
congruence – kongruent, ooreenstemmend
connotation – konnotasie, dieperliggende (emosionele) betekenis
conscientiousness – konsensieus, nougeset
consciousness – bewussyn
consensus – konsensus, eenparigheid
conservation – bewaring
consistency – konstantheid
constellationary – konstellasie, groepgebonde
construct – konstruk ('n abstrakte voorstelling), begrip
constructive alternativism – konstruktiewe alternativisme, veranderlikheid
consultation – konsultasie
consumer psychology – verbruiker-sielkunde
contagious violence – aansteeklike geweld
containment – inhou, insluiting
context – konteks, binne verband
contingency – gebeurlikheid, moontlikheid

continuity – aaneenlopendheid
continuous interaction – voortdurende interaksie
continuous variable – kontinue (ongelykmatige) veranderlike
continuum – kontinuum
convenience range – gerieflikheids-omvang
converge – konvergeer, bymekaarkom
convergence – konvergering, samekoms, samevoeging
convergent thinking – konvergente denke (spesifieke wyse van denke)
conversion disorders – konversie-versteurings
cooperative economics – gesamentlike ekonomie
coping skills – hanteringsvaardighede
core constructs – kernkonstrukte
corporative philosophy – korporatiewe- (bestuurs-) filosofie
corrective actions – korrektiewe -, regstellende handelinge
correlation – korrelasie, verwantskap
correlation coefficient – korrelasie-koëffisiënt
cosmology – kosmologie, wêreldkunde
counselling – voorligting
creative values – kreatiewe waardes
creative self – kreatiewe self
credibility – geloofwaardigheid
criterion – kriterium, standaard
critical periods – kritieke periodes
crystallization – kristallisasie, opklaring
cultural diversity – kulturele diversiteit
cultural values – kulturele waardes
culture-bound syndromes – kultuur-gebonde sindrome
cumulative stress – kumulatiewe -, aanhoudende stres
cyclothymic depressive – siklotimiese (veranderende) depressie
death instinct (thanatos) – doodsinstink (tanatos)
deceleration – afname, vermindering
decentralisation – desentralisasie
decision frame – besluitnemingsraamwerk

decision-making – besluitneming

decompensation – dekompensasie, disintegrasie

deduction – deduksie, spesifieke afleiding

defence mechanism – verdedigingsmeganisme

deficiency need – gebreksbehoefte

deindividuation – deïndividuasie, identiteitsverlies

delegation – delegering, afwenteling

deliberation – beraadslaging

delusion – delusie, waandenkbeeld

dendrite – dendriete, dendron (neuronvertakkings)

denial – ontkenning

denotative meaning – denotatiewe, saaklike betekenis

deoxyribonucleic acid (DNA) – deoksiribonukleïensuur (DNS)

departmentalisation – departementalisasie

dependent personality – afhanklike persoonlikheid

dependent variable – afhanklike veranderlike

depersonalisation – depersonalisasie

depressive disorder – depressiewe versteuring

deprivation – deprivasie, ontneming

depth psychology – dieptesielkunde (bv. psigoanalise)

descriptive statistics – beskrywende statistiek

desensitised – desensitiseer, gevoeligheidsafname

deterministic – determinerend, bepalend

developed cognitive ability – ontwikkelde kognitiewe vermoë

developmental tasks – ontwikkelingstake

deviant behaviour – afwykende gedrag

dexterity – handigheid (bv. regshandigheid)

diagnosis – diagnose, probleemanalise

diagnostic statistical manual (DSM) – diagnostiese statistiese handleiding

dichotomy – digotomie, tweeledigheid

differential reinforcement – differensiële versterking

differentiation – differensiasie, onderskeiding

discrete variable – diskrete (vaste) veranderlike

discretionary coalitions – diskresionêre koalisies

discrimination – diskriminasie

disease-prone personality – siektegeneigde persoonlikheid

disequilibrium – disekwilibrium, onewewigtigheid

disintegration – disintegrasie

disorder – versteuring

displacement – verplasing

disposition – disposisie, neiging

dissociative disorder – disassosiatiewe versteuring

dissociative fugue – dissosiatiewe fuga (verandering a.g.v. geheueverlies)

dissonance – dissonansie, onversoenbaarheid

distribution of practice – oefeningverspreiding

distributions – verspreidings

divergent thinking – divergente, buigsame denke

diversity – diversiteit, verskeidenheid

dizygotic – disigoties (nie-identies)

dominance – dominansie

drives – dryfvere, behoeftes

dyad – diade, paar

dynamic muscular activity – dinamiese spieraktiwiteit

dynamic – dinamiese trek

dynamics – dinamiek (ontwikkeling, motivering)

dysfunctional – disfunksioneel

dysthymic depression – distimiese depressie

eccentric – eksentries, snaaks

eclectic approach – eklektiese (saamgevoegde) benadering

eclecticism – eklektisisme, samevoeging

ecosystemic – ekosistemies

effectiveness – effektiwiteit

efficiency – doeltreffendheid, bekwaamheid

ego – ego, bewustelike self
ego-identity – ego-identiteit, persoonlike identiteit
egodystonic – ego-distonies, ego-onaanvaarbaar
eidetic reduction – eidetiese (detail) vermindering van ervaringe
emotion process – emosieproses
emotional intelligence – emosionele intelligensie
empathy – empatie
empirical – empiries, bewese (bv. kennis)
employee-centred – werknemer-gesentreerd
encoding – enkodering, verwerking
encounter group – ontmoetingsgroep
enduring belief – blywende oortuiging
enzymes – ensieme
epistemological – epistemologies (kennisbasis)
equilibrium – ekwilibrium, balans
equitable rewards – billike (vergelykbare) belonings
equity – billikheid
equivocality – dubbelsinningheid
ergonomics – ergonomika
erratic – deurmekaar, gedisorganiseerd
escalation commitment – toewydings-eskalasie
esteem needs – behoeftes aan agting
ethical codes – etiese kodes
ethnocentric approach – etnosentriese benadering
ethos – etos, gebruike
etiology – oorsaaklikheid
eustress – positief ervaarde stres
evolution – evolusie, ordelike ontwikkeling, veranderingsleer
exertion of power – magsuitoefening
exhaustion – uitputting, disintegrasie
existential living – eksistensiële lewe (ten volle lewe)
existentialism – eksistensialisme
expectancy – verwagting
expectancy theory – verwagtingsteorie
experiential learning – ervaringsleer
experiential values – ervaringswaardes
experimental – eksperimenteel

expertise – kundigheid
explanatory – verklarend
explicit values – eksplisiete, openlike waardes
exploitive orientation – ondersoekende instelling
external activators – eksterne aktiveerders
external stressor – eksterne stressor (spanningsfaktor)
extinction – uitwissing
extrasensory perception (ESP, psi) – ekstrasensoriese waarneming
extraversion – ekstraversie, na-buite gerigtheid
face validity – gesigsgeldigheid
facilitation – fasilitering, bevordering
facilitator – fasiliteerder
factitious disorders – denkbeeldige, nagemaakte versteurings
factor analysis – faktoranalise
fairness – regverdigheid, billikheid
faulty learning – foutiewe leer
feedback – terugvoering
feedback-control system – terugvoer-kontrolesisteem
femininity – vroulikheid
fight/flight – veg/vlug
figure–ground – figuur–agtergrond
five-factor model – vyffaktormodel
fixation – fiksasie
fixed ratio schedule – vaste ratio-, verhoudingskedule
fixedness – vasgesteldheid, rigiedheid
flexibility – buigsaamheid
flow (peak) experience – piekervaring, hoogtepunt
formal group – formele groep
formal leadership – formele leierskap
formal status – formele (toegekende) status
formative evaluation – vormende -, prosesevaluering
forming – vorming
fortigenesis – fortigenese, gesondheids-bronne
frame of reference – verwysingsraam-werk

free association – vrye assosiasie,
– gedagtevloei
free will – eie, vrye wil, selfbesluitneming
frequency – frekwensie, hoeveelheid
friendship group – vriendskapsgroep
frontal cortex – frontale korteks
functional autonomy – funksionele
outonomie
functional fixedness – funksionele
rigiditeit
functional specification – taakverdeling,
funksionele spesifikasie
functionalism – funksionalisme
gender identity – geslagsrolidentiteit
gene – gene, erflikheid
general wellbeing – algemene welsyn
generalisation – veralgemening
generalised anxiety disorder – veral-
gemeende angsversteuring
generating – generering, skepping
generativity – generatiwiteit, selfvoort-
bringing
genetic screening – genetiese sifting,
– evaluering
genetics – genetika, oorerwing
genotype – genotipe
germ cell – moedersel, kiemsel
Gestalt – Gestalt, geheel
Gestalt psychology – Gestalt psigologie
(sielkunde)
globalisation – globalisasie, geheelheid
goal achievement – doelbereiking
gradient – gradiënt, tempo van daling of
styging
gratification – bevrediging
group demography – groepdemografie
group dynamics – groepsdinamika
group identity – groepsidentiteit
group shift – groepdenkeverskuiwing
group think – groepdink
growth group – groeigroep
growth needs – ontwikkelingsbehoeftes
habituation – gewoontevorming
hallucination – hallusinasie, onrealistiese
waarneming/voorstelling
halo-effect – stralekranseffek
hassle – hindernis
hebephrenic/disorganised schizo-

phrenia – hebefreniese/gedisorgani-
seerde skisofrenie
heredity – oorerflikheid
heterogeneous – heterogenies,
gemengd
heterostasis – heterostase
(self-aktualisering)
heuristics – heuristiek, oplossings-
moontlikhede
hierarchy – hiërargie, volgorde
higher-order conditioning – hoërorde-
kondisionering
hindsight – nabetragting
histrionic – histrionies, histeries
hoarding orientation – versamel-
instelling
holistic perspective – holistiese, geheel-
perspektief
homeostasis – homeostase, balans
horizontal differentiation – horisontale
differensiasie
human relations approach – mense-
verhoudingsbenadering
humanism – humanisme
hygiene factors – higiëne faktore
hypochondria – hipochondries, siekte-
preokkupasie
hypothalamus – hipotalamus
hypothesis – hipotese, tentatiewe
navorsingstelling
hysteria – histerie
id-impulses – id-impulse, -instinkte
ideal self – ideale self
identification – identifisering
identity diffusion/confusion – identi-
teitsverwarring
ideographic – ideografies, individu-
gesentreerdheid
idiosyncracy – idiosinkrasie, eienaardig-
heid
illumination – opklaring, verheldering
illusions – illusies, foutiewe waarneming
imitation – nabootsing
immune system – immuniteitsisteem
implicit values – implisiete waardes
implied movement – geïmpliseerde
beweging
impression formation – indrukvorming

impulse-control disorder – impuls-kontrole versteuring
in-basket technique – in-mandjie tegniek
incentives – aansporingsmeganismes
incongruence – inkongruensie, verskillendheid
incubation – inkubasie
incumbent – ampsdraer, ampsbekleder
independent variable – onafhanklike veranderlike
individualism – individualisme
individuation – individuasie, geheelwording
induced movement – geïnduseerde (geskepte) beweging
induction – induksie, algemene afleiding
industrial psychology – bedryfsielkunde
industry – arbeidsaamheid
inertia – traagheid
inferences – gevolgtrekkings
inferential statistics – inferensiële (afleidende) statistiek
information-processing – inligting-verwerking
informed consent – ingeligte toe-stemming
inhibition – inhibisie, binne hou
innovation – innovasie, vernuwing
inputs – insette
instrumental – instrumenteel, behulp-saam
instrumentality – instrumentaliteit, nuttigheidswaarde
intellectualisation – intellektualisering
intelligence quotient (IQ) – intelligensie kwosiënt (IK)
interactionism – interaksionisme, wissel-werkingsteorie
interdependence – interafhanklikheid
interest – belangstelling, voorkeur
interest group – belangegroep
internal activators – interne aktiveerders
internal locus of control – interne lokus van beheer
internalised speech – geïnternaliseerde spraak
interpersonal – inter-, tussenpersoonlik
interval – interval, klasinterval

intervening variable – tussenkomende veranderlike
intervension – intervensie, ingryping
intrapersonal – intrapersoonlik (binne 'n persoon)
intrapsychic – intrapsigies (binne 'n persoon)
intrinsic values – intrinsieke, inherente waardes
introspection – introspeksie, self-beskouing
introversion – introversie, binnegerig
intuitive – intuïtief, aanvoelend
irrationality – irrasioneel
job-centred – taakgesentreerd
job characteristics model – werk-eienskappe model
job content – werkinhoud
job description – posbeskrywing
job design – werkontwerp
job dissatisfaction – werkontevredenheid
job enlargement – werkverruiming
job enrichment – werkverryking
job involvement – werkbetrokkenheid
job rotation – werkrotasie
job satisfaction – werktevredenheid
just-noticeable-difference – net-merk-bare (waarneembare) verskil
kurtosis – kurtose (skerpheid en afplatting)
labour relations – arbeidsverhoudinge
lactic acid – melksuur
laissez-faire – laat-maar-doen (bv. leierskapstyl, houding)
latent learning – latente leer
Law of Effect – Wet van Effek
Law of Exercise – Wet van Oefening
learned helplessness – aangeleerde hulpeloosheid
learned resourcefulness – aangeleerde vindingrykheid
legitimate power – wettige (toegekende) mag
leniency effect – toegeeflikheidseffek
lexical approach – leksikale benadering (volgens erkende woorde)
libido – libido, seksuele energie
life instinct (eros) – lewensinstink (eros)
life line analysis – lewenslyn ontleding

life span – lewenspan
limbic system – limbiese stelsel
linear – lineêr, reglynig
linguistic relativity – taalkundige relatiwiteit
locus of causality – lokus van oorsaak-likheid
locus of control – lokus (plek) van beheer, kontrole
longitudinal consistency – langdurige konstantheid
macro-system – makrostelsel
malingering – siektevoorwendsel
manic-depressive – manies-depressief
margin of error – foutgrens
marketing orientation – anderbevre-digende instelling
masculinity – manlikheid
mastery – bemeestering
material self – materiële self
maturation – ryping, volwassewording
maturity – rypheid, gereedheid
mean ($\bar{x}$) – rekenkundige gemiddelde ($\bar{x}$)
meaning systems – betekenissisteme (bv. konstrukte)
meaningful wholes – betekenisvolle gehele
measurement error – metingsfout
mechanism – meganisme
mechanistic – meganisties
median – mediaan, middelpunt
medulla oblongata – medulla oblongata, verlengde rugmurg
meiosis – meiose, chromosoomverdeling
mental abilities – verstandsvermoëns
mental age – verstandsouderdom
mental agility – verstandelike buigsaamheid
mental alertness – verstandelike helder-heid
mental demands – verstandelike eise
mental disorder – geestes- of sielkundige versteuring
mental imagery – denkbeelding, verbeelding
mental retardation – verstandelike vertraging
mentally challenging work – psigies-uitdagende werk

meso-system – mesostelsel (meso = middel)
meta-analysis – omvattende ontleding
metacognition – metadenke, metakog-nisie (denke oor denke)
metaneeds – meta-, oorkoepelende behoeftes
metaphysics – metafisika, realiteitstudie
metapsychology – metasielkunde
micro-system – mikrostelsel
midcareer crisis – middelloopbaankrisis
midlife crisis – middeljarekrisis
mind – psige
mirage – spieëlbeeld
misapplied constancy – misrekende konstantheid
mitosis – mitose, seldeling
mnemonics – mnemoniek, assosiasie en organisering (in geheue)
mode – modus (mees frekwente waarde)
modelling – modellering
moderating – modererende
modulation – aanpassing, buiging
monitoring – monitering, kontrolering
monocular – monokulêr (eenoogwaar-neming)
monophobia – monofobie, alleenwees-fobie
monozygotic – monosigoties (identies bv. tweeling)
moral – morele, moraal
morality principle – moraliteitsbeginsel
moratorium – beperking, oponthoud
motion parallax – bewegingsparalaks
motivators – motiveerders
motor (efferent) neurons – motoriese (efferente) neurone
multimodal – multimodale, meervoudige faktor
multiple determination – veelvoudige bepaling
mutivariate statistics – meerverander-like statistiek
myelin – miëlien
narcissism – narsisme, selfliefde
natural science – natuur- (like) wetenskap
nature – (menslike) natuur, aangebore
negative reinforcement – negatiewe versterking

neo-behaviourism – neo-behaviourisme (nuwe)

nervous system – senuweestelsel

neuroglial cell – neuroglia sel, senuwee-bindweefsel

neuron – neuron, senuweesel

neuroses – neurose, (ou begrip vir angs-gebaseerde versteurings)

nodes of Ranvier – knope van Ranvier (aksonvernouings)

nominal – nominaal (bv. metingskaal)

nomothetic – nomoteties, algemeen, groepgebaseerd

non-conforming – nie-konformerend

non-consciousness – nie-bewustheid

normal distribution – normaalverspreiding

normative – normatiewe, volgens verwagting

norming – normering ('n fase)

nurture (environmental) – omgewings-bepaald

observable behaviour – waarneembare gedrag

observation – observasie, waarneming

observational learning – waarnemingsleer

obsessive-compulsive – obsessief-kompulsief

occipital cortex – oksipitale korteks

occupational mental health – beroeps-geestesgesondheid

Oedipal conflict – oedipale konflik (teenoor teenoorgestelde geslag)

oneness – eenwees

ontology – ontologie, bestaanswese

openness to experience – oopheid vir ervaring

operant conditioning – operante kon-disionering

operational fatigue – operasionele vermoeidheid

opinions – opinies, beskouings

oral – orale (met mond te doen)

order effect – volgorde effek

ordinal – ordinaal

ordinate (y-axis) – ordinaat (y-as)

organisational citizenship behaviour – organisasieburgerskapgedrag

organisational commitment – organisa-sietoewyding, -verbondenheid

organisational diagnosis – organisasie-diagnose

organisational hierarchy – organisasie-hiërargie

organisational integrity – organisasie-integriteit

organisational psychology – organisa-siesielkunde

organisational rituals – organisasie-rituele

organisational trust – organisasie-vertroue

outputs – uitsette

overcompensation – oorkompensasie

oversight – oorsig

ovum – ovum, eiersel

pairing – afparing

panic disorder – paniekversteuring

paradigm – paradigma, denkwyse

paranoia – paranoia, vervolgings-waansin

paranoid schizophrenia – paranoïse skisofrenie

paraphilia – parafilie (tipe seksuele afwykings)

parasympathetic nervous system – parasimpatiese senuweestelsel

parietal cortex – pariëtale korteks

part learning – deelleer

pathogenic – patogenies, siekteveroor-sakend

pathological intoxication – patologiese intoksikasie, bedwelming

peak experience – piekervaring

peak performance – topprestasie

peer group – portuurgroep

peers – gelykes

percept – waarneming (konstruk)

perceptual distortion – perseptuele distorsie

performance – prestasie

performance ethos – prestasie-etos, - gedragskode

peripheral attitudes – perifere houdinge

peripheral constructs – perifere konstrukte

peripheral nervous system – perifere senuweestelsel

perseverative functional autonomy – perseverende (volgehoue) funksionele outonomie

person-centred – persoongesentreerd

person-situation-interaction – persoon-situasie-interaksie

persona – persona, persoonlikheid

personal hardiness – persoonlike gehardheid

personalise – verpersoonlik

personnel psychology – personeel-sielkunde

personnel turnover – personeelomset

personologist – personoloog/persoonlikheidskundige

personology – personologie, persoonlikheidstudie

phallic – fallies (met seksuele te doen)

phenomenological field – fenomenologiese veld

phenomenology – fenomenologie, ervaringsleer

phenomenon – fenomeen, verskynsel

phenotype – fenotipe, waarneembare eienskappe

phi-phenomenon – phi-verskynsel, stroboskopiese effek (m.b.t. skynbare beweging)

phobia – fobie

physiological needs – fisiologiese behoeftes

pituitary gland – pituitêre klier

placement – plasing

pleasure principle – plesierbeginsel

polygenetic heredity – poligene (veelvoudige) erflikheid

position power – posisiemag

positive regard – positiewe agting

positive reinforcement – positiewe versterking

positivism – positivisme, waarneembaarheidstudie

post-traumatic stress – post- (na) traumatiese stres

power distance – magsafstand

power inhibition – magsinperking

pragmatism – pragmatisme, verpraktisering

pre-conscious – voorbewuste

predictability – voorspelbaarheid

prediction – voorspelling

predisposition – predisposisie, voorafmoontlikheid

pre-emptive – vooruitbepaalde

prejudice – vooroordeel

pressure – druk, spanning, stres

presuppositions – voorveronderstellings

preverbal – voorverbale

primacy effect – voorrangeffek

proactive inhibition – voorafgaande inhibering

probability – waarskynlikheid

problem-focused coping – probleemgerigte hantering

process schizophrenia – prosesskisofrenie

procrastination – uitstel

progressive relaxation – progressiewe ontspanning

projection – projeksie, oorplasing

proliferation – proliferasie, indringing

propositional – voorstellende

propriate functional autonomy – propriale funksionele outonomie

propriate striving – propriale (eie) strewe

proprium – proprium, self

prosocial – prososiaal

proximity – nabyheid

psychoanalysis – psigoanalise

psychoanalytic school – psigoanalitiese skool

psycho-diagnosis – psigodiagnose

psychodynamics – psigodinamika

psychological contract – sielkundige kontrak

psychological optimality – psigologiese optimaliteit

psychometrics – psigometrika

psychopathology – psigopatologie, abnormale gedrag

psychopathy – psigopatie, sosiopatie

psychophysical – psigofisies

psychophysics – psigofisika

psychosexual – psigoseksuele

psychoticism – psigotisisme
punctuated-equilibrium model –
gepunktueerde ekwilibriummodel
purposiveness – doelgerigtheid
pyromania – piromanie, vuurmanie
pyrophobia – pirofobie, vrees vir vuur
Q-sort technique – Q-sorteringstegniek
qualitative – kwalitatief
quantitative – kwantitatief
radical behaviourism – radikale (klassieke) behaviourisme
range of convenience – gerieflikheids-
omvang
ratio – ratio, verhouding
rational emotive therapy – rasioneel-
emosionele terapie
rationalisation – rasionalisering
raw scores – rou tellings, onverwerkte
tellings
raw data matrix – roudataverspreidings-
diagram
reaction-formation – reaksie-formasie
(teenoorgestelde)
reactive schizophrenia – reaktiewe
skisofrenie
readiness – gereedheid
real self – ware self
reality principle – realiteitsbeginsel
receptive orientation – ontvanklike
instelling
receptor neurons – reseptor neurone
(ontvangs-)
recessiveness – resessiwiteit
reciprocal – wederkerig
reductionism – reduksionisme,
vermindering
referent power – referente (verwysings-)
mag
reframing – herdefiniëring (bv. 'n ander
verwysingsraamwerk)
refreezing – herbevriesing
regression – regressie, terugkeer
regression analysis – regressie-ontleding
reinforcement – versterking
relationship-orientated – verhoudings-
georiënteerd
reliability – betroubaarheid, konstantheid
religious – religieus, godsdienstig

remedial – remediërende
repertoire – repertoire, versameling
repetitive strain injuries – herhalende
ooreisingsbeserings
report level – rapporteringsvlak (deno-
tasie, saaklike betekenis)
repression – repressie, verdringing
research design – navorsings-
ontwerp
research methodology – navorsings-
metodiek
resiliency – aanpasbaarheid, herstel- of
weerstandsvermoë
resources – hulpbronne
respondent behaviour – respondente
gedrag
response style – reaksiestyl
retention – onthou, retensie
reticular activation system (RAS) –
retikulêre aktiveringstelsel (RAS)
retinal disparity – retinale dispariteit
(ongelykheid)
retrieval – herwinning
retroactive inhibition – retroaktiewe
inhibisie, nakomende inhibering
reward – beloning
role ambiguity – roldubbelsinnigheid,
rolonduidelikheid
role conflict – rolkonflik
role expectation – rolverwagting
role identity – rolidentiteit
role loading – rolbelading
role perception – rolpersepsie
safety needs – veiligheidsbehoeftes
salutogenesis – salutogenese (konsep vir
bronne van gesondheid)
sampling – monstertrekking
sanctioned aggression – goedgekeurde
aggressie
schema – skema, raamwerk
schizoid – skisoïde
schizophrenia – skisofrenie
schizotypical – skisotipies
school of thought – denkskool
screening technique – siftingstegniek
secondary trait – sekondêre trek
security needs – sekuriteitsbehoeftes
selection – keuring

selective orientation – selektiewe
  oriëntasie
self (ego) – self, ego
self-actualisation – selfaktualisering,
  potensiaalverwesenliking
self-concept – selfkonsep, selfbegrip
self-control – self-, persoonlike kontrole
self-defeating – selfverydelend
self-determination – selfbepalend
self-efficacy – selftoereikendheid,
  -doeltreffendheid
self-esteem – selfagting
self-fulfillment – selfvervulling
self-handicapping – selfhindernis
self-identity – selfidentiteit
self-image – selfbeeld
self-perception – selfpersepsie
self-realisation – selfwaardering
self-regulation – selfregulering
self-report inventory – selfantwoord-
  vraelys
self-schemas – selfskemas
self-sentiment – selfsentiment
self-serving – selfregverdigende
self-transcendence – selfuitstyging
semantic differential – semantiese
  differensiaal
sensation – sensasie, gewaarwording
sense of coherence – sin vir koherensie,
  samehang
sensitivity training – sensitiwiteits-
  opleiding
sensory adaptation – sensoriese aanpassing
sensory (afferent) neurons – sensoriese
  (afferente) neurone
separation anxiety – skeidingsangs
sex determination – geslagsbepaling
sex-linked genes – geslagsgebonde gene
sexual harassment – seksuele teistering
shadow – skaduwee, onderliggende
  gedrag (soos id)
shaping – vorming
shared spiritual essence – gedeelde
  geestelike belangrikhede
signal detection – seinherkenning,
  -nasporing
significance – betekenisvolheid

simple schizophrenia – eenvoudige
  skisofrenie
simplicity – eenvoudigheid, ongekom-
  pliseerdheid
simulator – simulator, nabootser
situational approach (situationism) –
  situasionele benadering
situational tests – situasietoetse
skewness – skeefheid
skill – vaardigheid
social isolation – sosiale isolasie
social loafing – sosiale (aanvaarbare)
  slaplê
social self – sosiale self
social support – sosiale ondersteuning
somatic – somatiese (liggaamlike)
somatic nervous system – somatiese
  senuweestelsel
somatotype – liggaamstipe
somnambulism – somnambulisme,
  slaaploop
source trait – oorsprongtrek
spacial differentiation – ruimtelike
  differensiasie
span of control – kontroleomvang
spatial summation – ruimtelike
  summasie
spill-over effects – oorspoelgevolge
spinal cord – rugmurg
spirit of the time – tydsgees
spiritual self – geestelike self
standard deviation – standaardafwyking
standardisation – standardisasie,
  eenvormigheid
static muscular activity – statiese
  spieraktiwiteit
stereotype – stereotipe, rigiede opvatting
stimulus-response (S-R) approach –
  stimulus-responsbenadering (S-R)
storming – storm ('n fase)
stream of consciousness – bewussyns-,
  ervaringsintegrasie
stress – stres (druk, spanning)
stressors – stresoorsake
stroboscopic movement – skynbare
  beweging (stroboskopies, phi)
structuralism – strukturalisme
sublimation – sublimasie, vervanging

subliminal perception – subliminale (onderbewuste) waarneming

submerged – onderliggende

subordinates – ondergeskiktes

substance dependence – substansie-, middelafhanklikheid

substance induced – middelgeïnduseerd (veroorsakend)

summative assessment – eindresultaat evaluering

super-ego – super-ego

surface trait – oppervlaktrek

survey – opname

suspended – uitgespreide, onderdrukte

SWOT analysis – SWOT-analise (sterk-punte, swakpunte, geleenthede, bedreigings)

syllogism – sillogisme, afleidende denke

symbolic rehearsal – simboliese her-haling

symmetrical – simmetries, ewewydig

sympathetic nervous system – simpatiese senuweestelsel

symptom bearer – simptoomdraer

symptom-focused – simptoomgerig

synapse – sinaps, (neuronekontakpunt vir impulsgeleiding)

syndrome – sindroom, siektebeeld

synergy – sinergie, samewerking

systemic – sistemies

systems model – sisteemmodel

task group – taakgroep

task identity – taakidentiteit

task-orientated – taakgeoriënteerd

task significance – taaksinvolheid

task simulation – taaksimulasie, taaknabootsing

taxonomy – taksonomie, indeling, klassifikasie

teaming – spanwerk, spanbou

teleological principle – teleologiese beginsel (toekomsgerigtheid)

telepathy – telepatie

temperament – temperament, geaardheid

temporal summation – temporale summasie

temporal cortex – temporale korteks

terminal values – terminale, eindwaardes

test bias – toetssydigheid

thalamus – talamus

theoretical – teoretiese

threshold – drempel

token economy – teken-, belonings-ekonomie

tolerance – toleransie, verdraagsaamheid

top-down – bo-na-onder

topographical – topografies

trait/factor – trek/faktor

transactionism – transaksionisme (inter-aksie tussen mens, omgewing en gedrag)

transcendence – transendensie, uitstyging

transfer of learning – leeroordrag

transference – oordrag

transformation – transformasie, vervorming

transition – oorgang

transparency – deursigtigheid

type A behaviour – tipe A gedrag

typology – tipologie

unconditioned stimulus – ongekon-disioneerde stimulus

unconscious – onbewuste

unconscious factors – onbewuste faktore

unconscious mental content – onbewuste psigiese inhoud

unfreezing – ontvriesing, desensitisering

unilateral – eensydige

unobservable behaviour – nie-waar-neembare gedrag

uplift – ophefffing

valence – valensie (aantrekkingskrag)

validity – geldigheid

values – waardes

variability – varieerbaarheid, veranderlik-heid

variable ratio – veranderlike ratio

variables – veranderlikes

variance – variansie, afwyking, varieer-baarheid

verification – verifiëring, aanvaarbaarheidsproses

vertical differentiation – vertikale differensiasie

vicarious learning – middellike leer, observasieleer

whole learning – geheelleer

wholeness – geheelheid

wholeness of experience – geheel van
   ervaring
will to meaning – wil tot betekenis
withdrawal – onttrekking
workaholism – werkolisme, werk-
   verslaafdheid
work centrality – sentraliteit van werk
work dysfunction – werkdisfunksie
work ethics – werketiek
workforce demographics – werkmag-
   demografie

working body posture – werkliggaams-
   houding
working conditions – werkomstandig-
   hede
work-related attitudes – werkverwante
   houdinge
work sample test – werkmonster-
   toets
work station design – werkstasie-
   ontwerp
zoophobia – soöfobie, dierefobie